YOU HEAR ME?

poems and writing by teenage boys

YOU HEAR ME?

poems and writing by teenage boys

edited by Betsy Franco

CANDLEWICK PRESS
CAMBRIDGE, MASSACHUSETTS

"The Baby She Loved Too Much to Keep" by Todd VanDerWerff was previously
published in *The Armour Chronicle*, November 10, 1998.

"There's a Harlem Renaissance in My Head" by Maurice E. Duhon, Jr.,
was previously published in *A Treasury of Famous Poems*
(Famous Poets Society, 1997).

First paperback edition 2001

The Library of Congress has cataloged the hardcover edition as follows:

You hear me? : poems and writing by teenage boys / edited by Betsy Franco.
—1st ed.
p.   cm.
Summary: An anthology of stories, poems, and essays by adolescent boys on
issues that concern them.
ISBN 0-7636-1158-1 (hardcover)
1. Adolescence—Literary collections. 2. Youths' writings.
[1. Adolescence—Literary collections. 2. Youths' writings.] I. Franco, Betsy.
PZ5. F925   2000
810.8'092836—dc21   99-057129

ISBN 0-7636-1159-X (paperback)

2 4 6 8 10 9 7 5 3

Printed in the United States of America

This book was typeset in Officina.

Candlewick Press
2067 Massachusetts Avenue
Cambridge, Massachusetts 02140

visit us at www.candlewick.com

For my sons, James, Thomas, and David

CONTENTS

PREFACE

P eople warned me that if I wanted to compile an anthology of stories and poems by teenage boys, I wouldn't receive any submissions. But in the summer of 1998, I felt compelled to launch the project *You Hear Me?* anyway. After all, I had three sons of my own, and I knew how important it was to hear from boys. Also, my experience compiling *Things I Have to Tell You,* a collection of writing by teenage girls, had taught me that it was worth the risk.

The focus and significance of *You Hear Me?* didn't become clear until I had received several dozen submissions and had spoken to a number of the authors. It became apparent that boys needed a forum to speak for themselves on issues that concerned them. One author was very relieved to hear that I wasn't going to be including commentary to clarify the work, or as evidence of a theory. He said he'd read a number of books in high school that supposedly addressed boys' issues . . . and he "couldn't relate."

My philosophy has been that people should speak for themselves. In the case of teenage boys, I've noticed that people tend to put words and feelings into boys' mouths, based on secondhand information and stereotypes. In *You Hear Me?* I wanted to present the uncensored accounts of teenage boys without the filter of adult sensibility

In collecting the pieces, my goal was to include all kinds of voices—from the suburbs to the heart of the city, from those who love to write to those who just have something to say, if someone will listen. The collection includes stories, poems, and essays from across the country. I advertised in creative writing journals, found an Internet site that linked me to forty-eight hundred classrooms, collected poetry from writing projects in Detroit, Houston, and Chicago, and invited individual boys to submit.

As the collection grew, I noticed a frankness and honesty, but also a sensitivity in the writing. *You Hear Me?* shows the inner and the outer sides of boys. I knew from my own sons that boys have a broad emotional range, but I wasn't sure that they would be willing to share their thoughts and feelings in a publication. I found out that they are willing, and the result is a powerful statement of who they are.

Betsy Franco

ACKNOWLEDGMENTS

So many people helped with this book. The first person I spoke to was Thomas Schellenberg, a gifted creative writing teacher, who let me talk to his classes at Palo Alto High School and helped me gather submissions for the book. Next I contacted Terry Blackhawk's InsideOut Writing Project, an outstanding program of poets in the Detroit schools. When she sent me her powerful selections, the book had a foundation. Throughout the project, Terry offered her advice, support, and enthusiasm. Poets-in-residence, teachers, and support staff connected to the InsideOut poets include John Aldrich, Therese Becker, Peggy Bodenmiller, Louis Carney, Dawn McDuffie, Helen Didley, Arbrie Griffin, Sheryl Heading, Stephen Jones, Mindy LePere, Ricardo Martin, Lenelle Parker, Dana Payne, Michael Phillips, and Joanne Sanneh.

Classroom Connect, an Internet site, linked me with forty-eight hundred classrooms. By advertising in *Poets and Writers Magazine* and with the Society of Children's Book Writers and Illustrators, I gained access to other individuals who would be interested in the project nationwide. Among the many people who helped me with submissions from across the country were Sheerly Avni of *YO!,* Nancy Barnby, Robert Boone of Young Chicago Authors, Paul Dunlap, Janet

Elliot, Gloria Evangelista, Jean Frankenfeld, Alfred Gomez, Meg Spencer Gorman, Traci Gourdine of the California State Summer School for the Arts, Steven Hulme, Joseph McCarren of Slippery Rock University, Judith Michaels, author of *Risking Intensity: Reading and Writing Poetry with High School Students,* Ann Munro, Christina Pacosz, Coach Parks, Alma G. Perez, Marsha Pittelkow, and Maura Vaughn. In the final stretch, Robin Reagler of WITS (Writers In The Schools) and her staff went out of their way to help me gather permissions from WITS authors in Houston.

Special thanks to my consultant Maria Damon, a writer and a professor of literature at the University of Minnesota, who was dedicated to the book and spent countless hours working on it with me. Thank you as well to my consultant Lorraine Bates Noyes, a writer, who generously solicited and evaluated submissions. Both Maria and Lorraine offered encouragement when I most needed it.

My sons — James, Thomas, and David — helped me keep my adult viewpoint out of each stage of the process and gave me advice about selections. My husband, Douglas Franco, offered valuable suggestions, and Marjorie Franco assisted with the editing of the stories.

Most important of all were my consultants in their teens and early twenties. Sam Doniach, Quantedius Hall, Stephan Johnson, Benjamin Martin, Sean McDonnell, Mike McGaraghan, Sean Mitchell, David Persyko, Daniel Raburn, and Shysuaune Taylor read and responded to each piece in the first draft. Their insightful feedback was integral to the selection process.

Working with my editor, Mary Lee Donovan, was a wonderful experience. She understood the book, was willing to take chances, and had a genuine respect and sensitivity for the authors. Associate editor Kara LaReau was insightful and supportive. Amy Rennert, my agent, understood my vision and believed in the project from the start.

Thank you especially to all the writers who trusted me enough to submit their poems, stories, and essays. Whether or not your work made it into the final collection, you played an important part in making this book possible.

YOU HEAR ME?

TIME SOMEBODY TOLD ME

Time Somebody Told Me
That I am lovely, good and real
That I am beautiful inside
If they only knew
How that would make me feel.

Time Somebody Told Me
That my mind is quick, sharp
and full of wit
That I should keep on trying
and never quit.

Time Somebody Told Me
How they loved and needed me
How my smile is filled with hope
and my spirit sets them free
How my eyes shine, full of light
How good they feel when they hug me tight.

Time Somebody Told Me

So, I had a talk with myself
Just me, nobody else
'cause it was time
Somebody Told Me.

Quantedius Hall, "Son of Reality," age 12

1

TOPIC 1: INTRODUCTIONS

Hi My Name is Tom
(Sounds good:
    Direct
    Honest
    Telling
    Humble)

My favorite Color is Blue
    (Yikes!
      No —
    Take back
    Lie
    Nerves
    Panic
    Upset
    Fluster)

I Like Blue
    (Okay!
    Good comeback)

How Are You?

Thomas Andrade, age 18

FRONT SEAT RIDER

Riding in a car,
I like to be the one to drive,
unlike my brother who always sits
in the back seat. He enjoys
just riding along, free to take in
scenes along the way, girls
and all that, rather than having
to watch where he's going.
He doesn't like
to ride with me, though.
He accuses me of doing
seventy-five to a hundred mph right in
the neighborhood. I admit I
drive fast, but not that fast, although
I like to get a whiff of burnt rubber
every now and then. I'd be
grounded for a year if my mother
caught me driving as fast as that.
I'm a front seat rider all the way.
If I ride at all, it's got to be
behind the wheel.

Triston L. Dunnett, age 15

Just because I love darkness
Doesn't mean I'm depressed
Doesn't mean I can't love
Doesn't mean I'm blind.
Just because I love my Mom
Doesn't mean I'm not a rebel
Doesn't mean I can't love others
Doesn't mean I'm a mama's boy.
Just because I act psycho
Doesn't mean I need medication
Doesn't mean I can't be compassionate
Doesn't mean I don't cry.

Marcel Mendoza, age 16

JOKER

You would be surprised
To know that the funny man
Is also the sad man
Like a clown fallen from his stilts.
> But this is his career
> Never will a joker feel secure in a serious environment
> He will keep telling jokes
> Never will a joker be secure in his insecurities
> He will keep telling jokes.
In the process of getting out of a hole
A hole I dug for myself
A bottomless pit
I will die . . .
Like the product of a pun
A misunderstanding.
The saddest joke . . .
> A clown lying by his stilts, full of regret.

Michael Tobias Bloom, age 16

5

DARK CELLAR

I like to hide in my dark damp cellar
Where rats scurry across the cold cement floor.
I don't know why I like to hide in my dark damp cellar.
All I know is that anger and sorrow
Evaporate into clouds of air
And bad thoughts disintegrate
When I'm there.

Every boy should have a cellar.

Joshua White, age 12

HE SHAVED HIS HEAD

He shaved his head to release his imagination.
He did it to get a tattoo on his shiny head.
He did it to lose his normality.
He did it to become a freak.
He did it because he was angry.
He did it to make people angry.
He did it for himself.

Rene Ruiz, age 13

BROKEN GLASS

crazy mad
mad like a vulture
no prey

i am a soldier
wounded in duty

i'm angry, man
you hear me?
angry
like a second place loser

loser, man

can you dig it?
can you feel me, winner?

i am not weird
i don't hold grudges
or sing in the shower
or chew rusty razors

do you?

i break glass
i cut it, man
i am able to cut glassy stares with sharper ones

believe me i'll do it
i'll handle it

i'm crazy mad

you can't stop the rain
or the reign

Joshua Bonds, age 17

INSTRUCTIONS FOR LIFE

Catch the football and make sure you score a touchdown; jump into the mud and make certain it is enjoyable; rip your jeans and tear your shirts; bleed on the field of glory and take it like a man; grind the grass stains into your clothes; order a hot dog at a baseball game; watch the Super Bowl and tell everyone about the play in the second half to prove you watched it; root for the home team; get hurt but don't cry; hide your emotions; pick yourself up when you are down; watch violent movies and crave blood and destruction. This is how to act tough on the outside; this is how you act in front of the guys. Slick your hair back with your father's gel just the right way to catch the eye of the girl next to you; don't burp; act like a gentleman; wear clothes that make you look cool; walk a walk that shows the girls how suave you are; act mature; protect your sister if she needs help. This is how you act in front of the girls. Do well in school; get straight A's because you have to get into a good college. This is how to succeed; this is how to be prosperous; this is how to be happy and live life to the fullest.

Brando, age 15

THE TORCH

Where was I when they were passing the torch
when they were all
getting some action out in the bush
getting some action behind a very green graffiti garage
getting some action out in the goddamned field
When they were all
getting their jock straps monogrammed gold
When they were all sipping sweaty, hard brews
Where was I when our fathers were teaching us
how to cover our cocks with barbed wire
teaching us how to make love
and orgasmic war
Where was I when we were boys becoming
greasy, bald-headed deacons and
finger-fucking commandos Praise the Lord
when we were boys becoming
fat-breasted, gold-buttoned, white-wig financiers
and the people who control the mail God bless America
Where was I when they were
boys sodomizing pilgrims and indians
and all the horses in between and leaving them for dead
Where was I when we were
playing spin-the-bottle at the never-ending parties
with girls in semen-colored dresses
pulled all the way over their heads and
who seemed to cum all night

11

Where was I when they were pissing inside
of their pretty alcoholic wives
When they were dancing naked homosexual rain dances
in the locker rooms all across the American galaxy and
smearing pricked fingers together swearing allegiance
to the covering of each other's ass
When they were taking shit breaks from the divine Law
as only real men can
When they turned Christ into toilet bowl cleaner
and Buddha into a synonym for the pussy hole and
Allah into abracadabra and
eventually a puff of cigarette smoke.
shit.
Where was I when we were growing invisible public hair,
taking the last drop of milk from the cow
graduating from Superman lunch boxes to
plumber's ass cracks and tool boxes
Where was I when all my brothers passed the torch before
me?
Where was I
and why can't I stop screaming?

Michael R. Jackson, age 17

MY POCKETS AIN'T THAT PHAT

I
   rotate to the rhythm
   of a ghetto
      grape
      jimbe
      voice
my step
is faaaaarrr to the left
and I
     don't
wanna keep up
   with Generation
       X-pense
       X-plore
       X-cite
       X-press myself
my groove
      clues of
reds, blacks, and blues

I
   don't
      wear nothing
of a

Nautica
Eddie Bauer
  Nike
  Fila
  Timbo-
  land
  Rockport
  Mike Jordan
        scent
  My clothes
        stay big
        Kmart cool
        Target fresh

I'm
 not a
hip hop
Dred
retro
  4-pierced brotha

Don't wanna be wrapped
up in '70s leather
polyester Afro
      zones

14

My hair is
        not
    tightly faded
    brown-skinned
    flawless, suave
My ride ain't
    a drop top
    bassed
    hydraulic
    screamin'
    pimp wagon
My tongue
        was not meant to
M.A.C.

My thoughts are
tightly wound
    about
makin'
    one
        Mrs.
            mine.

I'm cream
        neutral
        chills

of gray
     brown patterns
Forgive me for not
speaking.
      My dance of rejection
      freaks me
      breathless.

In a room of
      human collages
I'd rather sit
    and converse
with anger, happiness,
    my personality's
       offspring

I'm not
down with impressing
   anyone's impression
of an urban hip hop image
No, that stereotype
   doesn't move me
My words
    complement those
     that welcome
them.

'Til then
      they stay
colorfully quiet with
      a lot of a
      little
      to
      say!

Shysuaune T. Taylor, age 18

M.A.C. — flirt with every woman that comes my way

ODE TO MY HAIR TAIL

My hair tail is like a snake
wrapped around my neck.

It feels like a spider
crawling on my neck.

In the dark you cannot see
my hair tail because it's black.
In the sun it looks brown.

It decorates the back of my head.

When my sister tries to braid
it, she gets mad because it's long,
and it looks skinny from the
bottom, and she thinks she'll never
finish.

Some people think
that I am in a gang and
throw me gang signs.

In the mirror my hair tail looks
shiny, and I can see how
long it is.

I think I'll cut my hair tail
when it's a little bigger. I'll
save it and take it to
San Juan, Texas, and
leave it in a church.

Rigo Landin, 17

It all started in second grade. There was this kid and he would jump on my desk and chair. He also would call me inappropriate things. My teacher would say, Stay away from him. I said, *He* comes to *me.* She didn't care.

In third grade people were calling me a girl so I went down a hill and pulled down my pants to prove I wasn't. I was suspended for three days. After that it got a lot worse. Kids hit me and swore at me. One day at recess, some kids were chasing me and I went down a hill and about thirty kids beat me up big time.

In fourth grade, people were cooling down on me a little. But still, every time I went to the office to report on some kids, they wouldn't do anything. So I started saying things back to the kids. They went to the office and reported on me. I got in trouble. One time, the assistant principal carried me all the way to the office. My mom would check on me every day. At the end of the year things were starting to look up for me. I was going to go to a different school in fifth grade. The principal said that she would talk to the other kids that were going to the new school. During the summer I was diagnosed with Tourette syndrome.

In fifth grade I was in my new school. But the kids from my old school who were there spread everything that had happened. So most of the kids in the school were mean to me. I reported on them every day, but nobody did anything. When kids reported on me, I got in big trouble. Most of the time they would lie to the people in the office. I had maybe one friend in that school.

In sixth grade, it was bad again. I was beat up by some mean kid. People were calling me every bad word there is. They did a talk in my class to explain that I have Tourette and what it does to me. It helped a little at first, but it didn't last. In the bathrooms, there were no locks on the stall doors, so kids kicked in the door every time I went in there. I had to go to the bathroom in the nurse's office.

In seventh grade I was suspended two times the first week of school so I had to be in the quiet room at all times. People asked me why I was always in there. I told them, Because of you. It lasted until Christmas vacation. After Christmas vacation, I went to a special school program. It was good for the rest of the year.

1999–2000 I'm in eighth grade now in the program and it's great. I hope my story will show how hard it is to have Tourette syndrome.

Nick Sletten, age 13

Tourette syndrome is a neurobiological disorder. Symptoms include impulsive behavior, embarrassing tics, anxiety, and phobias. Verbal tics can include swearing and other socially unacceptable language. Understanding on the part of others, medical treatment, and learning coping strategies can lessen the anxiety for the individual with Tourette syndrome.

I AM

I am the hated one,
Spreader of the disease,
Carrying the blame unjustly.
I am the dying innocent.
I am the ungodly thing
Preached against in church —
Preached against in politics.
I am the loathed,
I am the shunned,
I am feared,
I am gay.

I am dying innocent,
I am Goddess,
I am God.
I am an unborn child.
I am a dying mother.
I am the blood from your wound.
I am living with you,
I am dying because of you.

James Balzer, age 14

CARABAO DREAMS

how how the carabao said to me in a dream
            refute the conspiring evils
            prove the strength that wills your breath
            hold tightly to poetry and loved ones
            as a book would bind its pages
            share your story through art and song
            fix your eyes on the stars so your voice
                can be heard
                    "taas noo, iho, taas noo!"

you *are* more than
            what they say
            what they think
            what they see

pinoy *is* more than
            brown and alibata
            barongs and tinikling
            pansit and Goldilocks
                you will understand
queer *is* more than
            cocks and A.I.D.S.
            white men and the Castro
            June and pride marches
                you will understand

life *is* more than

       angst and depression

       money and aspiration

       wanting and loneliness

          you will understand

how how the carabao said to me

          tell the people your story

          don't think an amendment frees your

          speech

          if they cover their ears and refuse to listen

          yell if you have to

          you do not have a choice

          this is not a request

          you need to be heard

how how the carabao said to me

          rush out into the world in perfect

          surrender

          give in to the sun as she licks your face

          and thighs

          offer no words when the winds

          whip at your backside

          respect the moon

          yield up limber arms in reverence to

          the stars

          for darkness is also a gift

          and silence can be a friend

go out into the world and do these things
and you will understand

how how the carabao said to me
                    sadness is not the absence of happiness
                    but your incapacity to witness its presence
                    your soul is not just a bird taking up
                    wings
                    your soul is the sea
                    your spirit is the shore
                    your mind is the black expanse
                    that births planets and consumes galaxies
                    you are not only part of the revolution
                    but you are the revolution
                    when you stop building comfortable walls
                    and notice that your feet are planted
                    on the same ground on which millions
                        have stood
                        you will understand
                            you will understand
                    you will understand

you *are* more than pansit
                    A.I.D.S.
                    and depression

how how the carabao said to me in a dream
                    this is just a dream

these are just my words
breathe life into them
assign them feet
make them real
how how the carabao said to me

how

how

Timothy Arevalo, age 18

carabao — water buffalo

"taas noo, iho, taas noo!" — "Look up, son, look up!"

pinoy — a Filipino person

alibata — ancient Tagalog script

barong — traditional Filipino shirt

tinikling — traditional Filipino dance

pansit — rice noodles

JUST LIKE ME

Black describes me.
My moods, my personality.
Black is a color that everyone likes.
Black is subtle,
Not too flashy, not too boring.
Black is power, authority.
Black moves like air.
Close your eyes, it's everywhere.
Black is nonchalant.
Black's carefree.
Nothing phases this color.
Black's hard as steel.

Black is my best friend.
Because we're just alike,
Plain, basic, understated,
Unlike a red or orange or yellow.
We don't brighten up a room.
We bring a coolness
That can't be produced by another.

Stone-faced is our expression.
Relaxed is our mood,
Our state of mind.
We stand alone,
But we can mix
With all people, all colors.

Lawan Mitchell, age 16

OUT OF MY LIFE

I want my grandmother
to stop sending me to the store
with fifty dollars worth of bottles
not sold in Michigan.

I want my grandfather
to stop telling the same war stories
that begin at breakfast
and end after dinner.

I want the Kool-Aid
to stop disappearing in one hour.
I want the ice trays
to stay filled.

I want the only bathroom
in the house
to be free for me
when nature calls.

I want big Ms. Whitaker
to stop wearing that frizzy wig
and pink dress that barely covers
what only her husband needs to see.

I want this to be
the last stanza of this poem
so I can burn this worn down pencil
and inhale the ashes.

Corey Edge, age 17

SLEEP

I woke up pissed this morning.
No motivation to get out of bed.
So many negative thoughts in my head.
I try to shake it off like everything is okay,
but the empty feeling in my gut won't go away.
My mind is at rest while I lie in bed,
which is better than lying to my soul outside today.
I roll over and retreat back to the safety of my dreams,
which will sedate the memory of
unfinished homework and a test at lunch.
Now I don't have to deal with the pain of fake smiles,
empty eyes, and pointless conversation.
Society seems to think I can't sleep my way through life,
albeit I had no regrets today.

Kyle Blanchard, age 16

I HATE SCHOOL

Fuck this shit, up the ass, I don't think I'll ever pass. It's fucking crap. I don't believe. I think that I'll just fucking leave. The teachers suck, the food just blows, society has reached new lows. We sit and stare all fucking day. And though it's public, we still pay.

I hate this fucking bullshit. I don't want to take it.

It's fucking bunk. We're not prepared. The grown-up world makes me scared. Inspirational posters on the wall— why won't that kitty fucking fall? A fight-free campus is required, but child molesters are not fired. They want the school clean and drug free, but I know a teacher who does speed.

I hate this fucking bullshit. I don't want to take it.

The PE teachers are insane, their methods can't be called humane. Smoking bud across the street, but hey— our football can't be beat! The jocks, they run the fucking school, chew dip all day, act real cool. Everybody annoys me. Someone is gonna get beat.

Kenny Weiss, age 17

I NEVER TOLD THIS TO ANYONE

There is a secret that I have told to no one.
The burning house that stood blazing on the hill,
the house that was occupied by a kind old man,
burned to the ground in front of my eyes.
No words were *ever* spoken
and only I know the truth.
I never told even this much to anyone.

Maurice Beaman, age 16

I'LL BE HERE

Go find yourself a listening ear,
And let it know all that you fear.

If the ear you seek cannot be found,
Don't shove your feelings to the ground.

Don't give up and run away;
Try again another day.

If nothing works and no one's there,
I know someone who will care.

I'll always be here for you,
Should you need someone to talk to.

Come and talk, come and cry,
Don't stop until your eyes are dry.

Once it's out, you've nothing to fear,
As long as you know, I'll always be here.

David Ho, age 16

FACES

Faces pass by at 35 mph
staring at you, laughing at you
wanting you, intrigued by you
loving you, hating you
giving you a smile that says, "Good morning"
giving you a look that says, "Stop looking at me."

You look for someone you know
your brother, your grandma, your ex-girlfriend
the president, your barber, Neil Armstrong,
Jon Voight, Michael Jordan, or Leslie Nielsen
the guy you saw in a Subway eating a tuna foot-long
the girl who sold you peanuts at Wrigley Field
the lover you wish for after a hard day
the asshole who stole your bicycle when you were nine.

But you're lost, a stranger among strangers
no idea who you are or why you're here
just that you're alone, lost in this city of faces.

Dan Gallagher, age 16

_____

In this darkness, I stand still,
Alone and cold.
The night drags on.
The sleep of over one hundred years.
No one seems to care,
But the darkness it will bear
The loves of time gone by.

People stare and ask
What my weariness means,
But they will never know,
No one will ever know,
Because all they do is stare
And see that I am going nowhere,
But never try to come along.

Jared Ryan Jackson Lowry, age 17

You've asked about me. I am a 20-year-old native Houstonian. I was a happy child from divorced parents. My parents divorced when I was two, but they always got along very well. One of the strangest things about my mother and father is that they were second cousins. I'm not *challenged* or anything. In fact, the probability that there will be a deformity from the coupling of second cousins is the same as people not related at all, 1 in 23.

My mother is a great person. An ex-hippie born and raised here in Texas, she has seen and done many things. She hitchhiked to California in 1969 at age 18. She saw the Doors, Led Zeppelin, and the original Black Sabbath in concert, not together of course. She has raised me well and has influenced me in many ways.

My father was a great guy. He was raised in El Paso, Texas, along with his identical twin brother and three other brothers and sisters. Like my mother, he had some hippie tendencies. His first vehicle was a Volkswagen microbus that he and his twin brother bought for $450. My father was pretty cool and quiet. A little over two years ago, a massive coronary killed him at the age of forty-three.

I was grief-stricken. Since the divorce, I had never seen my dad on a daily basis, but it was hard to deal with his really being gone. Shortly after his death, I was awarded $62,000 in life insurance. That money was my downfall.

Always a fairly poor person financially, I was overwhelmed by the money. Instead of saving it, or investing it, I spent it—in one and a half years. I bought a 1981 Jeep and a 1972 Volkswagen bus. I got Heavy into drugs. Cocaine, pills of all kinds went into my system, but the worst was heroin. That monster cost me all of my money and the trust of many of my friends. Since then, I've been to rehab, I'm going to college, and I have a good job. Hopefully, I'm now on the right track.

Jared Ryan Jackson Lowry, age 20

Jared wrote this essay in the spring of 1996. In the fall of 1997, the "monster" took him.

CHANT

smoke
choke
riverside dope
greens
funk
pump in the trunk
girls, boys
beer & liquor
cigarettes
hotels
weeds & strippers
fat girls
little girls
girls with whiskers
fine girls
pretty girls
girls with cute sisters
pimps, ballers
players & G's
just another day
in the D

Tommie Spivey, age 18

BLACK BOY BLUES

baby black boy learns his a,b,c's
baby black boy learns his a,b,c's
A,B,C,R,A,C,K Recipes
Boiling water, baking soda
Burning broken wire hangers.

mama don't know granny is into plague retail
mama don't know granny is into plague retail
Watch baby black hands trace
deadly outlines of overdosed
souls quivering on the floor

Baby black boy eyes watch
dream smoke rise
from glass
pipes
Baby black boy eyes watch
dream smoke rise
from glass
pipes
Burning away bills, food, hungry baby mouths

baby boy black learns his 1,2,3's
baby boy black learns his 1,2,3's
1,2,3 ounces of Cocaine
to be made into

        rock
            crystallized
                worlds
to be made into
        rock
            crystallized
                worlds

sing the song of make believe baby boy black
sing the song of make believe baby boy black
as you watch the gun
being put to granny's head
and she
clicks
and she
clicks
and she
clicks

    make believe
you are unaware
make believe
you are not scared
make believe
you don't know the recipe
for
        horror

Shysuaune T. Taylor, age 19

THERE'S A HARLEM RENAISSANCE IN MY HEAD

The trombones slap me in the face with their high-life
beats, and the piano's glamorous tunes tap me on my
shoulder and whisper in my ear. As I look down into the
Juke-Joint from my bedroom floor, rotted house, rotted
life, plain rotten seems forgotten as the music plays and
the beats go down to the rhythm of my heart's pound.
There's a Harlem Renaissance in my head, there's a Harlem
Renaissance in my head.

Through the floor a light, where the music roared,
overtakes the darkness that surrounds me as I look through
this floorboard. I can see the hoppin' and a dancin' and the
suave men a prancin' around the young ladies who stand
stunning on the floor . . .

The music stops, the poet stands up, and with each
turn of the page, his mind's thoughts he will emancipate
and everybody in the room he will captivate. His pen his
only weapon with which injustice he must eradicate. As
I look down into the Juke-Joint from my bedroom floor,
rotted house, rotted life, plain rotten seems forgotten as
the music plays and the beats go down to the rhythm of
my thoughts' pound. There's a Harlem Renaissance in
my head.

Let your ink run rampant, Langston Hughes. Let your fingers tickle the ivories forever, Duke. At every moment history being made in my own personal Juke-Joint. I lean my ears to hear even closer and find my mind in a past tense, opening my eyes to see beauty, but surrounded by pure silence. There's a Harlem Renaissance in my head, a Harlem Renaissance in my head.

Maurice E. Duhon, Jr., age 17

WHAT I AM

(IN THE EYES OF MY FATHER)

I am nothing
in the eyes
of my father.

When I get
good grades
he doesn't say

anything, not
one good word.
When I didn't

get into a top
high school
he said I was

nothing, never
going to be
nothing. I am

beaten down
from heaven
by the shaft

of my father.
It feels like
a bullwhip

going across
my back
every time

he puts me,
beats me
down, down.

Dwight Beavers, age 17

ODE TO CARING

Careless child I am
wandering off into the night
I make my mother stir at small hours
she makes herself
words in books fused together
like so many lies to soothe her angst
lies of where I've been
when I'll return
my father wishes my integrity
he doesn't know I wish the same
who knows in what completeness I'll return
but the propaganda is posted
and the party rages
someday the dissension will end
until then she'll read the lies

Benjamin D. Martin, age 17

———————

Sometimes
But not always
Well hardly ever it seems
Something is truly fulfilling.
A shame.

Michael Tobias Bloom, age 16

DOES MY MOTHER LOOK LIKE THIS?

Is she light-skinned
or is she brown?

Does she smile
or does she frown?

Is my mother tall
or is she short?

Is she a quitter
or a good sport?

Does my mother look like
a person who would

leave four sons and a daughter
and go to another place?

What does she look like?
Can you picture her face?

Seth Chappell, age 14

48

WORDS ON HANDS

(FOR LESLIE REESE)

Her voice danced black rhythms
Sunday dresses, old school tunes;
Funky Nassau, Temptations
That doo-wop group
That always hung
Out on the corner of
51st Street. Singin'
till the liquor store closed
45 records, 8-track tapes skippin'
skippin' until you
put that piece of paper
between the 8-track
and the stereo in a just-right position.

Her actions were painters splashing
Little black girls in pastels
Blue, yellow, pink Easter
Dresses, with white stockings
forbidden to run.
She taught me how to
write the smell of Grandma's greens,
chittlins, turkey whose reign
was always religious brown.

She wrote auntie's apple pie
like the sun going down, down
down till moonlight
shone on Uncle Junebug's bottle
of Cognac.

She made my brain sweat.
       Work out your
words with actions she said.
Make the tears of a
broken child smear
your ink, make the
joy of a grandmother
be the fragrance
of your voice. Hear Mama
smacking her child
with words that taste
like morning pancakes.
My performing teacher

pulled a me
       out of me
who was a dancer
an artist, whose actions
spoke words.

Shysuaune T. Taylor, age 17

MY DAD AND ME

I was a little curious about why my divorced parents had taken me to lunch on a hot, August day, but halfway through the lunch I found out. My father wanted to tell me he was gay, and that his friend Dave was actually his lover.

I was shocked. All I could do was concentrate on eating. Although I acted polite and understanding at the restaurant, my thoughts were really somewhere else, and it wasn't until my mother and I were alone that night that I began to unload my feelings.

"How could he do this to me?" I asked over and over. Though my mother and my father divorced when I was just seven, this new reality felt like too big a burden. How could I go anywhere with my father and Dave? What if someone I knew saw us? I could just imagine how cruel they might be, "Hey, did you know Jaime's dad's a fag?"

Not only was I afraid somebody might see us, I was afraid that my dad and Dave might display affection toward each other in front of me. To a sixteen-year-old boy, this would be disgusting.

As time went on, I decided that the best thing to do was to remain silent. I would not tell a soul, no matter what. After almost a year, however, I had to get this secret off my chest. I told my best friend, and to my surprise he didn't have a problem with my secret at all.

His reaction changed me. Was it such a big deal? Did the fact that my dad was homosexual actually matter? The more I thought about it, the more I understood, and the happier I became for my dad. He had found someone he cared about and loved.

Through the two years it's taken me to reach this point, I have discovered a lot about personal relationships. At first, I was always worried about what people would think of me. I have come to realize that I don't care what ignorant people think. Why would I want to be friends with anyone who would judge me based on prejudice toward my father?

Telling me about his relationship must have been one of the hardest things my dad has done. He placed himself at a crossroads of rejection or acceptance; a risk he took that shows me how much he truly loves me.

Jaime Daryl Marconette, age 18

I REFUSE

When I see the word *father*, the first person that comes to mind is myself. I am the father of a six-month-old girl who can light up the room when she smiles. Don't all parents feel this way about their children, or is it just me? All fathers don't stay around their kids, though. It seems to take bravery or some miracle for them to stick it out and see to their kids' well being. To be a father is more than a responsibility; it is a job. Tradition says that a father is the provider, not an easy role to play when you're still in high school, working low income jobs. Still, I do it for the good of my daughter, my creation, my seed. I refuse to be a deadbeat dad because no excuse is a good enough excuse to abandon your own creation.

Steven Hill, age 18

———

What happened Papa
What happened
Was it something I said
did
became?

Joshua Bonds, age 17

ASCENSION

My creation
was the solidification
of cries into pride
the first generation unadorned
by thorns
but when I was born
I was torn from my mother's chest

and they took me, melted my spirit
and squeezed until i was drained
morphing my frame
into a hollow lyric

I tightrope walk on rugged course
trying to fill myself back up
an empty volcano ready to erupt
holding hollow heart as cup
in hands
panhandling
for my spirit

but it cost too much to be a clone
so i took my hollow heart trying to pay
for what i thought was home
but they caught me sellin' nickel bags
of funk

in culture free zones
where the kids are drones
and have bones
made of dollar bills

and i spoke on these ills
and the police beat me until
i was unconscious enough to be read
my rights

then 6 knights
began to shine a light in my face
causing my subconscious to grate
dichotomous thoughts

separating cross from crucifixion
understanding the refractions of
mother's prism
putting false benedictions
under inquisition
and making the ultimate decision
to heal subconscious incision
made by colonizers
when they conspired
to take identity and land from fore
fathers
and morph it into tabula rasa

and they tried to make me cop a plea
and live my life in dependence
but fuck the 5th amendment
because I am the 7th descendant
of Truth

and my thoughts were dead until hope
made my words living proof
so the knights prepared the noose
and the scalpel for my castration
but their definition of manhood was so
complacent
they had not a clue to the gift i had
given

or the one i received
and they couldn't see
that this tree
was hanging on to me
and i was finally one with my brethren

so now i sit in the womb of heaven
telling GOD my story
and she rubs my head gently
and says you are loved
and can never be empty

Biko Eisen-Martin, age 16

––––––––––

I don't
Know what it is
I'll know when it comes
But I'll never be waiting here
For death.

Chorus Bishop, age 15

THE BUS STOP

When I woke up this morning I walked to my bus stop. A boy and a girl I kind of knew were arguing on the people's porch I set on every morning. The girl was raising hell about going to the doctor. I guess she was mad because no one took her to the doctor. She had a little baby in her arms. She left her house and walked down the street with the baby. Then the boy walked after her. I guess he stole the baby out of her arms. He walked back up the street holding the baby.

The next thing I saw, the girl came back to her house and took her baby from the boy. The boy said, "I got something for you!" He punched the girl and she fell with the baby in her arms. A couple of times. I was standing on the stair. "Hold my baby!" she said to me. I grabbed the baby and she punched the boy back in his face. Then the girl's brother came down the stairs and grabbed them apart. I gave the baby back to the girl. Then it started up again. It was a mess! The boy dropped his beeper. I picked it up and gave it to him. He said, "Thanks!"

My bus came.

Fred Brown, age 14

PEOPLE GOT MORE

Where me and Earnest went today,
seems like people got more
than what we have.
Black people down here won't
go to school or get jobs.
Those people get more money
put in their community.
They want us to stay back and live in the ghetto.
But it's not up to me.
It's up to *us* to stay in school
and get jobs
and make K.C. worth something.

Fred Brown, age 14

K.C. — Kansas City

60

I WANT

To know
If there's a ghetto
In heaven.

Troy Williams, age 16

ENVY

May I ask you something?
Why are you following me?
Every time I turn around
You are there telling me
something to wish for:

> his blue Mercedes
> his caramel girlfriend
> his Bloomfield house
> his paycheck.

Leave me alone.

Kyle L. White, age 17

MY LIFE

I live my life
Like quiet mice
Sometimes I think I'm way too nice.

I have no friends
But that's gonna end
I wish my uncle wasn't in the pen.

I have two sisters
One I don't like
Sometimes she makes me want to smack her all night.

I have a car
It's nice and blue
I like driving it 'cause it's fun to do.

One day I will drive it
From home to school
Oh I have a car that's nice and blue.

I love my mother
Like a son should
I'll always be there for her any way I could.

I have a job
For that I thank my aunt and God
I work very hard to keep my little job.

This is my life
I hope you think it's nice
If you don't I'll still be all right.

DeQon L Abner, age 16

BUMMING THROUGH PITTSBURGH? MAYBE NOT.

Hey, where are you going?
Where will you be in five to ten years?
Is it college, career, or do you really care
with your dark baggy clothing
and whacked out hair,
your face, an unfinished puzzle.
The moon only shines for those who request it.

Because the moon only shines for those who request it,
your face is an unfinished puzzle
with your whacked out hair
and dark baggy clothing.
Do you really care? Is it college, career —
where will you be in five to ten years?
Hey, where are you going?

Antony E. W. Kirkland, age 18

NEIGHBORHOOD WATCH

My neighborhood's filled with people who burn tires to show off in front of other people with sweet cars. Stray dogs run the street, pit bulls and rottweilers barking in backyards. People stand on the street corner for no apparent reason. Kids play football with pop bottles. My neighbor Mr. Huffman comes home every day at six with his dog at the fence waiting for him. My pit bull Damien in the basement barks, thinking someone's in the backyard or in the house who's not supposed to be. My brother Andre tells him to shut up 'cause he's trying to go to sleep. My uncle Clarence is in the back finishing the dog house. Pit bulls come in every color in the backyards on my block. People I've never seen before gamble on the porch. My mother fusses at Damien for not shutting up. People race up and down the street for entertainment. Weed smokers and dope dealers. At night, gunshots, police sirens, fire sirens echo from blocks away. Ms. Carter, an elderly woman, is outside almost every day watering the grass. Watch out: she'll fuss at you if you step on her grass.

Troy Williams, age 16

THE BEST CHRISTMAS OF ONASIS RODRIGUEZ

My best Christmas was two years ago because someone my dad knew at work invited us to his apartment to celebrate. When my dad and I got to the apartment, we marveled that it was so pretty. All the decorations were nice because the guy my dad knew from work had put a lot of effort into them. There were candles, presents, lights, and lots of food. My dad and I sat on the sofa. We met some people at the party we didn't know, friends and relatives of our host. We all ate chicken sandwiches and drank sodas. I couldn't help staring at the tree. It was decorated with lights, ornaments, a star on top, and especially, presents underneath.

When it was time to open the presents, my dad and I didn't have any to open because nobody really knew us. You might think that I was sad. But here's the best part of all: a lady at the party went to her room and came back with a present and gave it to me. I didn't know her but she was nice to me.

But I prefer a Gameboy or Playstation for a gift rather than a shirt. My dad didn't care about himself. He was happy that I got a present. My dad felt as good as I did.

At twelve o'clock, it was time for my dad and me to go home and go to sleep. On Sunday, I wore the shirt.

Onasis Hafid Rodriguez, age 15

As I sat, awaiting my match with the man known as Tripod, I had my "wrestling epiphany." My match with Tripod exemplified what I felt was the central dilemma in wrestling and made me realize that wrestling was not the sport for me.

The match with Tripod was no ordinary match—it was greatly complicated by the absence of his left leg. This complication made the bout one of the most intensely confusing experiences of my life. If I won the match, I would have faced the ignominy of having beaten up a disabled person. If I lost the match, I would have suffered the humiliation of having been out-wrestled by a guy with one leg. Surely, there could not be much dignity in either outcome.

The match was highly unorthodox. Tripod had an unusual repertoire of moves that effectively compensated for his disability. While Tripod used his specially designed pinning combinations on me, I succeeded in doing little but look shocked and confused. Tripod's competence as a wrestler was my only consolation as I returned, easily beaten, to my heckling teammates.

My match with Tripod taught me that I was not nor would ever be a wrestler and resulted in a temporary general distaste for athletic competition. Although wrestling a one-legged guy is not a common experience, the same dilemma presents itself in every competition. In victory you humiliate another, and in defeat another humiliates you. Realizing that wrestling can be a losing proposition in both victory and defeat changed my life significantly.

The world of sports organizes competition into wins and losses. Through my match with Tripod, I realized that winning and losing are only two of many possibilities and that each competition has the potential for an infinite number of outcomes. In my match with Tripod, the public outcome was less important than the outcome of my internal struggle. I now coach a Hillview Middle School girls' basketball team. Our primary goals, taught to me by the players, are pride, respect, and good sportsmanship.

Michael Kinsey, age 17

FIRST LOVE

Trained to return to my hand
like a yo-yo with no strings,
you burn nets to cinders,
kiss the backboard.

At night on the floor
next to me,
you press against desire,
waiting for the even rotation
of my touch.

I hear your voice calling me.
I am only twelve but
I can still grasp
the motion, the smoothness
of your bare skin,

how you love the way
my fingertips slide
softly across your body.
I am hypnotized every time
we touch.

This is not love, but addiction.
You blaze past my opponents,
but I am on fire.

Stephan Johnson, age 17

FOUL

Hearing cries of "Foul! Foul!" on the basketball court
Playing hard, sweating
Feeling dizzy and high, as if on crack
Leaving the court, funk in my nose
My funky, ball-playin', leaving-pop-at-the-hoop butt
Being chased by dogs out of oblivion
Mom telling me not to sit on the furniture
'Cause I'm even more funky now

Hussian Fry, age 16

I LOVE TO HEAR

how women say
my name—

"Tito . . ."
"Tito . . ."

—saying it
over and over

as if they don't want
to let go.

Tito D. Tate, age 15

THE GIRL I LIKE

I saw this girl on my way
home. She is everything
I want in a girl. A girl who
makes me smile when she smiles,
a girl who speaks what she feels.
She makes my heart skip like
a street beat, happy.

Ronnie Ross, age 16

AMOR DE DOS CULTURAS

Cuando en dos culturas
hay amor, que es diferente,
en las dos culturas encuentras paz y amistad
y cuando te enamoras
no importa de que sangre es, si no la sangre
que hay dentro de tu corazón.

LOVE BETWEEN TWO CULTURES

Between two cultures you find
a love that is different,
Between two cultures you find peace and friendship,
and when you fall in love
it doesn't matter of what blood, just the blood
that is in your heart.

Juan C. Medina Arias, age 18

Sunlight bouncing from hair
light walk, bright countenance
jealousy is mine

DTB, age 17

—————

I watch you
Undress me with your eyes
Take off my shirt
Kiss my chest
You'll use me
so.
I can't stop you
Unzipping my pants
You don't know
I cringe every time you touch me.

Bryan Phillips, age 16

SATISFACTION OF AN ORANGE

Two boys sat on the edge of the lawn next to their classroom. The sun was high, making small shadows on the grass around them. Other students lounged not far off, in small groups of three or four. One of the boys took an orange from his backpack, tearing into its skin with his uncut fingernail.

"The most satisfying thing in life is an orange," he stated, gently pulling the skin away, splitting the fruit in half.

"No it's not," argued the other.

The first boy pushed a whole slice between his lips. "It's soft and juicy and sweet in your mouth," he said.

"It's not the most satisfying thing," repeated the other, watching his friend caress a slice with his tongue.

"What is then?" the friend asked, chewing, turning to look at the other boy.

"Pussy," he stated, glancing at his pack, then back up at his friend.

"How would you know?" exclaimed the first, tearing another slice, popping it into his mouth.

"I dunno," shrugged the second.

"When you finish an orange, you don't feel like you need another one."

"You don't after some good pussy, either; you just feel good, and relaxed."

"At first, but eventually you need it again. And an orange doesn't have that tension while you're eating it," the first said, chewing two slices at once. "Want some?" he offered a piece to the other boy.

"Sure," said the second, taking the large chunk. He bit into it, carefully pulling the half in his hand away from his mouth. The two ate in silence for a moment. Chatter could be heard from across the field.

Swallowing, the second said, "Oranges squirt all over your clothes, if you're not careful."

"No comment."

Each took another bite. "Oranges don't play with your mind," said the first.

"Yeah. I dunno." The second shrugged his shoulders again. "Can I have another piece?"

Benjamin D. Martin, age 18

ME AND WOMAN KIND

How unfair,
you with your unpronounced,
unrecognized power.
Smooth sexy hips are your Gestapo,
erotic eyes your surveillance cameras.
The words you speak are more powerful,
more controlling than Big Brother.
Caught in the tangle of your hair,
I convince myself
I AM disloyal, I AM independent,
I control my freedom.
You, teenage queen, don't
own what I think,
nor lease my opinions.
But,
like a faithful pup,
I bound back,
sniffing for love,
competing for attention, distraction,
meaning.

Samuel Fox, age 17

———

a kiss

on

the

back of

the

neck

lying

next to

her

he

has felt her

breath

on his

neck; the soft

hairs

bristling

she stands and he lunges

to   grab   her

hand but

she

is

gone like every

thing else

and he
sits on
his bed
alone

Scott Baker, age 17

"So what's up between us? I don't want to call you my girlfriend. I don't want to call you anything. I don't want to mix you up with any fixed idea, with something that ought to be true. What am I scared of? I'm scared of being loved. Letting somebody love me, letting my guard down, showing you everything. I just want you to be there. Okay, so that's what I want. I'll see you again, right?"

Thomas Andrade, age 18

"JULIA"

What did we have?
      We had some pretty good times.
      and some great conversations
      about politics and the meaning of life
      and
      GOD
      (in all capital letters)
      although we never once discussed
      emotions.
      (But lord could you make me laugh.
      Like a downpour.)

And I ended it all
      Because of a cheap two-bit
      SLUT
      (In all capital letters)
      who liked to make me feel overly important
      and hated your guts
      for some reason
      until she won.

I miss you.

Todd VanDerWerff, age 18

"DANA"

Whatever love I have for you
is so rational that
I want there to be a car chase
or a wacky misunderstanding
or *some*thing
like where you turn out to be
     my long lost cousin
because the fact that everything
is going so gosh-darned flippin' expletive-deleted perfectly
just drives me *crazy*.
We seem dictated by the sitcom gods.

And yet there is a passion
in the way you grab my arm
or the way you wave good-bye to me as you drift away
that makes me want to wait around
to see what's there.

Todd VanDerWerff, age 18

84

OF EARTHWORMS AND YOU

sun's misplaced in the universe
galaxies fade
and planets disperse
every day is dark and drab
find my pleasure in
science lab
gone from the hope of your embrace
i stop and find
myself emasculate
dissect an earthworm
with a knife
and strike a point for
animal rights
saggy ascus and liverworts
i'd buy you back
but i'm afraid
iwishiwere
Omniscient
(don't ask me what it means)
sweatsocks and urine overpower me
as i walk into the rancid heat
you fell for gelboy and his hair
davy crockett shot a bear
i loved you and you loved me
gymnosperms grow inch by inch

(i suppose you wanted atticus finch
after all, gregory pecks a
hottie i guess)
disjointed ramblings
from a twisted brain
are all i have to hide the pain.
in a perfect world
x always equals three
if memphis is in tennessee
overwhelm me with self-pity
as mormons move to salt lake city
(i was never very good at history
but i'm worse without you)
give gelboy all my best
as for me I remain
Obsessed.

Todd VanDerWerff, age 16

―――――

Sort of a fly
On a pair of jeans
Without a zipper.
That's you.
Sort of a slit
In a wrist that's
Been roughly gashed.
That's you.
Sort of two lips
Without a mouth
To hold cigarettes
And talk.
That's you, in a way.

Ward Hoelscher, age 17

An easy clean-up
on the cold linoleum floor
after igniting my spark
on the bathroom's cool squares.
All it takes
is a Kleenex
to roll away my passion
and headstrong lust.
I feel empty.
Have I betrayed
God or
just myself?

Todd VanDerWerff, age 17

GUTS

With her he had some classes
And saw her every day.
His eyes always seemed to wander
Towards her general way.
Quite the crush had developed;
Within love he was enveloped.
He could have asked her right away,
But didn't have the guts.

If she peered a little left
And tilted her head correctly,
She could face the teacher, yet
Still watch him indirectly.
He was ever a distraction;
She couldn't even do subtraction.
All but three words she could say;
She didn't have the guts.

Just a single moment needed,
Yet many a moment passed.
While unrequited love grew deeper,
Quickly the years elapsed.

They thought their fears to be a crime
And made me write this sappy rhyme,
To warn you all this very day:
You'd better have the guts.

Kevin N. Gabayan, age 17

MAIL

Tomorrow I'm going to
seal up my heart
and send it to
my one true love.
When she receives it,
I hope she will sign for it
and send me hers.

Emmanuel E. Carter, age 14

FLOATING

—FOR ADRIEN

White blossoms at our feet
we walked a small even trail of sunlight
our jackets shielding us from the wind
our hands tightly gripping our book bags.
Every day this trail led us through our mysterious city
the sound of cars zooming by, horns pounding,
the distant chatter of grade school children,
a symphony in the city.
The weather here was never cold—
her smile is what kept me warm,
though the sun remained lost in the sky
leaking orange light.
A shower kept us pure,
infants in the breath of innocence.
We always talked on our walk home from school,
our thoughts sailing on an ocean of clouds and stars.
In twenty years, she would be a nurse and I a doctor, or
in her version, she would be the president
and I the first man.

We floated our dreams on clouds
until she moved away—
the photograph torn in half.
Now I walk this cold trail alone,
pacing the concrete
without her light to keep me warm.

Stephan Johnson, age 18

———

I need to do something,
Write a letter,
Let it go somehow.
My heart attaches
To things, people.
When there is collision,
I lose myself in it,
In confusion.
Why not have two hearts?
I don't understand love,
But I know it exists.

Thomas Andrade, age 17

SONG FOR MY FATHER

Death is a sad song that embraces even children.
If I could have known my father, my heart would mourn.
I can only wish to talk to the sky and imagine
hearing his voice.
He left me his name but no name at all.
I would use my only father as a raft to float
through these rivers.
At night I say "I love you" and hear no response.
The song of his silence is thrown down from pulsating stars
telling me to go on.

Stephan Johnson, age 17

The entire course of my life was determined for me one muggy summer day in 1980 before I was even born. Everything I have in my life, I have because of a woman I have never met.

In twenty days, I will be able to find her.

The feeling is odd. I have anticipated this moment since the time my mother sat me down and told me about how I came to South Dakota because "there were some people who weren't able to take care of a baby, so they decided to give it to someone else."

I imagine the moment it all happened. The woman peers down at the tiny bundle softly sleeping, and leans in to kiss the child's forehead, knowing she'll never see him again. A nurse takes the baby away and the young woman in Michigan lies weeping in her hospital bed, preparing for the awful and inevitable task of getting on with her life.

Seven hundred miles away, in a hog-shed in southeastern South Dakota, a woman in overalls receives a phone call from an office in Michigan, informing her that "we have a late Christmas surprise for you and your husband." She leans on the wall, crying tears of joy and praising God, then rushes off to find her husband. The calls go out to every corner of the nation. Uncles in Ohio and aunts in North Carolina, great-aunts in California and grandparents in Huron and Armour. Grandma dives into her yarn pile to begin crocheting baby jumpers and socks and blankets and afghans.

And so, I came into the world. My mom has all the newspaper clippings. I was mentioned in the church news and in a few thank-you ads. The baby cards fill an entire hundred-page scrapbook. It seemed everyone was happy.

But I wonder about the young woman from Michigan. I wonder where she is and if she thinks about me anymore. If she wonders whether or not she made the right decision. There's a ring of fatalism to my life. What ifs plague me like phantom hounds. What if she had decided to keep me? What if she had chosen adoptive parents who lived in Florida instead of here? What if she had had an abortion? But something stopped her from getting one. And for that, I thank her a million times over, though my echoes of gratitude fly out into emptiness.

She was courageous, thoughtful, and compassionate in a way that few people are today. It is impossible for me to hate her, no matter HOW hard I try. I love her in spite of myself. She loved me. I know it. I have the files that tell her story and how she wept when she gave me up.

And how can I hate someone who sent me here? For all of my complaining, I have found everything someone could ever want out of life in this town. In my scant seventeen years on Earth, I have found loving family, caring friends, success, and the kinds of people I will be loath to leave when I go off to college. I've confronted death, hope, faith, God, my own future, and love on the streets and windswept prairies of this town and I thank her for that.

But the time draws near that I will be able to seek her out. And I am afraid. What if she doesn't want to see me? What if she doesn't live up to my expectations? What if she has died? I don't know if I'm ready for any of that. And when people say to me, well-meaningly, naturally, "Todd, are you going to find your birth parents?" I am forced to say, "I don't know." They are always shocked at my response, but they don't understand what it's like to be haunted by the ghost of a woman out of my past that I have never met or spoken to. When the day comes that I am ready to seek her out, I will know. And that day will come eventually. Her voice still calls to me loud and clear through the mists.

And somewhere in Michigan, a thirty-something woman washes the dishes, grades some papers, and fixes a little supper for her kids. She always gets a little restless in November and nobody really knows why. Maybe it's the onset of winter or maybe it's the leaves falling off of all the trees, but only her closest friends and family will ever know that it's really something else entirely. For she is haunted by her past. And the baby she loved too much to keep . . .

Todd VanDerWerff, age 17

TIME LOST FOREVER?

On Mondays, he'd try to help me out on homework.
But I'm so independent, I'd get mad.
He'd clean my room for me on days he was off from work
and I'd get angry 'cause my things were misplaced.
He'd joke around with me on days I didn't want
to be bothered. Now we are separated,
my homework is all wrong, and my room is a mess.
If I could go back, I'd listen and laugh, but I can't.
When I go over to his house, he won't help
with my homework. He doesn't laugh with me at my jokes.
Yesterday, though, he chuckled at something I said.
That was the first time in a long time. Perhaps it was
the re-beginning of something spectacular.

John H. Taylor, age 17

DEAR GOD

I want to live my life
through peace and knowledge.
I want to grow up
without fear.
I want to be like
my mother and father.
I want to have my
brothers and sisters care for me.
I want to be a good person
to everyone.
I want to be a good person
to myself.
I want to wake up
to clean, fresh air
blowing in my face.
I want to sit in front
of my fireplace
just waiting
to see
what's going to happen.

John Merrell, age 14

A POEM FOR US

What god was it that plucked us
from heaven's branches
sewed us into our mothers' wombs
to sprout
to blossom
to be beautiful for us?

What god was it that slid us onto this planet
as slick as we are
with lightning for tongues
and gave us the task of poets?

I don't concern myself with things too much to think of
it's all irrelevant now, because

we are nothing less than great
but that's too much to believe, isn't it?

always trying to ease out of these bodies
I too know despondency
like I know the rolling, shifting
uneasy feeling of my spirit

I know discontent, as much
as my eyes know to retreat,
peeling back from the sight of my reflection

we are nothing less than great
but this truth we dread, waving blazing fists in its face
clenching doubt in our tender palms
because we are too afraid to love ourselves

how have we managed to travel so little
yet hate ourselves so much
Ginsberg said he saw the best minds of his generation
destroyed
I have seen the same

I have seen us in our rooms
foils and lighters in our hands
straw in our lips and our noses
chasing black dragons and snorting white cobras
because 10 dollars was cheap
for a double hit of joy

I have seen us hunched over toilet bowls
vomiting self-esteem down the drain
because *Vogue* and *Elle* always
dressed beauty in a size 3 and that
was only a heave-ho and upchuck away

I have seen us on the corner
complacent and numb
copping doom in dime bags
because we didn't know that
the grim reaper wore Filas and a hoodie

I have seen us swigging
golden poison because we
were fooled and made to believe that manhood
could be sold in 40-ounce bottles

I have seen us spread our legs like the horizon
because some man tricked us into believing
that love could only be found on our backs

I have seen
us
I have seen
us

and I am not a coward anymore
I see us for what we are
nothing less than great, because
we are the poets

the derelict cats who prance on fine lines of chance
the sky rips open for us, luck lands on our laps
we confuse the wind, dismiss it

and send it off to all directions
we tap-dance on the shoulders of waves
and give height to the tides
we walk and talk mountains
breathe hurricanes, hum earthquakes
and our kisses are wet haikus glistening on crimson pages

we are nothing less than great
more than divine
but great and divine are still just words
words still have walls
walls are nothing but limits
but we are limitless beyond articulation

the world is waiting, holding its breath, waiting for us
the poems are waiting, holding their breath, waiting for us
they are waiting for us
to speak our thunder
to claim the mountaintops
to siphon the sun into our pens
and illuminate the page

just take my hand
time is flying away on precious gilded wings
we cannot be cowards anymore
the stakes are too high
the poems are too many

just take my hand
there's a universe for us to write about
and stars for us to conquer
let's start right here on this mountaintop
where we are gods and goddesses
who do not know the meaning of defeat
take my hand if you want
and let's write these poems together

Timothy Arevalo, age 19

––––––––

The elements are at their peak.
Clouds raging, rain falling.
It's the kind of day that makes you think . . .

What does age bring, wisdom or confidence?
Will I ever know what I need to know?
Is there such a thing as an adult?
When I get there, if I get there . . . I won't forget.

Kyle Blanchard, age 16

A feeling,

    not necessarily of "I can."

    not even that "things will change."

    but undeniable courage

    to see the future through.

dr, age 18

THE KABUKI HANDBOOK

from

The Japan Foundation

THE KABUKI HANDBOOK

A Guide to Understanding and Appreciation,

with Summaries of Favourite Plays,

Explanatory Notes, and

Illustrations

by

AUBREY S. HALFORD

and

GIOVANNA M. HALFORD

CHARLES E. TUTTLE COMPANY
Rutland, Vermont   *Tokyo, Japan*

Representatives

For Continental Europe:
BOXERBOOKS, INC., Zurich

For the British Isles:
PRENTICE-HALL INTERNATIONAL, INC., London

For Australasia:
BOOK WISE (AUSTRALIA) PTY. LTD.
104-108 Sussex Street, Sydney 2000

Published by the Charles E. Tuttle Company, Inc.
of Rutland, Vermont & Tokyo, Japan
with editorial offices at
Suido 1-chome, 2-6, Bunkyo-ku, Tokyo

Library of Congress Catalog
Card No. 55-10618

International Standard Book No. 0-8048-0332-3

First printing, 1956
Fourteenth printing, 1986

Printed in Japan

This book is
gratefully and affectionately
dedicated to

ICHIKAWA EBIZO IX
and
ONOE BAIKO VII

whose acting first lifted us
above the conventions of
the Japanese stage

CONTENTS

CONTENTS

ILLUSTRATIONS

x

FOREWORD

by Faubion Bowers

People usually make two general remarks about Kabuki. One remark — made by Westerners — is that the story really doesn't matter because Kabuki is a spectacle. The other remark — this is what Japanese like to tell you — is that the stories are nonsense. Without setting myself either in judgment on or apart from such large numbers of people, I do feel a fundamental disagreement with both views, even though I know that each has some substantial truth in it.

Kabuki is essentially theatre and, no matter how glamorous or dazzling it may be to look at, or how synthesized with music, dancing, decor, and effects, it is primarily and basically the telling of a story. Whatever poetic or scenic flights Kabuki may indulge in, everything depends on the narrative. And too, regardless of the conventions which set Kabuki so strikingly apart from Western theatre, it is still, like all other theatre, the enactment of a plot and the unfolding of a series of affecting situations. These stories which underlie Kabuki, while being nonsense in a way (the Japanese say *nonsensu*, really meaning "illogical," "inconsistent"), still have meaning, emotion, and, often, historical fact behind them.

What I am trying to say in this discursive, roundabout way is that Vanna and Aubrey Halford's book of summaries tells us the stories of the one hundred odd best and greatest Kabuki plays and dances. This is extremely important. However much the spectator may delight in the exotic, or the connoisseur may quiver in the subtleties of polished, fragmentary details, the play's *story* is what everything is all about, and without understanding it no appreciation can go very far. This book makes it possible for the spectator to take that first step. This applies, oddly enough, not only to foreigners but to Japanese as well: Kabuki is now so old and today's audiences so young and new and modern that even the Japanese have trouble following the intricacies of the plot; nor does the archaic language help them either. Because of this book we can begin to understand what we are seeing, and on this foundation genuine delight and familiarity begin.

The complexity and incomprehensibility of many Kabuki plots are famous, and the little, abbreviated English-language program notes which are shyly sold around a pillar behind a counter of the Kabuki-Za are notorious at compounding confusion. As is only too well known, those program notes reduce the most thrilling story to a shambles of obfuscating, misleading, and disconnected information. Perhaps the best sample line, and one which well illustrates my point, is this: "Although she was lady in red lights she had heart of virgin which is courtesan's pride."

For some reason there has never been a book of summaries before. The need for one has been growing steadily wider as the outside world has become increasingly aware of this great theatre form. After reading this book with its lucid synopses and its crystal-clear explanations and interpretations of even the most difficult passages, I wonder how Kabuki got along before this book appeared. I cannot help thinking of all the many disappointed potential fans who have left Kabuki unconverted and puzzled — all because nothing guided them to the story they were seeing portrayed. And I cannot help remembering, too, all the times I have hurriedly explained in a taxi en route to the Kabuki theatre the plot, the story, the background, and all the other essentials. And then, after reaching the theatre, how many times have I distracted the entire area around me by whispering the rest of the story, which I didn't have time to get through during the taxi drive. Now, at last, these difficulties are at an end.

A copy of this book, earmarked the night before with the plays to be seen the next day, will tell the prospective spectator everything he needs to know to have a full, knowledgeable, intelligent, and sympathetic understanding of Kabuki.

The Halfords' book is an achievement. They, unlike the majority of foreigners, who are content simply to enjoy Kabuki for themselves, assiduously set about writing down the story and plot-action of every play they saw (they went to Kabuki at least twice every month, all day long, for almost two years — a formidable feat in itself!) and passed it along to any friends who asked for Kabuki help. Coupled with this, they added their own erudition and acquaintance with the theatre of the West. Most of all, practically speaking, they have turned the tangled web of Japanese history, convention, and thought patterns, which characterize Japanese theatre, into comprehensible form. For the first time ever, any Westerner who reads English can obtain a real insight into the plots and stories, the texts and characteristics of Kabuki dramas, and in terms which a Western-trained mind can readily understand. For this the entire Kabuki world must be grateful.

AUTHORS' PREFACE

It is said that every foreigner who goes to Japan wants to write a book about it. This is the book we wanted to write; not a history of Kabuki nor an aesthetic appreciation, but a playgoers' manual, a guide. It is a collection of synopses of the more commonly performed plays together with notes explaining many of the conventions and customs, some theatrical, some simply Japanese, which the foreigner finds confusing and often incomprehensible. In the synopses we have tried to tell the facts of what happens on the stage, where the characters " have their exits and their entrances," and, whenever possible, how they can be identified. It is the sort of book we ourselves should like to have had when we were first taken to see a Kabuki play.

The plays are arranged in the alphabetical order of their formal Japanese titles. Since these long titles are cumbersome to use, shorter ones, such as the name of the principal character, are often substituted. We have listed these alternative titles in the index together with the titles given to individual acts which are performed in isolation. Both are cross-referenced to the main title, and in the latter case the number of the act is given also. The notes are also arranged in alphabetical order, and Japanese terms will be found in the index with the appropriate cross references.

The Kabuki theatre divides its plays into various groups, and in this book the group to which each item belongs is given after the title. *Juhachiban* covers the exotic spectacles of virtuosity associated with the Ichikawa dynasty of actors, scenes concerning gods and superman. *Jidaimono* are the so-called classical plays of the seventeenth and eighteenth centuries, dramas of knightly valour and devotion. *Sewamono* or *kizewamono* are plays about the loves and sorrows of ordinary people, the people who largely composed, and still compose, the audience. *Shosagoto* are dances.

Most visitors to Japan are expected to " see Kabuki" on the grounds that it is " unique" and " exotic." All too often their friends think that it is sufficient for them to drop in for half an hour, rather as if it were a night club or a dress show. The Japanese themselves have adopted this point of view where foreigners are concerned. We have seen tourists dragged unwillingly from the theatre by their Japanese guides, who considered that they had been there long enough to enjoy the " show" but could not believe they might be interested in the drama. Kabuki is theatre, not a raree show. True, the " quaint" plays, the plays full of posturing and declamation, decked with fantastic costumes and make-up, are curious and picturesque ; but they are not all there is to Kabuki ; they are only a small part of the repertoire. To judge Kabuki by them alone is to place it on a level with devil dancing and other primitive spectacles. Yet it is these numbers which are almost always chosen for the entertainment of foreigners, largely because it is believed to be what they expect of an Eastern theatre. Kabuki plays are both dramatic and moving ; the characters are just as human as those of the Western stage, although not always actuated by the same motives. In particular the plays about " common people" give a fascinating insight in the life and emotions of pre-Meiji Japan. Newcomers to Kabuki find these plays easy to understand and nearly always enjoy them more than the spectacular ones. Yet these are the plays they are hardly ever allowed to see.

One feature which is hardly ever explained to a stranger is the composition of a Kabuki programme. He is told that the performance lasts from four to five hours and that he cannot possibly sit through the whole of it. He not unnaturally assumes that it is all one long play. He arrives in the middle of an act and has just reached the conclusion that the man in gold brocade with a blue face must be someone of importance, perhaps the hero, when the curtain is drawn. The next act brings on a set of characters in sad-coloured costumes and no one has a blue face at all. Instead of stamping about and making grimaces, they sit down and talk. He tries to read the English programme notes (if any are available), but has no idea where to start. He generally gives up in despair. What he does not know is that a Kabuki programme usually consists of a number of unrelated items: one or two acts from a highly conventionalized classical play; a dance or comic interlude; a " common people's play " in several scenes, acted straight; and possibly a short burlesque to finish. Translated into Western terms this would represent, say, the two best acts of *Hamlet*, the first part of *Swan Lake*, a condensed version of either *She Stoops to Conquer* or *Sweeney Todd, the Demon Barber*, and a harlequinade.

No one expects a newcomer to Kabuki to endure a five-hour performance, although a surprising number of foreigners learn to do so and indeed become such addicts that they will stay in the theatre from ten in the morning till ten at night. The programmes at the Kabuki theatres are published daily in the English-language press. We hope this book will enable prospective playgoers to look up the various plays and decide which they want to see. Any Japanese servant or hotel porter will ring up the theatre for them and ask at what time these plays are performed, so that the playgoer can see his choice as it should be seen, from the beginning, and enjoy an intelligible drama, not a bewildering curiosity.

Here also we hope our notes will be of service. We ourselves often puzzled over some stage property or piece of behaviour which we could not understand. For instance, we spent months trying to find out what was inside the odd-shaped lacquer case which figures in *Ichijo Okura Monogatari*.

It turned out to be a sword. We wondered why some men shaved their crowns and some did not; why people carried about severed heads in wooden hatboxes; why the loss of a sword, or, even more oddly, the loss of a tea-caddy, involved the loser in such dire penalties. The notes embody the answers to our questions. We hope they will save others from dwelling so much on some minor, but incomprehensible, point that the thread of the drama is lost.

In the notes will be found many of the Japanese technical expressions used in Kabuki together with explanations. We have deliberately omitted them from the text and have tried to make the synopses as readable as possible, although, when dealing with a theatre which uses the same situation again and again with only minor changes, it is hard to avoid being dull. Certain Japanese words we have been obliged to use since no English synonyms exist. Kimono and obi, samurai and geisha, are familiar to all, but *sake*, which is wine made from fermented rice, may be less so. *Hanamichi* is the technical term for the raised runway which goes from the back of the auditorium to the stage and, since such a feature does not exist in Western theatres, we have kept the original name. *Seppuku* is the expression used by the Japanese for what the West knows as *harakiri*, suicide by disembowelment; the latter word is considered vulgar.

We are very conscious that our transliteration of the Japanese will not satisfy the scholar. But apart from an inbred antipathy for diacritical marks, we intend this book, not for the scholar, but for the playgoer.

Not every play and dance of the Kabuki repertoire will be found in these pages, for they run into many hundreds. We have tried to choose those which form the backbone of Kabuki so that the reader will find included here two or three items, perhaps more, from any month's programme. The playgoer will notice that many of the plays are rarely, if ever, performed in their entirety. Isolated acts are put on; indeed, since in former days a single new play had to fill a whole day's bill and cater for all tastes, the acts frequently have very little in common, each being a self-contained drama. A play such as *Yoshitsune Sembonzakura* is really three different plays about three different sets of people. Thus it is that the hundred plays of our collection could be subdivided into twice that many individual programme items.

We have not attempted to make synopses of the plays by modern writers which are performed periodically as part of the Kabuki programme. These are mostly on historical themes and aim at a greater fidelity to fact than the classical plays; they are also a great deal duller. Many of these "new Kabuki" plays are never repeated. Fresh ones are constantly being written and space does not permit the inclusion of such ephemeral matter.

A word of warning. The playgoer may find that what he sees on the stage differs in minor details from our account of it. Kabuki plays are cut to suit the time limit and the number of star actors available, but the cuts do not worry the audience, which knows what has been omitted. Sometimes a modern adaptation of an old play is presented. In several cases a play has a number of alternative endings. There are also, in certain plays, bits of "business" which are the copyright of various acting families. Those who are familiar with the puppet plays of Chikamatsu, of which a number have been translated, will notice that the versions given here often differ considerable from the originals. This is because we have kept strictly to the Kabuki adapatations. We have based our synopses primarily on first-hand observation, but we have also consulted the standard texts and, where possible, compared these with the acting texts in the theatres. We are, nevertheless, only too conscious that there are bound to be discrepancies.

The cuts and alterations in the text may seem startling, but it should be remembered that the Kabuki is theatre, not literature. It is first and foremost an actor's theatre, and the text is of secondary importance. The Japanese audience, which knows the old plays by heart, goes to the theatre to see how an actor will interpret a famous rôle. This does not mean what we in the West call a "new production" with fresh costumes and innovations. In the traditional Kabuki repertoire the costumes and make-up of each character, even his gestures and the places where he must sit or stand, are crystalized. It may sound as if acting in Japan is mere stylized posturing, but this is not so. What the audience appreciates is the way in which a great actor, without altering by a hair's breadth the traditional performance handed down to him by his fathers, can yet inject into the character his own interpretation. It can be done. We have seen the same rôle played by three different men, each using the same stylized inflections of the voice and the same movements, down to the placing of a finger. But the personality presented differed in each case, each presentation being perfectly convincing. The secret of such performances is that the actors are familiar with the rôle from childhood. They have watched their fathers and grandfathers play it and no effort of memory is required for them to go through the ritual. They cannot remember learning the part; they absorbed it through their pores. They are therefore able to concentrate on the emotional interpretation. We once asked Ichikawa Ebizo what he throught about when he was acting the rôle of Moritsuna, the hero of one of the most stylized plays of Kabuki. The action concerns the conflict between two brothers and he answered, not "I think of my part," but very simply "I think of my brother."

It may be possible to appreciate the quality of Japanese acting without knowing what the play is about, but it is difficult. This is why we have written this book. We hope that the playgoer, already familiar with the main features of the plot, will be able to concentrate on the performance and appreciate the amazing virtuosity of this breed of actors who can perform in one day two gruelling emotional parts, each requiring a different idiom of acting, but with equal sincerity; and then also perform the principal rôle in a ballet and, perhaps, a comic turn thrown in for good measure. The Kabuki actor is a dedicated being and the Kabuki stage does more than hold its own with any other in the world. If this book in any way helps to put appreciation of this theatre into its proper perspective, we shall be content.

Our thanks are due to so many friends that it is difficult to know whom to single out for particular mention. But thanks must go first to Faubion Bowers for his foreword, his suggestions, and his friendship; to Professors Kawatake Shigetoshi and Miyake Shutaro for their encouragement and advice; and to Miss Kazuko Akaike for her help with the translations. Above all, however, we should like to pay tribute to those to whom we feel we owe the most — the actors, great and small, of the Nakamura Kichiemon, the Onoe Kikugoro IV, the Ichikawa Ennosuke, and the Kansai troupes.

Tokyo, January 1954 —
Tripoli, June 1956

SUMMARIES OF PLAYS

*An actor greeting his
audience upon receiving a new name*

An actor greeting his
audience upon receiving a new name

AMIMOYO TORO NO KIKUKIRI, or *Amimoyo Kiku Edozome;* commonly called *Kozaru Shichinosuke. Sewamono.* — Written by Kawatake Mokuami and first performed in July 1857. This play was put on on two subsequent occasions but never proved much of a success. It reappeared in 1921, slightly adapted and renamed *Amimoyo Kiku Edozome.* It is now regularly given in its original form and seems likely to remain permanently in the playbill. It is a melodrama about the adventures of that most popular of *sewamono* heroes, the "attractive scoundrel," found in so many of Mokuami's plays.

Act I

Sc. 1. *A room in the Shimazakiya, a brothel in Shinagawa, Edo.* A group of young men and girls are playing *ken.* The center of the group is **Yoshiro,** a *sake* merchant. Other guests arrive, bringing *sake,* and the party begins to get lively. When the courtesan **O Sugi** appears, however, a chill falls on the company. Yoshiro, who is hopelessly in love with O Sugi, says that he must be off. Drawing O Sugi aside, he learns from her that her debts have become so heavy as a result of her mother's illness that she has seriously been thinking of committing suicide. The only thing which prevents her is the thought that her death would aggravate her mother's condition. Softened by this tale, Yoshiro offers her twenty or thirty *ryo.* He will bring her the money shortly, and meanwhile gives her three *ryo* out of the seventy he has on him to pay his wholesaler. **Amiuchi Shichigoro,** a reprobate old gambler, overhears this conversation and when Yoshiro leaves sets out to tail him. **Kichizo,** O Sugi's accepted lover, arrives and receives the three *ryo* from his mistress. She gleefully tells him how easily she has deceived Yoshiro and promises him a further supply.

Sc. 2. *The ferry-boat terminal near the Eitai Bridge.* The ferry arrives from the Shinagawa side. Yoshiro and Shichigoro are among the passengers. Yoshiro realizes as he steps ashore that the packet of seventy *ryo* is no longer on his person. He accosts Shichigoro, who was sitting near him on the ferry. Shichigoro, who has stolen the money and hidden it in his hat, strips himself with an air of injured innocence and allows Yoshiro to search the bundles he is carrying. Finding nothing, Yoshiro apologizes, but Shichigoro turns nasty, kicks him down and beats him with his staff. In the scuffle the money drops out of the hat, and Yoshiro scrambles for it. Shichigoro strikes him senseless, but not before Yoshiro has torn off a sleeve of Shichigoro's kimono. The thief escapes with the money.

Act II

Sc. 1. *The Yahagi Bridge near the park of Okazaki Castle.* (This scene is not often performed, as it has little or nothing to do with the story. It was written to provide the variety required in a Kabuki programme of several hours. It depicts a meeting between Mashiba, later Toyotomi, Hideyoshi, who from humble beginnings rose to rule Japan, and the "field samurai," i. e., bandit, Hachisuka Koroku. But it also serves to explain something of the character of Shichinosuke, the hero of the present play, who has not yet been introduced to the audience.)

Mashiba Hideyoshi, then a beggar boy, is seen sleeping on a straw mat at the foot of the bridge. **Hachisuka Koroku,** accompanied by his gang, crosses the bridge at midnight, and in the dark Koroku treads on Hideyoshi's foot. The young hero leaps up and upbraids Koroku fearlessly. The bandit angrily asks who it is that dares to bar his passage and orders the boy to stand aside. Hideyoshi seizes the shaft of Koroku's spear and tells him that he shall not cross the bridge if he cannot keep a civil tongue in his head. Impressed by the boy's spirit and silencing his grumbling followers, Koroku falls into conversation with Hideyoshi. From him he acquires useful information about the magistrate of Okazaki, against whom he is carrying on a vendetta. In the end Hideyoshi joins the band. As every Japanese schoolboy knows, Koroku later became one of Hideyoshi's chief followers and in due course was made lord of many fiefs.

Sc. 2. *The Eitai Bridge across the Sumida at Edo.* (Except for the different sign post, this looks much the same as the Yahagi Bridge in the previous scene.) A man lies sleeping on a straw mat at the foot of the bridge. He is **Shichinosuke,** nicknamed "Kozaru" (Little Monkey), Shichigoro's ne'er-do-well son. He awakes, stretches, and exclaims: "Was it a dream? Or did it really happen to me?" He has just dreamed the preceding scene.

Takikawa, a pretty maid-in-waiting in the household of

the Lord of Chiba, enters escorted by **Yokome Sukehei,**
her master's chief retainer, and other servants. Takikawa's
sandal thong breaks and Sukehei mends it. Shichinosuke
listens to their chatter. Suddenly he approaches Takikawa
from behind, steals one of her hairpins, and escapes. The
party, much startled, continues its way down the *hanamichi*.

Yoshiro, looking distraught and still clutching Shichigoro's sleeve, totters onto the stage. He is desperate at the
loss of the seventy *ryo* and, after a little hesitation, jumps
into the river to drown himself. Shichinosuke, only faintly
interested by this tragedy, goes off in pursuit of Takikawa,
for whom he has conceived an irresistible passion.

Act III

Sc. 1. *The river bank near Fukagawa.* It is night. Two
men hurry past. They are in pursuit of O Sugi, who has
run away with Kichizo. From the other direction comes
Takikawa, in a palanquin, escorted by Sukehei and the
other servants. A violent thunder-storm breaks out. Sukehei and the others run in terror for shelter, leaving the lady
to her fate. One of the servants, however, stays behind and
reveals himself to be Shichinosuke. He drags Takikawa,
who is in a dead faint, from the palanquin and tries to
revive her. Finding it difficult to carry water to her, he fills
his mouth and forces the liquid between her lips. She regains consciousness. The moon comes out. Takikawa is
duly grateful to Shichinosuke for not having deserted her
and promises to reward him when they reach their journey's
end. He firmly corrects her misapprehension and declares
his love. He reminds her of their first meeting on the Eitai Bridge and produces her hairpin to prove it. Takikawa
protests that she is an innocent girl, serving in the household of a powerful lord, and moreover, betrothed. Shichinosuke becomes violent and finally she agrees to yield to
him at once, vowing to become a nun afterwards, but still
hoping they may be interrupted. They are, but it is Kichizo and O Sugi in flight. They have been sheltering from
the storm in a nearby hut which Kichizo is obliging enough
to point out to Shichinosuke. The two couples part, and
the stage is left deserted. After an interval Shichinosuke
and Takikawa reappear, the lady in some disarray. Shichinosuke is well pleased with himself. Takikawa has had
second thoughts about turning nun. She rather likes her

violent lover and has decided she will become his wife.

Sc. 2. *Further down the river bank.* Shichigoro and a boatman come along the bank and get into a moored boat. They push off and go fishing. Shichigoro casts a circular net. When he pulls it up, the ghost of Yoshiro, clutching Shichigoro's sleeve, is found in its folds. Shichigoro drops the net. The boatman remarks that the ghost looks just like a corpse that was fished out of the river under the Eitai Bridge ten days ago. They are both jittery by now, and when a fish jumps, the boatman loses his balance and goes overboard. Shichigoro tries to rescue him with an oar, but the body he brings up is still Yoshiro's ghost. He beats the phantom off, cursing its persistent vindictiveness, loses the oar, and finally makes for the shore paddling with a thwart.

Act IV

Sc. 1. *A brothel in Mikazuki, Edo, owned by Kuraganoya Gihei.* Three years later. Takikawa has sold herself into the establishment as a common prostitute in order to support Shichinosuke. She has changed her name to **O Kuma** and is nicknamed "Goshuden" (the Snare). She has brought prosperity to the house. As she sits smoking and gossiping with her colleagues, **O Same** and **O Nao**, no one would recognize the gentle, shy girl of the Chiba household. Sukehei has been searching for her ever since her disappearance, but when he finds her on this evening it is not he who

O Kuma

carries her away, but she who seduces him. A drunken priest, **Kaiten,** and his young assistant, **Kyoshin,** who are returning from a successful alms-gathering expedition, arrive at the house. Kaiten is determined to spend some of the money his young companion carries and finally prevails on him to enter. They are received by O Same and O Nao. Shichinosuke, posing as a countryman, comes to see O Kuma.

Sc. 2. *A ground-floor room in the same house.* The proprietor, **Gihei,** is being massaged by **O Nami,** Shichigoro's blind daughter. Shichigoro is ill and, in the absence of her brother Shichinosuke, the little girl struggles to earn enough to look after her father. Gihei's purse lies near the brazier, and as she works O Nami touches it and conceals it in her kimono. Gihei detects the theft and demands an explanation. Thus Shichinosuke and O Kuma, drinking *sake* in a room upstairs, overhear the story and realize who O Nami is. O Kuma, on her husband's whispered instructions, comes down and puts things right with Gihei. She takes O Nami up to her brother, who learns of his father's condition. He gives the child such money as he has for their father. As she leaves, Kyoshin bursts from O Same's room. He is determined to escape. Kaiten, hearing his protests, tries to prevent him and discloses in Shichinosuke's hearing that Kyoshin is carrying a good deal of money on him. Shichinosuke is now full of the idea of getting money quickly to help his father. Kyoshin has gone, but he has left his rosary behind him. Shichinosuke decides to run after him. As an afterthought he takes up a kitchen knife and secretes it in his belt.

Sc. 3. *On the bank of the Sumida River.* Shichinosuke overtakes Kyoshin and returns his rosary to him. He then demands his money. Kyoshin refuses. He protests that he has saved the money for his elder sister, who, he has learned, is in difficulties, having married a worthless husband. Shichinosuke threatens the priest with the knife, but Kyoshin is no coward and resists. In the scuffle Shichinosuke stabs and kills him. He takes the money and pushes the body into the river. A palanquin comes along the river bank. In order to escape detection, Shichinosuke strikes out the lantern. But the occupant is a samurai who is quite able to deal with footpads. Shichinosuke takes to flight, but not before the samurai has had a good look at him.

Act V

Sc. 1. *Shichigoro's house in Fukagawa.* The old man has been ill for three years and is haunted by the ghost of Yoshiro. He has sunk to the depth of despair. O Sugi and Kichizo share the house, but all they do is gamble and quarrel. The neighbours are hostile. Only the old boatman occasionally comes in to offer a few words of comfort.

O Nami comes home, tells her father of her meeting with her brother, and goes to bed. Shichigoro tries to pray for the repose of Yoshiro's soul. Shichinosuke, climbing over the roof-tops, comes to visit his father. He offers him the money taken from Kyoshin, but the old man refuses it and tells him to return it to its owner. Shichinosuke in some surprise asks why his father has changed his habits. Shichigoro breaks down and confesses all that is on his conscience, including Yoshiro's death. O Nami wakes up in a trance and, in a supernatural voice, prophesies Shichinosuke's punishment for his evil life. Much upset, Shichinosuke takes a tearful farewell of his father and leaves.

Sc. 2. *The lane outside Shichigoro's house.* O Kuma comes in search of her husband and meets him as he descends from the roof-tops. She is anxious because she has learnt from an amulet left behind by Kyoshin that he is her younger brother, whom she has not seen since he was a child. Moreover, since Sukehei has discovered her whereabouts, she dare no longer stay in the licensed quarter. She wants to finish with this life. Shichinosuke confesses that he has killed Kyoshin and begs O Kuma to kill him and avenge her brother. She refuses, and they decide to commit suicide together. The police, who have been put on Shichinosuke's track by the samurai he attacked by the river, surround them and take them prisoner.

BANZUIN CHOBEI SHOIN MANAITA, commonly called *Suzugamori. Sewamono.*—This is one act of a long play about Banzuin Chobei (see page 186) by Sakurada Jisuke, first staged at the Nakamura-za in 1789. At that time only this act was performed, the rest of the play being added later. The role of Chobei was acted by Matsumoto Koshiro IV and that of Gompachi (see page 62) by Iwai

Hanshiro V, an actor renowned in his day for his beauty.

Argument : When the curtain is drawn the scene shows the execution ground of Suzugamori, which lies beside the Tokaido, the highway between Edo and Kyoto, just outside Edo. It is night. Some palanquin bearers are warming themselves at a fire and complaining that business is bad. They have been forced to highway robbery as a side line, and one of their number complains that he has been swindled by his mate out of his share of a considerable sum of money taken from a courier. (These couriers belonged to accredited post-houses and travelled up and down the country carrying letters and valuables.) The others give him a drink to cheer him up.

A courier enters by the *hanamichi* carrying a letter-case. He is followed by a crowd of bearers who are pestering him to hire them, pointing out that he is in a dangerous place. The courier tries to drive them off with his sword, saying he has already been robbed by their fraternity. The bearers unite to attack and strip him. The courier, now without clothes or credentials, is utterly unnerved and, terrified lest they murder him, implores his tormentors to let him join the gang, offering as an " entrance fee " the letter-case he carries. The case contains a single document, which one of the bearers is able to decipher. It is addressed to the officials of the Shogunate in Edo and is from the chief magistrate of Inaba. It reports that one Honjo Suketayu has been killed by the son of Shirai Hezaimon, who is believed to have fled to Edo, where he must be discovered and arrested as soon as possible. The bearers realize that the murderer will have to pass this place on his way to the capital and they decide to try to catch him and earn the reward. One of them thinks he saw a young man wearing the Shirai crest engage a palanquin at Omori, which means he should shortly arrive. They call up reinforcements.

A palanquin bearing **Shirai Gompachi** comes down the *hanamichi*. It is set down, and he gets out, asking whether they have brought him to the seashore as he ordered. Gompachi is a handsome young samurai, hardly more than a boy. He tips the bearers generously, and they, thinking he is fair game, try to extort more money from him. When he refuses to pay, they swear to take all his money and his clothes as well. The bearers attack him, but are stopped by the leader of the other gang. Gompachi thanks his rescuer and is about to go on his way, but the gang-leader delays him, offering him a pipe. Gompachi refuses, saying he does not smoke, and turns to go, but the delay has given the gang the opportunity they needed to examine the crest on his coat. They are now sure he is the man they are expecting. They fall on him. The moon disappears behind the clouds, and in the darkness a macabre fight takes place in which Gompachi, single-handed, kills one of his attackers, wounds several more, and puts the rest to flight.

During the fight another palanquin comes down the *hanamichi*. The bearers take fright when they realize what is happening and, depositing their burden, make off as fast as they can. Gompachi, having got rid of his attackers, goes towards the palanquin and examines his sword by the light of its lantern. As he does so his eyes, travelling along the blade, meet those of the man seated inside. It is **Banzuin Chobei.** Gompachi is about to retreat, when Chobei calls to him to wait, saying he admires his fine swordsmanship. He gets out and, taking the lantern, hangs it on one of the pine trees bordering the road. He enquires why Gompachi is travelling alone and where he is going. Gompachi answers that he is on his way to Edo. The palanquin men took him by surprise; he had no intention of killing one of them. He tells Chobei a story about a cruel stepmother at home in Inaba, who caused him to be turned out of the house, and adds that he hopes to find employment in a samurai household in Edo. He asks whether Chobei, who is presumably a native of Edo, will help him. In reply, Chobei flings the body of the dead bearer into the bushes. Gompachi says : " I am Shirai Gompachi, a *ronin*." Chobei answers : " I am a humble merchant. Near the Sumida River they call me Chobei of Banzuin." Gompachi asks in amazement whether he is the famous Chobei who is known even in distant Inaba. Chobei, with humorous mock modesty, pretends that this is impossible, saying he is " just a man among men." He undertakes to help Gompachi in any way he can and begs him to come to his house in Edo. Chobei takes the lantern and is about to go on his way when he catches sight of the document on the ground. He picks it up. Neither he nor Gompachi knows what it is. While Chobei holds the light, Gompachi begins to read it aloud. He gets as far as : "The man who killed Honjo Suketayu on the 20th of March—" Then he stops. Chobei takes the paper from him and reads the rest. Chobei comments that it does not give the given name of the murderer, only his family name. He looks at Gompachi closely and, as he does so, holds the document so near the candle flame that it catches fire. He drops the flaming paper, saying: "Now all is forgotten." Gompachi exclaims that even a samurai could not do a finer thing.

Meanwhile one of the bearers has crept back and is watching them from the branches of a tree. Chobei sees him and gives a warning cry. Gompachi picks up a stone and flings it at the man, who falls. Gompachi seizes him and, at Chobei's bidding, kills him. As the youth wipes and sheathes his sword, he and Chobei exchange a look sealing their friendship. They promise to meet in Edo.

BENTEN KOZO. *Sewamono.*—Written by Kawatake Mokuami in 1862 for Onoe Kikunosuke V when he was nineteen years old. The whole play is rarely performed, but the last two acts are very popular, particularly the famous " Hamamatsuya Scene," often called " Benten Musume."

Kikunosuke was the son of a well-to-do cloth merchant of Kamakura, Hamamatsuya Kobei. His father placed him in the service of a man of rank, but the boy was caught pilfering and ran away. For some time he haunted one or other of the great temples in Kamakura, making such profit as he could out of the pilgrims who flock there. He was a handsome young man and had a certain talent for playacting. It amused him to disguise himself in different ways when he was carrying out his raids on the purses of the gullible. He called himself **Benten Kozo Kikunosuke.**

Act I

Before the Hatsuse Temple, Kamakura. Benten Kozo has come to the temple hoping to fall in with some well-to-do pilgrim. He is disguised as a young samurai and calls himself Shinoda Kotaro. This is the name of a young man whom he used to see in the house of his former master and of whose death he has recently heard. A fellow bandit,

Nango Rikimaru, accompanies him, posing as his servant.

A young lady, **Senju-hime,** comes to the temple with her attendants. She is the daughter of Benten Kozo's former master and was betrothed to the real Shinoda Kotaro. She has come to pray for her fiancé's soul and brings a valuable incense-burner as an offering. Senju-hime is struck by the appearance of the young samurai and sends her maid to ask who he is. When she hears that it is Shinoda Kotaro (whom she has never seen), she is amazed and overjoyed. Wonderingly, she asks the false Kotaro what he is doing here. Benten Kozo answers that he is in hiding and begs her to tell no one she has seen him. Senju-hime concludes that he must be hiding because he does not wish to marry her. She takes his sword and tries to kill herself, but Benten Kozo prevents her and convinces her that she is mistaken. He leads her away to a neighbouring tea-house to consummate their love.

At this moment a young man runs out of the temple pursued by two samurai. They had brought an offering of 100 *ryo* to buy intercessions for their late master's soul. The money has been stolen by the young man, **Akaboshi Juzaburo** (this rôle is traditionally played by an *onnagata*), who requires the money to assist the widow of his own former lord, the mother of the real Kotaro. The two samurai beat Juzaburo and retrieve the money. They go into the tea-house, but do not keep the 100 *ryo* for long, for it is stolen from them by a *ronin*, **Tadanobu Rihei.** Before ill fortune overtook him, Akaboshi Juzaburo was a high-ranking samurai, and Rihei was his retainer. Rihei steals the money to give it to Juzaburo.

Benten Kozo leaves the tea-house with Senju-hime. The latter, deeply in love, presents him with the incense-burner and begs him to take her to his home. Benten Kozo cocks an ironic eyebrow at his comrade Rikimaru. Then, taking the girl's hand, he leads her down the *hanamichi*.

Act II

In the mountains. Benten Kozo and Senju-hime stop to rest by a wayside shrine. Senju-hime asks to be taken to his home; she cannot understand why they have come to this remote spot. Benten Kozo tells her who he really is, and Senju-hime, overcome with shame that she should have given herself to a criminal, flings herself over a cliff.

From the shrine comes a priest, who accosts Benten Kozo, saying he has overheard their conversation. He tells Benten Kozo that he is the master-thief **Nippon Daemon.** He orders the young man to surrender the incense-burner. Benten Kozo refuses, and a fight follows in which Nippon Daemon overcomes his young opponent. The latter begs to be killed outright, but Nippon Daemon refuses to deprive himself of so promising a recruit. He forces Benten Kozo to join his gang and swear blood-brotherhood with him.

The stage is raised to show the valley below. Akaboshi Juzaburo, sick from the beating he received and ashamed of the depth to which he has sunk, comes seeking a place to commit suicide and stumbles on Senju-hime, who was only stunned by her fall. She revives. They tell each other their stories, and Senju-hime learns that Juzaburo was formerly her betrothed's retainer. Overcome once more by shame, Senju-hime succeeds in taking her life. Juzaburo is about to follow her example, when he is prevented by his servant, Rihei, who brings him the 100 *ryo* and persuades him it is better to live. Committed to a life of crime, they had better make such profit from it as they can.

The stage is lowered again. Rihei brings Juzaburo to Nippon Daemon and they also swear blood-brotherhood. They are joined by Benten Kozo's comrade Rikimaru, and by Nippon Daemon's sister **O Matsu.** The five bandits, known from now onwards as the " Five White Waves " (*Shiranami Gonin Otoko*), perform a special type of mime known as a *sewa-dammari*. (The name " White Waves " comes originally from the nickname given to a famous band of Chinese brigands, but has come to be a general term for bandits.)

Act III

Sc. 1. *The Hamamatsuya Scene (Hamamatsuya no Ba).* Nippon Daemon has an alias under which he is known when he poses as a respectable samurai : Tamashima Itto. He fears his neighbours may suspect that Tamashima has some connection with the underworld and is anxious to re-establish his reputation. He therefore arranges with his confederates to kill two birds with one stone. Two of them are to be caught thieving in a shop near Tamashima's house so that he can unmask them. At the same time they will be able to spy out the interior arrangements of the shop for a raid later.

The shop chosen is the Hamamatsuya cloth-shop, owned by Benten Kozo's father. Benten Kozo dresses up as a young lady of rank, the daughter of the samurai Hiyase. His comrade Rikimaru poses as a retainer who is escorting her. The two are respectfully received by the manager of the shop and his assistants. Rolls of silk and brocade suitable for wedding clothes are displayed before them, but Benten Kozo does not think much of the merchandise. While turning over a bundle of silks, he secretly drops among them a small piece of material which he then picks up again and clumsily stuffs into the front of his kimono. He is seen by one of the shop assistants and in the ensuing scuffle is wounded on the forehead by the manager. Rikimaru, as the "young lady's" protector, makes a terrible scene and proves to the manager that the piece of material does not come from his shop at all, even producing the bill for it from another cloth-shop. **Sawanosuke**, son-in-law of the owner, arrives and hears the story. He calls his father-in-law, **Kobei** (Benten Kozo's father), and a neighbour comes to mediate. Rikimaru holds out for 100 *ryo* as compensation for the wound on his "lady's" brow. After some haggling, during which the neighbour retires in disgust, Kobei is forced to pay up. The two bandits are about to make off with their booty when they are stopped by the arrival of Tamashima Itto (Nippon Daemon in disguise). The unfortunate affair is explained to him. He looks hard at the girl and her attendant and tells Kobei he has been fooled. He has caught sight of a pattern of cherry blossoms tattooed on the lady's shoulder and believes she is a man in disguise. He brusquely tells Benten Kozo to show his face and let them see who he is. This is the great moment of the play. With humorous *sangfroid*, Benten Kozo complies, making a famous "naming" speech as he does so. Neither his father nor his brother-in-law recognizes him. Rikimaru takes off his samurai dress, and Benten Kozo also removes as much of his disguise as he is able.

Nippon Daemon appears to be outraged by this plot to defraud an honest shopkeeper and offers to cut off the crooks' heads at once. Kobei is taken aback at this. He feels that the summary execution of two thieves on his premises is likely to cause a falling off of customers. He therefore says that, as they have stolen nothing, he is prepared to overlook the matter. He even gives Benten Kozo money to buy a plaster for his head. Benten Kozo kilts up his woman's clothes, and he and Rikimaru go off. Outside the shop they stop and divide the spoils. As the two go down the *hanamichi*, carrying the bundle containing the impedimenta needed for their hoax, they play an ancient game of which variants are found all over the world : each agrees to carry the bundle until they meet a bald-headed man, when it will be the turn of the other.

Sc. 2. *Kobei's house behind the Hamamatsuya.* (This scene is usually omitted.) Kobei invites Nippon Daemon to drink with him and presents him with a handsome coat. Nippon Daemon gets drunk and in a vainglorious speech reveals who he is. He draws his sword and demands Kobei's money. Sawanosuke throws himself between them, begging to die in the old man's place. Nippon Daemon is overcome by the young man's devotion, saying he once had a son who would be about his age. In the ensuing conversation he discovers that Sawanosuke is, in fact, his long-lost child, and Kobei learns that Benten Kozo is his son. These revelations are interrupted by the arrival of the police at the gate. Nippon Daemon, fortunately for him, is not too drunk to beat a hasty retreat.

Act IV

On the Bank of the Inase River (Inasegawa no Ba or *Shiranami Gonin Otoko no Ba).* This short act is purely a piece of attractive spectacle. The five bandits, Benten Kozo, Tadanobu Rihei, Akaboshi Juzaburo, Nango Rikimaru, and their leader Nippon Daemon, aware that the police are on their tracks, decide to disperse for a time. They travel together as far as the Inase River where, dressed in fantastic kimono and carrying paper umbrellas, they pose under the cherry trees, each in turn announcing his name and attributes. They are surprised by the police, but overcome their attackers and make good their escape.

Act V

Before the Gokuraku Temple, Kamakura (Gokurakuji no Ba.) *Ozatsuma* accompaniment. Benten Kozo comes to repent of his way of life. His treatment of Senju-hime in particular weighs on his conscience. He regains possession of the incense-burner which she gave him and determines to offer it on her behalf at the temple. But the police are at his heels, and as he comes to the temple gate, he is surrounded. They chase him onto the roof of the gate. After a spectacular fight he drives them off, but realizes that his hour has come. He shouts to them that he is the notorious thief Benten Kozo Kikunosuke, but that he now repents of his crimes and they shall see the end he will make. Standing upright on the roof, he commits *seppuku*. (This scene is considered a great test of the actor's powers. It is because of his repentance that the playwright allows Benten Kozo an honourable death at his own hand.)

The building is raised. Nippon Daemon is discovered in the upper storey of the temple gate. He was asleep but has been wakened by the uproar of the chase after Benten Kozo. Two of his servants, **Sanji** and **Gosuke,** come to tell him he is surrounded. It is, in fact, they who have betrayed him. They attack Nippon Daemon who kills them both.

The building is raised again. In the middle of the stage at the foot of the gate stands **Aoto Fujitsuna,** the Chief of Police. He informs Nippon Daemon that Benten Kozo is dead and the rest of the gang is captured. Nippon Daemon, seeing that there is no hope of escape, surrenders.

DATE KURABE OKUNI KABUKI, commonly called *Kasane,* being part of the play *Meiboku Sendai Hagi*. *Sewamono*. — This is the most famous of the Kabuki ghost plays. Its popularity has resulted in the incorporation of the word *Kasane* in the titles of a number of them.

The daimyo of Oshu, Ashikaga Yorikane, had in his service a devoted retainer, Kinugawa Tanizo, formerly a *sumo* wrestler. Yorikane was surrounded by many dangers, for his cousin was plotting to kill him and seize his property. Tanizo and his loyal servants implored him to take temporary refuge in a place of safety, but Yorikane refused, not wishing to desert his mistress, the courtesan **Takao.** Tanizo therefore killed Takao to set Yorikane free and compel him to seek safety. Yorikane and Tanizo took refuge in a distant village, where they lodged in a local shopkeeper's house. Neither of them was aware that the man was Takao's brother. Tanizo fell in love with Takao's younger sister

Kasane, and when his immediate duty towards Yorikane was discharged, he married her. They returned to his native village on the banks of the Kinugawa, where he changed his name to Yoemon and settled down to be a farmer until such time as his lord should need him again. But they were not destined to be happy. Takao's vengeful spirit laid a curse on Kasane, and the beautiful girl changed into a limping monster. Her husband succeeded in concealing this from her by forbidding her to look in the mirror. He now knew that his wife was Takao's sister and guessed the reason for her altered appearance.

Act I

Hanu Village, near the Kinugawa; Yoemon's house. Some farmers are helping Yoemon and Kasane sift soya beans. They tease one of their number about his sweetheart. The young man, in revenge, accuses Yoemon of making sheep's eyes at a pretty village girl. When the men have gone, Kasane asks in distress whether it is true that Yoemon is attracted by this girl. Even after Yoemon has firmly denied it, Kasane is still doubtful. She reminds her husband that, when he first assumed his farmer's disguise, he begged her never to look in a mirror. She has kept this promise faithfully, although often tempted to break it. People used to say she was very beautiful, " as beautiful as Hanshiro," (a reference to Iwai Hanshiro V, an actor renowned for his good looks, who first played the part). She cannot understand how he can prefer a coarse country girl to her. The singers comment that she is proud of her beauty, not knowing how changed she is. Yoemon, concealing his shrinking, assures her that he could never care for anyone else. His wife is lovely. Even in the Yoshiwara she would be second to none. Kasane is reassured. **Kingoro,** nicknamed the "Twister," arrives to speak privately to Yoemon. When Kasane has gone to fetch them *sake,* Kingoro asks about Yoemon's name in the days when he was a *sumo* wrestler, suggesting it was Kinugawa. Yoemon, taken aback, evades answering. Kingoro continues that he has heard the police are searching for a Kinugawa on a charge of murder. It would be a fine thing to catch him and earn a reward. Yoemon comments that no doubt this Kinugawa committed the murder for his lord's sake. Kingoro looks knowing and adds that he has a further piece

17

of news which makes him think that Kinugawa must be in the neighbourhood: yesterday he came across a beautiful young girl of about sixteen who was asking for Kinugawa. She had no one to look after her, so Kingoro took her in, planning to sell her in the licensed quarter, where she would fetch at least 100 *ryo*. The master of a tea-house was anxious to take her at once, but Kingoro felt he ought first to try to find this Kinugawa. Yoemon pretends to be so struck by the girl's description that he wants her for his concubine. Brushing aside the problem of Kasane, he promises to pay Kingoro what he would have received from the tea-house, but, since he cannot lay hands on the money immediately, he undertakes to bring it at midnight to the bridge across the Kinugawa, where Kingoro must hand over the girl. Kingoro agrees and leaves. Yoemon guesses that the girl must be the betrothed of Lord Yorikane, **Utakata-hime.** She is looking for himself for news of their lord. If Kingoro should find out who she really is, anything might happen. Since he has no prospect of raising the money, the only thing he can do is to kill Kingoro and then escort Utakata-hime to a place of safety. Yoemon rises to leave, but, as he does so, his feet become entangled in the string of his farmer's apron. He is reminded of Kasane and his promise to her brother never to forsake her. He decides to write to her and her brother jointly, explaining why he must leave her for a while.

As he writes it grows dark. When Kasane returns, he hides the letter. She asks what is troubling him. Yoemon invents a story that his father borrowed 100 *ryo* from Kingoro, who is now pressing for repayment. He has been forced to promise to find the money by midnight and, since he cannot possibly raise it, he will have to kill Kingoro. Kasane begs him to do nothing desperate: there must be some other way to get the money. She persuades him to rest in the inner room. Kasane weeps that her brother is too far away to help them. Then she recalls Yoemon's words about her beauty surpassing that of any girl in the Yoshiwara; she decides that, to save her husband from committing murder, she must sell herself. But she does not know how to set about it. She sits down and begins to make herself a new kimono while she ponders the problem.

Saibei, the master of the Hanaoniya, and his servant

come asking for Yoemon. They explain that they are looking for Kingoro, who is believed to be visiting her husband.
Kasane says he has already left, but, as they turn to go,
calls them back, asking whether Saibei is the proprietor of a
house in the Yoshiwara. Saibei admits it. Kasane asks
whether it is true that they pay money for the girls who
belong to such houses. Saibei admits this too. Kasane
hastily tidies her dress and hair and asks them into the
house, saying that Kingoro will be back presently. With
some embarrassment, she says she has a favour to ask.
Would it be possible to pay the money at once for a woman
who wished for employment in the Yoshiwara? Saibei,
mystified, asks who the applicant is. Kasane explains that
it is "someone" in urgent need of 100 *ryo* by midnight,
a young woman of about twenty-two who is so beautiful
that she is said to resemble "Yamatoya" (the *yugo* of
Iwai Hanshiro; see page 402). Saibei is delighted and surprised. He has the money on him and asks to see the girl.
Kasane says the girl has a husband and is not immediately
available. Saibei is prepared to wait for such a prize and
goes into another room, leaving Kasane rejoicing.

Yoemon comes in, and Kasane asks whether he still holds
to his threat to drive her from home if she looks in the
mirror. She intends to look now, she adds, because she
means to go and earn money for him in the licensed quarter.
Hiding tears of pity, Yoemon tries to dissuade her: he has
sworn to her brother never to part with her. But Kasane
is set on a divorce. A countryman arrives to summon
Yoemon to the village headman's office. Taking his sword,
Yoemon is forced to leave. As soon as he is gone, Kasane
calls Saibei and asks for the 100 *ryo*. He asks for the
young woman, and Kasane, in surprise, replies that, of course
it is herself. Saibei thinks she is joking and will not be
convinced that she is in earnest. He concludes that she
must be mad, and from what he and his servant say, Kasane
slowly realizes how hideous she has become. When they
offer her a mirror she cannot believe her eyes. She is overcome with shame and horror. Saibei and his man leave,
complaining that they have wasted valuable time.

Kasane now understands why Yoemon forbade her to
look in the mirror and weeps over his mistaken kindness.
She blames her sister's jealousy for her disfigurement. She

swears to drown in the river, but she cannot bear the thought of his marrying some pretty girl when she is gone. She implores him to remember her sometimes and to pray for her. Slowly she regains control. She takes a basket and a sickle and goes out. As she does so, she hears Yoemon returning and puts out the light. He calls to her, but she slips out of the house and, with a gesture of farewell, hurries in the direction of the river. Yoemon, who has felt her brush past him, turns to follow as the temple bell tolls.

Act II

The Bridge over the Kinugawa. It is night. Thunder rolls overhead and heavy rain falls. A statue of Jizo stands near some willows. Kasane enters. She longs to see Yoemon once more before she dies. She fills her basket with stones to serve as a weight when she throws herself in the river. At the sound of footsteps, she hides. Kingoro enters with a lantern and wearing a sword. He leads Utakata-hime, to whom he speaks of Yoemon, describing him as a handsome man tied to a monster of a wife and seeking a pretty concubine. He should be here at any moment. Kasane hears everything. Utakata-hime, who does not know that Yoemon and the wrestler Kinugawa are one and the same, begs to be taken to Kinugawa. Kingoro threatens to throw her in the river if she spoils his bargain.

When Yoemon enters, Utakata-hime at once recognizes his voice, but he silences her with a gesture. Kingoro's suspicions are, however, aroused. He now guesses not only the true identity of Yoemon, but that of the girl. Yoemon admits he is the wrestler Kinugawa and that he has not brought the money. He offers to allow Kingoro to beat him and hand him over to the police if he will only let him first place the girl in safety. Kingoro enjoys himself mal-treating Yoemon, but afterwards refuses to release Utakata-hime. Yoemon angrily draws his sword, and they leave fighting. Utakata-hime dares not follow them. Kasane comes out from her hiding place. She questions Utakata-hime (whom she does not, of course, recognize) about her relations with Kinugawa Tanizo. The girl does not know how to answer. Kasane, burning with jealousy, seizes her and, catching up her sickle, swears to kill her. Yoemon returns, and Kasane cries to him that it was cruel to conceal from her her disfigurement and yet to seek a handsome

mistress. Yoemon tries to explain, telling her Utakata-
hime's true identity. He begs Kasane to come with them
to Edo, where the princess will be married to their lord.
But the ghost of Kasane's sister Takao appears, still seeking
revenge, and stops Kasane from hearing what Yoemon is
saying. Ghostly music is heard and strange lights appear.
Kasane, beside herself, accuses Yoemon of infidelity and
deceit. He realizes that she no longer understands what
he says and guesses that Takao's evil spirit has come between them. He swears repeatedly that Kasane is his true
wife and he has never loved another. He begs her with
tears to understand him and help him protect the young
princess. Kasane is now utterly possessed by Takao's
jealous spirit. She tries to kill Utakata-hime, threatening
to give up Yoemon to the police for Takao's murder. He
again tries to convince her of his sincerity and swears on a
precious mirror given him by her brother that he loves her.
She thinks he is saying he deliberately caused her disfigurement by means of this magic mirror. She snatches it from
him and flings it in the river. Daring him to kill her, she
presses the sickle into his hand. Yoemon struggles to free
himself and accidentally wounds her. Takao's wicked
spirit now possesses him also. He sees before him not Kasane
but her sister and in a frenzy kills her and flings the body
from the bridge. Coming to himself, he realizes what he
has done. Utakata-hime has fainted. He revives her,
telling her he has been forced to sacrifice his wife for their
lord's sake. Utakata-hime says she was protected from
Kasane's attack by a holy charm which is found to be cut
in two.

Tansuke, Utakata-hime's servant, who has been searching for her, now rushes to them, overjoyed at finding his
mistress. He tells them how he escaped from the enemies
who held him prisoner. Yoemon begs him to take Utakata-
hime to a place of safety, saying he will follow. The two
leave. Yoemon watches them go. He picks up the mirror
from the shallow water where it fell. He puts it in his
breast. Kasane's ghost appears from among the willows
and drags Yoemon to her, declaring in Takao's voice that
she will be revenged and carry off both him and Kasane to
the other world. Yoemon exorcises her with the mirror,
and the ghost vanishes. Kingoro, who has been watching,

now enters with a young boatman (played by the actor who plays Kasane). All three pose; Yoemon, holding up the mirror, escapes along the *hanamichi*. He flings a stone at Kingoro, who screams "Thief!" after him as the curtain is drawn.

EHON TAIKOKI (*The Picture Book of the Taiko*). *Jidai-mono* of the Taiko Cycle (see page 467). — This play follows almost immediately on *Toki wa Ima Kikkyo no Hataage*. It was written for the puppets in 1799 by Chikamatsu Yanagi and others and is still performed by them. The play consisted originally of thirteen acts, one act for each day that passed between Akechi Mitsuhide's murder of Oda Nobunaga and his death at the hand of Toyotomi Hideyoshi. The tenth act is the only one which has survived. This act tells of an incident during the battle in which **Mitsuhide** was finally defeated.

When Akechi Mitsuhide determined to murder Oda Nobunaga, he laid his plans carefully. He chose a time when Nobunaga was in Kyoto with a bodyguard of not more than two hundred men, while his other forces were dispersed far from the capital. In particular, the two men Mitsuhide knew to be most likely to thwart his plans were, he trusted, in no position to resist him. Hideyoshi was away, laying siege to the castle of Takamatsu in Bitchiu, the last stronghold of Nobunaga's enemy Mori Motonari. Ieyasu was awaiting Nobunaga at Sakai with a small contingent. Mitsuhide arranged for Sakai to be surrounded at the same time as he made his own coup. Ieyasu escaped capture through the friendly warning of a local tea-grower. Mitsuhide had, however, underestimated Hideyoshi. Having brought Takamatsu Castle to its last gasp, Hideyoshi was able to conclude a speedy truce with Mori. He hurried back to Kyoto by forced marches, surprised Mitsuhide at Yamazaki, and defeated him. Legend has it that Hideyoshi killed Mitsuhide with his own hand, but, in fact, he was cut down by a peasant as he fled from the field.

The title of the play, literally "The Picture Book of the Taiko (Meritorious Prince)," refers to the title bestowed on Hideyoshi at the height of his power. The same variants of the principal characters' names are used as in *Hataage*.

Hideyoshi is called Mashiba **Hisayoshi.** Nobunaga is called **Harunaga.**

Act X, commonly called "The Amagasaki Scene," retains to a considerable degree the atmosphere of the puppet theatre. The *joruri* singers are more than mere narrators and in places perform the whole dialogue while the actors mime. The acting is modelled closely on that of the dolls.

Act X

At Amagasaki, near Osaka (Amagasaki no Ba.) It is a summer evening. The scene represents a poor cottage surrounded by thickets of bamboo. At one side there is a trellis supporting a gourd vine. Frogs croak in the neighbouring marshes. **Satsuki,** Takechi Mitsuhide's mother, is so horrified by her son's murder of his overlord that she has left his house and come to live in this cottage. Here she is visited by **Misao,** Mitsuhide's wife, and **Hatsugiku,** the betrothed of Mitsuhide's son **Mitsuyoshi.** They are distressed at the turn events have taken. While they are talking, a mendicant priest comes to the gate asking for a night's lodging. He brings news that things are going badly with Mitsuhide's side. Satsuki recognizes him as Hisayoshi, the most able and devoted of Harunaga's generals, and guesses that he is seeking Mitsuhide. She does not let it be seen that she has penetrated his disguise, but invites him in and offers him a hot bath after his travels. While Satsuki and Hisayoshi are in conversation Mitsuhide, who is on Hisayoshi's track, steals up to the house, sees them, recognizes his enemy, and retires into the bamboo thicket to bide his time.

Mitsuyoshi, although strongly opposed to the murder of Harunaga, must do his duty, particularly now that things are going badly, and join his father on the battlefield. He comes to receive his grandmother's blessing. Satsuki, who guesses that he does not mean to return alive, stipulates that he must first marry his betrothed, Hatsugiku. Mitsuyoshi is unwilling to do so. This is because it was considered shameful for a widow to re-marry and he did not wish to blight Hatsugiku's life. His grandmother leaves him with his thoughts.

(The act often starts at this point.) Mitsuyoshi believes his grandmother to be in the next room and, making respectful obeisance in that direction, he speaks aloud, saying that if he is killed he wishes Hatsugiku to be able to marry someone else. He knows that his refusal to marry her will cause her sorrow, but it will be best in the end. Sadly he mimes his grief and his firm resolve. The door opens, and Hatsugiku herself stumbles into the room, weeping. She stifles her sobs in her sleeve lest Satsuki should hear her. Mitsuyoshi must do as he thinks best, but for herself she will never in any circumstance marry another. Mitsuyoshi is moved by her devotion and finally promises that they shall be married before he leaves. He opens the chest containing his armour and, with the help of Hatsugiku, carries it into the inner room to arm himself. Hatsugiku, like all high-born girls in Kabuki, is so fragile that it is with the utmost difficulty that she lifts even the leg-pieces. The helmet defeats her altogether, and she is forced to drag it out of the room on her long sleeves.

Satsuki and Misao enter bringing ceremonial cups and *sake* for the marriage. They are followed by Hatsugiku, wearing wedding garments. Mitsuyoshi joins them, in full armour. The young people drink their wedding cups. Mitsuyoshi leaves for the battlefield, while the women weep. When he has gone, the priest comes from the back of the house to say that the bath is ready. His voice can be heard clearly in the nearby thicket. All go out, and as twilight falls, the silence is broken only by the croaking of the frogs.

Mitsuhide creeps out from behind the bamboo clumps. He is disguised in a farmer's straw cloak and hat. The

Mitsuhide

scar on his forehead has not yet faded. He watches the house and sees that a figure is moving about in the inner room. He is sure that this is Hisayoshi. He cannot safely reach this person with his sword so he cuts himself a spear of bamboo and steals into the house. He thrusts the spear through the paper door. A cry is heard. He withdraws the spear triumphantly, but it breaks off short. He flings the butt from him, thrusts open the door, and drags out the supposed Hisayoshi, intending to finish off his victim. To his horror he finds that he has stabbed, not his enemy, but his own mother. She sinks to the ground, and he does what he can to help her. Misao rushes into the room and supports the old lady, who now implores her son to give up his schemes to seize power and make atonement for the crime of killing his overlord. Mitsuhide refuses to listen to her. She tells Misao to plead with him, but he turns a deaf ear to her also.

There are sounds of fighting close at hand. Mitsuyoshi, mortally wounded, staggers down the *hanamichi* and collapses before the house. His father revives him with medicine and tells him to give an account of the battle. Mitsuyoshi describes how Mitsuhide's forces have been defeated and are already in retreat. He sinks down again, supported by his wife and mother, and finally dies in Hatsugiku's arms. His grandmother dies shortly afterwards. This tragedy upon tragedy is too much even for Mitsuhide. His self-control deserts him, and he weeps bitterly. He is recalled to himself by sounds of battle. *Here the stage revolves.*

Mitsuhide climbs to an eminence to see what is happening. The country-side is overrun by Hisayoshi's victorious troops, and his own are in full flight. *The stage revolves again, back to the first scene.*

Mitsuhide is about to rejoin his scattered forces but is confronted by Hisayoshi, who comes from inside the house, now in the full regalia of his rank and surrounded by his staff. A moment later Hisayoshi's second-in-command, **Kato Masakiyo,** appears on the *hanamichi*, in the van of the victorious army. Mitsuhide is caught between them. Masakiyo wishes to kill him on the spot, but Hisayoshi stops him and tells Mitsuhide that they will meet on the battlefield.

FUNA BENKEI (*Benkei in the Boat*). *Shosagoto.* —
Adapted by Kawatake Mokuami from the Noh play of the
same name. *Nagauta* accompaniment. The original of this
play is one of the many Noh dramas about the adventures
of **Minamoto Yoshitsune** (see page 418). The incident
depicted here takes place when Yoshitsune is escaping from
his brother's forces. The rôles of Shizuka Gozen and the
ghost of Tomomori are always danced by the same actor.
The set is the Kabuki version of the Noh stage.

Argument: Yoshitsune, accompanied by his concubine,
Shizuka Gozen, and five retainers headed by the warrior-
priest **Benkei,** arrives at Daimotsu on the shores of the
Inland Sea. From here he intends to take ship to Shikoku.
He is persuaded by Benkei to leave Shizuka Gozen behind
since the journey is hazardous. Yoshitsune and Shizuka
Gozen plight their troth by drinking *sake* together. Shizuka
Gozen dances a farewell dance and leaves them.

The party board their ship and are rowed away by a crew

*The ghost of
Tomomori*

of comic boatmen. These boatmen represent the interlude (*kyogen*) between the two parts of a Noh play and afford the necessary light relief.

On the very waters they are now crossing Yoshitsune has, not long before, finally defeated the Taira clan at the battle of Dan-no-Ura. A great storm arises. In the tumult of the elements Yoshitsune imagines that the ghosts of the drowned Taira soldiers are clamouring to attack him. Across the waters there rushes towards him a spectre, crying out that he is the ghost of the general **Tomomori** who drowned himself in the moment of defeat. Yoshitsune prepares to draw his sword, but is stopped by Benkei, who pulls out his rosary and, rubbing it between the palms of his hands, repeatedly drives off the angry spirit. Benkei prays fervently to Buddha, and at last the ghost vanishes. The storm abates, and they continue their journey.

GEDATSU (*The Release of Kagekiyo's Soul*). *Juhachiban.* —This is not a particularly good play, although the theme is old. It was given in Edo, according to the records, in 1744 and 1760. It was revived in 1914 and again in 1953 on the occasion of the 50th anniversary of the death of Ichikawa Danjuro IX.

The term *gedatsu* is derived from the Sanskrit *vimukta* and means "emancipation" in Buddhist terminology, signifying the freeing of the spirit from the trammels of earthly passion. Emancipation of this sort can apply both to living persons and to unhappy ghosts.

The time of the play is set at the close of the war between the Minamoto and Taira clans (see page 418), when the former were seeking out and destroying their vanquished enemies. The scene is the Todai Temple at Kamakura.

Argument: As the curtain is drawn, officials of the Shogunate discuss the curious happenings of the day. A service was to be held for the repose of the souls of the defeated Taira, but the great bell has lost its voice. Doubtless, the angry spirits of the dead have put a curse on it.

The light-blue curtain (see page 411) is whipped aside to reveal the belfry and the huge, silent bell. Two samurai enter by the *seriage* (see page 457). One is the Minamoto

Ema Koshiro. The other is not a man at all, but the ghost of the Taira general **Kagekiyo** (see page 122). Koshiro is at first suspicious and then convinced that the other is the spirit of Kagekiyo. He is joined by **Kajiwara Heita,** to whom he confides his discovery, and the two try to seize Kagekiyo. The spirit eludes them, however, and takes refuge under the bell, which lowers itself over him. The Minamoto try to move it, but it becomes so hot that they cannot even touch it. They retire, baffled, to fetch reinforcements.

From opposite sides of the stage enter a bell-smith called **Tarosuke,** who has been summoned to examine the bell, and a girl named **Hitomaru.** Tarosuke is in fact Kiyosada, the son of the late Taira no Munemori, and the girl is none other than Kagekiyo's daughter. The two have met before and had a fleeting love affair. Now brought together again in such unforeseen circumstances, they reveal their true identities to each other. Their confessions are interrupted by the return of Kajiwara Heita, supported by his subordinate **Yokosuke Gunnai** (a comic character). The two are attacked, overcome, and bound. Kajiwara orders them to be executed as Taira refugees, but is stayed by the ghost's voice saying "Wait, wait" from inside the bell.

The bell is lifted, and the fearful ghost of the dead Taira general emerges in its true shape. It seizes a huge grave-marker and runs amok amongst the Minamoto soldiery. All attempts to seize it fail. A local saint called **Monkaku** attempts to exorcise it in vain. The angry spirit dominates the stage, radiating a passionate hatred like an all-consuming flame. At the height of this impasse, the governor of nearby Chichibu, **Hatakeyama Shigetada,** arrives in haste to tell the wonderful news that the daughter of the late Taira no Shigemori, who had entered a nunnery, has been miraculously rapt into sainthood. A lady in waiting, **Shishu,** bears in the new saint's wadded silk garment and places it reverently about the ghost's shoulders. Immediately Kagekiyo's spirit is released from the toils of passion and hate.

GEMPEI NUNOBIKI NO TAKI, commonly called *Sanemori Monogatari.* *Jidaimono* of the Heike-Genji Cycle

(see page 418). — Written for the puppets by Namiki
Senryu (1695—1751) and Miyoshi Shoraku (1696
1775?) in 1749.   It was first staged at the Takemoto-za
in Osaka and later was adapted for the Kabuki.   The first
and second acts are now never performed, and the play is
usually known by the sub-title of the third act.   This bears
very strongly the imprint of its puppet origin — a reviving
corpse and a severed arm that is miraculously restored to
the trunk present no problem to doll-manipulators.

Minamoto Kiso Yoshinaka, the infant hero who is
born during the course of the play, was the first cousin of
Yoritomo and **Yoshitsune** and lived to achieve, briefly,
a fame almost as great as theirs (see page 421). His father
was **Yoshikata,** the brother of **Yoshitomo** (Yoritomo's
father) who, for the purposes of the play, is made to die at
the outset of the struggle between the Minamoto and the
Taira.   He was, in fact, killed some years earlier by
Yoshitomo's eldest son in a family quarrel.   It is true,
however, that little Yoshinaka grew up in hiding in the
mountains, tended by faithful retainers.   At the end of the
play, **Sanemori's** prophetic description of his own death
is based on fact.   It is told in the *Heike Monogatari* how,
during the battle of Shinowara (one of the several occasions
when the Taira were defeated by Yoshinaka), Saito Sanemori
was killed by **Tezuka no Taro Mitsumori.**   When his
head was displayed it was thought at first not to be his, for
Sanemori was known to be an old man, and the hair on
this head was black.   But when the hair was washed it was
found to be dyed; it was, in truth, white as snow.

Act III

*Sanemori Monogatari (Sanemori's Narrative).   The house
of Kurosuke.*   **Kurosuke,** a well-to-do farmer, has always
had connections with the Genji.   His daughter **Koman**
married a foot-soldier in Yoshikata's service.   After the
battle in which Yoshikata was killed, this man, although
severely wounded, succeeded in returning home, bringing
with him Yoshikata's widow, **Aoi Gozen.**   Shortly
afterwards, Koman's husband died of his wounds, but
Kurosuke continued to hide Aoi Gozen, who was expecting
a child.

When the curtain is drawn, **Koyoshi,** Kurosuke's wife,
is discovered spinning.   **Nisota,** Kurosuke's nephew, enters

and tells her that his uncle has just been to see him to ask his help in caring for the woman who arrived recently from Kyoto. He supposes she must be Kiso Yoshikata's widow. The old lady denies this, apparently quite shocked, adding that the woman is coarse, dark complexioned, and plainly of humble stock. She is probably her husband's mistress, and that is why he has brought her to have her baby here. Nisota is sceptical and they argue. In the end he declares that nothing will convince him that his aunt's story is not a lot of nonsense. He is sure this woman is Aoi Gozen and he intends to report the matter and obtain a reward. Koyoshi tries to persuade him to come into the house to wait for Kurosuke, but he refuses and goes off. Aoi Gozen comes from the inner room. She asks anxiously whether Koyoshi has any news of Koman, who is away from home. At that moment Kurosuke and Koman's little son **Tarokichi** come back from a fishing expedition. Tarokichi runs towards them crying that he has caught something very strange; it is in his grandfather's net. Kurosuke opens his net and takes from it not a fish but a human arm, the hand still clutching a white flag. The women are horrified by the sight of the smooth, white-skinned arm. Kurosuke tells them that Tarokichi found it in the river, just where it enters Lake Biwa. He dragged it to the shore, and they tried to disengage the flag, but the hand gripped it so tightly that they could not. Tarokichi then insisted on bringing it home. The two women and Kurosuke again try to release the flag, but in vain. Tarokichi tries and with no difficulty unclasps the fingers, one by one, and offers the flag to Aoi Gozen. In amazement Aoi Gozen recognizes it as the sacred standard of the Genji. Simultaneously she, Kurosuke, and Koyoshi know for certain that the white arm is that of the missing Koman.

Suddenly a friend of Kurosuke, **Tarobei,** a gentleman-farmer, rushes in and warns Kurosuke that a party of Taira samurai are making enquiries in the village. He advises Kurosuke to "clean up his house" and runs off. Kurosuke tells his wife privately that the Taira are out to exterminate the Minamoto: Aoi Gozen must be hidden with all possible speed. Koyoshi takes her and Tarokichi into the inner room.

Saito Sanemori and **Senoo Juro Kaneuji,** two high-

ranking Taira samurai, enter by the *hanamichi*, followed by
Tarobei, who points out Kurosuke's house. They enter
and seat themselves. Senoo questions Kurosuke, saying
that he is suspected of hiding Minamoto Kiso Yoshitaka's
widow who is known to be with child. Kurosuke denies
it, but Senoo tells him roughly that it is Kurosuke's own
nephew who has reported the matter and the only way to
save his skin is to surrender the lady. Kurosuke again
denies the whole story. Sanemori intervenes. As Kurosuke
has probably heard, the Taira intend to exterminate the
house of Genji, even unborn children. It is useless to attempt to conceal Aoi Gozen, but **Shigemori,** the eldest
son of Taira Kiyomori (who is now all powerful), is a humane
man and has decreed that, if Aoi Gozen's child is a girl, it
shall be spared. Kurosuke would do well to yield up the
lady, or the house will be searched, and Aoi Gozen may
be harmed. Kurosuke, after some reflection, admits that
the lady is here, adding that the baby is expected this month.
He begs them to allow her to remain where she is until
after the child's birth. Senoo refuses brusquely, saying they
have no time to waste; it will be better to kill the woman
at once and have a look at the child. The former is his
duty, he adds, and the latter Sanemori's: that is Kiyomori's
order. Kurosuke implores him to wait a month and so
spare two lives. Senoo again refuses. Kurosuke begs for
twenty days, or even ten days, but in vain. Senoo threatens
to go to look for Aoi Gozen himself.

Koyoshi's voice is heard calling to Kurosuke from the
inner room: Aoi Gozen's time is upon her. Kurosuke is
about to go to her, but is stopped by Senoo, who claims the
whole thing is a trick. A few minutes later Koyoshi enters
carrying a bundle in her arms. In tears she exclaims: "Oh,
unfortunate Genji!" Kurosuke asks anxiously whether it is
a boy or a girl. Koyoshi does not answer. Senoo assumes
from her silence that it must be a boy and orders her to
bring the baby for him to kill. But Sanemori again
intervenes: it is his duty to inspect the infant. Koyoshi
is made to show him the bundle, and Sanemori sees to his
amazement that it contains, not a child, but a severed human
arm. Senoo, from behind him, sees it also. Kurosuke,
turning on his wife, tells her that she has dishonoured Aoi
Gozen by this deception. But Koyoshi, weeping, declares

it is not a deception. She realizes now that she should have concealed the fact that the lady had given birth to such a monstrosity, but she was so flustered that she did not know what to do. Senoo asks; "Who ever heard of a woman giving birth to an arm?" But Sanemori answers that stranger things have been known to happen. Once in China there was a princess called Tokaku who suffered so greatly from the summer heat that she would constantly hold onto an iron pillar in the palace to cool herself and presently she gave birth to an iron bar, which, on the advice of the soothsayers, was forged into a famous sword called Kanshotakuya. Sanemori supposes that, on this analogy, Aoi Gozen must have been constantly massaged during her pregnancy and that the masseuse's hands brought about this strange birth. He intends, in commemoration, to rename this village Teharami-mura (the Village of the Severed Hand).

Senoo is baffled by Sanemori's smooth acceptance of the phenomenon. At last he declares he will tell Kiyomori what has occurred. Sanemori offers to take full responsibility if Kiyomori is displeased. Senoo makes a great show of going off, but, once out of sight of the house, he whistles up Nisota, and they conceal themselves in a neighbouring bamboo thicket.

Meanwhile, Aoi Gozen enters with Tarokichi and thanks Sanemori for saving her life. Sanemori tells her that before the Heike-Genji wars he served the Genji and that, although circumstances have now placed him on the other side, he cannot forget his former allegiance. The reason he volunteered for this duty was that by so doing he might be able to save Aoi Gozen and her child. As regards the severed arm, he believes it is the one he himself cut off when he and some other Taira warriors were crossing Lake Biwa by boat. Did the hand not hold a white flag? Aoi Gozen says she has the flag in her possession. She asks the age of the person holding the flag. Sanemori answers that it was a young woman of twenty-three or -four whose name, he believes, was Koman. Kurosuke and Koyoshi cry out that it was their daughter. Tarokichi bursts into tears. Kurosuke asks angrily the reason for Sanemori's cruel act. Koyoshi implores him to tell her where the body is. Sanemori agrees to tell the whole story.

(Now follows the "Sanemori Monogatari," for which the play is famous. It is considered a great test of the actor's powers. He illustrates the story with his fan.)

Munemori, the second son of Taira Kiyomori, wished to visit the shrine on Chikubu-shima, a small island on Lake Biwa. Sanemori was one of those who accompanied him. While their boat was crossing the lake, they saw a young woman swimming towards them with something white in her mouth. Sanemori wanted to rescue her, but none of the sailors was willing to leap into the bitterly cold waters. So Sanemori fastened a rope to an oar and flung it towards the swimmer, shouting to her to catch it. She did so and he drew her towards the boat and dragged her on board. He asked who she was and was told her name was Koman. Suddenly they heard a voice from the shore shouting: "She favours the Genji! She carries a white flag!" They saw a group of Taira samurai on the beach. One of the men in the boat attempted to wrest the flag from the girl's hands, but she refused to surrender it, declaring that, if she did so, the cause of the Genji would be forever lost. Sanemori, torn by conflicting loyalties, had no wish to be the instrument of the Genji doom. The girl declared that she would sooner die than relinquish the flag, so, to prevent its being taken from her by force, he killed her and, cutting off her arm, flung it, the hand still clutching the flag, into the lake, where it sank beyond the reach of the Taira. The body he carried to the shore.

Sanemori weeps as he tells the story. Kurosuke now understands why only Tarokichi was able to take the flag from the dead hand. Four fishermen enter carrying Koman's body, which they found on the shore. They say a prayer for her and leave. Kurosuke tells Tarokichi to look well at his mother, so that he will not forget her. Sanemori says gently to the child that his mother was very brave; even after her arm was cut off, she still held fast to the flag. Her heroic spirit entered into her arm which, miraculously, is still warm. Sanemori takes the Genji flag from Aoi Gozen and places it once more in the hand which closes upon it. He lays the severed arm by the corpse, to which it is rejoined, as if it had never been struck off. All cry "Koman" in wonder. Koman revives and Tarokichi rushes to her. She asks faintly if Aoi Gozen has the flag safely and, when assured that all is well, murmurs that there is something she wishes to say to Tarokichi. But she relapses into unconsciousness and dies before she can do so. Kurosuke knows what she wished to say. She wanted her son to know that she was not the real daughter of himself and Koyoshi. He found her by the lake-side when she was a baby, and with her was a dirk and a letter saying she was of Taira stock. He and his wife always expected someone to come to claim her, but no one ever did.

At this moment Aoi Gozen collapses: she is about to give birth to her child. She is helped into the inner room. Sanemori takes the white flag and sets it up at the gate so that the young heir may be born in a stronghold of his clan. Presently the cry of a baby is heard, and Kurosuke comes out to tell Sanemori that it is a boy. They give thanks, and Sanemori names him Komao-maru (later he became Kiso Yoshinaka). Kurosuke calls to Tarokichi and, giving him a short sword, sets him before Sanemori, asking that the boy be named the retainer of the new lord and made a samurai. Sanemori assents, renaming Tarokichi Tezuka no Taro Mitsumori and swearing that he himself will build a special shrine to Koman's loyal arm. (Tezuka means "the tomb of the arm.") He prophesies that the boy will be the right hand of the new Lord of Kiso.

Koyoshi enters with the baby in her arms. She brings a message from Aoi Gozen, who has overheard the foregoing conversation, to the effect that, although Tarokichi's father was a Genji and she herself loved Koman, nevertheless it is now known that Koman was a Taira, "perhaps even the daughter of Kiyomori," and therefore Tarokichi cannot become her son's retainer until he has proved himself. Sanemori agrees. Moreover, he adds, if Komao-maru is to be safeguarded from Taira vengeance, he must be taken as quickly as possible to his father's own fief, Shinshu, where Gonnosho Kaneto, his father's devoted retainer, will care for him. He bids Kurosuke prepare at once for the journey.

Senoo, who has overheard everything, leaps from the bamboo thicket and rushes upon them crying that he has Yoshikata's son in his power. Sanemori begs him to reflect that there are times when a samurai should show mercy even to his enemies. Senoo calls him a traitor and kicks Koman's body, declaring that he will kill the child out of hand. Tarokichi, hearing this and seeing his mother's corpse defiled, seizes the dirk Koman carried in her obi and attacks Senoo. He then unsheathes the sword given him by his grandfather and wounds Senoo with that also, crying; "Samurai, how dare you kick my mother?" As he falls Senoo calls to Aoi Gozen: "Now, surely, Tarokichi is worthy to be the retainer of Lord Komao-maru since he has killed a Taira."

Senoo then reveals that he was the Taira samurai who abandoned his child by the lake-side years ago. The dirk with which his grandson struck him he acknowledges as his own. He bids Tarokichi "take my head and win your spurs" and begs Sanemori's protection for the boy. Then, drawing his sword, Senoo cuts off his own head by holding the blade across the back of his neck. Kurosuke gives the head to Tarokichi to present to Aoi Gozen and her son, who now appear at the door of the inner room. Tarokichi obeys, but declares that, as he is now a samurai, he intends to avenge his mother's death by killing Sanemori. Sanemori tells him that, if he does so now, no one will believe him because he is only a little boy; but he promises that when Tarokichi is a fully grown samurai he will give him the opportunity to take his revenge.

Kurosuke's nephew, Nisota, comes out from the thicket declaring his intention to report all these treasonable happenings to the authorities. He runs off in the direction of the *hanamichi* but Sanemori kills him by throwing his short sword at him. The body is pushed down the well.

Sanemori prepares to leave by one road while the rest of the party take the other. Tarokichi renews his vow to avenge his mother's death when he reaches manhood. Sanemori bids the boy look at him well so that he may remember him. Kurosuke reminds Sanemori that by then he will be a grey-headed old man. Sanemori answers: "I shall dye my hair, so that he may recognize me." Then to Tarokichi: "We shall meet at Shinowara. Afterwards, if anyone doubts that it is the head of Saito Sanemori, wash my hair and show them the head again." Aoi Gozen intervenes to say that her son owes Sanemori a great debt and will do his utmost to prevent this vengeance. They all pose as the moon emerges from behind the clouds.

35

GION SAIREI SHINKOKI.

GION SAIREI SHINKOKI. *Jidaimono* associated with the Taiko Cycle (see page 467). — Written for the puppets in 1757 by Asada Itcho and Nakamura Ake. Later adapted for the Kabuki stage. Only one act, known as the "Golden Pavilion Scene," is still played.

This play concerns **Matsumaga Daizen,** an evil retainer of the Shogun Ashikaga Yoshiteru, who plots to destroy his master and seize his heir. Through Daizen's influence the Shogun takes as his mistress the courtesan Hanatachibana and gives himself up to pleasure. Hanatachibana is tricked by Daizen into murdering her lover, mistaking him for someone else. She afterwards takes her own life in expiation. On the Shogun's death, his infant heir is smuggled out of the palace by his faithful nurse, but Daizen seizes his late master's mother as a hostage and usurps power. Hanatachibana was a girl of good family who became a courtesan to support her mother and sister. This sister, **Yuki-hime,** is the heroine of the act summarized below. Sesson, the father of the two girls, was a famous painter. He possessed a magic sword, Kurikaramaru. He was murdered, and the sword was stolen, when he went to learn the ultimate secret of the art of painting from the dragon living beneath the Kancho Waterfall. Yuki-hime, who has inherited her father's gift, has vowed to find the sword and avenge her father. Since the sword is the symbol of the honour of her family, she keeps its loss secret, pretending that the treasure she seeks is a book on the art of painting.

Argument : *The Golden Pavilion Scene* (*Kinkakuji no Ba*). *Before the Golden Pavilion in Kyoto.* Matsunaga Daizen's retainers are on duty and reveal that, since their lord took up his quarters here and imprisoned the late Shogun's mother in the upper floor, he has given himself over to dissipation.

The sliding doors of the pavilion open. Daizen is disclosed playing *go* with his brother **Kitota.** Upon a sword-rest in the room lies the famous sword Kurikaramaru, formerly in the possession of the painter Sesson. At the end of the game Daizen discusses with his brother an awkward situation which has arisen. The late Shogun's mother, the nun **Keiju-in,** has expressed a wish to have a dragon painted on the ceiling of her room in the pavilion. She particularly desires to have the painting done by Yuki-hime or by her husband, **Kanonosuke Naonobu.** Daizen, wishing to propitiate the old lady, has had these two brought to him and has commanded first the one and then the other to paint the picture. Both have refused. Daizen, who has designs on Yuki-hime quite other than professional, has had Naonobu flung into prison, hoping to find the girl more amenable when alone. She is confined in the pavilion. Kitota thinks it foolish to take so much trouble over an old woman's whim. It would be simpler to kill her. Daizen answers that, so long as Keiju-in is in his hands, none of the late Shogun's loyal retainers will dare to move against him. His servants flatter him for his cunning. Daizen sends them away and tells his brother privately that a certain **Konoshita Tokichi,** formerly in the employ of one of his enemies, has expressed a desire to enter his service. He is vouched for by **Gumpei,** a retainer in whom Daizen has complete confidence, and should arrive shortly for an interview. (Both Gumpei and Tokichi are, in fact, faithful retainers of the Shogun in disguise and intend to rescue Keiju-in.) While waiting for Gumpei, Daizen causes the sliding doors between his room and that where Yuki-hime is imprisoned to be opened. She is weeping bitterly. Daizen assures her that he only desires her happiness. If she will paint the picture and become his mistress she shall command him in all things. Yuki-hime answers that the art of painting dragons is a secret belonging to her family. But the book containing the secret was stolen from her father and without it she cannot paint a dragon. As for the other matter, it was the Shogun himself who gave her in marriage to Naonobu, and therefore she can never give herself to another. Daizen, incensed, bids Kitota order Naonobu to be hanged in the garden well. Meanwhile, he adds, perhaps a little "torture by kindness" may make Yuki-hime change her mind.

Gumpei enters driving Tokichi before him, disarmed and with a drawn sword pointing at his throat. Daizen asks why he does this. Gumpei answers that, where his master's life is concerned, he trusts no man. Daizen says his zeal is excessive and, calling Tokichi to him, gives him back his swords. Tokichi formally offers his services. Daizen challenges him to a game of *go.* They play, watched by Yuki-hime. During the game, she is trying to make up her mind what to do. Gradually she comes to the conclusion that it is her duty to sacrifice herself to save her husband. After a final struggle, she tells Daizen that she will obey him and become his mistress. Daizen is much elated, but does not altogether trust so sudden a change of mind. As a precaution he orders Gumpei to proceed with Naonobu's execution. Yuki-hime threatens to retract her promise unless her husband is spared. Daizen countermands the order. He and Tokichi continue their game, and presently it is clear that Tokichi is the winner. Daizen is furious and threatens to strike him, but Tokichi asks for a return match. Daizen determines to try his skill in strategy by other means. He throws the box containing the *go* counters down the garden well, bidding Tokichi get it out without wetting his hands. Tokichi goes down into the garden and, taking a hollow bamboo pole, uses it to divert the neighbouring waterfall into the well so that it is filled to the brim with the box floating on the surface. He lifts out the box with his fan and, setting it on the upturned *go*-table, offers it to Daizen as if it were the severed head of an enemy, saying (somewhat cryptically) that thus he will serve his new master. Daizen formally accepts Tokichi's services and bids him go with Kitota and Gumpei to seal the bond and drink a pledge.

Left alone with Yuki-hime, Daizen orders her to paint the picture before they retire to his private apartments. Yuki-hime again tells him she cannot do it without her father's secret book. Daizen answers that he has the "book" in his possession. Taking up the magic sword Kurikaramaru, he goes with the girl into the garden. He holds the drawn sword over the waterfall. Immediately a golden dragon appears. Yuke-hime seizes Daizen's hand and stares at the sword, exclaiming that it is the treasure she seeks and Daizen must be her father's murderer. She attempts to kill Daizen, who flings her roughly to the ground, crying that she has no proof. Yuki-hime swears that the sword is proof enough. She knows it well. When it is held so that it reflects the rising sun, the God of Fire appears; when so that it reflects the setting sun, a golden dragon. This sword was stolen at the time of her father's murder, but his family concealed the loss, giving out that it was a book which disappeared. Only the murderer himself could know the truth. Daizen admits this, realizing that he can never now hope to be Yuki-hime's lover. Kitota and Tokichi return and bind Yuki-hime. Daizen orders Gumpei once more to execute Naonobu. Yuki-hime he will keep with him so that he may watch her suffer. He entrusts the magic sword to Kitota, who leaves with Gumpei. At Daizen's command, Tokichi ties Yuki-hime to a cherry tree in the garden.

(*Degatari* music. The musicians appear on the stage.) Yuki-hime is alone. The chorus sings of her loyalty and virtue and of Naonobu, who must soon die at this season when the world is full of life and beauty.

Naonobu, bound, is brought through the garden on his way to execution. He begs Yuki-hime's forgiveness for having failed to avenge her father and asks her to live on so that she can serve their late master's mother, Keiju-in. He is dragged away by Gumpei. (The following scene is performed as a *ningyo-buri*; see page 454.) After he has gone, Yukihime realizes that in her distress she has failed to tell him that Daizen is her father's murderer. She struggles to free herself, but in vain. Then she recalls an old story of a priest who, when he was a prisoner, turned himself into a rat and gnawed through his own bonds. She prays passionately to be turned into any sort of animal so that she may free herself, but no change takes place. She recalls another story about her own grandfather. As a boy he was once tied to a pillar in the temple because he drew pictures instead of studying. He drew a rat with his tears on the temple floor, and the rat materialized and freed him. Perhaps his grandchild may be able to do the same. With her feet she gathers into a heap the cherry-blossom petals which strew the ground and with her toe she draws in them the picture of a rat. In an instant a real rat appears and gnaws through her bonds. Yuki-hime is about to hurry after her husband, but Kitota emerges behind her and holds her fast. They struggle together. Yuki-hime's hand touches her adversary's dagger. She draws it to defend herself and kills Kitota.

Tokichi, splendidly attired in ceremonial dress and no longer concealing his true identity, now comes to her. Taking the magic sword from Kitota's body, he gives it to Yuki-hime, but, when she wishes at once to seek Daizen in order to avenge her father, he bids her have patience a little longer. Daizen is the enemy of all right-minded men, but his hour has not yet struck. Tokichi tells her Naonobu is safe. Gumpei is a friend in disguise and will not kill him. Tokichi sends her to join her husband while he himself frees Keiju-in.

Tokichi looks up at the windows of the room where Keiju-in is imprisoned. He sees a star shining above the roof and recognizes it as his lucky star. Some samurai try to prevent him from entering the pavilion, but he routs them all. He hears near at hand the drums of the army mustered by his colleagues, the late Shogun's faithful retainers. He climbs up into the branches of the cherry tree.

The stage is lowered to show the upper floor of the pavilion. The blinds are rolled up and Keiju-in is discoverd, seated in meditation. Tokichi enters, tells her who he is and that he has come to rescue her. She, who has utterly resigned herself to die, begs him to leave her to her fate. Tokichi reminds her that her duty to her infant grandson, the new Shogun, requires her to live. He lights a signal to inform the approaching army that she is safe.

The stage rises again to show the garden as before. Daizen enters brandishing a halberd and fights with the attacking soldiery. Tokichi and Gumpei appear with their retainers. They announce their true names — Mashiba Chikusen-no-kami Hisayoshi and Kato Kuranosuke Masakiyo — and surround Daizen, bidding him prepare to die. Daizen defies them and out of admiration for his courage his enemies agree to spare him a shameful death. All three swear to meet on the battlefield.

(Students of Japanese history will realize that Mashiba Hisayoshi is the stock theatrical version of the name of Mashiba, later Toyotomi, Hideyoshi. The approaching army is led by Oda Nobunaga. The character of Matsunaga Daizen is fictitious and so is his plot against the Shogunate.)

GOJU NO TO (*The Five-Storied Pagoda*). *Sewamono.*— The play is taken from an original story by Rohan Koda and describes the complicated interplay of loyalties and emotions amongst a group of architects and workmen. The central figure is **Kawagoe no Genta,** a famous architect who was responsible for the building of the Kaneiji at Yanaka in Edo, one of the most important Buddhist temples of the Tokugawa period. The temple was so famous and its abbot **Uda no Roen,** a saint and a prince of the Imperial family, was so renowned that pilgrims flocked to it from all over Japan. Their pious offerings soon made it possible to contemplate the building of a five-storied pagoda to embellish the precincts.

Act I

The lodgings of the Abbot Roen. The Abbot has summoned Genta in order to unfold his wishes to him. Genta is accompanied by one of his pupils called **Jubei,** whom he particularly loves because, of all his apprentices, he is the only true genius. Yet Jubei is idle and slapdash. He is known by his fellows as Nossori, the "sluggard." As the Abbot explains his project and asks Genta to estimate the cost, Jubei is seized with a passionate desire to build the pagoda himself, to achieve immortal fame for having been solely responsible for its design and construction. So lost is he in a daydream of his own future greatness that he fails to notice even that the interview is over and the Abbot has withdrawn. Called back to the present, he clumsily stumbles from the room.

Act II

Sc. 1. *Genta's house.* The apprentices and workmen are gathered to drink, smoke, and gossip. Genta's wife, **O Kichi,** learns of the new project from them. When Genta comes in, she asks whether he has secured the contract and is upset when he replies in the negative in an offhand manner. Genta has great talent, but he lacks inspiration, and for some reason he cannot wholly understand, the building of the pagoda does not fire his imagination. Jubei and his wife, **O Nami,** come to call. O Nami has learnt of Jubei's ambition and wants him to tell Genta about it. Jubei is half-ashamed and half-frightened. He does not want to steal a march on his old master, but yet he feels he must do this thing himself. And then again he fears that he cannot manage without Genta's help. O Nami forces him to talk. Genta encourages him, not realizing that Jubei wants to do the work on his own and thinking perhaps that Jubei will supply the inspiration he himself lacks. The conversation is rudely interrupted by **Seikichi,** a fanatically loyal, but jealous carpenter of Genta's who knows of Jubei's scheme. Genta quells Seikichi and gives his blessing to Jubei.

Sc. 2. *Jubei's house.* In his untidy, broken-down dwelling Jubei is hard at work making drawings of the pagoda. Genta calls with a gift, hoping to discover how Jubei's work is progressing. Jubei declines to show his plans, and Genta withdraws in a bad temper. Jubei has more or less completed his drawings, but he is puzzled to know how to present them to the Abbot in such a way that they will be accepted. His little boy breaks in with a crudely-made wooden model of a pagoda, and Jubei conceives the idea of making a small replica of the dream building he has designed and taking it to the Abbot. (In a subsequent scene, usually omitted, he presents his model to the Abbot and eloquently pleads for the contract.)

Act III

Genta's wood yard. Genta's workmen are going about their tasks. Jubei has become more absent-minded and aloof than ever. The other workmen mock him, but he takes no notice. Suddenly Seikichi arrives with the news that the Abbot has decided to give the contract to Jubei. Seikichi is furious and, seeing Jubei, attacks him with intent to kill. He is prevented by **Eiji,** the guild master, and O Kichi, who persuade him that Jubei has done nothing wrong, although his action must estrange him from Genta.

(Jubei throws himself heart and soul into the work, and by the end of the following January the pagoda is ready for dedication. On the very eve of the ceremony, however, a mighty storm of wind and rain rises and everyone fears lest the new structure, built on daringly modern lines, should not survive the buffeting. In two scenes, which are not usually performed, these fears are expressed to Jubei, first by the monks and then by the Abbot Roen himself. To the monks Jubei boastfully asserts that the pagoda will stand as firm as a rock. When he waits on the Abbot, however, the storm is raging more fiercely than ever. The Abbot is anxious, and Jubei begins to have doubts. Perhaps he has tempted Providence too far. Perhaps he was wrong to break away from Genta. Perhaps there was some secret of construction which he ought to have known and did not. He resolves to kill himself if the pagoda collapses.)

Act IV

Sc. 1. *The top storey of the pagoda against a storm-lashed sky.* Jubei is seen crouching against the doorway clutching a chisel to his breast.

Sc. 2. *Before the pagoda, the following morning.* It is calm and bright. Great trees lie in splintered ruin all around, but the pagoda stands. Genta appears. He too has watched all night in the neighbourhood. He examines the building with approval. The door opens, and Jubei staggers out more dead than alive. He sees Genta and throws himself on his knees before him. He realizes now that Genta's training has been responsible for his success, not his own genius. The two are reconciled. The priests arrive for the dedication ceremony. The Abbot Roen has written a memorial notice in his own hand and, because he is a saint to whom the hearts of all men are open, he has written thereon : " Jubei, a native of Kyoto, built this pagoda, but Genta made its accomplishment possible."

GO TAIHEIKI SHIRAISHI BANASHI. Sewamono. — Written for the puppets by Kino Jotaro and first staged at the Geki-za, Edo, in 1781. The original play was in eleven acts, of which Acts IV to VIII told the story of two sisters. This was based on a true incident in which a certain farmer from near Sendai was killed by a samurai and avenged five years later by his two daughters. Out of this long play only one scene is still performed. Although there is little or no action, it survives because it contains three excellent vehicles for actors. The actor playing Soroku must have a beautiful and persuasive voice. It has some affinities with the single act of J.M. Barrie's unfinished play *Shall We Join the Ladies ?* for here, as in the English play, the situation is set with skill and economy. We have the meeting of the two sisters and their decision to avenge their father. We realize, although they do not yet know it, that both the murderer and the man who will help them redeem their vow are under the same roof as they. How this is done can well be left to the imagination of the audience.

Argument : *The Yoshiwara Daikokuya Scene.* **Miyagino's** *room in the Daikokuya.* Miyagino is her professional name, taken from her native district near Sendai. She is so famous that the other courtesans of the Daikokuya use names derived from hers in the hope that it will bring them luck.

Miyasato and **Miyashiba** enter followed by Miyagino herself, accompanied by her maid. Miyasato and Miyashiba discuss two new clients who have just arrived. They are country samurai, and one is a handsome young man. The other "looks like a bear" and has an enormous moustache and large, protruding eyes. They wonder which will fall to their respective lots. They gossip about the new maidservant engaged the day before by the master of the house. She is a raw country girl who says she has come to Edo to look for her sister. Miyagino shows interest and Miyasato and Miyashiba go off to find the girl.

Presently they return with a shy little country girl called **Shinobu,** who is so afraid to enter the room that they have to push her over the threshold. She speaks with a strong northeastern accent, using country words and expressions. She stares round the room, commenting on the luxury of everything. The two courtesans laugh at her strange speech and ask her about herself. Shinobu bursts into tears and says she is from a village near Sendai. She was separated from her parents by tragic circumstances and came to Edo because she has heard it is a splendid place and because she has a sister who is a famous beauty of the Yoshiwara. The two courtesans can hardly understand what she says and wonder who her sister can be. Miyagino, who has been listening in silence, tells them not to make fun of the child: she can perfectly understand what she says. She bids them go and prepare to receive the guests. She sends her maid off on an errand.

As soon as they are out of the room, Miyagino calls Shinobu to her, asking her the name of her native village. When she hears it is Sakai, near Shirasaka, she asks whether Shinobu knows a man called Yomosaku. Shinobu exclaims in surprise that he was her father (she uses the north-country names for father and mother, "Da-san" and "Ga-san"). Miyagino tells her that in that case they are sisters. To convince her, she shows her a little charm which is identical with the one Shinobu wears round her own neck. They embrace and weep for joy.

Soroku, the master of the house, is in the next room and overhears their conversation. Miyagino asks for news

of their parents, and in tears Shinobu tells her that their
father has been killed by the *daikan* (a samurai in charge of
a district) **Shiza Daishichi,** because he, being a brave *ronin*,
stood up for the rights of the farmers. To the consternation
of her sister, Miyagino faints with grief and only revives
when Shinobu administers some medicine thrown into the
room by Soroku. Shinobu tells her moreover that she
herself witnessed the crime and would have been killed
as well if her uncle had not protected her. Their mother
died of grief, and Shinobu was taken into her uncle's household. But they treated her like a servant, and she ran away,
intending to find her sister and avenge her father. Miyagino
tells Shinobu how much she envies her for having been so
much longer with their parents. When she was twelve years
old, she sold herself to the licensed quarter to earn the
money needed to save her father, who had been imprisoned
for not paying his taxes. Since then she has lived in the
hope of returning to her native village and spending the rest
of her life caring for her parents. She used to dream of
marrying the man to whom she was betrothed as a child
and giving her parents a strong son; she has even heard that
this young man is in Edo and hoped to see him. But now
she must think only of revenge. She looks at the book
beside her and adds that they must seek inspiration from
the example of the Soga brothers in the old story. She
asks Shinobu whether she could recognize the murderer of
their father if she saw him again. Shinobu is sure that she
would, for he had big, protruding eyes and a flat nose.
Looking round nervously, Miyagino bids her lower her voice
"for walls have ears." They must escape from this place
and, remembering only that they are a samurai's daughters,
plan their revenge. They can creep out under cover of the
noise of the party next door.

The two girls go to the door. When they open it, they are
confronted by Soroku. Miyagino realizes that he must have
overheard their talk and, pulling out her razor, threatens
to kill him if he means to betray them. Soroku easily takes
away her weapon and bids her be calm while they talk things
over. She wants to imitate the Soga brothers. Picking up
her book, Soroku reads out a passage describing how Juro
and Goro sought their god-father's support in their mission.
If two boys needed help, says Soroku, how much more will

two girls! Revenge is a business which requires great patience. It is useless for Miyagino to try to run away; she is sure to be brought back immediately; she does not even know her way about Edo. She must not think him unkind, he goes on, but, after all, all courtesans love their parents, and if he let them do as they chose he would have to go out of business. Nevertheless, he feels it must be God's will which has brought Miyagino and Shinobu together and he will do what he can to help them. But they must be patient. How can Miyagino, who could not even scratch him just now with her razor, hope to kill a samurai? She spoke a few minutes ago of her betrothed. If she can find this young man to protect and help her, he, Soroku, will tear up her contract and let her go. But they must remember that the Soga brothers waited for eighteen years before they avenged their father. Miyagino, in tears, begs Soroku's forgiveness for attacking him and thanks him for his kindness.

At this moment, **O Masa,** the maid, summons Miyagino to the waiting guests. Soroku sends her to fetch his letter-case, and Miyagino, with a sigh, begins to make up her face for her evening's work. As Miyagino rises to go, Soroku takes from the letter-case two papers, her contract and a permit to leave the licensed quarter. He gives them to Miyagino, saying: "These are the two Soga brothers' passes." (See *Kotobuki Soga no Taimen*.) Miyagino takes them gratefully. She is about to go out, accompanied by Shinobu, but Soroku holds back the younger sister, saying: "She must not go; she is too young to know a man."

HEIKE NYOGO GA SHIMA, commonly known as *Shunkan*. *Jidaimono* of the Heike-Genji Cycle (see page 418). — Written for the puppet theatre by Chikamatsu Monzaemon and later adapted for Kabuki. It was the favourite play of Ichikawa Danzo III. The theme is taken from the *Heike Monogatari* and *Gempei Sesuiki*. The author was much influenced by the Noh play *Shunkan*, which portrays Shunkan's loneliness when abandoned on an island.

In the days when the Taira clan was paramount and Taira Kiyomori ruled Japan, there were many who resented his despotism. A number of abortive attempts were made to overthrow him.   One of these attempts was planned by three noblemen : a high priest whose name in religion was **Shunkan ; Taira Yasuyori**, lord of Hei ; and **Fujiwara Naritsune,** lord of Tamba. They were betrayed to Kiyomori, surprised, and taken prisoner at Shunkan's house at Shishi-ga-Tani, near Kyoto. They were all three exiled to Kikai ga Shima, a lonely island south of Kyushu. A few years later a general amnesty was granted on the birth of a son to the Empress, Kiyomori's daughter, and the exiles were allowed to return to the mainland.

Argument : The rocky shore of Kikai-ga-Shima, where Shunkan is living in a little hut of reeds. Shunkan is old and feeble but much loved and respected by his two companions. Yasuyori comes to tell him that Naritsune, hardly more than a youth, has fallen in love with a pretty fisher-girl of the island. Shunkan listens sympathetically and, when they are joined by Naritsune, gives his consent to the marriage. He bids him call the girl, **Chidori,** and presently she appears, overcome with shyness at finding herself in such noble company. Shunkan himself performs the ceremony, but since there is no *sake*, the bride and bridegroom pledge each other in sea-water. Shunkan tells Chidori that, if ever her husband is pardoned, she will be the Lady of Tamba. He wishes to perform an auspicious dance in honour of the young people and, having no fan, uses a paulownia leaf instead. But when he starts to dance, he is so weak from his many privations that he stumbles and falls. He laughs the mattter off, however, so as not to worry his companions.

At this moment they notice a vessel approaching the island, a sight not seen since they were marooned three years before. The ship enters the cove and from it disembarks Taira Kiyomori's messenger, **Senoo Taro Kaneyasu.** He announces that, to celebrate the birth of the heir to the throne, an amnesty has been granted. Drawing out the Imperial Rescript, he informs Naritsune and Yasuyori that they are pardoned and set at liberty. Shunkan waits to hear that he too is pardoned ; but there is no mention of his name. When Senoo Kaneyasu turns the document towards the pardoned exiles that they may read the order themselves, Shunkan, whose eye-sight is dim, creeps slowly towards it and assures himself, with bitter grief, that his name is really not there. (This scene is considered a great test of the actor). Senoo Kaneyasu looks on with heartless composure. But now a second messenger disembarks from the ship. He is **Tanzaemon Motoyasu** and he brings a second order. Because he was considered the ring-leader of the plot, Shunkan has been excluded from the amnesty, but, on the intervention of Komatsu, one of Kiyomori's chief councillors, his sentence has been mitigated and he may return as far as the Province of Bizen in Kyushu. Shunkan's joy as he verifies the good news with his own eyes is unbounded. Taking Chidori with them, the three exiles are about to go on board, when they are stopped by Senoo Kaneyasu : their orders permit them to embark only three people; the girl must be left behind. Shunkan, Naritsune, and Yasuyori all protest, Naritsune telling the messenger that Chidori is his wife. But it is of no avail. When Naritsune says that he will remain on the island, he is taken on board by force. Chidori is left alone on the shore.

Shunkan returns and tries to smuggle Chidori onto the ship, but he is pursued and prevented by Senoo Kaneyasu. Shunkan again appeals to his mercy, but Senoo mocks him and takes pleasure in warning him that he will not find his family awaiting him in Bizen: his wife is dead, and his son has long been missing. Overcome with grief and rage, Shunkan finds new strength and, wresting Senoo's sword from him, kills him after a grim struggle. He then thrusts Chidori on board, telling Motoyasu that, since he has now forfeited his pardon, Chidori can go in his place. All bid Shunkan a sad farewell and the ship sets sail. Shunkan clings to the mooring rope, his last link with the homeland until it is jerked from his hands. He watches the ship grow small in the distance and climbs from rock to rock trying to keep it in sight, until at last it vanishes over the horizon.

HIGE YAGURA (*The Tower for Whiskers*). *Shosagoto*.— Adapted by Miyake Tokuro from a *kyogen* of the same name. *Tokiwazu* accompaniment. The scene represents the Kabuki version of the Noh stage.

Argument : The lord **Hige no Saemon** has a magnificent beard and moustache of which he is inordinately proud. He receives a message summoning him to the Imperial Court and believes the appointment is largely due to his splendid whiskers. He boasts about it so much that his wife loses all patience with him. She calls together a group of her friends, who arrive carrying ancient pikes and halberds. She herself is armed with a large pair of scissors. Saemon takes fright at the sight of them and, to protect his beard and moustache, makes himself a wooden tower, into which he retires. This tower is represented by a sort of wooden box with doors which he hangs round his neck. The women chase him all over the house and eventually succeed in "entering" his fortress. Then, while her friends hold him down, his wife cuts off his whiskers with her scissors.

Saemon is left disconsolate and unable to obey the Imperial summons. The women retire along the *hanamichi*. The last to go is Saemon's wife, who performs a comic feminine version of a triumphant exit dance. Saemon catches cold, and the curtain is drawn on his sneezes.

HIKOSAN GONGEN CHIKAI NO SUKEDACHI, commonly called *Keyamura Rokusuke. Jidaimono.* — Written for the puppets in 1786 by Ume no Shiakaze and Chikamatsu Yasuzo. Later adapted for the Kabuki stage. Of the original eleven acts only four survive. Of these the most famous is Act VIII which is summarized below. The play is remarkable for the character of the heroine, O Sono, a "woman of chivalrous spirit" (*onna-budo*).

Yoshioka Ichimisai was the head of a famous school of fencing. He had two daughters, **O Sono,** whom he betrothed to his favourite pupil, **Keyamura Rokusuke,** and O Yuki, who was a widow and the mother of a little boy, **Yasamatsu.** Ichimisai was challenged to a fencing match by the head of a rival fencing school, **Kyogoku Takumi.** Ichimisai beat Takumi, and the latter was so filled with shame and anger that he murdered Ichimisai and fled. O Sono and O Yuki went in search of him to avenge their father. They took with them a faithful servant and little Yasamatsu. O Sono's mother set out for the home of her daughter's betrothed, Rokusuke, to bring him the news and obtain his help in the vendetta. While the two young women were on their travels, they were surprised by their enemy, Takumi, who murdered O Yuki. Their servant was killed, and the child, Yasamatsu, disappeared. O Sono, continued the search alone.

Keyamura Rokusuke was living in Kokura, in Kyushu, having taken service with the local lord. To this town Takumi (calling himself Mijin Danjo) also came. He saw a notice announcing that the lord of Kokura offered a prize of 500 bales of rice to anyone able to defeat Keyamura Rokusuke in a fencing match. Takumi knew who Rokusuke was, although the two men had never met. He determined to use this opportunity to get rid of a dangerous enemy. He found a sick old woman, the mother of a poor wood-cutter, and, forcing her to accompany him, went to Rokusuke and implored him to allow himself to be beaten so that "Danjo" might be able to support and care for his "mother." Rokusuke was so deeply touched by such filial devotion that he allowed his rival to win the match. As a result he was dismissed from his post, discredited, and reduced to poverty. He became a wood-cutter.

Act VIII

Rokusuke's cottage near Kokura. A child's kimono is hanging out to dry. Rokusuke, with a scar on his forehead from the wound received in the fencing match, enters and offers prayers for his master's soul. Yasamatsu, O Sono's little nephew, whom Rokusuke found wandering about lost (having escaped from Takumi) and for whom he cares as if he were his own child, returns from the village, and Rokusuke plays with him in the garden. Rokusuke laments that the grandchild of his master should have no better toys than stones. The little boy begins to cry for his mother. Rokusuke consoles him, and the child falls asleep and is carried into the house. Rokusuke watches beside him.

One of Takumi's minions, his face hidden in a straw mat, enters, stands for a moment gazing along the *hanamichi*, and then conceals himself among the trees. O Sono, disguised as a pilgrim musician, comes down the *hanamichi*. She is dogged by three local bad characters who intend to rob her. They attack her, but she has no difficulty in driving them off. She sees the child's kimono and recognizes it as belonging to Yasamatsu. She is convinced that the murderer of her sister and the kidnapper of the child must be living in this house. O Sono is not only brave, but so strong that she can lift a heavy tub (used for making *mochi* or rice paste). She goes to take the kimono, but the ruffians again attack her, shouting "Thief!" She once more routs them, watched with some interest by Rokusuke. She enters the house and tries to kill Rokusuke. He wards off the blow, completely mystified. The noise wakes Yasamatsu who comes running out. O Sono seizes him in her arms and again attacks Rokusuke. The latter, anxious not to frighten the little boy, tries to pretend that it is a game they are playing. He asks O Sono whether she is mad, telling her who he is and claiming that he is a fit person to have charge of the boy. Although they are betrothed, Rokusuke and O Sono have never seen each other. O Sono is so overcome with joy and relief at finding her fiancé that she forgets that he does not know who she is. She merely says that she is his wife and, shedding her disguise, begins to bustle about the house, lighting the fire and putting the rice-pot on to boil. (This contrast between O Sono's physical toughness and her womanly domesticity is the highlight of the play.) Rokusuke is still bewildered and suspicious. At last he discovers who O Sono is, and his joy is as great as her own. He insists upon her taking the most honourable seat in the room, while she tries to refuse. She is describing to him her many adventures when Takumi's accomplice, who has been all this time in ambush near the house, bursts in upon them and attempts to murder O Sono. O Sono overcomes him without difficulty but with considerable embarrassment, pausing now and then during the fight to assure her betrothed that, although her arm is strong, her heart is meek and gentle. Rokusuke watches her with respectful admiration. No sooner has the assassin been given his deserts than O Sono's mother, with Yasamatsu, comes from the inner room and begs Rokusuke to marry her daughter at once before continuing the vendetta. She presents him with her late husband's swords. While Rokusuke and O Sono are drinking their marriage cups, a wood-cutter, **Onoemon,** comes to the house to beg Rokusuke's assistance in avenging his old mother who has been brutally murdered. He shows the body to Rokusuke, who recognizes it as that of the "sick mother" of the man calling himself Mijin Danjo. He realizes how he has been tricked and deduces that this man must be none other than Kyogoku Takumi, the enemy both he and O Sono seek. His suspicions are later confirmed when O Sono's mother shows him a picture of Takumi, which clinches the matter. Rokusuke promises Onoemon that his mother shall be avenged. (Onoemon is the clown found in most puppet plays. Although he appears under tragic circumstances, his rôle is a comic one.) Rokusuke puts on the formal dress of a samurai. Yasamatsu begs to go with him to avenge his mother. Taking the child in his arms, he leaves in search of Takumi, carrying with him a branch of plum blossom bearing both red and white flowers to represent the two sisters, O Sono and O Yuki, and a branch of camelia to represent their mother.

HIRAGANA SEISUIKI. *Jidaimono.* — Written for the puppets by Takeda Izumo (1691—1756), Miyoshi Shoraku (1696—1775?), and Asada Kakei (1705?—1760?). First staged at the Takemoto-za in 1739. The original play was in five acts of which only two survive. The hero is **Minamoto Kiso Yoshinaka,** the cousin and, for a short time, the rival of Yoritomo (see Note on the Heike-Genji Cycle, page 421). For the purpose of the play he is accused of plotting to overthrow the Imperial power. Yoshinaka does not appear in person in either of the acts summarized below. The first is an entirely fictitious story concerning the sons of Kajiwara Kagetoki (see page 127). The second describes an attempt by a devoted retainer of Yoshinaka's to avenge his dead lord and has much in common with the revenge of Taira Tomomori in *Yoshitsune Sembonzakura,* written eight years later by the same authors.

Act I

The Disinheriting of Genta (Genta Kando no Ba).

Sc. 1. *The palace of Kajiwara Kagetoki at Kamakura.* **Kajiwara Kagetoki** and his elder son **Genta Kagesue** are away with the army of Yoritomo which, under Yoshitsune and his brother Noriyori, has taken the field against Kiso Yoshinaka. Today is Genta's birthday, and his armour and helmet are displayed in the *tokonoma* with offerings of wine and food on his behalf. Three maid-servants praise Genta's beauty, valour, and nobility. They compare unfavourably his younger brother **Heiji Kagetaka,** who is malingering at home instead of fighting alongside his father and brother. **Sado Junsai,** the family priest, enters and upbraids them for wasting their time gossiping instead of tending Heiji who is ill. The girls withdraw reluctantly. Left alone, Junsai reveals that he is Heiji's close confidant and expects to wield great power if the latter is able to supplant his brother and become lord of the household. While he is indulging in these dreams, **Yokosuka Gunnai,** a messenger sent by Kajiwara from Kyoto, announces Genta's imminent return. He himself would have arrived sooner, but he was delayed by bad weather. He has a letter from Kajiwara to their lady. Their young lord may arrive at any moment. Junsai looks gloomy at this news, but Gunnai assures him that all will turn out for the best and whispers something in his ear which cheers him. They go out together to bring the news to Heiji, to whom they refer obsequiously as "the young master." *The stage revolves.*

Sc. 2. *The bedroom of Heiji Kagetaka.* Heiji is lying in bed, smoking. The waiting-maids are noisily playing at "Poem Cards" in the room. Heiji asks crossly why they do not talk to him. He enquires where the waiting maid **Chidori** is. One of the other girls goes to call her from his mother's side and she enters, bringing Heiji's medicine. Chidori is a lovely girl and a favourite of her mistress. Heiji addresses her with clumsy gallantry, which she shows she does not like. He suggests that they should all have a party with plenty of drink and sends the other girls off to prepare for it, forcing Chidori to stay behind. He makes love to her, but she repels him, saying that, since she took service with his mother in order to ask a favour on her father's behalf, she cannot prejudice her position by carrying on an intrigue with her mistress' son. Heiji retorts angrily that she does not have the same scruples where his brother Genta is concerned. Chidori escapes from him and runs out of the room.

Gunnai and Junsai enter. Gunnai says he brings good news and begins in a mysterious manner : "Genta Kagesue Sama, riding on his black horse Surusumi—" He pauses and refuses to continue until he has received a "present" from Heiji. He then tells how at the battle of the Uji River, in which Kiso Yoshinaka was defeated, Genta, having vowed to be the first to cross the flood failed to do so. Another warrior was before him, and all the army mocked at him. Kajiwara was publicly shamed and would have killed his son out of hand; but that would be sacrilege in the capital. Genta is therefore being sent back to Kamakura, and there he will be ordered to commit *seppuku*. Kajiwara has issued instructions that he is to be treated with great severity. Gunnai adds that, when Genta is dead, Heiji will be his father's heir, and he and Junsai offer the young man their congratulations.

A voice announces the arrival of "the young master" (a title to which Heiji has, of course, no right while Genta lives). Heiji presents his coat to Gunnai as a reward and goes out, followed by his jackals. *The stage revolves.*

Sc. 3. *Inner room of the palace.* Genta Kagesue, a handsome young man wearing court dress, enters and asks to be announced to his mother. **Enju** comes to him joyfully, rejoicing that Yoritomo is victorious. Genta confirms this, adding that his father is well. Enju then asks him, with some surprise, why he has come home while fighting still continues. Genta answers that his father has ordered him to come, but has given no reason. He expected that his mother would have already heard from his father, but Enju shows him Kajiwara's letter still unopened, saying it has only just arrived and she has not yet had time to read it. She will do so at once. While she is reading, Chidori brings Genta refreshments ; it is plain from the way the young people greet each other that they are on intimate terms. Chidori comments anxiously on Genta's changed appearance ; he has grown thin and pale. Genta replies evasively and asks after Heiji. Chidori answers that he is, so far as she is concerned, in " far too robust health ." At this moment Heiji enters, asking Genta for news of the battle "in which, I suppose, you performed great feats of arms." Genta says quietly that he thinks he won his spurs, but will describe the battle later. Heiji presses him, and Genta does so in a dramatic narration (see page 443). The chanters tell how Kiso Yoshinaka angered the retired Emperor Go-Shirakawa by his overbearing behaviour, so that it was believed that he aimed to overthrow the Imperial House. Go-Shirakawa therefore commanded Yoritomo to destroy Yoshinaka, and an army of twenty-five thousand men was sent against him under Yoshitsune and Noriyori. Yoshinaka faced this army across the Uji River, not far from Kyoto, with only about five or six thousand soldiers. It was the end of the first month and the river was swollen with melted snow. Yoshinaka's warriors taunted their enemies and dared them to attempt the crossing, while they stood on the far bank with their bows strung and their arrows ready. At first no one would venture ; then he, Genta, decided to attempt the feat. He mounted his horse Surusumi, the gift of Yoritomo, and entered the river. Only one warrior, Sasaki Shiro Takatsuna, dared to follow him.

At this point Genta is roughly interrupted by Heiji, who says scornfully that, since the rest of the story will be painful to relate, he will tell it for his brother. Chidori bids him be quiet. Heiji retorts angrily that he knows the end of the tale : Takatsuna was the better man and crossed first, more shame to his brother. Chidori refuses to believe this. She is sure that, even though Yoshinaka's warriors must have placed stakes under the water to bring the horsemen down, Genta was first. Genta tells her she is right ; he won by a couple of yards. Heiji cries out that he is lying. He has had the true story from Gunnai. Takatsuna tricked Genta by shouting to him that his girths were slipping and, while Genta was tightening them, overtook and passed him, reaching the shore first. Personally, Heiji adds, he admires Takatsuna's cunning and considers his brother utterly disgraced. Genta is silent, while Chidori weeps.

Heiji asks his mother whether she has not had the true story from their father and whether Genta does not merit death. He tries to take the letter from her, but she strikes his hand away. She is in great distress. Heiji tells Genta that, if he had any proper feeling, he would have died before this of his own free will, instead of waiting to be ordered by their father. Since he lacks the courage to die, he, Heiji, will strike off his head and then, for the sake of the family honour, will give out that his brother committed *seppuku* as a samurai should. Heiji draws his sword, but Genta disarms him and beats him with the flat of the blade. Heiji escapes from the room. Genta asks Chidori to leave him alone with his mother. When she has gone, he implores Enju to believe that he is not afraid to die. She asks him to explain this extraordinary story, and with some hesitation, he does so. Some time ago his father, at archery practice, accidentally shot down the white standard of the Genji, which was considered a terrible omen of ill luck. Yoritomo was very angry, and Kajiwara wished to atone by committing *seppuku*, but Sasaki Takatsuna interceded with Yoritomo and saved Kajiwara's life. Genta himself was not present and, when he heard of it, he wished greatly to do Takatsuna some service to show his gratitude. Up to the time of crossing the Uji River no opportunity presented itself. When Genta was in the water he looked over his shoulder and saw who was following him. He realized that the opportunity to serve Takatsuna had come. He reined in his horse and allowed Takatsuna to reach the shore first. This he did deliberately. He feels no shame, for it was an act of filial piety. But he cannot explain this to his father; so he will now die, not because he has committed a fault, but for his father's sake.

Genta then lays his hand on his sword-hilt, but Enju stops him, asking why he did not tell all this to his father. Genta explains that, if he did so, he would nullify his tribute to Takatsuna by taking away his victory. He fears that he ought not to have told even his mother and begs her never to reveal this secret to anyone, even after his death. Enju implores him not to die, but Genta answers that he has no alternative. Enju then tries guile. She tells her son to think of his duty to Yoritomo, to whom he is especially bound since Yoritomo is his godfather. Genta has as yet had no opportunity to serve him. She reminds him that he, the eldest son, is called Genta (for the Genji) and not Heita (for the Heike, the clan to which the Kajiwara family had always been affiliated until Kagetoki joined Yoritomo) because of this special bond between his father and his lord. Genta has thought of all that, he answers, and, since a vassal must serve his lord in three lives, he will wait to do so in the next. Enju then sadly appeals to his love for herself: "We are mother and child in this life only. The child who wishes to die before his mother is cruel, and the husband who wishes to kill his son is crueller still. You are not only your father's son, but mine as well." She tears Kajiwara's letter into shreds.

Gunnai bursts into the room, crying that she is disloyal to their master and must force Genta to die. Genta replies proudly that he is fully prepared, but Enju says she will not permit it. She declares that since Genta has disgraced

their house, *seppuku* is too good for him. She has decided
to deprive him of his two swords and disinherit him, a far
more shameful punishment. She orders Gunnai to bring
her some old servant's clothing, and presently Heiji enters,
with Gunnai and Junsai, bringing the clothes. Heiji and
Gunnai strip Genta. Heiji mocks his brother : the new
clothes become him very well. Gunnai and Junsai, following
their master's lead, also scoff at and maltreat him, but his
quiet dignity shames them into silence, to the annoyance of
Heiji. Genta without a word bows his head and weeps,
while Enju, tears in her eyes, tries to pretend that she also
is deriding him. The noise attracts Chidori's attention. She
brands Enju as an inhuman mother. Looking at Heiji, Enju
answers that she hopes that this will serve as a warning to
Genta's brother. If Genta wishes to be reinstated, let him
prove his worth fighting the Heike. To Heiji she adds
pointedly : "Don't you agree, my son ?" Looking at Genta with loving eyes, she says that he will soon win his spurs
again. Genta in tears bows before her.

Heiji seizes Chidori, claiming that now she must give up
Genta and become his concubine. When Chidori refuses
angrily, he turns to his mother and claims that Genta and
Chidori are lovers and have disgraced her roof. Enju feigns
anger and drives Chidori before her into another room. Gunnai persuades Heiji that Chidori is not worthy of him,
having been Genta's mistress. Heiji, realizing that he has
lost the girl through his own fault, draws his sword and
attacks Genta, who strikes the weapon from his hand with an
exhortation to more worthy behaviour. Heiji, crestfallen and
shaken, is assisted from the room by Junsai. Gunnai also
tries to escape, but is recalled by Genta. He nervously
reminds Genta that he is Kajiwara's messenger and representative and therefore Genta owes him filial respect. Genta
agrees ; then, seizing Gunnai and wrenching his sword from
him, he cries : "It is your own sword that punishes you. Genta does not kill you. Only his hand strikes." When his enemy
is dead, Genta wishes to take leave of his mother, but realizes that it is better if he does not. He comforts himself
with the thought that he will soon return to her with some
great feat of arms to his credit. He is about to go when the
door opens and he sees Enju standing in it. She does not
look at him, but, indicating the armour in the alcove, com-

ments that, although she cannot give arms to a disinherited son, this harness, the gift of Yoritomo at Genta's birth, is his own property and no one can prevent him from taking it away. Genta takes the armour and finds Chidori concealed behind the chest. This, she explains, is also his mother's kindness. Enju has driven her away because of her sin of loving him. Now they may go together to Shikoku to fight the Heike. Solemnly they wish each other good fortune, bowing together in Enju's direction. They go towards the *hanamichi*. Enju comes out of the house. Standing with her back turned, she drops two packets of money, which they gather up, but she will not let them speak their thanks. She extinguishes her lantern to hide her tears, and they salute her silently as the curtain is drawn.

Act II *Sakaro*

Sc. 1. *The house of Matsuemon*. The boatman **Matsuemon** is in reality **Higuchi Jiro Kanemitsu,** the devoted retainer of Minamoto Kiso Yoshinaka and chief of his " four strong men " or personal bodyguard.

When the curtain is drawn, a priest and a number of farmers are reciting the rosary. **Gonshiro,** a fisherman, enters with his daughter, **O Yoshi,** Matsuemon's wife, and O Yoshi's son by a former marriage, **Tsuchimatsu,** (Tsuchimatsu is in reality **Komawaka,** the son of Kiso Yoshinaka). Gonshiro thanks the priest and farmers for their prayers, telling them it is the third anniversary of the death of Tsuchimatsu's father. He apologizes for the mean entertainment he offers them, but explains that they have been away on a pilgrimage and have had many heavy expenses. One of the farmers comments that Tsuchimatsu seems altered since their return. He is not so big and strong and he no longer plays with the other children. Gonshiro sadly tells them that they had a most unfortunate mishap while visiting the Mii-dera near Lake Biwa. They were spending the night at Otsu when the village inn was attacked by armed samurai. In the confusion Gonshiro had difficulty in finding the child, but they were at last able to escape to the mountains. It was only then that they realized that the child with them was not Tsuchimatsu. They returned to look for him, but it was hopeless : everyone was scattered. So they decided to care for this child as if he were their own and hope that someone else would do the same for the real Tsuchimatsu. O

Yoshi comments that her father has grown so fond of this little boy that he hardly seems to notice the difference, but she still prays that her own son may be restored to her. The priest and farmers leave.

Matsuemon comes down the *hanamichi* carrying an oar over his shoulder. He is a man of great physical strength. Gonshiro asks why he was called away so suddenly. They have been anxious about him. Matsuemon explains that he was sent for by no less a person than Kajiwara Kagetoki. He was first received by the Chief Counsellor, Banba no Chuta, who asked him about the art of *sakaro* (a method of manoeuvring ships in battle). Then Kajiwara himself entered, a large man with all-seeing eyes. He also questioned him about *sakaro*. Matsuemon explained that he knew the theory but, being a simple boatman who had never taken part in a battle, he had no practical experience. Kajiwara observed, however, that he had no one more competent available and therefore he would send certain of his sailors secretly that evening to Matsuemon to receive instruction. If Matsuemon performed his task well, he would be given the command of the ship which would carry the commander-in-chief of the army, Yoshitsune. Matsuemon thanks Gonshiro, who first taught him the theory of *sakaro*, for giving him this wonderful opportunity for advancement. Gonshiro comments that, although Matsuemon has only been with him two years, he never had an apter pupil. He calls for *sake* to drink to the good fortune of Matsuemon and to Yoshitsune's fleet. Matsuemon excuses himself, saying he had to drink at the palace and is sleepy. He picks up the boy and carries him off to the inner room "to keep him company." O Yoshi brings wine to her father and makes an offering to the God of Ships.

A young woman in travelling dress, **O Fude,** enters and enquires after Matsuemon. O Yoshi is not pleased to find a beautiful lady asking for her husband. Her father tells her not to be jealous : for all she knows it may be Matsuemon's sister ; they have never seen any of his family. Gonshiro invites the stranger to enter. O Fude explains that she does not know Matsuemon, but she has found a small travelling bag marked with the name "Tsuchimatsu" and this address. She herself lost a little boy at Otsu and found one whom she supposes to be theirs. Gonshiro tells her joyfully that her child is well and has been tenderly cared for. O Yoshi, thinking Tsuchimatsu must be outside, rushes to the door, calling his name and asking whether he has forgotten his home. O Fude says sadly that he is not there. In reply to their impatient questions, she reluctantly relates how on the night of the Otsu raid she and her party, which included an old man and a sick lady, O Fude's mistress, were not able to escape as quickly as Gonshiro and O Yoshi. Tsuchimatsu was torn from them in the fight, and all they found of him when the brigands withdrew was his headless body. Only then did they realize that it was not their child who was killed — their little lord, O Fude adds, for her mistress was his nurse. They prayed that he might have escaped, but they could find no trace of him. The sorrow was too much for her mistress, and the poor lady died. Then O Fude found the travelling bag and thought it might serve as a clue. She now begs Gonshiro to restore her little lord to her.

Gonshiro's grief turns to anger. The stranger boy is his grandson's enemy, and the life of the one must pay for the other's. The door opens and Matsuemon is discovered with the boy in his arms. He has heard the story and bids O Fude have no fear, for " our lord is safe in my keeping. When the time is ripe I shall reveal who I am." Gonshiro protests angrily, ordering Matsuemon to kill the child and avenge their son. When he refuses, Gonshiro bids O Yoshi summon the neighbours and drive Matsuemon from the house. He is no longer worthy to be her husband or his son. Matsuemon realizes that he must disclose his secret and trust to their personal loyalty. He places the child in O Fude's arms, saying that he recognizes him as Komawaka, the son of the great Kiso Yoshinaka. He himself is Higuchi Jiro Kanemitsu, the chief of Yoshinaka's bodyguard. To prove it, he speaks of her father, recently dead, condoling with her and praising her loyalty and devotion. He then tells his story. Before the battle of the Uji River, Kiso sent him off on a secret mission so that he was not present at his lord's death. When he learnt of it his one thought was vengeance , but he was alone against Yoritomo's forces and realized that his only hope was guile. He came, therefore, to this place, close to the palace of Kajiwara, Yoritomo's right hand man, and took service with Gonshiro, whose daughter he married. Thanks to Gonshiro's instruction, he was able to establish a connection with Kajiwara. Now the time for vengeance has come, for he will command the ship carrying Yoritomo's brother, Yoshitsune, the slayer of Kiso Yoshinaka. Knowing that his lord's son is safe, his joy is perfect, and he will now die content. Surely this is a sign from the gods, a reward to O Fude and himself for their loyalty. As a samurai he commands Gonshiro to spare the child and as a son he humbly begs him to do so.

Gonshiro raises his head and says " Since my son is a samurai I must be one also. My son's lord is my lord. Daughter, let us weep no longer. Tsuchimatsu has died as the son of a samurai should die, serving his master. You must give us a new Tsuchimatsu." Matsuemon thanks the old man, and O Fude restores the child to him since she has nothing more to fear. She must leave, for she intends to find her sister (Chidori, see Act I), who has become a courtesan in this neighbourhood, and with her to avenge their father. That done, she will return. She refuses their proffered hospitality even for one night and goes on her way. Gonshiro bids O Yoshi model herself on this fine woman. The three go to offer prayers for the repose of Tsuchimatsu's soul, carrying Komawaka with them. Some boatmen enter and call to Matsuemon. He comes out and they go off to the river.

Sc. 2. *The river bank where Matsuemon's boat is moored.* Matsuemon and the boatmen go on board. They carry oars. Matsuemon begins to instruct them in the art of *sakaro*. Suddenly the boatmen attack him. He overcomes them and flings them into the river, posing triumphantly.

Sc. 3. *Another part of the river bank, showing the back of Matsuemon's house and a large pine tree.* Matsuemon enters, followed by the fishermen of the village, who tell him that Kajiwara knows who he is and has ordered them to arrest him. Matsuemon cries out his real name and defies them to touch him. They close in, but he drives them off chasing them as far as the *hanamichi*. When they have beaten an ignominious retreat, Matsuemon climbs up to the pine tree and looks out over the countryside, seeing that he is surrounded on all sides by the Genji army. O Yoshi comes in great distress to say that her father has left the house without disclosing his destination. She fears that he may have gone to inform against Matsuemon. **Hatakeyama Shigetada,** the commander of the Genji troops, arrives and challenges

Matsuemon to fight. At the same moment Gonshiro returns, with Komawaka on his back. He admits that he indeed went to inform against Matsuemon, but he did it to safeguard the child and only when he knew that Kajiwara was already informed of Matsuemon's identity and whereabouts. By so doing he has been able to plead that the boy be spared as a reward for this service and also to point out that he is not the son of Matsuemon and so should not suffer with him. He believes Matsuemon will understand his motives.

Meanwhile, Matsuemon refuses to fight with Shigetada : only Kajiwara is a foe worthy of his sword. But, since he realizes there is no escape, he will die by his own hand, and Shigetada can carry his head to Kajiwara. Shigetada begs him to allow himself to be taken prisoner, adding that Yoshitsune is filled with admiration for Matsuemon's devotion and loyalty to his lord. Kiso Yoshinaka was a Genji and Yoshitsune's first cousin and, since it has now been shown that the prince was never involved in any plot against the Imperial Throne, but died without a stain on his honour, Yoshitsune urges Matsuemon to transfer his allegiance to him. This he can do without any shadow of disloyalty. Shigetada also hints that they know the child's real identity, but there is nothing to fear on his account. Matsuemon, after an inner struggle, puts up his sword and allows Shigetada to take him prisoner. He takes leave of O Yoshi and the boy, and is led away to Yoshitsune's presence.

HIYOKU NO CHO YUME NO YOSHIWARA

(*Lover's Nightmare in the Yoshiwara*), commonly called *Gompachi Komurasaki*. *Sewamono.* — Written by Fukumori Kyusuke.

The story of Gompachi and Komurasaki has had an immense success with the Japanese public. Gompachi is the type of handsome, courageous scoundrel who is much admired, if only because retribution is bound to overtake him some day. Komurasaki represents the beautiful courtesan who loves passionately and devotedly, against all logic.

Shirai Gompachi, whose story is told in detail in Mitford's *Tales of Old Japan*, was of samurai stock. At the age of sixteen, he accidentally killed a fellow-clansman in a dispute and was obliged to flee to Edo. According to one version, he was already betrothed to **Komurasaki,** whom he was later to find again in the Yoshiwara. According to another, the Komurasaki he found bore a striking resemblance to the fiancée he had left behind. In Edo Gompachi was befriended by Banzuin Chobei (see the play *Suzugamori*, page 8) and began the career of murders and robberies which ended in his execution. At first he seems to have been well-intentioned, seeking service with some man of rank. Either his search was hopeless or else he met Komurasaki too soon. As a result of family troubles, she had sold herself into a house in the licensed quarter and by her looks and wit had become one of the most popular courtesans of Edo. Gompachi could not raise the money to redeem her, and later on any such desire must have been forgotten. He gave himself up to a life of debauchery and supported himself by highway robbery and murder. He was a noted swordsman and owned one of the " bloodthirsty " swords made by Muramasa. For a time he prospered. But his crimes became more and more violent. Chobei broke off his friendship. Police spies were set to catch him. At last he was taken in the act and executed at Suzugamori like a common malefactor. Chobei is said to have relented and to have taken the body and its severed head to give them decent burial at the Tosho Shrine at Meguro. Here Komurasaki took her life before the freshly - turned earth. The priest buried her in the same grave and carved on the common tombstone a picture of the *hiyoku*, the legendary love-bird which only exists when it has found its mate. Lovers visit the grave to this day.

There have been several versions of this story or parts of it on the Kabuki stage. The present play gives a fanciful account of Gompachi's end.

Act I

The execution ground at Suzugamori, near Edo. — It is night. Along the *hanamichi* comes a macabre procession — torch-bearers, spearmen, and Gompachi, bound and dejected, mounted on a broken-down nag. They are met by two officials whose duty it is to see the execution performed. Gompachi is told to prepare himself for death. He kneels on the execution mat. His movements are slow and dream-like, as if he were in a daze. Suddenly Komurasaki comes running down the *hanamichi*. At first she is held away by the spearmen. But she pleads with the officials to be allowed to embrace her lover. Permission is at length granted, and together they recall all the happiness and sorrow of their life. They drink water together as a token of farewell. The fatal hour strikes. Suddenly Komurasaki draws a knife and strikes off Gompachi's bonds. Gompachi leaps to his feet as the stage is blacked out.

Act II

Sc. 1. *Komurasaki's house in the Yoshiwara.* Gompachi staggers into the room, rubbing his eyes and trembling with terror. Komurasaki follows him in alarm. He tells her of the hideous nightmare he has just dreamt at her side. She comforts him, but they are interrupted by the arrival of two police agents. Gompachi hides in the inner room while Komurasaki is interrogated about the young samurai who has been observed to visit her so frequently. She tries to make light of the enquiry. How should she remember one particular samurai among so many who frequent her house? The agents profess that they are satisfied with her explanations and withdraw. The two lovers realize that the net is closing. Gompachi decides to take flight in disguise. As a first and effective step, Komurasaki shaves off his front lock of hair. They take leave of each other, and Gompachi steps out into the street. He is attacked by the police, but beats them off by desperate courage and skilful swordsmanship.

Sc. 2. *On the bank of the Sumida River.* Here a ferry plies across the river. Gompachi runs down the *hanamichi* holding a straw mat round his head and shoulders. He unties the boat. Lights appear in the nearby hut, and the police fall on him. He drives them off and pushes away from the shore. Half-way across the river he sees that another body of armed men await him on the other side. He strips off the upper part of his kimono and, as the curtain is drawn, commits *seppuku* standing upright in the rocking boat.

HIZAKURIGE TOKAIDO CHU (*On Shank's Mare along the Tokaido*). *Shosagoto.* — The book *Hizakurige* by Jippensha Ikku is the great comic classic of Japan. It appeared in 1802 and was so popular that the author wrote a number of sequels. It is a humorous guidebook to the Tokaido, the great road which connected the Shogun's capital in Edo with the Emperor's capital in Kyoto. The journey is seen through the eyes of a couple of Edo ne'er-do-wells who decide to escape from their creditors by making the pilgrimage to Ise. Their numerous, and usually Rabelaisian, adventures are interspersed with accounts of the shrines, temples, inns, and gastronomic specialities of the places through which they pass.

Yajirobei and **Kitahachi** or, as they are called for short, **Yaji** and **Kita** consider that as natives of Edo they are greatly superior to everyone else. They are, nevertheless, constantly duped, cheated, and made to look foolish. Yaji is a great boaster, but chicken-hearted. Kita is slower witted and more good natured, an ideal butt for practical jokes. Yaji profits by this as much as anyone. It has become customary to stage scenes from *Hizakurige* during the summer when the regular Kabuki companies are on holiday. The young actors, who still have their names to make, put on a show at one of the minor theatres, and the adventures of Yaji and Kita give them plenty of scope to show their metal. A typical scene, which was played in his youth by the great Onoe Kikugoro VI, shows Yaji and Kita on the road between Akasaka-Namiki and Rantoba. Their appearance with staff, bundle, and pilgrim's hat is based on the original woodblock illustrations to the book.

Argument : The two travellers have separated for reasons of their own and have arranged to meet before a certain shrine at Akasaka. Kita arrives first and falls asleep on the steps of the shrine. Yaji, seeing him thus, creeps up behind him and frightens him by pretending to be a fox-spirit. When Kita realizes he is being fooled, he takes it in good part, as he always does, and the two of them go on their way.

Yaji, however, is to be paid back in his own coin. He is intensely nervous of ghosts and spirits, and many of their adventures turn on this. As evening falls they pass a graveyard, and the sight of some flapping grave-clothes before the sexton's shed so terrifies Yaji that he faints. No sooner has Kita revived him (with offertory water from a grave) than they see a figure approaching. Yaji is immediately convinced that this is a real fox-spirit. He and Kita attack it, but it proves to be a small boy, the son of a neighbouring farmer, sent to offer them *sake* and invite them to spend the night. The boy's father appears, in answer to his son's yells, and gives both Yaji and Kita a good drubbing. Kita escapes without too much damage, but Yaji gets a blow on the head and is stunned. The farmer thinks he is dead. He and the boy drag the body into the sexton's shed, dress it in grave-clothes, and make off, carrying Yaji's clothes and bundle with them. Yaji comes to and believes that he must be really dead. At this point the actor is at liberty to improvise. He usually takes off popular figures of the day, *sumo* wrestlers, his fellow Kabuki actors, or other notables, to the huge enjoyment of the audience. Finally he rushes down the *hanamichi* in pursuit of Kita.

A subsequent scene, sometimes played, shows their meeting. Kita is convinced that Yaji, still in grave-clothes, is a ghost and attempts to have him exorcised by the local priest.

HONCHO NIJUSHIKO (*The Twenty-Four Examples of Filial Piety*). *Jidaimono*. — Written for the puppets by Chikamatsu Hanji (1725—1783), assisted by Miyoshi Shoraku (1696—1775 ?) and Takeda Inaba (dates uncertain). First performed at the Takemoto-za, Osaka, in 1766 and later adapted for the Kabuki. The original play was in five acts. Only two survive, of which the second is by far the more famous and is frequently performed. The rôle of Yaegaki-hime in this act is considered one of the three more difficult "princess" rôles of the stage.

The play tells of various incidents in the feud between the Takeda and Uesugi. The Shogun Ashikaga Yoshiteru has recently been murdered, and the heads of these two noble houses deliberately take opposing sides in the ensuing civil wars, pretending to be bitter enemies in order to discover, in one camp or the other, the murderer. This they at last succeed in doing.

The first of the two acts here summarized is hardly ever performed on the Kabuki stage, but since it is still in the répertoire of the puppet theatre, it is included here. The second half of this act, which consists mainly of a series of fantastic explanations of the extraordinary happenings of the first half, is so involved that it is largely incomprehensible even to a Japanese audience. The authors have tried to simplify these explanations as much as possible so that the playgoer may have some idea of what is happening.

The chief points to bear in mind when seeing this act are : (1) the rival clans of Takeda and Nagao (as the Uesugi are called in the play) are both anxious to secure the services of the two sons of the famous strategist Yamamoto Kansuke, since both young men are reputed equally able ; (2) each of the sons has secretly committed himself to one or other of the clans, the elder, **Yokozo,** to the Takeda and the younger, **Jihizo,** to the Nagao ; (3) their mother, **Miyuki,** who plays an important part in the plot, is aware of the commitments of her younger son, but not of those of her elder.

In the first part of the act every effort is made to conceal the true situation, as tabulated above, from the audience. It is revealed only in the second half. The conduct of Yokozo and Jihizo is considered admirable, although to the Western playgoer they both appear to behave with extraordinary inhumanity towards the persons nearest and dearest to them.

Act I

The house of the widow of Yamamoto Kansuke. Yamamoto Kansuke never attached himself to any particular daimyo, although many were anxious to count him among their retainers. When he died his two sons were children, but his wife, Miyuki, girded on his two swords and took his name, teaching her sons all she could of their father's skill. Although, when the play opens, these two sons are grown men, she has not yet given either his father's name (which carries with it his renown) or his secret book of tactics. Meanwhile, the two young men live in seclusion with their mother, calling themselves Yokozo and Jihizo and supporting the family by hunting and fishing.

When the curtain is drawn the stage represents a wintry scene. Within the house **O Tane,** Jihizo's wife, is nursing a baby while two farmers are warming themselves at the fire. Of the two brothers they comment that the elder is a hard, cruel man, but the younger is kind and gentle. So is his wife, and both care for Yokozo's child as if it were their own. O Tane stops their criticism. Jihizo enters carrying a rod and his catch. He has been to fish for his mother's supper. The farmers remark that, in spite of Jihizo's devotion to her, the old lady always prefers her elder son. Left alone, Jihizo tells his wife to prepare the fish. He asks after his mother, who is asleep in the inner room, and the child, who is well. O Tane, in tears, cries out against Yokozo's cruelty in forcing them to abandon their own son Minematsu, so that she may nurse his son Jirokichi. She tells Jihizo that during his absence Yokozo has been trying to make love to her. Jihizo must tell her what he has done with their child. Jihizo silences her, adding that Minematsu is "happier than in this wretched house." (In an earlier scene, still occasionally performed by the puppet theatre, it is told how Jihizo abandoned his son, with a label bearing his name attached to his clothes, by the frontier post between the properties of the Takeda and the Uesugi.) Jihizo looks for his mother in the warm inner room; not finding her, he seeks her in the garden.

Snow is falling. **Nagao Saburo Kagekatsu** enters disguised as an ordinary man, wearing high *geta* and carrying an umbrella. He is followed by a band of retainers. He is the son of **Nagao Kenshin,** the head of the house of Nagao, and has come secretly to offer Jihizo the command of his father's army because he knows Jihizo to be an upright man and believes him to have inherited his father's skill and knowledge. Miyuki appears from the other side of the stage, leaning on a stick. Jihizo follows holding an umbrella over her and begging her to hurry into the house out of the snow. Miyuki speaks sharply to him, telling him not to order her about. She refuses the fish which he has caught : she really wants a dish of bamboo shoots. Jihizo answers mildly that in winter there are none. She rounds upon him saying that a dutiful son would find a way of obtaining some for her. She always hoped that one of her sons would follow in the footsteps of her famous husband and to this end she has taught them all she could of his secret art. But Jihizo is so stupid that she can get nothing into his thick head; he cannot perform the smallest task. All his pretended devotion is to cajole her into letting him assume his father's name and honours. Jihizo denies it in tears. Miyuki angrily tries to beat him with her stick, but stumbles and almost falls. When Jihizo tries to support her, she pushes him away. One of her *geta* slips from her foot and slides over towards the gate. Nagao Kagekatsu, who has overheard the whole conversation, picks it up and, coming forward, returns it to her. Miyuki thanks him repeatedly and, sending Jihizo away, invites Kagekatsu into the house. He tells her the purpose of his visit. Miyuki asks him which son he means to honour, and he names the elder, Yokozo. Miyuki says Yokozo is away at present, but finally promises his services to Kagekatsu. He gives her a mysterious box, but commands her not to open it. He makes her swear that if Yokozo does not become his retainer her head shall be forfeit. He leaves.

Yokozo returns carrying some game birds. His mother begs him to come in and warm himself, but he speaks roughly to her. Jihizo brings hot water to wash his brother's feet, but Miyuki insists on doing this herself. Yokozo, however, hints that he would prefer " the comforting touch of a young woman's hands " (i. e., O Tane). He orders the birds prepared for his own dinner. His mother leads him to the *kotatsu* in the inner room and makes him lie down under the quilt, but he complains that it is not warm enough because the old lady has been making use of it before him. When his mother wishes to rub his feet, he again says that he would prefer O Tane and calls to her, asking what she is doing and where her child Minematsu is. O Tane answers that Jihizo took him away, as Yokozo ordered, two days ago. Yokozo mocks her, saying that it was on her account that he drove his own wife away. He suggests that since O Tane is feeding his son (thus making it in some way her child also) it would be a good idea if he and Jihizo not only shared a child but a wife as well. He threatens that if O Tane will not consent he will ill-treat his old mother, to whom her husband Jihizo is so devoted. When O Tane shakes her head he immediately begins to abuse Miyuki for not waiting on him better.

A messenger announces that the prince **Takeda Shingen** is coming to visit Yamamoto Kansuke. Miyuki, in some doubt, orders Jihizo to entertain him suitably. Some retainers arrive at the gate, and presently **Karaori,** the wife of Takeda Shingen's chief retainer, enters carrying a child in her arms. Jihizo remarks in surprise that they were expecting a great lord, not a woman. Karaori shows them the baby who, she discloses, has been found and adopted as his heir by Takeda Shingen. Jihizo and O Tane recognize in him their own son Minematsu. Karaori tells Jihizo that in view of his reputation as a wise and great strategist the

young prince has come to enlist his services. Jihizo denies
any knowledge of strategy: unless he is granted the reversion of his father's name and given his secret book of
tactics, he will never take service with any lord. Karaori
pleads with him in vain. Then turning to O Tane, she tells
how the baby was found abandoned, with a label reading:
"This is Yamamoto's son." They have tried to feed the
child, but he will not suck and does nothing but cry. He
is already losing weight. Karaori guesses whose child he is
and begs O Tane to give "this general" the food he needs,
thus declaring herself and her husband on Takeda's side.
If she does not do so the baby will die. O Tane bursts into
tears, and the child, hearing her voice, leaps into her arms
and is suckled at her breast. But Miyuki commands Jihizo
to stop this; otherwise he will be committed to the Takeda
and so disobey his mother. Jihizo, true to his filial oath,
takes the child from O Tane and gives it back to Karaori,
telling his wife that Minematsu is theirs no longer. Karaori's renewed entreaties are in vain. O Tane begs to be
allowed to feed her son once more, but is prevented by Jihizo. Karaori goes out through the gate, which Jihizo locks
after her. He covers the lock with his tobacco case and
jams it on so tightly that it is difficult to remove it. Karaori leaves the baby outside the gate, saying: "The lord
Shingenko, son of Takeda Shingen, wishes to employ the
successor of Yamamoto Kansuke as his commander and
therefore he will not leave here until he has obtained his
wish. The life of the young lord is in your hands." She
hides in a thicket nearby.

The baby begins to cry, but when O Tane moves to go
to him Jihizo reminds her that even one step towards the
gate will be disobedience to his mother and he will divorce
her. He goes out to find some bamboo shoots for Miyuki.
Left alone, O Tane weeps over her husband's cruelty.
Again she hears her child crying, and her longing is too
much for her. She puts down Yokozo's son and goes out
to the gate. She cannot pull the tobacco case off the lock.
Jirokichi begins to cry, and she must return and rock him
to sleep. Her own child cries, and she returns to the gate.
At last she succeeds in forcing the lock and clasps her son
to her. As she stands nursing him, Karaori emerges and
declares that Jihizo is now committed to the Takedas. She

will tell her husband the good news. O Tane moves towards the house with her child at her breast. Suddenly a dagger is flung at the baby and kills him. The two women are frozen with horror. Yokozo comes out and, snatching up Jirokichi, carries him away. Finding her voice, O Tane swears that, as it must have been Yokozo who killed her son, she will be revenged on him. *The stage revolves.*

A bamboo thicket, covered with snow. Jihizo enters, wearing a straw raincoat, and begins to dig rather hopelessly for young shoots. Some doves hover round him. It occurs to him that they may be messengers from his father's spirit, and that the secret books of tactics may be hidden here. Yokozo enters and hides where he can watch him. Jihizo continues to dig. His spade strikes something hard. Yokozo jumps out and claims " the book buried there." They quarrel and come to blows. They pelt each other with snowballs, and then both fall to digging feverishly. They uncover a chest, but their hands are so cold that they drop it. They struggle for it, and their fight carries them onto the *hanamichi. The stage revolves.*

Miyuki's house. Miyuki opens the doors and calls to her sons : the time has come for them to take honourable service. She thanks Jihizo for fetching her " the bamboo shoots from under the snow" and commends his devotion. She commands him to guard the house. Jihizo withdraws. Yokozo places the chest before his mother. She promises him a good master and a fitting dress for his new station. She brings out an uncrested white robe and a dirk on a plain wooden stand, saying that he must die, for she has need of his head. She explains that she has learned that he, Yokozo, took service secretly with Nagao Kagekatsu when some days previously the prince saved his life. Yokozo therefore owes him a great debt. From the document found in the box Kagekatsu left in her charge she has discovered that Kagekatsu's life is forfeit and, since Yokozo resembles him closely, she believes the time has come for him to give proof of his loyalty to his lord and pay the debt he owes him. (This is the only reference in these two surviving acts of the play to the fact that the Nagaos and the Takedas are, in fact, both loyal supporters of the Ashikaga Shogunate and their supposed enmity is a ruse. The document in question is a solemn undertaking on the part of Nagao

Kenshin, Kagekatsu's father, to bring the murderer of the Shogun Yoshiteru to book within three years or offer, in expiation, the head of his own son.) He cannot escape, she adds, for the house is surrounded. He must commit *seppuku*. When Yokozo refuses, she threatens to kill him with her own hands. A dirk is flung onto the stage and falls at his feet. Yokozo stares at it and, exclaiming "The time has come!", seizes it and puts out his right eye, to his mother's great amazement. He tells her he now no longer resembles Kagekatsu and cannot act as his substitute. He proclaims that at this instant he succeeds to his father's honours and his name henceforth is Yamamoto Kansuke Haruyoshi. Upon him his father's genius has descended and his life is infinitely precious. He summons Jihizo, addressing him formally as "Naoe (the name of their mother's family) Yamashiro-no-kami Tanetsuna, the retainer of Takeda Shingen." Jihizo enters, wearing formal dress, and acknowledges the name, but denies allegiance to the Takedas. For some time he has secretly been in Nagao's service, but this was known only to his mother. Yokozo declares that he and his brother are enemies, for he has secretly pledged himself also, but to the Takedas. Through his lord he has been able to serve an even greater master, and, opening the doors, he calls : "Karaori, bring the young prince here!" Karaori is revealed, holding in her arms the infant Jirokichi. Yokozo explains that this is the son of the murdered Shogun whom he was able to preserve, pretending it was his own child. He opens the chest dug up in the bamboo thicket and takes out a white flag, the banner of the Shogunal house. He poses with the flag unfurled while Jihizo looks on in admiration and prophesies that the feud between their two lords will soon be at an end. He confesses that he himself killed his own son, Minematsu, because it was the only way he could preserve intact his loyalty to the Nagaos. His wife had, by suckling the child, made him a traitor (Minematsu was, as will be remembered, the adopted son of Takeda Shingen). Yokozo orders his mother to give his father's books of tactics to Jihizo so that they may share his honours. Jihizo accepts. Yokozo declares he owes a debt of gratitude to Kagekatsu, his brother's lord, for restoring her *geta* to his mother. He does not choose to be beholden to the enemy, so in the forthcoming battle he will wear one *geta* only. He and Jihizo will meet on the battlefield.

Yokozo fastens the white banner to a bamboo stem and poses once more, while the *joruri* sing in praise of his courage and loyalty.

Act II

The Incense-Burning Scene (Jisshiko no Ba). Takemoto accompaniment.

The palace of **Nagao Kenshin,** *near Lake Suwa.* Four ladies-in-waiting are discussing their young mistress, **Yaegaki-hime,** whose betrothed, **Takeda Katsuyori,** the son of Takeda Shingen, committed suicide on the eve of the wedding. He did this because of the violent enmity which sprang up between the young people's parents after the murder of the Shogun Yoshiteru (see introductory notes to the play). Yaegaki-hime has fallen into so melancholy a mood that her father, Nagao Kenshin, is at his wits' end. This evening he has arranged a concert of *koto* music to distract her. The ladies go out to prepare for the entertainment.

Katsuyori appears in formal dress, wearing his swords. He explains that, as he has been brought up in the country, he is not known in the capital. Hence, since he is believed to be dead by the people of the house, he has come disguised as a gardener, hoping to recover an heirloom of his family now in Nagao Kenshin's possession. This heirloom is a helmet entrusted by his father to the Suwa Hosho Shrine for safekeeping. It has now been bestowed by the priests upon his father's enemy.

On either side of the central room are two smaller rooms, the doors of which are closed. Those of Yaegaki-hime's room are now opened, and she is discovered within, contemplating a portrait of her dead fiancé. The doors of the second room are next opened to reveal **Nureginu,** Yaegaki-hime's chief lady-in-waiting, praying before a shrine for the soul of her dead husband, for this is the anniversary of his death. Seeing her, Katsuyori remembers that today is the anniversary of the death of the samurai who died in his stead. He also prays. (This samurai was in fact Nureginu's husband, who closely resembled Katsuyori. Nureginu is Katsuyori's accomplice.)

Yaegaki-hime speaks to the portrait, reminding her dead

73

betrothed that they were promised to each other by their parents when they were children. She will always be faithful and never marry anyone else. Taking a special incense called "Returning Soul," she burns it before the portrait and implores Katsuyori's spirit to speak to her just once, so that she may have a loving word to treasure all her life. In the garden Katsuyori hears Yaegaki-hime sobbing and guesses the reason. Nureginu is weeping also. She rises and comes out of her room. She sees Katsuyori and, calling him by the name he uses in his gardener's disguise, Minosaku, asks him the reason for his fine clothes. He replies that his master, Kenshin, has sent for him. Nureginu notices that the crest on his kimono is that worn by her husband on the day of his death. She again bursts into tears. Yaegaki-hime hears her weeping and looks out from her room. She recognizes Katsuyori, but believes that it is his spirit, called up by her prayers. Meanwhile, Katsuyori does his best to console Nureginu. Watching them, Yaegaki-hime begins to wonder whether he is not after all flesh and blood. She comes down from her room and stares at him, asking whether he is not Katsuyori. He answers that he is only the gardener Minosaku. Yaegaki-hime says he reminds her of her betrothed. She asks Nureginu whether she and the gardener are old acquaintances, since they seem so friendly. Nureginu, much embarrassed, answers that she never saw him before. Yaegaki-hime refuses to believe her and accuses them of being lovers. Nureginu fervently denies it. Yaegaki-hime goes on to say that, if Minosaku is not Nureginu's lover or her husband, she herself would like to become better acquainted with him and asks Nureginu to act as go-between. Nureginu looks at her in amazement, exclaiming that she always thought Yaegaki-hime a child. Now she has suddenly grown up. Yaegaki-hime confesses that she is in love. Nureginu promises, rather hesitantly, to do what she can to help her, provided the girl will give some proof that her love is genuine. Yaegaki-hime, mystified, offers to write Katsuyori a letter. Nureginu suggests that the best proof she could give would be the helmet brought from the Suwa Hosho Shrine. Yaegaki-hime at once exclaims that, if the young man wants the helmet, he must be Katsuyori. He again denies it. Yaegaki-hime, however, remains convinced that her lover has miraculously returned. She implores him to tell her the truth, saying that, though he may hide from all the world, he cannot hide from her. (This is sung by the Takemoto singers.) Katsuyori continues to reject her advances, reiterating that he is only the gardener. Yaegaki-hime's faith is shaken by his coldness. She begs Nureginu to kill her if this is in truth not Katsuyori. If she has offered herself to another man, her betrothed's portrait will never forgive her. Nureginu praises her faithful love and assures her that it really is her Katsuyori. She cannot bear to torture the girl any longer, and the two young people rush towards each other.

The voice of Nagao Kenshin is heard calling for Minosaku (Katsuyori), whom he intends to send to the town of Shiojiri, on the other side of Lake Suwa, with a letter. Katsuyori breaks away from Yaegaki-hime as Kenshin enters carrying a letter case. This he hands to Katsuyori, who leaves at once. Kenshin calls for his retainer **Shirasuga Rokuro,** and tells him that, since the lake is frozen over, they cannot go to Shiojiri by boat as planned, but must ambush Katsuyori on his return journey. Rokuro retires, promising to bring back Katsuyori's head. Kenshin sends another retainer, **Hara Kogunji,** to join him.

Yaegaki-hime, who has been listening, now asks, in great distress, what has happened; Kenshin tells her that he has recognized Katsuyori and is sure he intends to steal the helmet placed in his charge by the Suwa Hosho Shrine. Yaegaki-hime pleads with her father, but in vain. Kenshin calls Katsuyori the enemy of their house and accuses Yaegaki-hime of treachery. He drags the weeping girl into the house, Nureginu following. *The stage revolves.*

The garden of Nagao Kenshin's palace. (This scene is accompanied by *koto* music.) The helmet is kept in a small pavilion. There is also a pond. Yaegaki-hime comes alone into the garden and, while listening to the music, mourns over her lover, Katsuyori, who is going to his death. She has begged her father repeatedly to spare him, but it is useless. She would do anything to save him. If only the lake were not frozen over she would cross it by boat and so arrive before her father's retainers and warn Katsuyori of the ambush. But on foot a girl cannot hope to overtake men. All she can do is pray. She goes into the pavilion and prays for Katsuyori before the helmet, for she knows it was long treasured by his family. She takes it from the shrine and carries it out into the garden. Although it is heavy, she is miraculously able to hold it aloft. She suddenly notices that the moon's reflexion in the pond is blotted out by a fox face. Surprised, she puts down the helmet and stares into the water. Only her own reflexion gazes back at her. She lifts the helmet once more and looks again. Again she sees the reflexion of a fox. She recalls that the fox is the familiar of the god to whom the Suwa Shrine is dedicated and she guesses that fox-spirits are protecting the helmet. They seem to beckon to her. She remembers the old saying that if a fox can cross the ice when the lake is frozen it is safe for a human being to venture. She wonders whether her devotion to Katsuyori has touched the god, and he intends her to save her lover and restore the helmet to him. She puts on the helmet. Fox-fires blaze up around her as if to protect her and the treasure. Eerie drums are heard. The fox-spirits lead Yaegaki-hime away to guide her across the frozen lake.

Yaegaki-hime

HONZO SHIMOYASHIKI (*Honzo in the Detached Palace*). *Jidaimono.* — Written by Akeshiba Genzo. This play is rather more than one of the numerous plays written round the *Chushingura* theme. It is an appendix to *Kanadehon Chushingura*, since it fills in a blank in the original play, telling us what befell Kakogawa Honzo (the only entirely invented character in *Kanadehon Chushingura*) during the time when he was "detained by his lord's business," and his wife and daughter travelled alone to the house of Oboshi Yuranosuke in Yamashina. At the end of the play he sets out to join them and Yuranosuke wearing the *komuso* disguise in which he appears in Act IX of *Kanadehon Chushingura*.

Momoi Wakasanosuke mourns bitterly for Enya Hangan Takasada. He is young and hot-tempered, and he cannot forget that he was only saved from a like fate by what he considers unworthy conduct on the part of his chief councillor, **Kakogawa Honzo**. It is intolerable that Honzo should have stooped to bribery on his behalf. Moreover, although Honzo's well-meant efforts did indeed save his young master from Kono Moronao's insults, they only served to bring them down in an even more violent form on the head of the unfortunate Enya Hangan, giving rise to the events which ended with his death. Sore in spirit, Wakasanosuke places Honzo under house arrest in one of his country mansions, there to await his pleasure.

Argument : When the curtain is drawn, Honzo is discovered in the main room of the house, awaiting his lord's decision. Wakasanosuke's young sister, **Michitose-hime,** is also here in retreat. She was engaged to Enya Hangan's younger brother and heir, Nuinosuke, but as a result of the scandal the match has been broken off. She laments her misfortunes and finds sympathy and comfort with Honzo. **Inami Banzaemon,** another of Wakasanosuke's retainers, has conceived a plot to profit by this situation. He has poisoned his lord's mind against Honzo, whom he hates, but he also aspires to marry Michitose-hime. He knows that he cannot do this with Wakasanosuke's consent. He therefore prevails on Wakasanosuke to come to punish Honzo for his "conduct unworthy of a samurai," and once this has been achieved, he plans to kill Wakasanosuke himself. He arrives at the house and informs Honzo that their lord is on his way. He then contrives to put poison in his master's favourite *sake* pot. Honzo sees him making these arrangements without understanding what is afoot. Before he can enquire further, the arrival of Wakasanosuke is announced and Honzo is bound and removed to await his fate.

Wakasanosuke is so angry with Honzo, thanks to Banzaemon's insinuations, and has so far forgotten all that he owes his chief councillor that he condemns him to death. Since Honzo is not of high rank, the execution will take place in the garden; but, although he is not to be allowed the most honourable form of death, that by his own hand, he will not die as a felon; his lord intends to execute him himself. Honzo is led out and kneels on the execution mat. Wakasanosuke enters the room overlooking the garden and waits, his face inscrutable, while Banzaemon busies himself ostentatiously with preparations for the execution. Wakasanosuke draws his sword, purifies it, and advances. Then with one blow he decapitates the evil Banzaemon and cuts Honzo's bonds. He reveals that he has become aware of Banzaemon's plotting. He asks for *sake*, and it is brought to him in his own pot, but, before he can drink, Honzo realizes the meaning of what he witnessed earlier in the day and proves his fidelity by emptying the poisoned wine over a plant in the garden, which is immediately shrivelled up. Much moved, Wakasanosuke asks what he can do to reward him. Honzo humbly begs leave to resign from his master's service, saying that he blames himself bitterly for being the instrument of Enya Hangan's death. He wishes to make such amends as he can. He intends, therefore, to seek out Oboshi Yuranosuke, who is rumoured to be planning to avenge his lord. Honzo proposes to ask to be allowed to play some part in the vendetta. Wakasanosuke reluctantly grants his request and, in order that he also may play some part in the vengeance, although officially he cannot associate himself in any way with the *ronin*, he gives Honzo a plan of the layout of Kono Moronao's mansion in Edo. He offers Honzo *sake*, and the two drink to the success of Yuranosuke and his companions. Honzo puts on the disguise he will wear for the journey and takes up the flute which will declare him a *komuso* (travelling musician). He and his lord tenderly take leave of each other. Wakasanosuke sadly watches his faithful retainer go on his way. Honzo, covering his head with his wide wicker travelling-hat, sets out to repay the debt he feels he owes to the spirit of Enya Hangan Takasada.

HORIKAWA NAMI NO TSUZUMI (*The Echo of a Drum near the Hori River*). *Sewamono.* — Written for the puppets by Chikamatsu Monzaemon (1653—1724) and later adapted for the Kabuki.

Act I

The house of Nariyama Chudayu near the Hori River not far from Osaka. **O Tane,** the elder daughter of Nariyama Chudayu, is married to a samurai named **Okura Hikokuro.** Hikokuro is in the service of the local lord and his duties at the castle and elsewhere take him continually from home. At the moment, he is away in Edo, and O Tane has come to stay at her father's house until his return. O Tane bitterly resents her husband's long absences. She and Hikokuro have known and loved each other since they were children, and her wedding day was the happiest of her life. But now she hardly sees her husband ; he is often away for months and, even when he is at home, he has to spend half of every month on duty at the castle. O Tane broods over her loneliness and finds secret relief in drinking. She tries to fight against the desire for *sake*, for her father is a notorious drunkard, and her mother, on her deathbed, begged her children not to touch wine. One of O Tane's sorrows is that she has no children. She and her husband have adopted her younger brother **Bunroku** as their son.

When the scene opens, O Tane and her younger sister **O Fuji** are in the back garden of their father's house, cleaning and airing some clothes. O Tane is in a depressed state of mind and pours out her unhappiness to O Fuji. Hikokuro's kimono is hanging in the sun, and O Tane rather frightens O Fuji by pretending it is her husband, just returned, and fondling it. Presently Bunroku comes out of the house. He is a boy, still wearing his front-lock. He tells his "mother" that the new teacher, from whom he is to learn singing and how to play the hand-drum, has arrived from Kyoto. He asks O Tane to come and interview him. *The stage revolves.*

The teacher, a good-looking samurai named **Miagi Gen-**

emon, is waiting in the reception room at the front of the house, where Bunroku brings him tea. O Tane and O Fuji enter, and greetings are exchanged. Genemon and O Tane discuss the lessons, and she offers him *sake* to clinch the bargain. Genemon is impressed by the excellence of the *sake*. O Tane's weakness becomes apparent in the way she drinks and allows herself to be persuaded to take a second and then a third cup. Bunroku asks to be permitted to drink too, and she lets him have a sip, finishing the cup herself. Genemon gives a demonstration of his skill, and the party becomes lively. Night is falling. A servant comes to fetch O Fuji, who is staying with an aunt to make room for her elder sister at home. The house settles down for the night, but presently a samurai steals to the gate and, seeing O Tane sitting alone before her mirror, creeps up behind her. She catches sight of his reflection and turns, frightened, to find it is one of her husband's colleagues, **Isobo Shoemon.** She asks in surprise what he is doing there, and why he has not gone to Edo with the rest. He tells her that it is because of herself. Surely she must realize how long he has been in love with her. He has pretended to be ill so as to remain behind. He attempts to embrace O Tane, but she, although a little fuddled with the wine she has drunk, has her wits sufficiently about her to repel him firmly with her husband's kimono, which she has spread over her knees. Shoemon draws his sword and threatens to kill her and himself. At this moment the voice of the music teacher is heard in the next room. O Tane uses him as an excuse to persuade Shoemon to leave. He will not do so, however, until she has promised to meet him next day at her own house where they can be undisturbed. Shoemon goes, and O Tane bars the gate behind him. When she returns to the house, Genemon comes out of his room and tells her abruptly that he is leaving at once. O Tane realizes that he must have overheard the scene with Shoemon and, with an idea of somehow explaining the matter away and so preventing Genemon from spreading scandal about her, she implores him to stay and pours out all her troubles. She brings him *sake* and after a little accepts some herself. Genemon, overcome by the wine he has drunk, does his best to console her. O Tane puts Hikokuro's kimono over his shoulders and, drunkenly identifying him with her absent husband, allows him to lead her away to his room.

Shoemon is still suspiciously hanging about at the locked gate, but finally goes off, disgruntled. On his way he meets a priest from the Joshin Temple who recognizes him and asks whether he thinks it is too late to have a word with O Tane, for whom he has a message. Shoemon offers to deliver it for him and with this excuse goes back to the gate. O Tane comes from Genemon's room in a state of dishevelment and, learning that it is a message from the temple, does not trouble, as it is dark, to set herself to rights. Genemon comes out behind her. As soon as she unbars the gate, Shoemon bursts in. The three stumble about in the darkness, Genemon trying to reach the gate and escape. Before he does so, Shoemon catches hold of his sleeve and rips it out. He comes upon the trailing end of O Tane's obi and is not slow to guess what has happened.

Act II

The house of Okura Hikokuro. O Tane is expecting a child, and the scandal about her is known to the whole neighbourhood. Only Hikokuro is ignorant of it. He is happy to be home again and has brought presents from Edo for all the family. He has returned in company with his sister's husband, and now, to his astonishment, a gift of the long linen girdles associated with pregnancy is brought from her. Hikokuro thinks there is some mistake and is amused. Presently O Fuji comes into the room. She is anxious about O Tane, for in feudal Japan the unfaithful wife was punished with death. She has been trying to think of some way of inducing Hikokuro to spare her sister and has decided that, if she can persuade him to make love to herself, she may be able to shame him into forgiving O Tane. She therefore makes up a story about having long been in love with him and at the same time tries to slip a letter into his sleeve. Hikokuro merely tells her not to be ridiculous. He flings the letter on the floor and goes out, pursued by O Fuji. O Tane, who is in the next room, comes in, picks up the letter and reads it. A moment later O Fuji returns. O Tane furiously beats her young sister, and is only induced to stop by Bunroku. O Fuji confesses her stratagem, and O Tane is both touched and horrified. They are interrupted by the sound of voices, and hastily leave the room as Hikokuro enters with his sister, **O Yura.** O Fuji remains listening outside the door.

O Yura tells her brother the whole scandal. He at first refuses to believe her and says he has no intention of mentioning the matter to O Tane, but O Yura persists that the affair must be settled as otherwise her own husband is threatening to divorce her. She produces Genemon's torn sleeve as evidence. This is something Hikokuro cannot ignore. Catching sight of O Fuji he tells her to call her sister. O Tane comes slowly into the room. When she is taxed with unfaithfulness, she does not deny it. Hikokuro questions O Fuji and Bunroku and asks them angrily why they did not tell him sooner. Both he and O Tane know there is only one punishment for her and, taking up his swords, he commands her to follow him to the family shrine in the principal room of the house. *The stage revolves.*

Hikokuro and O Tane kneel before the shrine, the others remaining near the door. Before he draws his sword, he asks her whether she has anything to say to their ancestors. O Tane replies that she is guilty and deserves punishment. In spite of everything, she has never loved any man but her husband. "The spirit was not strong enough to resist the urging of the flesh," she adds sadly. As she speaks, O Tane, to spare her husband the terrible duty of taking her life, stabs herself under the heart. Hikokuro puts her out of her agony with his sword, thus ritually avenging his honour. Silently he cleanses the blade, covers the body with his crested coat, and sits beside it with bowed head. When he has regained control of himself, he tells his family that he now intends to go to Kyoto and take revenge upon his wife's seducer. They beg to go with him, but he points out that they must stay and mourn O Tane. As he is about to leave, he cries in an agonized voice: "Why did you not persuade her to go to the temple and become a nun? Then she would still be alive."

(A third act, never now performed, tells how Hikokuro fulfilled his vow, killed Genemon, and afterwards took his own life.)

IBARAKI. *Shosagoto.* — *Nagauta* accompaniment. Based on the Noh play of the same name, it is the sequel of *Mo-*

dori Bashi ; a recent adaptation, made for Onoe Baiko VI.

Argument : After the fight at Modori Bridge, in which **Watanabe Genji Tsuna** was nearly carried off by the demon Ibaraki, but saved himself by cutting off her arm, Tsuna locks the severed limb in a chest, hung about with holy symbols, and with his three companions takes turns to mount guard over it in his house. He is certain that Ibaraki will try to retrieve her arm.

One day when Tsuna is on duty, his aunt, **Mashiba,** to whom he is much attached, comes to the gate, having travelled from her distant home to visit him. She is a frail, gentle old lady. Tsuna is upset at having to deny her, but explains that he has sworn to let no one into the house and cannot break his vow. Mashiba is cast down and complains sadly of her weariness and her nephew's cruelty. As she stands begging at the gate, she seems all frail sweetness, but every now and then something quite different looks out of her eyes. Also, her kimono is curiously arranged, as if she had only one arm. Tsuna is adamant; he sits sternly on guard within the gate. The old lady prepares to return home. She slowly makes her way along the *hanamichi*, faltering and looking back over her shoulder. She is so pathetic a figure that at the very last minute Tsuna relents. He calls her back and invites her into the house. Mashiba returns with alacrity, and is offered food and drink. Tsuna's young sword-bearer, **Otowaka,** dances for her entertainment, and is followed by Tsuna, who performs a dance describing his fight with the demon. Finally, Mashiba herself rises and dances with great skill and grace. Tsuna is so touched and charmed that he asks her what he can do to show his appreciation. Mashiba replies that she is interested in his story and would very much like to see the demon's severed arm. Tsuna demurs, but finally consents. The chest is brought forward and unfastened. Tsuna turns his back while the old lady looks into the box. Suddenly she seizes the arm and stands clasping it to her, her face transformed by hate and triumph. Tsuna turns and realizes that Mashiba is Ibaraki in disguise. He draws his sword, but she evades him and he pursues her from the stage.

A comic interlude follows, performed by five of Tsuna's servants, who are terrified by the sounds of battle and the thunder and lightning which accompany it.

Ibaraki reappears in her true shape as a monstrous fiend, still clutching her severed arm. She defends herself from Tsuna's onslaughts with a witch's mallet and escapes with her trophy, bounding down the *hanamichi* in a triumphant *roppo*.

ICHI NO TANI FUTABAGUNKI (*The Chronicle of the Battle of Ichi no Tani*). *Jidaimono* of the Heike-Genji Cycle (see page 418). — Written by Namiki Sosuke and his assistants. The original play, in five acts, was first staged in 1751 at the Toyotake-za, one of the two great puppet theatres of Osaka. It was later adopted by Kabuki. The part of Kumagai is considered one of the greatest rôles of the live theatre.

Of the long play, only two acts are still performed and form a complete play in themselves. They tell the story of a dramatic incident during the battle of Ichi no Tani, the fight between the experienced Genji warrior Kumagai Jiro Naozane and the Heike boy-hero Taira Atsumori. The death of Atsumori is described in detail in the *Heike Monogatari* and is the subject of two Noh plays, *Atsumori* and *Ikuta*. The *monogatari*, the dramatized account of the fight given by Kumagai in Act II, follows the description in the *Heike Monogatari* very closely. It is some of the finest poetry to be heard on the stage and gains through the interpretation of the living actor. It is interesting that it is in no way lifted from either of the Noh plays. In these, the two accounts of the fight dwell rather upon incidents before the battle and only briefly recount Atsumori's death.

Seventeen years before the play opens, **Fuji no Kata,** a lady-in-waiting to the Emperor, had among her ladies one named **Sagami.** Sagami fell in love with a warrior of the proscribed Genji faction, **Kumagai Jiro Naozane.** For a lady of the court to take a lover was an offence punishable by death, or at the best exile, and Kumagai was, moreover, of the enemy clan. Sagami was already with child, and her plight was desperate, but her mistress took pity on her. With the help of Fuji no Kata the pair were able to fly to Western Japan. They vowed eternal gratitude to her. Fuji no Kata was also at that time pregnant by her lover, who was the Emperor himself. She was married shortly afterwards to **Tsunemori,** the nephew of the all-powerful Taira **Kiyomori.** Her child, **Atsumori,** was brought up as Tsunemori's son. The debt of gratitude owed by Kumagai and his wife to Fuji no Kata was known to **Yoshitsune.** He also knew that in Atsumori's veins ran Imperial blood. On the eve of the battle of Ichi no Tani, Yoshitsune sensed that an inescapable destiny would cause Kumagai and Atsumori to meet on the field. Because of his debt, Kumagai must not kill Atsumori, nor must he shed Imperial blood. Yet as a soldier it would be shameful for him to spare an enemy. Therefore Yoshitsune determined to suggest to Kumagai the tragic but only way out of the dilemma. He caused the priest **Benkei** to write a notice and place it against a young cherry-tree growing before Kumagai's headquarters. The notice read : " Anyone lopping a branch from this tree must have a finger cut off." There is here a play on the words, " one branch," " one finger," and " one son," the hidden meaning of the notice being : " Anyone killing a son must kill his own son."

Act I

Before the Heike Camp at Suma Beach (Suma no Ura Kumiuchi no Ba). It is a moonless spring night. **Kumagai Kojiro Naoie,** the son of Kumagai Jiro Naozane, appears before the gate of the camp. He is a boy, still wearing his long forelock. This is his first battle, and he is in the van of Yoshitsune's attack on the Heike camp. He hears music from inside the stockade. He stands listening, entranced, murmuring to himself that what he has heard is true — these Heike are such courtiers that even on the battlefield they play music. He begins to feel a little ashamed of his own rough, soldierly upbringing. Out of the darkness a voice challenges him. Kojiro recognizes it as that of **Hirayama Sueshige,** a fellow general of his father's. He calls him by name. Hirayama Sueshige comes forward and praises the boy for being the first to reach the camp, adding that they will enter together. Kojiro bids him wait a moment and listen to the wonderful music, but Hirayama tells him to beware as it may well be a trick. They must attack at once. Kojiro goes forward and strikes upon the gate, crying his name. Heike soldiers rush from the camp and Kojiro is dragged inside, struggling and fighting. Hirayama makes no attempt to assist him. Kumagai enters, seeking his son. Hirayama tells him that he is inside the Heike camp and claims that he did his best to stop the boy from entering in so foolhardy a manner. Kumagai rushes to the rescue, crying to Hirayama to follow him. But Hirayama prefers to remain outside until Kumagai should have shortened the odds a little. Kumagai returns carrying the wounded Kojiro in his arms. He calls to Hirayama that he will take the boy behind the lines and return. Meanwhile Hirayama can carry on the fight. The latter still hesitates, but suddenly there emerges from the gate a troop of Heike warriors, among them young Taira Atsumori. Atsumori, who is on horseback, attacks Hirayama and they fight fiercely. *The stage revolves.*

A rocky part of the sea-shore. The voice of **Tamaori-hime,** Atsumori's betrothed, is heard calling his name. She comes down the *hanamichi* with a sword in her hand, seeking her love. Hirayama, who has fled from Atsumori and is hiding among the rocks, accosts her. He is an old suitor and now declares that, since last he saw her in Kyoto, he has obtained her parents' consent to their marriage, and she must come with him at once. Tamaori-hime says firmly that, no matter what her parents may have said, she is Atsumori's bride and would prefer to die with him than live with Hirayama. Hirayama tells her roughly that Atsumori is dead, killed by himself. Tamaori-hime weeps ; then, drawing her sword she turns upon her tormentor, vowing to be revenged. Hirayama disarms her without difficulty and threatens to kill her if she will not submit to him. Tamaori-hime says proudly that never, in any circumstances, will she do so and Hirayama, in fury, stabs her.

Sounds of fighting can be heard near at hand. Hirayama hastily hides the body of Tamaori-hime among the rocks, and makes off. Far out at sea ships appear. Atsumori comes down the *hanamichi* on horseback. Presently he can be seen riding out into the sea. Kumagai's voice is heard calling to him. Kumagai enters, also on horseback, carrying his war-fan. He shouts to Atsumori to turn back and fight. He pursues him into the water where the two can be seen fighting. Atsumori is dragged from the saddle and Kumagai dismounts to deal the deathblow. Kumagai's horse rushes in terror down the *hanamichi*, but Atsumori's remains near his master. Kumagai stands over Atsumori and asks his name and whether he has any last wish to make before he dies. Atsumori answers that he came to the battlefield prepared for death. His only regret is that he cannot say farewell to his parents. He asks Kumagai to send his body to them. He proclaims himself Atsumori, Tsunemori's son. Kumagai hesitates to strike, wishing to spare the boy. Without warning a body of soldiers rushes upon the scene and at the same time Hirayama comes out from among the rocks. Hirayama shouts scornfully that to spare an enemy is the act of a traitor. He orders the soldiers to attack Kumagai as well as Atsumori. The soldiers advance threateningly and Atsumori begs Kumagai to kill him, saying he wishes to die by his hand. He closes his eyes, joins his hands and prepares to die. Kumagai takes his place behind him, saying in an agonized voice that he can no longer save him. He raises his sword, but cannot bear to strike. Atsumori implores him to do so, adding that if he does not, he will take his own life. He looks full at Kumagai who says slowly that he has a son of the same age as Atsumori. He well understands what his parents' feelings will be. The boy bows his head, and with one blow Kumagai cuts it off. Taking the head, he holds it up and cries to Hirayama and the soldiers to bear witness that Kumagai has slain Atsumori. Hirayama and the soldiers retire. Kumagai is left alone on the stage, sunk in thought. Suddenly from behind the rocks comes the faint voice of Tamaori-hime, who has regained consciousness in time to hear Kumagai proclaim that Atsumori is dead. Kumagai finds the dying girl, and she begs to see the head of her betrothed. Reluctantly he brings it to her, but death has already dimmed her eyes, and she cannot distinguish the face. She dies calling Atsumori's name. Kumagai wraps the boy's body in the caparison of his horse and binds it upon the horse's back. He casts Tamaori-hime's body into the sea. Then, taking up the head, he returns to his headquarters.

(The explanation of the above scene is that the boy whom Kumagai carried away from the Heike camp was, in fact, Atsumori. Kumagai's son, Kojiro, disguised himself in Atsumori's armour and sacrificed himself so that his father might pay the debt of honour he owed to Atsumori's mother, Fuji no Kata.)

Act II

Kumagai's Camp (Kumagai Jinya). The act opens just after the arrival of Kumagai's wife, Sagami, at her husband's headquarters, before which stands the cherry tree with its cryptic message. She has come for news of Kojiro who has just fought his first battle. Kumagai has not yet returned, but to her astonishment a woman appears. Sagami recognizes her as Fuji no Kata, whom she has not seen for sixteen years. Fuji no Kata tells Sagami that she has heard that Atsumori, her son, is dead by the hand of Kumagai. She has come to avenge him. She commands Sagami to assist her, and Sagami remembering the great debt she owes to her former mistress, reluctantly consents.

(The following short scene is generally omitted, but is interesting as it provides a logical explanation of the curious incidents at the end of the play.) **Kajiwara Kagetoki,** one of Yoritomo's most trusted generals, is announced. He has come to consult Kumagai, but is told that he has gone to pray at a neighbouring temple. He orders his retainers to bring in an old stonemason, **Midaroku,** whom he has taken into custody for erecting a monument to Taira Atsumori. He questions Midaroku closely. Who ordered this monument? Midaroku answers that it was Atsumori's ghost, adding that the stingy spirit never gave him a penny for it. Kajiwara is invited by Kumagai's chief retainer **Gunji** to enter and rest until his master returns. Kajiwara does so, handing over Midaroku to Gunji for safekeeping.

A shout announces Kumagai's return. He walks slowly along the *hanamichi* deep in thought. He no longer wears armour, but is in ceremonial dress. He carries in one hand a rosary. As he advances, the chorus sing : " Kumagai has slain Atsumori in the flower of his youth. He knows now the vanity of this world. He has drunk the cup of sorrow to the dregs." Kumagai pauses, his hand falls to his side, and the beads tinkle against his sword sheath. He comes out of his rêverie and, after hiding the rosary, enters the camp.

Kumagai shows his displeasure at finding his wife there and asks her why she has come. Before she can answer, Fuji no Kata rushes upon him with a drawn dagger. Kumagai knocks the dagger from her hand and looks at her in amazement. When he realizes that it is indeed Fuji no

Kata, he makes deep obeisance, offering her his sword in homage. Fuji no Kata bids Sagami make good her promise and kill Kumagai. Sagami, weeping, cannot bring herself to do it. She asks her husband what can have possessed him to kill the son of their benefactress. Kumagai replies that on the battlefield no distinction can be drawn between enemies. He offers to describe to them what happened.

Kumagai begins the famous narrative (*monogatari*) which is one of the highlights of the play. Using only his fan and his sword, he describes the fight between himself and Atsumori. As he tells the story his open fan becomes first the two horsemen approaching each other. Then, as he speaks of the fighting, the closed fan imitates the strokes of the sword. When he has unhorsed Atsumori and thrown him down, he uses his sword to show how he raised the boy and brushed the dust from his clothes. He describes his emotions at the sight of Atsumori's youth, and how the lad begged for death, since he was already defeated. He was about to spare the boy when Hirayama, his fellow general, appeared and cried to him (Kumagai acts this dramatically) that to spare an enemy was the act of a coward. He realized then that he had no alternative and asked Atsumori whether he had anything to say before he died. Atsumori answered that although he sorrowed for his mother, he wished only for death. Kumagai stops speaking and Fuji no Kata tragically echoes his last words. She is brokenhearted, but has abandoned all thought of vengeance. Sagami tries to console her.

Kumagai retires to put on ceremonial dress before carrying Atsumori's head to Yoshitsune. Fuji no Kata asks to burn incense for the repose of her son's spirit and, while doing so, plays on a flute belonging to the boy. As she does so, a shadow appears on the closed paper doors of the inner room. Fuji no Kata breaks off in amazement, and the shadow vanishes. She flings open the doors to find only a suit of armour inside.

Yoshitsune himself is announced. He has come to identify the head in the privacy of Kumagai's headquarters, because he does not know how Kumagai may have interpreted his message delivered through the notice. Kumagai comes to receive him. He knows now that he can no longer spare the two women. That they should be present at the head inspection is something which he had no reason to expect. Reluctantly he prepares to present the head, but first he takes the notice-board from the cherry tree and places it before Yoshitsune. Slowly Kumagai lifts the cover of the head-box, but a cry from his wife makes him quickly replace it. (It is only at this point in the play that Sagami's cry tells the audience for certain that Kumagai has in fact adopted Yoshitsune's solution and has sacrificed his son.) Sagami struggles to approach the head-box, but Kumagai, in a sort of frenzy of grief, drives her off with the notice-board. He poses for a moment, while Sagami and Fuji no Kata (who still thinks the head is Atsumori's) weep together. Kumagai once more removes the cover and, his eyes fixed upon Yoshitsune, presents the head. He continues to gaze at his young commander throughout the inspection, partly because he cannot bear to look at his son's face, partly because he is not at all certain that this is, in fact, what Yoshitsune intended him to do. Yoshitsune slowly opens his fan and looks down at the head through the ribs, his face concealed. At length he closes his fan: "You have done well. This is indeed the head of Atsumori." Kumagai signals to Sagami that she may now approach the head and show it to Fuji no Kata. Sagami, caressing it with loving hands, bravely pretends that she believes it to be Atsumori's. Fuji no Kata can do no less than further the deception. Her joy is the easier to conceal

Kumagai

since she reads in Sagami's face the sacrifice which has now repaid her own kindness of long ago. They are interrupted by the sudden entrance of Kajiwara Kagetoki. He threatens to expose the deception to Yoritomo, who has ordered the most ruthless extermination of the family of Taira Kiyomori. Kajiwara goes off down the *hanamichi* full of anger. A moment later a scream is heard off-stage.

The old stone-mason, Midaroku, enters. Like Scott's " Old Mortality," he spends his last years erecting and caring for memorials to the heroes of his clan, and he has come to the battlefield to give decent burial to the fallen Heike soldiers. He now informs Yoshitsune that he has killed Kajiwara by throwing a dirk at him. This he has done that Yoshitsune's hands " may not be sullied by base blood." He is about to go on his way when Yoshitsune stops him, calling him " Munekiyo." When Midaroku pretends he does not know to whom Yoshitsune is speaking, the prince relates how the great Heike warrior Munekiyo saved the lives of his mother, his brothers, and himself when they were caught in a snowdrift in the mountains. Yoshitsune adds : " Although I was an infant then, I have never forgotten your face." Midaroku admits that he is indeed Munekiyo. It is in an attempt to atone for his fault in sparing the life of one destined to become the instrument of the Heike's downfall that he gave up his samurai rank in order to care for the Heike dead. Yoshitsune does not resent his words. He recognizes the debt he owes Midaroku and sees in it the means of solving the one remaining problem of smuggling the living Atsumori out of Kumagai's headquarters. He therefore orders a large case, ostensibly containing armour, but in which Atsumori is hidden, to be brought and presented to Midaroku.

Kumagai returns in full armour. Solemnly he begs Yoshitsune to absolve him from his warrior's vow and to allow him to relinquish his command. He lays before his lord the tightly bound lock of hair which marks the soldier and removing his helmet and cuirass reveals himself in the habit of a shaven-headed priest. The shock of the terrible action forced upon him by duty and honour makes it impossible for him to continue in the profession of arms. All he wishes to do is to spend the rest of his life praying for the release of his son's spirit. Yoshitsune, deeply grieving, grants his request, and Kumagai turns away to take up the palmer's hat and staff. Yoshitsune bids him look once more on his child's face. From the depth of his sorrow Kumagai cries out: "Alas, the sixteen short years of his life have passed in a moment, like a dream—like a dream!"

As the curtain is drawn, Kumagai remains alone on the *hanamichi*. He sinks down beneath the burden of his grief.

IKUTAMA SHINJU (*Double Suicide at Ikutama*). *Sewamono*. — Written for the puppets by Chikamatsu Monzaemon. The plot of this play is almost identical with that of his first great double suicide play, *Sonezaki Shinju*, the difference lying in the characterization.

Act I

The Shimizuya Tea-house near the Temma Shrine at Osaka. A wealthy country bumpkin from Yamato, **Hikosaku,** has become infatuated with **O Saga,** a courtesan at the Kashiwaya, and, having purchased her services, is now impatiently awaiting her arrival at the tea-house. The tea-house maids know O Saga and are aware that she is in love with a young china-merchant, **Koheiji,** whom she hopes to meet here before she goes to her client. They therefore persuade Hikosaku, who is already rather drunk, to wait in the inner room.

O Saga arrives in a palanquin and is greeted sympathetically by the girls. She confesses how anxious she is about Koheiji, who has not been near her for weeks. She is afraid he is in some trouble. Presently Koheiji arrives in disguise. O Saga cannot conceal her joy at seeing him again, but she tells him how unhappy his neglect has made her : she fears he no longer loves her. Koheiji is in a depressed state of mind. He assures O Saga that he loves her as much as ever, but things at home are becoming difficult. As she knows, his father recently set him up in a china-shop of his own near the Yamato Bridge. But since meeting O Saga he has been neglecting his business, and the fees at the house which owns her services have eaten up all his ready money ; he is, in short, in debt, for he owes one **Idenya Chosaku** 300 *ryo*. These facts have come to his father's ears and his father is angry. He has forbidden his son to see O Saga again and, to get him out of his

financial embarrassment, has arranged for him to marry O
Kiwa, a young woman with a handsome marriage portion
which will set the family on its feet again. Koheiji is in
despair for there seems to be no way out of his difficulties.
O Saga, when she knows the full story, readily forgives him
and does her best to comfort him. There are sounds of
people approaching. Koheiji and O Saga take refuge in the
palanquin.

Koheiji's sister, O Riku, enters, leading by the hand her
younger brother, Ikumatsu, who is afflicted with an eye
complaint. They have followed Koheiji and now sit down
to rest. While tea is being brought, O Riku pours out the
family troubles : her poor brother is badly in need of treatment for his eyes but, unless her elder brother brings money
into the family by marrying well, they cannot afford it. O
Saga emerges from the palanquin and joins them. A conversation full of double meanings takes place, for O Riku
guesses who O Saga is and suspects that Koheiji is also
inside the palanquin. She therefore talks at them, harping
on the disgrace it would be if her brother should elope with
a courtesan and his wickedness even in thinking of such a
step when duty and family feeling so clearly forbid it.

O Saga is called to her impatient client, and O Riku and
Ikumatsu start for home. Idenya Chosaku comes to the tea-
house and says he must speak to O Saga. She comes out
to him, and he tells her roughly that her lover is in his debt
and, if she does not want Koheji exposed, she must make
herself agreeable to him. Koheiji emerges from his hiding
place and implores Chosaku to be patient, swearing he will
find the money shortly. Chosaku mocks him, calling him
a poor-spirited swindler. Koheiji angrily springs to his feet
and attacks Chosaku, but the latter is the stronger, and in
the ensuing fight Koheiji is badly beaten up. Chosaku goes
off, well pleased with himself. Hikosaku comes out of the
tea-house and insists on taking O Saga away. It has started
to rain. As O Saga is carried off in her palanquin, gazing
anxiously at the prostrate Koheiji, she flings towards him a
covering to protect him from the downpour.

Act II

Koheiji's shop at the Yamato Bridge. Some days later.
During this time Hikosaku, the rich country bumpkin, has
announced his intention of ransoming O Saga and taking

her away. This is the final blow to Koheiji. Since he cannot hope to raise the money to ransom the girl himself, the two run away together.

When the curtain is drawn two servants from the Kashiwaya arrive at the shop door and find it locked. They are hunting for the fugitives, but are told by **Sobei,** the dyer who lives next door, that the house is empty. The men go on their way. Shortly afterwards Koheiji and O Saga come down the *hanamichi*. Koheiji fumbles with the door of his shop, which he had left unfastened, but finding he cannot open it, he tries to knock off the lock with a stone. There is a sound from the dyer's house. O Saga hides herself as old Sobei, who is not only Koheiji's neighbour but his landlord, appears and produces the key, chiding the young man for his carelessness. After he has gone, Koheiji and O Saga steal into the little house and, when a light is struck, sit down forlornly to take stock of the situation. O Saga urges that the only thing for them to do is to commit suicide together. If they are caught, she points out, people will despise Koheiji, saying that he had not the courage to die, preferring to live in misery under the stigma of having defrauded the brothel which owned her. But Koheiji hesitates, hoping that they may still have time to steal a little happiness in this life.

They are interrupted by a knock at the door, and Koheiji hears the voice of his father, **Gohei,** calling his name. O Saga climbs out of the window and hides herself on the little landing-stage at the waterside below the house. Koheiji conceals her slippers and then admits his father, who is accompanied by O Kiwa, the rich bride the old man has found for him. Gohei implores the young man to give up his mistress and settle down respectably. Everyone knows that O Saga must be with him, and unless he returns her to the Kashiwaya immediately, he is in danger of arrest. If he will do this and marry O Kiwa everything shall be smoothed over and his debts paid in full. Koheiji will not consent, although his father's pleadings reduce him to tears. Finally, as a last resort, the old man draws his sword and, saying that since his son is so undutiful he has no wish to go on living, is about to kill himself. In horror Koheiji stops him and at last, with bitter tears, consents to his father's plan. Gohei says the betrothed couple must drink together and, when Koheiji objects that there is no *sake* in the house, adds that he has brought with him all that is needed. Koheiji brings him an ordinary wine-cup, but Gohei demands something much bigger and into a large dish pours from his *sake*-bottle not wine but a heap of gold coins. These, he tells Koheiji, are to pay his immediate debts and to settle matters at the brothel when he takes back O Saga. Koheiji is overcome by such generosity and promises to do as his father wishes provided he may have a little time to arrange matters. Gohei presents his sword to Koheiji, as a reminder of the solemnity of the promises exchanged, and leaves with O Kiwa.

As soon as they are gone, Koheiji goes to the window beneath which O Saga is huddled. She has overheard the whole conversation and now, with the unselfishness of real love, tells him he did right to obey his father. She must return to the brothel and he to his family. "It is too late for us to die together," she ends sadly. Koheiji, speechless with grief, is about to help her climb back into the room when again there is a knock at the door. It bursts open and in rushes Chosaku with two or three roughs. The dish full of gold coins is lying on the floor. Koheiji hurries to conceal it, but it has already been noticed by one of Chosaku's friends. In the ensuing scuffle Chosaku and his confederates get possession of the money, which is consid-

Koheiji and O Saga

erably more than Koheiji owes, and make off, although Koheiji in his despair breaks most of his stock-in-trade over Chosaku's head, wounding him with a broken plate. When he finds his money gone, Koheiji seizes the sword left behind by his father and rushes after them. But the noise of the fight has aroused the dyer, Sobei, who now comes from his house with his apprentices and locks Koheiji into the shop, saying that to return home and then immediately disturb the whole neighbourhood with a brawl is too much. Koheiji must cool his heels till morning. Koheiji tries to explain through the locked door what has happened and implores Sobei to let him out, but in vain. The dyer and his men settle down on guard before the china-shop.

Koheiji has now lost the money entrusted to him by his father. He cannot face the old man or the world and, above all, he realizes that he cannot bear to part from O Saga. There is only one fate left for them. Taking his father's sword, he climbs down beside O Saga onto the little landing stage, which is connected with the other bank of the river. When he tells her that they must die together, she calmly, almost joyfully, consents, and hand in hand they go away to the Shrine at Ikutama.

(Here the play ends. But the chorus chant the story of the last scene. Upon the holy ground of the shrine, Koheiji kills O Saga by stabbing her in the throat. He is about to wipe the sword before killing himself when he recalls that it was given him by his father as a keepsake. To use it against himself would be the crowning offence against filial piety. He unwinds O Saga's sash from about her body and hangs himself.)

IMOSEYAMA ONNA TEIKIN (*An Example of Noble Womanhood*). *Jidaimono.* — Written for the puppets by Chikamatsu Hanji and his assistants. First staged in 1771 and later adopted by the Kabuki. The original play was in five acts, of which two are still performed. The first of these is remarkable not only for its lavish scenery but because it is in fact two separate plays performed simultaneously. It makes use of two *hanamichi* and is the only play which uses two sets of *joruri* singers, one on each side of the stage. It is a popular play for the months of March and April, the time when Japanese girls display the sets of dolls which have an important part in the story.

Background : There are two mountains called Imoyama and Seyama, which are separated by the Yoshino River, famous for its cherry blossoms. On these two hillsides are built two country palaces, one belonging to the daimyo Daihanji Kyozumi, the other to the daimyo Dazai Shoni. There is an ancient feud between these families over the property along the banks of the Yoshino. The feud might easily have been healed, but, for political reasons, the two families find it expedient to be at enmity. **Soga Iruka,** the chief minister, rules with an iron hand and suspects any daimyo who appear to be on friendly terms of plotting insurrection. Iruka's ambition is known to be unbounded. It is believed that he even aims to depose the Emperor and seize the Throne. Daihanji Kyozumi and Dazai Shoni are both loyal to the Emperor, but neither feels himself strong enough to try conclusions with the arch-enemy.

Daihanji Kyozumi's young son, **Koganosuke,** is a page at the Imperial Court. Soga Iruka has cast covetous eyes on a beautiful concubine of the Emperor's, but Koganosuke helped the lady to hide herself from him. To save his son from Iruka's anger, Kyozumi shuts the boy up in his remote country palace on Seyama.

Dazai Shoni's daughter, **Hinadori,** is very lovely. Iruka desires her also, but so far her parents have saved her from his clutches, making the excuse that she is ill. She has been sent to recuperate at the palace on Imoyama. Hinadori's illness is not entirely feigned, for she is deeply and, as she believes, hopelessly in love with Koganosuke, who returns her love. Her mother suspects this and, being secretly in sympathy with her child, arranges that the two young people should thus be neighbours.

Soga Iruka has issued ultimata to the two families. Hinadori is to become his concubine, and Koganosuke must take service as his retainer (in this way he hopes to be able to wrest from the boy the secret of the hiding place of the Emperor's mistress). The girl's mother and the boy's father are to carry these commands to the children. If Hinadori consents, the mother is to throw a branch of flowering cherry into the river ; if she refuses, a dead branch. The same signal is to be made by the father for the boy.

Act I

The two country palaces. When the curtain is drawn, the doors of the two houses are closed. Those of Hinadori's room open, and she is seen seated before the *tokonoma*, in which are displayed the traditional dolls and ornaments of the *hina-matsuri* or Girls' Festival. Presently the doors of Koganosuke's room are opened, and he is also seen reading the *sutras* (Buddhist scriptures).

Hinadori is teased by her maids and her nurse, who guess that she is in love. She is induced to write Koganosuke a letter which the maids throw into the river. It floats across to the other bank and attracts the attention of Koganosuke, who leaves his reading and comes down to the water's edge to see what it is. The maids drag Hinadori from her room, and the two young people confront each other. Hinadori (who, like all high-born young ladies of Kabuki, is not at all backward in expressing her feelings) is the first to overcome the shyness which has seized them both. She tells Koganosuke how much she has missed him: it is because of him she has been ill. Koganosuke is too tongue-tied to make any proper reply, beyond enquiring politely about her health. Hinadori's mother is announced and, a moment later, Koganosuke's father. Both children return to their rooms.

Hinadori's mother, **Dazai no Koshitsu Sadaka,** comes down the *hanamichi* as Daihanji Kyozumi approaches along the *kari-hanamichi*. There follows a famous passage, both soliloquizing on the problems which beset them. Sadaka tells Kyozumi she has come to fetch her daughter to be Soga Iruka's bride (the position of concubine or secondary wife was, of course, perfectly respectable). Kyozumi informs her in return that his son is to take service with Iruka. Neither expresses his real thoughts, for both are determined to do their utmost to prevent these developments.

At this point the play turns into two simultaneous plays. Kyozumi enters his house, greets his son, and informs him of Iruka's proposal. Koganosuke without hesitation declares that in no circumstances will he take service with such a lord. He would prefer to die. His father agrees that, if he refuses Iruka's offer, death is indeed the only alternative. He praises his son's courage and resolution. Koganosuke prepares to die, and Kyozumi brings him the white robe of death and the dagger. The boy commits *seppuku* according to the prescribed form. Before he dies he asks his father to fling a flowering branch of cherry into the river so that Hinadori may not be grieved by the knowledge of his death.

Sadaka enters her house, greets her daughter, and tells her she must reconcile herself to her fate. Hinadori is unwilling to go to Iruka, but, when her mother tells her that, by doing so, she will save Koganosuke from the great minister's vengeance, she consents. Sadaka bids her prepare for the marriage ceremony. Hinadori takes down her hair to have it dressed. When she has done so, she looks across at her dolls seated in the *tokonoma* and, with tears in her eyes, says she envies them their happy tranquility. She accidentally knocks the dolls from their stand, and the head of one falls off and rolls across the floor. Both Hinadori and Sadaka stare in silence at this omen. Sadaka points to the head and, in a strangled voice, says that this is a better fate than to become Iruka's concubine. Hinadori joyfully thanks her for allowing her to take this honourable course. Sadaka answers that in her heart she never imagined her daughter would wish for any other fate. It was for death, not for marriage, that she has taken down her hair. "If you die now," she adds, "it will be as if you died the wife of Koganosuke." Hinadori declares there can be no greater happiness and prepares to die. But she begs her mother, after her death, to throw into the river a flowering branch of cherry so that Koganosuke may not be grieved by the knowledge of her death. Sadaka then cuts off her head. The two branches of cherry blossoms go floating down the river.

The parents open the doors facing across the river and discover what has happened. Amazed and touched to find that the child of the other has preferred death to dishonour, they vow to end the feud between their two houses. Sadaka begs, since Hinadori regarded herself as Koganosuke's wife and it is the bride who goes to the groom's house for the wedding ceremony, that she may send her daughter's head to him as a symbol of this marriage and as a token that all enmity is at an end between them. She places her daughter's head on the girl's own *koto*, inverted to serve as a boat. The dolls in the *tokonoma* recall too many memories. She arranges them and their gear round Hinadori's head so that they represent the wedding procession of a daimyo's daughter. Thus accompanied, the head floats across the river. Kyozumi draws the *koto* to the bank, accepting this bride for his son. Taking the head, he says: "This is the child for whom you wished a thousand years of happiness." He praises the children: their courage will be an example to himself. He must delay no longer, but overthrow the wicked Iruka or die in the attempt. Since Koganosuke and Hinadori have the consent of their parents, this is a true marriage. Even now they are together on the road of death. "When you pass through the court of the King of the Underworld," he apostrophizes the dead children, "walk proudly and say: 'We are an example to all mankind.'" Kyozumi recites the *sutras* for the repose of departed souls. Standing by the river bank, the parents exchange reminiscences of their children's lives. Evening falls. The sound of a temple bell is heard through the rushing waters.

Act II

O Miwa's Scene (O Miwa no Ba). The palace of Soga Iruka at Mikasayama. Surrounded by his court, Soga Iruka is feasting in his palace. He boasts of his power and the glory of his name. His retainers flatter him obsequiously, saying that with him has dawned a new age of the gods.

Iruka's greatest rival was formerly **Fujiwara Kamatari,** at one time Minister of the Interior. Since Iruka is now supreme, Kamatari has gone into hiding, and is believed dead by Iruka. A young fisherman now enters giving his name as **Fukashichi.** He is in reality **Kanawa Imakuni,** Fujiwara Kamatari's retainer. He brings Iruka a gift of *sake* and a letter from Kamatari. The letter reads: "As you are now become the undisputed ruler of the whole world, I must bow to your power. I therefore pledge myself to your service and send this *sake* as a token of my loyalty." Iruka reads the letter, but refuses to believe that it is written in good faith. He is convinced it is a trick to put him off his guard. He orders the fisherman to be arrested. Iruka will not touch the *sake*, fearing poison. Imakuni, to prove its innocence, drinks it before all the company. Iruka is, however, still unconvinced. He retires with his suite.

Imakuni is not ill-pleased with his stratagem, for it has enabled him to get into the palace. He and his lord's son, **Nakatomi Tankai,** intend to kill Iruka and put an end to his tyranny. An attempt is made to stab Imakuni through the floor with spears, but this he foils. Next a group of ladies-in-waiting bring him food and *sake*. Imakuni suspects such courtesies shown to a prisoner and pours the *sake* on a bed of chrysanthemums, which withers immediately. **Gemba,** a retainer of Iruka's, and some soldiers rush from the palace and, seizing him, drag him away to be questioned.

Ladies from the household of Iruka's sister, **Tachibana-hime,** enter in search of their mistress. Presently she joins them, coming down the *hanamichi*. Tachibana-hime has fallen in love with a handsome youth of whom she caught sight at a festival. She does not know who he is and fears she will never see him again. Her ladies exclaim that her dress is wet with dew: she must change at once. One of them notices a thread attached to the sleeve. She begins to wind up the thread, which, to her surprise, is much longer than she expects. Presently the thread tightens and down the *hanamichi*, winding up the same thread, comes a young man. Tachibana-hime recognizes him at once as the man to whom she has lost her heart. He tells the ladies that his name is Motome and explains, rather lamely, that he found this spindle of thread in the road and followed it out of curiosity. In fact, he also has fallen in love at first sight and, anxious to discover who the lady is, has attached the thread to her dress so that it may lead him to her. Now realizing that he is standing in the grounds of Iruka's palace, he guesses who she must be. He asks her whether she is not Iruka's sister. She at the same moment guesses that he must be Nakatomi Tankai. Tankai is in great distress for he has sworn to be revenged on the whole house of Soga and, if he is true to his vow, he must now put her to death. Tachibana-hime confesses her love and declares she would rather die by his hand than live without him. Tankai is torn between love and honour. Finally he hits on a solution. Part of his vow is that he will recover from Iruka a precious sword, which the tyrant seized when he came to power. If Tachibana-hime will help him to this sword, his debt of gratitude will be sufficient reason for sparing her life. Then, when Iruka is overthrown, they may be able to marry. Tachibana-hime, who hates her brother (who is trying to force her into a marriage profitable to himself), undertakes to help Tankai. That very night she must dance before her brother's guests at a banquet. She will try at the same time to steal the sword. The lovers part, but Tachibana-hime bids Tankai come secretly to her apartments, where they may exchange marriage vows.

When the princess and Tankai have gone, a young woman appears, holding a spindle, the now broken thread of which had been attached to Tankai's kimono. This is **O Miwa**, the daughter of a merchant in the neighbouring village with whom Tankai (whom, of course, she only knows as Motome) has been having a passing love affair. Like her high-born rival, she is deeply in love with him, and jealousy has made her follow him. She is rather put out to find he has entered so grand a palace, but is determined to discover what he is doing. She calls to attract attention. Tachibana-hime's old nurse, **O Mura,** comes by and asks her business. O Miwa explains that she is looking for Motome. The nurse finds this very amusing and tells O Miwa that the man she seeks is the betrothed of her princess. O Miwa goes from door to door desperately trying to find a way into the palace. Some of Tachibana-hime's ladies enter and are also amused when they learn for whom she is looking. To tease her they explain that Motome is a great lord and she must learn how to behave in his presence. They make fun of her, pretending to teach her how to offer *sake*, sing, and dance. O Miwa's eyes turn constantly towards the door from which she hopes her lover will appear. The farce becomes one of the most tragic passages in Kabuki, mental and physical cruelty culminating in one of the ladies striking her down. The heartless band pull her clothes about, tie a wooden stand to the end of the thread on her spindle and desert her.

O Miwa revives to find how she has been treated. These insults on top of all the rest fan her mortification and jealousy to a flame. From inside the palace she hears the voices of the ladies-in-waiting offering, she thinks, good wishes to the newly married Tankai and Tachibana-hime. Burnt up with jealousy, she rushes in the direction of the sound. Imakuni, coming from the palace, meets her and in a flash draws and wounds her mortally. He cries out that she must rejoice that in this way she can serve her lover. O Miwa asks how this can be. Imakuni replies that Mo-tome is in reality the young lord Nakatomi Tankai who has sworn to kill the tyrant. But Iruka bears a charmed life and neither steel nor poison can touch him. There is one way, however, in which he can be killed. Iruka's father, Soga Emishi, was many years without a son and, as he desired one above all things, he consulted a fortune-teller who told him that, if his wife drank the blood taken from the heart of a living white doe, she would conceive. Iruka was born as the result of such a potion, and his father named him "the Stag." At his birth, the same fortune-teller foretold that he would only die if he drank the fresh blood of a jealous woman mixed with the powdered hoof of a black stag. As he speaks, Imakuni catches O Miwa's blood in his flute and thanks her for the service she has done his master. O Miwa is now happy to die, since her death will profit the lord who for a short space honoured her with his love. Already her sight is failing; she gropes about until she finds her spool of thread, the end of which she believes is still attached to Tankai's kimono, and, winding it desperately in her hands, she dies.

Imakuni announces that now he and his master can be sure that their plans will be successful. He hides the flute in his breast and is about to go to find Tankai when Iruka's retainers rush upon him. He overcomes them all and, as the curtain is drawn, poses triumphantly.

IPPON GATANA DOHYO IRI (*The Wrestling Ring and the Sword*). *Sewamono.* — The play, by Murakami Motozo, was taken from the novel by Hasegawa Shin and popularized by Onoe Kikugoro VI. It is of the type known as *kizewamono*, dealing with gamblers, gangsters, prostitutes, and other small fry of the underworld of the late Tokugawa era.

Act I

Sc. 1. *Before the Abikoya, a low-class restaurant at Toride Juku on the Mito road.* Business is slack. Waitresses and townspeople loaf in front of the house. **Funado no Yahachi,** a local bully, picks a quarrel with a young married couple. They escape thanks to the intervention of a horse-coper called **Kyutaro.** Yahachi looks for another victim and finds him in **Komagata Mohei,** who tried to be a *sumo* wrestler but was kicked out for incompetence and is now trudging the streets in the last stages of physical exhaustion. Yahachi miscalculates, however, and in the end is butted in the stomach for his pains. He retires, swearing vengeance. This scene has been observed from upstairs by **O Tsuta,** a waitress. She is drunk and sentimentally takes pity on the half-starved wrestler. He tells his story, and she gives him all the money she has, as well as a comb and a hairpin. He accepts, promising to repay her some day, and goes on his way. Yahachi and some roughs follow him.

Sc. 2. *The Tone River ferry.* The ferry leaves. Mohei, gnawing a yam, enters and awaits its return. Yahachi and his thugs set on him. They abuse O Tsuta. Mohei, angry and with something in his inside for the first time in days, thrashes them soundly.

Act II

Sc. 1. *Ten years later ; a small ship-building yard near the River Fuse.* Mohei, now the chief of a successful gang of gamblers, has come some distance to repay his debt. He learns from the ship-builders that the Abikoya has gone bankrupt and O Tsuta has disappeared. He is attacked by members of a gambling gang run by **Nami Ichiri no Giju,** who mistake him for **Tatsusaburo,** a woodcarver and O Tsuta's husband. Tatsusaburo has deserted his wife and child for many years, but is now returning to them. He has won money from Giju's gang the night before by cheating, and they are now looking for him. Mohei violently disabuses them of their error and continues his search. Tatsusaburo sneaks in, throws his loaded dice into the river and makes for O Tsuta's house.

Sc. 2. *O Tsuta's house.* O Tsuta ekes out a living for herself and her little girl, O Kimi, by making sweetmeats. As night falls, she prepares to put the child to bed. Some of Giju's gang come to the house, looking for Tatsusaburo. They manhandle her and leave. It is the first she has heard of her husband in years. Tatsusaburo comes and there is a touching family reunion. They decide to decamp and are making their few preparations when there is another knock at the door. Mohei comes in, thanks O Tsuta for her kindness of ten years ago, and lays a roll of money before her. O Tsuta in her present distress cannot remember him. Hardly able to conceal his disappointment, Mohei leaves, but almost immediately returns to warn them that Giju's gang are coming for Tatsusaburo. The thugs attack, and Mohei butts one of them in the stomach with his head. Then O Tsuta recalls the Abikoya incident. *The stage revolves.*

Sc. 3. *Outside O Tsuta's house.* Mohei takes on the gang a..d lays them all out, including Giju himself. He tells Tatsusaburo to escape with his wife and child while they can. They do so, with many tearful expressions of gratitude. Mohei watches them go, reflecting with some gratification that, though he was never able to reach champion status in the ring, he was able to put up a first-rate show for O Tsuta's sake.

IREZUMI CHOHAN (*The Tattooed Gambler*). *Sewamono.* — The original story by Hasegawa Shin is a study of social conditions in the early part of the 19th century, particularly of the floating population of ne'er-do-wells who migrated from town to town, living by their wits and their quick fingers. These *toseinin* were loosely organized into groups owning allegiance to regional bosses; the groups were often at variance with each other; those who were not enrolled in such a group might fare ill at the hands of the bosses unless they recognized their authority and paid the appropriate dues. The hero of this play, **Hantaro,** an expatriate from Edo, to which he longs to return, is such an independent vagrant and lives mostly by gambling.

Act I

Sc. 1. *The landing place at Gyotoku, Shimosa province.* Hantaro is hanging about with nothing particular to do on a fine moonlight night. He quarrels with **Arakida no Kumasuke,** a fellow gambler, who taunts him with the report that Hantaro's love, **Hiraiya no O Sada,** has cast him off out of disgust. Hantaro throws him into the river. Then he hears a second splash and goes to the rescue.

Sc. 2. *Lower down the riverbank.* Hantaro has rescued a girl called **O Naka,** one of those wretched chattels who pass from tea-house to tea-house without hope of ever again attaining freedom. O Naka has several times tried to commit suicide. Each time she has been rescued and each time she has become the mistress of her rescuer until he has tired of her and has sold her back into a tea-house. She naturally assumes that Hantaro will do the same thing. He is not interested, however, and reproaches her for her immodest behaviour. Instead he gives her money and goes off. O Naka is deeply moved and follows him.

Sc. 3. *A dilapidated house.* Kumasuke and another ruffian break into the house, where Hantaro lives, and, after fumbling about in the dark, lie in wait for him. He enters, but is able to ward off the attack and, in the ensuing scrimmage, kills Kumasuke. He decides he had better leave and is discovered making his preparations by O Naka. She asks to be allowed to go with him, and he agrees.

Act II

Sc. 1. *Two years later; Hantaro's house in Shinagawa, Edo.* Hantaro and O Naka lead a miserable existence. Hantaro will not earn a decent living and squanders such money as he gets by gambling. O Naka has fallen seriously ill. The doctor can offer little hope of her recovery; indeed he lets her understand that her days are now numbered. When Hantaro returns, she pleads with him to reform and finally prevails on him to let her tattoo a pair of dice on his arm to remind him of his vow to give up playing games of chance.

Sc. 2. *Near the six Jizo.* An old man and his wife on pilgrimage pass across the stage. After a short prayer to Jizo for their lost son, they continue on their way. Hantaro staggers in pursued by the gang of the local boss, **Masagoro.** He will not submit to Masagoro, and so he has been beaten up. He tells the story of his life, and they jeer at him when he relates the circumstances of his vow to O Naka. Masagoro offers to throw dice with him — if Hantaro loses, he must acknowledge Masagoro; if he wins, Masagoro will give him money. Hantaro has little choice but to break his vow. He throws — and wins.

IRO MOYO CHOTTO KARIMAME, commonly called *Kasane. Shosagoto.* — By Tsuruya Namboku; about 1820; a rehash of the popular *Kasane* (see page 16). Only the *michiyuki* dance, embodying the plot, remains today.

Argument: The samurai **Yoemon** has lost a valuable heirloom and, fleeing his lord's anger, is overtaken at a river by his mistress, **Kasane,** who begs to die with him. He at last agrees and they are saying farewell, when a skull floats by with a sickle stuck in it, the same one, he realizes, that he used to slay a jealous husband long ago. (Though Yoemon is unaware of it, Kasane is the child of his former lover and her murdered husband, Suke.) Suke's vengeful spirit enters Kasane, disfiguring her with the same wounds inflicted on him by Yoemon. Two police agents leap out, but Yoemon drives them off and finds a notice proclaiming him Suke's murderer. Kasane runs up and clings to him, but, realizing who she is, he tries to escape and wounds her with the sickle. Making her look in a mirror, he confesses his crime, saying they can never be happy together even in death. Kasane, now completely possessed by her father's spirit, is pursued by Yoemon. He kills her with the sickle and tries to flee, but her beckoning ghost drags him back to the scene of the crime, where his dead love lays ghostly hands on him.

ISE ONDO KOI NO NETABA (*The Dance of Death at Ise*). *Sewamono*. — Written by Chikamatsu Tokuzo for the puppet theatre and first staged in Osaka in July 1796. It is essentially a summer-season play. The story is based on an actual case of mass murder at Furuichi, in Ise. Chikamatsu Tokuzo's play appeared within two months of the crime and was set in the same locality, but to give it additional local colour he connected the murderer with the Grand Shrines at Ise. The play is still very popular.

The plot concerns a valuable sword made by the smith Shimosaka and possessed by a bloodthirsty spirit. The original play was in three acts, but only a short scene from Act I and the whole of Act III are now regularly performed. The rest of the play is extremely involved and a summary of the essential features is given below since, otherwise, the isolated scenes are incomprehensible. Portions of these obsolete acts are occasionally performed, usually freely adapted and turned into a dance or a comic scene for stock buffoon characters.

The daimyo of Awa had in his service a samurai to whom he entrusted a precious Shimosaka sword. This sword caused the death of the samurai and also that of his son, who inherited the trust. The son left an only child, a little boy, whose mother was already dead. The boy's aunt, terrified of the evil sword, disposed of the weapon secretly and fled from Awa with her small nephew to settle under an assumed name in the Ise district. The boy, **Fukuoka Mitsugi** (who is the hero of the play), was adopted by a priest of the Grand Shrines and grew up in the service of the Shrines, but he never forgot that his first allegiance was to the daimyo of Awa and more especially to the daimyo's Chief Counsellor, who had been his father's immediate superior. Meanwhile, the daimyo of Awa died and was succeeded by a child. This boy's uncle, **Kajikawa Daigaku,** plotted to usurp the daimyate, but was thwarted in his plans by the loyalty of the Chief Counsellor. Daigaku therefore determined to discredit him and one of the several plots he devised concerned the Shimosaka sword. Word came to the Chief Counsellor that this sword, his lord's heirloom, was for sale in the town of Furuichi in Ise. He therefore sent his son, **Imada Manjiro,** to buy it and bring it back to Awa. Manjiro was a charming youth of weak character. He bought the sword, but then fell victim to the attractions of **O Kishi,** a courtesan of Furuichi. Instead of returning home he remained with his love and to pay his debts was forced to pawn the Shimosaka sword, although retaining the certificate which proved its authenticity. The spies of the wicked Daigaku were watching Manjiro. The chief of these, a samurai named **Tokushima Iwaji,** plotted to secure both the sword and the certificate so that Manjiro would be unable to fulfil his mission and his father would be disgraced through him. Iwaji succeeded by a trick in stealing the certificate from Manjiro, but could not lay his hands on the sword because both the pawnbroker and the weapon had disappeared. At this point Fukuoka Mitsugi enters the story. As has been said, he was by birth the retainer of the Chief Counsellor of Awa. He learned of Manjiro's predicament and received permission from his present master, who was a friend of Manjiro's father, to go to the youth's assistance. Mitsugi decided that the first thing was to get Manjiro out of harm's way; then he could hunt for the sword and the certificate.

At this point occurs the short scene often performed. Its popularity is largely due to its stage effects. It takes place on the sea shore near the Ise Shrines at Futami-ga-Ura, where two sacred rocks emerge from the sea. The sun rises exactly between these two rocks, which are "married" by a sacred rope, on New Year's Day. The scene is in the form of a *sewa-dammari*, a mimed dance.

Act I

Sc. 3. *Futami-ga-Ura Scene (Futami-ga-Ura no Ba).* Mitsugi comes to the beach with Manjiro whom he is escorting to a place of safety. Mitsugi has already had a skirmish with Iwaji's spies in the course of which he has secured possession of a piece of valuable evidence, half of a letter from Daigaku to Iwaji, which proves conclusively that Daigaku is plotting against his nephew, the young daimyo. The spies are on his track, but in the darkness the two parties run into each other unawares. There follows a general scrimmage of the sort greatly appreciated by Kabuki audiences. Both sides receive reinforcements in the shape of Mitsugi's servant **Rimpei** and another spy who have been carrying on a private fight. The spies are overwhelmed. Mitsugi wrests from one of them the other half of the torn letter which makes his evidence complete. He sends Manjiro off in charge of Rimpei and then, holding down his struggling antagonists, waits for the sun to rise between the two rocks so that he may have light enough to make sure that he has obtained the right paper. The curtain is drawn as he poses triumphantly.

Between this scene and the famous "Aburaya Scene" which closes the play there is an act which takes place within the precincts of the Ise Shrine. In this Mitsugi recovers the lost sword. It is brought to him by his aunt who has come across the absconding pawnbroker, recognized the sword and insisted on redeeming it. She tells Mitsugi the sword's history and commands him to restore it to Awa, warning him earnestly, however, that if the blade leaves the sheath it will not return until it has tasted blood. Mitsugi now needs only the certificate to complete his mission.

Act III

The Aburaya Scene (Aburaya no ba). Tokushima Iwaji has in his possession the certificate and is still searching for the sword. He does not, of course, know that the incriminating letter from Daigaku is in Mitsugi's hands. He is staying at the Aburaya Tea-house at Furuichi in company with two merchants, **Jirosuke** and **Kitaroku.** As a precaution, he and Kitaroku have exchanged clothes and identities. The real Kitaroku is courting O Kishi, the courtesan with whom Manjiro is infatuated, while Iwaji is courting the beautiful **O Kon.** But he makes little progress, for O Kon is deeply attached to Mitsugi who has been her chosen lover for some time. The chief maid of the establishment, **Manno,** is an evil woman in Iwaji's pay. She is determined to put an end to the relationship between Mitsugi and O Kon so that her patron may gain the lady's favours.

The act opens with a short scene between Manjiro, who is in hiding at a near-by temple, and O Kishi. He learns from her that Mitsugi is in Furuichi searching for him and has been several times to the Aburaya. He leaves a message with her that he will return and meet Mitsugi later in the evening. (*When this act is played alone, this scene is usually omitted*).

Mitsugi enters by the *hanamichi*, carrying the Shimosaka sword, and receives Manjiro's message from O Kishi. She tells him also that she is afraid that Iwaji and his friends intend to ransom herself and O Kon and take them away. She begs his help in preventing this. Left alone, Mitsugi reflects that he has been watching the so-called Iwaji closely and is convinced that he is an impostor. The man calling himself Kitaroku must be the real Iwaji in disguise. Iwaji has the certificate belonging to the sword, but tonight he, Mitsugi, will wrest it from him. He is discovered by the maid Manno who at once puts into operation her plan to bring about a quarrel between Mitsugi and O Kon. She declares that O Kon is too busy to see him and will only allow him to remain in the tea-house on condition that he chooses another courtesan to keep him company. Mitsugi is forced to comply, since he dare not risk missing his *rendez-vous* with Manjiro. He tells Manno to send him anyone she likes. It is one of the rules of the establishment that swords must be left in a rack at the entrance. Manno tries to take Mitsugi's sword from him. Mitsugi declines to give it up to a woman, but in the end hands it over to the tea-house cook, **Kisuke.** This Kisuke is the son of a former retainer of Mitsugi's father, is devoted to him and fully in his confidence. When Manno has left the room he begs Mitsugi to leave the place as it is dangerous. Mitsugi tells him that he has found the lost sword, which is the one now in Kisuke's hands, and believes the missing certificate to be in this very house. He has come to retrieve it, not for amusement. They go out together unaware that Manno has overheard their conversation. Iwaji presently comes from the house carrying his own sword and Mitsugi's, which Manno has just told him is the Shimosaka weapon. He unrivets the two blades from the hilts and exchanges them. Kisuke sees him doing so.

Mitsugi returns, looking for Manjiro. He is followed by the courtesan **O Shika,** whom Manno has bribed to discredit him in O Kon's eyes. O Shika flings herself tearfully upon Mitsugi asking why he treats her so coldly after all that has passed between them. In this situation they are discovered by O Kon, as Manno intended. Before Mitsugi can say a word, the doors open to reveal Iwaji, his two confederates and O Kishi, before whom O Kon accuses Mitsugi of infidelity and deceit while O Shika declares that he has written her love letters and borrowed money from her. Mitsugi attempts to deny everything, but the evidence is too cleverly arranged. O Shika produces the letters and Manno swears she delivered the money into his hands. In spite of the insults of Manno, Iwaji and his companions, Mitsugi tries to keep calm. But O Kon refuses to listen to his explanations. When Manno calls him a swindler, his self-control snaps and he threatens to strike her. O Kon turns away from him towards Iwaji, who bids Manno eject the troublesome fellow. Mitsugi calls angrily for his sword, but Manno tells him to fetch it for himself. It is brought to him by Kisuke, who hides the hilt with his sleeve, for it is the Shimosaka sword with Iwaji's hilt which he carries. Mitsugi snatches it without looking and accepts his coat from O Kishi, who has taken no part in the quarrel. As he reaches the gate, O Kon calls after him : " This is the end." At the sound of her voice, Mitsugi instinctively turns back, but O Shika comes between them. Mitsugi strikes first her and then Manno, who pushes him through the gate. When peace is restored, Iwaji, pleased with the rout of his enemy and rival, offers to marry O Kon and make her a samurai's lady. He explains that he is the real Iwaji and that through him his master will shortly become daimyo of Awa so that he will be a person of great importance. O Kon has not really been deceived by Manno's stratagem ; she loves Mitsugi too well to mistrust him. She has pretended to turn against him because she hopes thereby to be able to help him. She appears to fall in with Iwaji's plans, but then suddenly asks him suspiciously about a small packet he cherishes in his bosom, declaring that it must be the document ransoming some other courtesan. Iwaji, taken by surprise, lets out that it is the certificate of the Shimosaka sword. He tries too late to cover up his mistake and refuses to let her see the paper. O Kon makes a jealous scene and swears she will never be his wife until she has seen it. She is about to flounce out of the room when Iwaji, to pacify her and believing that she is too stupid to understand the document, gives her the packet, bidding her look at it privately in her room and then return it to him.

Iwaji and his confederates are left alone. While they are planning how to murder Mitsugi quietly, Manno rushes in to tell them that Mitsugi has gone off with Iwaji's sword. She thinks that he has accidentally left behind the Shimosaka sword, but to her chagrin learns that it is just the other way about. Mitsugi has the Shimosaka sword in spite of everything. No one suspects Kisuke, who is called in and rated for his carelessness. He is sent off to return Mitsugi's sword and recover the other. Kisuke salutes the company respectfully, but as he goes down the *hanamichi* he puts out his tongue at them, shouting "Baka." (fools).

The stage is empty. The music of the dance called "Ise Ondo" is heard. Mitsugi comes hurrying back calling for Kisuke and Manno; he has noticed the strange sword hilt. He frantically checks over the swords in the rack, but the one he seeks is not there. He shouts that he has got the wrong sword. O Kon appears at an upper window and throws down a letter, saying that she hates him and this letter is to sever their relationship for ever. She closes the window. Mitsugi picks up the paper and finds enclosed in it the certificate belonging to the sword. O Kon's letter reads: "Many people are watching us so you must pretend to be in despair. I know you did not cheat O Shika. Manno and she were bribed by Iwaji to discredit you and make me give you up. Now they trust me, thinking I have broken with you. Iwaji and the merchant Kitaroku have exchanged identities. They are Daigaku's emissaries. I never want to be separated from you. I shall be faithful always."

Mitsugi puts the certificate in his bosom and wonders remorsefully how he could ever have doubted O Kon. All his fury is turned against Manno, who at this moment comes out demanding the return of her patron's sword. Mitsugi refuses to give it until he sees his own. Manno tries to snatch it from him, but he beats her off with the sheathed weapon. The scabbard splits and the blade wounds Manno in the back. Mitsugi grasps the sword and the blood-thirsty spirit of the Shimosaka blade takes possession of him. He puts his hand over Manno's mouth to stifle her screams and runs her through. Iwaji's confederate Jirosuke appears, sees Manno's corpse and shouts "Murderer!". Mitsugi instantly cuts him down, although without killing him. A crowd of young men rush out to try to disarm him and are put to rout. A little maid from the tea-house who comes out with a lantern to see what is happening is killed by the sword which Mitsugi can no longer control. Moving like one in a dream, he goes upstairs. He finds Kitaroku asleep in bed and cuts off his head, covering the body with a quilt. On his way down he meets Iwaji and wounds him. A moment later O Shika appears in her night clothes. Terrified by Mitsugi's bloody sword and expression she tries to escape, imploring his forgiveness, but he kills her as she hides behind a screen. *The stage revolves.*

The garden of the Aburaya, spanned by a wooden bridge. A number of young girls dance over the bridge, but are frightened away by the uproar in the house. Mitsugi appears, covered with blood. He is set upon by Iwaji and Jirosuke, both wounded. When he has dispatched them he looks about for more victims. O Kon comes out to him, the only person who has courage to do so. Mitsugi sees her, his face changes and he beckons her to him. He tries to lay down the sword, but his fingers will not relax their grip. Again and again he tries; as a last resort he strikes his elbow on the ground until the pain numbs his fingers and the sword flies from his grasp. (Some actors strike their hands against the edge of a stone water-basin.) He begins to thank O Kon for the certificate, but she begs him to escape at once. He replies that he cannot do so and by a gesture indicates that he intends to commit *seppuku.* O Kon implores him to wait. Kisuke hurries in, asking anxiously whether Mitsugi is hurt. Mitsugi rates him for giving him the wrong weapon. Since he has lost the Shimosaka sword there is nothing left for him but to die. Kisuke holds up a lantern and bids Mitsugi examine the blade with which he has just done such execution. Mitsugi recognizes it as the Shimosaka sword. Vowing to carry the treasure with all speed to the country of his forefathers, Mitsugi poses, with Kisuke and O Kon, as the curtain is drawn.

KAGAMI JISHI (*The Dancing Lion*). *Shosagoto.* — Written by Fukuchi Ochi and first staged in 1893. *Nagauta* accompaniment. The rôles of Yayoi and the lion spirit are danced by the same actor.

Argument: A room in the Shogun's castle at Edo. Here there is set out a stand with offerings and lion masks, used in certain dances performed to frighten away evil spirits. It is customary to choose one of the waiting-women to perform these dances and on this occasion the Shogun's retainer **Sandayu**, in consultation with the lady-in-waiting **Koshiji**, chooses **Yayoi**. The lady-in-waiting and another woman-servant lead in Yayoi, who is shy and frightened. She tries to escape, but they bring her back and shut her in the room with the lion masks to practise her dance.

Yayoi begins to dance rather tentatively, overawed by her surroundings. First she performs a temple offering dance. Then she dances with one and two fans. She becomes absorbed in her dancing, but slowly the lion masks on their stand begin to exert a curious influence on her. She is conscious of them all the time and cannot keep her gaze from wandering to the stand. At last she goes over to it and, kneeling, takes one of the masks in her hand. She claps the jaws experimentally and then begins to dance, carrying the mask. Slowly the mask takes charge of her. It is no longer Yayoi who is working the jaws. She cannot control the mask. Neither can she remove it from her hand. It drags her round the room. Two butterflies appear and the mask pursues them. Yayoi fights in vain to free herself. She is forced to go with the mask which pursues the butterflies down the *hanamichi*. They all disappear.

There follows an interlude of a New Year dance performed by two young page-girls, first with drums and then with tambourines. After they have gone, the music becomes more and more restless. Great bushes of tree-peony are set up on the stage. Finally the curtain of the *hanamichi* is drawn and the personified spirit of the lion appears.

The lion rushes down the *hanamichi*, retreats back into its lair and then comes on again, with fierce, animal head-shakings and gestures. He dances proudly on the stage and then crouches down among the peonies, which have a soporific effect on him. While he sleeps the girls, who now become two butterflies, return. They tease him until he awakes and rushes at first one and then the other, trying to drive them off. The butterflies irritate him to a frenzy, and he dances, swirling his great mane around him like a whiplash.

KAGAMIYAMA KOKYO NO NISHIKIE (*The Women's Chushingura*). *Jidaimono*. —

Written by Yo Yodai in 1783. Yodai was court physician to the Shogun and could write with authority about palace life. The play is based on a scandal which occurred at the Tokugawa court but, in the usual Kabuki manner, it has been set in a remoter age. This does not, however, prevent the author from referring in the dialogue to the current theatrical success, *Chushingura*. Partly on account of this reference, partly because the themes of the two plays are similar, this play is popularly known as *Onna Chushingura* (*The Women's Chushingura*).

Act I

The Cherry-Blossom Scene. (This act is rarely performed and is mainly spectacle.) *At the Hatsue Temple*. A scene of bickering and teasing between maids-in-waiting and pages in the service of the daughter of the Shogun **Yoritomo**. Their conversation suggests the unrest in the household and also informs the audience that the princess was betrothed to her cousin, Minamoto Yoshitaka, who has been murdered for political reasons by her father. She now wishes to enter a convent to spend the rest of her life praying for the soul of her lover.

Act II

The Princess' palace. It is the day of the Girls' Festival. Branches of peach blossoms are brought to the **Princess**. The chief lady-in-waiting, **Iwafuji**, and the other ladies offer their greetings. The Princess enquires after **Onoe**, the second lady-in-waiting who has been away on a mission for her. Onoe enters. The Princess asks eagerly for her father's answer. Onoe says that Yoritomo has given permission for her to take vows and has sent her a nun's habit as a token of his approval. The Princess rejoices and shows her a small image of the Buddha which was the gift of Yoshitaka. The Princess loves and trusts Onoe above her other ladies. She now charges her to place the image in the temple where both Yoshitaka and his father, Yoshinaka, are buried.

The senior lady-in-waiting, Iwafuji, is jealous of Onoe. She speaks spitefully to her, sneering at her for being the daughter of a merchant. One of the other ladies, more kindly disposed, points out that Onoe has reason to be proud of her father's wealth, since he has been able to assist the Shogun himself. This is why Onoe has been received into the Princess' household. Iwafuji remarks that since Onoe, in spite of her lowly birth, holds a position worthy of a samurai's daughter she is no doubt acquainted with the use of those noble weapons, the halberd and the sword. Onoe is silent. Iwafuji challenges her to a fencing match. **Motome,** a young samurai, reminds Iwafuji in whose presence she is. Iwafuji counters that every samurai's daughter should know how to use the sword. She herself has instructed the maids-in-waiting in her charge. Let Onoe choose any one among them as an opponent. **O Hatsu,** Onoe's personal attendant, enters, seeking her mistress. Onoe orders her to retire at once, since she has no business there. O Hatsu is roughly stopped by Iwafuji, who asks how she was allowed to enter the presence chamber. O Hatsu replies that no one " allowed " her ; she just came. She wishes to ask something. Iwafuji bids her do so. O Hatsu explains that, although her mistress is a merchant's daughter, she is expert in the use of the halberd and the sword. Onoe instructed O Hatsu herself and she suggests that it would be more correct for her, O Hatsu, to fence with Iwafuji's pupil. Iwafuji is taken aback, but consents. Motome is delighted. With the Princess' permission, the match is arranged. The girls fence with bamboo swords. O Hatsu easily beats all the maids-in-waiting. Iwafuji, ill-pleased, offers to take her on herself. O Hatsu at first demurs, as she is too low in rank to fence with Iwafuji. But when Iwafuji suggests that in that case Onoe had better fight instead, O Hatsu hastily accepts. Iwafuji and O Hatsu fence. O Hatsu strikes Iwafuji on the hand, numbing it, so that she drops her weapon. Onoe stops the match. O Hatsu returns Iwafuji's sword to her, and Iwafuji, in a rage, attacks O Hatsu unawares, striking her repeatedly. She then claims to have won the match. O Hatsu answers hotly that it was only out of respect for Iwafuji's rank that she did not strike the decisive blow when she dropped her sword. Iwafuji mocks at her and the quarrel grows angrier until Onoe parts them, reminding O Hatsu that she is in the Princess' presence. She dismisses O Hatsu and asks Iwafuji to excuse her rudeness. The Princess, however, admires O Hatsu's devotion.

Motome tells the Princess the hour has come for her to take her nun's vows. The ladies-in-waiting mourn to think that such beautiful hair must be sacrificed. The Princess leaves with all her ladies for her private oratory. O Hatsu returns, but finds Onoe gone. She muses that it is sad so lovely a young princess should become a nun. All her household are good and kind, except for Iwafuji, who is jealous of Onoe. No one likes her. Iwafuji, who has lingered behind, hears all this from her place of concealment.

Act III

The Scene of the Sandal. A room in the Palace. The ladies-in-waiting, including Iwafuji, are discussing the flowers presented by Iwafuji and Onoe to their mistress. They obsequiously make disparaging remarks about Onoe's flowers. A messenger **Danjo,** a retainer of Yoritomo, is received by Iwafuji. He announces that a holy priest will administer the final vows and conduct the Princess to her convent. For this ceremony a special incense, called *Ranjatai,* must be used. The Princess has this incense in her keeping. Iwafuji sends for Onoe, to whom it has been entrusted. Onoe appears hurriedly, carrying a casket which she delivers to Danjo. Danjo opens it and asks in amazement whether this is really what was entrusted to her. Iwafuji watches with an air of triumph. Onoe looks into the casket and sees that the precious treasure she has been guarding has become a sandal. Onoe, weeping, declares that the incense must have been stolen by a person of ill will. Iwafuji makes a great show of indignation when one of the older ladies identifies the sandal as hers. Iwafuji's personal attendant hurries in, declaring that, unable to find her mistress' sandals, she has just discovered one of them in Onoe's room. Iwafuji accuses Onoe of deliberately planning to incriminate her. Let her confess what she has done with the incense. The more Onoe denies having touched it, the more Iwafuji taxes her.

Danjo rules that Onoe has failed in her duty and asks Iwafuji, as chief lady-in-waiting, to hold an enquiry. Iwafuji asserts that Onoe is unquestionably the thief and, taking up the offending sandal, strikes her with it (see page 476). The ladies try to stop her, but Iwafuji warns them that if they interfere they will become parties to the theft. Onoe agrees that the responsibility is hers alone; and she should be punished. Iwafuji continues to beat her with the sandal until Onoe, weeping, seizes her hand and cries that she has been punished enough. Iwafuji again screams "Thief!" and throws the sandal in her face. Danjo leaves to report to the Shogun. Iwafuji and the ladies-in-waiting follow. As the curtain is drawn, Onoe sits with the sandal in her hand, her face expressing all the humiliation and shame of her position.

Act IV

Onoe's apartments. O Hatsu is waiting anxiously for her mistress. Some of the ladies of Iwafuji's party come to taunt her, making veiled remarks which she does not understand. Something has obviously happened between Iwafuji and Onoe. Night has fallen. O Hatsu, almost beside herself, comes into the corridor outside her mistress' room. At last she sees Onoe's disconsolate figure approaching. O Hatsu runs to her. Onoe makes no answer to her anxious enquiries. They reach the door of Onoe's room, and as they enter, Onoe draws the sandal from her bosom.

Onoe's room. O Hatsu busies herself about her mistress, but Onoe refuses food and even tea. Onoe tells her not to worry. She was taken ill, but is now better. She refuses O Hatsu's offer of medicine, but asks her to rub her shoulders. Onoe questions the girl about her father who was, she knows, a samurai. She pities O Hatsu for having to take service with a merchant's daughter. O Hatsu indignantly rebuts this suggestion. Onoe should not let her mind dwell on her father's rank. She ought to amuse herself more, perhaps, by going to the theatre. They talk about plays and actors. O Hatsu, watching her mistress

shrewdly, says her favourite play is "Chushingura." Onoe
agrees it is a fine play, adding that she detests the character
Moronao. O Hatsu asks whether she thinks Enya Hangan
was justified in attempting to kill him. Onoe thinks he was.
O Hatsu disagrees. Enya Hangan should have thought of
his family, on whom his action brought utter ruin. He
should have thought of his parents, she adds meaningly.
They exchange a long, understanding look, and O Hatsu,
greatly relieved, withdraws.

Alone, Onoe confesses that, in spite of O Hatsu's kindness, she cannot bear the burden of such terrible disgrace.
She will write to her parents, tell them everything, and then
die. O Hatsu interrupts her, and she sends the girl to find
her lacquer letter case. When O Hatsu returns with it,
Onoe hides her scissors and sends her to find them. Onoe
finishes her letter and puts it, with the sandal, in the letter
case. When O Hatsu returns, Onoe asks her to take it to
her mother at once. The girl, on pain of dismissal if she
delays, reluctantly takes the letter case and goes.

O Hatsu has changed her obi for one suitable for a visit.
She is anxious about Onoe and prays for her. As she goes
along the *hanamichi*, Onoe calls her back. But it is only to
tell her to take good care of herself. Alone again, Onoe
weeps, as she thinks with gratitude of O Hatsu's devotion.
But she is glad that the girl does not realize she has seen
her mistress for the last time. She thinks of her parents,
whose forgiveness for dying before them she has asked in
her letter. She will say her last prayers and prepare to
die. She withdraws into her oratory.

Act V

The Scene of the Crow. It is a dark, rainy night. O Hatsu enters, accompanied by a boy with a lantern. Her
anxiety about Onoe is such that she sends the boy back to
the Palace with a message for a friend, asking her to see
whether Onoe needs anything. The boy is unwilling to
leave O Hatsu alone, and while they are arguing, his lantern
goes out—a bad omen! At last he goes back. O Hatsu is
in two minds about going on herself. A crow croaks
suddenly—another bad omen! O Hatsu is tempted to
open the letter case to see what is in it. But it is sealed.
She stumbles, hurting her foot. At this moment one of
Iwafuji's confederates, **Ushijima Chikara**, enters. He has

the stolen incense which he intends to hide in a safe place. He is pursued by **Datehei,** a man of integrity in the Princess' service, who has guessed what is in Chikara's box. He now attempts to wrest it from him. Chikara flings the box away and in the struggle in the dark Datehei finds the letter case dropped by O Hatsu and thinks it is the incense box. Chikara makes the same mistake. The three of them struggle for it, the cord of the case is broken and the letter and sandal drop out. O Hatsu picks up the letter and sees the words " My will." Meanwhile Datehei has discovered the incense box and Chikara draws his sword. He and Datehei pose.

Act VI

Onoe's apartments. Onoe, dressed in white, lies dying. She has stabbed herself. A letter addressed to the Shogun is on her writing desk. Behind her stands Iwafuji with a drawn dirk in her hand. She has come to gloat over her dying rival, and now orders her to give up the image of the Buddha entrusted to her by the Princess. When Onoe refuses, Iwafuji takes it from her by force. She boasts that she and her brother Danjo arranged the theft of the incense. Now they have the image also. Iwafuji leaves at the sound of approaching footsteps. (*The scene may start here.*) O Hatsu rushes into the room with the letter and sandal. Onoe, almost spent, tells O Hatsu that Iwafuji has stolen the image. O Hatsu in tears swears to recover it and avenge her. Onoe dies in her arms. A thunderstorm breaks overhead. This is O Hatsu's opportunity. Under cover of the storm she will creep across the garden to Iwafuji's apartments. She notices the wistaria (*fuji*) in full bloom. It reminds her of Iwafuji (wistaria rock) and she angrily rips off a branch. She goes out into the garden.

Act VII

The Revenge. The palace garden. Night and frogs croaking in the pond. A young page, **Umpei,** enters and flings a pebble against the door of Iwafuji's apartments. When Iwafuji comes, he tells her he has buried the " little doll " at the north end of the garden near Onoe's rooms, as she ordered. (This is part of a curse Iwafuji has put on Onoe.) Iwafuji rewards him. She shows him the Buddha which he tries to seize from her, but she beats him off with her sword and he runs away. (*The scene may start here.*)

Iwafuji is about to go back, but suddenly realizes that the frogs have stopped croaking. She waits to see who can have disturbed them. When she sees O Hatsu, she asks her curtly who gave her permission to come into her private garden. O Hatsu answers as she did in Act I. "No one allowed me. I wish to ask you something." Her mistress has fainted, and she needs help. The medicine she has tried has done no good. She knows that Iwafuji has a wonderful charm which she is sure will revive her mistress. She begs Iwafuji to lend it to her. Iwafuji denies having any charm of the sort. O Hatsu replies that she means the precious image of Amida Buddha. Iwafuji pretends not to understand. She offers to go with O Hatsu to visit Onoe, but not immediately : "because she has a headache." "Oh," cries O Hatsu, "I have an excellent cure for headaches!" and, drawing the sandal from her bosom, places it on Iwafuji's head. Iwafuji strikes it off and screams abuse at O Hatsu. She manages to slip the image of the Buddha into her closed umbrella. She strikes O Hatsu with the sandal, promising her the same treatment as Onoe. She draws her sword and O Hatsu catches up the umbrella to defend herself. The precious image falls to the ground. O Hatsu sees it and, picking it up first, declares that now she can avenge Onoe. O Hatsu draws her sword and kills Iwafuji. In tears, O Hatsu strikes the body repeatedly with the sandal, crying that her mistress is avenged.

Motome appears. He reveals that it has now been discovered that Iwafuji was plotting, with her brother, against the life of the Shogun himself. O Hatsu has therefore served both the Shogun and her mistress. O Hatsu gives him the image and Onoe's last letter, together with a paper written by Iwafuji which was with the image. She begs him to show them to their lord. Motome tells her that the incense has been recovered and her mistress' spirit can now be at rest. O Hatsu, her mission accomplished, intends to kill herself and join her lady, but Motome prevents her, telling her he has a message for her. The Princess, deeply moved by O Hatsu's loyalty, as a reward promotes her to the position formerly held by Onoe. She will henceforth be known as Onoe II. Motome bids her go to the Princess at once.

As O Hatsu is about to leave, Umpei, the wicked page,

attacks her, but is himself killed in the struggle. O Hatsu and Motome pose triumphantly.

(*Koto* music accompanies the second half of this act.)

KAGEKIYO. *Juhachiban*. — Not now often performed, this play is described here solely as an example of *semeba* (see page 456).

Argument : Kagekiyo was one of the great Heike or Taira generals (see also in *Gedatsu*). After his final defeat by the Minamoto, he was confined in a cave prison where he ultimately died.

The set shows the barred entrance to the cave. Kagekiyo, wearing the exaggerated *kumadori* (see page 437), bushy hair, and gold brocade of the " loyal warrior," glowers through the grille at the outside world. His wife and children are led in, in bonds, so that he may taste the full bitterness of defeat. He is let out of his prison, and his fetters are removed. He sits on a great rock in the center of the stage. The Minamoto warriors cluster round him, mocking and gloating over his downfall. Kagekiyo relates the misfortunes of the ill-starred Tairas in a famous *monogatari*. He declares his unshakeable loyalty and his faith. The soldiers torture his wife and daughters before his eyes, but, though he weeps for them, he will not retract a word of what he has said. His son is thrown into the prison cave, but he still refuses to admit Minamoto superiority. The soldiers then tempt him with food and drink, but he scornfully kicks it from him. He then turns on his tormentors and, shouting his defiance, roots up the great boulder on which he has been sitting and hurls it into their midst. They disperse in terror and Kagekiyo poses, brandishing a huge wooden beam which he has snatched up for the fight. (Cf. the grave marker which he uses in *Gedatsu*.)

KAGOTSURUBE SATO NO EIZAME, commonly known as *Sanno Jirozaemon*. *Sewamono*. — Written by Kawatake Shinhichi III and considered his masterpiece. First staged in 1889. Acts VI and VIII are frequently performed.

Background : Sanno Jirozaemon is the innocent victim of a curse put on his father by a woman he had wronged. As a result Jirozaemon is hideously disfigured by smallpox and believes no woman can ever love him. He learns swordsmanship from a skilled fencing master who on his deathbed bequeathes him his long sword made by the famous swordsmith Muramasa. He warns him that it will bring him good fortune only so long as he does not draw it. Once the sword is out it cannot be sheathed until it has tasted blood.

Act V

The Naka-no-cho of the Yoshiwara. Jirozaemon's business has prospered and he is now a wealthy man. He comes to Edo with his servant **Jiroku,** and they visit the Yoshiwara to see the sights. The courtesan **Yatsuhashi** passes with her attendants. Jirozaemon, who has never loved a woman, is struck by her beauty and forgets his good resolution not to waste his money. Yatsuhashi pauses on the *hanamichi* to execute a long and derisive laugh at his boorishness.

Act VI

Sc. 1. *The Tachibanaya Tea-house.* Jirozaemon has become Yatsuhashi's regular client, meeting her at the Tachibanaya " at least once in three days." He is at last in love and believes that in spite of his disfigurement Yatsuhashi returns his love. He is about to ransom her and meanwhile endears himself to the tea-house staff by lavish presents.

Tsurigane Gompachi, Yatsuhashi's " father," (i. e., owner,) comes to the tea-house to borrow money from the proprietor on the expectation that this " daughter " will be ransomed shortly by her new patron. The proprietor refuses because Gompachi already owes him a large sum. Gompachi leaves resentfully. Jirozaemon enters with two silk merchant friends, **Tambei** and **Josuke.** He offers to find them each a charming courtesan. Yatsuhashi arrives and welcomes Jirozaemon. His friends are impressed by her beauty and her affection for her pock-marked client.

Sc. 2. *The house of the ronin Shigeyama Einojo.* **Einojo** is Yatsuhashi's favoured lover, but he is poor and cannot hope to ransom her. When the scene opens he is at the public baths. Yatsuhashi's maid brings the gift of a splendid kimono from her mistress. Einojo returns with Gompachi, whom he has met on the way. Gompachi has been turning over in his mind how best he can do a bad turn to the proprietor of the Tachibanaya and has decided to make trouble between him and Jirozaemon. He tells Einojo that Yatsuhashi will shortly be ransomed by her new patron and commiserates with him on her heartlessness. Einojo refuses to believe him, but Gompachi assures him that the whole Yoshiwara, " even the palanquin-bearers," are talking about it. Einojo is upset. Yatsuhashi has sworn to be faithful to him, and they have exchanged many written vows. He received a new one from her only the day before. (Written love-tokens exchanged between a courtesan and her love were a regular practice and reaffirmed at least spiritual fidelity.) If she is really planning to marry Jirozaemon, he will break with her at once. Gompachi persuades him to come to the Yoshiwara and find out for himself. Einojo refuses to wear Yatsuhashi's gift.

Sc. 3. *The Tachibanaya.* Jirozaemon has provided two courtesans, **Kokonoe** and **Nanakoshi,** for his friends. They await Yatsuhashi's arrival. Einojo and Gompachi come to the tea-house also asking for her. Jirozaemon is told that Gompachi's companion is his servant. The young man's appearance arouses his suspicions. Jirozaemon tries to follow them, but is prevented by the mistress of the house.

Sc. 4. *A small room in the Tachibanaya.* Yatsuhashi comes joyfully to Einojo, but he treats her coldly. He charges her with infidelity and reviles her for allowing herself to be ransomed by Jirozaemon. Yatsuhashi denies it. (She loves Einojo, but is also fond of, and sorry for, poor ugly Jirozaemon. He, unaccustomed to the ways of the world of pleasure, believes her feelings to be stronger than they are.) Einojo angrily accuses her of lying. He reminds her that they have loved each other since they were children, long before she came to the Yoshiwara, and that he has always wished to make her his wife. Yatsuhashi tearfully reiterates that she knows nothing about any ransom. Gompachi, who has been listening outside the door, comes in and assures her that everything is arranged between Jirozaemon and the tea-house proprietor. Einojo tells her he will only believe she really knows nothing of the transaction, if she will promise never to see Jirozaemon again. Otherwise it is all over between them. Yatsuhashi is caught in a dilemma. While eager to prove how much she loves Einojo, she knows she will never be allowed to deny the wealthy Jirozaemon.

Sc. 5. *A large banqueting room in the Tachibanaya.* Jirozaemon, Tambei, Josuke and their courtesans are having a
rowdy party. Jiroku brags about the beauty of his master's
courtesan. Yatsuhashi appears, excusing her lateness by saying she feels ill. Jirozaemon offers to send for a doctor, but
she explains she is " sick with annoyance," and the sight of
Jirozaemon makes her worse. She orders him not to speak
to her and never to see her again. She absolutely refuses to
be ransomed by such a revolting looking creature. (Yatsuhashi has decided that the only way to keep her promise to
Einojo is to insult Jirozaemon in the hope that he will give
her up of his own accord.) Jirozaemon pleads with her,
offering everything he can think of, even a house in Edo.
The tea-house proprietor protests; the arrangements for the
ransom are completed. Everyone is surprised, for Yatsuhashi
has never before given any hint of disliking her patron.
Yatsuhashi remains firm in her refusal. The other courtesans
try to reason with her, but she will only repeat; " I hate
him." Tambei and Josuke make fun of Jirozaemon, but
Jiroku defends him and tells Yatsuhashi she should give
back all the money Jirozaemon has spent on her.

(During the rest of the scene special music on a *kokyu*, a
kind of fiddle, is played.)

Jirozaemon persists that he intends to ransom Yatsuhashi
whether she is willing or not. If she dislikes him so much,
she should have told him so from the beginning; now it is
too late. Gompachi looks into the room to see how his plan
is progressing. Jirozaemon remembers seeing him earlier in
the evening with a companion. He is suddenly certain that
the young man must be Yatsuhashi's lover. Yatsuhashi
admits it. The news that all the time she was in love with
someone else overwhelms Jirozaemon. He gives up all claim
to her. Yatsuhashi, shamed by his magnanimity after her
bad behaviour, leaves the room.

Jirozaemon's friends try to console him with drink. Jiroku
wishes to kill the girl. The tea-house proprietor offers to try
to arrange matters, but Jirozaemon refuses to have anything
more to do with Yatsuhashi; he intends to return to the
country at once.

Act VII

Jirozaemon arrives at his brother's house where he tells
his family that he is taking service with a great lord, who

will make him a samurai because of his skill with the sword. He proposes to transfer all his property to his brother and marries Jiroku to his niece. He gives all his ready money to the girl as a dowry. He asks his brother to arrange for prayers on his behalf " for I do not know how soon I may be called upon to die." Jiroku brings him his sword, which has been newly sharpened. He leaves, with the sword in his hand.

Act VIII

Sc. 1. *The Tachibanaya, four months later.* Jirozaemon enters, carrying his sword, and is made welcome. He is told that Yatsuhashi regrets her bad behaviour and is anxious to see him. He sends a message to her.

Sc. 2. *A room in the courtesans' house.* Kokonoe, Yatsu-hashi's friend, tells her that it is rumoured that Jirozaemon is in Edo. She advises her to make her peace with him. Yatsuhashi agrees that she ought to ask his pardon ; her conscience troubles her about the unkind things she said to him. But she fears she will not have the opportunity. At this moment the message is brought from Jirozaemon at the Tachibanaya. Kokonoe offers to go with her.

Sc. 3. *An upper room in the Tachibanaya.* Jirozaemon distributes presents to the tea-house servants. Yatsuhashi arrives and asks his forgiveness. Jirozaemon tells her that the past is forgotten ; they will look upon this as their first meeting. Yatsuhashi begs him to stay the night to show he has really forgiven her, but he refuses, pleading "urgent business." He asks to speak to her privately. When they are alone, Jirozaemon offers her *sake*, to drink " for the last time in this life." Yatsuhashi drops the cup, startled, sees the expression on his face and tries to escape. He catches her, telling her that she has guessed right ; he has not for-given and will never forgive her. He has come for revenge, not reconciliation. Yatsuhashi again tries to escape, but he holds her by her hair. He draws his sword and stabs her repeatedly, stifling her cries with his hand and saying, "You shamed me before all the world ! " A maid comes in with a candle, sees what has happened and is about to give the alarm when Jirozaemon kills her also. He looks down at his gleaming sword and smiles.

Sc. 4. *The roof-tops.* Jirozaemon climbs onto the roof, carrying his sword. A servant comes after him, but cannot

catch him. Voices are heard shouting : " Murderer ! " Jirozaemon climbs from roof to roof. Firemen in the street below
hose the roof to make it slippery. They climb after him
and he fights six at once. He loses his footing on the wet
tiles and falls.

Sc. 5. *The street below.* The firemen are searching for
Jirozaemon. Einojo and Gompachi are passing and learn of
Yatsuhashi's murder. Einojo, beside himself, wishes to rush
to the Tachibanaya to see her body when Jirozaemon
appears crying : " I'll show you Yatsuhashi ! I'll give her
a companion in death ! " He and Einojo fight.

Sc. 6. *The gate of the Yoshiwara.* The Chief of Police
is receiving a report on the fight, in which Einojo has been
killed. He orders Jirozaemon to be captured at all costs.
A party of firemen bring him in, still struggling. He is only
mastered when someone strikes him with a ladder and he
drops his sword. The Chief of Police has him bound.
Jirozaemon, calm again, quietly asserts that now he is satisfied. (Note : the last three scenes may be rearranged
according to the needs of the production.)

KAJIWARA HEIZA HOMARE NO ISHIKIRI (*The
Stonecutting Feat of Kajiwara*). *Jidaimono* of the Heike-Genji
Cycle (see page 418). — Written by Bunkodo and Hasegawa
Senshi for the puppet theatre. First staged in 1730 at the
Takemoto-za, Osaka. Later adapted for the Kabuki.

Kajiwara Kagetoki is an historical figure and appears in
a number of the plays about Yoritomo and Yoshitsune. He
was a notable Taira warrior who did, in fact, desert from his
own side and join Minamoto Yoritomo. It is this change
of allegiance, or " double-heartedness " as it is termed in
Kabuki, which is the fundamental theme of the play.

The incident which finally made Kajiwara decide to join
the Minamoto is pure drama. Yoritomo had been forced
by circumstances to appear in open rebellion some months
before he actually planned to do so. As a result, he had
very few adherents and crossed the Hakone Pass to advance
on Sagami in September, 1180, with only three hundred men.
He was confronted at Ishibashiyama (Stone-Bridge Hill) by
Oba Kagechika (who appears in the play) with a force of
over three thousand and, after a desperate fight, was defeated.

Yoritomo escaped into the hills and one of those sent out to hunt for him was Kajiwara Kagetoki. At one moment, when his pursuers were close at his heels, Yoritomo hid inside a hollow tree. Kajiwara looked into the tree, saw whom it contained and, telling his men there was no one there, directed the search away from Yoritomo's hiding place. A couple of months later Yoritomo, now at the head of twenty thousand men, was able to march upon Kamakura, where Oba Kagechika had his headquarters. It was at this time that Kajiwara joined him. Oba Kagechika was driven from Kamakura and for the first time Yoritomo established himself in what afterwards became his capital. Kajiwara became one of his most trusted advisers and served him with devotion to the end of his life.

Argument : *Before the Hachiman Shrine at Kamakura.* (The time of year has been altered, for theatrical reasons, from late summer to spring.) **Oba Kagechika** and his staff are celebrating their recent victory at Ishibashiyama and are viewing the cherry blossoms. With Oba Kagechika is his younger brother **Kagehisa.** They are joined by **Kajiwara Kagetoki** and his suite, who bring *sake* to contribute to the festivity. The two drink ceremonially, but it is noticeable that relations between them are strained, and their profound courtesy towards one another has a brittle quality. Kajiwara does not enter into the cheerful mood of his fellow general, but remains preoccupied.

An old man and a young woman come down the *hana-michi.* They are **Rokurodayu,** a worker in inlay, and his daughter **Kozue.** Kozue is married to a young man who is an adherent of the Minamoto. Now that Yoritomo is in such dire straits after his recent defeat, this young man wishes to do what he can to help the cause. He has in his possession an ancient sword which he decides he must sell to raise money for Yoritomo's army. He asks his father-in-law to arrange the sale, since he is a quiet old man who will not by suspected by the Taira. Rokurodayu has, therefore, some days previously, offered this sword to Oba Kagechika, asking for it the sum of three hundred *ryo* in gold. Kagechika realizes the sword is an excellent one, but the price is high and he wishes to think the matter over. He has told the old man to bring the sword on this day to the Hachiman Shrine, when he will give his answer.

Oba Kagechika now tells Kajiwara about the sword and says that, before making up his mind, he would be glad to have the latter's opinion of the weapon, since he is a noted expert. The sword is presented to Kajiwara who examines it with due ceremony and at last exclaims that it is indeed an excellent one. Oba Kagechika's brother, Kagehisa, is sceptical. He says that it is impossible to judge the temper of a blade merely by looking at it. The only true test is to try it out on human bodies. A really good sword should be able to cut through two men. He suggests that two criminals be brought from the jail and the sword tested on them. Oba Kagechika agrees and orders the criminals to be brought. But the jailor reports that only one is available. Kagechika is still undecided about buying the sword for he thinks the price is high. He now begins to hedge, saying that if the test cannot be arranged, he cannot consider making the purchase.

Rokurodayu is becoming more and more uneasy. He sends off his daughter on an errand and, when he has watched her out of sight, comes forward and offers to take the place of the second convict on condition that the three hundred *ryo* be handed over to his daughter after his death. Kagehisa finds the idea highly amusing. Oba Kagechika asks sharply whether the old man realizes what he is proposing. Rokurodayu answers that he is in great and urgent need of the money and will do anything to obtain it.

Meanwhile, Kajiwara has been lost in thought and has not followed the conversation. When he is told of the old man's offer, he is shocked and refuses to take part in any such test. Rokurodayu pleads with him, repeating that he is in desperate need of the money. A messenger, **Kikubei,** arrives bringing Oba Kagechika a despatch. Yoritomo, with a considerable force, is even now approaching Kamakura. The news appears to bring Kajiwara to a decision. It also throws the rest of the party into confusion. The officers of Oba's staff leave hastily to return to their posts. Oba Kagechika himself and his brother remain to conclude the business of the sword.

Kajiwara now speaks earnestly to Rokurodayu and assures himself that the old man's offer is genuine. He then declares himself ready to take part in the trial. The criminal is brought in and, in a deliberately comic scene, is introduced to Rokurodayu. He is then dragged away to prepare for death. Kozue returns and is aghast to find her father kneeling bound on the execution mat. She tries wildly to go to him, but is prevented and finally sinks in a faint on the ground. Throughout this scene Kajiwara sits like a statue, with lowered eyelids. Rokurodayu lays himself on the mat and the condemned criminal is brought in and laid on top of him. Kajiwara purifies himself at the stone water-trough which stands at the gate of the Shrine. He draws the sword, but when the blow is struck, only the criminal's body is found to be severed in two. Rokurodayu is untouched, although the blade has cut the cords that bind him. The old man is revived by his daughter, while Kajiwara, in silence, cleanses the sword and returns it to its sheath. Oba Kagehisa says scornfully that this cannot be a very remarkable weapon since it can only cut one man in two. He certainly has no intention of paying three hundred *ryo* for such a sword. He and his brother leave, mocking at the old man.

Rokurodayu, in despair at losing the money, wishes to commit suicide. He is prevented by Kajiwara who dismisses his attendants and tells the old man and his daughter that the secret of the sword is known to him. As soon as he examined it, he recognized it as an heirloom of the Minamoto family. He has purposely deceived Oba Kagechika as to its excellence so that it might not pass into the hands of the Taira. Rokurodayu and Kozue cannot understand him, since he is himself a Taira general. Kajiwara then tells them that he has determined to abandon his own side and join Yoritomo. In an elaborate mimed narrative (*monogatari*) he describes how he came upon Yoritomo when the latter was in hiding and, having him in his power, raised his arm to strike off his head. But his arm became numb, and he could not lift his sword. He realized then that some divine power protected Yoritomo and that he must throw in his lot with him. He now intends to join Yoritomo with all speed and he will take the sword to restore it to its rightful owner. It shall bring a better gift to the Minamoto than three hundred *ryo*, since it brings Kajiwara himself.

Rokurodayu still has doubts about the sword. He cannot believe it was skill alone that saved his life, nor that the weapon confided to him is really so great a treasure. To convince him Kajiwara looks round for something upon which to test the blade. His eyes light upon the stone water-trough. He offers to cut it in two to prove the quality of the sword and does so with a single blow. When he examines the blade afterwards, he finds it unblemished. Rokurodayu, now convinced, gladly entrusts the sword to Kajiwara, who leaves to join Yoritomo's advancing army.

KAMAKURA SANDAIKI (*The Kamakura Trilogy*). *Jidaimono*, associated with the Taiko Cycle (see page 467). — Written for the puppets by Chikamatsu Hanji and his assistants. First staged in 1761. The original play was in ten acts and was a sequel to *Omi Genji Senjin Yakata* by the same author (see page 240). It recounted further incidents in the career of Sasaki Takatsuna, the brother of Sasaki Moritsuna.

Only Act III survives, but this is frequently performed both by the puppets and on the Kabuki stage. It might well be called *The Female Moritsuna* after a Kabuki fashion which has produced *The Female Chushingura*, *The Female Shibaraku*, *The Female Kirare Yosa*, etc. The choice between loyalties imposed upon the heroine, Toki-hime, is even more painful than that to which Moritsuna is subjected. Like him, she believes death to be the only solution. It is noteworthy that her way of solving her problem is similar to that chosen in real life by a twelfth century heroine, Kesa Gozen, who deceived her lover into killing her when he intended to kill her husband.

The rôle of Toki-hime is considered one of the three most difficult *onnagata* rôles of the type known as *o hime sama* (see page 394). The names chosen to disguise the two factions, the Tokugawa and the Toyotomi, whose struggle for the possession of Osaka Castle is the background of this play, are the same as those used in *Omi Genji Senjin Yakata*.

Act III

Kinugawa Village (*Kinugawa Mura no Ba*). A cottage belonging to **Sakamoto Miuranosuke Yoshimura**. This young man is a near relative of Minamoto Yoriiye and is married to Hojo Tokimasa's daughter. Now that the Minamoto and the Hojo factions are at war, he finds himself compelled to take up arms against his father-in-law. He is away at the moment, fighting with his lord at the defence of Sakamoto Castle, the last stronghold of the Minamoto. His wife and mother have come to live in this humble dwelling to be within the castle's protecting shadow.

Nagato, Miuranosuke's mother, is ill in bed. She is cared for by neighbouring peasant women, while her daughter-in-law **Toki-hime** is away shopping in the village. Two ladies-in-waiting from the household of Toki-hime's father, Hojo Tokimasa, arrive with their attendants. They inform the old lady that they have been sent to fetch Toki-hime home to her father's palace, since Tokimasa does not choose that his daughter be the wife of an enemy. Nagato, however, refuses to give her consent, since neither she nor her son wishes to divorce the girl. The ladies insist that it is their lord's command and go to the gate to await Toki-hime's return.

Toki-hime enters by the *hanamichi*, carrying a tray of *sake* and bean-curd. When the ladies greet her, she tells them that she already knows their errand, for she has had a letter from her father. But, as she has been brought up to believe that an honest woman considers her husband's house her only home, she cannot go with them, particularly as her mother-in-law is ill and needs her care. She brushes past them and goes to the old lady, bringing her her medicine and closing the window lest she be in a draught. The ladies, touched by Toki-hime's devotion, decide to remain and help her. Toki-hime bids them think well what they are doing. They will find things very different from the palace; they will have to live like ordinary people and learn to speak the peasant dialect. She sets about preparing supper for Nagato, although she does the work unskilfully. She goes to the well to wash the rice, but one of the peasant women has to help her draw the water. She lights the fire and returns to nurse Nagato. The ladies, deeply shocked, decide that they ought to kill the old lady and take Toki-hime home by force.

They go into the garden to make plans and there meet a samurai in their master's employ. This man, Adachi Tozo, is in fact **Sasaki Takatsuna,** the brilliant and daring general commanding the Minamoto forces defending Sakamoto Castle. (In a previous act it is explained how he tricked Hojo Tokimasa into believing that he was not Takatsuna, but a farmer who resembled him closely. It is the head of this farmer which plays a prominent part in *Moritsuna Jinya*, see page 244. To avoid confusion in the future, Tokimasa causes Takatsuna to be tattooed on the brow so that the Hojo faction may know he is a friend. Tokimasa further makes the supposed farmer a samurai and sends him off to bring Toki-hime out of the Minamoto camp, promising him her hand as a reward.) Takatsuna shows the ladies a sword given him by Tokimasa and bids them leave the affair in his hands. They leave while Takatsuna hides among the trees.

(It is at this point that the scene usually opens.)

Miuranosuke, who has heard of his mother's illness, has seized this opportunity during a lull in the siege to come to see her. He is already badly wounded, but, as he staggers down the *hanamichi*, he is able to drive off a posse of enemy soldiers who pursue him. He sinks down at the gate where Toki-hime finds him unconscious. She revives him and he is amazed to find his own wife tending him, for he did not know that she was with his mother at the cottage. They describe in mime their emotions at this unexpected meeting. Miuranosuke asks after his mother and the two creep into the house to peep at her, believing her asleep. But Nagato is awake. She is a fierce, strong-willed old lady and now refuses to look at, or take any notice of, Miuranosuke, on the grounds that it cannot really be he. It must be a fox-spirit wearing his appearance because she is sure that her son would never leave his lord's side in this crisis. If it really is he, she will disown him, for her one remaining desire is to carry to her husband in the next world a good report of his son. Miuranosuke pleads with her in vain. He turns away sadly to leave, while Toki-hime implores him to stay with her just one night. ("Surely that is not against the way of the samurai!") She is convinced that he will not survive this engagement. He shakes her off and goes as far as the *hanamichi*, then looks back at her and hears his mother coughing. He hesitates, his private feelings get the upper hand and he returns to the house. Toki-hime helps him to disarm and he takes from her the tray on which his mother's medicine is prepared. *The stage revolves.*

A thicket near the house. **Tonda Rokuro,** another of Tokimasa's retainers, enters. He has been sent to keep an eye on the newly created samurai, Adachi Tozo. He is now approached by **O Kuru,** one of the peasant women who appear at the beginning of the act. This O Kuru is the widow of the farmer whose close resemblance to Sasaki Takatsuna

caused his death. She guesses who has assumed her husband's identity and, in order to be revenged upon Takatsuna,
offers to help Rokuro and show him how to enter the cottage
unobserved. (This incident is usually omitted.) *The stage
revolves to show the scene as before.*

Toki-hime is alone. She stands holding a short sword
sent her by her father, who, to test her filial piety, has ordered her to kill Nagato. She loves Nagato and has nursed
her devotedly ; now she does not know whether to obey her
father or her heart. She is still in this dilemma when Takatsuna appears. He shows her her father's sword to prove his
identit y and bids her come with him at once. Toki-hime
refuses ; she will not go to an enemy's house, even if it be
her own father's. Takatsuna tells her roughly that her
husband is as good as dead and his cause is hopeless. She
had better cut her losses and return to her father so as presently to marry himself. He attempts to embrace her, but
Toki-hime escapes from him, threatening him with her
sword. This incident makes her reach a decision ; she cannot
obey her father. She will neither kill Nagato nor accept any
other husband but Miuranosuke. Sooner than submit she
will kill herself and, drawing her sword, she is about to do
so. Takatsuna has gone, but at this moment Miuranosuke
appears in time to prevent her death. He praises her fidelity,
but begs her not to die until she has avenged his own death.
Toki-hime asks upon whom she must take revenge and

Toki-hime

Miuranosuke answers that it is her father. The Genji general, Sasaki Takatsuna, has been foiled in his attempt to kill the arch-enemy, but with her it is a different matter. She can return to Kamakura and there kill both her father and herself. If she loves her husband and obeys him as a wife should, she must do this. Toki-hime, after a terrible struggle, consents.

Suddenly Rokuro and O Kuru emerge from the house, declaring they have heard everything and will report the matter at once to Tokimasa. As Rokuro is about to make good his threat, he is killed by a spear which appears mysteriously from the mouth of the garden well. From this hiding palace Takatsuna climbs, at a call from Miuranosuke. He is now dressed as befits his rank. He tells Toki-hime the story of his adventures at her father's camp, explaining the tattoo mark on his forehead and adding that now, with her help, he hopes at last to turn the tide of battle. The matter is in her hands, for he and Miuranosuke must return to the fighting. Toki-hime implores Miuranosuke not to die. He opens his body-armour, and shows her that the wounds he has already received are mortal. He puts her away from him and prepares to go. Takatsuna salutes him; Miuranosuke can die serene, for his head shall never become an enemy's trophy. He, Takatsuna, will be in the forefront and will himself strike off his head and return it to his kindred. The two men pledge themselves to meet in the next world. Inspired by their example, Toki-hime is confirmed in her belief that, even as it is a samurai's duty to follow and obey his lord, so it a wife's duty to follow and obey her husband. She takes up Takatsuna's discarded spear and makes an experimental pass with it at a stone water-basin near the house. The blade is caught through the window by Nagato who stabs herself with it so that she may accompany her son on the road of death and Toki-hime may be able to tell her father she has obeyed him. She praises the two young people for their loyalty and promises to await them in the other world.

Takatsuna goes to a point of vantage and looks out over the landscape. It is dawn, and he can see the lanterns and banners of Hojo Tokimasa's army approaching Sakamoto Castle. Crying to Miuranosuke that they must hasten, if they intend to take part in the last engagement, he, Miuranosuke and Toki-hime pose as the sound of fighting is heard, and the curtain is drawn.

(The end of the story is as follows : It was arranged between Toki-hime and Takatsuna that she should not attempt to kill her father with her own hand, but should inform Takatsuna, who was, as has been said, in the Hojo ranks, when a suitable opportunity arose. Shortly after her arrival at her father's camp, word was brought to Toki-hime that Miuranosuke had died in battle and the Genji were utterly defeated. Takatsuna's strategy had served no purpose, but Toki-hime considered she must carry out her promise. She sent word to Takatsuna that her father, wearing armour of a certain pattern, would pass a given spot that night unattended. Takatsuna went to the rendezvous and struck off the head of the warrior who appeared. When he carried it into the moonlight to examine his trophy, he found that he had killed, not Hojo Tokimasa, but Toki-hime herself. Overwhelmed by her sacrifice and realizing his cause was doomed, Takatsuna took his own life.)

KAMI NO MEGUMI UAGO NO TORIKUMI, commonly called *Megumi no Kenka. Sewamono.* — Written by Takeshiba Kisui, Kawatake Mokuami's best pupil, with his master's assistance. The play was a vehicle for Onoe Kikugoro V and was first performed in 1890. The fight between the firemen and the *sumo* wrestlers has always been popular with Edo audiences. The play has a New Year setting and is often given in January.

Act I

The upper floor of the Shimazakiro Tea-house in Shinagawa, Edo. Some samurai are entertaining their favourite *sumo* wrestler, **Yotsuguruma** (Four-Wheeler) **Daihachi.** The party becomes noisy and a guest in the next room protests. He is a member of one of the forty-eight firemen's companies of Edo. A quarrel breaks out and shows signs of turning into a fight, when **Tatsugoro,** the chief of his company (the " Megumi," i. e., the " Me " Company, each company taking a character of the Japanese syllabary for identification purposes) appears and does his best to settle the matter amicably. Tatsugoro can control his own subordinates, but he cannot pacify Yotsuguruma, who insults him grossly. Tatsugoro, determined to avoid a fight, leaves the tea-house.

Act II

A street in Shinagawa, the same evening. Tatsugoro, smarting under the insults put upon him, lies in wait for Yotsuguruma as he returns from his party. Tatsugoro kicks out the lantern and attacks Yotsuguruma in the darkness, but the *sumo* wrestler is too strong for him. **Kisaburo,** Tatsugoro's friend and the head of the fire service of Edo, is involved in the scrimmage and picks up a tobacco pouch dropped by Tatsugoro. (This scene takes the form of a special type of mime called *sewa-dammari.*)

Act III

Outside the Kuzuiza Theatre. Some members of the Megumi are watching the New Year Kabuki performance. Tatsugoro's wife, **O Naka,** and their little boy wait for Tatsugoro outside the theatre, but are advised to go home as there is trouble brewing. A fight starts in the theatre between some of the *sumo* wrestlers and the firemen, who are kicked out by Yotsuguruma and his friends. The fight is about to be continued outside when Tatsugoro arrives and again tries to settle matters peaceably.

Act IV

Kisaburo's house. Tatsugoro comes to ask Kisaburo's advice about the feud with the *sumo* wrestlers. He deplores the whole business and explains that he has done all he can to prevent a serious clash. O Naka comes to consult Kisaburo, hears her husband's voice and listens outside the door. She gathers that Tatsugoro intends to continue his policy of passive resistance and that Kisaburo approves. She does not understand the inner meaning of his remark that, " if anything should happen to him," he hopes Kisaburo will care for his wife and child. She hurries away. Kisaburo lets Tatsugoro know he understands and thinks him no coward by returning his tobacco pouch. They drink together.

Act V

Tatsugoro's house. O Naka is shamed and offended by Tatsugoro's pacifism. When he comes home, pretending to be drunk to discourage her from asking questions, she demands a divorce, hoping to shame him into defending his honour and that of his company. Tatsugoro appears to acquiesce. He asks for a cup of water (a symbol of farewell) and offers it to her. At first she will not accept it, but is persuaded to do so by their little son. Suddenly she realizes that her husband intends this to be their last pledge on earth. He has always intended, as a last resort, to avenge the wrestlers' insults, and his plans are now ripe. Afterwards he means to commit suicide as a protest against the overbearing behaviour of his enemies. The three drink together and say good-bye. Tatsugoro's apprentices come to fetch him, and they go off, carrying the Megumi's standard.

Act VI

Near the sumo ring at Shimmei. The firemen and the wrestlers meet and a tremendous fight takes place. It is stopped by Kisaburo. He reconciles the two parties and, producing two workmen's jackets, one bearing the crest of the firemen, the other of the *sumo* wrestlers, claims to be able to speak for both.

KANADEHON CHUSHINGURA (*The Treasury of Loyal Retainers*). — Written by Takeda Izumo (1691—1756), Miyoshi Shoraku (1696—1775?), and Namiki Senryo (1695—1751). First staged as a puppet play in 1748, but very shortly after adapted for the Kabuki stage. It superseded a number of earlier plays on the same theme, the earliest of which appeared in 1706, only three years after the occurrence of the incident on which the play is based. *Chushingura* has remained throughout two centuries one of the most popular plays, if not *the* most popular play of Kabuki. It is regularly performed every year in Tokyo and Osaka, and either the whole play or scenes from it are always put on in December, the month in which the vendetta occurred. A number of subsidiary plays about incidents connected with the main theme are popular, and a version of the story which keeps closely to the historical facts and uses the real names of the people concerned is sometimes given under the title *Genroku Chushingura*. An English rendering of *Chushingura* was made by John Masefield and called *The Faithful*.

The events upon which the play is based took place in Edo in the years 1701 to 1703. (See Mitford's *Tales of Old Japan*.) The synopsis of the play which follows is based mainly on the original text. In certain scenes, however, where various alterations have permanently superseded the original, both versions are given. The companies performing the play make such cuts as seem good to them and often interpolate new dialogue, so that the playgoer is unlikely to see *Chushingura* in the exact form here given.

Although many liberties are taken with the text after the immemorial fashion of the Japanese theatre, the sets and costumes always remain the same, except in so far as they may be more or less rich and elaborate according to the means of the company. Enya Hangan's black *haori*, Kampei's light blue kimono, and Honzo's travelling dress are now as much part of the play as the plot itself.

Owing to the strict censorship enforced by the Tokugawa Government, the play is ostensibly set in the 14th century, and the names of the characters are disguised, more or less thinly. Thus Asano Takumi-no-kami Naganori becomes Enya Hangan Takasada and Kira Kozukenosuke Yoshitaka, Kono Musashi-no-Kami Moronao. The characters of lesser rank are easily recognizable: Oboshi Yuranosuke for Oishi Kuranosuke, Hayano Kampei for Kayano Sampei, Amakawaya Gihei for Amanoya Rihei.

Act I

The Hachiman Shrine (Tsurugaoka Hachiman-gu no Ba). In the year 1338 the Shogun Ashikaga Takauji sends his younger brother, **Tadayoshi,** to preside at the opening of a new shrine to the war-god Hachiman at Tsurugaoka, near Kamakura. The opening scene shows the reception of the Shogun's deputy by the Governor of Kamakura, **Kono Moronao,** and the two daimyo appointed to assist him, **Yasuchika Wakasanosuke** and **Enya Hangan Takasada.** Tadayoshi announces that the Shogun wishes the helmet of Nitta Yoshisada, a noble enemy recently defeated and killed in battle, to be laid up in the new shrine, which commemorates this victory. The helmet was presented to Yoshisada by the late Emperor. Kono Moronao and Wakasanosuke differ on the propriety of treating an enemy's helmet with such respect. These two are at odds with each other, and Moronao is taking advantage of his position to browbeat his young colleague. The matter is smoothed over by Enya Hangan.

Moronao asks with a sneer how it is possible to identify the helmet, since it may be any of a large number gathered on the battlefield. Tadayoshi replies that he has had all the helmets packed in the chest they see before them. He understands that Enya Hangan's wife was, before her marriage, a maid of honour at the court of His Majesty and was one of those in charge of the armoury. He has therefore summoned her to see whether she can identify the Imperial helmet.

Lady **Kaoyo** now enters. As soon as she appears, Moronao shows that he is attracted by her. Kaoyo is asked whether she can identify the helmet. She replies that she has handled it frequently and, besides, Nitta Yoshisada, before he wore it, caused it to be perfumed with a valuable incense.

The chest is opened, and one by one the helmets are displayed. Kaoyo shakes her head at all of them, until at last a great dragon-helmet is brought out. A rich perfume fills the air. Kaoyo declares this to be the Imperial helmet, and Tadayoshi orders Enya Hangan to carry it to the shrine treasury. He thanks and dismisses Kaoyo and leaves, followed by his suite.

Only Moronao remains behind. Kaoyo is just going when he catches her sleeve and, on the pretext of asking her advice on a poem he has written, slips a love letter into it. Kaoyo, greatly embarrassed, but not wishing to make an enemy of so powerful a man, removes the letter and drops it on the ground. Moronao picks it up and tells her plainly that her husband's career depends on herself. Moronao can make or mar Enya Hangan in the Shogun's eyes. If she will yield to his love, she shall command him in all things. Moronao attempts to take her in his arms and, as she struggles to prevent him, they are interrupted by Wakasanosuke. Wakasanosuke takes in the situation, and at a word from him Kaoyo makes good her escape. Moronao, furious at being caught in such a situation by one he already dislikes, abuses Wakasanosuke for presumption. Wakasanosuke, being young and quick-tempered, can hardly restrain himself. He is already gripping his sword hilt when the return of Tadayoshi and his suite forces him to stay his hand.

Act II

Sc. 1. *The Palace of Momoi Wakasanosuke (Momoi-Yakata no Ba).* The act opens with a recapitulation of the previous act in the form of a conversation between some gardeners. (This is omitted when the play is given as a whole.) They are sent about their business by Wakasanosuke's chief councillor, **Kakogawa Honzo**. To him is brought word that **Rikiya**, the son of **Oishi Yuranosuke**, chief councillor to Enya Hangan, has arrived with a message. Honzo bids his wife **Tonase** receive the young man.

Rikiya is betrothed to Honzo's daughter, **Konami**. Her mother knows that Konami is longing to see her lover and arranges for the girl to receive him in her place. Rikiya is seventeen, still wearing his boy's forelock. He is conscious of his responsibility, but disconcerted to find he must deliver his message to his betrothed. They blush as their eyes meet, but Rikiya collects himself and repeats what he has been instructed to say, namely the hour Wakasanosuke and Enya Hangan must be at the Palace next day. Then he and Konami are again struck dumb with shyness. The situation is saved by Tonase who emerges from behind a screen and formally thanks Rikiya for the message. Rikiya leaves.

(In the original text it is Wakasanosuke who comes in just as Rikiya finishes his errand and the scene between him and Honzo follows immediately. Very often, however, this scene is played separately.)

Sc. 2. *Kenchoji Shoin no Ba.* Wakasanosuke is in retirement at a temple where he is living during his court duty. Honzo comes to deliver Enya Hangan's message. Wakasanosuke, smarting under the insults put on him by Moronao, tells his chief councillor, with tears of rage, that he has made up his mind that, come what may, if Moronao insults him again he will kill him, even in the Palace itself. Wakasanosuke seems to expect his councillor to do all he can to dissuade him. Indeed, he tries to make him swear not to interfere even before he tells him what he means to do. To his surprise Honzo agrees that he cannot with honour bear such treatment and applauds his decision. Wakasanosuke thinks Honzo is not taking him seriously. Honzo assures him that he is mistaken. To convince his master he draws his short sword (or sometimes his fan) and hacks a branch from a small pine tree. This he wordlessly offers on his fan as a symbol that thus Wakasanosuke should deal with his enemies. (In the original version,

Honzo withdraws, calls for his horse, and mysteriously leaves the house in haste.)

Act III

Sc. 1. *In front of the gate of the Ashikaga Palace (Ashikaga Yakata Monzen no Ba).* The palace of Ashikaga Tadayoshi, the Shogun's brother. Next morning before daybreak. Kono Moronao arrives in a palanquin at the West Gate accompanied by his retinue. The act opens with a recapitulation in the form of a conversation between Moronao and his confidential retainer **Bannai** (a comic character) but, as in Act II, this may be omitted. One of the palace guards announces that Honzo is asking to speak to Moronao. Moronao suspects that Wakasanosuke has sent his retainer for no good purpose and tells Bannai to be ready for trouble. Bannai instructs the footmen how to attack Honzo on a pre-arranged signal. Honzo enters and causes to be set down several trays of gifts before Moronao. Then bowing respectfully, he makes Moronao a most obsequious speech. On behalf of his master's wife, himself, and Wakasanosuke's other retainers, he has come to thank Moronao for all the trouble he has taken in instructing their young lord in his unaccustomed duties. He has ventured also to bring some small presents and will be greatly honoured if Moronao will accept them. Honzo hands a list of the presents to the stupefied Bannai who reads it out. Honzo has collected all the ready gold and valuables of his own he can find and is offering them as coming from Wakasanosuke's wife and household. In this way, although to grovel to such a man as Moronao is bitter to him, he hopes to avert a catastrophe and save his lord from his own impetuosity. Moronao is notorious for his avarice. Once he has set eyes on the gold, he has no intention of refusing it and Bannai, on his master's behalf, makes an effusive speech to Honzo about Wakasanosuke's great ability. Moronao sees, of course, through Honzo's stratagem and begins to realize that his tongue has led him into a greater danger than he knew. As an extra precaution against Wakasanosuke's anger, he insists upon taking Honzo into the palace with him.

Enya Hangan enters accompanied by his young retainer, Hayano Kampei. Enya Hangan goes into the palace, but just as Kampei is to follow him, a girl appears outside the gate with a message. She also belongs to Enya Hangan's household. Her name is **O Karu** and Kampei is in love with her. She gives him a letter-case sent by Kaoyo which the latter wishes Enya Hangan to present to Moronao. O Karu tells Kampei that she undertook this errand in the hope of seeing him. Their conversation is interrupted by Bannai, who informs Kampei that his lord is asking for him. Kampei takes the letter-case and hurries away. Bannai meanwhile tries to make love to O Karu. After a few minutes Bannai is also called away and Kampei returns, laughing, to say he has fooled Bannai with his own trick. He and O Karu wander off together into the privacy of the garden.

Sc. 2. *The Pine-tree Room Scene (Denchu Matsu-no-Ma no Ba). Inside the palace.* Wakasanosuke appears, smouldering with fury against Moronao. He sees his enemy approaching and braces himself, but to his amazement Moronao rushes towards him and, throwing down his sword, apologizes abjectly for his behaviour of the previous day. Wakasanosuke is stupefied by this turn of events. He cannot now fight Moronao, but he also cannot bear to be fawned upon by one who has so recently insulted him. He escapes from Moronao by feigning illness. Honzo, watching, heaves a sign of relief.

Moronao has not enjoyed humbling himself before a youth half his age who so clearly lets it be seen how greatly he despises such behaviour. He now longs to humiliate someone in his turn and so restore his self-esteem. As ill luck will have it, Enya Hangan appears at this moment. Enya Hangan is a quiet man of great self-restraint. Moronao has even come to believe he is lacking in spirit. This is mainly because Enya Hangan, who knows and trusts his wife, has never seemed to pay the slightest attention to Moronao's advances to Kaoyo. Moronao is, therefore, convinced in his own mind that here is a man he can insult with impunity, particularly within the palace precincts where brawling is a capital offence. Moronao immediately starts rating Enya Hangan for being late. The letter-case is brought, and Enya Hangan gives it to Moronao, saying his wife has sent it. Moronao is annoyed that Kaoyo should use her husband as a messenger. He is still more annoyed when he finds in the case, not a love letter, but part of an old poem condemning "unlawful love." This new frustration makes him lose all sense of judgment. He abuses Enya Hangan for neglecting his duties and insinuates that the latter dare not trust his wife out of his sight even for a moment.

Enya Hangan keeps his temper, mystified by this outburst. He tries to pass the matter off by asking whether Moronao has been drinking. Moronao brushes the remark aside and returns to the rankling subject of Kaoyo. He makes a famous speech in which he compares Enya's trust in his wife with the stupid contentment of a carp in a well. The carp believes nothing exists beyond his prison and then, on being thrown into the river, has a rude awakening. These insinuations against his wife's virtue are more than Enya Hangan can bear. He asks Moronao sharply whether he is mad. Moronao enjoys the spark he has kindled, since he is certain he can quench it. He tells Enya Hangan arrogantly to remember to whom he is speaking. Enya, restraining himself with great difficulty, asks whether these insults are then deliberate. Moronao enquires what he will do, if they are. Enya lays his hand on his sword, but again restrains himself, remembering where he is. Moronao taunts him, now more than ever convinced that his victim dare not retaliate. But Enya Hangan has reached the end of his patience. In a flash his sword is out and he strikes at Moronao, wounding him on the brow. Moronao tries to escape. Enya, in a white-hot fury, pursues him, but is caught and restrained by Honzo who rushes in from the next room. Enya, now as wild as he was quiet before, struggles like a madman while various daimyo and Imperial servants help Honzo hold him.

The scene returns to the West Gate. The noise of the disturbance within the palace can be plainly heard. Kampei, who has forgotten time and duty in O Karu's company, is brought to his senses by the sound and rushes to the gate. There he is told of the quarrel between his master and Kono Moronao. His master has been arrested and has been sent back to his house under guard. Kampei is beside himself. He has failed his master in a crisis and is utterly disgraced. His first thought is that there is nothing left for him but to commit suicide. He is restrained by O Karu, who persuades him that the best thing will be for them both to go to her parents' home in the country and await an opportunity to ask their lord's pardon. Kampei agrees, saying that when Enya Hangan's chief councillor, **Oboshi Yuranosuke,** returns to Edo he will go to him, confess everything and ask him to intercede with their master. The lovers are sadly creeping away when Bannai bursts upon them with a band of servants. They attack Kampei thinking him easy prey, but he, in his fury, puts them all to flight and is about to kill Bannai when O Karu begs him not to spoil his chance of pardon by killing Moronao's servant. While Kampei hesitates, Bannai escapes. The two lovers set off on their journey.

It is not at all unusual to cut all the scenes dealing with Kampei and O Karu. Their love story, Kampei's despair and attempted suicide, and the fight with Bannai are performed instead as a *michiyuki* (travel dance) at the end of the following act. (*Totsuka Sanchu no ba.*)

Act IV

The Seppuku Scene (Enya Yakata no Ba). The house of Enya Hangan, a few days later. The act opens with the arrival of two envoys, come to acquaint Enya Hangan with the Shōgun's judgment. They are received by two senior samurai of the household, **Ono Kudayu** and **Hara Goemon.** The envoys are **Ishido Umanojo,** whose sympathies are with Enya, and **Yakushiji Jirozaemon,** a jackal of Kono Moronao. They enter without exchanging greetings and seat themselves at one side of the room.

Enya Hangan comes in by another door. He wears a long black *haori*. He has regained the quiet self-control that typified him earlier in the play. He greets the envoys, who proceed to read the Shōgun's order. Enya Hangan listens in the correct attitude of respect and betrays no emotion. The order reads: "Whereas Enya Hangan Takasada did, out of private hate and malice, attack and wound the Governor of Kamakura, Kono Moronao, and cause a disturbance in the palace, his domains are confiscated and he is ordered to commit *seppuku*."

Enya Hangan, in a steady voice, declares himself ready to submit to the Shōgun's will and offers refreshment to the envoys "after their heavy duty." He is rudely silenced by Jirozaemon who tells him he should be thinking about preparing himself for death, not empty courtesies. Jirozaemon rates him for wearing an elegant *haori* when he is no better than a common criminal. With an echo of Enya's own words to Moronao, he asks whether he is drunk or mad to dress himself like that. Enya Hangan smiles and replies quietly that, since he was expecting the sentence, he is fully prepared. He takes off his *haori* and reveals that beneath he is wearing the white, uncrested garments of death. Jirozaeman relapses into sulky silence. Umanojo tells Enya Hangan he has all his sympathy, but that the sentence must be carried out immediately. Enya Hangan thanks him and declares that, since the moment he drew his sword, he expected no other fate. Then suddenly he looks full into Umanojo's face and, behind his outward impassivity, it can be seen that the rage kindled by Moronao still burns fiercely. His voice is as quiet as ever, but it is charged with passion as he adds: "My only regret is that I was held back by Kakogawa Honzo from killing Moronao. This I shall never forget. I shall return to life again and again until my vengeance is accomplished." These words are the clue to the second half of the play.

In the adjoining room Enya Hangan's retainers are assembled and beg through the closed door to be allowed to see their master once more. He says they may not do so, unless Yuranosuke comes. Enya Hangan shows that he is anxious to see his chief councillor before he dies. In the subsequent scene the relationship, almost that of father and son, between these two men is brilliantly and rapidly revealed. The love and trust they bear each other is far beyond that of lord and vassal.

Enya Hangan turns his back upon the room and in silence the preparations for his death are made. When the thick white mat is laid, with branches of herbs at the corners, Enya Hangan turns and takes his place. He slides from his shoulders the winged shoulderpieces of the *kataginu* and tucks the long ends firmly under his knees so that the drag of the cloth will force his body to fall forward after death. To fall backwards is considered unseemly. Goemon helps his lord slip off the top part of his kimono, beneath which he wears another, also white. At a silent signal, Rikiya enters bringing the prepared dirk on a wooden stand. As he places it before Enya Hangan, Enya raises his eyes for the first time since he took his place on the mat and

looks with entreaty at the boy who sadly shakes his head —
his father has not come.

Enya Hangan continues his preparations, but slowly, so
that Jirozaemon grows restive. At last there is nothing
further to do. Enya breaks the silence in a voice greatly at
variance with his impassive exterior. He cries to Rikiya the
name of Yuranosuke. Rikiya must again answer that his
father is not here. Enya Hangan regains control of himself
and says he can wait no longer. As he drives home the
dirk, there is a stir and Yuranosuke comes hurrying down
the *hanamichi*. The chief retainer prostrates himself at the
entrance, while the rest of the retainers crowd into the room
and take their places behind their master. As soon as Enya
Hangan sees Yuranosuke, it is as if for him the worst is
already over. He says, "I have long been waiting for you,
Yuranosuke." Yuranosuke goes to his side and they speak
a few intimate words, the elder man in a steady voice bidding the younger die bravely. Looking into his chief retainer's face, Enya Hangan draws the dirk across his belly and
turns it upward. He tells Yuranosuke that with this dirk he
must avenge his death. With a last effort he withdraws the
weapon from his side, cuts his jugular vein, and falls forward.

In the silence that follows, Yuranosuke takes the dirk
from the dead hand and, wrapping it carefully, puts it in his
bosom. He then straightens his lord's body. The two
envoys formally inspect the corpse. Jirozaemon begins to
bluster at the retainers, but Umanojo silences him, bidding
Yuranosuke perform the proper funeral ceremonies and then
make ready to hand over his late master's property. He
adds a word of sympathy and leaves to make his report at

*Yuranosuke and
Enya Hangan*

the palace. Jirozaemon says he will wait in another room to make sure "these new *ronin*" steal nothing.

Enya Hangan's body is placed in a palanquin. Kaoyo enters with her women, all in mourning clothes, and she burns incense before it. She is followed by the chief retainers, who also burn incense. She then offers a lock of her hair cut off to show she has taken religious vows. The palanquin is taken up and, escorted by Rikiya and some of the retainers, is carried away, the ladies following.

The senior samurai remain behind to discuss what must now be done. It soon appears that there are two schools of thought. One, headed by Ono Kudayu, next in rank to Yuranosuke, and his son **Sadakuro,** is in favour of rifling Enya Hangan's war chest and making off. The other, headed by **Sanzaki Yagoro,** wishes to resist the order to hand over the mansion and die defending it. Yuranosuke has been lost in his own thoughts, but, when asked his opinion, supports Yagoro's plan. Old Kudayu is indignant and leaves with his son, declaring he will have nothing to do with such nonsense.

When they have gone, Yuranosuke tells those that remain that he agreed with Yagoro only in order to test Kudayu's loyalty. He persuades them that it would be useless to fight the Shogun's troops. They had better give up the property quietly, for their quarrel is not with the Shogun. Later they will meet together and make plans to avenge their lord. As he speaks, Jirozaemon returns and orders them to clear out. The retainers bid him check over their master's belongings to be sure they have taken nothing. Then, sadly looking their last on the familiar rooms, they leave. *The stage revolves.*

The scene shows the great gate of Enya Hangan's mansion, heavily barred. The retainers emerge by a small postern and stand before the gate. There they are joined by Rikiya and the samurai returning from their lord's funeral. They all clamour to fight the Shogun's troops. Yuranosuke and his companions persuade them with some difficulty that it is better to disperse quietly and mature their plans. As they are talking, they hear the bolts within the gate being shot, and Jirozaemon's voice taunts them with their masterless state. The younger samurai can hardly bear it, but Yuranosuke restrains them, asking whether they do not wish to avenge their lord. They disperse, leaving Yuranosuke alone before the gate.

Yuranosuke takes the dirk from his bosom and silently renews upon it the pledge he made to Enya Hangan. Then, turning, he gazes long at the house which has been his home and his father's before him. He sinks down, overwhelmed with grief.

Act V

The Shotgun Scene (*Yamazaki Kaido Teppo Watashi no Ba*). Some months have passed. Kampei is still living in the house of his parents-in-law, isolated among the hills. To keep himself and his family he has turned hunter. It is nightfall. The heavy rain of a summer shower is pouring down as the scene opens, and Kampei, with his gun in his hand, takes shelter under a tree. The rain has extinguished his match, and he is wondering what to do, when a traveller comes hurrying in his direction, shielding a small lantern under his coat. Kampei asks to be allowed to relight his match, explaining that his tinder is damp. The traveller is suspicious, but when Kampei offers to hand over his gun while he takes the light, he looks at Kampei more closely and recognizes him. As the traveller utters his name, Kampei realizes that this is one of his fellow samurai in Enya Hangan's service, Sanzaki Yagoro. Haltingly he begins to try to explain his failure to be at his master's side in the hour of need and his subsequent disappearance. He tells Yagoro how, when the news of Enya Hangan's death first reached him, his only thought was to follow his lord as quickly as possible. But he felt himself too unworthy. While he was debating what he could do to redeem himself, he heard a rumour that Yuranosuke and Goemon were planning revenge. Now his greatest desire is to join their league, and he begs Yagoro to help him. Yagoro is moved by Kampei's remorse, but does not feel sufficiently sure of him to tell him what is planned. He therefore makes up a story about a monument to Enya Hangan which he says Yuranosuke and some others are anxious to erect. He tells Kampei that, as they are all now *ronin*, any monetary help will be most welcome. If Kampei cares to subscribe, he will tell Yuranosuke. Kampei, understanding the implications of this tale, eagerly declares himself most willing. He confesses that he has not a penny to his name and his father-in-law is as poor as he, but, he assures Yagoro, somehow he will find some money and bring it to him in a few days. Yagoro gives him Goemon's address and tells him to take it there. Kampei, carefully protecting his relighted match, goes off into the woods. *The stage revolves to show another part of the same area. Rice hangs drying on bamboo frames.*

An old man is seen approaching down the *hanamichi*. It is O Karu's father, **Yoichibei,** who comes trudging along through the rain talking to himself the while. He has been on a sad errand to Kyoto. He has sold his only daughter to a brothel in Gionmachi in order to raise money to help his son-in-law redeem his honour. He and his wife and daughter concocted the plan without Kampei's knowledge, because they could think of no other way of helping him. Yoichibei, weary from his long journey, decides to shelter a little under the drying poles. While he rests there, he takes from his bosom a purse of striped cloth which contains 50 *ryo*, half the price of his daughter's service. A moment later a hand shoots out between the bundles of rice-ears and seizes the bag. Yoichibei reels back, clutching at his treasure, and there comes out a man with a drawn sword who quickly puts an end to the old man, twisting his blade brutally in the wound. The thief kicks the body into the un-

Sadakuro

dergrowth and, turning, shows himself to be Sadakuro, the ne'er-do-well son of Ono Kudayu. He puts the purse in his bosom and is about to make off when he hears sounds in the woods nearby and takes cover once more behind the screen of rice-ears. A shot rings out and a wounded wild boar charges across the stage; it is followed by Kampei who, aiming at the noise made by the beast since it is too dark for him to see, fires at the very spot where Sadakuro is hiding. Sadakuro staggers out and collapses. Kampei, thinking that by a lucky chance he has got his boar, hurries forward and feels about in the dark for the quarry. To his horror he finds the body of a man. He is about to retreat when his hand lights on the bag of coins. This is an opportunity he cannot miss. He takes it and puts it in his breast; then he makes off as fast as he can in the direction of Goemon's lodging.

Act VI

The Scene of Kampei's Seppuku (Kampei Seppuku no Ba).
The house of Yoichibei, the next morning. His wife and O Karu are anxiously awaiting his return. O Karu repeatedly assures her mother, **O Kaya,** that she has no regrets about the sacrifice she is making for Kampei's sake ; she only regrets the trouble it gives to her father. O Kaya reminds her that, since their son was also in Enya Hangan's service, Yoichibei could do no less.

A palanquin arrives before the door. From it descends the mistress of the brothel to which Yoichibei has sold his daughter. She is accompanied by her man of business who asks for Yoichibei and is surprized to hear he has not yet reached home. He and the woman explain that the old man hurried off as soon as the bargain was concluded with half the money. They now propose to pay the other half and take O Karu away. O Karu protests that they cannot do so until the old man returns. A wrangle ensues. In the end the women are forced to accept the balance of the money and O Karu is dragged out and pushed, weeping, into the palanquin. As the little procession sets out, it runs into Kampei who stops it peremptorily, amazed to see his wife going off in this fashion. They all return to the house. Kampei asks what is happening, but O Karu and O Kaya, putting off the evil moment, press about him with homely attentions. Here, under his father-in-law's roof, Kampei is once more a samurai and behaves with the instinctive dignity and authority of his class. He changes out of his wet clothes into a faded kimono which still bears the crest of his dead lord. O Karu hands him his two swords and brings out his special pipe and fire-box.

O Kaya explains the arrangement made without his knowledge. She tells him that now the brothel-keeper has come to take O Karu away, but Yoichibei, who is supposed to have the rest of the money, is still absent. Kampei takes the matter with surprising calm, saying that he is grateful for his father-in-law's kindness and feels sure they should not let O Karu go until he returns. Kampei adds that he has also had some luck of which he will tell them later; O Karu may not have to stay long in Gionmachi. The man of business becomes indignant and an argument starts between him and Kampei, because he thinks Kampei is throwing doubt on his good faith. He tells, angrily and at great length, the whole story of the transaction and finally, to add a last touch of verisimilitude, says that they gave Yoichibei a cloth bag in which to put the money. Kampei starts and asks about this bag. The brothel-mistress then produces the piece of material in which she had brought the second 50 *ryo* and says it was made out of the same stuff. Kampei examines it closely. Then under cover of knocking out his pipe, shielding himself with his kimono sleeve, he brings out the bag he took from the dead man. He compares the two and realizes with horror that they are made of identical cloth. (This pose and the play of expression required of the

Kampei

actor is considered one of the highlights of Kampei's part.)

Convinced now that he has murdered his father-in-law, Kampei's whole demeanour changes. He is only anxious to get the pair from Gionmachi out of the house; he would rather send his wife with them, than let her discover what he has done. He therefore surprises O Karu and O Kaya by saying he supposes, after all, that she must go. To silence her protests at leaving without seeing her father, he makes up a lame story about having met him himself that morning and not knowing when he will come home. The women are amazed at his not mentioning this before. Before they can make further enquiries, the brothel mistress and her attendant are in a bustle to be off. Kampei appears to pay scant attention to O Karu's departure. She tries not to mind this sudden coldness. O Kaya overwhelms her with tenderness and advice and at last, with many tears, O Karu is carried away.

O Kaya returns to the house and tries to console Kampei whose strange silence she believes due to this sudden parting. Then she begins to question him about her husband. Kampei's replies become more and more vague.

They are interrupted by the arrival of four hunters bringing Yoichibei's body which they have found by chance. Kampei does not move. O Kaya is at first overwhelmed by her grief. Then she turns again to Kampei with a further torrent of questions about the supposed meeting. Her grief turns to suspicion and anger. Finally she tears the money bag, stained with blood, from his kimono bosom and cries that this accounts for his dazed attitude. He must have murdered her husband. Kampei, who believes the same thing, tries to explain, but she quells him, abusing and beating him. He bears it in silence.

Two samurai knock at the door, announcing themselves as Goemon and Yagoro. Kampei hastily hides the body behind a screen and, pulling himself together, admits them. They have come, they say, from Yuranosuke. He was at first pleased that Kampei should offer so much money for the "monument," but he later decided that his lord's spirit might not approve since Kampei had been faithless. They therefore return the money to him. Kampei is overwhelmed. Hearing what Goemon says, his mother-in-law comes out and, reviling Kampei, pours out her story. The two samurai

are horrified and join her in abusing the young man.
This is too much for him. His wife has been torn from
him, his gift refused and he believes himself a parricide.
His character may be weak, but he is still sufficiently a
samurai to take the only course he considers open to him.
He draws his sword and commits *seppuku*. His action takes
the other three by surprise. They listen in silence while he
tells them the story of the chance shot in the darkness.
Then Yagoro rises and goes to examine Yoichibei's body.
He calls out to them that the old man has died from a
sword wound, although the sword has been turned in it so
that it could easily be mistaken for a bullet hole.

Goemon then recalls that they passed the body of a man
killed by gun shot on their way here. They identified him
as Sadakuro, who was known to have turned highwayman.
It must have been he who murdered Yoichibei. Kampei's
shot avenged his father-in-law's death. O Kaya is now beside herself with remorse and clings to Kampei. He says
quietly that, since his name is cleared, he will die content.
Goemon tells him that, as he has shown himself willing to
die to wipe out his fault, he shall now see the covenant of
the loyal *ronin* who have sworn to take revenge on Moronao.
He places a scroll before Kampei, showing him that his
name stands upon it. He bids him seal it with his blood.
Kampei begs him in return to take both the sums of money
as his contribution. Goemon does so, afterwards returning
it to O Kaya to be used for prayers for the dead and, seeing that Kampei is nearly spent, the two samurai leave.
Kampei dies in O Kaya's arm.

Act VII

Ichiriki Tea-house Scene (Gion Ichiriki no Ba). The tea-house
called Ichiriki at Kyoto. Some months later. This place
has become the haunt of Yuranosuke who has apparently
given himself up to dissipation since the death of his lord.
Ono Kudayu and Moronao's retainer, Bannai, arrive to spy
on Yuranosuke and see whether he is really as altered as
rumour has it. Kudayu has sold himself to Moronao. They
are shown into a room in the garden, since Yuranosuke has
engaged all the other rooms for a party. When they are
gone, three of the faithful *ronin* come to the tea-house in
search of Yuranosuke, accompanied by **Heiyemon,** O
Karu's brother, who was a footsoldier in Enya Hangan's

service. The samurai ask impatiently for Yuranosuke, but
are told that he is so drunk that, even if he came to them,
they could get no sense out of him. A moment later Yuranosuke blunders into the room playing at blind-man's-buff
with the tea-house girls. His former companions try to sober
him, but without success. Heiyemon pleads with him to
be allowed to join the league to avenge their lord. Yuranosuke tells him that he is talking nonsense ; there is no
such league ; they all decided it was too risky. Heiyemon
thinks he is being put off with this story, because he is not
a proper samurai. He explains humbly that he only wants
to carry the luggage of his betters in the great enterprise.
But while he speaks Yuranosuke appears to fall asleep and
the three disgusted samurai are about to kill him when
Heiyemon stops them, suggesting that Yuranosuke's wits
must have been turned with sorrow and this has driven him
to drink. All four go out.

(The act often starts here.) Down the *hanamichi* hastens
Rikiya hot-foot from his home. He sees his father asleep,
but dares not call him. He hides outside the gate and
gently rings his sword-guard against the sheath. Instantly
Yuranosuke is alert. He comes to the gate and, with his
back to his son, so that he may watch the tea-house, asks
the reason for this visit. Rikiya gives him a letter sent secretly by Kaoyo. The letter contains news of Moronao's
movements. Yuranosuke bids him return home. (The act
may start here).

Unknown to father and son, Kudayu has been spying on
them. Now, as Yuranosuke is about to read the letter, he
reappears, for the little scene he has witnessed has aroused
his suspicions. He questions Yuranosuke closely, but can
get nothing from him. He offers him more *sake* and then
as a final test, a piece of octopus meat. As Yuranosuke,
thanking him, is about to eat it, Kudayu stays his hand,
reminding him that it is the eve of the anniversary of Enya
Hangan's death. Yuranosuke asks what difference that
makes and — to Kudayu's amazement — calmly eats the fish.
Then he staggers to his feet and reels off into the tea-house
calling to Kudayu to follow him. When he is gone, Bannai
returns, and he and Kudayu decide that Yuranosuke must
have given up all ideas of revenge ; otherwise he would certainly be fasting on this particular day. Bannai can reassure

Moronao. Yuranosuke has left his sword behind, and they find it, its blade covered with rust. This is still further proof of Yuranosuke's condition. Kudayu enters his palanquin and Bannai continues to talk to him. Getting no reply, he lifts the curtain and is astonished to see a stone inside. A voice calls to him in a whisper from beneath the verandah. It is Kudayu who tells him he intends to hide there, because he is still uneasy about the letter brought by Rikiya.

Bannai and the palanquin leave. A courtesan appears at the window of an upper room, overlooking the verandah. She is O Karu, not yet fully accustomed to her new life. She has come to cool her flushed face, for too much *sake* still makes her feel giddy. Yuranosuke re-enters, looking for his sword. Finding the place empty, he decides to use this opportunity to read his letter. He goes to the lantern hanging at the corner of the verandah and reads by its light. O Karu, looking down on him, thinks it must be a love letter, and, intrigued, tries to make out the characters. But she cannot read them easily for they are the wrong way round. She fetches her mirror and finds she can read them reflected in it. At the same time Kudayu, down below, is able to peruse the long letter which, as Yuranosuke unrolls it, hangs down over the edge of the verandah.

Suddenly a pin drops from O Karu's hair and Yuranosuke looks up, sees her and quickly rolls up the letter. Part of the end, which Kudayu was holding, is torn off. Yuranosuke realizes that at least two people beside himself have had access to its secrets. He asks O Karu to come to him and helps her climb down by a ladder. She admits to him she saw him reading a letter and he guesses she knows something of its contents. To her surprise he suddenly offers to ransom her and adds that, if she has someone else she loves, he will not come between them. At the end of three days she will be free. O Karu is beside herself with joy, but can scarcely believe her ears. Yuranosuke goes off, saying he will settle the business at once while she waits for him.

O Karu starts to write the good news to Kampei. She is interrupted by her brother, Heiyemon. (Heiyemon fills the rôle of the traditional clown of the puppet theatre. The scene which follows, although fundamentally tragic, affords moments of comedy which are intended to relieve the tension of the drama.) She is surprised to see him, but he tells her he has been with their mother and knows the whole story of her removal to Gionmachi. O Karu informs him joyfully that she has now been redeemed by none other than Yuranosuke. Heiyemon asks whether Yuranosuke knows she is Kampei's wife. She thinks not. Her brother then adds that in that case Yuranosuke must be as bad as everyone says he is and is certainly not dreaming of revenge. O Karu defends him hotly and whispers to her brother what she read in the letter. To her horror, Heiyemon immediately draws his sword and tries to run her through. She escapes from him, asking him what she has done to anger him and swearing that all she longs for in the world is to see her parents and husband again. Heiyemon clumsily tries to break gently to O Karu the news of her father's and husband's deaths and then revives her when she faints at the terrible news.

When O Karu is recovered, Heiyemon explains that he quite understands why Yuranosuke has offered to ransom her. Since she has read the secret letter, he is doing so in order to put her to death. Heiyemon thinks it would be better for her to die by her own brother's hand. O Karu is willing to die now that she knows she will be going to join Kampei, but, for her mother's sake, she feels she should kill herself, rather than be killed by Heiyemon. As she takes his sword a voice calls to her to stop and Yuranosuke appears. He praises her and her brother for their loyalty but adds that, although her husband Kampei joined the league before he died, he had no opportunity to kill a single enemy. This, he says, shall now be put right. Placing in O Karu's hand his own rusty sword, he drives the blade through the floor of the verandah and wounds Kudayu in the shoulder. Heiyemon drags the old man out and flings him down before Yuranosuke. The latter, catching him by the hair, pours out all his pent-up rage and chagrin. He tells the faithless *ronin* that, while he is fawning on Moronao, others are thinking only of revenge. He bitterly recalls how Kudayu forced him to break his fast on this sacred day. Yuranosuke, in his grief, beats his enemy's head on the ground and bids Heiyemon inflict on him any torture he can devise. But he must not kill him here, he adds, lest it cause talk. Heiyemon hoists Kudayu on his back and drags him off to throw him into the river. (As he goes, the three loyal samurai appear from a neighbouring room and beg Yuranosuke's forgiveness for doubting his loyalty. This incident is, however, usually omitted to allow for a spectacular curtain pose.)

Act VIII

The Bridal Journey (*Michiyuki Tabiji no Yomeiri*). This act is a *michiyuki*. It adds nothing to the plot and is often omitted when the whole play is performed. It is, however, frequently played separately. It describes the bridal journey of Konami, the daughter of Honzo and the betrothed of Rikiya. The action is mimed, while the singers describe the events of the journey and the places through which the travellers pass. It is now autumn, eighteen months having passed since Enya Hangan's death.

Konami has become so restless and moody since Rikiya and his father became *ronin* and left Edo that her mother decides she will take her to Yuranosuke's new home at Yamashina and put through the marriage without more delay. They set out on foot, without any escort, because Rikiya is now a poor man. At one point on their journey they meet a daimyo's procession and Konami reflects sadly that, had circumstances been different, she might herself have travelled to her wedding in such state. Each place through which she passes makes her think of her lover. She wonders whether her happiness will vanish like the snow-dust on Mount Fuji. Crossing the Oi River she remembers the saying that a stream and a man's heart are fickle — will her lover's heart ever change? Then a chance-heard country song seems to her a good omen and cheers her spirits. They take the ferry to Atsuta in a hailstorm. They pass the junction where the roads to Ise and to Kyoto divide. Here the very stones remind her of her lover. (In real life the name of Oboshi Rikiya was Oishi Chikara. Oishi means "large stone.") At last they come to the village of Yamashina.

Act IX

Yuranosuke's House in Yamashina. (*Yamashina Kankyo no Ba*). Yuranosuke returns from Kyoto, apparently very drunk. He is accompanied by girls from the tea-house. It has snowed heavily and he makes an unseemly exhibition of himself trying to build snowmen. Then he goes into the house and falls asleep, leaving his wife to get rid of the other revellers. As soon as they are gone, Yuranosuke, now

his normal self, asks his son Rikiya what he makes of the
snow piles that stand in the garden. Rikiya tries to evolve
a comparison between "snow and loyalty." Yuranosuke
tells him he should rather say "snow and loyal patience."
In the shadow snow will not melt; they themselves live in
the shadow and their loyalty is unwavering. The family go
inside.

(The act often begins here.) Outside the gate appears
Tonase, Honzo's wife. She wears two swords like a man.
Konami, in a palanquin, waits a little distance off. Tonase
asks for Yuranosuke and bids the servant tell him who is
at the door. Then she calls her daughter. They are asked
to enter and are joined by Yuranosuke's wife, **O Ishi.** She
treats Tonase with distant ceremony. Tonase tries to bring
the conversation onto a more friendly level and refers to the
betrothal of Konami and Rikiya. But O Ishi continues to

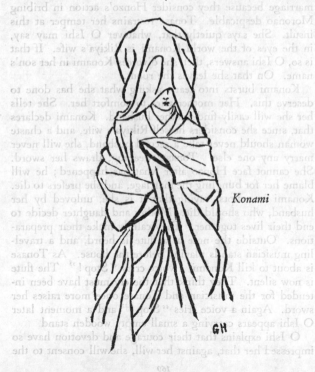

Konami

talk about the sights of Kyoto as if they were ordinary visitors. Finally Tonase says firmly that they have come about the marriage. It has taken her some time to discover where Yuranosuke and his family went to live after Enya Hangan's death, but as soon as she knew she set out to bring her daughter to her betrothed. Honzo, she adds, should have come himself, but he was detained on his lord's business. She has put on her husband's swords, which are his soul, and is acting as his deputy. She asks to see Yuranosuke, to arrange for the wedding ceremony. O Ishi replies that she thought all idea of the marriage had been given up on both sides. Now that her husband is a *ronin* and a poor man, Rikiya would no longer be a fit husband for Konami. Tonase explains that she and Honzo do not feel like that about it. O Ishi then shifts her ground and says that she and her husband have changed their minds about the marriage because they consider Honzo's action in bribing Moronao despicable. Tonase restrains her temper at this insult. She says quietly that, whatever O Ishi may say, in the eyes of the world Konami is Rikiya's wife. If that is so, O Ishi answers, then she divorces Konami in her son's name. On that she leaves the room.

Konami bursts into tears, asking what she has done to deserve this. Her mother tries to comfort her. She tells her she will easily find another husband. Konami declares that, since she considers herself Rikiya's wife, and a chaste woman should never take a second husband, she will never marry any one else. Tonase, weeping, draws her sword. She cannot face Honzo after what has happened; he will blame her for bungling the marriage, and she prefers to die. Konami interrupts, saying that it is she, unloved by her husband, who should die. Mother and daughter decide to end their lives together. They calmly make their preparations. Outside the note of a flute is heard, and a travelling musician stands playing before the house. As Tonase is about to kill Konami, a voice cries "Stop!" The flute is now silent. They think that the cry must have been intended for the musician and Tonase once more raises her sword. Again a voice cries "Stop!" and a moment later O Ishi appears carrying a small empty wooden stand.

O Ishi explains that their courage and devotion have so impressed her that, against her will, she will consent to the marriage. But she expects Tonase to place an unusual wine cup for the ceremony on the stand. Tonase, not understanding her, offers the two swords. O Ishi returns them scornfully saying that what is required is Honzo's head. She adds that the real objection to the marriage is that it was Honzo who prevented Enya Hangan by force from killing Moronao, so that their lord died full of bitterness.

While mother and daughter sit in stupefied silence, a voice outside cries that Honzo's head is here. The musician comes in at the gate, removing his hat, and shows himself to be Honzo. He turns to O Ishi declaring that he is the one who has a right to object to the marriage, not she. He will not, he says, give his daughter to the son of a cowardly samurai who gets drunk instead of avenging his lord. O Ishi flares up at this and, seizing a halberd, attacks Honzo. He fends her off and disarms her. As he does so, Rikiya rushes in and, picking up the fallen weapon, attacks and wounds him mortally. Before Rikiya can give the finishing stroke, Yuranosuke enters and stops him. Turning to Honzo, he says that he hopes he is now satisfied. He has fallen by the hand of his son-in-law, as he wished to do.

Honzo then tells Yuranosuke the whole story of his reason for bribing Moronao and his bitter remorse at the unexpected outcome of his action. Realizing that his well-meant interference between Enya Hangan and Moronao would stand between his daughter and her betrothed, he begged his lord to dismiss him and let him come to Yuranosuke to make atonement. Yuranosuke says gently that all is forgiven. Since he and Rikiya must certainly die as soon as the vendetta is accomplished, he and his wife wished to spare Konami the sorrow of being a widow as soon as she was a wife. Tonase and O Ishi weep together and beg each other's forgiveness. Honzo declares that it will be a great honour for his daughter to marry the son of a man of such unswerving loyalty. He has a wedding-gift to offer. He gives Rikiya a plan of Moronao's house. Yuranosuke is overjoyed and explains to Honzo how they intend to make the attack. He mentions that they will force the shutters of the verandah. Honzo objects that the shutters are strongly bolted and the noise of breaking them down will rouse the household. Yuranosuke tells Rikiya to show what they intend to do. Rikiya goes into the garden and, catching a strong

bamboo near the house which is bowed down by a load of
snow, he puts the top end under the lintel of the verandah
window. When he shakes off the snow, the bamboo stem
tries to spring up straight, lifting the lintel just enough to
allow the shutters to fall bodily out of their groove. Yuranosuke explains that they will carry two bows of bamboo
ready strung so that, on cutting the string, the same effect
will be achieved and the shutter forced to collapse inwards.
Rikiya asks his father's permission to leave at once to make
the final arrangements for the attack, but his father tells him
that he intends to go himself. Rikiya will remain behind
and set everything in order. Next day he is to join his father.
They all realize that Yuranosuke is doing this in order to
allow the young lovers these few short hours of married happiness. Honzo, dying, looks at him in gratitude. Yuranosuke gathers up Honzo's discarded disguise and puts it on.
O Ishi, though she knew the day must soon come, realizes
with despair that she is seeing her husband for the last time.
He, without a backward glance, goes on his way.

Act X

The Amakawaya Scene (Amakawaya no Ba). (This act is
almost always omitted when the whole play is given, but is
sometimes played alone.)

The shop of **Amakawaya Gihei,** a merchant of Sakai.
Gihei has just dispatched a number of heavy chests which
have been stowed on board a trading vessel. His apprentice
and his small son, **Yoshimatsu,** are alone in the shop.
Yoshimatsu cries for his mother, who has recently been sent
away by his father, for no good reason. They are interrupted
by the arrival of Goemon and Rikiya, who ask for Gihei.
Gihei comes out to them, and they discuss the shipment of
arms and equipment which Gihei has been making on their
behalf. He explains how he was able to collect the stuff
without arousing suspicion and how he has sent his wife
back to her father and dismissed his servants so that they
should know nothing. Goemon and Rikiya thank him for
his assistance. When they leave, Gihei's old father-in-law,
Ryochiku, enters complaining about his daughter's return
home and saying that if she is to stay there, Gihei must
divorce her properly. Gihei is very loth to do so, but finally
writes the letter of divorce. Ryochiku then tells him that
he intends to marry his daughter, **O Sono,** to a wealthy

suitor. Gihei, very angry and mortified, kicks him out.

That night Gihei's house is surrounded by the police and he is arrested on the charge of supplying arms to be used by Enya Hangan's ex-retainers to avenge their dead lord. Gihei denies the charge stoutly. The police then bring in a box which they have taken off a ship about to set sail. Gihei recognizes it at once as one of those he has dispatched. When the police are about to open it, he breaks loose from his guards and leaps upon the lid. He makes up a story about the contents being the private property of a great lord's wife and not to be handled by common folk. The police then fetch little Yoshimatsu and threaten to kill him, if Gihei does not tell all he knows about the *ronins'* plans. But Gihei remains silent. The police threaten to torture him, but he mocks at them. At that a voice is heard inside the box, and when Gihei descends, the lid is lifted, and Yuranosuke himself emerges. The police reveal themselves to be some of the other loyal *ronin* in disguise. Yuranosuke assures Gihei that he himself never doubted his good faith, but as some of the others who did not know him were doubtful, this trial was devised. They now all thank him for his great loyalty and courage. Gihei welcomes them without malice and bids them stay to supper. Yuranosuke consents, sending Goemon and Rikiya ahead with an advance party.

When they have gone into the back of the house, O Sono comes to the door. She is unhappy at being sent away by her husband and cannot bear the thought of marrying another. She longs to see her child. She makes the apprentice call out Gihei, who treats her roughly, thinking she is a willing party to her father's plans. O Sono tries to make Gihei take back the letter of divorce, but he refuses. He realizes, however, that she does not wish to exchange him for a worthless husband and tells her to make the old man see reason. In the spring he, Gihei, will be able to bring her home again. O Sono declares sorrowfully that nothing will stop her father remarrying her. She is about to go away when a strange man rushes on them with a drawn sword, cuts off her hair, robs her of her hair-ornaments and vanishes. While she and Gihei stand dumbfounded, Yuranosuke comes out of the house and offers Gihei a gift. Gihei spurns it, thinking it is money, but the packet falls open. It contains O Sono's hair, combs and ornaments.

Yuranosuke explains that, since O Sono is now temporarily a nun, her father cannot force her into a marriage. By the time her hair has grown again, the vendetta will be accomplished, and Gihei can take her back as his wife. Meanwhile he advises Gihei to engage "this nun and nurse" to care for his child. Gihei and O Sono are full of gratitude. Yuranosuke tells Gihei that, when the attack is launched, they will use his trade-name "Amakawaya" as a battle-cry so that in name as well as in spirit he will be present.

Act XI

The Vendetta Scene (Koke Uchiiri no Ba.) This act consists of a long series of fights, each one almost a dance. It ends with the killing of Kono Moronao. The forty-seven *ronin* appear before Kono Moronao's gate. Each wears armour and the blue and white coat for which they are famous. Each carries a wooden tag inscribed with one of the 47 characters of the Japanese syllabary. These are identification badges. (This is the explanation of part of the title of the play : "Kanadehon" means "syllabary book.") The gate is forced, and a number of quick scenes show the prowess of the various *ronin* during the fight to get possession of the house. Rikiya has a spectacular scene to himself. The other actors are given opportunities to display their skill in sword-fighting.

One scene, however, although not in the text, is based on a real incident which took place in the actual vendetta. We are told that three brave retainers of Kira Kozuke-no-suke (the original Kono Moronao) stood guard before the door of his private room and drove off every attack. Finally Chikara (the Rikiya of the play) was commanded by his father to kill them or die in the attempt. Chikara slipped on the snow-covered edge of a pond and fell into it. Handaiyu leant over to finish him off, but Chikara cut his adversary in the leg and made him fall. Then he crawled out of the pond and killed him. The other two men, Kobayashi Hehachi and Shimizu Ikkaku, were meanwhile dispatched by others of the *ronin* (See Mitford's *Tales of Old Japan*).

In the play the incident by the pond is dramatized. The youth is not Rikiya, but another young *ronin* and the name of Moronao's loyal retainer is Kobayashi Hehachi, not Waku Handaiyu.

The wicked and cowardly Bannai is given his deserts

and finally the loyal *ronin* gather in the courtyard. The house is in their hands, but they have failed to find Moronao. A small charcoal-shed stands at one side of the courtyard. The quick ears of Yazama Jutaro catch faint sounds of movement within. He breaks open the shed and drags out Moronao who is in his night clothes. The *ronin* bow respectfully to their enemy's rank and Yuranosuke, drawing from his breast the dirk used by Enya Hangan, offers it to Moronao and begs him to die by his own hand as a samurai should. Moronao pretends to agree and then attacks Yuranosuke, who wrenches the blade from him and kills him. The head of Kono Moronao is cut off and attached to a halberd. Bearing it aloft in triumph, the 47 loyal retainers set out to take this offering and lay it on the tomb of their lord.

KANJINCHO (*The Subscription List*). *Juhachiban*. — This play is perhaps the most popular of the Ichikawa collection. It was adapted from the Noh *Ataka* by Namike Gohei III (1789—1855) and was first performed in 1840 by Ichikawa Ebizo (Danjuro VII). Danjuro IX improved the text with certain refinements and in 1887 had the unprecedented honour of being commanded to perform it before the Emperor.

As an example of classical drama, *Kanjincho* ranks very high. Its theme is the presence of mind of a loyal retainer. But it has many other attractions — generosity on the part of an enemy, a touching reconciliation scene, a riotous drinking bout, and some excellent dances — in short all the best ingredients of a masterpiece.

The story of the play revolves round **Minamoto Yoshitsune** at the time when, accompanied by the faithful warrior-priest Benkei and a handful of loyal servants, he was fleeing from the wrathful jealousy of his elder brother, Minamoto Yoritomo (see page 425). After seeking refuge in vain in the island of Shikoku, Yoshitsune decided to make a break for Mutsu in the North, where he had grown up as a boy, and could count on the friendly support of certain local notables. The journey, however, involved passage through the length of the territory controlled by Yoritomo. The latter foresaw that in the end Yoshitsune would try to go North and, in order to hinder him, set up barriers at strategic points on the way. In mountainous country it was impossible to avoid these road-blocks, even while travelling on foot. On the other hand, once the first barrier was negotiated, it was psychologically easier to pass any subsequent ones. This play tells how Yoshitsune and his companions surmounted the first hurdle successfully.

The single scene of the play is the traditional Kabuki version of the Noh set. The musical accompaniment is provided by a *nagauta* orchestra.

Argument : **Togashi Saemon** enters, accompanied by his sword-bearer and three soldiers. He explains that he is the guardian of this new barrier set up to intercept Yoshitsune and his party, who are believed to be fleeing to the North disguised as wandering priests. He enjoins his soldiers to be vigilant, and they tell him that they have already killed three priests on suspicion. He commends their zeal and takes his seat stage left.

The musicians sing a song describing Yoshitsune's journey. While this is in progress, Yoshitsune enters by the *hanamichi*. He is dressed as a porter, has a wide straw hat and a staff and carries a sort of portable shrine containing a holy image on his back. He is followed by four retainers who pass him and kneel facing stage left. Benkei enters and takes up a position facing Yoshitsune. The young prince says that he would prefer to die by his own hand rather than be killed by nameless men (alas ! a prophetic remark), but he will consider Benkei's plan for getting through the barrier. The four retainers point to their swords and offer to fight their way past it. Benkei observes that violence will not serve. There will be other barriers to pass and they cannot risk calling attention to themselves by feats of arms. They must rely on cunning. That is why he has advised Yoshitsune to disguise himself as a humble porter. He now asks him to pull his hat over his eyes and enter the barrier with dragging feet some distance behind the others.

To the ominous taps of a drum, Benkei followed by the four retainers stalks onto the stage towards Togashi. Yoshitsune kneels down stage right, hat over eyes and both hands clasped on the staff resting on his shoulder. (This is a famous pose borrowed directly from the Noh). Benkei announces that they are priests wishing to pass the barrier.

Togashi and his soldiers register excitement. Benkei explains that they have been sent out to collect funds for the restoration of the Todai temple at Nara and are to tour the Hokurikudo district. Togashi replies that they may not pass and tells them the reason. Benkei says that he understands that they are seeking for disguised priests, but surely genuine ones may pass. The three soldiers explain that they are taking no chances and are killing all priests on suspicion. Benkei asks whether Yoshitsune was indeed among the priests they claim to have slaughtered a few days before. Togashi is embarrassed and refuses to discuss the matter further. Benkei turns to his companions and, in a loud aside, comments that he never expected to find such sacrilege, but there is no help for it; they must all prepare to die. Togashi begins to feel very uncomfortable, for killing priests, Yoritomo or no Yoritomo, is no trifling matter. The four retainers form a square in the middle of the stage. Benkei stands in the centre and they dance, rubbing their rosaries. They end in a kneeling position, their hands folded in prayer. The musicians describe the action.

Togashi is unnerved by this performance and feels he must use great caution. He therefore asks Benkei whether, since they claim to be collecting funds, he has a *kanjincho*. This is usually translated as a " subscription list." It is a pious exhortation issued by some holy man setting out the merits of subscribing to the particular charity or restoration fund. The language of such documents was extremely difficult to understand, but the more pompous it sounded the better it was thought to be. Benkei is rather taken aback by this request and Togashi, noting his momentary confusion, is confirmed in his suspicions. The musicians comment that of course Benkei has no *kanjincho*. Benkei goes to the back of the stage and returns with a scroll which he starts to unwind. Now follows one of the great moments of the play. As Benkei unwinds the scroll and begins the preliminary address, Togashi advances deliberately towards him. Suddenly he starts forward, glances at the scroll and retreats as Benkei catches him in the act. He says nothing, but he must show that he has seen that the document is a fake, but that nevertheless he admires Benkei's courageous ingenuity and is prepared to let him go on with the deception. Benkei shows that he realizes that any faltering now will ruin the chances of success and that he feels that Togashi is going to be magnanimous. In a sonorous voice, he recites a long and suitably impressive exhortation to the pious and generous. He rolls up the *kanjincho* with a snap.

Togashi, having made a decision to let them pass, is now enjoying himself. He questions Benkei about the costume and equipment of this kind of priest. Benkei answers with firmness and clarity. Togashi declares himself satisfied and begs to be allowed to make his own offerings to the fund. His servants bring in money and other gifts. Benkei thanks him gravely and asks him to keep the gifts against the party's return in April. He takes the money at once, however.

Benkei gives the order to pass the barrier. The musicians sing. Benkei is half-way down the *hanamichi* with the four retainers following and Yoshitsune well in the rear, when one of Togashi's soldiers calls his attention to Yoshitsune. Togashi much as he might like to do so cannot ignore this. He cries out, hand on sword, and Benkei and the others rush back onto the stage. Togashi and Benkei glower at each other. Benkei abuses Yoshitsune for holding up the march. Togashi retorts that he has detained him because he resembles " a certain person." Benkei roars with laughter when Togashi says that this person is Yoshitsune. He then simulates anger and rates Yoshitsune for his laggardly dawdling. Finally he seizes Yoshitsune's staff and beats him

Benkei and Togashi

with it. Yoshitsune escapes from him, but the soldiers will not let him pass. The four retainers group themselves in support of Benkei, and there follows a famous dance, again lifted directly from the Noh, in which the two sides alternately advance on, and retreat from, each other. Benkei at last raises his staff above his head and declares that, if the porter is suspect, Togashi is welcome to keep him together with the presents until they return.

This offer turns the balance once more. Togashi is sure that the porter is Yoshitsune. Yet he has watched Benkei beat his master and he knows what a strain it must have been on his loyalty. When Benkei again offers to beat the porter to death, if necessary, Togashi begs him to restrain himself. Admiration mixed with embarrassment has got the better of his judgment. They may all go on their way.

Togashi and his men withdraw from the stage by the "hurry-door" up left. Yoshitsune crosses to down left and seats himself. Benkei passes him with bent head and kneels down right. The retainers sit in a line between them. The ensuing scene is justly celebrated, after the hurly-burly of the preceding dances, for its pathos and dignity. Yoshitsune thanks Benkei for saving his life. The retainers extol Benkei's cunning and resource. Benkei apologizes for beating his master. His arm was numb, but he felt he must do it. He bursts into tears for the first time in his life. He

Yoshitsune

and Yoshitsune advance towards each other, weeping. The prince laments his unkind fate and the musicians recount his adventures with Benkei in the service of Yoritomo. They all rise at last and move towards the *hanamichi*.

Suddenly Togashi re-appears and calls to them to wait. He is accompanied by servants carrying *sake*. He seats himself down left, a stand and *sake* saucer are placed before him, and he drinks. He apologizes to Benkei for having suspected him and invites him to drink, too. Benkei accepts. Two soldiers pour a little *sake* into the saucer. He looks at it wryly and drinks. Then he beckons to the third soldier to bring the lid of a lacquer tub. The soldiers fill it and he swallows down the huge draught of liquor to everyone's amazement. The musicians sing. Benkei, in relief, relaxes and clowns with the soldiers. He has several refills and finally ends with the lid on his head. He rises and dances the " game of the winding stream," an old Chinese game in which wine cups were floated down a stream while the players competed to compose the best poems as the cups passed them. Benkei is now fairly drunk, but does not forget his manners. He offers *sake* to Togashi, who begs him to dance for them all. He then performs a " dance of longevity." As the music quickens and the dance grows wilder, Benkei signals to his party to move. With Yoshitsune leading, they hurry away along the *hanamichi*. Togashi stands up and poses with his men. It is a tragic moment for him—having betrayed his trust, he has now no alternative to suicide. Benkei staggers to the end of the *hanamichi* and the curtain is drawn leaving him in front. He raises an arm above his head, smiles slowly and spares a thought for Togashi. He then goes out along the *hanamichi* performing what is a tour de force, even on the Kabuki stage, namely a *tobiroppo* or " flying *roppo* " (see page 403).

KATAKIUCHI TENGAJAYA MURA (*Revenge at Tengajaya*), commonly called *Tengajaya Mura*. *Sewamono*. — Written for the puppets by Naka Kamesuke I in the late eighteeth century and revised by Naka Kamesuke II. It was a popular Kabuki vehicle for Otani Tomoemon IV.

The Hayase brothers, **Iori** and **Genjiro,** have a twofold mission — to recover a lost treasure (a painting) entrusted to them by their lord and to avenge the death of their father at the hands of their fellow samurai, **Toma Saburouemon.** They are assisted by Iori's wife, **Somenoi,** and by Genjiro's betrothed, **Hazue,** and by their two servants, the brothers **Adachi Motoemon** and **Adachi Yasuke.** The whole party goes to Osaka in search of Toma and the treasure.

The play depicts the depravity of a servant whose misfortune it is to fall from his master's favour. His former loyalty becomes hatred and his good qualities are turned to roguery and violence.

Act I

Before the gate of the Shitennoji at Osaka. Somenoi and Hazue arrive in travelling dress to pay their respects at the temple. They are followed by Iori, Genjiro, and their servant Yasuke. The brothers observe a samurai whose face is hidden by a straw travelling hat, but whose dress bears the crest of their enemy Toma Saburouemon. They conclude it must be he and attack him. He beats them off and they realize that they have made a mistake. They apologize and withdraw into the temple. Another samurai, similarly dressed, who is, in fact, Toma, appears with his servant **Udesuke.** While they are discussing plans, Motoemon arrives. Udesuke accidentally drops a letter which Motoemon retrieves and from which he guesses Udesuke's identity. He attacks him, but is struck down by Toma. Udesuke revives him with liberal draughts of *sake* and Motoemon falls into a drunken stupor. As Toma and Udesuke are leaving the two ladies come out of the temple. Toma conceals himself, and the first samurai appears at the same moment. Somenoi and Hazue make the same mistake as the men. They set upon the samurai, convinced it is Toma. When they discover their mistake, they are also forced to apologize and withdraw. Iori and Genjiro return and discover Motoemon. They are enraged at his disgraceful behaviour. He is stripped of his livery and left lying in the street. Yasuke hangs back and leaves a little money in his brother's belt before hurrying after his masters. As soon as all is clear, Udesuke returns with a litter, and Motoemon is bundled into it and carried away. The two samurai meet, remove their hats, and reveal themselves in a triumphant pose as Toma and his brother Taizo.

Act II

The Hayase brothers' poor dwelling behind the Toji Temple. Some months later. Both the searches have proved vain. Genjiro has contracted an eye infection which makes him almost blind. Yasuke is loyally trying to make ends meet. Motoemon, disguised as a blind masseur, comes to the house to spy on the brothers. He has transferred his allegiance to Toma and his sole desire is to be revenged on his former masters. He is recognized by Yasuke, but tells a pathetic hard luck story which induces his brother not to betray him. At that moment Iori calls to Yasuke. In a panic Yasuke hides Motoemon in a cupboard. The Hayase brothers and Somenoi enter and are lamenting their lack of success when **Izutsuya Isaburo,** an old family servant turned brothel-keeper, arrives with the news that he has discovered the missing picture in a curio shop where it is on sale for two hundred *ryo*. Iori goes at once to bespeak the picture. While he is away, Isaburo's sister, **O Kichi,** appears, and in the course of conversation, the suggestion is put forward that Somenoi should sell herself into Isaburo's brothel for the two hundred *ryo*. The deal is rapidly concluded and Isaburo pays out one hundred *ryo* as a deposit to Genjiro. Somenoi takes a tearful leave and is carried away in Isaburo's litter. Genjiro goes to bed, hiding the hundred *ryo* under his quilt.

Yasuke releases Motoemon, gives him some old clothes and a little money, and bids him be off. Motoemon shuffles away, but as soon as he reaches the *hanamichi*, he opens his eyes and reveals himself to the audience as the scoundrel he has become. (This is the great moment of the scene). He creeps back to the house, but the door is locked. He climbs onto the roof and awaits an opportunity to enter. Yasuke, upset by his brother's appearance, tries to solace himself with *sake*, but he dislikes the taste and at last lies down comfortless on his bed to sleep. Motoemon forces an entry through the roof. With the utmost care, he slides back the doors of Genjiro's room, finds the money, and steals his sword. He tries to strike off Genjiro's head, but cannot swing the long blade in the small room. Realizing that he cannot kill Genjiro quietly and quickly, he decides to murder Yasuke first. He stabs him through the heart. Genjiro is aroused, but at that moment Iori returns. Motoemon strikes out Iori's lamp, wounds him in the thigh, and makes good his escape.

Act III

Sc. 1. *The woods near the Fukushima Tenjin Shrine.* Some months later. The Hayase brothers have sunk so low that they now live in a wretched reed-mat hut in a colony of outcasts. Genjiro's eyes are cured, but Iori is a helpless cripple. They live by doing odd jobs normally only performed by outcasts. Iori sits by a boggy patch of road and hires out high wooden clogs to the passers-by. Udesuke, Toma's servant, comes to the place disguised as an outcast, recognizes them, and hastens to report. Genjiro goes away to find work. Two strolling comic players stop a moment to talk to Iori and try to cheer him by performing their dance. Iori is left alone. Motoemon and Udesuke arrive by the *hanamichi* and attack Iori, who defends himself as best he can. Toma appears soon afterwards and in the ensuing scuffle is wounded in the wrist by Iori. This incident throws Toma into a paroxysm of rage and he and his creatures murder Iori by slow degrees. When the wretched cripple is dead, Toma goes off by the *hanamichi*, striking a pose of fiendish triumph. Genjiro returns and discovers his brother's mutilated corpse. He is stricken with grief, but pulls him-

Motoemon

self together, digs a grave, buries his brother, and says a prayer for his soul. He collapses in a torrent of tears. He is attacked by a band of roughs in Toma's pay and thrown into the neighbouring river.

Sc. 2. *The opposite bank of the river.* Genjiro creeps out of the water more dead than alive and is helped by a kindly passer-by who takes him into his care.

Act IV

The woods outside the village of Tengajaya, near Osaka. Somenoi has served her time in the licensed quarter. She, Genjiro, and Hazue (now Genjiro's wife), supported by **Kouemon,** a brave merchant who has taken pity on them, arrive by the *hanamichi* and explain that they have learnt that Toma, now the holder of a high office under the government, is to pass through Tengajaya that day. Dressed in pilgrim white, they ask permission of the local governor, **Akashi Kamon,** to carry out their vendetta. It is granted. Toma and Motoemon appear. The latter is quickly overpowered by Kouemon and bound to a signpost. Toma faces the three others, is struck down, and stabbed to death by them all. Motoemon is released and at first begs abjectly for mercy. Then he treacherously tries to kill Genjiro, but is borne down and put to death.

KICHISAMA MAIRU YUKARI NO OTOZURE (*Ki-chi's Strange Homecoming*). *Sewamono.* — This play is based on an incident in a novel by Kawatake Mokuami. The hero is a young samurai, the heir to a large estate, but he is something of a lay-figure, for Mokuami's genius does not lie in the portrayal of virtuous young men. The most vivid characters are a parcel of disreputable scoundrels who become indirectly involved in the drama. It is upon their story that the play is based.

On the death of his father, **Kobori Samonnosuke** becomes head of his house and heir to great wealth. But, since he is still a minor, the estate is administered by his uncle, **Yaheiji,** who stands next in the succession. As the time approaches when his nephew will be of age and he will have to hand over the estate to him, Yaheiji begins to think how convenient it would be if the young man were to die. He therefore decides to starve him to death and imprisons him in a stone-built storehouse. One winter night **O Sugi,** a maid-in-waiting who loves her young lord, secures possession of the keys and releases Samonnosuke, who is smuggled out of the mansion. By ill luck O Sugi drops a hair ornament near the storehouse which is found by **Kyusuke,** one of Yaheiji's retainers. O Sugi is tortured in order to make her confess Samonnosuke's whereabouts. She commits suicide to prevent herself betraying him. Yaheiji and his henchmen find themselves in an awkward situation with a corpse on their hands of which they do not know how to dispose.

Yaheiji has taken as his concubine a girl named **O Mitsu.** O Mitsu loathes Yaheiji, but was forced to enter his household by her brother, a disreputable priest named **Benshu.** She is in love with one of Benshu's friends, **Kichisaburo (Kichisa** for short) who earns his living by selling shrouds and by other less reputable means. Benshu has on more than one occasion been of service to Yaheiji, and it is to him the latter now entrusts the business of getting rid of O Sugi's body, paying him fifty *ryo* for the job. Meanwhile O Mitsu has told Kichisa the whole story including her brother's part in it and the amount of money he is being paid for disposing of O Sugi's body. Benshu, who knows nothing of all this, decides that the best way of disposing of the corpse is to have it cremated under a false name. To do this he must have a proper cremation permit, a wooden ticket issued by a temple. He decides that the best person to procure this for him is Kichisa since, being a dealer in shrouds, he has access to the office inside the temple precincts where the tickets are sold.

Act I

Sc. 1. *Before the gate of the Ryonen-ji, Edo.* Benshu meets Kichisa and puts the problem to him, offering, with a great show of generosity, to pay him ten *ryo* for the ticket. Kichisa appears to consider the matter and then demands twenty-five *ryo* for such a difficult task. Benshu declares he could not possibly lay hands on so large a sum, but Kichisa points out to him that he happens to know that Benshu is getting fifty; it is half and half or nothing doing. Benshu threatens to expose Kichisa's relations with O Mitsu, but Kichisa retorts that this is more likely to damage Benshu and his family than himself. After a good deal of wrangling, Benshu is forced to accept Kichisa's terms, for he knows of no one else who can get him the ticket. Benshu retires, grumbling, and Kichisa goes off on his errand.

Sc. 2. *The priests' quarters in the Temple.* In the back premises **O Tora,** a low class servant, is complaining to one of the priests, who is her lover, that the cremation ticket he sold her is not properly made out ; it is for a woman instead of a man. She produces the ticket, attached to the white cloth which is placed over the burial-tub before the last rites, and the two quarrel about it. Kichisa arrives at the back door and hears the argument. He sees in it an opportunity to get hold of the necessary ticket without having to bribe the priest. He comes in, asks what the trouble is, and, when the matter is explained to him, observes that the ticket can easily be altered without anyone being the wiser. He sends the two away to make up their tiff over a cup of *sake* and then picks up the cloth with the ticket and makes off.

Sc. 3. *Outside the temple walls.* Benshu and Kyusuke, with the burial-tub, are waiting impatiently for Kichisa. They are relieved when he appears with the necessary permit. The white cloth is draped over the tub with the ticket on top and Benshu sends Kyusuke off to arrange for the cremation as quickly as possible. He is about to follow him when Kichisa calls him back, demanding his fee. Benshu starts to prevaricate and refuses to pay the twenty-five *ryo,* going back to his first offer of ten. Now that he has the cremation ticket in his possession he feels on safe ground. But Kichisa stands firm, telling Benshu that if he does not pay up — and, upon reflexion, Kichisa has now decided to raise his fee to forty *ryo* — he will go straight to the police with the whole story. He emphasizes that he has nothing to fear since there is nothing to link him with the permit. Benshu becomes frightened and angry, and eventually, since Kichisa will only answer " Forty *ryo* " to all his threats and cajolings, he is forced to hand over the money. Kichisa counts it with great deliberation while Benshu goes off vowing to get even with him. As he reaches the *hanamichi* Kichisa calls after him ironically : " Benshu ! Forgive me for causing you so much trouble." (*Benshu ! Go-kuro !*)

Between the first and second acts there is a considerable lapse of time. Young Samonnosuke comes out of hiding and obtains redress. His uncle's plot against his life and the torture and death of O Sugi are exposed. Yaheiji commits

suicide and all those concerned in his crime, including
Benshu and Kichisa, are wanted by the police. Yaheiji's
household is dispersed, and O Mitsu, who has lost touch
with both Kichisa and her brother, disappears into the
underworld.

Act II

Sc. 1. *A greengrocer's shop in Hongo, Edo.* The owner of
this shop is a worthy old man named **Kyushiro** who has
an attractive only daughter, **O Shichi.** It was here that Samonnosuke was concealed when he fled from his uncle, and
he and O Shichi have, unknown to her father, fallen in love.
Before she knew the real identity of her lover, O Shichi
hoped to marry him, but now that he is revealed to be a
great lord and has returned to his proper sphere she does
not expect ever to see him again. It is summer. The scene
opens to show the front of the greengrocery, facing onto the
street. Kyushiro's servant and apprentices are in charge.
Presently a young samurai approaches, wearing a wicker
travelling hat. He calls the maidservant out to him and
reveals himself to be Samonnosuke. The maid smuggles him
through the garden to the back of the house where O Shichi
is. Evening is falling, the apprentices have gone off, and the
shop is empty. Kichisa, who is in hiding from the police
and intends to leave Edo as soon as he can, comes cautiously
to the entrance. The forty *ryo* are long since vanished. He
must have money for his journey, and having heard that old
Kyushiro is prosperous, he intends to enter the house and
rob the till. He is about to do so when a sound from the
inner room disturbs him. He hides behind the vegetable
baskets as Kyushiro enters and settles down to his accounts.
The stage revolves.

Samonnosuke is seated in the inner room of the house,
where he is joined by O Shichi. The sight of him in his
fine clothes and with his two swords quite overcomes her;
he seems like another person. He assures her that his love
for her has not changed, and they renew their vows. O Shichi realizes that he can never marry her, but for a girl of her
class to become a concubine in a great lord's house is no
disgrace. Samonnosuke leaves promising to visit her again
soon. His departure is hastened by a message to O Shichi
from her father saying that he wishes to speak to her. *The
stage revolves.*

O Shichi comes to her father in the shop, where he has now finished with his books. Kyushiro tells O Shichi that, since she is his only child, he can have no secrets from her. He is in grave difficulties and needs her help. He speaks sadly of his son who was kidnapped as a child and never heard of again. O Shichi asks about her brother and what he was like, but Kyushiro, shaking his head, replies that, since he was hardly more than an infant when he disappeared and now must be twenty-four, it is impossible to say what sort of a man he has become, if indeed he is still alive. Probably the only way he, his own father, would be able to recognize him is by the curious mole on his left fore-arm. He returns to the subject of his difficulties and explains to O Shichi that he owes a certain **Kamaya Buhei** the sum of a hundred *ryo* which he cannot repay. Buhei is, however, prepared to take O Shichi as his wife and cancel the debt. O Shichi is compelled by her duty to her father to consent to the proposal, but when Kyushiro leaves the room she breaks down and weeps bitterly. She cannot bear to give up Samonnosuke to become the wife of an old man like Buhei; she would rather die. She writes a letter to her father explaining everything and begging his forgiveness. Then she takes the knife from her writing-box and is about to kill herself when Kichisa leaps out from among the vegetable baskets and prevents her. The sound of voices and of a struggle brings Kyushiro from the next room with the maid-servant at his heels. Kyushiro thanks the stranger repeatedly for saving his daughter. Kichisa appears almost as greatly upset as the old man and, when Kyushiro tries to reward him with a gift of money, refuses it brusquely and tells him that he came to the house to steal. Kyushiro is taken aback and questions the young man about himself, but, beyond eliciting that he is about twenty-four years old, receives only evasive answers. Prompted by the maid-servant, O Shichi thanks Kichisa for his intervention, addressing him naively as " Mr. Thief " and commenting that she never thought robbers looked like that. Kichisa prepares to leave, startling the family still further by undertaking to put into Kyushiro's hands next day the hundred *ryo* he needs to pay his debt. Kichisa accidentally uncovers his left fore-arm, and upon it the old man sees the mole which he recognizes. Kichisa rushes from the house before anyone can stop him, ashamed that his father and sister should know that he has fallen so low.

Sc. 2. *Outside the Tennin-ko incense shop in Koishikawa, Edo.* It is raining. Kamaya Buhei, O Shichi's suitor, is walking home late in the evening. He is accosted by a young woman who asks to share his umbrella. She is O Mitsu, who has changed her name to O Kan and serves as a courtesan at the Yushima house of assignment. She has quarrelled with her employers and wants to escape from Edo. She realizes from his conversation that Buhei is well off and, taking him unawares, she succeeds in winding him and knocking him out so that she may steal his purse. Out of the darkness a voice calls to her from the roof above. O Kan is frightened, but her fear turns to joy when the owner of the voice reveals himself to be her lover. Kichisa has just robbed the incense shop and has the hundred *ryo* he needs for his father. He and O Kan report all that has happened since they last saw each other and plan to escape together. Kichisa climbs down from the roof by way of the waterbutt, but as he jumps to the ground the package containing the hundred *ryo* falls out of the front of his *kimono*. At that moment Benshu, who is of course also on the run, comes round the corner of the house and hears Kichisa tell O Kan what has happened. He recognizes their voices. The three all start searching in the darkness for the money. Benshu comes on it, but at the same time runs into Kichisa who realizes that there is a third person present. He recognizes Benshu who escapes from him and runs off. Kichisa sets out in pursuit, O Kan following. As they go, the alarm is given inside the shop and the apprentices rush out searching for the thief. They find Buhei and beat him up, thinking he must be their man.

Sc. 3. *The approach to the Suidobashi in Koishikawa.* Here by the outer moat of the city Kichisa catches up with Benshu. Since the money is for his father, Kichisa is determined to get it back without blood-shed, if possible. He explains to Benshu why he needs the sum and asks him to return it. Benshu answers that he intends to keep the money as compensation for the forty *ryo* Kichisa had off him for the cremation ticket. Kichisa tries to persuade him by appealing to his better feelings, but Benshu, taking advantage of the darkness, puts some stones in his *tenugui* and, while Kichisa is arguing, strikes him on the head. Kichisa is not stunned and, controlling his temper, makes one more appeal to Benshu, the blood streaming down his face. Benshu whips out his knife and attacks him. He and Benshu fight desperately in the darkness.

Here the play ends. Kichisa kills Benshu and recovers the money. He succeeds in sending it to his father and he and O Kan are about to escape from Edo when they are caught by the police.

KIICHI HOGEN SANRYAKU NO MAKI (*Kiichi Hogen's Book of Tactics*). *Jidaimono* of the Heike-Genji Cycle (see page 418). — Written for the puppets by Bunkodo, Hasegawa Senshi and their assistants. First staged in 1731. The original play was in five acts, but of these only two are still performed. The plot is set in the period when the Genji clan was proscribed and the Heike in power. Both the surviving acts deal with the stratagems employed by the secret adherents of the Genji. **Minamoto Yoshitsune** appears as a young boy, newly escaped from Heike tutelage. He is still called by his "boy's name," **Ushiwakamaru,** and wears the boy's long front lock of hair. His mother, the beautiful **Tokiwa Gozen,** is for the sake of the plot, married to a supposed half-wit. (According to the authorities, when **Taira Kiyomori** cast her off, she became the wife of a Fujiwara nobleman who was Kiyomori's Minister of Finance). Two of the band of followers who remained with Yoshitsune throughout his life appear as the principal Genji agents engaged in the stealthy co-ordination of the clan's reviving strength. They are the brothers **Yoshioka Kijiro** and **Yoshioka Kisanta.**

Act III

The tale of Okura Ichijo (Okura Ichijo Monogatari). **Okura Ichijo Nagashige** is believed to be feeble-minded. Although of a family which in the past supported the Genji faction, he is unmolested during the Heike domination. Taira Kiyomori even decides that he is so harmless that he will make a suitable second husband for Tokiwa, widow of Minamoto Yoshito and mother of three of his four surviving sons. The youngest of these sons, Ushiwakamaru (Yoshitsune) has escaped from the Taira and is somewhere in hiding. Kiyomori is not particularly troubled by this, since Ushiwakamaru is still only a boy and, in any case, he holds not only Tokiwa Gozen's other two sons, but, far more important, their elder half-brother, Yoritomo, the heir to the Minamoto honours. The latter seems perfectly content to live in comfortable exile in Izu.

Yoritomo is not as idle as he seems, however, and young Ushiwakamaru has gathered a band of followers whose object is to organize Genji resistance. Okura Ichijo has in his possession a sword, a Minamoto heirloom, which, in the hands of Ushiwakamaru, would strengthen his position with the clan. Ushiwakamaru decides to send Yoshioka Kijiro to ask Tokiwa Gozen to obtain it from her husband.

Kijiro, although realizing the importance of the mission, is prejudiced against Tokiwa Gozen from the outset. For a widow to marry again is considered, in Japan, a shameful breach of faith. Tokiwa Gozen has not scrupled to save the lives of her parents and children by becoming Kiyomori's concubine. Kijiro feels that the least she should do is to kill herself or retire to a nunnery. Instead of which she lives in comfortable splendour under the hated Taira's wing.

Kijiro and his wife, **O Kyo,** come secretly by night to Okura Ichijo's palace. They make their way to Tokiwa Gozen's apartments and are scandalized to find her not, as she ought to be, praying for the unfortunate Genji, but amusing herself by practising archery. Kijiro is so filled with indignation that he forgets his mission. Accusing her of treachery to his lord, he rushes upon her with intent to kill. But Tokiwa Gozen, with great dignity, tells him he is mistaken. Taking an arrow, she throws it at the target set up across the room. The outer covering falls. Beneath it there is a portrait of Kiyomori, pierced by her arrow. She explains that as she shoots each arrow, she curses Kiyomori and prays for his downfall. As she speaks, a man bursts into the room crying that he has heard their treasonable talk and, tearing down the disfigured portrait, declares that he will show it to Kiyomori himself. This is **Yatsurugi Kageru,** ostensibly one of Okura's retainers, but, in fact, a spy placed in the household to watch Tokiwa Gozen. He is followed, as a witness, by his wife. Before he can leave with this incriminating evidence and Kijiro can make a move to prevent him, the curtain of the inner room falls and

Okura Ichijo, a lacquer case in his hand, stands before them.

Okura Ichijo performs a piece of elaborate mime to illustrate his madness. Then his whole expression changes. He is no longer deranged, but a man of noble aspect and serious purpose. He draws towards him the case and takes from it the precious sword. Solemnly he entrusts it to Kijiro, who receives it with joy and respect. (Okura Ichijo's change from madness to sanity is indicated not only by his expression, but by an elaborate change of costume, called *hikinuki*, see page 426). Up to this point Kageru has regarded Okura's actions as all part of his lunacy. He thinks it useless to say anything to the poor creature about his wife's conduct and is waiting for him to withdraw so that he can make off with the evidence. He cannot leave the presence of his lord without permission, nor can Kijiro attack him. It now occurs to him that he is witnessing not the irresponsible mouthings of a half-wit, but a most cunning act of treason. Looking into Okura's face, he sees that here Kiyomori has an enemy as dangerous as he is unexpected. He tries to run from the room, but, striking like a snake, Okura Ichijo seizes a halberd and runs him through. Okura solemnly declares that he has vowed to be revenged upon Kiyomori and commends Tokiwa Gozen for her patience and fidelity. It is to bring about the restoration of the Genji to power that she consented to become his wife. But, although one spy is dead, there may be others. He dare not for long reveal his true nature. He pretends to have killed Kageru accidentally in a fit of madness, and, slashing off the spy's head with his sword, he sits playing with it in his arms, laughing idiotically, as the curtain is drawn.

Act V

The Chrysanthemum Garden (Kikubatake). **Yoshioka Kiichi Hogen,** although belonging to a family which had served the Genji for many generations, quarrelled with his father when he was little more than a boy and ran away from home. He took service with the Heike and, when the two clans came into conflict, fought on their side. He became a successful general and a noted strategist but, because of his Genji connections, never received from Taira Kiyomori the recognition he considered his due. He retired into private life and spent his leisure hours composing the three-volume Book of

Tactics of which the play treats. As he grew older he came to regret that he had abandoned his ancient family allegiance. Rumours of activity among the Genji came to his ears, in which the names of his two young half-brothers played no small part. Meanwhile, **Ushiwakamaru** and the younger of Kiichi's two brothers, **Kisanta,** have heard of the distinguished old strategist and his Book of Tactics. They decide to take service in his household and, since Kiichi is believed to be out of favour with Taira Kiyomori, they hope they may persuade him to give them the benefit of his knowledge, together with the book. The book they are determined to have in any case, even if it means stealing it. Kisanta has no idea, of course, that Kiichi is his half-brother.

When the act opens, Kisanta, who goes by the name of Chienai and wears the livery of a servant, is found sweeping his master's garden. Or rather, he is sitting very comfortably on a bench shaving himself while the other servants do the work. The servants sense his superiority and are curious and resentful. They suggest he must be a dirty Genji spy and he thrashes them for their pains. A lady of Kiichi's household enters carrying a cushion. She tells Kisanta to prepare a suitable seat for her master, as he is coming to view the chrysanthemums. Kisanta prepares the seat and withdraws.

Kiichi and his attendants arrive by the *hanamichi*. He inspects the flowers closely and says a word of praise to Kisanta whom he summons. He sits down and begins to ask his new man servant about himself. When Kisanta mentions the name of his province, Kiichi tells him that he also comes from that province and adds some details of his own youth. During the ensuing conversation it becomes clear that Kiichi realizes Kisanta's identity and purpose. He suggests in veiled terms that he is prepared to give his book to a worthy Genji leader, but, although he has suspicions, he is not yet sure of the identity of his other new servant, the boy who goes by the name of Torazo. Kisanta, while understanding the trend of Kiichi's remarks, is far too cautious to commit either himself or his young lord. He still has no idea that Kiichi is his brother, in spite of the various hints thrown out. Kiichi is afraid that the young man's manner might give him away, in which case he himself would have no alternative but to arrest him as a spy.

Ushiwakamaru returns from an errand of some delicacy to

Taira Kiyomori. Kiyomori has expressed a great desire to see the famous Book of Tactics. Kiichi, knowing that, once it got into the Taira's hands, it would be lost forever, has sent his daughter, **Minazuru-hime,** escorted by Ushiwakamaru, to explain that the book is not immediately available. They have failed in their mission of appeasement, for Ushiwakamaru reports that Kiyomori is angry. He sends word to Kiichi that the book must be in his hands next day without fail. Further, adds Ushiwakamaru in a clear voice, since Kiichi is closely related to the rebels Yoshioka Kijiro and Yoshioka Kisanta, he is suspect and Kiyomori is sending a representative to enquire into his conduct. Kiichi sees the crisis looming ahead faster than he expected and decides to find out at once whether this boy is in fact the young Minamoto Prince. He pretends to be angry with "Torazo" for bungling his errand and, throwing his staff to Kisanta, tells him to give the lad a good beating. Kisanta has now realized that the "two young brothers" to whom Kiichi has referred so pointedly must be Kijiro and himself. He momentarily forgets his rôle and his face betrays the indignation he feels at being given such an order. He quickly grasps the stick and raises it. But his natural instincts are too strong for him. He cannot bring himself to strike his lord. Kiichi, now certain of the identity of "Torazo" and anxious to allay any suspicions which Kisanta's behaviour may have aroused in the rest of the household, pretends to be in a great passion. Seizing the stick from Kisanta, he is about to beat Ushiwakamaru himself. At that moment his daughter returns and, catching hold of his raised arm, begs him on her knees to spare the boy. Her father is glad to have a good excuse to do so and allows himself to be persuaded, although for the benefit of the other servants, he angrily dismisses the two young men.

Kiyomori's representative, **Kasahara Tankai,** is seen approaching majestically along the *hanamichi*. He has come to examine Kiichi and take charge of the Book of Tactics. Kiichi receives him with courtesy. Tankai is much struck with the charms of Minazuru-hime and so far forgets his mission as to attempt some ill-judged gallantries. Kiichi does not discourage him, since, if he is paying attention to Minazuru-hime, he is the less likely to look closely at the two men-servants bowing respectfully in the background.

Indeed, Kiichi begins to wonder whether he might not use his daughter as the means of saving not only Ushiwakamaru, but the Book of Tactics as well. He ushers Tankai affably into the house and drags the unwilling girl after him.

Left alone, the young men are despondent. The Book of Tactics appears to be lost to them for ever, and, although Kiichi's public dismissal of them gives them a good reason to disappear, they are loth to leave the old man and his daughter in Kiyomori's clutches. Suddenly Kisanta has an idea. He proposes to Ushiwakamaru that they steal the precious book. Kiichi will not then be implicated in any way, particularly as his household can bear witness that he was on bad terms with both of them. If, however, Tankai is not prepared to swallow this story, they will kill him and carry off Kiichi and Minazuru-hime to a place of safety.

Ushiwakamaru agrees to this plan and they are about to put it into execution when Minazuru-hime returns to the garden. Ushiwakamaru is angry at this interruption and sits down with his back to her. Minazuru-hime puts a different interpretation on his action. She herself has fallen in love with him and now proceeds coyly to declare her love by means of a conversation full of double meanings carried on with Kisanta, but directed at Ushiwakamaru. Kisanta is at first mystified by her allusions and then amused to find that she intends him to act as go-between. The young lady picks a chrysanthemum and asks Kisanta to offer it to "Torazo." The prince, preoccupied with other matters and, in any case, not yet of an age to enjoy flirtation, refuses the flower flatly, even when Minazuru-hime offers it herself. Determined to shock him out of his indifference, she throws discretion to the winds and tells the two young men that she has guessed who they are, naming them aloud. Kisanta's first instinct is to seize and kill her, lest she betray their secret. But as he moves, the gate is flung open and Tankai strides out, crying that he has overheard the girl and now knows who they are. Even as he speaks, Ushiwakamaru has drawn his sword and, before Tankai can lay his hand on the hilt of his own weapon, the boy cuts him down. Kisanta triumphantly wipes his lord's blade.

Ushiwakamaru tells Minazuru-hime that she has nothing to fear and charges Kisanta to take her and her father to a place of safety. The girl directs his attention to the open door of the house. There on the threshold of the inner room her father waits to place in the hands of his true lord the precious Book of Tactics.

KIWAMETSUKI BANZUIN CHOBEI (*The Last Days of Chobei of Banzuin*). *Sewamono.* — Written by Kawatake Mokuami. First staged 1882. Chobei of Banzuin was a famous historical character who flourished during the Edo period. He was an *otokodate* (see page 448 and Mitford's *Tales of Old Japan*). He figures in many stories, notably those of Shirai Gompachi and Nagoya Sanza. Though powerful and well-loved, he had many enemies, chiefly among the *hatamoto* lords (see page 455) and more especially in Mizuro **Jurozaemon,** Kondo **Noborinosuke,** and Abe Shirogoro. The first never forgave him for a piece of magnificent impertinence on the occasion of their first meeting, but was not for many years able to achieve his revenge.

The present play is a somewhat fanciful version of Chobei's end.

Act I

The Murayama Theatre in Negi Street. A performance is in progress on an old fashioned stage, modelled on the Noh stage, with four pillars, a tiled roof, a *hashigakari*, and a row of kneeling musicians at the back. The play is taken from the Genji legends. The youthful Minamoto Yoriyoshi and his wife are in conversation with the saintly Abbot Higashi-yama Manryo when they are interrupted by the entrance of the popular hero, Sakata Hyogonosuke Kimpira, who blus-ters and storms and beats the old priest over the head with his own rosary. The acting is burlesque of the best kind.

Suddenly a drunken servant causes an uproar in the theatre. The play stops, but goes on when one of the assistant stage-managers has bundled the drunkard uncere-moniously out into the street. Soon afterwards an upper servant of the same house (which is now seen to be Jurozae-mon's) enters along the *hanamichi* and demands an apology with drawn sword. The actors cower back, particularly the rumbustious Kimpira, and the priest falls to telling his beads. No one has the courage to face the naked blade. A mod-estly dressed commoner climbs onto the stage, crosses to the *hanamichi* and with the skill of a trained swordsman disarms

the intruder, throws him to the ground and holds him down.
It is Chobei. The servant, thus discomfitted, withdraws,
muttering dark threats. Amid the applause of the audience
and the thanks of the actors Chobei returns to his place. But
as he passes one of the curtained boxes from where the samurai
used (illegally, but with impunity) to watch Kabuki performances, the bamboo screen falls, revealing Jurozaemon livid
with rage and glowering on Chobei.

Act II

Chobei's house in Asakusa. A few days later. The apprentices are sitting round gossiping, their day's work done.
One of them, **Detchiri Seibei,** relates the happenings at
the Murayama theatre. Chobei's wife, **O Toki,** listens with
misgiving. When Chobei enters, he chides them for their
idle talk and sends them about their business. A visitor
approaches along the *hanamichi*. It is **Hosho Mushanosuke,** one of Jurozaemon's henchmen. Though usually blus-
tering in manner, he has no stomach for the present job,
which involves entering the house of his lord's enemy. He
is, however, courteously received and delivers his message,
which is that Jurozaemon invites Chobei to dine with him
that night. With little hesitation, though he guesses that
some treachery is afoot, Chobei accepts. Mushanosuke
retires, overjoyed at the apparent success of the plot. Chobei
is in a cleft stick. After the rebuke he has administered to
Jurozaemon, he will lose face if he refuses the invitation. He
must go to prove his courage. At the *hatamoto's* house, he
will either be killed by treachery or he will kill Jurozaemon ;
in either case his life will be forfeit. His wife and his apprentices, headed by the faithful **Token Gombei,** seek to dissuade him. After all, nobody doubts his courage, why
sacrifice himself uselessly? But that is not the point. Chobei cannot himself act below the standards he has set. And
he might kill a villain in the *mêlée*. He dresses himself for
a formal party, takes leave of his wife, his son **Chomatsu,**
and his apprentices, telling Token Gombei to send a burying
tub round to Jurozaemon's house on the morrow, and strides
away down the *hanamichi*.

Act III

Sc. 1. *The reception room of Jurozaemon's house in Kojima-
chi.* The retainers are preparing for Chobei's reception. An
atmosphere of nervous hilarity prevails. Chobei is shown

in, and Jurozaemon enters. A cup of wine is offered. Chobei is asked and agrees to show a few feats of swordsmanship. A clumsy maidservant spills *sake* on his clothes. He is offered a bath and change of raiment. He demurs, hinting that nakedness is a poor defence. Jurozaemon enquires who would possibly wish him ill in his house. (The audience, if a good one, should here yell the name of the actor playing Hosho). Chobei sees no escape and agrees. *The stage revolves.*

Sc. 2. *The bathroom.* Chobei, wearing only a *yukata* (see page 409), is ushered in by the servants and all the usual preparations for bathing are made. Suddenly Jurozaemon appears, armed with a spear. Chobei defends himself with the wooden handle of a water-ladle. He is borne down by half a dozen servants, but disposes of them one after the other. Finally Noborinosuke enters and strikes him down from behind with a sword.

(There is some historical evidence for this story. It seems probable however, that Chobei's death was less heroic. He was lured into the bathroom and there imprisoned. The bath water was heated from outside until he could no longer sit in it — and so enjoy the protection of the metal tub — and, when he stepped out of it, spears were driven through the thin walls of the room until he was unable to evade them any longer and so died in great agony. When Gombei arrived next day to claim the corpse, his murderers could not help but express admiration at this proof of Chobei's cold courage. Chomatsu and the apprentices tried valiantly to be revenged on Jurozaemon, but the matter was taken out of their hands by the treacherous lord himself who, falling foul of the authorities, was forced to flee and take his own life in the temple called Kaneiji at Ueno.)

KOI HAKKE HASHIRAGOYOMI (*The Almanack of Love*), commonly called *O San Mohei. Sewamono.* — Written for the puppets by Chikamatsu Monzaemon during the period of his association with Gidayu (1705—1714), it has suffered many changes since its adoption by the Kabuki theatre, and it is quite usual to play only excerpts from the original. The following account therefore must be read with this important reservation in mind. The theme of the play is how two morally innocent young people can be caught in a cruel net of circumstances not of their own making.

Act I

The House of Ishun, the Almanack Publisher, at Karasumaru in Kyoto.

Sc. 1. *The principal room of the house.* It is November 1st, the day on which the New Year's almanacks are being distributed. **Ishun** has returned from calling at the Imperial Court and the houses of the princes and nobles. He has accepted much hospitality and now is sleeping off its effects. The chief clerk, **Sukeyemon,** is in charge. He is a mean type, domineering and envious. He chides **O San,** Ishun's pretty young wife, abuses the maid, **O Tama,** threatens what he will do to the clerk **Mohei** when the latter returns, and finally goes off to deliver almanacks. In a charming dialogue, O San reveals to O Tama that she is not happy in her married life, and the maid discloses that she is in love with Mohei. O San leaves the room. Ishun awakes and makes advances to O Tama. The situation is saved by the arrival of O San's mother to offer her congratulations on the firm's most important day of the year. Ishun retires to the inner room, and O San joins her mother. Mohei enters accompanied by a servant. He too has been distributing almanacks and is tired and a little bemused with *sake*. O San calls to him and confides to him that her father is in financial difficulties as a result of having mortgaged his house to two different creditors. A settlement is in sight, however, if only he can lay hands on fifteen *ryo* by the end of the month. O San says she has been forbidden to speak to her husband; Sukeyemon is too proud and suspicious; and, in short, she looks to Mohei for help. The clerk (who is respectfully in love with his mistress and in whom the *sake* is still working encouragingly) offers to obtain the necessary funds on his master's credit. He has Ishun's seals and can at once draw a bill of exchange. O San goes out to tell her mother this good news. Mohei is surprised in the act of making out the bill by Sukeyemon who rouses the household. Mohei refuses to divulge the reason for his attempted embezzlement despite threats and abuse. O San returns and is trying to screw up her courage to confess her part in the affair when O Tama comes forward and pretends that the " loan " was being made on her behalf. While this relieves O San, it infuriates Ishun, who, having at first been sceptical of Suke-yemon's charges, now turns against Mohei and orders him to be locked up until the morrow. Begging O San's mother to stay with her, he goes out with his servant, ostensibly to visit his father-in-law, saying he will return late.

Sc. 2. *O Tama's bedroom, near the kitchen. Midnight.* O San enters and finds O Tama still awake. She thanks her for her help and asks how she knows that her mistress is in trouble. O Tama confesses that she acted solely out of love for Mohei whom she hopes to put under an obligation to herself. She goes on to tell O San of Ishun's advances. She is lying awake because she is afraid he will come home presently and pester her. O San decides to teach her husband a lesson. She persuades O Tama to change places with her; if Ishun comes to O Tama's room, he will be received and unmasked by his wife. In the meantime, Mohei has broken out of confinement and thinking to thank O Tama, of whose devotion he has plentiful evidence, steals to her bedroom. This may be his last night on earth and the least he can do is to try to repay O Tama's kindness by making her happy for once. He is received by O San who thinks it is Ishun and returns his endearments. They are interrupted by the noisy return of the master of the house. "What! Is it O San-sama?" "What! Are you Mohei?"

Act II

A cottage at Okazaki, near Kyoto. *Some days later.* O Tama's uncle, **Akamatsu Bairyu,** a *ronin,* makes a living by reciting heroic ballads. The scene opens with a group of townsmen applauding the end of such a recital. They disperse, gossiping. A palanquin is carried in, followed by Sukeyemon, who beats on Bairyu's door and offensively tells him to open. Bairyu appears. Sukeyemon says that he has brought O Tama home. She is to remain in her uncle's charge until O San and Mohei, who have eloped, have been captured, brought to justice, and executed. For her suspected part in the intrigue O Tama may well lose her head too. Bairyu protests vehemently at Sukeyemon's manner and requires that his niece be handed over with proper ceremony. O Tama, bound, is dragged from the palanquin. She protests her innocence and charges Sukeyemon with being in love with O San. It is his jealousy that has magnified the present incident into a crime. Bairyu is incensed at finding O Tama bound and beats Sukeyemon with the pole of the palanquin. He forces him to release the girl, takes her into his house, and slams the door. Sukeyemon, muttering revenge, is carried away in the palanquin.

Act III

Travel-Dance (Michiyuki). O San and Mohei, moving as in a dream, have wandered far and wide and at last find themselves in Okazaki. O San is worried about O Tama's fate and what her parents think. Mohei admits that he has brought her here on purpose to learn what they can from Bairyu. They listen at the door and hear Bairyu reciting heroic verse. He is in fact advising O Tama to have nothing to do with O San and Mohei if they should come to her for help. It will only give substance to the rumour that she has been the lovers' go-between. The only kindness she can show them is to be harsh to them. O Tama agrees, despite her love for Mohei and her affection for her mistress. The lovers listen and weep. At this moment O San's parents, **Dojun** and his wife, pass by. O San throws herself at their feet. Dojun angrily denies her, rebuking her for lingering near the scene of her crime. O San protests her innocence and declares her readiness to die, now that she has seen her parents once more. Her mother gives her money and begs her to leave the neighbourhood, sparing them the knowledge of her death. Mohei offers to shoulder all the blame if only O San's parents will take back their daughter. O San loyally refuses to desert him. They decide to flee to Mohei's native village in Tamba province. The moon rises as the lovers and the old people take leave of each other. Dojun bids Mohei look after his daughter. They part as the temple bell tolls.

Act IV

Kaibara Village in Tamba Province. It is spring. Some comic dancers perform before the cottage where O San and Mohei are living. Their leader remembers seeing her in Kyoto, and she is forced to bribe him to keep quiet. Mohei returns and tells her that he has heard that Sukeyemon is on their track and is combing the neighbourhood. They decide to flee at once, as soon as Mohei can recover a sum of money he left with their landlord for safekeeping. The landlord, when asked to repay the sum, refuses, saying it is lent out on interest. Their urgent pleadings make him suspicious. He leaves the house ostensibly to try to recover the money, but returns soon afterwards with the police. The lovers submit to arrest with dignity. Sukeyemon appears and presumes to give orders to the officers about their prisoners. The police speak roughly to him. Bairyu arrives to testify to the lovers' innocence. He says that the whole trouble has been caused by his niece's indiscretion. He has punished her, and produces her head in evidence. The chief of police declares that Bairyu's rashness in removing a material witness may well cost the lovers their lives. He bids his men convey them to Kyoto. Bairyu tries to kill Sukeyemon so that he may die with the lovers. Weeping, O San and Mohei ride to their doom. *The stage revolves.*

A road leading to the execution ground. A crowd of spectators is gathered. The lovers arrive, bound. O San's parents offer themselves in her place, but their plea is rejected. The priest **Togan** of the Kurodani Temple intercedes for the prisoners. Although his authority is great, the police officers are unbending. Finally Togan prevails and claims O San and Mohei as his disciples. The crowd is sympathetic, and the lovers are released and placed in Togan's charge, to spend the rest of their lives in holy orders making atonement for their unwitting sin.

(In another version, the lovers are executed. In yet a third, they evade arrest and, after Mohei has settled accounts with Sukeyemon, commit suicide together.)

KOI HIKYAKU YAMATO ORAI (*Love's Messenger on the Yamato Road*), commonly called *Umegawa-Chubei*, or *Ume-Chu. Sewamono.* — The original puppet play, *Meido no Hikyaku* (*The Messenger from Hell*), was written by Chikamatsu Monzaemon, probably in 1706, during the period of his association with Gidayu (1705—1714). It is still performed by both the puppet theatre and the Kabuki. A number of versions exist, some stopping short at the flight of the lovers, others adhering to the original tragic climax. The adaptation used on the Kabuki stage is by Suna Senusuke. He makes the character of the hero, Chubei, less weak and more sympathetic than it is in the original and supplies the play with a villain, thus bringing it more closely

in line with the conventional type of "double suicide."

Chubei is a young man, who, with all the advantages, takes the wrong turning. He is the son of a well-to-do farmer who has given him a fair portion. He has been adopted into a prosperous express agency business as the heir to the owner, the widow **Myokan.** (The play, incidentally, throws an interesting light on the system of financing commercial exchanges in early eighteenth-century Japan.) He has been to Edo on several occasions. He is adept in the tea-ceremony, a poet and calligrapher, handsome, and able to carry his liquor. But, to belong to the *jeunesse dorée* of Osaka means cutting a figure in the licensed quarter of Shimmachi and this proves to be Chubei's downfall.

Act I

The Courtesans' House in Shimmachi (Aneya no Ba).

A room in the Izutsuya tea-house in Shimmachi, owned by **Tsuchiya Jiyemon.** A servant is preparing the room for a wealthy client. Voices are heard outside greeting this guest, who enters with a party of friends. **O En,** the tea-house mistress, summons **Umegawa,** the courtesan they have bespoken. She makes an excuse not to accompany the party immediately to their private room upstairs and, when they have gone, confesses the reason to O En. Until a few days ago she was happy because her lover Chubei had promised to ransom her and had paid the first deposit. But he had been unable to raise the balance and the date fixed for the final payment expired yesterday. Consequently, Chubei's chief rival and enemy, **Hachiemon,** now proposes to ransom her out of spite. O En remarks sympathetically that she has heard Chubei's adopted mother keeps him short of money and Umegawa voices a fear that he may be tempted to commit some folly. She has not seen him for ten days and has sent him word to come secretly this evening, but has had no answer.

While the two women are talking, Chubei comes along the *hanamichi.* He confesses he cannot raise the money to ransom Umegawa ; it would be better for her if he gave her up so that she might be happy with someone else. Yet if Hachiemon ransoms her, Chubei does not know how he can bear the insult to his manhood. He peeps into the house, unnoticed, and watches Umegawa, wondering jealously whether in these ten days she has changed and now prefers

Hachiemon. Perhaps she has sent for him merely to tell him so. This thought makes him turn to leave, but he stops again and returns to the gate, coughing to attract attention. Umegawa and O En hear him, but at that moment a servant comes to fetch Umegawa, saying her client is impatient. Hearing this, Chubei hides himself. O En, to spare Umegawa, says that the courtesan is unwell and must rest a little in the inner room. Umegawa agrees readily and goes out, imploring O En with her eyes to go to the gate. As soon as she is alone, O En calls Chubei in and they whisper together. O En goes towards the inner room. *The stage revolves.*

The inner room facing the garden. Chubei enters from one side as O En, leading Umegawa, enters from the other. O En leaves them, reminding them to talk in low voices. During the tender little love-scene which follows Chubei confesses how ashamed he is that he has not been able to raise the ransom money and begs Umegawa not to hate him. She assures him that she will never change. (An incident which may be omitted : they are interrupted by the rich client upstairs who pushes open the window declaring he is drunk and must get a mouthful of water from somewhere. He drinks from a hanging bucket by the window, chokes, and spatters Umegawa and Chubei, who spring apart.) A moment later O En returns, bidding them separate. She whispers to Umegawa who smiles and whispers to Chubei. *The stage revolves.*

The outer room once more. Some time has passed. The wealthy client and his guests, all drunk, have come downstairs and are about to leave. They go off to have one last drink to fortify them on the road. Tsuchiya Jiyemon arrives, asking how business is and whether Umegawa is here. Umegawa and O En enter and he tells Umegawa that the affair of her ransom must be settled this evening once and for all. He knows Chubei is Umegawa's favourite, but he has failed to keep his undertaking and now it is her duty to agree to Hachiemon's offer. Umegawa implores him not to force her to accept Hachiemon since all the world knows he is Chubei's rival and she will appear heartless and fickle. She believes Chubei has now raised the money and if only Jiyemon will wait a few hours longer all will be well. Jiyemon, who is good-hearted, complains that Chubei has been making him lose money over Umegawa for the last four years, but he supposes that if she insists he will have to give way. He does not want to force her to take a man she hates. While Umegawa is thanking him, Jiyemon's creditor, **Yoshibei,** arrives, demanding the 100 ryo owed to him and reminding Jiyemon that he undertook to surrender one of his courtesans if he failed to honour the debt. When Jiyemon asks him to wait a few days longer, since Umegawa will shortly be ransomed, Yoshibei retorts that he prefers to take Umegawa himself. The argument is interrupted by Hachiemon, bringing the 250 ryo to ransom Umegawa. In spite of the difficulties in which he now finds himself, Jiyemon is true to his promise. He refuses to yield Umegawa to a man who, he says, has insulted him by not following the etiquette laid down for such transactions. Both Hachiemon and Yoshibei revile Jiyemon, while Umegawa weeps. Hachiemon abuses Chubei, asserting that he could never hope to raise 250 ryo honestly; even the deposit of 50 ryo which Chubei paid was stolen money, money sent from Edo to Hachiemon himself through Chubei's agency. O En loyally defends Chubei; Hachiemon says such things from jealousy because no one in the quarter cares for him, but even the kitchen-maids love Chubei.

Chubei has crept upstairs and now looks down on this scene from an upper window. He cannot bear to see Umegawa suffer. When Hachiemon accuses him of embezzling the money of his mother's firm, he puts his hand in his breast, remembering that he carries 300 ryo belonging to a client. He is tempted to make use of it to redeem Umegawa, but thrusts the idea from him.

Downstairs Hachiemon continues to speak ill of Chubei, prophesying that once he has taken the wrong turning he will come to a bad end. He advises Jiyemon to refuse the young man admittance; it is but a short step from theft to murder. Umegawa, in despair, longs for a sword to kill herself, rather than be forced to listen to such talk. Chubei can no longer resist the impulse of his heart. He rushes down, shouting to Hachiemon that he will make him eat his words. It is true that he once borrowed 50 ryo from him, but he can produce Hachiemon's receipt proving that he returned it in full. He shows the receipt to all the company, swearing that he would kill Hachiemon on the spot, if it would not be doing an ill turn to Jiyemon. His father, Chubei continues, is a wealthy farmer in Yamato and has recently sent him a gift of 300 *ryo*. He takes the paper-wrapped rolls of money from his breast. Hachiemon slaps down his 250 *ryo* with a sneer about farmer's money being nothing but pebbles. Chubei strikes him on the brow with a roll of gold pieces and the two quarrel noisily, Chubei, in his rage, beating on the floor with the money roll. Suddenly the seal on the paper breaks and the coins are scattered. Chubei stares at the gold, realizing fully for the first time the crime he is committing; then he bids Hachiemon look at it well and see for himself. Hachiemon bends over and, quickly picking up the wrapper with its seal, hides it in his sleeve. He again hints that Chubei, whose trade is to deal in other people's money, has turned thief and, with a crude gesture, threatens him with a halter. Chubei springs forward to attack him, but Hachiemon rises and leaves. At the gate he takes the sealed wrapper from his sleeve and examines it, well content.

Chubei pays Jiyemon the balance of 200 *ryo* required for Umegawa's ransom. He makes a present of 50 *ryo* to O En, thanking her for her kindness. O En joyfully sets about preparing the marriage feast, but Chubei stops her, asking

Chubei

her rather to hasten the formalities for Umegawa's release since they must leave at once. When they are alone, he bids Umegawa prepare for a long journey. In answer to her startled question he shows her the broken seal of the second roll of coins; saying that his head is forfeit, he asks whether she is willing to die with him. Umegawa replies that, since she is the cause of all his troubles, she is "not willing but joyful." All she stipulates is that she may be his wife for just three days. They decide to remain alive until their money is exhausted.

O En returns to say that everything is settled and they may leave the licensed quarter. As the two go out, Chubei distributes presents to the tea-house servants, asking them to "pray for us," but quickly correcting himself to "I mean, drink our health."

(The foregoing scene may be played somewhat differently according to the actor's taste. One popular version makes Hachiemon deliberately incite Chubei to break the seals. Chubei then ends the scene in panic.)

Act II

Ninokuchi Village (Ninokuchi Mura). A blue curtain conceals the stage, and before it the village headman discusses with some farmers the search being made for a runaway couple. As they leave, Chubei and Umegawa enter by the *hanamichi.* The curtain falls to reveal the village street, under heavy snow. Chubei tells Umegawa that this is the place where he was born. He has brought her here so that, before they die, they may go together to the grave of his real mother; then, in the next world, she and Umegawa can greet each other as parent and child. Umegawa thinks of her own mother far away in Kyoto. Chubei dares not go to his father's house and decides to seek shelter in that of **Chuzaburo,** an old friend who is his father's tenant. Chuzaburo has been called away from home by the village headman. His new wife does not know Chubei, although she is full of the scandal about him. She goes off to fetch her husband, telling them to mind the rice-pot for her. As they stand by the gate they see a group of villagers passing in the distance. Among them Chubei recognizes his father **Magoemon,** and bids him a silent farewell. They take refuge in the house, fearing to be recognized, just as old Magoemon comes along the *hanamichi.* He slips on the icy road, his sandal-thong breaks and he falls in the snow. Chubei checks his impulse to rush to his father's aid, but Umegawa hurries out, offering to wash the old man's feet and mend his sandal. Magoemon is surprised to receive such attentions from a stranger, but Umegawa answers that he reminds her of her own father-in-law. She asks for some of his paper (which he has taken out to make a new thong) as a souvenir and at her words Magoemon guesses who she is. He tells her in veiled terms that it is not safe to remain as the police are searching the village, adding that his love for his son is unchanged. Within the house Chubei bows to the ground. Magoemon informs Umegawa that Chubei's adopted mother has been thrown into prison because of his theft. He feels it is Chubei's filial duty to save her by giving himself up, even if it costs him his life. But he must not do it before the eyes of his poor father, who would do anything within honour to save him. He offers Umegawa money to aid their escape, which she accepts with tears. Chubei gazes at his father with love and remorse, mourning that they can be parent and child in one life only.

Magoemon once more reiterates that, if he sees his son, his duty will compel him to hand him over to justice. But Umegawa understands the longing behind the words and, covering the old man's eyes with a cloth, beckons to Chubei who comes out and silently takes his father's hand. The tramp of feet is heard. Magoemon begs them to fly and turns from them without a backward glance. But it is too late, the police rush on to the scene and arrest Chubei as the curtain is drawn.

(This act may be performed in a modified form as a dance, with the suggestion that the lovers commit suicide together.)

KOI MINATO HAKATA NO HITOUCHI (*A Slight Case of Love in the Port of Hakata*), commonly called *Kezori*.

Sewamono. — Chikamatsu Monzaemon wrote the puppet play called *Hakata Kojoro Namimakura* for the chanter Masatayu, probably about 1716 or 1717. It was later adapted, with a new title, for the Kabuki stage. The first two scenes are still popular for their scenic effects and the robust spirit of swashbuckling adventure that animates them. Like many of Chikamatsu's plays, these first scenes are homely and simple in language and situation; the later scenes move into the realm of metaphysical poetry and are now rarely performed. The character of the hero Soshichi is not well drawn. The laurels must go to the gusty smuggler captain, Kezori (Close Shave), after whom the play is generally known.

Act I

Sc. 1. *The roadstead off the " International " Port of Shimonoseki. Towards sunset.* A ship lies at anchor, ready to sail. On deck are the captain, **Kezori Kuemon,** and some of his crew, **Yaheiji, Denne, Niza,** and **Heizaemon.** They are fit and tough, but have a wary look in their eyes. Kezori enquires whether **Ichigoro** and **Sanzo** have returned. If all goes well, they will sail that night, slip into the port of Hakata, ransom some girls, and then make off to Osaka. He has given a passage to a Kyoto merchant and his servant and bids one of his men bring the merchant up for a chat. **Komachiya Soshichi** presents himself. He is making a yearly trip to Hakata. Introductions are made and some exotic refreshments are brought. Kezori boasts how he once bested a drunken Satsuma samurai in Nagasaki. Soshichi, when pressed for a tale, can only admit that he has fallen in love with a courtesan in Hakata named **Kojoro** and is even now on his way to ransom her. This provokes scornful laughter which offends Soshichi. He retires. The boat with Sanzo and Ichigoro arrives. Bales and packages and pots of contraband goods are transferred to the ship — for the company are smugglers dealing in valuable merchandise from China and Holland — and the ship drops away with the tide to sea. Unfortunately for Soshichi, he has seen fit to look out of his porthole while the transfer is going on. Kezori has seen him and now orders his men to throw the young man and his servant into the sea. After a short scuffle they are pitched into the waves. The ship changes course, swinging round on the revolving stage so that her prow points out into the audience. She goes round further and disappears. Soshichi is supposed to have swum under water and now reappears by the trap in the *hanamichi* and clambers into a fisherman's boat. He paddles her away with a floor-board as the curtain is drawn.

Sc. 2. *The front room of the Okudaya in Yanagi street,*

Hakata. **Yokuichi,** a blind minstrel, is playing while two girls practise their dances. There is a slight altercation broken up by the master of the house, **Shirozaemon.** Kezori and five of his merry men, dressed in an outlandish mixture of foreign and Japanese garments, arrive. He gives orders to have half-a-dozen girls ransomed from neighbouring houses and heaps presents of clothes, *ginseng*, and ornaments on the household. All retire for a meal.

Soshichi, pale, haggard and shabbily dressed, appears outside the gate. He is so ashamed of his condition that he dares not call on his friends for help. He cannot now ransom Kojoro, but is drawn to her willy-nilly by the bond of love. A servant harshly bids him begone, but **Shigenojo,** one of Kojoro's maids, recognizes him and makes him enter the house. Kojoro comes to him with her toilet half completed. There follows an affecting scene in which Soshichi relates the tale of his misadventures. She protests that so long as he is alive, nothing else matters. They withdraw to an inner room. *The stage revolves.*

A large banqueting room where Kezori's party is assembled. Kezori relates the " secret " of his wealth, the famous comic passage called "The Millionaire's Bible " or " The Bell of Muken" (this speech may be omitted). Kojoro enters and recognizes in him a kindly patron who has promised to help her in time of need. Kezori is astonished at her request to help her lover, but accedes to it. Kojoro begs to be allowed to bring him to thank Kezori in person. She calls in Soshichi. There is an ugly moment. The smugglers are for killing Soshichi, but Kezori quietens them down and sends them all into another room. He then, pleadingly but with his hand on his sword-hilt, offers to ransom Kojoro for Soshichi, give him money and set him up again, if he will join the gang. His reason for this generosity is, he frankly admits, that he believes Soshichi to be unusually lucky and he, Kezori, can always use luck. Soshichi is torn between duty and love (and self-preservation). Kojoro, who is unaware of the nature of Kezori's business, pleads with him to accept the offer. Soshichi at last yields. The gang is reassembled and they all drink on the pact. The bill is paid and a final drink is being enjoyed when the alarm is given that the police are searching the quarter for a murderer. The gang trembles with apprehension, but there is no escape. Fortunately, the hunt stops at the house next door with the arrest of the wanted man. Amid sighs of relief, but now somewhat subdued, the smugglers leave, with their girls, down the *hanamichi*, Kojoro leading Soshichi and Kezori triumphantly bringing up the rear.

(The remaining two acts of the original puppet play tell how Soshichi was disinherited by his father when he learnt of his son's joining the smugglers, quarrelled with Kezori, took flight with Kojoro and finally killed himself as he was being arrested by the police.)

KOKAJI (*The Swordsmith*). *Shosagoto*. — Based on the Noh play of the same name and adapted for the Kabuki by Kimura Tomiko. *Gidayu* accompaniment. For the significance of swords, see page 464.

The Emperor Ichijo, who reigned at the end of the tenth century, dreamed one night that he received a divine command to have a sword forged by a certain smith named **Kokaji Munechika** of Sanjo in Kyoto. He sent his vassal **Tachibana Michinari** to order the smith to make the sword.

It is at this point that the play opens.

Sc. 1. *Before the Inari Shrine at Kyoto.* Kokaji Munechika is troubled by the Emperor's order. He has no assistant of sufficient skill to wield the counter hammer. In despair he comes to the Inari Shrine to pray to his patron, Inari Myojin, the God of Grain. There he is accosted by a young boy carrying a bunch of rice ears. To Munechika's surprise, the lad calls him by name and tells him that he need have no fear of obeying the Imperial order, a skilled assistant will be forthcoming. Munechika asks in amazement how the boy knows of his task. The boy replies in a famous passage : "Heaven has a voice which is heard upon earth. Walls have ears and stones tell tales. There are no secrets in the world. The flash of the blade ordered by Him who is above the clouds is quickly seen." He tells Munechika to go home and prepare his forge. He then vanishes.

Sc. 2. *Before Kokaji Munechika's house.* (This scene is the equivalent of the *kyogen* of the Noh play.) Munechika's two apprentices and his maidservant return from the shrine bringing the bamboo poles, ropes, and prayer papers to consecrate the forge, and an offering of rice cakes. They each dance a comic dance.

Sc. 3. *The forge of Munechika.* All preparations have been made. The Imperial messenger Tachibana Michinari arrives to take delivery of the sword. Munechika awaits the arrival of the promised assistant.

Suddenly on the *hanamichi* there appears **Inari Myojin** in the guise of a fox, the animal sacred to him. He joins Munechika and together they forge the blade. When it is done, Munechika engraves his name on one side and offers it to his assistant, who places his on the other. He prophesies that this sword will bring peace and prosperity. He then vanishes. When Munechika examines the blade to discover the name written there, he finds "*Kogitsune*" (Little Fox). It is by this name that the sword is known ever after. Joyfully Munechika delivers the weapon to the Imperial messenger. (The boy of Sc. 1 and the fox of Sc. 3 are played by the same actor.)

Inari Myojin, God of Grain

KOKUSENYA KASSEN (*The Great General's Battle*). *Jidaimono.* — Written for the puppets by Chikamatsu Monzaemon and first performed in 1710. The original play is very long, taking fourteen hours. The acts which survive have been transformed by the Kabuki into a play in *aragoto* style. The hero is half Japanese and half Chinese. The costumes in the Chinese scenes are the eighteenth-century Japanese idea of Chinese dress.

This is the most famous of Chikamatsu's historical plays and the only one still performed regularly.

The play concerns the downfall of the Ming Dynasty in China at the hands of the Tartars and its subsequent restoration to power. It tells how the Emperor Shiso gave himself over to pleasure and neglected the affairs of the Empire. The Tartar King was able to undermine the loyalty of the Chinese nobles, so that when the Tartars invaded China the Emperor found himself without support, except for a single loyal general, Go Sankei. The Tartar hordes overran China, and the Emperor was murdered. The Empress was killed accidentally, while escaping from the invaders, but her new-born son was rescued and spirited away by the faithful Go Sankei. At this point occur the acts which are usually performed.

Act II

The seashore at Nagasaki. At Nagasaki there lives a man named **Tei Shiryo** who was formerly one of the Ming Emperor's generals, but incurred the Imperial displeasure and fled to Japan. He married a Japanese wife who bore him a son named **Watonai**. Watonai studied tactics under his father and became famous in all Japan. He and Tei Shiryo have heard of the war being fought in China and are anxious to go to the Emperor's assistance.

One day when Watonai and his wife **Komutsu** are walking by the seashore, they see a snipe and a clam fighting in the shallows. The clam holds the snipe captive by the beak. Neither can free itself. While they watch the struggle, Watonai concludes that it is a sign that the time has come for him to cross over to China and put an end to the deadlock there. Suddenly he notices a small boat drifting out at sea. He brings it to the shore. In it is a lady who turns out to be the younger sister of the late Emperor Shiso, the Princess **Sendan**. Watonai calls his parents and the

Princess tells them the terrible story of her brother's downfall and murder. Komutsu, who does not understand Chinese, is filled with jealousy for the beautiful stranger to whom her husband listens with such attention. When Tei Shiryo hears that the Tartars have overrun his native land, he determines to return and do what he can to help drive out the invader. He sets sail with Watonai and his wife, leaving the Princess to follow with Komutsu, now much ashamed of her jealousy.

Act III

Sc. 1. *Before the castle of the Chinese general, Kanki.* When they arrive in China they find that **Kinsho,** Tei Shiryo's daughter by a former wife, is now married to **Kanki,** formerly in the Emperor Shiso's service, now the most important Chinese general serving under the Tartar King. After many adventures Tei Shiryo, his wife, and Watonai arrive before Kanki's castle. The general is away from home, but they have an interview with Kinsho. She recognizes her father from a portrait of him in her possession. They convince her that, since her family has always served the Ming Emperors faithfully, it is her duty to persuade her husband to abandon his allegiance to the Tartar King and assist her father to restore the rightful dynasty. Kinsho dares not admit her father or her brother into the castle. She takes her stepmother with her, although the guards insist on binding the old lady. Kinsho promises to signal to the men outside the outcome of her interview with her husband. If she is successful, she will drop white face-powder from the castle window into the moat below; if she has failed, she will drop rouge.

Sc. 2. *A room in the castle.* Kanki returns home. He listens to the appeal made by his wife and mother-in-law and after considering the matter agrees that it is his duty to join Watonai and Tei Shiryo. As he speaks, he draws his sword and is on the point of killing Kinsho when the old lady, horror-struck, intervenes. Kanki explains that, if he joins Watonai, it will be said that he allowed his judgment to be swayed by his wife. It is well known how deeply he loves her. Therefore, before he openly declares himself, his wife must be dead. He begs Kinsho to sacrifice herself for the sake of his honour. She answers that she is willing. But her stepmother is not so resigned. Every time Kanki raises his sword, the old woman, still bound, catches his sleeve in her teeth. She implores him to spare Kinsho on the grounds that it would be an everlasting disgrace not only to herself but to Japan, if it were known that a Japanese mother had acquiesced in the death of her Chinese daughter.

A deadlock has been reached. Kanki regretfully informs the two women that he will be obliged to fight against Watonai. Kinsho goes to give the agreed signal for failure.

Sc. 3. *Beneath the castle walls.* Watonai waits impatiently by the bridge for the signal. Suddenly he sees the water turn red and knows his sister has failed. He becomes anxious for his mother's safety and forces his way into the castle.

Sc. 4. *The same room in the castle.* Watonai enters, finds his mother and cuts her bonds. He confronts Kanki and demands his answer. Kanki refuses to speak to him. Kinsho staggers into the room with a blood-stained dagger in her hand. She reveals that she has stabbed herself and that the colour which stained the water below the castle wall is her own blood. She begs that her death may serve to unite her husband and her brother, and dies in Kanki's arms. Kanki swears to grant her wish and immediately undertakes to join Watonai. He bestows on him the name of Kokusenya, "Great General," and offers him a magnificent suit of armour. Watonai's mother kills herself with Kinsho's dagger so that she may accompany her daughter on the road of death and prove the devotion of a Japanese mother. She dies urging Kanki and her son to regard the Tartar King as the murderer of herself and Kinsho and to be revenged on him, at the same time restoring the Ming Dynasty. Watonai and Kanki pose triumphantly.

(In the final acts of the play, Watonai, Kanki, and Tei Shiryo raise a mighty army and are able to drive out the Tartar hordes after the great battle which gives the play its name. They restore the Ming Dynasty in the person of the infant Emperor, who is produced at the right moment by the loyal Go Sankei.)

KOTOBUKI SOGA NO TAIMEN (*The Soga Brothers Confront Their Enemy*). *Jidaimono* of the Soga Cycle (see page 462). — Written by Ichikawa Danjuro I. Played in *aragoto* style with *joruri* accompaniment. Juro's kimono is patterned with flying plovers and Goro's with butterflies. These motives are associated with these two characters in all the plays about them.

Soga Juro and **Soga Goro** were young children at the time of their father's murder. Only eighteen years later are they able to carry out their long meditated revenge. When the time is ripe, they wish to announce their intention to their father's murderer, the daimyo **Kudo Suketsune.** By so doing, the vendetta will be officially recognized and so will not count as a crime. They have a friend, **Kobayashi Asahina,** who is a retainer of Suketsune's. Through this friend they arrange to attend the daimyo's New Year reception.

Argument: The audience hall of Kudo Suketsune's palace where his vassals and retainers are assembled. Kudo Suketsune appears attended by his household and also by two beautiful courtesans, **Oiso no Tora** and **Kehaizaka no Shosho.** These two ladies are the mistresses of Juro and Goro. They play hardly any part in the present story, but are associated with them in many of the other plays.

Asahina, at a signal from Suketsune, summons the two brothers. They appear on the *hanamichi* carrying the traditional New Year gifts of pine, plum, and bamboo branches. Juro, the elder, advances slowly. Goro, the younger, shows at once his impetuous character and is with difficulty restrained from rushing forward and attacking Suketsune on the spot. Goro swallows down his rage and they present their gifts. Suketsune offers them in return ceremonial cups of *sake,* first drinking himself. Tora carries the cup to Juro, who drinks as good manners require. Goro declares he will not drink, but is brought to reason by Juro. Goro comes forward, his feelings expressed in every gesture, and kneels to receive the wine brought by Shosho. But when he raises the cup to his lips, he cannot drink. He dashes it to the ground and cries out loudly that Kudo Suketsune is his father's murderer. He and his brother intend to be revenged upon him and here and now publicly declare this intention.

Suketsune treats this speech with scorn. He derides the brothers for having waited so long. He regrets that, owing to official business, he cannot " place himself at their disposal immediately," but he imagines they will not mind waiting a little longer. Finally, to show his contempt for them, he offers to give them the opportunity they seek. Later in the year he intends to hold a hunting party at which the Shogun himself will be present. It will be held at Suketsune's private preserve at the foot of Mount Fuji. To enter the grounds it is necessary to have a pass. He now flings two of these wooden passes to Juro.

Goro once more springs forward, but is restrained by his brother. Juro picks up the passes and promises to take Suketsune at his word.

KUMO NI MAGO UENO NO HATSUHANA, commonly called *Kochiyama. Sewamono.* — Written by Kawatake Mokuami and first staged in 1881. This play is the first part of *Kochiyama to Naozamurai,* but the two parts are rarely, if ever, played together and are so tenuously linked that they must be considered separate plays. The second part, *Naozamurai,* will be found on page 383.

Kochiyama Soshun, a priest, is the leader of a gang of petty criminals in the Ueno district of Edo. One day, when he is looking over the stock-in-trade of a local pawnshop, the pawnbroker tells him, with sorrow and indignation, that his daughter, who is in service as a waiting maid in the palace of **Matsue Izumo-no-kami,** is being kept there against her will. Her father wishes her to return home and marry a suitable husband he has chosen for her, but her master wants to make her his concubine and will not release her. Kochiyama decides to make use of this story for his own ends. He looks forward not only to blackmailing Matsue Izumo-no-kami but to making him look a fool as well.

Act I

A room in the palace of Matsue Izumo-no-kami. As the curtain is drawn, **Namiji,** the waiting-maid, enters the room pursued by her master. Matsue is angry because she will not yield to him and he threatens to kill her. He is prevented from doing so by one of his pages, **Kazuma.** Matsue has in his service a certain **Kitamura Daizen,** a samurai of evil character and doubtful antecedents. Daizen takes advantage of his master's rage to poison his mind against Kazuma, saying that he and Namiji are lovers. Matsue summons his chief councillor, **Takaiki Kozaemon,** but before he can give orders for an enquiry, a messenger from the Prince-Abbot of the Kanei Temple at Ueno is announced. Matsue refuses to see him and retires to his private apartments, muttering that it is odd that a person of such importance should arrive without warning.

Act II

Another room in the palace. Kozaemon and Matsue's other retainers receive the visitor. They explain that their master is ill. The Abbot's messenger, who announces himself as Kitadani Dokai but is really Kochiyama in disguise, appears gravely displeased; he is unaccustomed to such rudeness and will leave at once. (He speaks in elaborate ecclesiastical language.) At this moment Matsue, who has remembered his good manners, enters and Kochiyama allows himself to be appeased. He asks for a private interview. When he and Matsue are alone he informs him that the Prince-Abbot has heard from private sources that Matsue is refusing to release a young girl in his service, whose family wish her to return home. The Abbot is highly scandalized by such behaviour and has commanded Kochiyama to enquire into the affair and personally conduct the young woman to her parents. Matsue replies haughtily that his private affairs do not concern the Abbot. Kochiyama hints that the Abbot may feel it his duty to make the scandal public if his wishes are not obeyed. He succeeds in making Matsue so uneasy that eventually he undertakes to let Namiji go. When their lord has withdrawn, the retainers offer Kochiyama food and drink. He refuses both, but asks instead for " a cup of golden tea " by which he makes it clearly understood that he means a considerable present of money. It is brought to him by the page Kazuma, who thanks him for saving both Namiji and himself from their lord's displeasure. Kochiyama, who never wastes an opportunity to acquire useful information about people in high places, draws out the young man and hears the whole story of Daizen's false accusation. Left alone, Kochiyama drops his saintly mask for a moment in his anxiety to find out the exact amount of Matsue's gift. (This is the great moment of the scene.) *The stage revolves.*

The porch of the palace. Kochiyama, the money safe in his bosom, is about to make a stately departure when he is stopped by Daizen. The latter once had dealings with Kochiyama's gang and recognizes the priest by the mole on his cheek. Kochiyama tries to brazen the matter out, but realizes that it is useless. Shedding his saintly manner, he admits who he is and makes a famous speech to the assembled retainers, describing how he came to the palace "entirely out of pity for the poor girl kept there against her will" and how very much their lord's reputation will suffer if he, Kochiyama, is arrested and the story becomes public. (This speech is in highly coloured Edo dialect and is the climax of the scene.) Furthermore, he adds, he could tell the police many interesting facts about the past of his accuser, Daizen. His remarks are overheard by Kozaemon, who now appears, followed by Kazuma. He realizes that Kochiyama is right; for their master's sake they dare not have him arrested. He apologizes profoundly to the "saintly messenger" for the grave error committed by Daizen and, thanking him for his godly counsel, begs him to go on his way. Kochiyama, resuming his former manner, takes his leave. As he reaches the *hanamichi* he pauses to look back in triumph. Matsue appears in the porch and Kochiyama utters the one word : "Fool !"

(As a result of Kochiyama's visit, Kozaemon is able to persuade his lord to send Namiji home, lest he lay himself open to further attempts at blackmail. When he has done so, Matsue sets the police on Kochiyama's track and the priest is at last arrested with all his gang.)

KURAMA JISHI (*The Lion of Kurama*). *Shosagoto*. *Kiyomoto* accompaniment.

After the death of Minamoto Yoshitsune (see page 425), his faithful concubine, **Shizuka Gozen**, goes mad and wanders among the mountains of Mutsu, where Yoshitsune passed much of his boyhood and where he died. She carries with her a halberd which Yoshitsune left in her care. **Yoshioka Kisanta**, a retainer of Yoshitsune, follows her, disguised as a strolling playing, complete with lion's mask, drum, and Buddhist prayer bell.

One day on the slopes of Mount Kurama, Kisanta comes to her. She does not recognize him, but takes him for a lion-spirit and begs him to recall her lover Yoshitsune. To humour her, Kisanta begins to dance his lion dance. During the dance Shizuka Gozen snatches from him his prayer bell and shakes it wildly in the hope of attracting the attention of her lover's spirit. Kisanta tries repeatedly to regain it from her, but she refuses to give it up and finally hides it, threatening him with her halberd. To distract her, Kisanta continues his dance and she follows him about in a kind of dream. Her wild looks frighten him. He tries to escape from her, but she pursues him. She has dropped her halberd, and Kisanta now calls her attention to the abandoned keepsake. She goes back to fetch it and, while she is doing so, Kisanta disappears. Shizuka Gozen, who has already forgotten he was ever there, gathers up the halberd and, cradling it in her arms, falls into a rêverie.

KURUWA BUNSHO (*Tales of the Licensed Quarter*), commonly called *Yugiri Izaemon*. *Sewamono*. — Written by Chikamatsu Monzaemon in 1679 for the actor Sakata Tojuro. This was the first of his plays of the common people. The characters are more stylized than in his later puppet plays; Izaemon is the typical Osaka hero, concealing his skill in all the warlike arts beneath a cloak of effeminacy, while Yugiri is the prototype of all the courtesans of the stage, superlatively beautiful and monolithic in character.

Only one scene of the play is still performed. The plot from which it is taken is briefly summarized: **Izaemon** is a rich and pampered young man. He is in love with **Yugiri,** the most celebrated courtesan of the licensed quarter of Osaka. Izaemon's father had built up a prosperous business by his own efforts. His widow, alarmed at her son's improvidence, decides on drastic action. She disinherits Izaemon and turns him out of the house with only the paper kimono his father wore in the days of poverty. He wanders aimlessly about for some time and then, learning that Yugiri is ill, determines to go to her. When he arrives in Osaka he is told that Yugiri has recovered and has taken a samurai client, Aira Hiraoka, who has adopted the child born to Yugiri and himself. Yugiri and Izaemon meet, quarrel and are reconciled. O Yuki, the wife of Hiraoka, comes to beg Yugiri to allow the child to be legally adopted as her husband's heir. Yugiri and Izaemon (who has disguised himself as one of her palanquin bearers) see their child for the last time. Yugiri falls desperately ill and all seems lost when suddenly fortune smiles again. O Yuki, touched by Yugiri's motherly love, sends enough money for her ransom. At the same time Izaemon's mother relents, softened by her son's sufferings. She also sends money to ransom the courtesan. Yugiri's child is restored to her and the three, happily united, start a new life.

The act which survives is that of the quarrel and reconciliation, to which has been added a "happy ending."

Sc. 1. *Before the Yoshidaya, a tea-house in Shimmachi, Osaka. The last days of the old year.* Servants and a country samurai client are pounding rice to make the New Year rice-cakes. Izaemon enters by the *hanamichi*. He is wearing a sedge hat and the famous paper kimono. He is cold, hungry, and distraught. The servants think he is a beggar and start to manhandle him, but **Kizaemon,** the master of the house, intervenes and recognizes in this forlorn figure the rich young patron of former days. He heartily bids him welcome and tells Izaemon that Yugiri has indeed been ill, but has now recovered. Izaemon confides to him the sad circumstances to which he is reduced and Kizaemon persuades him to enter the house.

Sc. 2. *A room in the Yoshidaya.* Izaemon is asleep under a quilt. He awakes and mimes his misery. He alternates between despair and jealousy, for he has heard that Yugiri has a new patron and believes them to be together in the adjoining room. His emotion almost gets the better of his good manners and he nearly bursts in on the couple. A sound makes him fly back to his quilt and he pretends to

Izaemon

be asleep. Yugiri comes to him. She is gentle and understanding and humours her lover as a mother might treat a small child. Izaemon is cold and angry, abruptly rejecting all her peace offerings. Yugiri patiently lets his jealousy work itself out and then they are reconciled. At that moment a train of porters bearing heavy boxes approaches down the *hanamichi*. They bring the money sent by Izaemon's mother who has relented and wishes him to ransom Yugiri. The maids of the house hasten to dress her in a wedding robe and prepare a feast. Izaemon puts on a silk coat worthy of a wealthy merchant's son and the curtain is drawn on a triumphant pose.

MEIBOKU SENDAI HAGI (*The Disputed Succession*). *Jidaimono.* — Written by Naka Kamesuke in 1777 for the puppet theatre, this play was taken over soon after by the Kabuki, and various interpolations were made. Two acts which form a separate play are performed under the name of *Kasane* (see page 16).

The plot is based on an incident which occurred rather over a century before the first production, when a dispute arose over the heirship of the House of Date. The third act of the play (sometimes called *Masaoka*) is frequently performed and is considered one of the classic "loyalty plays" of the Japanese theatre, but the whole play is of great interest, particularly as it is customary to act each scene in a different style.

Act I

The Hanamizu Bridge at Kamakura. The daimyo of Oshu, **Ashikaga Yorikane,** is so entirely given over to dissipation and pays so little attention to the administration of his estates that his vassals have become gravely dissatisfied. **Oe Onitsura,** the head of a minor branch of the Ashikaga family, who would succeed to the daimyo's honours should Yorikane and his little son disappear, fosters this discontent with the help of his nephew **Nikki Danjo.** He has in his pay a high Government official, **Yamana Sozen.**

One night he organizes an attempt on his kinsman's life. Yorikane is returning late from the licensed quarter. His palanquin is attacked near the Hanamizu Bridge and he and his servants are overpowered. The malcontents are about to put him to death when **Kinugawa Tanizo,** Yorikane's retainer, bursts upon the scene, puts the attackers to flight and saves his lord's life.

Act II

The Bamboo Room in the palace of the Ashikaga. (This act is performed in the classical style.) Because of his dissipation and his general unpopularity, Yorikane is forced to withdraw from public life. His son **Tsurukiyo** is a young child and Oe Onitsura, his ambitious cousin, believes that to get rid of the boy will not be a serious problem. Oe Onitsura's niece **Yashio Gozen,** the sister of Nikki Danjo, is introduced into the child's household as chief lady-in-waiting, but she finds that she has no free access to the little lord because of the ever watchful devotion of his nurse, **Masaoka.**

When the scene opens, Tsurukiyo is playing with his small foster-brother **Senmatsu,** under the eye of the latter's mother, Masaoka. She fears that an attempt may be made on her charge's life, for she guesses that evil influences are at work. She particularly hates and fears Yashio Gozen. She has therefore given out that Tsurukiyo is ill and cannot leave his room. She insists on preparing all his food herself, instead of giving him what is brought from the kitchens.

Yashio Gozen suspects that the boy's illness is a ruse on Masaoka's part and makes up her mind to get rid of the nurse. She arrives unexpectedly, accompanied by two other ladies-in-waiting, and forces her way into the room to visit the patient. She questions Masaoka closely about the child's illness and his lack of appetite. Masaoka makes evasive replies. Yashio Gozen then announces that she has brought with her **Komaki,** the wife of the physician Ono Doeki, who is very skilful. Komaki is brought in and suggests various treatments. Masaoka opposes them all, but allows Komaki to feel the child's pulse. Komaki pretends to be disturbed by evil influences in the room and asks Masaoka to bring her charge outside. Masaoka complies and Komaki feels his pulse again, declaring it to be perfectly normal. She then announces that there is a wicked person hidden somewhere in the room who menaces the young lord's life.

Yashio Gozen, with the other ladies-in-waiting and servants, searches about and, taking a halberd, strikes the ceiling just outside the door. Through the hole tumbles a

man of sinister appearance whose name is given as **Katota.**
Under pressure he reveals that he is in Masaoka's pay and
was hidden in the roof to murder Tsurukiyo. Masaoka
denies this hotly.   **Matsushima,** one of the two ladies
accompanying Yashio Gozen, but who is not in the plot,
questions Katota closely and proves his story false. Yashio
is furious at being foiled, but contains herself. She produces
what purports to be a treasonable document written by Masaoka showing that she is scheming to kill her charge and
substitute her own son. The second lady-in-waiting, **Okino-
ishi,** examines the paper, compares it with one in Masaoka's
writi ng and declares it to be a forgery. Yashio Gozen, in
spite of this second set-back, is determined to get rid of
Masaoka somehow. She now exercises her authority as the
child's relative and chief lady-in-waiting, a person greatly
superior to the nurse, who is a mere samurai's wife. She
declares Masaoka to be a woman of evil reputation, not fit
to have charge of their little lord, and attempts to drive her
from the room. But this time she is defeated by Tsurukiyo
himself. The boy is angered when he sees his dear Masaoka about to be taken from him. Laying his hand on his
sword, he orders her to return to his side, saying he will
have no one but her. Yashio Gozen is forced to yield to
his command. Masaoka retires into the inner room, taking
both children with her.

*Masaoka, Tsurukiyo,
and Senmatsu*

Yashio Gozen consults her minion, Katota, about the next move in the game.

Act III

An inner room of the palace overlooking the garden. (This act is performed in imitation of the puppets with *joruri* accompaniment.) Masaoka is seen standing between the two boys, still holding the tray of food which she has carried with her from the Bamboo Room. She sets this aside, although the children look at it longingly, for it is long past their usual mealtime.

Telling them to play quietly, Masaoka unlocks the tea ceremony apparatus in a cabinet and sets about preparing rice. She is so afraid of poison that she tests everything first on her own child, even the water in which the rice is to be cooked. She has trained Senmatsu to taste everything offered to Tsurukiyo. While she is busy she makes him repeat this "lesson," his duty to his lord.

Masaoka is unnerved by the ordeal through which she has just passed and fears that in the end Yashio Gozen will succeed in getting rid of her. But lest Tsurukiyo should realize his danger, she tries to appear cheerful. The boys grow too hungry to play and keep asking when dinner will be ready. Masaoka sets them to play a singing game, singing herself, although her voice is strangled with tears. Senmatsu does his best to keep his foster-brother happy. The two children throw grains of rice to the birds in the garden, but watching them peck only makes them hungrier.

At last the rice is cooked and Masaoka divides it into two portions. First she makes Senmatsu eat and when he shows no ill effects, she allows Tsurukiyo to eat his share. When the meal is over Senmatsu withdraws. Almost immediately a servant announces that **Sakae Gozen,** wife of the eminent government official Yamana Sozen, has arrived bringing a gift to Tsurukiyo from the Shogun Yoritomo himself. Yashio Gozen and the other ladies of the household enter. Masaoka is powerless to deny them.

Sakae Gozen approaches in state and offers a box of elegant cakes. Yashio Gozen receives them on behalf of the little lord, exclaiming at their excellence. She places them temptingly before the child, but Masaoka restrains him from helping himself. At this moment Senmatsu returns. He sees that the cakes are set before Tsurukiyo and automatically does as his mother has trained him. Before anyone can make a movement, he takes one of the cakes and eats it. Something about the flavour warns him that the cakes are not what they should be, and, to prevent Tsurukiyo touching them, he kicks over the box.

The cakes are poisoned and Yashio Gozen's plot has gone wrong, since the wrong child has eaten them. She must get rid of Senmatsu before the poison begins to work. She seizes the child, crying out that it is a grave offence to treat the Shogun's gift in such a fashion. Pretending to be beside herself with rage, she draws her poignard and cuts his throat. Masaoka sits as one turned to stone, shielding her nurseling. Sakae Gozen watches her intently from behind her fan.

Masaoka's self-control is such that, until her charge is safe, she will not allow herself even to look towards her own child. Yashio Gozen goes out, leaving the little corpse on the floor. The other two ladies, whom Masaoka can trust, are permitted to lead Tsurukiyo away. Sakae Gozen remains. She is amazed by Masaoka's fortitude. She concludes that the whole affair has been arranged beforehand. Masaoka must be in the plot and has exchanged the children's clothes so that it is Tsurukiyo who has been killed and not her own Senmatsu. She therefore praises Masaoka for her cunning and gives her a list of the conspirators.

When Sakae Gozen has left, Masaoka allows herself to give way to her grief. She gathers her child into her arms and mourns over him, although she is proud that he should have died so honourable a death, saving the life of his lord. (The acting of Masaoka here follows closely the movements of the puppets. It has great beauty and pathos.)

While Masaoka is weeping over her son, Yashio Gozen reappears armed with a halberd and attempts to murder her, but Masaoka turns upon her and succeeds in killing her instead. In the struggle the list of conspirators drops from the nurse's sleeve. Suddenly a large grey rat appears running about the floor. It seizes the document and darts away with it before anyone can catch it.

Act IV

Below the floor of Tsurukiyo's room. (This act is performed in *aragoto* style.) **Arajishi Otokonosuke,** a devoted retainer of Yorikane and Tsurukiyo, has been kept away from his little lord by the machinations of Yashio Gozen and the conspirators. But although he is not allowed to see the child, he does his best to guard him and has taken up a post below the floor of the boy's room. He is waiting there on the alert when he sees a large grey rat come down through the floor carrying a roll of paper in its mouth. Otokonosuke puts his foot on the rat and tries to kill it with his iron fan. He wounds the beast on the head, but it wriggles away from him and escapes.

The rat vanishes in a cloud of white smoke and in its place is revealed Nikki Danjo, who has occult powers, clad in grey garments and with the document between his teeth. He has a fresh wound on his brow. He traces the character for "rat" in the air with his finger.

Otokonosuke is powerless against him. Danjo goes off triumphantly having achieved his object of regaining possession of the list of conspirators.

Act V

The Court of Justice. (This act is performed in the naturalistic *sewamono* style.) Since Oe Onitsura has failed to get rid of Tsurukiyo by foul means, he decides to dispute the boy's legal right to the lordship. He is supported by his nephew, Nikki Danjo, and the presiding judge, Yamana Sozen, is his ally. He has little doubt of winning his case.

When the court assembles, it is announced that the second judge, **Hosokawa Katsumoto,** who should attend, has been delayed. Yamana Sozen decides to hurry on and give judgment before his colleague, Katsumoto, who is not privy to the plot, can arrive. Oe Onitsura appears with Danjo and other supporters. Tsurukiyo is represented by a body of loyal retainers headed by **Watanabe Gekizaemon (Geki),** and his son, **Mimbu.** Geki opens the case by presenting, first of all, a letter written by Danjo to his uncle, advising Onitsura to arrange for Tsurukiyo to be deposed from the headship of the clan. Danjo denies that he wrote the letter. Geki then accuses Danjo of trying to poison Tsurukiyo. Danjo laughs at this, saying that, since Onitsura is the child's legal guardian, it is unnecessary to kill him. He counters by accusing Geki of placing a spy under the floor of the boy's room to do him mischief. Geki makes no reply to this, but produces a note to himself written by Danjo and asks to have the writing verified. Danjo admits that he wrote the letter. Geki then produces a third letter signed and sealed by Danjo which contains directions for the purchase of a quantity of poison. Danjo, of course, declares this letter to be a forgery. Geki asks for the letters to be compared, but the judge, Sozen, says he is convinced the letter is forged and accuses Geki of contempt of court.

At this point Geki's son, Mimbu, enters and informs his father that he has just received the "secret letter." Unfortunately, however, it is torn and the superscription is lost. It will, nevertheless, be of use. Geki takes the letter and reads it. He insists that the judge read it also, but the latter says angrily that, since there is no superscription, it is not evidence and flings it back to Geki. Sozen now orders their swords to be returned to Oe Onitsura and his supporters as a sign that they have won the case. He then burns the letter about the poison on the grounds that it is a forgery. Geki is thus deprived of his chief piece of evidence.

Just as Sozen is about to declare the court closed, the second judge, Hosokawa Katsumoto, appears, apologizing for his lateness. Yamana Sozen says he has given him up, and the case is closed. Katsumoto asks to hear the judgment, but Sozen is reluctant to reopen the case. He tells Katsumoto merely that it has been proved that Geki brought false evidence. Geki protests about the unorthodox destruction of part of his evidence and begs to be allowed to show the "secret letter" to Katsumoto. Katsumoto silences him in a peremptory manner. He then turns to Danjo, congratulates him, and asks whether he may put a question. He wishes to know whether Danjo was aware of the disreputable life led by his kinsman and overlord, Ashikaga Yorikane. Danjo answers that he was never in Yorikane's confidence. Katsumoto comments that he ought to have made it his business to know the company his lord kept. By skilful questioning he forces Danjo to admit that he has failed in his duty. (Katsumoto uses a lengthy simile concerning the preservation of a precious fan.) He suggests that in the circumstances Danjo ought to set his lord a good example by committing suicide.

Katsumoto then passes to another subject. He asks Danjo whether he favours Tsurukiyo as heir to Yorikane. Danjo says that he does, but that Onitsura must be his guardian. Katsumoto suggests that Danjo himself would be a better candidate for this post. He requests Danjo to write a letter at once, applying for the guardianship of the boy. Rather mystified, Danjo complies and gives the letter to Katsumoto who asks him to seal it. This Danjo does. Katsumoto then asks to see Geki's "secret" letter. He reads part of it aloud, as follows : "now is the time to put a curse on young Tsurukiyo; please do your utmost. If you do your work well, you will be well rewarded. I have made the straw image as you ordered and buried it under the boy's room." Katsumoto then tells the assembly that he has in his possession the missing portion of the letter, upon which he has chanced on his way to the court-room. It is addressed to a certain mountain hermit. It is signed and sealed by Nikki Danjo. He proves by demonstration that the two pieces belong to the same document. Danjo still tries to declare that the letter is a forgery and asks to have the seals compared. He has put a hair under the seal he made in the court's presence, so that it does not look the same as the other. But Katsumoto sees through this ruse also.

Danjo demands that he and Geki be put to the torture to prove which is telling the truth. At this Katsumoto becomes angry and says that it is a shameful suggestion which no true samurai should make, for to force a samurai to submit to the indignity of torture is a deep disgrace. He guesses that Danjo has proposed it because he knows he is younger and stronger than Geki and less likely to succumb. Katsumoto declares that his mind is made up and since new evidence has been brought into court he proposes to reverse the judgment. Danjo, still protesting, is forced to submit. Katsumoto orders the *kataginu* (see page 415) of Onitsura, Danjo, and their supporters to be removed as a sign of disgrace. They retire angrily.

Geki thanks the honest judge and leaves the court with his party. Sozen attempts to make away with the " secret letter," but is prevented by Katsumoto and slinks out. Katsumoto is left triumphant. *The stage revolves.*

(This scene is sometimes omitted). In another apartment Geki is writing letters. His companions come to rejoice over the success of their petition. They praise Katsumoto. Geki tells them that he has written to the daimyo's council informing them of the verdict and orders that the letter be sent by special messenger. He gives his son a separate letter for Masaoka.

219

Left alone, Geki gives solemn thanks to the gods for his victory. While he is praying, Danjo enters. Geki is amazed to see him, but Danjo explains that he now bitterly repents of his crimes and offers to place in Geki's hands a document signed by all the conspirators in their own blood, with the name of his uncle, Onitsura, at the head. He asks Geki to take this to Katsumoto and beg him to allow Danjo to commit *seppuku* instead of dying a dishonourable death at the hand of the public executioner. Geki, out of charity for a fellow samurai, consents to do this. Danjo approaches him with the roll of paper in his hand. There is a dagger hidden in the roll, and, as Danjo holds it out to Geki, he stabs him in the side. Geki tries to defend himself with his fan and escapes from the room. *The stage revolves.*

(This scene is performed as a dance-drama.) Geki staggers down the *hanamichi*, still clutching his torn fan. He falls in a swoon behind a screen. Danjo enters in pursuit and they struggle together. Geki's son and supporters, who have rushed in at the sound of the commotion, take on Danjo and finally overcome him. Geki is revived and, assisted by his son, gives the *coup de grace* to Danjo.

Mimbu binds up his father's wound with his *kataginu*, but the old man is faint from loss of blood. At this moment Katsumoto enters, bearing a cup containing a reviving draught. He offers the cup to Geki, praising his courage and devotion. Geki is concerned that a great lord like Katsumoto should see him in so dishevelled a condition and begs his forgiveness. Katsumoto tells him gently that it is of no consequence. He bids him drink the medicine and orders Danjo's body to be removed. Tsurukiyo is fortunate, he adds, to have so loyal a retainer. Now the boy's title to his inheritance is assured. He draws out the certificate of inheritance and gives it to Geki who, as he dies, thanks him and asks leave to return home. Katsumoto offers him his own palanquin. Geki tries to rise, but is too weak and must be assisted by his son. Katsumoto watches him sadly, but again wishes him joy of his triumph.

MEIGETSU HACHIMAN MATSURI (*The Full Moon on the Hachiman Festival*). *Sewamono*. — The original story of this play is by Kawatake Mokuami and was adapted for the stage by Ikeda Daigo in 1918. It is a favourite play for the summer months and, as it is set in a festival period, gives an opportunity for impressive scenic effects and dancing.

Act I

A room of a house in the Fukagawa district of Tokyo on the bank of the River Sumida. It is a summer evening. Boats move up and down stream. The fishmonger **Uo-so** and his wife **O Take** come into the room behind their shop and relax in the fresh coolness of the evening. They receive a visit, half pleasure, from **Shinsuke,** a cloth retailer from Niigata Prefecture. While he is trying to interest them in his latest patterns, the courtesan **Miyokichi** is seen in a boat being poled across the river. Shinsuke falls a victim to love at first sight and is rooted to the spot when he learns from the fishmonger's shouted conversation with Miyokichi that she is on her way to see **Sanji,** a boatman who is her lover.

Act II

Miyokichi's house. The courtesan is both selfish and extravagant. She is heavily in debt and not as confident of her patronage as she was. She has taken to drinking and is apt to fall into bad-tempered, sulky moods. In such a state, we see her quarrel with her lover Sanji from whom she has borrowed money and who is himself a man of violent passions. Left alone and feeling more desperate than ever, Miyokichi receives a visit from Shinsuke. To her surprise, he declares his love for her. Nevertheless she agrees, if he will raise 100 *ryo* for her, that they shall marry and retire together to the country. Shinsuke is overjoyed with this unexpected success. He hurries away to collect the money. Miyokichi is not best pleased with this solution of her difficulties, but it is the only one which offers at the moment. Presently however, she receives another visitor — the trusted servant of a samurai patron of hers, named **Fujioka.** The samurai has decided to break off his liaison with Miyokichi and as a parting gift sends her 100 *ryo*. The courtesan, though abandoned by her wealthy patron, is glad to have won a reprieve from marriage with Shinsuke. Sanji, her lover, breaks into the house at this point. He is drunk and angry with her. He has a confused intention of cutting her throat or robbing her of the money he is sure she has hidden or both. Miyokichi handles him with considerable skill, gives him a present of money and invites him to have a drink. Sanji forgets his bad temper and they are all having a gay little party when Shinsuke comes back with the money he has raised. Miyokichi has almost forgotten who he is and treats him with tactless contempt. Sanji mocks him for a fool. The shock to Shinsuke's mind is so violent that he reels away from the house unconscious of the direction he is taking.

Act III

Sc. 1. *A back street of the Fukagawa district on the night of the festival.* People in holiday mood are everywhere. Only Shinsuke, crazed with disappointed love, behaves like a spectre at the feast. He rails against Miyokichi to all and sundry, he tosses handfuls of gold coins at passers-by and in general behaves like a lunatic. He is not so mad, however, as to miss the opportunity of stealing a dirk from the belt of an official he meets in the crowd.

Sc. 2. *In front of a geisha-ya.* Miyokichi and other professional ladies are dancing for the amusement of the holiday crowd. Suddenly news is brought that the Eitaibashi over the Sumida has collapsed under the heavy traffic caused by the festival. The crowd moves off to see what has happened. Shinsuke enters, his clothes torn, his hair dishevelled, the naked dirk in his hand. He drives away the other girls and after a prolonged struggle, stabs Miyokichi to death.

Sc. 3. *A back street off the river.* It gets lighter as the full moon rises. There is a confused noise of people shouting. Shinsuke emerges from behind a pile of timber. He is seen by some fishermen, one of whom courageously disarms him. Seized by the crowd and borne shoulder high, Shinsuke is carried off to arrest, laughing like a demented devil.

MEKURA NAGAYA UME GA KAGATOBI (*The Wicked Masseur and the Fire Department*). *Sewamono.* ── One of the last works of Kawatake Mokuami, this play was first produced in 1886. The original version of seven acts has two themes. The first deals with the misdeeds of a masseur called Dogen. The second tells of the rivalry between the Edo fire-brigade and the fire-fighters employed privately by Maeda, a daimyo of Kaga, whose palace was at Hongo where Tokyo University now stands. Fire has always been the greatest latent danger in the wood-built towns of Japan and, while most cities had their municipal fire-brigades, the daimyo who had extensive properties in the towns maintained their own teams. There was a good deal of rivalry, not always well-intentioned, between these private groups and the municipal companies.

Nowadays it is customary to give only the Dogen scenes, but one scene from the fire-brigade sequence is still very popular for its spectacular effects and also because it is traditional that the actor playing Dogen should also play for contrast the rôle of one of the leading fire-men.

Act I

On a dark, snowy night a traveller is passing through the deserted district of Ochanomizu in Hongo. He is a countryman called **Tajiemon.** Tired and cold, he is suddenly taken ill and sinks helpless to the ground. In this position he is found by **Kumataka Dogen,** a masseur of great resource, but negligible morals. Instead of helping the sick man, Dogen kills him and robs him of his money, but in doing so, he drops his own tobacco pouch beside his victim. The corpse and the tobacco pouch are later found by **Hikagecho Matsuzo,** a senior fireman of the Edo Brigade.

Act II

This is the single scene from the fire-brigade story to which reference is made above. As a result of several insults put upon them, the Edo fire-men have been working up for some time for a show-down with the Maeda brigade. Matsuzo sympathizes with them, but the decision to fight rests with **Umekichi,** their chief, who is even now making a reconnaissance of the enemy camp. He is late and the fire-men have got themselves into a state of high excitement. Umekichi at last returns and begs them to calm down and do nothing while negotiations for a settlement are in progress. The fire-men are indignant at the delay and Umekichi is in the end forced to appeal to their personal loyalty to himself to prevent violence. He declares that any attack will have to be made over his dead body. Matsuzo supports him in this stand and the fire-men at length grudgingly disperse.

Act III

Sc. 1. *Dogen's house at Kikuzaka.* Dogen's wife O Setsu is the sister of the murdered Tajiemon. She is, however, unaware of his death. Dogen's niece O Asa, who works as a maid in the Iseya pawnshop, lives with her uncle and aunt. She tells O Setsu that her master, Yohei, out of pity for her, has given her five *ryo*, a fair sum of money in those days. O Setsu is uneasy about this revelation and fears that the girl may have stolen the money. Dogen who has overheard this conversation puts a darker interpretation on Yohei's action and at once sets about evolving a plan to blackmail him. He sends off O Setsu to make some further enquiries. He is joined by his mistress, an evil woman called O Kane, and together they force O Asa to sign a confession that Yohei violated her. They have arranged in any case to sell O Asa to O Tsume, a brothel-keeper, who now arrives to claim O Asa. Dogen at first pretends that he knows nothing about the transaction, but in the end he agrees to entrust the girl to O Tsume's care. He and O Kane leave to call on Yohei.

Sc. 2. *The Iseya pawnshop at Takecho.* Dogen and O Kane try to blackmail Yohei and demand 100 *ryo* to keep quiet about his " generosity " to O Asa. The pawn-broker is indignant, but realizes that he is helpless. Through the intermediary of his clerk, Sagobei, he agrees to pay 50 *ryo*. At this point, fortunately for him, Matsuzo walks in, sizes up the situation at a glance and is able to prove that O Asa's confession is a fake. Dogen tries to brazen it out, but Matsuzo has not finished with him yet. He produces the tobacco pouch he found near Tajiemon's body and mentions that he saw a masseur, who he broadly hints was Dogen, hurrying from the scene of the crime. Dogen's bluff is called. He accepts a gift of 10 *ryo* and bows himself out with O Kane.

Act IV

Sc. 1. *Dogen's house.* O Asa has escaped from O Tsume and Dogen suspects that O Setsu has had something to do with her disappearance. He and O Kane have tied up O Setsu and are now trying by torture to make her confess. O Setsu is saved by the arrival of Kihei, the landlord, who brings the news that a dog has scratched up a blood-stained kimono under Dogen's house. Dogen recognizes it as the one he was wearing at the time of Tajiemon's murder, but he denies all knowledge of it. Kihei is not satisfied and, taking O Setsu with him, goes off to report the affair to the police. Dogen confesses to O Kane that he did murder Tajiemon and the two make hurried plans for flight They are surprised by the police and, though O Kane is taken, Dogen escapes.

Sc. 2. *The main gateway of the Maeda palace.* (The gate still exists as the Red Gate of Tokyo University.) Dogen thinks that he has outwitted the pursuit. He is mistaken, however. The whole area is surrounded by the police. After a desperate fight, he is arrested.

MIGAWARI ZAZEN (*The Substitute*). *Shosagoto.* — Adapted by Okamoto Shiko from a *kyogen.* *Tokiwazu* and *nagauta* accompaniment. The scene represents the Kabuki version of the Noh stage.

Argument : A young daimyo, **Yamakage Ukyo,** is married to **Hananoi,** a lady of forceful character. Before his marriage he had a beautiful mistress called **Hanako.** He is now never able to visit her because his wife is jealous and watches him closely. One day he receives a letter from Hanako begging him to come to her. He decides he must do so at all costs.

Ukyo tries to think of a way of escaping his wife's vigilance. He announces to her that he intends to visit the family tomb, hoping in this way to be allowed out alone, but his wife will not hear of it. He then says that he will go and pray in the Buddhist temple attached to his house, adding that he intends to stay there for seven days and seven nights. His wife is suspicious even of this, but finally gives her consent for one day only. Ukyo retires to the temple and sends for his servant, **Tarokaja.** He disguises Tarokaja in his own coat and tells him to stay there till he returns. He goes off triumphantly to visit Hanako.

Ukyo has, however, underestimated his wife's vigilance. Soon after he leaves, Hananoi appears, ostensibly to bring him food. She quickly discovers what has happened, and to save his skin, Tarokaja gives away the whole plot. Hananoi sends him off and herself takes his place under the coat.

Ukyo returns, joyfully overcome by *sake* and Hanako's

225

charms. He looks particularly ridiculous because he is wearing a woman's coat over his other clothes. He thinks the shrouded figure is Tarokaja and describes in great detail exactly how he has spent his time and how much he has enjoyed himself. This he does in a mimed dance in which he acts both himself and Hanako. He takes off the coat, explaining that Hanako gave it to him. Hananoi listens in silence, only the tapping of her foot occasionally betraying her rage. Finally Ukyo playfully twitches the coat off the supposed Tarokaja and discovers how dearly he will have to pay for his night out.

MODORI-BASHI (*Modori Bridge*). *Shosagoto*. — Based on the Noh play of the same theme entitled *Rashomon*. The original story is told in the *Heike Monogatari*. *Nagauta* accompaniment.

Minamoto Yorimitsu, Commander of the Cavalry of the Imperial Guard and guardian of the Imperial Palace, has in his service four warriors of matchless bravery known as the "Four Heavenly Kings." One of these, **Watanabe no Tsuna,** he sends on a journey. Since he loves him, he gives him a famous sword from the Minamoto treasury, "Higekiri," the "hair-splitting" sword, to preserve him during his travels.

Argument: The play opens to show Tsuna returning, his mission completed. He has reached the Modori Bashi, the bridge across the Horikawa at Ichijo in the outskirts of Kyoto. Night has fallen, and Tsuna hurries along with his two retainers, for the Modori Bashi has recently acquired an evil reputation as the haunt of a malevolent demon. It is April, and a gust of wind rustles the fresh green tendrils of the willows by the water-side. The sound makes Tsuna glance behind him, and he sees a young girl coming towards him. She is entirely alone, which is most strange at such an hour and in such a place. It crosses Tsuna's mind that she may be the demon in disguise and, being a courageous man, he decides to wait for her. If his suspicions are correct, he hopes to capture her, thereby bringing back a worthy trophy to his lord and ridding the city of a scourge. He tells his retainers to hide themselves.

The girl advances falteringly, while the singers express

the timidity and fear she wishes to convey to Tsuna in her approach. Tsuna emerges from the trees and asks her where she is going. She explains that her home is in Gojo, a district of Kyoto, that darkness has overtaken her on her way from Omiya, and that she is frightened. Tsuna agrees to escort her home and she accepts gratefully. The moon comes out from behind the clouds and they look at each other for the first time. Tsuna realizes that the girl is beautiful, but a moment later he catches sight of her reflection in the river and sees there her true shape; she is indeed the demon.

The two go on their way together, down the subsidiary *hanamichi*, across the back of the theatre to the *hanamichi* and so to the stage again. The girl appears to flag. She uses the sudden call of a cuckoo (a night-singing bird in Japan) as an excuse to stop. In answer to Tsuna's enquiry she admits she would be glad to rest. They fall into conversation.

Tsuna finds her more and more attractive and begins to doubt his earlier conviction. He asks about her father. She tells him he is a folder of fan papers in Gojo and also an expert in classical dancing. She says she herself has been taught by her father and offers to dance for Tsuna, first borrowing his fan. She dances exquisitely to a song of cherry-blossoms. Tsuna is more captivated than ever. Presently she asks him whether he is married and expresses disbelief when he says he is not. Tsuna poses as a simple country-man turned soldier. The girl, however, lets slip that she knows who he is and is aware of his distinguished reputation. This arouses all Tsuna's dormant suspicions. The girl tries to explain away her knowledge by saying she has long been in love with him, but he sternly taxes her with occult powers. He accuses her outright of being the evil spirit whose reflection he saw in the water.

At this the demon reveals her true self. Tsuna's retainers, who have been following, leap upon her, but she shakes them off. The spirit declares she comes from Mount Atago and her purpose is to kidnap Tsuna. Tsuna fights with her and is anxious to take her alive. The demon seizes him by the neck and attempts to fly away, carrying him with her. Tsuna, with one stroke of the sword "Higekiri," frees himself by cutting off her arm. He falls to the ground with the arm still clutching his shoulders. The demon vanishes, flying like a shooting star towards Mount Atago.

MOMIJI-GARI (*The Maple-Viewing Party*). *Shosagoto.* — Adapted from the Noh of the same name by Kawatake Mokuami, for Ichikawa Danjuro IX. *Nagauta* accompaniment.

Argument : **Taira Koremochi,** a young warrior, has come from Kyoto to hunt deer on Mount Togakushi. He is accompanied by a single retainer and has been entrusted by the Emperor with a secret mission. It is mid-autumn and the maple leaves are at their best. In the heart of the mountains he is surprised to meet a lovely young princess and her attendants, who accost him and invite him to view the maple leaves with her. Koremochi hesitates, but she persuades him to remain, pointing out that their unexpected meeting in so remote a place must be predestined. The party sits down among the mossy rocks, and his hostess offers Koremochi *sake.* He knows that he ought to refuse and keep his wits about him, but the combined attractions of a lovely girl and the autumn landscape are too much for him. He drinks cup after cup and finally falls into a heavy sleep. The princess glides away, mockingly wishing him " sweet dreams."

While he sleeps, there appears to Koremochi an attendant spirit of the God of War, Hachiman, the titular deity of the place, which informs him that the young woman is **Kijo,** the demon of Mount Togakushi, in disguise, and that she intends to kill him. Koremochi then reveals that his purpose in coming on this expedition is to find and slay the demon, but this adventure has put the matter out of his head. Hachiman's messenger presents him with a sacred sword on behalf of the god and tells him to awake.

Koremochi wakes with a start to find the sword at his side. He springs up as Kijo reappears in her true shape. She rushes upon him, but Koremochi draws the sword and stands his ground. The fiend tries repeatedly to overpower him, but he wounds her and holds her at bay. Kijo grows afraid of the sword. She tries to escape by leaping onto a rock, but Koremochi drags her down, thrusting her through the body.

MUSUME DOJOJI (The Maiden at the Dojo Temple).
Shosagoto. — Adapted from the Noh play *Dojoji.* First
staged in 1753. *Takemoto* and *nagauta* accompaniment.
This is the original version of the dance-drama and the one
which follows the Noh story most closely. Various others
exist, however — dances by two girls, by a man or a man
and a girl. The original is perhaps the greatest and most
difficult play in the whole repertoire. Certain of the properties used by the actor, such as the hand-towel and the
drum, are traditionally marked with his personal crest,
which is also embroidered on his obi.

Argument : The scene represents the precincts of the
Dojoji, dominated by a great hanging bell. A number of
priests enter. They are celebrating the dedication of a new
bell. For many years the temple has been without one.
Long ago the Dojoji had a bell like other temples. There
was a handsome young priest with whom Kiyo-hime, a girl
from a neighbouring village, fell in love. He rejected her
advances, since he had taken vows of celibacy. She pursued
him mercilessly and finally her hate and jealousy turned her

Hanako

into a serpent. The terrified priest ran to the temple and hid beneath the bell, which the abbot caused to be lowered over him. The serpent, finding itself frustrated, coiled itself round the bell and from its jaws poured out flames until both bell and priest were destroyed. Because of this story, the present abbot has given strict instruction that on no account should any woman be allowed into the precincts at this time.

While the priests talk, however, a beautiful young girl knocks at the gate. She explains that she is **Hanako,** a temple-dancer, travelling about to collect funds to rebuild a temple destroyed by fire. She has heard of the new bell and has come specially to see it dedicated. She is cast down when she is refused admittance, but her disappointment touches the priests' hearts. She offers to perform a special dance in the bell's honour and they allow her to enter.

Hanako dances, first with a hat she borrows from the temple, then with other properties, a set of seven travelling hats, a small hand towel, a drum and tambourines. (These dances may be interpreted as the phases of a woman's life from infancy to maturity.) The watching priests begin to feel there is something strange about her. During the dance she nine times changes her costume. With each change the uncanny aura about her increases. The priests are frightened and remember that the serpent is reputed to slough its skin nine times. Finally they decide to seize and drive her from the temple, but she eludes them and climbs onto the bell where she poses in triumph, revealing herself to be Kiyo-hime, the serpent-demon, returned to injure the new bell.

The version most commonly performed ends at this point. In the full version the girl disappears under the bell which falls upon her with a crash. The priests think there has been an earthquake and dance a comic interlude. Then the bell is raised and the serpent-demon emerges in its true form. It fights with a band of armed men and is finally subdued by the local governor, **Saba Goro,** armed with a large bamboo pole. They all pose as the curtain is drawn.

NARUKAMI. *Juhachiban.* — This curious play was first staged by Ichikawa Danjuro I in 1684. It is noteworthy as being a play written directly for the Kabuki stage rather than adapted from the Noh or the puppet theatre. The climax is a seduction scene which is as salacious as it is profound, a weird mixture of bawdiness and Buddhism.

The holy recluse Narukami has made a petition to the Emperor which has been refused. To have his revenge, Narukami, by a judicious mixture of prayer and magic, has captured the God of Rain and confined him in a rock pool beneath a waterfall. No rain falls. The country is on the verge of drought and starvation. The farmers are at their wits' ends. As a last resort, **Taema-hime,** a princess of the Imperial house, offers to sacrifice herself by going to Narukami's mountain retreat to try to seduce and overpower him.

Argument : Narukami's hidden hermitage. Women are banned from the area and **Taema-hime** is refused admittance by two comic priests. She tries to trick them by telling the story of her sad love and is so far successful that **Narukami,** who has been praying nearby, is attracted and permits her to enter. She goes on with her story and Narukami becomes visibly more excited until he swoons with emotion. The princess revives him with delicate feminine attentions. Suddenly she complains of a violent pain. This is the climax of the play. Narukami says that he is a doctor as well as a priest and will cure her. He examines her thoroughly, very thoroughly, interlarding his comments on her physical charms with metaphysical glosses. At last he confesses himself driven out of his senses by her beauty and his desire. The spell is broken. Narukami is turned into a devil as Taema-hime severs the sacred straw rope guarding the mountain retreat. The Rain God in the form of a small dragon escapes up the waterfall. The rain begins to fall as the curtain is drawn.

(The play *Fudo* which is not now performed tells how the ghost of Narukami haunted Taema-hime until she was rescued by the miraculous power of the god Fudo.)

NATSU MATSURI NANIWA KAGAMI (The Summer Festival), commonly called *Natsu Matsuri. Sewamono.* —— Written for the Osaka actor Kataoka Nizaemon I by Takeda Koizumo (d. 1754), Miyoshi Shoraku (1696—1775) and Namiki Senryu (1695—1751). It was later adapted for the puppet theatre and staged at the Takemoto-za in

1746. The original play was in nine acts, but it is now customary to use the third act as the first and follow it with acts VI, VII, and occasionally Act VIII.

Act I

Outside the Sumiyoshi Shrine, near Osaka. The act opens with a short comic scene in which a doctor is trying to get a needy actor to pay his bill.

A fishmonger, **Tsurifune** (Fishing-boat) **no Sabu,** enters with **O Kaji,** the wife of his friend and colleague **Danshichi Kurobei** and his little son, **Ichimatsu.** They rest before the shrine, and Sabu tells O Kaji how glad he is that her husband is going to be released from prison today. O Kaji confesses that she feared that Kurobei would be sentenced to death and can still hardly believe that he will be set free. She and Ichimatsu intend to give thanks at the shrine while they are waiting for him. Sabu enquires why O Kaji's father, **Giheiji,** is not with her. O Kaji replies hastily that he is not well, but Sabu is sceptical. O Kaji and the child go into the shrine, saying that afterwards they will get a meal at the Kobuya. Sabu promises to wait for them.

A palanquin stops before the shrine. From it emerges **Tamashima Isonojo,** a young man of good farmer stock whose father was formerly Danshichi Kurobei's employer. The bearers want to set him down here and demand their money. He refuses to pay them till they reach Osaka. He tries to overawe them by saying he is a samurai, but they point out scornfully that he has forgotten his long sword and call him a swindler. They overturn the palanquin and tip Isonojo out, threatening to take his clothes in lieu of payment. Sabu intervenes and asks what the cost is. The bearers tell him it is 250 *mon,* but Sabu says they cannot fool him, the correct fare is 100 *mon* and that is all they will get. He flings them the money and they retire, crestfallen. Isonojo thanks Sabu and asks his name and address so that he can reward him. Sabu is evasive, but says that he heard Isonojo mention that he was going to the Nagamachi (Long Street) in Osaka and asks what number he wants there. Isonojo answers that he is looking for the house of Mikawa Giheiji whose daughter, O Kaji, he is anxious to see. (It should here be explained that Isonojo's father, who owned the village of Takashima, had apprenticed him to a curio dealer in Kyoto and Giheiji, for reasons of his own, had sought out the young man.) Sabu exclaims that he must be Isonojo-sama and, when the youth has recovered from his surprise at being recognized, explains that he is a friend of Kurobei and that O Kaji is here at this very shrine waiting to welcome her husband, who is to be released from prison. He tells Isonojo that he need have no further worries, for Kurobei will look after him. He advises him to go to find O Kaji. Isonojo goes off in the direction of the Kobuya, and Sabu decides to while away the time by a visit to a neighbouring barber's shop.

A drum is heard. A crowd gathers. Danshichi Kurobei is led in by a police escort, still wearing his blue prison dress. He is ordered to sit down, and the crowd stares at him. **Tonai,** the chief of the escort, removes the prisoner's bonds and reads the order of release. It states that Danshichi Kurobei attacked and wounded a retainer of the samurai Oshima Sagaemon last September. Both were arrested and the retainer died of illness in prison. Consequently, Kurobei should have received the death penalty, but the Court has been merciful. He is released, but is banished from his native town of Sakai. If he dares to return there or in any way attracts the attention of the police, he can expect no mercy. The police escort march off, and the crowd disperse. Kurobei gives thanks for his release and makes a vow that in gratitude to **Heitayu-sama** (Isonojo's father), who procured his pardon, he will always care for and protect Isonojo.

Sabu calls to him and comes out of the barber's shop. They greet each other joyfully. Sabu assures Kurobei that he need feel no shame at having been in prison, "for he who has never been to prison or to Edo cannot call himself a man." He tells Kurobei that his wife and child have also come to meet him, but advises him to tidy himself up before he sees them. Sabu has brought some clothes for Kurobei and suggests that he go and change in the barber's shop. While Kurobei is thanking Sabu, he notices that he wears a rosary hanging over his ear and comments that he must have taken to religion. Sabu tells him seriously that he is now a changed man; he has given up fighting and, when he loses his temper, he folds his hands and says "Namu Amida Butsu!" He keeps the rosary hanging on his ear as a constant reminder. He then tells Kurobei of

Isonojo's unexpected arrival; the young man is now at the Kobuya with O Kaji. When Kurobei shows signs of wishing to rush there at once, Sabu stops him saying he must first make himself handsome to please his wife; he cannot meet her with those whiskers. Kurobei enters the barber's shop with the bundle Sabu has brought him. Sabu tells him he will find money and tobacco in it as well as clothes and then remembers with some chagrin that he has forgotten to put in a loin-cloth. However, he says, his own was clean this morning, and, drawing out the end through his sleeve he passes it through the window of the shop, unwinding it from around his body. He calls out to Kurobei that he will await him at the Kobuya. As he is about to leave, he starts to tuck up his kimono, remembers that he has nothing under it and hastily pulls it down again.

Sabu has got no further than the *hanamichi* when he sees a young girl running towards him. She is **Kotoura,** a courtesan and Isonojo's lover. She is escaping from the samurai **Oshima Sagaemon** (Isonojo and Sagaemon are old rivals and enemies), and has fled to this shrine because she once visited it with her lover. Sagaemon is close behind her and now catches her. He holds her prisoner by her sleeve and curses her for running away, telling her that he has learnt from her master that Isonojo has ransomed her, but she is not likely to find life with him very pleasant, as his father has just disinherited him for dishonourable conduct. She would do far better to break with him and return to Sagaemon. Kotoura refuses angrily and struggles to free herself. Suddenly Sagaemon's arm is caught by a hand which emerges from the barber's shop. A moment later Kurobei comes out, shaved and in a fine kimono, with a towel over his shoulder. Sagaemon recognizes him and makes disparaging remarks about the " gaol-bird." Kurobei retorts that Sagaemon should be ashamed to attempt to force himself on a girl. He asks Kotoura whether she comes from the Otaiya and whether she knows Isonojo. Kotoura has no idea who Kurobei is and denies any knowledge of Isonojo, but Kurobei tells her he is in his service. She then pours out her story. Kurobei, who is shocked that she is quite unattended, promises to look after her and take her to her lover, who is near at hand. During this conversation Sagaemon twice attacks Kurobei, trying to catch him off his guard, and is twice repulsed. Both Kotoura and Sagaemon enquire where Isonojo is. Kurobei seizes Sagaemon and presses his hands over his ears while he tells the girl how to find the Kobuya. Sabu, he adds, will care for her. As she leaves, Kurobei releases Sagaemon and proceeds to give him an elaborate set of false directions, which he illustrates with various punches all over the wretched samurai's body. Finally Sagaemon escapes from his tormentor and Kurobei, not displeased with his first enterprise since his release, goes into the shrine to give thanks.

Kurobei is called back, however, by **Issun Tokubei,** a retainer of Sagaemon, who now enters accompanied by the same palanquin bearers who attempted to cheat Isonojo. They tell Kurobei blusteringly that they have come to get Kotoura and he had better hand her over. They attack him, encouraged by Tokubei. When Kurobei has dealt with them, he and Tokubei close to continue the fight, but O Kaji rushes between them crying that he should be ashamed of himself for quarrelling and fighting even before he has seen his wife and child. O Kaji recognizes in Tokubei the beggar she saw the other day. She explains to Kurobei that this man saved Isonojo from a gang of thieves a few days previously and received a reward of money and clothing from Isonojo's mother. O Kaji supposes that these presents enabled him to take service with Sagaemon. Kurobei turns furiously on Tokubei, saying that he hated him before, but now he hates him doubly because, having received favours from Isonojo's family, he is now serving their enemy. He is about to attack Tokubei again, but Tokubei begs him to wait. He had no idea of the identity of the young man he rescued from the robbers. Had he known he would never have entered Sagaemon's employ, for he comes from Tama-shima, the village of Isonojo's father. He will therefore immediately leave Sagaemon's service and seek that of his rightful master. Kurobei commends Tokubei for his loyalty, and the two swear to serve Isonojo faithfully, each ripping a sleeve from his kimono which they exchange as a pledge (here there is a complicated play on words). O Kaji tells them that Sabu has taken Kotoura to his house and will also find a suitable lodging for their young master. Kurobei is relieved and the three of them are about to take the road to Osaka, when they are once more attacked by the palanquin bearers. They are routed by Kurobei and Tokubei who pose triumphantly as the curtain is drawn.

Act II

The house of Tsurifune no Sabu. (It is this act which gives the play its title.) It is the evening before the Kozu Shrine festival in Osaka. This takes place in the month of June when the rainy season has started. **O Tsugi,** Sabu's wife, is preparing food for the festival, and Kotoura and Isonojo are helping her. The lovers are bickering because Kotoura is jealous of Isonojo's supposed flirtation with the daughter of his former master, from whose house he has been dismissed for dishonesty, since he has mislaid a sum of money entrusted to him. The two palanquin bearers enter, wearing lion masks in honour of the festival, and offer the customary congratulations. Sabu returns home, carrying his rosary. He has been to settle the matter of the stolen money with Isonojo's former master, the curio dealer. He says that all is now arranged, but it is necessary for Isonojo to leave Osaka till the scandal has died down. He cannot think where to send the young man, but no doubt he will find some way of safeguarding him. Meanwhile he begs Kotoura to go into the back of the house lest she be seen by passers-by in the street. The young people retire.

O Tatsu, Tokubei's wife and a woman of great beauty, comes to the gate. She asks for Sabu. She and O Tsugi recognize each other, and she is invited in out of the rain. O Tatsu thanks Sabu for extending his friendship to her husband. She hopes that his quick temper did not give too much trouble. The two women gossip about the quarrel-someness of their husbands. O Tsugi explains about Sabu's rosary and how it helps him keep his temper. Sabu enquires after Tokubei. O Tatsu says she is on her way home to Tamashima, and her husband will be joining her there in a few days' time. O Tsugi is struck by her words and asks O Tatsu whether she will do her a favour. She explains that Isonojo has been living with a merchant family in Kyoto, but now, for private reasons, must leave this part of the country. She asks O Tatsu to take charge of him and let him go with her to his home in Tamashima. O Tatsu consents, saying it will be a pleasure, as his father is her cousin. O Tsugi is about to call in Isonojo, but Sabu stops her, saying the plan is not consonant with his honour. At first he will not tell the women his objections, but in the end he is forced to say that he considers O Tatsu far too beautiful to be put in charge of a young man like Isonojo. He could not be responsible to Tokubei for the outcome. O Tatsu looks at him reproachfully and then, before either Sabu or O Tsugi realizes what she is doing, she takes the red hot tongs from the fire-box and presses them to her face. She does not utter a word, but, when she has disfigured herself, she faints from the pain. When she revives, Sabu praises her noble spirit and begs her to take Isonojo with her " even as far as China." O Tsugi leads O Tatsu into the inner room to ease the pain and Sabu remains praying before the family shrine.

The two bearers return once more and ask for Sabu. He tells them he is busy but, as it is festival time, he bids them help themselves to the food and drink set out in the room. The bearers try to blackmail him, saying that they know that Kotoura is in the house. They have been told by "a certain samurai" to find the girl, but, for a considerable sum of money, they are prepared to keep their knowledge of her whereabouts to themselves. Sabu asks whether the samurai is Sagaemon. They can tell their master, then, that Kotoura is with her betrothed, Isonojo. The two men try to force their way into the house and are roughly treated by Sabu, who is rapidly losing control of his temper. O Tsugi rushes out to discover the reason for all the noise. He shouts to her that he is sorry to be forced to break his vow, but the provocation is too great. He tears his rosary in two, saying that this is how he would like to treat these two fellows. Now nothing binds him any longer; he is his old self; he can kill any two men with his bare hands. He orders his wife to bring him his sword as he intends to visit Sagaemon. He leaves by the *hanamichi* driving the bearers before him, watched anxiously by his wife.

Giheiji, the father of Danshichi Kurobei's wife O Kaji, enters, followed by another palanquin. He tells O Tsugi that his son-in-law is worried about Kotoura and has sent him to fetch her in order to relieve O Tsugi of the responsibility. O Tsugi gladly goes to fetch the girl, who is told that she is to go to Kurobei's house for a few days. Kotoura answers that she would rather go with Isonojo, but is made to realize that that would endanger her lover. When she has been carried away, Isonojo and O Tatsu come out to begin their journey, the young man entreating O Tsugi to send him news of Kotoura, for he is reluctant to leave her behind. As they leave, O Tsugi heaves a sigh of relief.

A moment later Kurobei, Sabu, and Tokubei all come along the *hanamichi*. His friends have prevented Sabu from attacking Sagaemon, and O Tsugi rejoices to see her husband safe and sound. They enter the house and Kurobei asks for Isonojo and Kotoura. O Tsugi explains that Isonojo is on his way to Tamashima with O Tatsu and that Kotoura has, of course, gone with Giheiji. Kurobei, much upset, declares he knows nothing about this and asks which way they went. He pushes the astonished O Tsugi out of his way and runs to the *hanamichi*. He sees that O Tsugi has fallen as a result of his roughness. He takes his tobacco pouch from his belt and throws it to her, saying that there is medicine in it, and then runs on his way. (His action signifies that he is in such a hurry that he has not even time to take the medicine from the pouch.)

Act III

A back street off the Nagamachi near a well. (Throughout this scene the festival procession on its way to the Shrine is passing through the rejoicing crowds at the back of the stage.) Giheiji comes hurrying down the *hanamichi* with the palanquin containing Kotoura. Kurobei calls to him from the back of the theatre and comes running after him. He catches up with the palanquin and orders the bearers to carry it back to Sabu's house. Giheiji shouts to them to pay no attention. An argument follows, and the bearers set down the palanquin until the matter is settled. Kurobei angrily accuses his father-in-law of stealing Kotoura in order to sell her to Sagaemon and so dishonour his family. He knows now, he says, that it was Giheiji who stole the money from the curio-shop in Kyoto, the theft for which Isonojo was blamed. That affair has been settled, but, he, Kurobei, will not allow any further evil practices. Kurobei again tells the bearers to go and again Giheiji bids them remain. Giheiji, who is a thorough old rascal, now attempts to turn the tables on his son-in-law by accusing him of ingratitude ; he needs money to pay what he owes Giheiji for caring for O Kaji and Ichimatsu while Kurobei was in prison. Kurobei, who is well aware that he does indeed owe a debt of gratitude to the old man, controls his rage and promises to earn money for Giheiji if only he will let Kotoura go. Giheiji, however, has by now persuaded himself that he has been deeply wronged by his ungrateful son-in-law, and begins to beat and kick Kurobei, who submits in silence. He swears he will never again interfere with the old man, if he will only now do as he asks. He offers him 30 *ryo* as compensation. Giheiji is tempted and saying grudgingly that he would have got at least 100 *ryo* from Sagaemon, he accepts. Kurobei quickly tells the bearers to take the lady back whence she came. As they go on their way, Giheiji asks to see the money. Kurobei, who has not, in fact, yet thought how he is going to raise the sum, hesitates and then tells the old man that he will fetch it from home. Giheiji is at once suspicious and, seizing him, calls him a thief and a swindler. He again begins to kick and beat Kurobei, who does not attempt to retaliate. Kurobei has his straw sandals tucked into his belt; one of these falls out and Giheiji, who is beside himself, snatches it up and strikes him in the face, screaming abuse. This insult is too much for Kurobei, who lays his hand on the hilt of his sword. Giheiji calls him a parricide and dares him to draw the blade. At last, Kurobei, unable to control himself any longer, does so and makes a pass at Giheiji, wounding him slightly. Giheiji, now thoroughly frightened, attempts to escape, screaming "Murderer!" but Kurobei pursues him and runs him through the heart, sobbing out a plea to be forgiven for this crime. The festival procession is slowly approaching. Kurobei hastily conceals the body and washes himself at the well. The temple shrines pass across the stage followed by the holiday crowd. Kurobei mingles unobtrusively with it. As he goes off, Tokubei enters at the rear of the procession. He sees Kurobei's sandal lying in the road and picks it up, recognizing to whom it belongs by the mark on its side.

(The fourth act—the eighth in the original play—can be briefly summarized: Kurobei becomes ill from remorse, and O Kaji guesses what he has done but, since she knows her father's character, cannot find it in her heart to blame him. She lives in daily dread that the police will arrest him. Tokubei, who has, of course, also guessed Kurobei's secret, tries to persuade Kurobei to come with him to Tamashima and, when he refuses, succeeds in tricking O Kaji into making her husband divorce her, thus severing the blood relationship between Giheiji and Kurobei and making his crime less dreadful in the eyes of the law. He and Sabu take O Kaji and Ichimatsu away as a posse of police surrounds the house to arrest Kurobei. Tokubei returns and persuades the officer in charge of the guard that Kurobei is so strong and dangerous that he had better let someone like Tokubei, who knows him, go into the house and trick him into surrendering. The police officer consents. The stage revolves to show the roof of the house, where Kurobei is at bay. The house is surrounded except on one side where there is a river. Tokubei joins Kurobei on the roof. They look into each other's eyes, and, leaping into the river, are able to swim to safety and escape to Tamashima.)

OMI GENJI SENJIN YAKATA (*Moritsuna's Camp*), commonly called *Moritsuna Jinya. Jidaimono,* associated with the Taiko Cycle (see page 467). — Written for the puppets in 1769 by Chikamatsu Hanji. Only one act, Act VIII, survives out of a long play. It was adapted for the Kabuki within a few years of its first production and has now become essentially an actor's vehicle, the rôle of Moritsuna being considered one of the finest in Kabuki. The play concerns the siege of Osaka Castle (here called Sakamoto Castle) and the final defeat of Toyotomi Hideyori.

Act VIII consists of a subplot about two brothers and can therefore stand alone. **Sasaki Moritsuna** and **Sasaki Takatsuna** (in real life Sanada Nobuyori and Sanado Yukimura) are generals on the opposing sides. Takatsuna, the more able and daring of the two, is fighting on the losing side, that of Minamoto Yoriie (Toyotomi Hideyori). He plans a desperate stratagem to try to retrieve the position. He knows that his reputation as a commander stands high and he believes that, if the enemy think him dead, they may well relax their stranglehold.

The character of Takatsuna, who never appears on the stage, dominates the whole play. He is a man of great ruthlessness and brilliance, with the power of holding the devotion of lesser men. His little son is prepared to die for him. His brother's love for him is the theme of the play. He can read Moritsuna like a book and it is because of this that his stratagem succeeds. Takatsuna's personal magnetism makes some sort of sense out of a series of incredible events.

Moritsuna's character, on the other hand, has an almost feminine streak in it. When he tries to interpret his brother's motives, all he can imagine is what he himself would feel and do in like circumstances. Takatsuna knows this and counts on it. It is because of this "partial" outlook that Moritsuna is the less able of the two. Personal feelings obscure his judgment, not only in the final scene, but at the beginning of the play when he believes his brother may be making a desperate attempt to rescue the boy, Koshiro. This is what he would undoubtedly have done himself. Had he really understood his brother's nature, he would have known that such a surrender to emotion on Takatsuna's part was impossible.

Act VIII

Sasaki Moritsuna's camp near Lake Biwa. Moritsuna's crest is prominently displayed on the walls of his headquarters.

In a short scene, now never played, Moritsuna returns victorious from battle accompanied by his little son **Kosaburo** and his nephew **Koshiro,** whom Kosaburo has captured. They are received by Moritsuna's wife **Hayase** and his mother **Bimyo.** Moritsuna wished to kill Koshiro on the battlefield to spare him the indignity of capture, but his commander-in-chief **Hojo Tokimasa** (Tokugawa Ieyasu) ordered the boy's life to be spared. Moritsuna commits Koshiro to the charge of Bimyo and retires to remove the traces of battle.

(Here the act begins.) Word comes that **Wada Hidemori,** a commander under Takatsuna, has arrived asking for a parley. Moritsuna is amazed, but receives him. His surprise turns to suspicion when Wada begs him to release Koshiro. Moritsuna cannot understand why this officer should be so anxious about a boy who, from the military point of view, is insignificant. He feels there must be some stratagem behind this request. To give himself time to think, he answers evasively, laughing scornfully at Wada for demeaning himself for the sake of a boy. But Wada persists earnestly. Moritsuna begins to wonder whether this request originates not from Wada himself, but from Takatsuna. He dismisses it brusquely; Koshiro is unimportant but, nevertheless, he cannot be released without the permission of Hojo Tokimasa. When Wada still insists, Moritsuna adds that any attempt to seize the boy by force would be useless. To prove his point he summons his guard.

Wada at last gives up and leaves to carry his plea to Tokimasa himself. When he reaches the *hanamichi*, he pauses to express his satisfaction. For Koshiro's release is not his object. He has come to implant in Moritsuna's mind the notion that Takatsuna's love and anxiety for his son might obscure his judgment. In this he has clearly been successful.

Left alone, Moritsuna tries to think the matter out. The more he reflects, the more possible it seems to him that anxiety for his child has clouded his brother's reason. The idea takes hold of him that Takatsuna might make dishonourable terms to save the boy, might even turn traitor for his sake. The thought appalls him. He wonders whether Tokimasa has guessed this and whether this was the reason why he was anxious that Koshiro be taken alive. Koshiro is making a coward of his father. If Koshiro were dead, his father would not be tempted. So reasons Moritsuna, judging Takatsuna by himself, Koshiro must die to save his father from dishonour. Moritsuna cannot put to death a captive he has been commanded to preserve. He ponders and then finds the solution. Koshiro must commit suicide. He must be persuaded that death is better than the shame of capture in his first battle. The person who must do this is his grandmother, Bimyo, since Moritsuna cannot tamper with the boy himself.

Moritsuna braces himself and lays the matter before his mother. To convince her that only her grandson's death can prevent her son's dishonour, he uses all the charm and persuasiveness of his nature. He woos her with almost loverlike pleading. Yet he is fully aware of the dreadful nature of the request he is making. Finally Bimyo gives way and consents to undertake the task. Moritsuna gives her his sword, telling her that, if Koshiro is craven, she must kill him. Both weep with sorrow. The evening bell sounds in the camp and Moritsuna says sadly, thinking of the boy : " The short day is almost over." He and Bimyo leave by different ways. The stage is empty.

Takatsuna is not sure how well Wada may have succeeded in his mission. He is determined to convince Moritsuna of his desperate anxiety for his son. He therefore sends his wife

Kagaribi, Koshiro's mother, to further the stratagem. She appears disguised as a soldier and shoots an arrow into a tree near Moritsuna's headquarters. To the arrow is attached a message ostensibly for Koshiro, actually directed at Moritsuna, which reads : " Would that I might see him come in secret ! " (a quotation from a well-known poem). Takatsuna intends that this message should convince his brother that he is urging the boy to escape. While Kagaribi stands at the gate, Hayase comes from the inner room. She sees the arrow and reads the message. She recognizes both the hand and the messenger, but is uncertain what answer to make. So she attaches to the arrow a cryptic poem : " Whether to go or to stay the Osaka barrier knows not," and shoots it into a tree outside the gate. Kagaribi, interpreting it as a sign to wait, lingers in the hope of catching a glimpse of her child. Hayase goes back into the house.

Koshiro now appears, a pathetic little figure. He is followed by his grandmother who sets about the dreadful task of persuading him it is his duty to commit suicide. But Koshiro will not yield. She offers him a dagger, but he shakes his head, saying that he wants to see his parents again and chop off a few enemy heads before he dies. He escapes from Bimyo, who follows him, sword in hand. She threatens to kill him if he will not die, as a samurai should, by his own hand. Koshiro pleads with her and she cannot bring herself to strike. In the end she bursts into tears and embraces the child, declaring that she cannot perform so terrible a task. At this point Koshiro catches sight of his mother outside the gate and tries to go to her, but Bimyo will not allow it and drags him back into the house.

Kagaribi breaks open the gate and is about to run to her child when a battle drum is heard. Hayase rushes out with a halberd in her hand and prevents Kagaribi from entering. Moritsuna appears, alarmed by the sound. He sends his son Kosaburo to find out what is happening.

A messenger, **Shinraku Taro,** arrives hot-foot. He announces that Takatsuna, frantic with grief for his son, has launched a desperate attack on the camp, but his force is so small that he is bound to be beaten off with heavy losses. Moritsuna believes that Takatsuna must inevitably be killed. A second messenger approaches with news that the attack has already been beaten off. Tokimasa is coming to the camp.

Moritsuna goes to make ready to receive his lord. (This messenger, **Ibuki Tota,** provides some comic relief at this moment of tense emotion by his miming of the battle.)

Tokimasa arrives by the *hanamichi* with his suite. He tells Moritsuna that his brother has been killed. He has brought Takatsuna's head so that Moritsuna may identfy it. The head-box is placed before Moritsuna. How dreadful the task is to him is apparent from his face. He cannot bring himself to uncover the head until urged roughly by Tokimasa. Koshiro quietly opens the door of the inner room and watches the scene. When Moritsuna at last raises the lid of the box, he sees the head and, crying out " My father ! " draws his sword and commits suicide. Moritsuna replaces the lid of the head-box without having seen the head. Any thought that it might not be that of his brother is dispelled by Koshiro's action. He asks with a harshness bred of suffering why the boy has done this now. Koshiro answers that he only wished to live to see his father again. Tokimasa again impatiently urges Moritsuna to identify the head. Slowly Moritsuna lifts the lid once more and with closed eyes proceeds with the ritual cleansing of the head before identifying it. He cannot bear to open his eyes and see his brother's face. At last he forces himself to look. This is the great moment in the play and the actor should, in complete silence, portray the following seven emotions : — 1) grief and revulsion at the duty imposed upon him ; 2) amazement at discovering that the head is not his brother's : 3) mystification ; 4) joy that his brother is not dead ; 5) speculation as to why

Moritsuna and Koshiro

Koshiro should have committed suicide, since the head is clearly not his father's (at this point the actor should make it apparent that he slowly unravels the whole plot—Takatsuna's series of stratagems to give colour to his supposed death with, as a final touch, Koshiro's heroic sacrifice) ; 6) admiration for Koshiro in conflict with his own duty to Tokimasa ; 7) his final decision that he cannot nullify the gallant child's sacrifice. Moritsuna says deliberately : " In spite of the arrow wound on the brow, this is undoubtedly the head of my brother Takatsuna." Koshiro raises his eyes and stares at him. Moritsuna takes the head and displays it before Tokimasa. The latter thanks him and departs after presenting him with a chest of armour as a reward for his services.

Left alone with his family, Moritsuna tells his wife and mother that the head was false and that Takatsuna lives. Turning Koshiro's face towards him, he gazes at the boy with sorrow and admiration and speaks feelingly in his praise. He calls Kagaribi from her hiding place to say farewell to her child. Koshiro dies in his mother's arms.

After Koshiro's death, Moritsuna realizes the enormity of the thing he has done. He has allowed his emotions to lead him into exactly that act of betrayal from which he wished to preserve his brother. Unable to bear the burden of such dishonour, Moritsuna prepares to kill himself, not reflecting that this will stultify Koshiro's action as completely as if he had never given false testimony. He is oblivious to the entreaties of his wife, but before he can draw his sword, Wada Hidemori reappears. He has remained hidden in the camp to report to Takatsuna on the success of the plot. Wada cries to Moritsuna to hold his hand. He carries a pistol which he points at Moritsuna, then suddenly he turns and fires into the chest of armour left by Tokimasa. From the shattered chest leaps a spy concealed inside to watch Moritsuna. Tokimasa apparently knew his general's weakness. The spy falls dead. Wada tells Moritsuna that it is not yet time to die. Soon they will meet on the battlefield and there Moritsuna may find an honourable death without sullying his devotion to his own flesh and blood.

O NATSU KYORAN. *Shosagoto.* — A dance drama with *tokiwazu* accompaniment. First staged in 1914 by Onoe

Baiko VI who included it among his " Ten Favourites."
The story is based on an incident in a well-known novel, *Five Women in Love*, by the seventeenth-century novelist Saikaku.

Argument : **O Natsu** is a spoiled and beautiful young girl whose parents have denied her nothing. She considers she may do just as she pleases, even in the matter of choosing a husband. She falls in love with an elegant young ne'er-do-well from Osaka, a former samurai, called Seijuro, famous for his success with the courtesans of Shimmachi. He persuades her to rifle her father's strong-box and run away with him. The two are arrested ; Seijuro is charged with enticement and theft, and executed. O Natsu goes mad with horror and grief.

The dance shows O Natsu wandering through the autumn rice-fields perpetually seeking her dead lover. She carries a pilgrim's banner and has a great bunch of prayer papers tucked into her obi. These papers are twisted so that when she flings them into the air they float like grass-seeds in autumn. Four children come upon her and tease her with heartless innocence, making her think that Seijuro is at hand. She meets a drunken horse-dealer whom she mistakes for her beloved, but he runs away terrified when he realizes she is mad. Weary with her search, she falls asleep and wakes in the half light of evening to see two old pilgrims praying before a neighbouring shrine. She hastens to them, peering beneath their wide straw hats to see whether either of them is Seijuro. The old people go off indignantly, leaving O Natsu, who has already forgotten their existence, gazing down the twilit road, convinced that at last she really sees her lover approaching.

OSHI NO FUSUMA KOI NO MUTSUGOTO, commonly called *Oshidori*. *Shosagoto*.—*Nagauta* accompaniment. The *oshidori,* love-bird or mandarin duck, is regarded in Japan as the symbol of conjugal devotion. If the bird loses its mate, it is said to pine away, never seeking another.

In the days when the Genji and Heike strove for power, there lived two noble youths, **Kawazu Saburo Sukeyasu** and **Matano Goro Kagehisa,** who loved the same lady, the beautiful courtesan **Kisagawa.** Sukeyasu belonged to the Genji, Kagehisa to the Heike faction. Kisagawa favoured

Sukeyasu, but since neither young man would yield to the other, they decided to settle the matter by a wrestling match. The loser was not only to give up all pretensions to the lady, but was to pledge himself to support the victor's clan.

Argument : When the curtain is drawn, the stage represents a garden by the side of a lake. Sukeyasu and Kagehisa appear, accompanied by Kisagawa, who is to act as umpire. She carries an umpire's fan. The young men announce their intentions and the terms of the match. Kisagawa prepares the ring and gives the signal to begin. Sukeyasu is the more skilful and succeeds in throwing his rival. Kagehisa is forced to admit defeat and Sukeyasu goes off in triumph with the lady.

Left alone, Kagehisa sees on the lake a pair of mandarin duck who suggest to him all too vividly the happy couple who have just left him. There is an ancient belief that if a man drinks a potion made with the blood of the male bird, the female bird, in the wildness of her grief, will bewitch him. Kagehisa remembers this and believes that, if he can make Sukeyasu drink such a draught, it will be easy to kill him when he is bewitched. Kagehisa therefore draws the little knife from the scabbard of his sword and throws it at the bird. The female duck dives under the water. Kagehisa gathers up the body of the male and carries it away.

The spirit of the female duck (now represented by the actor who played the part of Kisagawa) re-emerges from the waters of the lake. In an exquisite dance, she mourns bitterly for her mate. She climbs from the bank into the garden, following the bloody traces of her companion. Suddenly the gate of the garden opens and Sukeyasu staggers in. He has drunk the magic potion and it draws him towards the lake. Because he has drunk the blood of her mate, the female duck identifies Sukeyasu with her dead love. They dance together, he becoming more and more dazed, she more and more amorous. Kagehisa, who has been watching the outcome of his stratagem, thinks that he now has Sukeyasu at his mercy. He leaps from his hiding-place to kill his rival, but at that moment Sukeyasu is transformed into the spirit of the male mandarin duck. The two bird spirits turn upon Kagehisa and punish him for his cruelty.

SAIKAKU GONIN ONNA (*Saikaku's Five Women*).

Shosagoto. — Scenes from a famous novel by a writer of the late seventeenth century, Ibara Saikaku. *Tokiwazu* and *nagauta* accompaniment. The book appeared in 1683 and a quarter of a century later it was still so popular that at least two of the stories it contained were elaborated and dramatized by famous playwrights. *O San and Moemon* inspired Chikamatsu Monzaemon to write his great puppet play *Koi Hakke Hashiragoyomi* (*The Almanack of Love*) which is still frequently performed both by the puppets and on the stage (see page 188). *O Shichi and Kichiza* was dramatized by Chikamatsu's rival, Ki no Kaion, under the title *O Shichi, the Greengrocer's Daughter* and is also still popular.

Each scene is only a fragment. They are, in fact, a series of dances in contrasting styles fitted into frames already familiar to the audience.

Sc. 1. *O Natsu and Seijuro* (compare *O Natsu* on page 245). **Seijuro** is a handsome young clerk from Osaka travelling on business for his firm. **O Natsu,** the younger sister of one of his clients, thinks him a coxcomb and declares her dislike for that sort of effeminate beauty in a man. Her old nurse, to tease her, tells her what a successful lover Seijuro is and how all the courtesans of Osaka write him love-letters. O Natsu begins to see Seijuro in a new light.

The dance represents O Natsu's wooing of Seijuro. It is a sophisticated dance in the amorous Osaka style to which the inversion of the male and female rôles adds piquancy. Seijuro is not slow in responding to O Natsu's attentions, but they are interrupted by the old nurse calling her charge. Here also it is the girl who takes the initiative. Holding Seijuro by the hand she leads him away down the *hanamichi* with the gesture used as a rule by a lover leading his mistress. The nurse appears still calling O Natsu and searches for them in vain.

Sc. 2. *O Shichi and Kichiza.* The style of this dance is in marked contrast to the previous one. It has about it a feeling of youthful innocence. It is winter and the roofs and trees are laden with snow. A strolling musician, disguised in a straw travelling hat, pauses before a prosperous looking house and begins to play. A window opens and **O Shichi,** the greengrocer's pretty daughter, looks out.

The musician removes his hat and she sees with joy that

it is **Kichiza,** a page at the Kichijo Temple. They became acquainted when O Shichi and her family were forced to take refuge in the temple after their house burned down. They fell in love, but she feared that he had forgotten her.

Closing the window, O Shichi hurries out to her lover, and they reaffirm their vows. They are interrupted by her father calling her name. Sadly she leaves Kichiza, who just as sadly takes up his disguise and tears himself away. Standing in the doorway, O Shichi watches his figure till she can see it no longer.

Sc. 3. *O Sen and the Cask-maker.* A comedy perfomed in the manner of the *kyogen* of the Noh theatre. Two women servants employed by a maltster in Osaka are on a pilgrimage to the Ise shrine. **O Sen** is young and comely. **Kosen** is old and staid and keeps a sharp eye on her companion. They have met a young cask-maker, **Shosuke,** and he and O Sen have fallen in love.

O Sen has another suitor, a servant in her master's house, called **Kyushichi.** She does not favour him at all and was glad to escape from his attentions. To their dismay, Kyushichi turns up unexpectedly just as they are approaching Ise. He believes O Sen cannot really dislike such a fine fellow as himself and dances vaingloriously before her. He repeatedly makes advances to her, but is always foiled by Kosen, who knows, of course, where the girl's affections lie. While Kosen and Kyushichi are involved in what is practically a fight, watched and assisted by a crowd of passers-by, Shosuke and O Sen slip quietly away. Kyushichi, Kosen, and the others go off holding onto each other in a comic follow-my-leader.

Sc. 4. *O San and Moemon.* This is an elaborate piece of mime. It is an excellent vehicle for an accomplished actor for he is able to play the rôles of both hero and heroine. **O San** is the wife of a wealthy maker of almanacks, picture-scrolls, and similar wares. She is distressed by her husband's infidelities; he is even now trying to force his attentions on their maid, **O Tama.** She knows that O Tama is in love with her husband's clerk **Moemon,** although Moemon has never taken the slightest interest in her.

O San, in a last effort to win back her husband's affections, one night persuades O Tama to exchange sleeping places. Her husband is out drinking and, when he returns, O San

suspects that he will go and pester O Tama. O Tama consents and lays out the bedding behind a screen in her usual
corner. She helps her mistress to bed and then takes off her
apron as if she were going to bed herself. She remembers
in time and goes off to her mistress's room, but leaves the
apron on the floor. O San lies waiting. After a while she
falls asleep. Meanwhile, Moemon, who was been having
twinges of conscience about O Tama's devotion, makes up
his mind to go to her. In the darkness he creeps to her
sleeping place and, finding her apron on the floor, is sure
that she has gone to bed. He stretches out his hand behind
the screen and whispers "O Tama!" A hand catches his.
He does not notice that it is smoother and slenderer than
O Tama's hand.

Sc. 5. *O Man and Gengobei.* This is a popular type of
nostalgic dance-drama. **O Man** is the prototype of the loyal,
self-sacrificing woman; **Gengobei** of the man who has
brought his misfortunes upon himself. It is typical that
Gengobei, a samurai by birth, although he is now compelled
to earn his living as a strolling player, scorns to take the
first and most obvious step towards disguising himself, that
of discarding his long sword. The *ronin* turned actor was a
common feature of Saikaku's age and several of the great
acting families today trace their descent from a *ronin* ancestor.

Gengobei passionately loved a beautiful boy whose sudden
death plunged him into despair. Because of the scandal, he
was disinherited by his family. His betrothed, O Man,
feared that he would take his life. Since he would not look
at a woman, she disguised herself as a boy and was able to
comfort him and win his love.

At the time of the cherry-viewing at Kagoshima, O Man
and Gengobei, now strolling players, arrive, hoping to profit
by the holiday mood of the crowd. O Man, in boy's clothes,
carries Gengobei's short sword at her belt and a spear such
as is used in certain dances. A young samurai in the crowd
throws her some money. Gengobei recognizes him as **Sangobei,** a former friend. He is filled with shame that anyone
who knew him then should see him now. O Man comforts
him; she does not care how many old acquaintances she
meets so long as she and he are together. Gengobei, still
more shamed by O Man's loyalty and devotion, makes an
effort to throw off his bitter mood and each in turn dances

to entertain the crowd. Sangobei returns and shows Gengobei that he is still his friend. A crowd of young people surround the three of them, crying out for a general dance, which is performed by the whole company.

SANNIN KICHIZA KURUWA NO HATSUGAI
(*Three Men Called Kichiza*), commonly called *Sannin Kichiza*. *Sewamono*. — Written by Kawatake Mokuami for the actor Ichikawa Kodanji IV. First performed in 1860. Like many of Mokuami's plots, the original play, in seven acts, consisted of two stories loosely linked together. One story, that of a wealthy lumber-merchant called Kiya Bunri and his love for the courtesan Hitoe, is based on a popular novel of the period. The other concerns three bandits, of the type Mokuami loved to portray, who all bear the name of Kichiza. Only this second plot is performed nowadays.

The theme of the play may be described as "honour among thieves," for the three Kichiza, who have sworn blood-brotherhood, have one redeeming characteristic — loyalty to each other. Because of this, in spite of the crimes they commit, the playwright allows them to escape the public executioner and die a more honourable death. The three Kichiza are: **Osho Kichiza**, a priest; **Ojo Kichiza**, a young pickpocket who because of his girlish appearance often disguises himself as a woman; and **Obo Kichiza**, a ronin. The story has a moral: the evil which the same sum of money can cause if wrongfully acquired.

Act I
By the Sumida River, Edo. **Sojuro**, a clerk employed by the lumber-merchant Kiya Bunri, is in love with a young courtesan, **Otose**. One night when he visited her he had with him a hundred *ryo* belonging to his master. He thoughtlessly left this large sum behind in the girl's room.

When the curtain is drawn, Otose is searching for Sojuro, intending to return the hundred *ryo* to him. She has come to this place because it was here that they met the night before. She sees another woman approaching. This is Ojo Kichiza in disguise. He discovers that the girl has money on her and robs her, knocking her out in the struggle. He throws her unconscious body into the river.

This scene is observed by the *ronin*, Obo Kichiza. Not

realizing that he has to deal with a young man, he attempts to gain possession of the money. Ojo Kichiza produces a serviceable sword from his woman's clothes and they fight. Osho Kichiza, the priest, who happens to be passing, hears the clash of steel and hurries to intervene. He takes charge of the purse and persuades the other two that it will be more profitable for all three to go into partnership. The fact that they all bear the same name she that their meeting has been decreed by fate. The three Kichiza swear blood-brotherhood.

Act II

Danshichi's house in Shinyoshiwara. Otase is rescued from the river and carried to a neighbouring house belonging to **Danshichi,** the father of Osho Kichiza. Here also is brought the unconscious body of Sojuro, who has tried to drown himself rather than confess he has lost the hundred *ryo.* Both recover, but their joy at being reunited is turned to dismay when they learn that they are brother and sister, Danshichi's children, abandoned in babyhood at a time when their father's fortunes were low.

Osho Kichiza, who is, of course, their elder brother, comes secretly to his father's house. He has recently been having twinges of conscience about his neglect of the old man and he now brings him the self-same hundred *ryo* as a gift. Danshichi, who suspects that his ne'er-do-well son has not come by it honestly, refuses to accept it. Neither father nor son will touch the money and it is left lying on the floor when Osho Kichiza leaves. An apprentice, **Kamiya Takebe,** sees and steals it. Danshichi, catching him in the act, pursues him out of the house. *The stage revolves.*

Danshichi succeeds in overtaking Takebe and recovering the money. As he is returning home, he meets Obo Kichiza, who, not knowing he is the father of his confederate, robs and murders the old man. It should here be mentioned that Obo Kichiza, though a *ronin,* nevertheless considers himself bound in fidelity to his former lord. It is indeed on account of his lord that he has turned bandit. He at once carries the money to his master, who is in great need of it.

Act III

The Kichijoin Temple. The police are close on the heels of Ojo Kichiza and Obo Kichiza, who come to the temple to ask Osho Kichiza's help. He hides them.

Sojuro and Otose come to see Osho Kichiza and tell him of Danshichi's murder. They beg him to avenge their father and add that, because of the terrible sin they have committed, they intend to commit suicide. Osho Kichiza says there may be a better way of making expiation. He realizes that the police have surrounded the temple and he and his friends have small hope of escape. He persuades his brother and sister to allow themselves to be killed and then presents their heads to the police, saying they are those of the two notorious thieves for whom they are searching. The police, however, discover the imposture before the three Kichiza can make their escape. *The stage revolves.*

Outside the temple is a fire-watcher's tower. At its foot the three Kichiza stand at bay. They beat off their immediate attackers, and Ojo Kichiza, in an attempt to create a diversion, climbs the ladder and beats the alarm drum. They hope to escape in the confusion, but the police are on the watch and close in on them again. In order to escape a felon's death, the blood-brothers, true to their oath, kill each other.

SATOMOYO AZAMI NO IRONUI, commonly called *Izayoi Seishin. Sewamono.* —Written by Kawatake Mokuami. First performed in 1895. The *kiyomoto* music in the first act is by Tayu Enju and is very famous. The original play was in four acts, of which two are still performed.

Act I

The *Hyapponkui* (*Dike of the Hundred Posts*) *by the Inase River.* **Izayoi,** a courtesan of the Ogiya, a house in the licensed quarter, comes down the *hanamichi.* She looks anxiously behind her (for she has run away from her employers) and then towards the walls of the Gokurakuji, which can be seen in the distance among the trees. She explains how some time before she fell in love with a young priest of this temple, **Seishin,** who returned her love. They met in secret, but one day the temple authorities discovered the affair, and, since Seishin had violated his vows, he was expelled. Deeply troubled by the shame and sorrow she has brought upon him, Izayoi is searching everywhere for her lover.

While Izayoi is trying to repair a broken sandal, Seishin enters from the opposite direction. He walks with downcast

eyes and his head is covered, for since his expulsion from
the temple he dare no longer shave his head and his hair is
only partly grown. Izayoi runs to him and tries to catch his
sleeve. But Seishin wards her off, keeping his eyes averted.
When Izayoi begs him to show her a little tenderness,
he tells her he is determined to redeem himself. He intends
to live a life of austerity and to becomes a novice at some
temple in far-away Kyoto, where he is not known. Izayoi
pleads with him, reminding him of their love. (This scene
is mimed to *kiyomoto* music.) At last Seishin can resist her
no longer and responds to her entreaties. Izayoi tells him
their only hope of happiness is to commit suicide so that
they may be born together to a new life. When Seishin
hesitates, she attempts to throw herself in the river. Seishin
stops her and, overcome by her devotion, promises to die
with her. They make their preparations, purify themselves,
repeat the appropriate prayers, and go down to the bank of
the river to throw themselves in, their sleeves weighted with
stones. *The stage revolves.*

A stretch of the river. A boat is moored in midstream
and in it sits fishing **Byakuren,** a poet, attended by a servant.
His net is spread over the side and, Byakuren is smoking
and enjoying the evening cool when he becomes aware that
something is caught in the net. He and his man haul it in
and find Izayoi, unconscious, entangled in its meshes. They
revive her and she immediately tries to fling herself into the
water again. Byakuren prevents her, saying the fates do not
intend her to die tonight. He tells his servant to make for
the shore at once for the girl will catch cold in her wet
kimono. As they are poled away, he makes a caustic comment on the excellence of their catch.

Act II

Another part of the Hyapponkui. Seishin genuinely meant
to die with his love, but once in the water, his skill as a
swimmer and his lack of moral fibre (which is the key to
his character) make it impossible for him to drown. Almost
without knowing what he has done, he finds himself once
more on the bank. He is filled with shame at his own cow-
ardice and tries once more to throw himself into the water,
but cannot do it. He makes the excuse that he hears someone
coming and to his relief he does, in fact, catch sight of a
boy approaching in the distance. The boy comes down the

hanamichi and pauses. There follows a passage of the rhythmic prose for which the playwright is famous (see page 429). It is spoken alternately by the two characters, each of whom is unaware of what the other is saying. Seishin flagelates himself for his indecision and mourns for Izayoi, who may already have found another companion on the road of death. The boy, **Kiozuka Motome,** says that he is a temple page. He has a sister who, to assist her parents, has become a courtesan. His father has just heard that a priest who was kind to his sister is now disgraced because of his association with a woman of the licensed quarter. He has therefore collected all the money on which he can lay his hands and has sent Motome to find the priest and give it him.

As Motome comes towards Seishin, he is suddenly taken with a violent cramp in the stomach. Seishin hurries to help him and, while rubbing his stomach, feels the bag of money in the boy's belt. When Motome is recovered, Seishin asks him whether he has not a large sum of money on him. Motome admits that he has fifty *ryo* which he is carrying to someone in great need. Seishin helps him to his feet and sets him on his way. But as he watches him go, desire to get possession of the money takes hold of him. With such a sum he could buy many services of intercession for the repose of Izayoi's soul ; surely the money could be put to no better use. He runs after the boy and drags him back, saying he only wants the money as a loan. Motome protests and refuses to surrender it. They fight and Seishin snatches the bag from the lad's bosom. In the ensuing scuffle he finds to his horror that he has strangled him with the purse-string which was round his neck. Seishin's first instinct is profound remorse. He replaces the bag of money, lays out the body and says prayers for his victim's spirit. The only expiation he can make is to die, and, taking the boy's sword he prepares to commit *seppuku*. But again he has not the courage to kill himself. Faintly he hears the laughter of a company of merry-makers in a neighbouring garden. From behind the clouds the moon appears. Seishin lifts his head and his face is seen to have changed. Since he cannot take the honourable way out, he will give himself up to evil. " There is no one but the moon and I who know of this murder. Why should I let my conscience make life a burden to me, when I might be as carefree as those whose laughter I hear ? "

The clouds blot out the moon and rain begins to fall. Seishin tips Motome's body unceremoniously into the river and is about to make off when a group of people approach with a lighted lantern. They are Byakuren with Izayoi and his servant. Seishin kicks the lantern from the servant's hand and, never realizing how close he is to his love, makes his escape as the curtain is drawn. (This last scene is mimed in the style called *sewa-dammari.*)

(Seishin turned bandit and took the name of Seikichi no Oniazami, the Thistle. Izayoi escaped from Byakuren, who wished to make her his mistress, and became a nun in order to pray for her lover's soul. She went on pilgrimage to Hakone and there met Seishin. This time it was his turn to persuade her to abandon the religious life. Her love for him was such that she followed him and became his confederate in crime. They attempted to blackmail Byakuren only to discover that he was Odera Shohei, the head of a notorious band of thieves. Seishin and he found that they were, after all, brothers, but this did not prevent Shohei from gleefully telling the lovers that the boy Motome, whom Seishin murdered, was Izayoi's brother. Filled with remorse, Seishin and Izayoi repented of their wickedness and committed double suicide, this time successfully. Shohei was finally arrested and executed.)

SESSHU GAPPO GA TSUJI (*Gappo and His Daughter Tsuji*). *Sewamono.* — Written for the puppets by Suga Senshu in 1773. Later adapted for the Kabuki. The play has always been contentious and was indeed banned as late as 1937 on the grounds that a stepmother's love for her stepson was immoral. There are two interpretations : the first, that the heroine's love for her stepson is nothing more than a ruse to save his life ; the second, that the heroine's love for her stepson is genuine, but her motherly duty prevails over her affections.

Gappo, the samurai, has retired to become a priest. His wife **O Toku** accompanies him into the country. His daughter **O Tsuji** has been married to Fujiwara Michitoshi Takayasu, a local magnate, and is now known as **Tamate Gozen.** She has two stepsons, **Shuntokumaru,** son of her husband's first wife and heir to the title and property, and an elder half-brother, **Jiromaru,** born out of wedlock, but adopted into the family. Jiromaru plans to kill Shuntoku-maru and so succeed to the inheritance. O Tsuji is only nineteen and has fallen in love with Shuntokumaru. A scandal is caused when O Tsuji, apparently out of jealousy of Shuntokumaru's fiancee, **Asaka-hime,** gives Shuntokumaru a poisonous concoction of wine and abalone juice which causes a loathsome leprosy to break out on his face. Disfigured, he flees with his fiancée to Gappo's retreat in the country.

The action takes place in Gappo's house.

Argument : As the curtain is drawn, Gappo and O Toku are discovered offering prayers for their dead daughter, since, having disgraced herself, she is dead to them. While they are thus engaged O Tsuji arrives at the outer gate and calls softly to her mother. Gappo hears and is startled, but seeing that O Toku has not heard, ignores the call. O Tsuji calls again and this time her mother hears. She tries to go to the gate, but Gappo stops her. He reminds her of O Tsuji's misconduct and suggests that she must already be dead, that it is an evil spirit, a fox, a badger, or even her ghost at the door. O Toku nevertheless tries to admit O Tsuji and Gappo warns her that, if O Tsuji is allowed inside, he will have to kill her. O Tsuji pleads through the gate, saying that she has a reason which she may not disclose before others. Gappo relents, on the fiction that it is only O Tsuji's ghost and can do no harm.

Mother and daughter are joyfully reunited. O Toku asks whether the reports of O Tsuji's misconduct are true. To her surprise, O Tsuji confesses her love for Shuntokumaru in lyrical terms. Her mother is revolted and Gappo goes off to find his sword. On his return he reminds O Tsuji of his own virtuous career and his indebtedness to her husband. Even if O Tsuji is in love, her duty requires her to suppress her passion. Yet she dares to ask to be married to Shuntokumaru. Gappo has no alternative but to kill her himself. O Toku stays his hand by suggesting that nothing will be gained by O Tsuji's death. It is Gappo's duty to persuade his daughter to become a nun. O Tsuji declares that she would much prefer to become a courtesan and so captivate Shuntokumaru with her beauty and her finery. Her father again makes to kill her, but O Toku holds him off, by promising to persuade O Tsuji to give up her love. Gappo retires and the two women go into the dressing room.

Irihei, a footman loyal to his young mistress, arrives at the gate and finds one of O Tsuji's sandals there. He hides himself in case he is needed.

Shuntokumaru and Asaka-hime enter. He believes that, if O Tsuji sees him now, blind and disfigured, she will forget her passion for him. At that moment, his stepmother rushes into the room and embraces him. He strives, unsuccessfully, to disentangle himself. O Tsuji tells him that she it is who gave him the poisoned wine so that he should become hideous to see and Asaka-hime should reject him. She makes amorous advances to him. He is horrified. Asaka-hime loses her temper and upbraids her. Irihei enters and pleads with her to behave fittingly. O Tsuji persists in her declarations of love. Gappo hurries in and stabs her in the side.

O Tsuji begs leave, before she dies, to explain the reason for her behaviour. She discloses the plot Jiromaru has made with Tsuboi Heima to kill the rightful heir. She has made love to Shuntokumaru only to drive him from his father's house and to safety. Gappo questions her closely. Why did she not reveal the plot to her husband? She answers that then her husband would have ordered Jiromaru to commit suicide. After all, he too is her stepson. "I have tried to save both my stepsons at the risk of my life. I am their mother." Why, then, has she pursued Shuntokumaru even after he has fled from his father's house? "If I had not seen him again, throughout all his life he could not be cured of his affliction." She then discloses that she has the antidote for his illness. Leprosy caused by poison can be cured if the patient drinks the life blood from the liver of a woman born at the hour, on the day, and in the month of the year of the Tiger, provided he drinks it from the vessel in which the poison has been administered. She herself was born at the specified time and she now produces the abalone shell she herself used for the poisoned wine. Her father and Asaka-hime beg her forgiveness. Irihei bemoans her ill luck. Neither Gappo nor Irihei has the courage to perform the last office for O Tsuji; she herself drives the sword in deeper and catches the blood in the shell. Gappo tells his beads and strikes the prayer bell. Shuntokumaru respectfully drinks the blood and is suddenly restored to health. Everyone rejoices and O Tsuji dies without regret, saying, "Tomorrow I shall see the moon from the lotus flowers of heaven."

SHIBARAKU (*Wait a Moment*). *Juhachiban.* — Probably the finest example of the *aragoto* style, this play was first staged by Ichikawa Danjuro I in 1697. The essential idea is the dramatic exploitation of the *deus ex machina* — a tense situation is resolved by the unexpected appearance of a new character who by sheer weight of personality overcomes the powers of evil which are temporarily in the ascendant. One simple early version tells of a person of high rank set upon by rogues and rescued at the eleventh hour by a valorous stranger. This theme saw many elaborations before the play reached its present form, and these changes explain some of the curious features of today's version — the mysterious ledger, the sword called the "Thunderer," and even the manner of the hero's entry. The story is complicated and now only of secondary importance. The main interest today lies in the play's association with the *kaomise* ("face-showing") ceremonies and its many allusions to theatrical customs and traditions. Some attempt will be made here to indicate where these esoteric subtleties occur.

Argument : The scene represents the precincts of the Tsurugaoka Hachiman Shrine at Kamakura. **Kiyohara no Takehira,** an ambitious and evil lord, has succeeded in contriving the disgrace of **Minamoto no Yoriyoshi,** governor of the eastern provinces, by stealing his seals of office. The theft has also encompassed the disinheritance of Yoriyoshi's son, **Yoshitsuna,** who had the safe-keeping of the seals. Takehira, moreover, desires Yoshitsuna's betrothed, **Katsura-no-mae.** Judging the time ripe for the fruition of all his plans, he proposes to announce publicly his assumption of power at a ceremony of dedication when he will offer a precious sword to the temple. Such an act without Imperial sanction amounts to high treason, and, indeed, Takehira's ambitions do not stop at the eastern provinces; he is one of the megalomaniacs of the Kabuki stage. He does not know, however, that he is himself spied upon by his chief lady-in-waiting, **Teruha,** who is the cousin of the hero of the play, **Kamakura no Gongoro Kagemasa.**

To the sound of *kagura* music, servants with feathered spears announce that it is the *kaomise* month (November). Some samurai enter and congratulate themselves on serving such a master as Takehira. A second group enters with Yoshitsuna and Katsura-no-mae. Yoshitsuna has presented a ledger to the temple, but Takehira has seen fit to question his right to do so and will examine the case personally. Yoshitsuna, as a loyal subject of the Emperor, cannot understand why his offering made in good faith for the prosperity of the nation should have been removed from the shrine. He and his brother, **Yoshisato,** protest. The samurai retort that from now on Takehira will call the tune in Kamakura. Yoshitsuna had better stay in his shop with his ledger as all good shopkeepers should. Thereupon, a quarrel breaks out.

Takehira arrives as the singers chant a triumph song (lifted from a Chinese poem and not entirely appropriate to the season). His creature, **Togane Taro,** carries the ledger, and servants bear in *sake,* plum blossom and other congratulatory emblems. He announces that, pending the Imperial assent, he will today mark his assumption of power by dedicating the sword called the "Thunderer" to the temple. A priest makes a comic good-luck speech, and *sake* is served. Takehira orders everyone to swear allegiance to him. Yoshitsuna and Yoshisato refuse and charge him with treason. Takehira tells Yoshitsuna that his hatred for his father descends to him, but, if he will give up Katsura-no-mae and acknowledge his suzerainty, he will find favour even with Takehira. Yoshitsuna and Katsura-no-mae flatly refuse and make to leave for Kyoto to report to the Emperor. They are obstructed by the retainers who clamour to kill them. Teruha points out that the shrine must not be defiled, but she is overruled by Takehira who orders his henchman, **Narita Goro,** to be fetched to execute them. Goro enters by the *hanamichi* and *kagura* music is played as he prepares himself. The other retainers perform a *haradashi* ("bellyshowing" dance). Takehira drinks.

A voice is heard shouting "Shibaraku—wait a moment" from the back of the audience. Takehira pays no attention and urges his men to hurry. Goro says the voice sends cold shivers down his spine. The retainers ask each other who the newcomer can be and confusion reigns. (This incident has its origin in a quarrel on the stage between Ichikawa Danjuro II and Yamanaka Heikuro. Heikuro, out of jealousy, tried to spoil Danjuro's entry by not taking his cue and Danjuro kept shouting "Shibaraku" from the back of the theatre until he was red in the face with anger. The audience loved it and it has been played in this way ever since.)

Kamakura no Gongoro Kagemasa enters to the approving comments of the singers. He stops on the *hanamichi* and proclaims his identity in the celebrated *serifu* of which a rendering is given on page 457. Takehira recognizes Gongoro and asks the reason for his interference. Gongoro counters by questioning Takehira's removal of the ledger from the shrine and in an elaborate play of words shows that it is a particularly auspicious offering. Takehira angrily orders one of the priests to take away the ledger at once. Gongoro will not let him pass, even when Teruha's help is invoked. (She addresses him as "Narita-ya san," the *yago* of the Ichikawas, see page 396. If a Matsumoto plays the rôle, "Koraiya-san" is, of course, substituted). Gongoro cuts a terrifying *mie* at her. Two retainers fare no better. When eight servants make an attempt, he threatens to tie tails on them and use them as kites (*yakko dako*). A samurai attack is mounted by Goro, but Gongoro generously offers to come to them and at last stalks onto the stage. They prepare to fight. Takehira asks him to restrain his youthful impetuos-

Kamakura no Gongoro Kagemasa

ity. Gongoro taxes him with treason. They argue about the propriety of the sword offering. Gongoro demands back Yoriyoshi's seals of office. Teruha intervenes and hands the seals to Yoshitsuna. She offers the "Thunderer" to Gongoro who presents it to Yoshitsuna. The young man can now be considered as reinstated and free to marry Katsura-no-mae. His friends clap their hands in congratulation. Takehira's retainers do the same in defiance. Teruha reveals the double rôle she has been playing and warns Takehira that she knows all his secrets. Takehira cries for vengeance, but his retainers are cowed by Gongoro. Yoshitsuna, Katsura-no-mae, his brother, and Teruha leave. A group of soldiers try to overpower Gongoro when he is off-guard, but he draws his enormous sword and slices off all their heads at one blow. Gongoro poses before the curtain and makes his exit while *sarashi* (triumphal *aragoto* music) is played.

SHIMBAN UTAZAEMON (*The Strolling Minstrel's Song Book*), commonly called *O Some Hisamatsu*. *Sewamono.* — Written for the puppets by Chikamatsu Hanji (1725—1783). The theme has been used by various authors, but this version is the most famous. The only act still performed is the third.

O Tsune is the widow of a well-to-do pawnbroker in Osaka. Since her husband's death she has competently carried on the business with the help of her two clerks, **Kosuke** and **Hisamatsu**. She has a lovely young daughter, **O Some,** who will inherit the shop in due course. Hisamatsu, the younger of the two clerks, is a handsome youth, still wearing his boy's forelock. He and O Some fall in love, and the match seems suitable in every way, but Kosuke has designs on O Some's dowry. He is jealous of his young rival and, in order to be rid of him, makes it appear that Hisamatsu has stolen a considerable sum of money from his employer. He also spreads slanderous rumours about the young couple.

There is another complication in Hisamatsu's life. As a child he was betrothed to the daughter of an old friend of his father's. When the parents of this girl, **O Mitsu,** died, she was brought up by Hisamatsu's parents so that the two children were like brother and sister. She continues to live at his home in Nozaki village, expecting him to return and marry her. Hisamatsu intended to visit his parents, explain matters and ask O Mitsu to release him. He has not told O Some about O Mitsu, and, now that he is involved in a scandal, it is too late to do so.

Act III

Nozaki Village. Before the house of **Kyusaku,** *Hisamatsu's father. It is just before New Year.* When the curtain is drawn, O Mitsu is standing at the gate. A pair of strolling minstrels enter and try to sell her a new song, called "O Natsu and Seijuro" (see page 248). She tells them she has no time for singing as her mother is ill. Finally she is persuaded to buy a copy. When the singers have gone, O Mitsu stands looking at the song and thinking of Hisamatsu, to whom she expects to be married in the New Year. But her serenity is clouded by rumours which have reached her that Hisamatsu has fallen in love with an elegant town-bred beauty called O Some.

Kosuke and Hisamatsu now approach the house. Kosuke asks for Kyusaku and is told that he is away. Kosuke says he will wait for his return and forces Hisamatsu through the gate with him. O Mitsu recognizes Hisamatsu and is overjoyed to see him. She bustles about, offering tea, but Kosuke roughly refuses it, saying he has not come to exchange courtesies. Hisamatsu has stolen 500 *ryo* from their mistress and that is why he has come to see his father. O Mitsu repeats that their father is away. Kosuke refuses to believe her and loses his temper. He begins to bluster, saying that Hisamatsu has been making love to their mistress' daughter and living above his station — as a result of which he stole the money which he was sent to collect from a client, substituting copper coins for the gold in the packet. O Mitsu begs Kosuke to lower his voice as their sick mother is in the next room, but Kosuke shouts that he wants to tell the whole world about Hisamatsu's thieving. O Mitsu now explains that Kyusaku has gone to offer New Year's greetings to Hisamatsu's employer, O Tsune. Kosuke retorts that he knows that is a lie. If it were the case, they would have met the old man on the road. He tries to force his way into the house, Hisamatsu does his best to stop him and a struggle ensues.

Greatly to O Mitsu's relief, Kyusaku suddenly returns. He gives Kosuke a push and makes him fall. Kosuke is angrier than ever, but Kyusaku asks him how " an old man like myself" could possibly have knocked him down. He explains that, hearing of their arrival, he has returned home. He offers hospitality to Kosuke, who shouts out his accusations against Hisamatsu and claims that, as his father, Kyusaku is responsible. If he does not refund the money, Kosuke will call the police. Kyusaku tells him to calm down and discuss the matter over a meal. When Kosuke refuses, Kyusaku takes a package from his bosom and offers it to him. To Kosuke's astonishment it contains the required sum of money. Kyusaku bids the clerk take it and be off. He has been slandering Hisamatsu at the top of his voice in his own village and he is lucky to escape without a drubbing. Kosuke leaves, muttering : " I hope this money won't turn into frogs on the way home ! "

Hisamatsu asks his father in amazement how he comes to have so large a sum of money. Kyusaku says it was something he put by for his children's marriage. He was on his way to ask O Tsune to release Hisamatsu, as he is needed at home. As things have turned out, that is no longer necessary. The best thing will be to hold the marriage ceremony that very evening, as it is an auspicious day. Hisamatsu asks in obvious embarrassment whether his father really intends him to marry O Mitsu while he is under a cloud. Kyusaku says that, if O Mitsu has no objection, he sees no difficulty. Since he himself intends to take religious vows as soon as they are married, so far as he is concerned, the sooner everything is settled the better. They have New Year food and *sake* in the house ; everything is prepared. He continues to make cheerful plans while Hisamatsu stands dumbfounded and O Mitsu is overcome with shyness. He sends Hisamatsu off to see his sick mother, while O Mitsu prepares the meal. (*The act may begin here.*) Left alone, O Mitsu is blissfully happy. She carefully arranges her hair before her mirror and then neatly chops up the *daikon* (Japanese horse-radish) for the coming feast.

While O Mitsu is thus engaged, O Some, accompanied by her maid **O Yoshi,** comes down the *hanamichi*. They are looking for Hisamatsu's house and have been told that they will know it by the plum-tree in the garden. O Some is anxious about Hisamatsu. When they have identified the house, she sends O Yoshi back to await her in the boat which has brought them, for she does not want a witness to the coming interview. O Some approaches the gate and calls. O Mitsu, annoyed at being disturbed, tells her shortly to come in, if she has business with anyone. O Some asks for Hisamatsu. O Mitsu looks up and sees the beauty and elegance of the caller. Staring at her she says roughly that she "has never heard of such a person." She tells O Some to be off. O Some thinks O Mitsu must be a stupid country servant and offers her a present of money, which she puts in a small incense-box. O Mitsu angrily flings it to the ground.

Kyusaku and Hisamatsu return. Kyusaku complains that all this excitement has given him a headache. He asks O Mitsu to massage his back and shoulders. He thinks an application of *moxa* (a herb burnt on the skin to relieve rheumatism) would help him. Hisamatsu, who does not yet know that O Some has arrived, offers to massage his father while O Mitsu prepares the treatment. O Mitsu first shuts the door in O Some's face and puts a bundle of brush-wood against it, ostensibly to keep out the draught. She then goes to attend to the old man, who roars with pain as the *moxa* (to which, however, he attributes his hearty old age) is applied. Hearing all this noise, O Some pushes open the door and peeps in. She is seen not only by O Mitsu but by Hisamatsu. O Mitsu is about to slam the door again when Kyusaku stops her, saying that she is shutting out all the light. He complains that Hisamatsu is not massaging him properly and crossly bids him pay attention to what he is doing. Hisamatsu, speaking to his father, but intending his words for O Some, answers: "I am paying attention. This a bad time for not minding one's own business." His father cannot think what he means and accuses him of impertinence. O Mitsu says angrily that Hisamatsu must be ill to behave so rudely to his father and to invite strange girls in smart clothes to the house. She would like, she says, to apply an extra-large moxa to Hisa-matsu to see whether that would cure him. She and Hisamatsu bicker, old Kyusaku having the worst of it as both pummel him to relieve their feelings. At last he has had enough of their ministrations and scolds them for quarrelling in this ridiculous way just before their wedding. He forcibly drags O Mitsu off into the inner room.

As soon as they are gone, O Some runs into the house. She tells Hisamatsu that she has come because of the letter he left for her. It is all very well for him to say she must forget him and marry her other suitor, Yamazaya. She cannot do it and she will not give him up. Hisamatsu answers that she should think of her mother. O Some then accuses him of concealing his betrothal to O Mitsu. If he marries this other girl, she will kill herself. As she says this, she draws a razor, but Hisamatsu catches her hand. Weeping, O Some asks him whether he has forgotten their vow to die together if they cannot marry. Hisamatsu, overcome by her devotion, swears he will die with her, if they can find no other way out of the dilemma. As they sit sadly holding hands, Kyusaku, who has overheard the whole conversation, comes into the room. He tells them he has something particular to say. Turning to Hisamatsu, he tells him he is really the son of a samurai named Sagara Jotayu. Kyusaku's sister was his nurse. When his father fell on evil days, Kyusaku took charge of the child and, in due course, sent him to Osaka to learn a trade. It was wrong of Hisamatsu to repay his employer's kindness by making love to her daughter behind her back. It was even more wrong to steal his employer's money, which Kyusaku could only replace with great difficulty. Kyusaku tells O Some that he and his wife have always looked forward joyfully to the time when Hisamatsu and O Mitsu would marry. Now she has come between them and has brought sorrow on his house. He begs her not to make the last years of his old wife and himself miserable by holding Hisamatsu to his promise, but to renounce both the young man and her vow.

The lovers weep and can make no answer. O Some at last says she is prepared to give up Hisamatsu and marry her other suitor. Hisamatsu, not to be outdone, undertakes to marry O Mitsu and make his parents happy. But, unnoticed by Kyusaku, the two look into each other's eyes as they speak and make a secret vow. Kyusaku then calls to O Mitsu, who enters wearing a formal bridal head-dress. Kyusaku remarks that, since no-one else has any proper clothes for the wedding, she had better take it off. He himself removes it and all see that O Mitsu has cut her hair like a nun. She confesses she has heard the whole story and has guessed that, although O Some and Hisamatsu have outwardly consented to give up each other, they have really determined to die together. She has therefore renounced marriage and determined to become a nun. She opens her kimono beneath which she is wearing a white nun's robe. Kyusaku, overcome with sorrow, weeps bitterly. O Mitsu tries to comfort him, saying she never believed she would marry anyone like Hisamatsu. For a little while she was able to deceive herself and be happy, but now it is all over.

Cut to the heart, O Some asserts that it is all her fault. She attempts to commit suicide, but is prevented by Kyusaku. Hisamatsu claims that, on the contrary, the blame is his. He also tries to take his life. Kyusaku stops him and declares, in exasperation, that, if no one will consider him, he will kill himself. He is prevented by Hisamatsu and they all promise each other in tears to continue to live.

Kyusaku remembers O Some's mother and tells the girl she must go home to relieve the lady's anxiety. As he speaks, O Tsune arrives in person in a palanquin to fetch her daughter. She says she knows the whole story and thanks Kyusaku and O Mitsu for their generosity towards her child. She offers Kyusaku a cake-box, saying she has brought a gift for his sick wife. Kyusaku clumsily drops the box, and from it falls a packet of coins. He recognizes it as the money he gave to Kosuke. O Tsune explains that that affair is now settled, and Hisamatsu is not to blame. She wishes to offer the money to the " new nun " as a dowry. She invites Hisamatsu to return with O Some and herself to celebrate the New Year festival with them. Kyusaku, wishing to make some gift in return, offers O Tsune a branch of plum blossom in bud. She accepts it, trusting it is an omen that all will be well by the time the plum tree flowers. Since it would not be correct for O Some and Hisamatsu to travel in the same conveyance, she arranges to take her daughter home by boat and tells Hisamatsu to use her palanquin. He is reluctant to use so elegant a form of transport, but O Tsune kindly insists. *The stage revolves.*

O Tsune and O Some leave, seen off by Kyusaku and Hisamatsu. O Mitsu watches them from the window and wishes O Some all happiness. Turning to her, Hisamatsu asks her pardon, adding that this must be fate against which no one can fight. O Mitsu tells him not to grieve. Now that she is a nun, she has put away worldly passions. She and Hisamatsu say good-bye. O Tsune and her daughter are rowed away while the chorus sings a gay song in praise of the plum-blossom. Hisamatsu is carried away in the palanquin while O Mitsu and Kyusaku stand watching at the cottage door.

(Although this act ends happily, the Kabuki convention will not permit Hisamatsu to go unpunished for his betrayal of O Mitsu; her sacrifice is in vain. O Some and her lover are so much oppressed by the slanders spread about them by the vengeful Kosuke, from which they believe they can never clear themselves, that they finally commit suicide together in the storehouse built as a sign of rejoicing at the time of her birth.)

SHINJU TENNO AMIJIMA (*The Love Suicide at Amijima*), commonly called *Tenno Amijima*, or *Kamiji*, or *Jihei*. *Sewamono*. — Perhaps the best and certainly the most popular of Chikamatsu Monzaemon's masterpieces, this play was written for the chanter Masatayu, probably in 1715, at any rate in the last phase of Chikamatsu's long career. It has been extensively altered by adaptors. All Chikamatsu's domestic plays are variants on the theme of the conflict between duty and humanity, but it would be a mistake to think them all the same. The situations vary little, but the dramatist's real genius is revealed in the diversity of his characters. **Jihei,** the hero of this play, is a mature businessman with a devoted wife and children. He knows that his attachment to **Koharu** is wrong and threatens to encompass his ruin. He makes the effort to pull himself out of the morass. Curiously enough, it is his own wife who pushes him back into his predicament, motivated by pity for Koharu and the idea that Jihei, with a position to keep up, ought to be able to afford a mistress the same as anyone else. From that point onwards, Jihei's doom is sealed.

Act I

The Kawasho Tea-house in Shinmachi, Osaka (*Kawasho no Ba*). Serving-maids are preparing for the day's guests. A courtesan, **Koito,** asks whether her friend **Koharu** of the

Kinokuniya has arrived. She is told that someone has been sent to fetch her and that orders have been given that special precautions be taken with regard to her. Presently Koharu enters, looking very downcast. Koito asks her anxiously whether she is in trouble about Kamiji-san (the paper merchant, i. e. Jihei). Koharu admits it and Koito begs her to do nothing rash, reminding her that she has already once unsuccessfully tried to commit suicide with Jihei. Koharu is evasive and Koito leaves her reluctantly. (The act often starts here.)

Sangoro, Jihei's apprentice, comes with a letter for Koharu, but, to her surprise, it is not from his master, but from **O San,** Jihei's wife. Sangoro explains importantly that it is a secret letter about which his master knows nothing. Koharu reads it with many tears and finally, after repeated urgings, writes an answer. She hides her note in a charm-bag and, after some hinting on his part, gives Sangoro a tip. Alone once more, she bursts into bitter weeping and is so discovered by another courtesan, **O Sugi,** who, like Koito, asks whether there is more trouble about Jihei. Koharu answers indignantly that the story about herself and Jihei is a piece of malicious gossip put about by one of her clients, **Tahei,** and his friends. O Sugi comments that, although Tahei is unattractive, he is rich, and Koharu ought to consider herself lucky to be ransomed by him. Koharu exclaims that she would sooner keep company with an ox. Her words are overheard by Tahei and his friend **Zenroku** who have just arrived at the house and now burst in, drunk and angry. Tahei threatens Koharu with all kinds of penalties when she is his wife. Zenroku makes a ribald speech about "Waste-paper," as he calls Jihei, poking fun at Koharu for taking an interest in a miserable shop-keeper, with a wife and two children hanging round his neck, who can never hope to scrape together enough money to ransom her. Tahei also jeers at Jihei, saying that money is better than a handsome face and, if "Waste-paper" has bespoken Koharu for tonight, he will have him thrown out of the house as he intends to have Koharu to himself. O Sugi explains that tonight Koharu is engaged not to Jihei, but to a samurai client. Tahei answers that in that case he'll throw out the samurai and says scornfully of samurai in general "take away their

swords and what's left?" He and Zenroku start drinking,
Zenroku sings a rude song about Kamiya Jihei, Tahei
accompanying him on a broom. Presently they see someone
approaching the house, and, convinced that it must be Jihei,
they stagger out to intercept him. **Magoemon,** Jihei's
brother, enters disguised as a samurai. Tahei swaggers up
to him shouting: "Pay me the money you owe me!" He
is very disconcerted when he sees Magoemon's two swords
and beats a hasty retreat, bowing respectfully. (For brevity's
sake, the whole Tahei episode may be omitted.) Magoemon
enters the house and is immediately accosted by **Tasuke,**
the servant in charge of Koharu, who insists on seeing his
face. O Sugi, in some confusion, explains that Koharu's
master requires them to make certain that any visitor is not
Kamiji Jihei in disguise. She makes the guest welcome,
while Koharu, plunged in her own thoughts, pays no attention. Magoemon tries to start a conversation with Koharu
who only answers with lugubrious questions about the
different methods of committing suicide. O Sugi, scandalized, hurries Magoemon into the inner room to listen to
some music, obliging Koharu to accompany him.

Jihei comes along the *hanamichi.* He has heard that
Koharu is entertaining a samurai client, but he cannot keep
away. He stands by the window and sees Koharu's shadow
on the thin paper door of the next room. He longs to call
to her, but the next moment he sees another shadow and
hears a man's voice. He shrinks out of sight as Magoemon
comes back into the outer room with Koharu, but he can
hear their conversation through the open lattice. Magoemon
assumes a paternal air and tries to dissuade Koharu from
any thought of death, offering her money to help her out of
her difficulties. Koharu confides to him that her master
has forbidden her to see anything more of Jihei and that,
since Jihei is poor and cannot hope to ransom her, they
have resolved to commit suicide together. But, she admits,
she does not really want to die and begs Magoemon to save
her from her lover. Jihei can hardly believe his ears. He
is wild with rage and jealousy. When Koharu rises and
approaches the window he suddenly draws his sword and
thrusts at her through the bars. Koharu retreats unhurt,
but Magoemon disarms Jihei and, seizing his hands, ties
them to the window bar. Koharu has recognized the sword

and begs Magoemon to let Jihei go, but Magoemon answers that it will do him no harm to cool his heels and takes Koharu back into the inner room. Jihei is left weeping with fury. At this moment Tahei and Zenroku return, even drunker than before. They see Jihei and, after making quite sure that this time it is really he, demand the 20 *ryo* he owes, producing his note of hand. They try to drag him off to the police, but find he is tied up. They are delighted to find him pilloried like a petty thief. They kick and beat him while a crowd gathers. Magoemon comes suddenly from the house and flings Jihei's tormentors roughly aside. He demands proof that Jihei is a "thief" and Tahei, humble and respectful before the samurai, produces the note of hand. Magoemon tears it up and pays the money, flinging it on the ground so that Tahei has to grovel to pick it up. He forces from him and Zenroku a statement that they have nothing further against Jihei and sends them slinking away, the sniggering crowd at their heels.

Magoemon frees Jihei and reveals who he is. He forces him into the house. Koharu is amazed to discover Magoemon's true identity. At the sight of her all Jihei's fury returns. He abuses her fiercely, and is only prevented from kicking her by Magoemon, who tells him he was a fool to trust a courtesan and should rather kick himself. He reads Jihei a lecture on his family duties, warning him that his father-in-law is threating to take his wife home, if he does not mend his ways. Jihei bursts into tears and begs his brother's forgiveness; he abuses Koharu for making him undutiful. He quotes examples of her "devotion" to himself to prove her perfidy. When Tahei offered to ransom her, she begged to die with her lover and made all the preparations. He shouts "Fox! Badger!" (Kitsune! Tanuki!) at her; he never wants to see her again. Magoemon reminds Jihei that he has so often said the same thing before that he wants something more concrete. Jihei, with some reluctance, produces from a charm bag a number of vows of love written by Koharu on sacred paper. He confesses that he and Koharu exchanged one such written vow every month for the last three years, thirty in all. By returning hers to Koharu he irrevocably gives her up and he asks his brother to get from her those he himself wrote so that he may burn them. Magoemon offers the papers to Koharu

and demands the return of Jihei's written vows. Koharu
denies having them. Magoemon first tries persuasion, but
finally forcibly takes the papers from her bosom. With
them is the letter sent to Koharu by Jihei's wife. Magoemon glances through it curiously and then conceals it before
Jihei can see it. Koharu tries to snatch it from him, but he
puts it away with the rest of the papers, promising her,
however, to burn it also. Magoemon's whole attitude towards Koharu changes. Since Jihei is now becoming
curious about this letter, he sends him out of the house,
making an excuse to remain behind a moment himself. He
tells Koharu how much he admires her self-sacrifice and
promises not to betray her to Jihei. Jihei calls his brother
impatiently and Magoemon hurries out to him, for he is
now apprehensive lest Jihei should attempt to do Koharu
some bodily injury, perhaps even murder her. He speaks
soothingly to him, trying to lead him in the direction of
home, but Jihei breaks away and rushes back into the house.
Jihei seizes Koharu by the throat and raises his hand to
strike her. His brother shouts in dismay, and Jihei lets his
hand fall, but as Koharu sinks down he kicks her in the
face, abusing her. Koharu bears it in silence. When Magoemon has succeeded in pacifying Jihei, she offers him her
comb so that he may tidy Jihei's hair. Jihei snatches it
from his brother and is about to fling it at Koharu when
Magoemon prevents him. As the two men go out, a look
of understanding passes between Koharu and Magoemon.

Act II

Kamiya Jihei's House (*Kotatsu no Ba*). (Several versions
exist of the first part of this act. The one summarized below
follows most closely Chikamatsu's original text. In another
version Magoemon comes alone to visit Jihei and finds O
San's father already there. Jihei is asleep in the next room
and does not appear at all. The old man refuses to believe
that Jihei has reformed, but finally is persuaded by O San
and Magoemon to give Jihei another chance. He insists,
however, on taking his grand-daughter home with him as a
kind of surety.)

Ten days later. Jihei is asleep under a quilt spread over
the *kotatsu* (a wooden frame placed over a small fire of
charcoal embers). His wife, O San, is busy about the house.
Their son, **Kantaro,** comes in, followed by the servant San-

goro carrying their daughter, **O Sue**. O San suckles the child while Sangoro tells her that her mother and Magoemon are on their way to call. O San rouses Jihei, who goes into his shop and pretends to be busy with his ledgers. He comes out with a preoccupied air to welcome the visitors. They refuse refreshment (a sign that their errand is an unpleasant one) and Magoemon declares that, despite Jihei's renunciation of Koharu they now hear that he is after all planning to ransom her. Jihei denies it, but his mother-in-law insists that the rumour is all over the town. Her husband is determined to fetch O San back home before Jihei sells her to a tea-house to raise money. Jihei swears that it is not he but Tahei who is ransoming Koharu. This relieves the tension. Jihei writes a sworn statement to the effect that he has broken with Koharu forever. His brother and mother-in-law leave satisfied. (The act may begin here.)

Jihei creeps back under the quilt. Presently O San lifts the cover from his face and finds that he is weeping bitterly. O San realizes that he cannot forget Koharu, but Jihei protests that he no longer loves her, saying she "has refused to die with me, and I have awakened from my three years' dream." But he is humiliated that Tahei should triumph. His rival will not fail to slander him in every commercial house in town. O San, much upset, lets fall that she is sure Koharu will never allow Tahei to ransom her, she

O San and Jihei

would sooner kill herself, and it will be O San's fault. She confesses that she wrote to Koharu begging her to break with Jihei for the sake of his family. She knows Koharu loves him and is true to him. She implores Jihei to go to Koharu at once and ransom her to prevent a tragedy. She has 80 *ryo* set aside to settle some business debts and offers to sell her clothes and the children's to make up the 150 *ryo* needed for the ransom. She makes Jihei change into his best clothes, telling him that, if only for the sake of his reputation as a merchant, it is necessary for him to save Koharu and forestall Tahei. They will think later what is to be done with the girl. O San ties up her most cherished possessions in a bundle and Jihei is about to leave when his father-in-law, **Gozaemon,** arrives. The old man seizes the bundle and demands the release of O San. Jihei pleads to be allowed to keep her as his wife and promises again to reform and make good. But Gozaemon is adamant. He discovers that the chest-of-drawers is empty and O San's clothes are in the bundle. He is sure Jihei is stripping his wife to pay for his dissipations. He will listen neither to his daughter nor to Jihei. If Jihei will not divorce O San he will take her away and make a public scandal. He drags off O San, leaving the weeping children with Jihei.

Act III

Before the Yamatoya Tea-House (*Yamatoya no Ba*). It is a bitterly cold night. A palanquin arrives at the tea-house to fetch Koharu, but is sent away. **Dembei,** the master of the house, is heard saying that Jihei is about to leave and Koharu should be roused. Jihei steps out into the cold, telling Dembei not to disturb her. He is going to Kyoto on business and leaves money with Dembei to settle certain debts. He finds that he has forgotten his sword. Dembei fetches it for him and they say "goodnight." Jihei goes off, but at once returns quietly and hides himself in the shadow of the door, watching a lighted window on the floor above. Magoemon enters, followed by Sangoro carrying Kantaro. He asks Dembei whether Jihei and Koharu are there, and is told that Jihei has gone to Kyoto and Koharu is asleep. Puzzled but reassured, Magoemon goes off, lamenting little Kantaro's ill-luck, cold and deserted by his father. Jihei is deeply affected by his brother's devotion and the thought of the distress his family is going to suffer. The watchman passes again. At last the light is extinguished and a moment later Koharu is struggling to open the house door. The lovers' fingers tremble so much that they have difficulty in doing so. Jihei tenderly wraps Koharu in his own coat and they set out on their journey.

Act IV

The Lovers' Journey (*Michiyuki*). Jihei and Koharu appear on the *hanamichi*, uncertain which way to go. Sombre thoughts revolve in their minds — the inevitability of their fate, the shameful publicity of the morrow, the dark cold of the night, the shortness of their happiness compared with the eternity of their sorrow. Jihei tries to cheer Koharu with the thought that they will be together in their next life and the one after that and so on until they both reach Buddhahood together. Dawn is breaking when they reach the Daicho Temple at Amijima. Koharu is full of remorse that she has broken her word to O San. Jihei reassures her; word came to him that O San has become a nun and therefore is no longer his wife. They stop near a sluice gate and Jihei asks Koharu for her sash. He fastens one end of it to the cross-bar of the gate, thinking sadly as he does so of his children. A crow croaks in the day. The temple bell tolls. They wipe the tears from their faces and repeat their last prayers. At the last moment Jihei's courage fails. Urged by Koharu, he stabs her clumsily at first, but then to a finish. He lays the corpse out according to the rites and then, murmuring "Ichiren Takusho Namu Amida Butsu" (May we two come to rebirth together within the lotus — praise be to Amida Buddha) he hangs himself from the sluice gate. Fishermen find their bodies in the dawn.

Act III (Alternate Version)

(There exists an alternative version of Act III which is also frequently played and is therefore summarized below. It follows Act II without an interval and links up with the scene in which Gozaemon takes away his granddaughter. See note to Act II.)

Kamiji Jihei's house. After the departure of O San and her father, Koharu appears at the gate. She explains that she has come secretly, with the connivance of the mistress of the tea-house, to say good-bye because Tahei is going to ransom her. Kantaro runs to her thinking it is his mother. She tells Jihei she has overheard all that has just taken place. She praises O San's unselfishness and hints that she intends to kill herself because of the sorrow she has caused her. Jihei answers that he will die with her and so expiate his sin against his wife. At this moment Sangoro comes with *sake* cups, saying O San bade him do so, that they might make their marriage vows. As there is no *sake* in the house, they will have to make do with water (this is the equivalent of preparation for death, and Jihei and Koharu regard it as an omen.) They drink. Gozaemon creeps up to the gate leading O Sue, dressed as a nun and leaves her there. She is brought in and shows Jihei that there is writing on her white dress. It is a message from O San saying that she saw Koharu hiding by the gate. Because of Koharu's devotion she wishes to give up Jihei and therefore she and O Sue have both become nuns. She begs Koharu to be a good mother to Kantaro. There is a further message on the dress from Gozaemon begging Jihei's forgiveness for not returning to him a large sum of money which Jihei lent him secretly six years ago. (It was to conceal this loan that Jihei began to frequent the licensed quarter, pretending he had spent the money there, and so met Koharu). Gozaemon writes that Jihei will find 150 *ryo*, sufficient to ransom Koharu, in the drawer from which O San's clothes were taken. Koharu and Jihei weep with joy and sorrow. They are disturbed by the entrance of Tahei and Zenroku looking for Koharu. They threaten to kill Jihei who, hastily sending Sangoro off with the children to his father-in-law's house, draws his sword to defend himself. In the struggle Tahei and Zenroku accidentally wound each other mortally and are finished off by Jihei. Realizing that their happiness is now in any case compromised, Jihei and Koharu go hand in hand to seek death at the temple at Amijima. (This act may be followed by Act IV, the *michiyuki*.)

It follows Act II without an interval and links up with the scene in which Gozaemon takes away his granddaughter.

SHINKEI KASANE GA FUCHI (*The Music Mistress' Ghost*). *Sewamono*. — The ghost story is popular with Japanese audiences and it is customary to present one or two ghost plays during the hot summer months (the idea being that the spectators will shiver with horror). This is the tale of a middle-aged music mistress called **Miyamoto Toyoshiga** who dies of love and returns to haunt her young lover.

Act I

Toyoshiga's house. The poor lady lies sick with a loathsome skin disease. She is tenderly cared for by a pupil, **Shinkichi,** with whom she is in love. The local doctor **Shunkai** can do nothing to cure her, and she is in despair. Already at a disadvantage because of her age, she feels that her disease must ruin any chance of winning Shinkichi's love. The young man, unaware of her feelings, nevertheless does his best for her. Toyoshiga is visited by **Habuya Yoemon,** a fancy goods retailer, his second wife **O Kiyo,** and her daughter **O Nobu** and **O Hisa,** Yoemon's daughter by his first wife. O Hisa is badly treated by her stepmother and instinctively feels herself drawn to Shinkichi, whose fate seems not dissimilar from her own. Toyoshiga is at once conscious of their mutual attraction and becomes insanely jealous. The guests leave, Shinkichi makes Toyoshiga comfortable for the night and then decides to go out for a breath of fresh air. He meets O Hisa on the *hanami-chi* and they leave together. Presently Toyoshiga wakes up, calls for Shinkichi, realizes she is alone, and, while trying to get herself water to drink, collapses.

Act II

A room above a sushi-shop. Shinkichi and O Hisa enter and order tea and *sushi.* They tell each other of their sad bondage and sigh for freedom. They are drawn to each other by their common miseries, but just as they are on the point of declaring their love, the spiteful ghost-face of Toyoshiga appears at the window. Shinkichi incontinently leaves his lady and flees.

Act III

The house of Shinkichi's uncle, Kanzo. The old man is turning in for the night when Shinkichi arrives, breathless, to tell him what has just happened. Kanzo pooh-poohs the story and tells his nephew that his duty is with Toyoshiga. He must return to her at once. At that very moment, a palanquin arrives, and Toyoshiga gets out. She looks very strange and her hands are icy cold. Shinkichi is terrified. She says that she has come to bid him goodbye. He persuades her to rest in the inner room. A professional story teller, called **Sancho,** comes bursting with the news that Toyoshiga has been taken very ill. He urges them to return with him and at last goes off by himself. Uncle and nephew, in utter perplexity, decide that Toyoshiga had better go back home. They persuade her to get into the palanquin. Sancho comes back with the news that Toyoshiga has just died a wretched death. Kanzo and Shinkichi shout out "What utter nonsense! She is in that palanquin." They draw aside the curtain and see that the palanquin is — empty.

SHINOBIYORU KOI WA KUSEMONO (*The Witch Princess*), commonly called *Masakado. Shosagoto.* — *Tokiwazu* accompaniment. Towards the middle of the tenth century, when the Fujiwara family dominated Japan, Taira Masakado organized a rebellion and succeeded in making himself master of all the eastern provinces. He believed himself to be divinely inspired and declared himself Emperor under the title of "New Sovereign." The Fujiwara Regent, Takahira, sent an army against him. Masakado was defeated and was shot down by Tawara Toda, a famous warrior of the Fujiwara, as he was flying from the field. Masakado's son, Yoshikado, later attempted to rally his father's supporters. He was driven into the mountains, and troops were dispatched to exterminate not only him, but Masakado's whole family.

Argument : Oye Taro Mitsukuni is one of those sent to make an end of Taira Masakado's family. He is a young warrior of great personal beauty. In the course of his search he comes one rainy night to a ruined palace, once a favourite retreat of Masakado, hidden in the heart of the mountains not far from Soma, near Sendai. He takes shelter in the deserted palace and falls asleep.

In this ruin a daughter of Taira Masakado is now hiding. She is called **Takiyasha-hime** and has magic powers. She learns who has taken refuge in the house and lays her plans accordingly. She has in her possession, through enchantment, a letter written by Mitsukuni to his mistress, a courtesan named Kisaragi, of Shimabara in Kyoto. She disguises herself as this courtesan and appears before the ruined palace. Mitsukuni awakes to find her there. He is suspicious, for courtesans could not leave the licensed quarter and travel freely. To convince Mitsukuni that it is indeed his lover, the false Kisaragi dances a description of their first meeting. Kisaragi went with a group of other courtesans to the annual cherry-blossom viewing at Arashiyama, near Kyoto. There she saw Mitsukuni and fell in love with him at first sight. He appeared not even to notice her, so that she returned to Shimabara desolate. But later he came looking for her there and visited her constantly.

This description does not, however, entirely lull Mitsukuni's suspicions. He has heard it rumoured that this place is inhabited by a member of Taira Masakado's family. He determines to test her, and to do so, he describes Masakado's death in a dance. Takiyasha-hime cannot restrain her tears and, guessing that he has seen them fall, she redoubles her efforts to persuade him that she is indeed Kisaragi. But Mitsukuni now knows the truth. He resists her and, when she accidentally drops a banner of Soma brocade belonging to her family, he accuses her of being Masakado's daughter. She admits it, telling him her name.

Takiyasha-hime has come intending to kill Mitsukuni, but now that she has seen him, she realizes why Kisaragi lost her heart to him. She tries to induce him to abandon his allegiance to the Fujiwara and join her brother. But Mitsukuni scorns her overtures. Takiyasha-hime, angry and humiliated, threatens to kill him by sorcery. He summons his followers to take her prisoner, but she drives them off. Mitsukuni tries to seize her himself, but she recites a spell and vanishes. There is an earthquake. The old house crumbles, burying Mitsukuni in the ruins. Takiyasha-hime appears triumphantly on the roof accompanied by her familiar, a huge toad. Mitsukuni succeeds in digging himself out, for his strength and courage are such that even magic cannot touch him.

Takiyasha-hime poses defiantly with Masakado's flag in her hand, foiled in her attempt to kill Mitsukuni.

SHINREI YAGUCHI NO WATASHI, commonly called *O Fune*. *Jidaimono*. — Written for the puppets by Hiraga Gennai (1729—1779) and first produced at the Hizenza, Edo, in 1770. Later adapted for the Kabuki stage. The fourth act is still frequently performed.

Background : During the reign of the Emperor Go-Daigo, the wicked **Ashikaga Takauji** attempted to dethrone the Emperor and set up a pretender in his place. A great battle was fought on the Plain of Musashino, near what later became Edo. The commander of the Imperial army was **Nitta Yoshioki,** a famous soldier. He and his troops fought courageously, but were defeated through the treachery of a man whom Yoshioki believed to be his friend. Yoshioki himself was murdered by this same false friend at Yaguchi, where a ferry crossed the Tama River.

Nitta Yoshioki had a younger brother named **Yoshimine** who did not take part in the battle. Yoshimine had been ordered to remain behind and guard the Emperor. In his charge his brother left the family heirloom, two magic arrows which had once been the property of Minamoto Yorimitsu, the ancestor of the Nitta family. Ashikaga Takauji desired to gain possession of these arrows and his spies succeeded in making Yoshimine drunk and stealing them while he slept. Yoshimine, in despair, tried to commit suicide, but was dissuaded by his devoted concubine, **Utena.** The two set out together to seek the lost treasure. While they were upon the road, they heard the news of the defeat of the Imperial army and the death of Yoshioki. Yoshimine determined to rally his brother's troops and march against Ashikaga. He therefore turned his steps towards his ancestral home at Nitta as being the best point of assembly for fugitives from Musashino. On their way, he and Utena came to the ferry at Yaguchi, where Yoshioki had died.

Act IV

The house of the ferryman, Tombei, at Yaguchi. **Tombei** is a wicked old man, in the pay of the traitor Ashikaga Takauji. He took part in the murder of Nitta Yoshioki and for this service was richly rewarded. As a result he has become greedy for more gold. His house overlooks the ferry, and Tombei has been ordered by Ashikaga to watch carefully for fugitives from the Imperial army. Captures will bring a further reward. He is to watch in particular for Nitta Yoshimine. It is arranged that, if Tombei learns of the presence of a fugitive, he is to fire a rocket to alert the countryside. If he actually captures or kills one he is to beat the great drum. Both drum and rocket are kept ready for immediate use.

When the curtain is drawn Tombei is away from home. Yoshimine and Utena arrive at the ferry. They come to the house and ask for a boat, but find only Tombei's daughter, **O Fune.** O Fune tells Yoshimine that there is no one to put them across the river and offers to let him spend the night in the house, since there is no inn. She has fallen in love with the young man at first sight and, when he thanks her and brings forward Utena, she is bitterly disappointed. Nevertheless, she shows them into the inner room.

(O Fune's monologue, which follows, is usually played as a *ningyo-buri*, see page 454). O Fune meditates on the charm and good looks of Yoshimine, thinking that this is just the sort of man she would like for a husband. But she fears that the beautiful lady with him must be his wife. If this is so, there will be nothing left to live for. Her thoughts are interrupted by the return of Yoshimine who has decided to try to persuade O Fune to get them across the river somehow that night. When O Fune questions him about his companion he realizes that she has fallen in love with him. He does not wish to antagonize her at this critical moment so he tells her the lady is his sister. When O Fune makes advances to him, he does not repulse her. She is a lovely girl and her attractions are not wasted upon him. He takes her in his arms, but the movement dislodges the Nitta banner which he is carrying in his bosom. It rolls across the floor and O Fune realizes who he is. Yoshimine hastily retreats into the inner room.

Rokuzo, Tombei's assistant, comes down the *hanamichi*. He is the traditional clown who figures in most puppet plays. He has long courted O Fune who has always repulsed him. He enters the house and catches sight of the shadows of Yoshimine and Utena on the sliding paper door of the inner room. He at once suspects that they are Nitta fugitives and that the young man may be Yoshimine himself. He is about to break in upon them when he is stopped by O Fune. She persuades him that the capture of a fierce warrior is too dangerous a task for him. If he really wants to marry her, she adds archly, he must take care of himself. He had better go and consult her father. Rokuzo, delighted at this sudden change in O Fune, hastens off to do so. O Fune, although she knows that she can never hope to marry a great lord like Yoshimine, determines to save his life.

Night falls. Tombei and Rokuzo creep up to the house intending to surprise and capture Yoshimine. Tombei sends

Rokuzo to guard the back and then, finding the door locked, breaks into the house. (*The stage revolves*). He gets below the floor of the inner room and thrusts his sword up through the boards intending to kill Yoshimine as he sleeps. A shriek is heard. Tombei flings open the doors and finds not the young warrior but his own daughter, bleeding from a mortal wound. She confesses to him that she has assisted Yoshimine to escape because she loves him and because he promised her that, if she would expiate her father's crime of murdering Yoshioki, he would make her his wife in the next world. Beside himself with rage, Tombei strikes his daughter repeatedly. Then, thrusting her aside, he leaps down from the house and fires the rocket signal in the yard. He rushes off in pursuit of Yoshimine.

O Fune knows that the rocket will rouse all the troops for miles around. She is in despair, convinced that Yoshimine will be captured. Then she remembers the drum. If she can beat the drum the signal will cancel the rocket alarm and Ashikaga's men will think the fugitive has been either captured or killed. Painfully she drags herself to the drumtower and feebly succeeds in striking the drum. Rokuzo hears her and hurries in to prevent her giving the signal. O Fune loses the drum-stick, but she pulls Rokuzo's short sword from his belt and in the ensuing struggle she stabs him, and he falls into the river. O Fune, with the last of her strength, beats the drum with the empty scabbard. As she falls dead a small boat, rowed by her father, appears on the river. Tombei is rapidly approaching the further bank when an arrow wings its way from out of nowhere and strikes him dead.

Here the scene ends. The arrow which kills Tombei is, of course, one of the two magic arrows of the Nitta come miraculously to Yoshimine's aid. The second arrow kills Rokuzo who, in spite of his wound, is swimming across the river. Thus Yoshimine recovers the family heirloom and is able to rally the Imperial troops and lead them to victory.

SHINSARAYASHIKI TSUKI NO AMAGASA (*O Tsuta's Death*) *Sewamono*. — This play, drawn from the original story by Kawatake Mokuami, belongs to the group of *sewamono* depicting the uneasy relations between the upper and lower

classes in the late 18th century. It is not a particularly good play, but it is often performed because it affords the chief actor a splendid opportunity in the scene where he breaks his vow and takes to drink again. Usually only this scene and the succeeding scene are performed.

Act I

Sc. 1. *Isobe's mansion at Atagoshita.* The high-ranking samurai **Isobe Kazusanosuke** has a beautiful concubine called **O Tsuta,** the younger sister of the fishmonger **Sogoro.** One of his retainers, **Iwagami Tenzo,** has designs on the girl and makes advances to her. She repulses him, however, in a somewhat tactless manner, and he vows vengeance. Tenzo is, in any case, plotting to ruin his master and thinks he can involve both Kazusanosuke and O Tsuta in a general catastrophe. The chief obstacle in his path is the head retainer **Urado Juzaemon.** Tenzo plans to slander O Tsuta to her master by half-proving that she is having an affair with Juzaemon's son, **Monzaburo.** This will probably result in a quarrel between the Urado's and Kazusanosuke and the dismissal of O Tsuta who may then be more amenable to Tenzo's offers.

Sc. 2. *Before the Benten Shrine in the garden of Isobe's mansion.* Tenzo contrives a meeting between O Tsuta and Monzaburo in the garden at which Kazusanosuke shall be present in hiding. The samurai is suspicious of Tenzo's story, but wishes to reassure himself. He is by nature violent, overbearing, and impulsive. The innocent meeting between O Tsuta and Monzaburo rouses him to uncontrollable anger. Tenzo's plot has succeeded too well. Kazusanosuke throws himself on the two young people. A fight starts in which Kazusanosuke kills O Tsuta in the most brutal manner. He orders her body to be thrown down the well. Monzaburo, though protesting both his own and O Tsuta's innocence, is dismissed from his lord's service. Kazusanosuke retires to decide what he must now do about Juzaemon.

Sc. 3. *The old well in the garden.* O Tsuta's ghost cannot rest, as she has been so wrongfully done to death. In a puff of smoke, her haggard, grey wraith emerges from the well and haunts the house, her unearthly movements appearing as shadows on the paper of the sliding doors and windows.

Act II

Sc. 1. *Sogoro's shop at Shiba-Katamonmae.* The news that

O Tsuta has been killed by her master in the very act of disgracing herself with Monzaburo has cast a deep gloom over the household. Sogoro, his wife **O Hama,** his old father **Tahei,** and even the irrepressible apprentice **Sankichi** feel the shame and the sorrow of it the more, since affairs have prospered for Sogoro and it has been a great honour that his sister should have been chosen by a samurai for his concubine. Sogoro is a big, burly man with a violent temper which he can only control so long as he abstains from alcohol. He knows his failing and, since he has become respectable and a person of consequence in the neighbourhood, he has scrupulously refused to drink. Various visitors come to offer their condolences, not all of them with the best motives, as for instance, **O Mitsu,** the proprietoress of the Kikujaya tea-house who takes some pleasure in saying that she always thought that no good would come of O Tsuta's aspiring to a station above her proper one. Sogoro, kneeling before the family shrine and intoning a prayer for O Tsuta, pays little heed to such malicious hints. O Mitsu and her maid, **O Shige,** withdraw. A small barrel of *sake* is brought by a boy, followed shortly by the donor. **O Nagi,** a maid in Kazusanosuke's house and one of O Tsuta's friends, arrives.

Sogoro

After some hesitation she tells the family the true facts of the case. Everyone is dumbstruck. Then Sogoro electrifies them all by asking someone to give him some *sake*. His wife, his father, and even the apprentice try to dissuade him, but he has his way. He very rapidly disposes of the entire contents of the gift cask and then, peeling off his outer kimono, swears he will break into Kazusanosuke's house and have his revenge. They all try to stop him, but he is as strong as an ox and inflamed with drink. He belabours his wife and his father and wounds the apprentice on the forehead. Reeling, he staggers away down the *hanamichi*. O Hama follows him to try to prevent any further mischief.

Sc. 2. *The front door of Isobe's mansion.* Sogoro enters, closely followed by O Hama. The servants try to subdue him and a general scrimmage ensues. Tenzo appears and directs operations with the result that Sogoro is at last overcome and bound. The fishmonger falls into a stupor. Juzaemon enters and, learning of the circumstances, orders Sogoro to be unbound. He bids O Hama look after him until he is sober.

Sc. 3. *The garden of Isobe's mansion.* Sogoro, prostrate on the ground, slowly regains consciousness. O Hama tends him. Juzaemon who has meanwhile informed Kazusanosuke of what has been happening comes to enquire how Sogoro does. The fishmonger is covered with shame and apologizes to Juzaemon for his outrageous behaviour, begging him to punish him. The head retainer, on the other hand, declares that it is for him to apologize to Sogoro since he and his son are in some measure to blame for the present situation. Presently Kazusanosuke, whose violent anger has given way to remorse, enters and tells Sogoro that his feeling of resentment is entirely justified. Tenzo has been unmasked in all his wickedness and suitably punished. Kazusanosuke then takes the unusual step of apologizing to Sogoro, who accepts the samurai's gesture (and a considerable present of money) and returns home with his wife.

SHIN USUYUKI MONOGATARI (*The Tale of Usuyuki*). *Jidaimono*. — Written for the puppets by Takeda Koizumo and his assistants. First staged in 1741, later adapted for the Kabuki stage. The whole play is still performed and is considered one of the finest of the classical dramas.

Act I

Cherry blossom viewing at the Kiyomizu Temple, Kyoto. **Usuyuki-hime** and her ladies come down the *hanamichi* to visit the temple at the height of the cherry blossom season. Her chief lady-in-waiting, **Magaki,** brings an offering on behalf of her mistress. Usuyuki-hime composes a poem on the cherry blossom which is tied to the branch of one of the trees. The party goes up onto the terrace before the temple. Magaki discloses that a young samurai, **Sonobe Sayemon,** will be coming to the temple shortly to offer a precious sword on behalf of the Shogun. She hints that Usuyuki-hime is in love with him and that her mother approves. A man approaches, but turns out to be an elderly samurai in a wicker travelling hat. At last the real Sayemon appears accompanied by his servant **Tsumahei,** and a famous swordsmith **Rai Kuniyuki,** the maker of the sword. They are met by the chief priest, to whom Sayemon offers the sword. When the ceremony is over he asks whether he may gather a branch of cherry for his mother. The chief priest assents and withdraws with the swordsmith. Sayemon catches sight of the poem, greatly admires it, and gathers the branch to which it is attached. Usuyuki-hime, who has returned, sees him do so and is covered with confusion. Magaki approaches Tsumahei to ask for the return of the poem but he, being in love with Magaki and believing her to be trifling with him, refuses to take a message to his master. Magaki is forced to ask Sayemon herself for the poem which he reluctantly returns. Usuyuki-hime begins another poem, but then declares she cannot think how to finish it. Magaki carries the paper to Tsumahei, telling him that his master must complete the verse. Tsumahei first offers to do it himself. A comic scene follows in which he tries to compose the missing line, one moment shouting : "I have it !" and the next : "No, it's gone !" Finally he is compelled to take the poem to his master. Sayemon reads : "No branch, however high, is beyond the grasp of him who means to reach it. Hopeless love —" to this he adds : "— these words do not exist for the true lover." Magaki bids her mistress thank Sayemon, but she is overcome with bashfulness. Once more Magaki acts as spokes-

man and asks the young man whether he is prepared to help
her lady. He swears earnestly that he is. Magaki tells him
that Usuyuki-hime wishes to become his wife. Greatly
taken aback, Sayemon protests that she is far above him in
birth, and he must have time to think the matter over.
Magaki calls upon Tsumahei to help her : both are anxious
to promote the match. Magaki whispers to Usuyuki-hime
that if she wishes to win her lover she must pretend she is
going to kill herself. Usuyuki-hime, an apt pupil, takes up
Sayemon's sword and is about to draw it when he catches
her hand. She vows she must die because of his cruelty.
Sayemon, who is secretly in love with her, finds that the
only escape is to consent to marry her. Magaki and Tsumahei offer to teach them how to make love. A comic scene
follows in which they demonstrate what to do and say.
They induce the lovers to hold hands and finally to embrace,
to the consternation of a young priest sent to summon
Sayemon to the temple. At Magaki's instigation, Usuyuki-
hime writes a message inviting Sayemon to visit her secretly.
The letter, consisting of their two names together with a
drawing of a sword and the character for "heart," is
attached to a cherry branch. Sayemon interprets it aright
and promises to obey. The lovers part. Magaki and
Tsumahei have made up their quarrel and also arrange a
meeting.

Usuyuki-hime and her maids go to pray in the temple,
leaving Magaki alone. **Shibakawa Toma,** a retainer of the
wicked lord **Akizuki Daizen,** enters. He has been courting Magaki and now tries to take her in his arms. In the
ensuing struggle Magaki informs him that she cares only
for Tsumahei, beats him with her umbrella, and escapes.
Toma guesses that, if Magaki is in love with Tsumahei, the
chances are that Usuyuki-hime is in love with Sayemon.
He knows that his own master wishes to marry Usuyuki-
hime. He argues, therefore, that if he, Toma, kills Sayemon, he will not only serve his lord, but throw Tsumahei
out of a job, so that he cannot marry Magaki. Toma conceals himself to watch for an opportunity.

Kunitoshi, the son of Rai Kuniyuki, enters by the
hanamichi. He wears penitential dress, for he has been disinherited by his father and has come to ask his forgiveness.
His father appears from the temple. When he sees him, he

is about to withdraw, but Kunitoshi catches him by the sleeve calling: "Father!" Kuniyuki replies angrily that he has no son. Kunitoshi implores his forgiveness, swearing he has repented of his former extravagant way of life. Kuniyuki is touched and says that if he really wishes to earn forgiveness he must learn to be a swordsmith, making up for the time when he was too idle to profit by his father's teaching. When he can bring a fine sword as proof of his repentence, he shall once more bear his father's name.

When father and son have gone, **Masamune Dankuro,** the son of another great swordsmith, comes hurrying from the temple precincts. He follows his father's profession but has taken to evil ways and is now in Daizen's pay. He carries the sword-case offered by Sayemon to the high priest. He takes out the sword and, using his professional knowledge, he damages and curses the blade. Rai Kuniyuki sees this crime perpetrated, comes out, and accuses Dankuro of sacrilege. In the fight which follows Kuniyuki stumbles and falls, and is killed by Dankuro. At this moment Daizen appears from inside the temple, accompanied by his retainer, Toma. Dankuro informs him that the sword is damaged as he commanded. Daizen first wishes to kill Dankuro so as to eliminate the only witness to the crime, but then decides to spare him when Dankuro, to prove his loyalty, offers his neck for the sword. Daizen sees Usuyuki-hime's message, which is still hanging from the cherry tree. The sight of her name and Sayemon's fills him with jealousy. He hides the paper in his bosom and leaves, bidding Toma dispose of Kuniyuki's body and then spy upon Sayemon and Usuyuki-hime. Toma waylays two of Usuyuki-hime's maids and tries to discover whether Sayemon is still with their mistress. He is interrupted by the return of Magaki. He tries once again to press his unwelcome attentions upon her, but Tsumahei enters in time to save her. They quarrel. Toma accuses Tsumahei and Magaki of defiling the temple precincts by carrying on a love affair. He promises to make Tsumahei drink "a marriage cup he will never forget." At a signal from him, menservants rush in carrying buckets of water and surround Tsumahei. They attempt to douse him, but Tsumahei routs them. Toma draws his sword and tries to take Tsumahei unawares. The two are fighting as the curtain is drawn.

Act II

The palace of Usuyuki-hime's father, Saizaki Iga-no-kami.
Usuyuki-hime receives a message from Sayemon which falls
in the garden attached to the tail of a kite. It announces
that he will visit her secretly that night. Evening falls.
Sayemon arrives at the gate and is received by Magaki, who
leads him to her lady's apartments.

Toma, his face covered in bandages as a result of his fight
with Tsumahei, enters by the *hanamichi*. He asks for **Hagi-
no-kata,** the wife of **Iga-no-kami** and Usuyuki-hime's
mother. While he is waiting for her he catches sight of the
shadows of Sayemon and Usuyuki-hime on the paper doors
of the next room. Hagi-no-kata appears and Toma informs
her that he comes as a go-between for Daizen who wishes
to marry her daughter. Hagi-no-kata refuses to answer
until she has consulted her husband, who is away from
home. Toma angrily threatens that, if she gives an
unfavourable answer, it will be the worse for all the family.
He hints that Usuyuki-hime has a secret lover and is a
disgrace to her parents. Hagi-no-kata, deeply insulted,
drives him from the house. She then flings open the door
of her daughter's room and discovers Usuyuki-hime and
Sayemon. She is not angry with them, but comments that,
since it is plainly high time that her daughter were married,
and she has always wished Usuyuki-hime to marry Sayemon, they had better celebrate the wedding at once.
Magaki and the maids prepare for the ceremony and the
two exchange cups of *sake*. Suddenly the return of Saizaki
Iga-no-kami is announced. The articles used for the wedding are hastily removed. Iga-no-kami enters and greets his
household and Sayemon. He is particularly glad to see the
latter since he has a proposal to make to him. He and his
wife have long ago decided that Sayemon would be the most
suitable husband for their daughter. Now he has reasons
for wishing to expedite the matter. He asks Sayemon to
accept Usuyuki-hime as his wife.

The general rejoicings are interrupted by the unexpected
arrival of **Katsuraga Mingu,** the Shogun's representative
in Kyoto. He is accompanied by Akizuki Daizen and
Sayemon's father **Sonobe Hyoe.** A retainer carries a sword
box. Mingu tells Iga-no-kami that he and Daizen have
come to enquire into the conduct of Usuyuki-hime and

Sayemon, who are accused of practicing black magic against the Shogun. When Sayemon denies it, Mingu produces the damaged sword with the curse marks on it. To make such an offering to the Buddha on behalf of the Shogun is plainly an attempt to do harm. Hyoe tells his son that he hates and disowns him. If he had any sense of honour he would have killed himself long ago. Iga-no-kami asks how his daughter's name comes to be connected with the matter. Daizen produces Usuyuki-hime's message, bearing her name and Sayemon's with the drawing of a sword and the character for "heart" (see Act I). When asked what it means, Usuyuki-hime can only answer incoherently that it is a love letter. Daizen brushes her words aside, explaining that the message is an order to damage the middle (or heart) of the sword. Sayemon swears that, if there is any blame, it is entirely his, and Usuyuki-hime has no part in it. He begs Mingu to summon the swordsmith Rai Kuniyuki, who can testify that the sword left Sayemon's hands undamaged. Mingu consents, but as he speaks two priests from the Kiyomizu Temple carry in Kuniyuki's corpse, which they have discovered in the temple grounds. They have been sent on from Mingu's house. Sayemon with tears begs the corpse to clear him of guilt and asks Mingu to examine the wound. Mingu declares that Kuniyuki has been killed by a skilful swordsman. Few have the skill to inflict such a wound apart from his colleague Daizen (there is no love lost between these two, for Mingu is a just and upright man.) Daizen counters by accusing Sayemon. The latter offers to kill himself in witness of his innocence, but is stopped by Mingu, who does not believe Sayemon is expert enough to inflict such a wound and therefore will not accuse him of the crime. However, since he and Usuyuki-hime cannot clear themselves of the charge of treason they will have to be punished. Iga-no-kami and Hyoe ask to be allowed to speak together privately. They go onto the *hanamichi*. Iga-no-kami suggests that they ask Mingu to let each act as gaoler to the child of the other while they are enquiring into the charge. They return and make their request. Daizen objects, but Mingu grants permission. He calls Sayemon and Usuyuki-hime to him, allows them to say good-bye, and then entrusts the young man to Iga-no-kami and the girl to Hyoe. Magaki is allowed to accompany

her mistress. The two fathers vow to treat their prisoners
with the utmost severity.

Act III

The house of Sonobe Hyoe. (This act is known as " The
Scene of the Three Laughs "— Sannin Warai no Ba.) The
garden of Hyoe's house. Sayemon's mother, **Ume-no-kata,**
tries to console Usuyuki-hime, telling her she is convinced
that both she and Sayemon are innocent. Hyoe comes to
speak privately to Usuyuki-hime. He tells her that he looks
upon her as his own child and believes her guiltless. He
asks whether she is prepared to obey him as a father;
Usuyuki-hime promises to do so. Hyoe continues that,
although Daizen is deeply suspect, there is no proof against
him, and it is likely that Usuyuki-hime and Sayemon may
suffer for the crime. He has therefore decided to let her
escape. She and Magaki are to start at once, escorted by
Tsumahei. Usuyuki-hime thanks Hyoe for his generosity,
but refuses because she does not wish to escape without
Sayemon and she cannot allow Hyoe to pay the penalty for
her flight. Magaki endorses her mistress' words. Hyoe
asks sternly whether Usuyuki-hime has forgotten her
promise of obedience. If she refuses she will no longer be
his daughter (and therefore no longer Sayemon's wife).
Cowed by the feigned displeasure of Hyoe and Ume-no-
kata, Usuyuki-hime and Magaki at last consent to leave
with Tsumahei.

Ume-no-kata asks her husband anxiously how this decision of his will affect their son. Hyoe tries to reassure her,
but at that moment a messenger from Iga-no-kami enters,
carrying a sword case. He informs Hyoe that Sayemon has
confessed to the crime of wilfully damaging the Shogun's
sword and that Iga-no-kami has been obliged to execute him.
He sends the blood-stained sword as a token that Hyoe
should execute Usuyuki-hime so that the lovers may be
joined in death. Iga-no-kami will come shortly, bringing
Sayemon's head, so that the two of them may go together
to report to the Shogun's deputy. Hyoe, with outward
calm, accepts the sword and undertakes to produce Usuyuki-
hime's head in due course. When the messenger has left,
Ume-no-kata snatches up the sword to kill herself, but Hyoe
prevents her. He stares long at the blood-stained weapon.
When Iga-no-kami is announced, Hyoe bids his wife be

brave and receive him. He himself withdraws. Iga-no-kami
enters, carrying a head-box, and asks Ume-no-kata whether
his daughter made a brave end. She cannot bring herself
to speak to him and both fall silent. A temple bell tolls.
Sayemon, his face concealed, comes down the *hanamichi*.
He calls to his mother who rushes to the gate in amazement, but is held back by Iga-no-kami who assures her that
what she sees must be a fox or badger spirit come to torment
her. He recites exorcisms at Sayemon, who takes the hint
and hides himself. Hyoe returns, also carrying a head-box.
The two men open the boxes simultaneously. Each contains
no more than a letter. Iga-no-kami smiles, saying : "I see
you have taken my meaning aright." The boxes will hold
their own heads, not those of their innocent children. Hyoe
strips off his outer garment and reveals that he has already
committed *seppuku*. He knows, he says, that Iga-no-kami
has done the same since the sword he sent was stained not
for the whole length of the blade, as it would be after a
beheading, but only at the point. Iga-no-kami in turn
removes his outer garment and shows the silk bandages
about his body red with blood. Ume-no-kata weeps bitterly. Her husband tells her to be brave and rejoice that their
troubles are now over and the children safe. He bids her
laugh with him and Iga-no-kami because they are free from
all care. The three laugh in turn, choking back their tears.

Hagi-no-kata comes through the garden, having followed
her husband. The two women weep in each other's arms.
Hyoe and Iga-no-kami rise and, taking the head-boxes,
prepare to confront the Shogun's deputy.

Act IV

The house of the swordsmith Masamune Gorobe. Kunitoshi
(see Act I), now calling himself Kichisuke, has become
Gorobe's apprentice. He and Gorobe's daughter, **Oren,**
have fallen in love. Gorobe's son Dankuro (see Act I) has
arbitrarily ousted his father and rules the household. He
claims that the old man is lazy and spendthrift — he
frequents the licensed quarter and has his hair dressed every
day.

When the scene opens, Dankuro returns home with some
friends, installs himself in the best room, and orders his
sister about. Gorobe appears at the gate and Dankuro's
friends attempt to bring about a reconciliation (for which the

son now seems anxious) but the old man refuses to accept "forgiveness." When the friends have gone it becomes apparent why Dankuro wishes to come to terms with his father. He has been ordered by Daizen to make a sword to replace the one "damaged by Sonobe Sayemon" and alone he is not competent to do so. He shows the damaged sword to Gorobe, who recognizes it as the work of Kuniyuki and undertakes to make the new blade. Dankuro insolently orders him to go and bathe "to remove the stink of the licensed quarter." Oren leads her father away.

Shibakawa Toma comes to the gate to summon Dankuro to Daizen's presence. He tells him that Usuyuki-hime is believed to be hiding in the vicinity. *The stage revolves.*

The bathroom of Masamune Gorobe's house. Kunitoshi is preparing his master's bath, helped by Oren. He tells her that he cannot hope to marry her unless her father teaches him the innermost secret of his craft, which is the correct temperature of the water for tempering a blade. This secret Gorobe has imparted to no-one, not even Dankuro. Gorobe enters and complains that the water is not hot enough. Kunitoshi stokes the fire. Gorobe again tests the water, then takes Kunitoshi's hand and dips it in, bidding him remember the temperature as it is the correct heat needed to temper a sword; this is the secret of his craft. He has recognized Kunitoshi as the son of the great swordsmith Kuniyuki, whose father taught Gorobe all his skill. Kunitoshi tells the story of his disinheriting, his father's death, and his own vow to avenge him and be worthy to take his place. Gorobe appoints Kunitoshi his assistant in the forging of the new sword and gives his blessing to his marriage with Oren. *The stage revolves.*

The forge. Gorobe, in ceremonial dress, is seated in the centre with Dankuro and Kunitoshi as his assistants. (For the procedure used by swordsmiths, see page 465). Gorobe prays and begins to forge the sword. When the moment comes to temper the blade, Dankuro tries to discover his father's secret by dipping his hand in the water. Gorobe turns upon him and wounds his right arm with the half-made sword. This he does to punish Dankuro, whom he knows to have committed the crime of damaging the Shogun's sword. When he looked at the blade, he saw upon it a mark showing it was under a curse, but it was not the secret curse mark of the swordsmith Kuniyuki, who made the sword; it was the secret curse mark of the Masamune family. Only Dankuro could have put it there. Dankuro is unworthy to be his son and, although he still loves him, he disinherits him. Perhaps in time, now that the skill he used for evil purposes is taken from him, he may repent and become a good man. Gorobe begs Kunitoshi and Oren to care for him and makes Kunitoshi his heir in the craft.

Usuyuki-hime and Magaki enter by the *hanamichi* and beg for shelter. They are recognized by Gorobe and Kunitoshi. Dankuro repents of his former wickedness and confesses his part in Kuniyuki's murder. He offers to help Usuyuki-hime by way of expiation. When Toma reappears at the gate, Dankuro tells him that his association with Daizen is at an end. Toma attempts to have him and Kunitoshi arrested by his followers. In the ensuing fight, Dankuro seizes the newly forged sword in his left hand and defends himself gallantly. Kunitoshi kills Toma, saving Dankuro's life. All pose triumphantly as they express their intention of going at once to report Daizen's evil doings to the Shogun's deputy and to demand permission to be revenged on him.

SHOJO (*The Baboon*). *Shosagoto*. — Adapted from the Noh play of the same name. *Nagauta* accompaniment. The *shojo* was a supernatural creature which appeared in the shape of a large baboon. It was a lucky omen to see one, for it only appeared to the virtuous and in time of prosperity. It lived in rivers or the sea and was said to be fond of *sake*. Various versions of this dance are performed by one, two, or five *shojo*, but the basic theme remains the same. The tale is of Chinese origin.

The scene represents the Kabuki version of the Noh stage. Sometimes a giant *sake* jar is placed in the centre, but the classic version, which keeps most closely to the Noh and allows for one *shojo* only, dispenses with all properties.

Argument: A youth enters and announces that he is **Kofu** of the village of Yangtze at the foot of Mount Kanekin in China. He keeps a *sake* shop near the river Shinjo. One night he dreamed that a *shojo* came to him and presented him with a flagon of *sake* which would never run dry, saying

294

that it was a reward for his virtue and filial piety. When Kofu awoke he found the flagon at his side and with its help became a wealthy man. Recently he again dreamed of a *shojo* who this time came up from the river asking for drink. As he owes his good fortune to the *shojo*, he has hurried down to the river bank with the miraculous flagon.

Kofu then sits down stage left, the position taken in the Noh plays by the secondary character. The *shojo* appears and Kofu pours *sake* for him. The *shojo* drinks greedily and then performs an auspicious dance which promises peace and plenty in the land.

SHOUTSUSHI ASAGAO NIKKI (*The Diary of Morning Glory*), commonly called *Asagao Nikki. Sewamono.* — Written for the puppets and, in particular, for the *gidayu* singer, Takemoto Shigedayu, by Chikamatsu Tokuso (1753—1810) in about 1804. The play did not, however, become really popular until a Kabuki version was made in 1850 by an unknown author using the penname " Yamada-no-Kakashi " (Scarecrow in a Mountain Rice-field). This version was staged with great success by the actor Sawamura Tanosuke II and gave rise to a craze for patterns incorporating the morning-glory (*asagao*) on clothes, fans, hair-ornaments, etc. The third act remains a perennial favourite and is frequently performed.

Act I

The Uji River, near Kyoto. The Uji is famous for the fireflies which may be seen there on a summer evening. It was, and still is, fashionable to picnic in a boat on the river and enjoy the evening cool while " viewing " the fireflies. When the curtain is drawn, a large pleasure-boat, with the bamboo curtain lowered, is seen anchored in the stream. A smaller boat containing a party of youths ties up near it. The host of this party is a young man named **Miyagi Asojiro**. Asojiro and his friends settle down to drink *sake* and enjoy the fireflies, but suddenly a gust of wind blows some papers and pieces of silk out of the large boat. A lady's head-covering drops into the small boat near Asojiro who politely returns it to the maidservants who appear from behind the bamboo screens. He and his friends are invited on board the pleasure boat. The curtains are rolled up, and they meet their hostesses, **Maki-no-kata,** the wife of a wealthy samurai, and her daughter **Miyuki.** The head-covering belongs to Miyuki, and she is admonished by her mother to thank Asojiro. The two young people look into each other's eyes and fall instantly in love. Maki-no-kata suggests that to commemorate this pleasant meeting Asojiro might write a verse on her daughter's fan. Miyuki offers it shyly and, after a moment's thought, Asojiro writes the following poem in the old *saibara* form : " The morning-glory blooms in the dew of the dawn, but the sunshine withers its beauty. If a gentle rain were to fall, the flower would keep its fragrance a little longer."

The young men thank Maki-no-kata for her hospitality and return to their own boat. Holding the fan in her hand and lost in a happy rêverie, Miyuki watches the boat disappear in the distance as the fireflies dance in the evening air.

Act II

The house of Miyuki's father, Akizuki Yuminosuke. Some months have elapsed since the previous act, and during the interval Miyuki and Asojiro have met again on the beach at Akashi on the Inland Sea. They scarcely had time to do more than exchange vows, but, as they parted, Miyuki threw to Asojiro as a keepsake the fan on which he wrote the poem.

Since her return from Akashi, Miyuki has become more and more pensive. When the scene opens, her maids are discussing her with her old nurse, **Asaka.** Miyuki enters and sits dreaming about her lover. When she has retired to her own apartments, **Yuminosuke,** her father, comes home and, sending for her mother, announces that the most flattering proposals for Miyuki's hand have been made to him through his lord. The young man in question is a well-to-do samurai, the adopted son of a friend of their lord. His name is **Komazawa Jirozaemon.**

Yuminosuke knows nothing about his daughter's infatuation and does not trouble to mention that, before he was adopted, the young man's name was Miyagi Asojiro. His wife, however, knows Miyuki's heart and is distressed when Yuminosuke orders her to inform their daughter of her good fortune. Yuminosuke leaves and Maki-no-kata sits wondering how she is to break the news to Miyuki. At length she sends for her daughter and tells her she is to be married. Miyuki weeps bitterly, but it does not occur to her to protest, even to her mother.

It is evening, and the household is settling down to rest. Left alone, Miyuki decides to run away and find Asojiro. But she only makes this decision after much heart-burning. She writes a farewell letter to her parents and leaves it by the lamp, which she extinguishes. Then she steals out by the garden gate. A moment later her nurse's voice is heard calling in the next room that Miyuki is not in her bed. The girl crouches outside the gate as her parents and nurse hurry in, light the lamp and discover the letter. While her father is reading it, she takes silent leave of them and hurries off down the *hanamichi*.

Act III

Sc. 1. *The Ebisuya, an inn at Shimada Juku.* Several months have passed. Miyuki's disappearance has, of course, put an end to the marriage plans, and Asojiro, now called Jirozaemon, is heart-broken. He has no idea why Miyuki should have run away, but suspects that it is with another lover. Nevertheless, he still cherishes the fan.

Jirozaemon, with another samurai of his clan, **Iwashiro Takita,** and a suitable escort, is travelling to Edo on his lord's affairs and stops the night at the Ebisuya at Shimada Juku. They are shown into the best room overlooking the garden, and there to his surprise Jirozaemon sees pasted on a screen a fan paper bearing the verse he wrote for Miyuki. He draws the real fan from his breast and compares them. Then he sends for the inn-keeper, **Tokuemon,** and asks him about the paper. Tokuemon tells him that a poor blind girl, calling herself Asagao, has come to live in the neighbourhood and keeps herself by singing this song and others to the inn guests. Jirozaemon wonders whether this can possibly be Miyuki, fallen for some reason on evil days. He tells the inn-keeper to send for the young woman. His companion, Takita, protests that they do not want a dirty beggar in the room. It is settled that she shall play to them outside in the garden. A country girl appears carrying Asagao's *koto* (thirteen-stringed zither) and presently the blind girl herself comes feeling her way with a stick. Jirozaemon recognizes her at once as Miyuki, although she is terribly changed. She settles down before her *koto* and Jirozaemon asks her to sing the " morning-glory " song. She does so in a sad voice and is chidden by Takita for not singing better. He orders her to sing another, more cheerful, song, but Jirozaemon, moved and fearing that it will be too much for this emaciated shadow of the lovely Miyuki, vetoes the idea. Takita then suggests that she entertain them by telling them her story, which the inn-keeper has hinted is pathetic. She does so, and Jirozaemon learns that it is for his sake alone that she left her parents, that she has been seeking him in vain and has gone blind from weeping. He does not like to tell her who he is before Takita and plans to do so as soon as he can get her alone. Shortly after Miyuki has left, one of their escort comes to say that they must continue their journey at once if they want to reach Edo, for heavy rains have swollen the Oi River, which they must cross and soon it will be impassable. Since he is on his lord's business, Jirozaemon is obliged to acquiesce. Takita goes out to arrange for their immediate departure and Jirozaemon summons the inn-keeper and asks to see Asagao. To his dismay he is told that she has gone home and it is impossible for her to be fetched before he leaves. Jirozaemon hastily writes an explanation of his change of name on the back of the fan he has been cherishing and gives it to Tokuemon with a considerable sum of money and a special medicine to cure blindness, asking him to convey them to Asagao. The medicine, he adds, must be administered in fresh blood. He then hurries after his companions.

Jirozaemon has no sooner left than, to Tokuemon's surprise, Miyuki returns, saying that she has had a premonition that she is needed. He gives her the gift left by Jirozaemon. She asks him to keep the money for her, but keeps the medicine. When she touches the fan, she at once feels something familiar about it. She begs Tokuemon to tell her whether there is anything written on it and he reads out to her the " morning-glory " poem and, on the reverse side, the words: " Miyagi Asojiro, now called Komazawa Jirozaemon ". Miyuki is almost beside herself and, half laughing, half crying, sobs out again and again " And I didn't know " (Shirananda). When she realizes that Jirozaemon has already gone, she insists on following him, although heavy rain is falling, and Tokuemon assures her that he will have already crossed the river. Miyuki shakes off the inn-keeper and rushes away wildly, stumbling and falling, in the direction of the ferry. *The stage revolves.*

Sc. 2. *The bank of the Oi River.* The last ferry has

crossed, carrying Jirozaemon and his party, and the river swirls fiercely between its banks. Miyuki comes reeling through the rain. The ferryman shouts to her that no boat can live in the waters. This cruel extinguishing of her new-found hope drives her to despair. She is sure her lover is now lost to her forever; there is nothing left for her but to drown in the cruel river. She fills her sleeves with stones, making sure where the water is deep by casting pebbles into the stream. Then she repeats her last prayers and prepares to throw herself in. She is prevented in the nick of time by a passing traveller who is none other than **Sekisuke,** a retainer of her father's, one of those sent out to search for her after her disappearance. He recognizes her, amazed. A moment later Tokuemon, the inn-keeper, comes hurrying along the bank and learns from Sekisuke that the blind girl on whom he took pity is none other than his own daughter's nurseling, his old master's child. He tells Sekisuke of the strange events which have brought about Miyuki's present plight and begs the girl not to despair. With Sekisuke's help she will find her betrothed again and, moreover, she carries upon her the cure for her greatest affliction, her blindness. Miyuki suddenly remembers the medicine. Tokuemon asks for the loan of Sekisuke's short sword and before the others realize what he is about, plunges it into his side, thus providing the fresh blood necessary for the administration of the drug. Sekisuke catches it in his cup and, mixing the medicine, gives it to Miyuki. She drinks it and faints, but, when she revives, finds to her incredulous joy that she can see again. She and Sekisuke thank Tokuemon for his loyal sacrifice and, as the sun rises, he dies supported by Sekisuke while Miyuki prays beside him.

Act VI

Michiyuki (Travel dance). This act, which has nothing to do with the plot and is simply a dance relating some incidents during Miyuki's journey, is usually omitted. Miyuki and Sekisuke are seen on the highway leading from Kyoto to Edo, where she expects to find her betrothed. They dance singly and together to express their joy and hope. Sekisuke carries over his shoulder a pilgrim's pole hung with *sutras*, and Miyuki is dressed as for a pilgrimage. They meet a crowd of young people on the way and dance with them.

SOGAMOYOO TATESHINO GOSHOZOME, commonly known as *Otokodate Gosho no Gorozo. Sewamono.* — Written by Kawatake Mokuami for the actor Ichikawa Kodanji IV and first performed at the Ichimura-za in 1864. This play is a classic example of typical Edo Kabuki, all violence and stylized poses. The hero is an *otokodate,* and the *otokodate,* or chivalrous commoner, was something peculiar to Edo, (see page 448).

The first act of the play is never performed nowadays. It concerns the household of the young daimyo **Asama Tomoenojo** who takes a concubine, named Hototogisu, the daughter of a tea-ceremony instructor. Tomoenojo's wife, Yuri-no-kata, is jealous and beats the girl to death.

This first act bears only indirectly on the main theme. Asama Tomoenojo has in his service a retainer named Suzaki Kakuya who, because of the strength of his hands and his skill in swordsmanship, is nicknamed **Gosho no Gorozo** after the famous captor of Soga Goro (see page 376). Gosho no Gorozo is the lover of Tsuji, a waiting maid in the Asama household. Their love affair is strictly against the rules governing a daimyo's retinue. They are betrayed by **Hoshikage Doemon,** a samurai also in Tomoenojo's service, whose advances Tsuji has repulsed. Tomoenojo is forced reluctantly to dismiss both Gosho no Gorozo and Tsuji. Such is the feeling against Doemon in the household that he also leaves his master's service and sets up as a fencing instructor.

Seven years have passed. Gosho no Gorozo and Tsuji are married. At a moment when their fortunes were at a low ebb, Tsuji, to help her husband, sold herself to be a courtesan in the Yoshiwara, taking the name of **Satsuki.** Gosho no Gorozo becomes an *otokodate* of high repute.

Act II

The Naka-no-cho in the Yoshiwara. Gosho no Gorozo and Doemon enter, each accompanied by his personal followers. It is their first meeting since they both served Asama Tomoenojo. Their followers have recently been involved in a fight in which Doemon's samurai were worsted. Both groups are anxious to be at each others' throats again and throughout this scene are with difficulty restrained by their masters. Gosho no Gorozo and Doemon at first exchange courtesies, speaking of the beauty of the spring (the poetry of this

passage is famous—see page 429). Then Doemon says he
learns that the celebrated Satsuki is none other than Tsuji who
treated him in so cavalier a fashion long ago. Now that she
is serving in the Yoshiwara, he intends to buy her company
every night to compensate himself for what he suffered in
the past. Gosho no Gorozo, restraining his temper, replies
that Doemon may not realize that Satsuki is his wife. Since
she is a courtesan of rank, she is able to choose her own
clients and, as no doubt Doemon knows, it is etiquette for
a courtesan known to have a husband to be expected to
entertain only guests of her own choosing. Doemon,
laughing, retorts that he knows no such thing. He intends
to buy Satsuki in any case, even if it costs him a million *ryo*
a night. Gosho no Gorozo boils at this insult, particularly
as it is offered to him in public. He and Doemon are
about to draw their swords, but are stopped by **Yogoro,**
the proprietor of the Kabutoya tea-house outside which they
are standing and where Satsuki is employed. Yogoro begs
them not to make a disturbance outside his premises just at
the moment when people begin to throng to the Yoshiwara.
It is cherry-blossom time and Yogoro thinks they have been
drinking, for he knows nothing of their past histories. He
invites them into his house to drink an amicable cup together.
Gosho no Gorozo refuses, saying brusquely that he is pressed
for time. Yogoro tells Doemon to set Gorozo a good example. Doemon, who feels he has come off best in the
altercation, opens his fan and offers it to Gosho no Gorozo
who takes it reluctantly. (The exchange of some such
objects as wine cups, swords, or fans was a recognized
indication that a quarrel was ended or at least had been
postponed).

Act III

Sc. 1. *The inner room of the Kabutoya giving on the garden.*
The two principal courtesans are Satsuki and **O Shu.** O Shu
is the sister of Asama Tomoenojo's unfortunate concubine,
the girl murdered in Act I. Tomoenojo has fallen in love
with her because of her resemblance to his dead mistress and
spends most of his time in her company. He has wasted his
patrimony and is now deep in debt. He owes the master of
the Kabutoya two hundred *ryo* and, unless he can raise this
sum, he will no longer be able to see O Shu. Gosho no Gorozo hears of his former master's embarrassment and, remain-

ing loyal despite his dismissal, determines to try to find the money for him.

When the curtain is drawn Satsuki, wearing the magnificent regalia of a courtesan of high rank, is reading a letter from her husband begging her to help him raise the money Tomoenojo requires by midnight. Satsuki is pondering this problem, when Doemon enters. He has overheard her and offers to give her the sum. Satsuki is taken aback by his unexpected kindness, but accepts joyfully. He lays the bag of money within her reach, but as she is about to pick it up, observes that there is one condition attached. He will give her the money, if she will write her husband a letter of divorce and come with himself that night to a house of assignation. Satsuki refuses indignantly, but ultimately, because the money is for her lord and Gorozo, she accepts, privately vowing to commit suicide rather than give herself to Doemon. She writes the letter and Doemon calls in his followers to celebrate his victory. Doemon tells one of them to deliver the letter to Gorozo. No one is anxious to perform the errand, but before it has been decided who shall go, the notes of a flute are heard and Gorozo is seen passing the house. Satsuki is taken aback by this unexpected development, for she counted on being able to let Gorozo know privately that she has written the letter only for the sake of their lord, her devotion to Gorozo remaining unchanged. She hastily withdraws behind a screen and writes a note explaining the situation. This she wraps up with the money. Doemon's followers hail Gorozo and the letter of divorce is handed to him. He reads it in angry disbelief. Doemon's jackals jeer. Doemon forces Satsuki to declare that she is indeed the author. She tries to make Gorozo take the money (and her explanation), but he refuses it flatly and, pulling out his flute, is about to beat her with it, when O Shu rushes in and stops him. (This scene, called an *enkiri-mono* or " severing of marital relations," is a famous example of a common situation in this type of play).

O Shu, who knows for whom the money is intended and feels responsible for all the trouble, persuades Gorozo to hold his hand. Satsuki again implores him to take the money, but he again refuses to touch " the dirty stuff " and reviles her for her faithlessness. He goes off down the *hanamichi*, vowing vengance.

Doemon tells Satsuki that it is time for her to redeem her promise and go with him to the house of assignation. Satsuki is sick with anxiety and O Shu persuades Doemon not to press her. O Shu offers to go in Satsuki's place, wearing her long outer garment. (Except for the colour of these coats the two courtesans are dressed similarly, the elaborate arrangment of their hair etc. being the badge of their profession). No one will know the difference, she says, and Doemon's victory will be complete. Privately she realizes that Gorozo means mischief and intends to sacrifice herself for Satsuki. Doemon consents. The exchange is made and he and O Shu leave. Left alone, Satsuki gathers up the rejected money. Her first instinct is to go to find Gorozo. But as a courtesan, she is not free to leave the Yoshiwara. In despair she determines to commit suicide.

Sc. 2. *Outside the Hanagataya house of assignation.* Gorozo enters with his drawn sword in his hand. It is now late at night. He extinguishes the lamp which burns before the gate and hides near by.

Doemon and O Shu come down the *hanamichi,* the courtesan escorted by her retinue. A servant goes before her carrying a lantern (usually painted with the crest of the actor playing Satsuki.) By this light Gorozo is able to distinguish the colour and design of the coat she is wearing. At the gate of the Hanagataya, Gorozo springs on them and knocks out the light. He slashes at O Shu, and the servants take to flight. Doemon seeks refuge in the house, thinking O Shu will follow him. Gorozo cannot see O Shu's face in the darkness. He pursues her and stabs her to death. Then, when he bends over the body, he discovers his mistake. He begs pardon of her spirit and, knowing he can make no atonement in this world, challenges Doemon to come out and fight. Doemon appears, and they engage in a duel to the death. (Gorozo kills Doemon and then himself.)

SONEZAKI SHINJU (*Double Suicide at Sonezaki*). *Sewamono* — Written for the puppets by Chikamatsu Monzaemon (1653—1724). First staged in 1703 at the Takemoto-za by the great *joruri* singer Gidayu, and later adapted for the Kabuki stage. It was the first of the many *shinjumono* written by the author and is deservedly famous for the clever dramatization of Act II, Sc. 1, and the moving poetry of Act II, Sc. 2. In other respects, the pattern is familiar.

Act I

A tea-house in the precincts of the Ikutama Shrine. **Gihei,** a countryman with money to spend and his toady, **Sampei,** are discussing with **Hikomaru,** a professional clown, how they shall spend the evening. They hit upon the idea of buying the famous courtesan, **O Hatsu** of the Temmaya, and taking her out for a party. O Hatsu, however, pleads that she has been made to drink too much and has a frightful headache. Gihei and his friends go off, leaving her to her sad reflections. She is in love with **Tokubei,** a clerk at the Hiranoya oil shop, and she is unhappy because her lover has not been to see her for so long. However, the maids of the tea-house cheer her up by giving her a message from Tokubei to the effect that he is coming to see her that very day. Presently Tokubei appears, and O Hatsu upbraids him for his fickleness and the suffering he has caused her. She cannot understand why he is so quiet and aloof, but at last he tells her all his troubles. His employer is his uncle, **Kyuemon ;** pleased with his nephew's honesty and application, he arranged for him to marry his second wife's niece, a considerable heiress. When Tokubei refused to comply, he discovered that his aunt had received the dowry money in advance and had used it for her own purposes. This money must now be returned to the girl's parents and Tokubei was sent to collect it from his uncle's clients. On his way home with the money, he fell in with a friend named **Kuheiji** who was in desperate need of cash and persuaded Tokubei to lend him the money entrusted to him. To make matters worse, since he refuses to marry his aunt's niece, his uncle now insists that he should settle his debts with him and leave Osaka for ever. This, he explains to O Hatsu, is why he has not been to see her for so long. O Hatsu is overjoyed to find he still loves her and seeks to comfort him in his anxiety. At this point, the same Kuheiji enters, accompanied by a party of friends and all apparently the worse for drink. Tokubei goes to him and presses him to repay the loan, but Kuheiji denies all knowledge of it. Tokubei produces a note of hand, but Kuheiji declares it to be a forgery and is supported in this by his friends. A crowd gathers. Tokubei, in despair, attacks Kuheiji and a lively scuffle takes place.

The country-man Gihei, who has returned to see the fun, catches hold of O Hatsu, who has followed her lover into the thick of the fight, and forces her to leave in a palanquin with him. The combined strength of Kuheiji and his supporters is too much for Tokubei, who is struck on the head and knocked out. When he recovers his enemy has gone and only the curious crowd surrounds him. Tokubei, limping and with blood streaming down his face, retires weeping with frustration.

Act II

Sc. 1. *A room in the Temmaya.* O Hatsu weeps in despair as her fellow courtesans **O Naka, O Chiyo,** and **O Katsu** whisper unkind things about her lover. Kyuemon comes to the door and asks for her. She goes out to speak to him in the street. He pleads with her to give up Tokubei, telling her that she is putting ideas into his head, spoiling the advantageous match arranged for him, and driving him to squander money which is not his to spend. O Hatsu denies his charges and swears that her love for Tokubei is true and lasting ; she also denies any knowledge of the whereabouts of Tokubei, who, his uncle says, has disappeared. Kyuemon goes into the Temmaya to have a smoke and chat with the proprietor, an old friend of his. O Hatsu remains looking anxiously down the street, troubled about Tokubei who, she fears, may have been killed in the fight at the shrine. But, to her great joy, she sees a disconsolate figure in a battered sedge hat approaching. O Hatsu and Tokubei embrace tenderly and she tells him of his uncle's visit. Something, she says, must be decided at once. They are interrupted by the arrival of Kuheiji and his friends who are fortunately too pleased with themselves to notice Tokubei in the dark street. O Hatsu is forced to go back into the house as they have come specially on her account, but she manages to smuggle Tokubei in with her and hides him under the veranda while she sits on the step above. Kuheiji has come with the intention of ransoming O Hatsu with the money stolen from Tokubei. O Hatsu can see no way out of this culminating dilemma but death. She makes it clear during the ensuing conversation, in which her answers, addressed to Kuheiji, are really intended for Tokubei, that she is ready that very night to join her lover in putting an end to their unhappiness. In her anxiety to make sure that Tokubei understands, she taps her *geta* on the stone step to give emphasis to her words and stretches out her naked foot in Tokubei's direction. He caresses her foot to show that he understands her intention and draws the instep across his throat as if it were a sword to show that he also is ready to die. Kuheiji, who thinks she must be drunk to talk in this extraordinary way about preferring to die, brandishes his money-bag under her nose and goes off to conclude the bargain. O Hatsu is forced to go to her room without speaking directly to Tokubei. The house settles down for the night.

A bell tolls. O Hatsu creeps out of her room, dressed in white and clutching a rosary and a razor. She makes the latter flicker in the lamp-light and so attracts Tokubei's attention. She puts out the lamp and in the darkness the lovers grope towards each other. Their stumblings awaken **Sobei,** the master of the Temmaya, who comes in telling the maid-servant to relight the lamp. Before this is done however, the lovers get safely away. They have hardly gone when **Mohei,** Kuheiji's servant, comes to the door calling for his master. Their conversation reveals Kuheiji's wicked plot to defame Tokubei, for Kuheiji has foolishly neglected to give his man the promised share of the stolen money. Kyuemon, who has overheard their talk, angrily bursts into the room and beats Kuheiji, who is now deserted by his friends and supporters. A servant is sent to fetch O Hatsu and see whether she knows where Tokubei is hiding. She returns with O Hatsu's last letter and Kyuemon, deeply affected, immediately organizes a search for the lovers, running out ahead crying, "Tokubei, don't kill yourself!"

Sc. 2. *The woods of Sonezaki.* This scene is renowned for the moving quality of its *joruri* music and singing. The dark sky is spasmodically illuminated by fitful flashes of lightning. A temple bell tolls mournfully. The two lovers, unaware of the change in their fortunes, make their last preparations. Asking the forgiveness of their friends and relatives, they start on their journey to the other world.

SUGAWARA DENJU TENARAI KAGAMI (*The Secret of Sugawara's Calligraphy*). *Jidaimono.* — Written for the puppets in 1746 by Takeda Izumo, Namiki Senryu, and Miyoshi Shoraku. The play is based on the life of Sugawara

Michizane, the known historical facts of which are as follows: Sugawara was born in the middle of the ninth century. Because of his poetic genius he gained favour with the Emperor Usa and was appointed Privy Councillor, mainly to check the power of the Fujiwara family. When the Emperor abdicated, Sugawara and Fujiwara Shihei were made regents for his young heir. Shihei became increasingly jealous of Sugawara's influence. He succeeded in convincing the young Emperor that Sugawara was plotting with Prince Tokiyo, the heir presumptive, to seize the throne. Sugawara was condemned to exile in Kyushu where he died, broken-hearted, at the age of fifty-nine. After his death so many catastrophies occurred in Kyoto that they were attributed to the "curse of Sugawara."

Sugawara was a man of great integrity and virtue. He was one of the master calligraphers of Japan and created the "Kanke" style of writing. Twenty years after his death he was posthumously reinstated and elevated in rank. Later he was deified as the God of Calligraphy and patron saint of writers.

The authors of the play have woven a love story into these facts, but the real appeal of the cycle lies in the characters of the three brothers who are the retainers of Sugawara, Prince Tokiyo, and Shihei respectively. At the time when the authors were working on the play, a great stir was caused in Osaka by the birth of triplets. It was therefore decided to make use of triplets in the new production and thus it was that Matsuomaru, Umeomaru, and Sakuramaru came into being.

For the purposes of the story, the triplets are the sons of Sugawara's retainer, Shirodayu. When they were born, Sugawara stood sponsor to all three and named them after the trees he loved best, Matsuo (Pine), Umeo (Plum), and Sakura (Cherry). On their father's retirement, Umeo took his place as Sugawara's personal retainer. At the same time his two brothers were found equally worthy employment, one as the retainer of Prince Tokiyo and the other in the household of Sugawara's colleague, Fujiwara Shihei. When Shihei's jealousy brought about Sugawara's downfall, the triplets became the victims of divided loyalties. The play is essentially the depiction of this intimate family struggle; its theme is separation.

Act I

On the banks of the River Kamo (*Kamo Tsutsumi*). Prince **Tokiyo,** the Emperor's brother, is attracted by Sugawara's daughter, **Kariya.** His retainer, **Sakuramaru,** who has access to Sugawara's palace, arranges a meeting between the lovers. The Prince comes to the tryst in a carriage, attended by Sakura. Kariya arrives, heavily veiled, with her maid, **Yae.** They retire into the carriage, and Sakura courts Yae nearby. They are disturbed by the arrival of a court official and his retinue. Sakura is drawn away by a running fight, and during his absence some of the attackers return. The official peers into the carriage and recognizes the Prince and his sweetheart. He is, of course, the minion of Shihei and is not averse from picking up evidence to use against Sugawara. He retires, calling off his men. Prince Tokiyo and Kariya, greatly alarmed, take flight, leaving a letter for Sakura explaining what has happened. Sakura returns, realizes the significance of the incident and sets off after the prince. The maid, Yae, is again attacked by the soldiery who wish to seize her as a material witness. She drives them off, however, and removes by her own efforts the one vital piece of evidence, the carriage.

Act II

The Mystery of Calligraphy (*Hippo Denju*), written by Miyoshi Shoraku.

Sugawara has taken great pains to train his favourite retainer, **Takebe Genzo,** in the art of calligraphy. It should be noted that, following the Chinese tradition, calligraphy (which implies a great deal more than beautiful brushwork) was considered the first qualification for high government service. Sugawara never had a more gifted pupil. But Genzo fell in love with **Tonami,** a lady-in-waiting in Sugawara's household. This was a serious offense, and Sugawara dismissed them both. Genzo left Kyoto with his wife and became a village schoolmaster.

The Emperor has now commanded Sugawara to impart the ultimate secrets of his calligraphy to a chosen pupil who will be his successor. He considers none of those at present in his household sufficiently gifted and has sent to recall Genzo from exile.

The scene opens to show a room in Sugawara's Palace. **Mareyo,** his pupil and one of his assistant ministers, is

practising calligraphy. He has repeatedly presented speci-
mens of his skill, hoping to be chosen as the successor, but
in vain. He now obliges a reluctant lady-in-waiting, **Minase,**
to carry yet another example to Sugawara, who is meditating
in the inner room. Sugawara's wife, **Sonoo-no-Mae,** enters
with their little son, **Kan Shusai.** Mareyo tries to find out
from her what has happened to her daughter, Kariya, who
is believed to have eloped with the Emperor's brother, Prince
Tokiyo. Sonoo-no-Mae does not know for certain, but thinks
that they may have taken refuge in the house of Sugawara's
aunt, **Kakuju.** This lady is, in fact, Kariya's mother since
the girl is only the adopted daughter of Sugawara and herself. She confesses that she has not yet had the courage to
tell her husband about the elopement.

Genzo and his wife, Tonami, are announced. Sonoo-no-
Mae receives them kindly, dismissing Mareyo. Presently
Genzo is summoned to Sugawara. *The stage revolves* to show
a very simple room.

Sugawara is seated with writing materials before him.
He asks Genzo whether, since the severing of their relationship, he has forgotten all he knew. Genzo answers that he
now teaches calligraphy for a living, but is no longer worthy
of his former master. Sugawara commands him to give an
example of his work. Mareyo enters and does all he can to
hinder Genzo. In spite of Mareyo's insinuations, Genzo copies
two of Sugawara's poems. The master praises the calligraphy,
calling it the answer to his prayers. He undertakes to appoint
Genzo his official successor, but refuses to forgive him for
what he still regards as a betrayal of trust ; he will not allow
Genzo to re-enter his service. Genzo declares that he cares
more for Sugawara's forgiveness than for Imperial favour.

A messenger comes to summon Sugawara to the Emperor's presence. He retires to make ready. Sonoo-no-Mae
enters with Tonami hidden beneath her long outer coat.
Sugawara reappears in Court dress. He summons Genzo
to him and presents him with a book containing the secrets
of his calligraphy, thus appointing him his successor. At
the same time he commands him never to appear before him
again. Sonoo-no-Mae stops Mareyo from driving out Genzo
forthwith and allows him and Tonami to remain a little
longer in her husband's presence. Sugawara, torn between
love for Genzo and determination not to forgive him,

pretends not to notice. Sugawara goes out with Mareyo and his retinue. Mareyo returns and tricks Genzo into giving the book of calligraphy into his hands " that he may pay respect to it." He tries to steal it, but Genzo recovers it, threatening to kill him. Genzo and Tonami take their leave, begging Sonoo-no-Mae to intercede once more for them with her husband. *The stage revolves.*

Outside the gate of Sugawara's Palace. **Umeomaru** enters in great distress, announcing that Sugawara has been arrested on his way to the Imperial Palace. Some supporters of **Fujiwara Shihei** (Sugawara's chief enemy) enter with Sugawara in their midst. He has been convicted of treason and is sentenced to perpetual exile. Mareyo appears and offers to transfer his allegiance to Shihei. He seizes a pole and is about to strike his master when Umeo intervenes. Sugawara parts them and enters the gate, which is barred behind him. Mareyo joins Shihei's supporters.

Genzo and Tonami come out from their hiding-place, having witnessed this scene. Genzo attacks Mareyo and routs him and Shihei's supporters. When they have gone, Genzo knocks at the gate, calling Umeo. He says he longs to accompany Sugawara into exile, but knows he will not be permitted to do so. He begs Umeo to smuggle out little Kan Shusai so that he may hide him from his enemies, who will surely seek to exterminate the house of Sugawara. Umeo, filled with admiration, brings Kan Shusai and hands him over the garden fence. One of Fujiwara's spies is discovered by Genzo and killed before he can report what he has seen. Umeo commends Kan Shusai to Genzo and Tonami.

Act III

At the Domiyo Temple, near Osaka (Domiyoji no Ba), written by Miyoshi Shoraku.

Sugawara has been permitted to break his journey into exile to say good-bye to his aunt Kakuju (mother of his adopted daughter Kariya).

Since she and her lover, Prince Tokiyo, were captured and forcibly separated, Kariya has been in the charge of her elder sister, **Tatsuta-no-mae,** the wife of a magistrate of this district. The two sisters enter and Kariya says how much she longs to beg her father's forgiveness and how anxious she is over her lover's fate. Tatsuta-no-mae's husband, **Sukune Taro,** comes to inform them that Sugawara will be leaving next day at cock-crow. Tatsuta-no-mae promises to try to arrange for Kariya to see her father before he goes.

Kakuju comes from the inner room. She is a fierce and terrible old lady, passionately devoted to her illustrious nephew. She blames Kariya for all the misfortunes which have befallen him and belabours her with her stick. Tatsuta-no-mae tries to stop her, but the old lady then beats them both. From the inner room Sugawara's voice is heard, begging her to stop and promising to see Kariya once more. Kakuju bursts out weeping, saying that she only beat Kariya to spare him the pain of punishing his adopted child. She leads the two girls to the inner room, but, when the doors are opened, all that they see is a wooden statue of Sugawara. Kariya sinks down in despair, taking this as a sign that her father will never forgive her. To comfort her Kakuju says that this statue is his parting gift; she must look upon it as himself.

Evening falls. Sukune Taro returns, accompanied by his father, **Haji Hyoe**. When the women have withdrawn, the two whisper together mysteriously. Hyoe and Taro are both secret retainers of Fujiwara Shihei. They plan to murder Sugawara this night. They intend to trick him by coming with a palanquin and an escort of their own hirelings, ostensibly to take him to his ship for Kyushu, actually to kill him in a convenient out-of-the-way spot. It is necessary for Sugawara to be removed before the real escort arrives at cock-crow and Hyoe has brought a cock which he intends to cause to crow early. Tatsuta-no-mae overhears their plotting and, coming out to them, implores them to give up their plan. Hyoe pretends to yield to her entreaties but, as she turns to go back to the house, he signals to Taro to kill her. Taro does so, gagging her first with a piece of cloth torn from his sleeve. The body is thrown into the neighbouring pond. Hyoe makes use of his daughter-in-law's corpse to further his plot, for it is an ancient belief that, if a cock perches above a corpse, it will crow. By holding the cock over the pond Hyoe is able to give the false signal.

Taro summons the palanquin and escort. Sugawara comes out and is carried away. Kakuju asks for Tatsuta-no-mae; a search is made and her body is recovered from the pond. Taro makes a great show of grief and zeal to discover the murderer, but Kakuju has already recognized the cloth stuffed in the dead girl's month. She borrows Taro's sword and, taking him unawares, stabs him mortally. At this moment the real escort, headed by **Terukuni**, the chief magistrate of the district, arrives. At first he believes that Kakuju has connived at Sugawara's escape, but the old lady is sure there has been foul play and is finally able to persuade him of her innocence and induce him to go off in pursuit. As Terukuni is about to leave, to the amazement of all, Sugawara's voice is heard from inside the house. At the same moment the false escort returns; they have been tricked for they have found only a wooden statue in the palanquin. When the palanquin is opened, however, Sugawara himself emerges. Terukuni arrests all the conspirators and old Hyoe, finding that his son is on the point of death, confesses and is beheaded by Terukuni. Sugawara mourns that he should have been the cause of Tatsuta-no-mae's death. He is about to leave with Terukuni when Kakuju reappears followed by her maids carrying a large basket covered with Kariya's outer coat. She offers it " to keep out the cold," but is interrupted by Sugawara, who, in a speech full of double meanings, asks Kakuju to keep " this dress " (i. e., Kariya) as her own to replace the one (Tatsuta-no-mae) she has lost. Kakuju begs him to give his child one glance. Kariya emerges from the basket and is able to see her father once more. He makes a gesture of farewell and goes towards the *hanamichi* as the girl sinks down in tears. (The explanation of Sugawara's conduct towards Kariya is not, as she believes, that he cannot forgive her for unwittingly causing his exile, but that he wishes at all costs to save her from being involved in his disgrace.)

Act IV

Stopping the carriage (*Kuruma Biki*). (This act was not in the original puppet play, but is a Kabuki interpolation, played in the *aragoto* style, see page 403. It is now, nevertheless, performed by the dolls, who on this occasion imitate the style of the live actors. It is in this scene that the three brothers appear together for the first time. Although they are triplets, in fact, both in character and appearance they are very different. Their relationship is indicated by their costume which is similar except that each has worked on his kimono the emblem of his name. Matsuo is the eldest. He is also the bad one of the three, although he redeems himself later in the play. He speaks in a deep bass voice and his make-up in this scene is that of a villain. Umeo is the next in age. His voice is deep and manly and his make-up indicates that he is a loyal warrior. Sakura is the youngest. The part is usually taken by an *onnagata* and requires a boy's voice and the unlined, white make-up associated with women and young men.)

The act opens to show the entrance to the Yoshida Shrine in Kyoto. Two samurai arrive wearing large straw travelling hats. They reveal themselves as Umeo and Sakura, now both *ronin* owing to the disgrace of their masters. They denounce the wickedness of Fujiwara Shihei. They grieve that their brother, Matsuo, brought up in the shadow of Sugawara, should continue to serve one who has shown himself to be Sugawara's bitterest enemy.

A steward announces that Shihei, who has been worshipping at the shrine, is now approaching. Close on the steward's heels comes **Matsuomaru** bearing his master's standard. Umeo and Sakura round on their brother, accusing him of disloyalty to the benefactor of their family. Matsuo replies that, since he has taken service with Shihei, it is his duty to remain true to his master, no matter whose enemy he becomes. A fierce quarrel breaks out and the three come to blows. They are interrupted by the arrival of Shihei's carriage. Umeo and Sakura turn on it and drag away part of the sides so that Shihei is forced to reveal himself. When they see the great Minister of State, the two brothers are

Umeomaru

overcome with ~we. Shihei rebukes and scorns them. Matsuo mocks at them, but reminds them they will all soon have an opportunity to continue their quarrel, as they will be meeting at their father's house for his seventieth birthday.

Act V

The Seventieth Birthday (Ga no Iwai), written by Namiki Senryu.

Matsuo and Umeo continue to act in *aragoto* style, but wear a modified make-up. Matsuo has shed most of the indigo paint which marked the baser side of his character. The *aragoto* in this scene was not, of course, in the original puppet version; it was introduced because of the success of the previous act. This example of *aragoto* has also been adopted by the puppets.

Shirodayu, the father of the triplets, lives in rustic retirement at Sato village. It is his seventieth birthday and his three sons are expected to come to congratulate him. His three daughters-in-law have already arrived when the act opens. **Chiyo,** Matsuo's wife, and **Haru,** Umeo's wife, are busy preparing for the festivities while the old man is giving thanks at the temple.

Umeo and Matsuo arrive severally and, while they are waiting for their father's return, the quarrel breaks out again. They are both in a dangerous mood and their wives, after trying in vain to pacify them, take away their swords, in order at least to prevent bloodshed. Matsuo and Umeo fight with their bare hands and then with the rice bales in the porch. During the bout, they accidentally break a branch of the flowering cherry tree their father particularly loves. Neither has achieved any advantage when Shirodayu is seen returning, accompanied by Sakura's wife, Yae. The brothers hastily put themselves to rights and greet their father respectfully. Yae lingers at the gate looking down the *hanamichi* for her husband. She comes at last into the house and takes a place near her father-in-law.

The brothers draw from their bosoms two documents which they present to their father. They are not, as they ought to be, congratulatory addresses, but petitions that he should indicate how he intends to bestow his property. Since the brothers are triplets, the ordinary law of primogeniture does not hold good. Shirodayu is displeased with them both, but against Matsuo his anger boils over. He accuses him of disloyalty and ingratitude; he should long ago have broken his connection with Shihei. The ancient loyalty of his family to the house of Sugawara should be more to him than this new allegience. Matsuo tries to justify himself, but his father silences him. Taking off his cap he flings it at him saying that, since he has asked what his portion will be, he shall have it at once. That cap is all he will ever get from his father. Matsuo rises and slowly leaves, wounded and moved by his father's words. His wife follows him sadly.

Shirodayu next turns on Umeo, chiding him for his passionate impatience. He had better go, too. Umeo and Haru do so, abashed. The old man withdraws into the inner room. Yae goes once more to the gate to look for Sakura. While she is standing there, her husband enters quietly from the back of the house where he has been hidden all the time. She runs to him. He tells her that he has come to a decision. He feels himself in great part responsible for Sugawara's disgrace and exile. He promoted the love affair between Prince Tokiyo and Kariya which was the pretext for Sugawara's downfall. The only atonement he can make is to die. His father has given his consent. He intends to commit *seppuku*.

Shirodayu enters carrying the ceremonial knife on a stand. Sakura is his favourite child, but he will not dissuade him from dying, since he also believes him blameworthy. Sakura makes his formal self-accusation in the presence of his wife and father. The old man, taking three fans painted with pine, plum and cherry, laments the fate of his children, Matsuo disloyal, Umeo passionate and Sakura doomed to die before his time. Yae tries in vain to dissuade her husband. Sakura breaks from her and disembowels himself, dying with great calmness and fortitude while his father prays. Yae seizes Sakura's sword and is about to kill herself also when Umeo and his wife rush in and prevent her. Umeo is overcome by the combination of his brother's sacrifice and his own unworthiness. Shirodayu decides that he must set off to visit Sugawara in exile and report to him all that has happened. He sets out, bowed with grief, leaving Umeo to perform the last rites for his brother.

Act VI

The Village School (Terakoya), written by Takeda Izumi. (A French rendering of this act has been made by Professor

Florenz and an English one, entitled "The Pine," by John Masefield. The acting in this scene is in the straight classical style. Matsuo no longer wears *kumadori* make-up, but retains the pine symbol on his kimono.)

During the time that has passed between this and the previous act a change has come over Matsuo. He left his father's house hurt and angry at the treatment he received, but also shaken in his self-confidence. He now begins to wonder whether the code he follows is right after all. While he is debating this problem, the news comes that Sakura, whom everyone loved, has committed suicide. That Sakura should thus atone for conduct, which at the time he could not possibly have foreseen would harm either his prince or his father's patron, fills Matsuo with a crushing sense of his own unworthiness. If Sakura had to die, how much more should he, who continued to adhere to his lord after he knew his lord's conduct to be perfidious! Matsuo's first instinct is to follow his brother's example. Before he can do so, however, a greater sacrifice is demanded of him.

Fujiwara Shihei is still uneasy about the enemy he has apparently crushed so effectively. Sugawara himself is a sick man, unlikely to give further trouble, but the thought of Sugawara's family is a gnawing worry. When Kariya escaped, Shihei thought that Sugawara's wife and son were with her. Then suddenly he learns that the boy is in hiding with Sugawara's retainer, Takebe Genzo (see Act II), who gives out that the child is his own. Shihei decides to exploit the interdict issued against Sugawara's family at the time of his disgrace. He will have the village where Genzo lives surrounded and then demand of this *samurai* turned schoolmaster the head of Kan Shusai.

Shihei sends for Matsuo, knowing his previous connection with Sugawara's household, and tells him that a cordon has been put round Genzo's village. The Imperial Messenger is about to depart to enforce the interdict and Shihei orders Matsuo to accompany him to identify the head of Sugawara's son. Matsuo realizes that no mere *seppuku* can now save him from the taint of his master's guilt. If he leaves his service and takes his life, it will not preserve Kan Shusai. He must find some way to save the boy and redeem himself in his own eyes and in those of his father and brother. Then he thinks of his own little son, of the same age as Kan Shusai.

And he thinks of the problem that will shortly face Genzo, about whom the trap is already closing.

It is at this point that the act opens.

The curtain is drawn to show Genzo's house in the little village of Seriu. Genzo has been called from home by the village headman, but Tonami, his wife, is supervising the work of some little boys who are all copying characters more or less busily. Kan Shusai is among them, and, although plainly dressed, is at once set apart by his aristocratic appearance.

A lady comes to the gate with a little boy and a servant carrying a desk and school box. Tonami goes out to her and the lady asks whether the schoolmaster has had her message asking him to accept a new pupil. Tonami says he has, but he has been called away urgently. The lady (she is Matsuo's wife Chiyo, but Tonami does not know her) says that in that case she will leave her little son as she is pressed for time. She will return later and see the schoolmaster.

The child's belongings are carried into the school and Chiyo distributes sweets to the scholars. She bids Kotaro be good; she will return presently. He makes no spoken answer, but can hardly bear to see her go. Chiyo leaves, but comes back at once asking for her fan. Tonami, surprised, points out that it is in her hand. Chiyo apologizes and once more says good-bye to Kotaro, who still remains silent. Tonami thinks he is shy and tells Kan Shusai to be kind to him. (The act often begins here.) Genzo returns, walking slowly down the hanamichi. He comes into the schoolroom and sinks down, wrapped in painful thought. He abruptly calls the names of one and then another of his pupils, but finds no satisfaction.

Tonami is worried by his look and, thinking to cheer him, tells him that the new pupil has arrived and seems a promising child. She brings Kotaro forward to meet his schoolmaster. Genzo does not even glance at him. It is not until the little boy, making obeisance, says in a sweet treble that "it is very kind of you to take me under your protection" that Genzo turns suddenly, struck by the voice. He stares at the child, resolution hardening in his face. His wife is glad to see that the cloud has lifted and asks whether he does not agree that this new pupil looks intelligent. Genzo replies, wonderingly, that he must be of aristocratic parentage. He hastily dismisses the class, bidding the boys go and play quietly. Tonami takes away Kan Shusai and Kotaro and returns. Genzo tells her that the summons to the headman's office was a pretext to make sure of his whereabouts. He has learnt that Fujiwara Shihei now knows where Kan Shusai is hidden. The village is already surrounded and an official messenger is on his way to demand their charge's head. The messenger is accompanied by the traitorous Matsuo who can only too well identify it. Tonami asks what they are to do. Genzo replies that at first he thought there was nothing for them but to die with their little lord. But now, since the arrival of the new pupil, he sees his way clear. He must sacrifice this child of birth and breeding to save his master's son. It is a terrible thing to have to do, but loyalty demands terrible sacrifices. Tonami protests, but Genzo asks how else they can save Kan Shusai. This new child seems to have been sent by heaven; no one in the village even knows he is there; he resembles Kan Shusai more than a little and is the same age. Tonami, weeping, asks what they are to do when the mother returns. Genzo says swiftly that they will have to kill her if she asks to see the child. They cannot have her spoiling the plan. Tonami unwillingly agrees. Genzo is determined to carry out this ruse, although he is aware of its full horror.

The Imperial Messenger, **Shundo Gemba,** arrives with his retinue. Matsuo follows in a palanquin, for he has given

Genzo

out that he is ill. Behind them come, fearfully, the fathers
of Genzo's rustic scholars. They kneel respectfully along the
hanamichi. Gemba summons Genzo to deliver up the head
of the traitor Sugawara's son. The fathers of the village beg
to be allowed to take their children home and the boys are
called out one by one, scrutinized by Matsuo and Gemba
and released. (This small comic scene serves as the traditional slackening of tension found in most tragedies of puppet
origin.) When all are gone and Kan Shusai is not among
them, Gemba and Matsuo enter the schoolhouse. Gemba
gives Genzo the head-box, bidding him delay no longer.
Matsuo adds, warningly, that "not even an ant can escape."

Genzo stares at the head-box for a moment in silence, then
takes it up and goes into the inner room. Gemba, looking at
the array of writing-desks against the wall, questions Tonami
suspiciously about the number of scholars. There seems to
be one desk too many. Kotaro's new desk still stands
conspicuously in the middle of the room. Tonami readily
admits it is Kan Shusai's, but Matsuo recognizes it, and now
knows for certain that his son is in the school. Will Genzo
make the right decision?

A sound comes from the inner room. Matsuo makes a
convulsive movement, but controls himself (this pose is considered one of the great moments of the play.) The silence
drags on. At last, slowly, Genzo returns with the head-box
and sets it before Matsuo. He himself kneels near his wife,

Matsuo

watching Matsuo intently, his hand on his sword hilt. If Matsuo seems about to deny that the head is Kan Shusai's, Genzo intends to cut him down. Meanwhile Gemba's guard closes in on Genzo with their weapons drawn, ready to kill him if he has attempted a fraud. (This tableau is another great moment of the play.)

Matsuo slowly lifts the cover off the head-box. He is not certain what he will find there—the head of Sugawara's son, in which case his atonement will have come to nothing, or that of his own child. When Kotaro's head is revealed he gazes upon it, his face unchanged, only his eyes, which are hidden from Gemba, revealing his pride and his agony. Then he replaces the cover and says in a firm voice : " This is indeed the head of Kan Shusai. There is no mistake." Genzo relaxes a fraction and darts one questioning look at his wife. The guards sheathe their knives.

Gemba takes the box and makes ready to go, telling Genzo that, in consideration of his prompt surrender of his charge, he will neither be executed as a rebel nor imprisoned. He tells Matsuo he has deserved well of his lord. Matsuo answers that he is a sick man and this is the last service he will do Shihei. He asks Gemba so to inform him. Gemba and his retinue depart. Matsuo goes off alone in a different direction.

When they are gone, Genzo and his wife give way to their pent-up emotions and, calling Kan Shusai from his hiding place, weep with relief that he is alive. Tonami leads the boy away.

Chiyo is seen approaching the gate. She asks permission to enter, enquires whether Genzo is the schoolmaster and explains that she is the mother of his new pupil. Genzo replies shortly that the boy is with the other children. Chiyo calls " Kotaro ! " Genzo, in desperation, draws his sword. She snatches up her son's school box and holds it as a shield between them. As she does so, the lid falls off and on the floor are scattered, not toys and clothing, but the grave-clothes of a little child. Genzo stands back, dumbfounded, as Chiyo kneels and tenderly gathers them up. Genzo asks : " Whose child was this ? " and from the gateway Matsuo's voice answers : " Mine." As he speaks he flings into the room a pine branch to which is attached a poem composed by Sugawara when Shirodayu visited him in exile. He speaks the first lines: " The plum blossom is scattered. The cherry blossom is withered. How can the pine-tree remain untouched by the storm ? "

Tonami returns and learns of the sacrifice Matsuo and Chiyo have made. They talk of the parting that morning. Chiyo could hardly bear to tell Kotaro she would return, knowing she would never see him again, but she was afraid he would make a scene if she did not reassure him. Matsuo reveals that Kotaro knew why he had come to the school ; he himself had told him. He asks Genzo whether the boy died worthily. Genzo answers : " Like a samurai. When I told him he must die, he smiled."

Chiyo begs for her child's body and Tonami, gathering up the graveclothes, goes out. The side door opens and Kan Shusai comes in, asking whether it is true that his new playfellow has died in his stead. Matsuo looks long at him and going to the gate, summons his palanquin. From it steps Sonoo-no-mae, Sugawara's wife and Kan Shusai's mother. Mother and son comfort each other as Tonami reappears with the body of Kotaro in her arms. She carries it out and lays it in the palanquin. She lights a sacred fire, while Genzo prepares incense. He offers it first to Kan Shusai and his mother that they, who owe so much to the dead boy, may be the first to honour his spirit. When the ritual is over, Matsuo and Chiyo, who have removed their dark outer garments and are in mourning clothes of white and pale turquoise, rise to escort their child's body to its resting place.

(The final act of the play is never now performed. In it we learn that Umeo went to tell the dying Sugawara that his wife and son had joined his daughter in safety. Sugawara died lamenting that his enemy, Shihei, was all-powerful. After his death, Shihei was haunted by the ghosts of Sugawara and Sakura. Kan Shusai and Kariya returned secretly to the capital and with Umeo's help killed Shihei and avenged their father. At their petition, the whole question of Sugawara's guilt was again examined and his innocence established. His honours were posthumously restored to him.)

SUKEROKU YUKARI NO EDO-ZAKURA, commonly called *Sukeroku. Juhachiban.* — This famous play ties for second place with *Shibaraku* amongst the Ichikawa collection. It was written in 1713 and first staged by Ichikawa Danjuro II. In 1716 it was assimilated into the Soga brothers' "world" (see page 462). Sukeroku became Soga Goro Tokimune, Shimbei became Soga Juro Sukenari and the villain, Ikyu, was renamed Heinai Saemon Naganori. This sort of re-attribution of successful plays was fairly common. The Soga brothers are hardy perennials even today and their box office draw in the early eighteenth century attracted to them a number of quite unconnected adventures to which their names alone were thought to add lustre. But "Sukeroku" would have been a success in any case, because it is a good play on its own merits and it had a particular appeal to the play-going public of Genroku Edo. The hero, Sukeroku, is an *otokodate* (see page 448) with all the qualities of courage, resourcefulness, bravado, and physical charm which the lower classes admired. Played by Ichikawa Danjuro II, he epitomized all the aspirations of the humble, romantic townsfolk. He even went so far as to wear a head-band and socks dyed with a certain purple dye which, because of the enormous cost of importing it from China, only the Shogun himself had hitherto been accustomed to use. "Sukeroku" in eighteenth century Edo can be compared with Beaumarchais' "Barbier de Séville" and "Noces de Figaro" in eighteenth-century France; it gave dramatic expression to a certain stirring of the social consciousness of the common people. The present form of the play dates from about 1749. There is also a 'pirated' version which Onoe Kikugoro VI put on in 1915. The text is the same, but a new *kiyomoto* accompaniment was substituted for the original *katobushi* music. This and changes in various symbols were apparently enough to get round the Ichikawa copyright. The version is called *Sukeroku Kuruwa no Momoyogusa* and belongs to the Onoe family.

Argument : The single act is set in the Naka-no-Cho, the centre of Edo's licensed quarter, before the Miuraya, one of the famous houses of assignation. Two fire watchmen do their rounds. The celebrated courtesan, **Agemaki,** and her attendants, enter by the *hanamichi*. Her colleagues await her outside the Miuraya and comment unkindly on her drunken appearance. Agemaki protests that, while it is true that she has had to run the gauntlet of proffered *sake* cups all the way to the Miuraya, she requires more drink than that to unsteady her. She stumbles, nevertheless, and her attendants make her drink some sobering medicine and lead her to rest on a bench. (The following scene is often omitted.)

Manko, Sukeroku's mother, enters. She has come a long way and is consulting a slip of paper on which Agemaki's crest is drawn. She patters about, comparing the paper with the lanterns outside the various houses. The servants and attendants try to drive her away, but she insists that she must find Agemaki. The latter finally reveals herself to the old woman and when Manko says that she has come from Sukeroku, Agemaki finds an excuse to send her chief attendant, **Kasuke,** off on an errand. The others she bids await her in her room. Alone with Manko, Agemaki discloses that she knows who the old lady is. Manko is embarrassed, but makes her plea, nevertheless, that Agemaki shall cast off her son. She explains that Sukeroku is supposed to be avenging his father's murder, but he comes constantly to the licensed quarter and wastes his time and substance in unseemly brawling and dissipation. Agemaki agrees that Sukeroku, once so gentle, has become a quarrel-seeker. There have been several unpleasant incidents of late to his discredit. But she loves him so deeply that she cannot bear to pass a night without seeing him; if she casts him off, it will break her heart. Manko is impressed by her devotion and finally capitulates. She gives her sanction to their marriage, but begs the courtesan to try to dissuade her son from brawling. The attendants return, and Kasuke comes back, announcing that the elderly samurai, Ikyu, an admirer of Agemaki's, is on his way to visit her. She bids her attendants take Manko indoors and look after her. Left alone, she soliloquizes on the sad fate of lovers. (End of the scene which may be cut.)

Shiratama and other ladies of the district enter and **Ikyu,** followed by his retainers, comes down the *hanamichi*. He is a dissolute and vicious old man, famous in the quarter for his huge, white beard, but he has money and is one of Agemaki's best clients. She hates him and rebuffs him, whenever possible, but he seems rather to enjoy it and tries to make her jealous by having affairs with all and sundry. He descants on Agemaki's loveliness, while Shiratama, Agemaki's confidential friend, chides him for his evil way of life. He exchanges a good deal of banter with the assembled courtesans and then presents himself to Agemaki. (If the scene with Manko is omitted, Agemaki at this point receives a letter which she reads and pretends is from Sukeroku but is in fact from his mother.) Ikyu at once begins to abuse Sukeroku to her, calling him a pickpocket and a thief. Agemaki admits that she is perhaps foolish to be in love with Sukeroku, but calling him a thief is too much. Ikyu points out that Sukeroku has not a penny to his name and warns her that, if she goes on associating with him, she will start thieving herself, to supply him with cash. They will both come to a bad end. Agemaki retorts with a magnificent speech, comparing the courtesan's feelings for her patrons with the devotion she has for her chosen lover. She dares Ikyu to strike her for her outspokenness. Ikyu, furious, tells her to go to her lover and be damned. Shiratama tries to patch up the quarrel, but Agemaki declares that she will never have anything to do with Ikyu again and withdraws, followed by Shiratama and her attendants.

The sound of a flute is heard off-stage. **Sukeroku** enters by the *hanamichi*. He wears a black kimono adorned with

Sukeroku

the "Sukeroku *mon,*" a chrysanthemum flower and leaves, but his obi (following the precedent set by Danjuro II) is woven with the crests of the actor playing the part. Into the back of his obi is tucked his flute. The singers chant a love-song as he dances with his umbrella (this is of a colour between indigo and black with a broad white band and symbolizes Mount Fuji and Mount Tsukuba). The ladies of the quarter call attention to his purple head scarf. They applaud him and crowd round him as he steps onto the stage, offering him their pipes. Ikyu, annoyed at finding himself suddenly deserted, says loudly that he wishes to smoke too, but Sukeroku insolently points out that all the pipes are in use. He seems bent on provoking his rival and, after boasting vaingloriously of his power over women, he offers Ikyu a pipe, holding it between his toes. Ikyu is boiling with rage, but curiously enough prefers not to take up Sukeroku's challenge, pretending that it is beneath contempt. Sukeroku reels off a string of offensively apposite insinuations and then warns the ladies of the appearance in the Yoshiwara of a white-bearded, lice-infested snake who stinks of aloes.

Fortunately for Ikyu a diversion occurs at this point, for one of Ikyu's retainers, **Kampera Mombei,** comes out of the house shouting furiously that he has been cheated by the attendants who put him into a bath and left him to stew without joining him there. He is mocked by the ladies. While he is describing his ill-treatment, **Fukuyama,** a *soba*-seller (buckwheat noodles), enters and bumps into him. Kampera will not accept his apology and begins to talk big. Fukuyama loses his temper and offers to fight, but Kampera sidles away from him. Sukeroku intervenes, twists Kampera's arm and treats him with contempt when he tries to boast of the wealth and importance of his master and himself. He buys a dish of *soba* and, when Kampera refuses to eat, breaks the dish on his head. Kampera's cowardly screams bring in another of Ikyu's retainers, **Sembei,** with a crowd of young toughs who attack Sukeroku. He routs them with hardly more than a scowl. Sukeroku then makes a famous "name-saying" speech in which he claims to be without equal in arms and in love and that he is feared and admired throughout the length and breadth of the Yoshiwara. He is the chosen lover of the most famous courtesan of the district and his chief pride is in being known as "Agemaki's Sukeroku." Ikyu's two retainers attack him again, but he throws them down before their master, challenging Ikyu to draw and fight. Ikyu remains silent. As a culminating insult, Sukeroku takes off one of his *geta* and puts it on Ikyu's head (see page 476). Ikyu still refuses to be drawn. His retainers protest at his cowardliness, but he replies that his sword is too noble to be soiled with a thief's blood. Sukeroku contemptuously slices in two the arm-rest on which Ikyu is leaning and puts up his own sword. Ikyu, his followers and the courtesans withdraw into the house. When they have gone, the band of roughs return and again set upon Sukeroku, who again disperses them. Among them is his brother, **Shimbei,** disguised as a *sake*-seller. Shimbei hides on the *hanamichi*.

When the roughs have fled, Shimbei calls to Sukeroku and there is a comic exchange between them, until Shimbei discloses his real identity. He then protests to Sukeroku about his behaviour and reminds him of his oath, given eighteen years before, to be avenged on their father's murderer. Sukeroku tells his brother that there is a reason in his madness. His sword, Tomokirimaru, has been stolen from him and he comes to the Yoshiwara, where all classes of people meet, in the hope of finding it. He picks quarrels with all and sundry to make them draw their swords. But, if his brother disapproves, he adds, he will give up fighting and turn priest. Shimbei apologizes and offers to help him in the search. Sukeroku tells him that he believes Ikyu must have the sword, since he is the only one who has refused to fight. He then gives Shimbei a lesson in the way he should insult strange samurai and provoke them to brawling. They try it out on some innocent passers-by and together make them crawl between their legs. (This allows for much comic improvisation.)

Agemaki's voice is heard off-stage. She lets Manko, hidden under her straw travelling-hat, out of the house. Sukeroku tries to pick a quarrel with this supposed samurai and is dumbfounded when he discovers it is his own mother. Shimbei has the same experience. Manko upbraids her two sons for their scandalous behaviour and declares her intention of repairing to her husband's grave and there taking her life. Sukeroku, at Shimbei's request, explains the reason for his conduct. Manko is overjoyed to find her faith in her sons justified. (This incident may be omitted. Since she still has some secret doubts about her wild Sukeroku, she presents him with a charmed jacket which will protect him in all his fights, if only he will govern his temper, for she suspects that his brawls are not always inspired by filial piety. If he loses his temper, she says, the jacket will split and so will his mother's heart.) She leaves, escorted by Shimbei.

Ikyu is heard calling for Agemaki and a moment later comes out of the house with Shiratama and the others. Sukeroku hides behind Agemaki's voluminous skirts, as she sits on a bench. Seating himself beside her, Ikyu, who is rather drunk, claims that Agemaki has promised to let bygones be bygones. He tries to take her back into the house. Agemaki asks to be allowed to enjoy the fresh air a little longer. When Ikyu gallantly says he will keep her company, Sukeroku cannot resist pinching his legs. Agemaki's little page-girls are blamed and sent indoors. Ikyu starts to make heavy love to Agemaki and Sukeroku pinches him again. Ikyu now guesses who must be under the seat and abuses Sukeroku, calling him a ditch-rat. At this Sukeroku emerges from his hiding-place. Ikyu, calling him by his real name, Tokimune, reviles him for haunting the licensed quarter when he should be avenging his father. He strikes him with his fan. Sukeroku, controlling his temper, observes that Ikyu is lucky to be able to strike his enemy-in-love, even with a fan, when he and his two brothers have had to wait eighteen weary years for a chance to strike at their enemy. Ikyu now attempts to trick Sukeroku into making treasonable statements against the Government, which he hopes to use as a means of getting rid of his rival permanently. Drawing an example from a three-legged incense burner standing near him, Ikyu suggests that, so united, they could not only strike at their enemy, but at the Shogun himself. If they would do so, he adds, he himself would be prepared to join them. But separated —carried away by his metaphor, Ikyu draws his sword and slices the burner in two. Sukeroku stares at the sword, Ikyu tries too late to hide it and goes quickly into the house. The sword in Ikyu's hand is " Tomokirimaru." Sukeroku's mission is accomplished. He whispers to Agemaki that he will wait for Ikyu tonight. She understands and retires into the house while, as the curtain is drawn, Sukeroku goes off down the *hanamichi*.

(There is a final scene called the " mizu-iri " which is not often played. When Ikyu and his retainer Sembei leave the Miuraya, Sukeroku attacks them and demands the sword. He kills them both but, as he draws the blade to examine it, a crowd arrives shouting " Murderer ! " Sukeroku hides in a barrel full of water — and it is real water — and Agemaki assures the pursuit that the murderer has fled. Sukeroku comes out of the barrel and climbs up a ladder onto the roof over which he makes his escape.)

SUMA NO UTSUSHIE (*Suma Memories*), commonly called *Matsukaze to Murasame*. *Shosagoto*. — This play, with *nagauta* accompaniment, is inspired by the Noh play *Matsukaze,* where the ghosts of two sisters re-enact the story of their love for the same man. The Kabuki dance gives the same story in dramatic form.

Arihara Yukihira, a great poet of the Heian Era and a prince of the Imperial blood, was exiled for three years to Suma, a place on the shores of the Inland Sea. While there, he amused himself in the company of two lovely fisher girls, sisters called **Matsukaze** and **Murasame,** who both fell in love with him. When he was recalled from exile he could not bear to say farewell and left behind him a poem promising that, if " like the pine-tree of Inabayama " they awaited him faithfully, he would return. He never did.

Argument : The scene opens to show Yukihira on the sea-shore at Suma. He has just received the message recalling him to the capital. It is evening and the moon has risen. Matsukaze and Murasame enter, carrying their water-buckets, and dance the "water-carrying dance" which is also a feature of the Noh play. Looking into her pail, Matsukaze sees the moon reflected in the water and calls her sister's attention to it. Murasame looks into hers and sees the moon reflected there also. Thus is symbolized their love for Yukihira. The sisters dance with Yukihira, vying with each other for his attentions. Murasame shows a more fiery, jealous temperament than the dreamy, poetic Matsukaze. Suddenly from seaward a flight of plovers takes wing. Yukihira recognizes that the tide is turning and that his ship is about to set sail. Gently he extricates himself from the sisters' hands and bids them await him in their little hut nearby. When they have gone, he writes his farewell poem, and, attaching it to his cloak and court hat, hangs it on the branch of a pine tree growing by the shore. He leaves.

The two girls are seen at their toilet inside the hut. When they emerge, they find the cloak, hat and poem and realize that their lover has left them. They wait, hoping he may return, but a fishmerman, **Konohei,** comes and tells them that Yukihira's ship has already set sail. The sisters are plunged in grief. Konohei has long desired Matsukaze, but while the Prince remained in Suma he had no chance of success with her. Now he sees his opportunity. He sends the the younger sister off on the hopeless errand of trying to find a boat to pursue Yukihira. When she has gone he attempts to make love to Matsukaze. But she, clasping her lover's cloak, pays no heed to him. The shock of Yukihira's sudden departure has unhinged her wits.

Putting on her lover's cloak, Matsukaze dances the story of her tragic love and faithful waiting. Sometimes it seems to her as if Yukihira has returned and is by her side; then he is gone again for ever. The fisherman Konohei grows jealous and impatient. He attacks Matsukaze with his sword but she, in her mad wanderings, evades his onslaught and escapes. Wrapped in her inner vision, she seeks her lost lover among Suma's rocks and pine-trees.

(The roles of Yukihira and the fisherman are usually played by the same actor. A shortened version of this dance, consisting of the " water-carrying dance " performed by Matsukaze alone followed by her mad dance and the struggle with the fisherman, is often performed. It is called *Hama-matsukaze Koi no Kotonoha* or *The Love Song of Matsukaze*.)

SUMIDAGAWA (*Sumida River*). *Shosagoto*. — Adapted from the Noh play of the same name. *Kiyomoto* accompaniment.

Argument : A woman of strange and dishevelled appearance is wandering along the bank of the Sumida River. She stops uncertainly near a ferry, where the boatman laughs at her. She bursts into tears and begins a rambling story which makes him realize she is mad. The boatman is sorry and listens to her tale. She is a widow whose only child disappeared from the temple where he was being educated. He was believed to have been kidnapped. She has been searching ever since, but has found no trace of him. The boatman, overcome by her story, tells her, in an elaborate mimed dance, that the boy was caught by a slaver who intended to ship him to the West, but he fell ill and, when they reached this very ferry, the slaver abandoned him. He was carried to a nearby village where the villagers cared for him, but it was too late and he died, calling his mother's name. The boatman tells her that the villagers so loved the boy that they erected a monument and held services for the repose of his soul. He offers to take her to the spot and puts her across the river in his boat. The mother prostrates herself beside the grave. Her child's ghost appears and she tries to clasp it in her arms. (In the Kabuki version the ghost is seen only by the mother, but in the Noh it is visible to the audience as well.) She sinks down by the grave, to spend the rest of her life there in prayer.

SUO OTOSHI (*Dropping the Robe*). *Shosagoto.*— Adapted from a *kyogen* by Fukuchi Ochi. First performed in 1882. *Nagauta* accompaniment.

Argument : A young daimyo decides to go on pilgrimage to the Ise Shrine. His uncle having offered to go with him, he instructs his servant **Tarokaja** to go to his uncle's house and enquire whether it would suit him to leave at once. He tells Tarokaja to return without delay.

Tarokaja sets off, walking round the stage to indicate his journey. He arrives at the house of his master's uncle and learns that he is not at home. The uncle's daughter receives him and hears his message. She tells him that she is sure her father will be unable to come as he is extremely busy at the moment.

Tarokaja ought, of course, to return to his master. But the young lady invites him to drink to her cousin's auspicious journey and he is persuaded to remain. *Sake* is brought, but, when Tarokaja has drunk two ceremonial cups, he finds it so good that he complains that the cup is too small. The lady's attendants bring him the lid of a lacquer tub and he twice drains this large vessel. He asks the lady whether her servants will not dance to entertain them. Two of them do so.

Tarokaja himself, now very drunk, is then invited to

dance. He gets unsteadily to his feet, but controls himself and performs the famous narrative dance called "Yashima." This dance commemorates the battle fought between the Genji and the Heike on the beach near Yashima in 1185 (see page 423). In particular it recalls a remarkable feat of archery performed by a young Genji warrior. The incident is vividly described in the "Heike Monogatari." The sun was sinking at the end of the long day's fighting. The Genji warriors were on the shore while the Heike ships dominated the bay. Suddenly, a small boat was seen rowing towards the land. When it was within thirty yards of the water's edge it swung broadside on and was seen to contain a young girl, dressed in white and scarlet, who took a red fan with a rising sun on it and tied it to a pole fastened to the gunwhale. The Genji guessed that it was a trick to induce their leader, Yoshitsune, to come within bowshot of the ships. Yoshitsune called to a young man renowned for his skill with the bow. His name was Yoichi Munekata and he was barely twenty years old. He carried a Shigeto bow and a quiver of twenty-four arrows feathered with black

Tarokaja

and white and one turnip-headed arrow pointed with staghorn. Yoshitsune bade him shoot down the fan. The boy demurred, saying he feared that, if he failed, it would be a reproach to the Genji. But Yoshitsune ordered him again to shoot. Munekata mounted his black horse and rode into the sea. The wind was blowing strongly and the waves were running high on the beach. The fan fluttered in the breeze. Both armies looked on in silent expectation. Munekata closed his eyes and prayed to Hachiman, the God of War, vowing to put an end to himself if he failed. When he opened his eyes again the wind had dropped a little so that the fan made an easier mark. Munekata took the turnip-headed arrow, fitted it to his bow, and let it fly. The arrow went straight to the target. The fan leapt into the air and fell into the sea. The waiting hosts saw its scarlet gleaming in the rays of the setting sun as it danced upon the crest of the waves. The Heike in their ships applauded, while the Genji on the shore rattled their quivers in triumph. All this the dancer must convey. In the Noh tradition, his own fan is an important stage property.

Tarokaja's dancing impresses the young lady, who again offers him *sake* and the gift of a handsome ceremonial coat (*suo*) which Tarokaja, with a good deal of false modesty, accepts. Tarokaja sets out for home carrying the robe. Then he remembers that his master is a covetous miser. He decides to conceal his present for fear the daimyo should take it. After trying first one place and then another, he at last puts it under his sleeve. As he is about to enter his master's house, he almost collides with him and his sword-bearer **Dontaro**. He tries to conceal his drunkenness, but his tongue continually trips him up when he is repeating the young lady's message. He excuses himself by saying he has been forced to drink *sake*. His high spirits get the better of his prudence and he offers to show his master what a fine dancer he is. The coat in his sleeve gets in his way and he tries to find somewhere else to put it. However, he can find no better place than his sleeve. In his maudlin state the coat falls to the ground and is seen by the sword-bearer who quickly picks it up and shows it to the daimyo. They laugh uproariously and decide to make fun of Tarokaja. Dontaro hides the coat behind his back. Tarokaja suddenly realizes that his present is no longer in his sleeve. He looks for it frantically and begins to suspect that one of the others must have it. He searches the sword-bearer, who manages to prevent him seeing it. He would like to search his master, too, but does not dare do more than try to feel among his clothes as if by accident. Then suddenly he catches sight of the garment in Dontaro's hands. The daimyo and his attendant amuse themselves by passing the coat from one to the other while Tarokaja blunders after it. Finally they stand back to back with the coat between them and Tarokaja is completely mystified. At last he succeeds in catching hold of a corner. They all three pull it this way and that and in the end the daimyo and Dontaro go off triumphantly with the prize pursued by the disconsolate Tarokaja.

TOKI WA IMA KIKKYO NO HATAAGE (*The Standard of Revolt*). *Jidaimono* of the Taiko Cycle (see page 467). — Written by Tsuruya Namboku IV for Matsumoto Koshiro IV in the early nineteenth century. The play deals with the events which led up to the murder of Oda Nobunaga in 1582.

Among the many able generals with whom Nobunaga surrounded himself was **Akechi Mitsuhide.** He had been a *ronin* before entering Nobunaga's service. His ability was such that he rose rapidly and achieved great possessions. He is said to have been a man of immense ambition and, in the event, Nobunaga came to suspect his loyalty. Mitsuhide fell from favour and feared that his lands were about to be taken from him. His suspicions were confirmed by a number of deliberate insults heaped on him by Nobunaga. He was twice charged with providing official banquets at his own expense to which the guests never came, and, when he expostulated, Nobunaga, who was drunk at the time, beat him on the head with his iron-ribbed fan. These incidents and his personal ambition decided Mitsuhide. He seized an opportunity, when Nobunaga's other generals were engaged in military operations far from the capital, to fall on Nobunaga who was in Kyoto with only a small bodyguard. Nobunaga was mortally wounded and committed suicide. His eldest son and his favourite page, to whom he had promised the reversion of Mitsuhide's lands, were also killed in the general massacre. In the play the chronology of events has been considerably simplified and distorted.

Act I

The Honno Temple in Kyoto. **Oda Harunaga** has returned from military operations in the interior of Japan. He is accompanied by **Akechi Mitsuhide,** of whose ability he is both jealous and suspicious. Harunaga and his son are to receive an Imperial message of congratulation, and the arrangements for the messengers' reception and entertainment are put into the hands of Mitsuhide and Harunaga's favourite page **Rammaru.** Mitsuhide makes sumptuous preparations. Rammaru protests that he is not being consulted. The two quarrel and are about to come to blows when Harunaga appears. Rammaru accuses Mitsuhide of treason, pointing out as proof that the hangings of the banquet hall bear Mitsuhide's own crest instead of that of his lord. Harunaga seizes upon this as a pretext to dismiss Mitsuhide summarily. Holding him down on the floor with his own hands he bids Rammaru strike Mitsuhide on the brow with his iron-ribbed fan until the blood runs. Mitsuhide submits in silence.

Act II

A courtyard of the Honno Temple. Mitsuhide requests a further interview with Harunaga, which he at length achieves through the good offices of his sister **Kikyo,** a lady-in-waiting in Harunaga's household. Harunaga receives him with angry coldness. The wound on Mitsuhide's forehead is still unhealed.

Mitsuhide protests against the treatment he has received. To his surprise, Harunaga orders him to be served with wine, but when the cup is brought it is not a small cup, such as should be offered to a man of rank, but a large lacquer tub used to wash horses' legs. Mitsuhide chokes back his indignation and drinks from this vessel. He is then informed that his present lands, from which he draws his revenues, are to be exchanged for others. He is given a box containing the new title deeds. When he opens it, the box is empty. Harunaga tells him that his new lands are, in fact, still in the possession of the enemy, and he will have to go and fetch the title deeds for himself. Meanwhile, tossing him a horse's bridle, Harunaga says that here is something with which to check his ambitions.

Alone, Mitsuhide sits in silent fury, while his sister weeps. At last he takes up the empty box and leaves.

Act III

An Inn on Mount Atago. Mitsuhide has withdrawn from the capital with his family and retainers. He is brooding over Harunaga's insults. His wife **Misao** and his sister Kikyo are discussing the situation. Kikyo describes the dreadful interview with Harunaga and blames herself for arranging it. Misao comforts her. Mitsuhide comes in and indicates that he is contemplating open rebellion. Misao does her utmost to dissuade him.

Messengers from Harunaga are announced. Mitsuhide retires to change into ceremonial dress and Misao leads away her weeping sister-in-law. She returns presently to receive the guests, whose manner is cold and haughty.

Misao leaves and Mitsuhide enters. The messengers, **Asayama Taro** and **Nagao Yataro,** inform him that their lord has delivered sentence against him. The sentence is then read, Mitsuhide assuming the correct respectful posture. It declares Mitsuhide to be a traitor and condemns him to death. Nagao places before Mitsuhide a plain wooden stand such as is used to offer the dirk to a man condemned to commit *seppuku.* And upon it is not a dirk, but a wooden sword. This is the ultimate insult, for a wooden weapon indicates that Mitsuhide must die by beheading instead of honourably by his own hand. He protests angrily. Asayama and Nagao fall on him, but he beats them off with the wooden sword, springs to his feet and, drawing his own weapon, runs them through. At this moment his chief retainer, **Shioden Tajima-no-kami,** arrives and announces that the moment to strike Harunaga has come; the tyrant is in the capital with hardly any troops. Mitsuhide in a triumphant pose declares that he will raise the standard of revolt and revenge himself.

(In this play the character of Mitsuhide is on the whole a sympathetic one, but in the more famous *Ehon Taikoki*, see page 22, he is depicted as a complete villain. This is because his motive in killing Harunaga was not simply to avenge the insults heaped on him. If he had killed Harunaga and then committed suicide, he would have been a hero. Because he wished to seize Harunaga's power he is a villain.)

TORIBEYAMA SHINJU (*Double Suicide at Toribeyama*). *Sewamono.* — Written by Kido Okamoto in 1915 for Ichikawa Sadanji II.

Sc. 1. *A tea-house in Gion, Kyoto.* The Shogun has come to the capital on a prolonged visit. Among the samurai of his bodyguard is a young man called **Kikuchi Hankuro** who, idling in the soft, refined atmosphere of Kyoto, has fallen in love with a courtesan named **O Some.** O Some is only seventeen and Hankuro is her first lover; she is as deeply in love as he. They put off from day to day the painful decision of what they are to do when the time comes for Hankuro to return to Edo. But at last they find themselves unexpectedly faced with the problem, for the Shogun has decided to cut short his visit, and his bodyguard are under orders to leave the capital. Hankuro, realizing that he cannot bear to be parted from O Some, promises, in some way or other, to raise the money for her ransom.

It is a hot summer evening. The scene opens with the arrival of O Some's father **Johei,** bringing his daughter a parcel of new kimono she has ordered. Among them is a beautiful man's dress which she intends to offer to her lover as a wedding gift. When Johei has gone and she has put away the clothes, Hankuro enters, somewhat the worse for drink. He says he believes he has solved the problem of the ransom money. He lies down to sleep off the *sake* while O Some prepares him a cup of tea. Presently they are joined by Hankuro's intimate friend and comrade-in-arms, **Sakata Ichinosuke,** and Ichinosuke's mistress, the courtesan **O Hana.** Ichinosuke is also rather drunk. He wakes Hankuro and in the course of their conversation we learn that Ichinosuke has long coveted a sword of Hankuro's which the latter has now suddenly offered to sell him. Although he is anxious to own the sword, Ichinosuke will not clinch the bargain because he suspects his friend's motives. Hankuro refuses to tell him frankly why he wants the money, saying merely that it is "to release a bird from a cage." Ichinosuke guesses the truth and declares that it would be shameful to sell a valuable sword for such a purpose. The argument is interrupted by the arrival of Ichinosuke's elder brother, **Sakata Genzaburo.** Like the two young men he is also in the Shogun's bodyguard, but he is much older and more staid. He strongly disapproves of their dissipations, which he considers contrary to the strict samurai code and he regards Hankuro as Ichinosuke's evil genius. He now attempts to remove his brother from this haunt of vice. Ichinosuke refuses to go and the two are on the point of a fierce family quarrel when Hankuro intervenes. He succeeds in pacifying Genzaburo and persuades him to leave, promising to follow immediately with Ichinosuke. When Genzaburo has gone, his brother goes off with O Hana to another part of the house and both young men forget all about him. Hankuro and O Some fall into a pleasant rêverie about the happy life they are going to lead together, although O Some has some qualms about the sale of her lover's sword. Their idyll is rudely shattered by the return of Genzaburo. He demands Ichinosuke and abuses Hankuro for breaking his promise. Hankuro tries once more to pacify him, but this time has no success. Genzaburo insults him and O Some until at last Hankuro, still rather fuddled, can stand it no longer. He seizes his sword and swears to make Genzaburo eat his words. In spite of O Some's pleas, the two men go off to have the matter out.

Sc. 2. *The dry bed of the Kamo River at Kyoto.* Hankuro and Genzaburo draw and fight by moonlight. Genzaburo is killed and Hankuro flings his body into the river. O Some, who has followed them, now comes to him. Hankuro tells her that he has no alternative but to commit *seppuku*, since he has killed a comrade in the licensed quarter while both were on duty with the Shogun. He begs her forgiveness for the pain he must cause her. O Some answers that she wishes to die with him for she will never take another lover. They decide to die at Toribeyama, a hill above Kyoto which is the cremation site for the city. O Some remembers the new clothes she has prepared for so different an occasion, and she and Hankuro return to the tea-house to put them on and make ready for death.

O Some's maidservant and Hankuro's retainer, **Hachisuke,** enter from different ways, seeking their master and mistress. They compare notes and then continue their search. Hankuro and O Some return. Hankuro has discarded the distinctive samurai features of his dress (full, pleated trousers and long sword) and wears O Some's gift with his short sword thrust through the belt. The two tenderly take leave of each other and of the beautiful, moonlit world before their eyes. Then, hand in hand, they make their way towards Toribeyama.

The chorus tells us that Ichinosuke and the two servants, who have at last got upon the track of the lovers, witness their suicide from afar, but are too late to prevent it.

TSUCHIGUMO (*The Ground Spider*). *Shosagoto.* — Adapted by Kawatake Mokuami from the Noh play of the same name. First acted in 1881 by Onoe Kikugoro V. *Nagauta* accompaniment.

The central human figure in this play is the lord **Raiko**. This is a stage name for Minamoto Yorimitsu who flourished early in the eleventh century at a time when the House of Fujiwara held supreme temporal sway in Japan and the Minamoto were their trusted henchmen. The Regent Fujiwara Michinaga nicknamed Yorimitsu and his brother, Yorinobu, his "Teeth and Nails." Yorimitsu, who commanded the cavalry of the Imperial Guard, had in his service four devoted warriors known as the "Four Heavenly Kings," who all appear at the end of this play. The Minamoto family possessed two famous swords which were forged by a Chinese swordsmith for Yorimitsu's father, Mitsunaka. They were "Hizamaru," the knee-cutting sword, capable of lopping off a man's head and cutting through both knees as well, and "Higekiri," the hairsplitting sword. The little ground spider of Japan still makes its nest in a mound of earth as did the legendary spider, seven feet high, of the story.

The set represents the Kabuki version of the Noh stage.

Argument: When the curtain is drawn, Yasumasa, Raiko's chief retainer, enters and announces that his master has been ill for some time and no medicine can help him. However, services of intercession are being held at various temples on his behalf, and now he is thought to be improving. This suggests that his illness is of supernatural origin. Raiko enters and assures Yasumasa that he is feeling better. He tells Yasumasa to rest.

Kocho, a woman attendant, enters, bringing a special preparation for Raiko from the apothecary. She enquires after his health, and he repeats that he is feeling better. To cheer him and help his recovery, Kocho dances a description of the beauties of the autumn landscape. Raiko thanks her and tells her to withdraw.

When Raiko is left alone, attended only by his sword-bearer, he is seized with a terrible fit of trembling. The light suddenly grows dim, and from the shadows comes a priest, rosary in hand. Raiko, in surprise, asks how he came there. The priest explains he has heard that Raiko wishes for services to be held for his recovery, and he has come to help. Raiko thanks him, and the priest approaches to begin his intercession. Suddenly the sword-bearer exclaims that the priest has a strange look. At that the light fails altogether and with a burst of demon laughter the priest advances on Raiko trying to cast a web about his body. (The web is symbolized by fine paper streamers). Raiko, in spite of his weakness, manages to draw his sword, "Hizamaru." He slashes at the priest and wounds him. The faithful Yasumasa rushes in, but the monster has already vanished. Yasumasa finds traces of blood leading from the room and, with Raiko's permission, sets off with the "Four Heavenly Kings" to track the spider-fiend to its lair. (At this point there follows a comic interlude which has no connection with the main theme. It serves to divide the play in the traditional Noh manner and give the actor time to change his costume and make-up.)

The set remains exactly the same for the scene which follows, except that a wooden framework thatched with moss is brought onto the stage. This represents the ancient tomb in which the spider has taken refuge.

Yasumasa, accompanied by the four warriors, arrives before the tomb following the bloodstains. They hear a groan inside the ruin and guess that the spider is hidden there. They cry out their names and attributes as a challenge. The spider-fiend emerges. It accepts their challenge, crying out that it schemes to destroy their lord as a first step to dominating the whole world. They will be powerless against it as its strength is superhuman. It weaves its web about them, binding them more and more closely. The five warriors struggle against it undaunted. At last the wounded monster begins to tire, and Yasumasa swiftly deals the death blow. The heroes pose triumphantly beside the body of their enemy.

In commemoration, Raiko's sword "Hizamaru" was renamed "Kumokirimaru" (the spider-slaying sword.)

TSUCHIYA CHIKARA. *Sewamono.* — Written by Watanabe Katei. This tale is an offshoot of *Chushingura*. The action takes place mainly in the house next door to that of Kira Kozuke-no-suke Yoshinaka (the Kono Moronao of *Kanadehon Chushingura*) in Edo, on the night of the vendetta. The owner of this house is Tsuchiya Chikara, a well-to-do samurai, something of a poet, and an intimate friend of Shin Kikaku, a notable poet of the day.

Act I

Sc. 1. *The house of Shin Kikaku.* It is a winter evening. A messenger arrives from Tsuchiya Chikara inviting Shin Kikaku to attend a *haiku* party (see page 416). Kikaku accepts and is about to leave for his friend's house when a visitor appears, a *ronin* to whom Kikaku has always been a good friend. This **Otaka Gengo** was until eighteen months before a retainer of Lord Asano Takumi-no-kami Naganori (the Enya Hangan of *Kanadehon Chushingura*). Kikaku, whose mind is full of the coming festivity, tells his friend about the invitation. Gengo appears momentarily taken aback; then he quickly covers his surprise by telling Kikaku that he also is acquainted with Tsuchiya Chikara. The sister of one of his fellow *ronin,* Katsuda Shinzaemon, is employed there as a maid-in-waiting. He pauses a moment and then goes on to tell Kikaku that he has come to say goodbye. He has at last decided to take service once more and is leaving shortly to become the retainer of a lord in Western Japan. He thanks Kikaku for all his kindness and says that he fears it will be long before they meet again. **Ochiai Kigetsu,** a young poet and a disciple of Kikaku, is present during this conversation. He is a fiery and romantic youth. He is disgusted to hear Gengo, who was a retainer of the much wronged Lord of Ako, speak so lightly of seeking new employment while his dead master is still unavenged. He reviles Gengo, calling him faithless and mean-spirited, and strikes him. Gengo does not retaliate. He quietly picks up a sheet of paper on which Kikaku has written the first half of a *haiku* (see page 416) : "As the year's ending is likened to a rapid flowing stream, so is a man's golden

340

opportunity—" After a moment's thought he adds the finishing line : "— likened to a treasure-ship which comes but once in a life-time and leaves him in a twinkling." He takes formal leave of his friend and goes. Kigetsu reads Gengo's closing verse, but can see in it only proof that the writer puts personal ambition before all else. Even Kikaku, while defending his friend, begins to doubt whether Gengo still remembers the shameful death his lord died. *The stage revolves.*

Sc. 2. *The house of Tsuchiya Chikara.* Night is falling. Kikaku, accompanied by young Kigetsu, arrives and finds Chikara awaiting him, attended by the girl **O Sono** who is playing to him on the *koto.* Kikaku asks whether this is the sister of Katsuda Shinzaemon and, when informed that it is, apologizes for his curiosity, telling the story of Gengo's visit and repeating the poem he completed. Chikara is interested by the poem and falls into a rêverie. Then suddenly, to Kikaku's mystification, his face lights up, as if some obscure point has been made clear. Meanwhile, Kigetsu, still brooding angrily over the faithlessness of Asano Takumi-no-kami's retainers, casts hostile glances at O Sono. At last he rises, saying he cannot bear to sit in the same room as the sister of one of these despicable creatures, and goes out, followed unwillingly by his master, Kikaku. O Sono, wounded by Kigetsu's insulting remarks about her brother and Gengo, tries to kill herself, but is prevented by Chikara, who persuades her that her brother and his friends are in reality anything but faithless.

While he is speaking, a hubbub is heard next door. Kikaku and Kigetsu return, having been prevented from making their way home. They tell Chikara and O Sono that Kira Kozuke-no-suke's mansion has been attacked, it is believed by a band of loyal retainers of Asano Takumi-no-kami, led by Oishi Kuranosuke (Oboshi Yuranosuke). The sound of fighting continues. Presently Gengo, now in armour and wearing the badge adopted by the *ronin,* asks leave to enter. He comes on behalf of his leader, Kuranosuke, to apologize for the disturbance. Chikara receives him with deep respect, telling him that he understood the hidden meaning of his poem. Kikaku, on the other hand, is filled with shame at his own obtuseness and begs his friend's forgiveness for having doubted him. Kigetsu is overwhelmed by the way he has misjudged Gengo and, remembering how he insulted him a short while ago, implores Gengo to kill him. Gengo answers that, since he wished to be misjudged, Kigetsu's treatment of him was flattering rather than otherwise. O Sono, who is in love with Gengo, sits silently watching him. Chikara tells him of her act of faith. When Gengo is about to leave, she cannot bear to see him go to what must inevitably lead to his death. She tries to detain him, clinging to his sleeve, but he, although he loves her also, puts her sternly aside. He hastens away to join the rest of the forty-seven loyal retainers, watched in silent admiration by Tsuchiya Chikara and his companions.

TSUMORU KOI NO SEKI NO TO (*The Love Story at the Snow-Covered Barrier*). *Shosagoto.* — *Tokiwazu* accompaniment.

Background : The Emperor Nemmei had two devoted retainers, brothers named **Yoshimine Munesada** and **Ginosuke Yasusada.** Munesada was betrothed to a lady of high rank, **Ono no Komachi.** Yasusada loved a courtesan, **Kurozome,** who had magic powers. The brothers had a bitter enemy, **Otomo Kuronushi,** a man eaten up by ambition who dreamed of seizing the reins of government. Munesada had more than once thwarted his plans, but, owing to his favour with the Emperor, Kuronushi had been unable to be revenged upon him.

When the Emperor died, Kuronushi saw his opportunity. He went into hiding, assuming the disguise of an official in charge of the newly erected barrier on Mount Osaka. Here he waited for his plans to mature. Meanwhile, he sent his retainers to ambush Munesada, who was living quietly during the mourning period in a house belonging to Ono Takamura, his future father-in-law. In fact, it was Munesada's brother Yasusada who was living there. Munesada had moved to a little cottage just inside the Mount Osaka barrier, near the tomb of his master, the late Emperor. He and Kuronushi were living side by side without recognizing each other.

Kurozome was the incarnate Spirit of the Black Cherry Tree. She learnt through magic of the dangers besetting

Munesada and warned Yasusada that the innocent-looking barrier-keeper was none other than Kuronushi. Before Yasusada could carry the news to his brother, Kuronushi's retainers attacked. Yasusada, in order that Munesada might be believed dead and so be in a better position to overcome their enemy, gallantly pretended to be his brother and was killed in his stead. Before dying he sent a warning to Munesada. Ripping out his kimono sleeve, he wrote on it in his own blood : " Two brothers in the same boat." This is a line from a Chinese poem about two brothers, one of whom is killed in mistake for the other. Tying this to the leg of a favourite hawk, he loosed the bird.

Argument : *The barrier on Mount Osaka.* Munesada is playing the *koto* in his house. Outside, under the branches of a great black cherry-tree, in full bloom amid the snowy wastes, sits Kuronushi, drinking *sake* and chopping firewood to keep himself warm.

Ono no Komachi comes to the barrier and is refused admittance. Munesada, however, hears her voice and, coming out, vouches for her. She is allowed to pass. The lovers are happily reunited. Kuronushi, whom the *sake* has made benevolent, thinks they are planning to elope and decides to help them. While the three are talking, the Imperial seals, which Kuronushi has stolen and is hiding against the moment that he brings off his plot, fall from his sleeve. Kuronushi succeeds in recovering one, but the girl hides the other in her bosom. Kuronushi is angry and leaves the lovers to themselves. When he is gone, the hawk bearing Yasusada's bloody sleeve comes to Munesada. Munesada realizes what must have happened. A cock crows. Munesada is divinely inspired by the Spirit of the Black Cherry to shift a stone embedded in the ground nearby. Beneath it lies hidden a mirror which he recognizes as an heirloom of Kuronushi's family. He becomes suspicious and sends off Komachi to bring help from her father.

Evening is falling, and the hour has arrived when Munesada is accustomed to pray for the repose of the late Emperor's soul. Tonight he wishes to join to that of the Emperor the name of his gallant young brother. He makes his preparations and lays the bloodstained sleeve on the incense stand. Then it occurs to him that this relic may defile the Emperor's soul. He hides it in his *koto*.

Kuronushi reappears and Munesada tries to confirm his suspicions by adroit questioning. Kuronushi feigns drunkenness to escape from this awkward interrogation. Munesada retires into the inner room. Kuronushi sits with his *sake* bowl in his hands and sees reflected in it the stars that now stud the night sky. He reads in them a favourable omen and is filled with a desire to build a shrine on the spot. He looks about for material and decides to cut down the ancient cherry tree that stands by the barrier.

Kuronushi takes his great axe and sharpens it. To test the edge, he chops Munesada's *koto* in two and the bloodstained sleeve falls from it. Kuronushi reads the message and realizes that his plan has miscarried. But his enemy is here at his mercy. From the folds of the sleeve drops the Imperial seal which Komachi had entrusted to Munesada for safe-keeping. Before Kuronushi can pick it up, however, it miraculously flies into the cherry tree.

Kuronushi attacks the cherry tree with his axe, but his hand is stayed by a magic power. He gives up and falls into a doze. Immediately the Spirit of the Tree appears in the form of Yasusada's lover, Kurozome. Kuronushi is aroused, and suspects her at once. He questions her closely about her life as a courtesan. She answers without hesitation. She gathers up the sleeve and weeps. Kuronushi is mystified and tries again to make her reveal her identity. Kurozome counter-attacks until he, overcome by her strange attraction, tells her who he is and the ambitions he nurses. Kuronushi appears before her in his proper dress. She also changes. The courtesan is gone and in her place stands the Spirit of the Black Cherry. She declares that she will frustrate his wicked designs and avenge her lover. Kuronushi attacks her with his great axe, but she defends herself with a branch of the cherry tree and overcomes him.

TSUYU KOSODE MUKASHI HACHIJO (*The Old Story about the Wet Wadded Silk Coat*). *Sewamono.* — This play is an adaptation from an original story by Kawatake Mokuami and is notable for the appearance of the popular hero Chobei, the "father of the *otokodate*" (see page 448).

Act I

Sc. 1. *The house of the late Shirakoya in Edo.* **O Kuma,**

old Shirakoya's only daughter, is in love with **Chushichi,** one of the shop assistants. However, they are desperately in debt, and she has no alternative but to yield to her mother's wishes and agree to marry a suitable party of **O Tsune's** choosing. Faced by this inevitable engagement, she plots to elope with her lover. Their plans are overheard, however, by a scoundrel of a barber called **Shinza** who for some time has secretly been in love with O Kuma himself. In order to further his own interests, he draws out the two lovers and encourages them in their project. The three leave together.

Sc. 2. *At the foot of the Eitai Bridge.* The lovers and Shinza appear. Without warning Shinza attacks Chushichi, throws him into the river, and drags O Kuma away.

Act II

Sc. 1. *Shinza's house.* Shinza is holding O Kuma a prisoner, when he is unexpectedly visited by one **Yatagoro Genshichi,** who has saved Chushichi from drowning and, having learnt from him the circumstances of O Kuma's abduction, has come to rescue her. Shinza abuses him for his impertinence and sends him packing. The story of the abduction has, however, already gained currency in the district. Shinza receives a visit from his neighbour and landlord **Chobei,** who reasons with him at length in an effort to induce him to repent of his wickedness. Shinza refuses at first and Chobei withdraws. But such has been Chobei's eloquence and so great is his personal prestige that Shinza changes his mind.

Sc. 2. *Chobei's house.* Shinza appears with O Kuma and hands her over to the safekeeping of the famous apprentice guild-master.

Act III

The Emma-do Bridge. Genshichi has not forgiven Shinza for his treatment of him when he attempted to rescue O Kuma. He has in fact been waiting for a chance to even the score. On this day, the two meet on the bridge, and, in the ensuing scuffle, Genshichi kills Shinza.

UKIYOZUKA HIYOKU NO INAZUMA, commonly called *Nagoya Sanza. Sewamono.* — Written in 1824 by Tsuruya Namboku IV for Ichikawa Danjuro VII. This play links up with the Banzuin Chobei Cycle. The original story may be found in Mitford's *Tales of Old Japan*. The samurai Nagoya Sanza was entrusted by his lord with a precious sword which was stolen from him by his enemy Banzaemon. Sanza was disgraced and eventually murdered by Banzaemon. Sanza's son was befriended by Chobei and with his help avenged his father and recovered the sword. The Kabuki version differs somewhat. Two acts are perennial favourites. In the third the *kakeai* dialogue is justly celebrated (see page 429).

Act I

Before the Hase Kannon Temple at Kamakura. (This act is rarely performed.) **Nagoya Sanza** has been entrusted by his lord, **Sasaki Keinosuke,** with a precious scroll which is deposited for safekeeping in the temple. His fellow retainer, **Banzaemon,** is jealous of this favour. He also desires Sanza's betrothed, **Koshimoto Iwahashi.**

Iwahashi comes to the temple one rainy day. She is pestered by Banzaemon, but escapes from him, losing her sandal in the mud. One of Banzaemon's accomplices steals and opens the casket containing the scroll, substitutes Iwahashi's sandal for the scroll, and restores the box to its place. Banzaemon kills this minion so that there may be no witness to the crime. Sasaki arrives to inspect his treasure. The sandal is discovered. Sanza is accused of theft, but Iwahashi recognizes her sandal and recounts how and when she lost it. Since Sanza is responsible, although Iwahashi's evidence tends to show he is not the thief, and since Banzaemon is clearly compromised, Keinosuke degrades and banishes them both. Sanza leaves with Iwahashi.

Act II

The Story of the Face Like Lightning (*Sono Omokage Inazuma Zoshi*). *Sanza's humble house in Asakusa, Edo.* Sanza tries to keep up his dignity as a samurai and is loyally served by a devoted maid called **O Kuni.** There is nothing to eat or drink, the roof leaks, the house is always full of the fishmonger, the green-grocer, the *sake* seller, and the rice merchant all clamouring to be paid. O Kuni has an ugly birthmark on her cheek (like a lightning flash) and has long been the butt of all the wits in the neighbourhood. She is in love with her master, who seems to her to be as handsome as the most famous actors of the day. She is a pathetic and lovable little figure. Sanza's wife Iwahashi has sold herself into a brothel in order to help him prosecute his search for the lost scroll and for his enemy Banzaemon. She has become the famous courtesan **Katsuragi** and commands an extensive *clientèle*. Whenever she can, she comes to Sanza to comfort and encourage him. Pressed by his creditors, Sanza determines to go to the licensed quarter that night to try to borrow some money. He dispatches O Kuni to fetch his party clothes from the pawnbroker, sending the best of the household effects in their stead. While she is gone, Katsuragi comes to visit him. She comes down the *hanamichi* surrounded by her attendants, a glittering contrast to the misery in which her husband lives. Katsuragi brings news. She has learned in the Yoshiwara that one of her clients, known as "the daijin" (the millionaire), is none other than Banzaemon. Sanza can find him that very night. Having delivered her message, she leaves with her attendants. In the meantime, other plots are afoot. O Kuni's old father, **Ukiyo Matahei,** is always hanging about the place. He is a petty thief and a thoroughly bad character. **O Tsume,** the mistress of the brothel which employs Katsuragi, now approaches him. She is in Banzaemon's pay and he has suborned her to get rid of Sanza, which she is not unwilling to do, a husband being a great handicap to a successful courtesan. For a small bribe, Matahei agrees to put poison in Sanza's drink. The two prepare the mixture.

O Kuni returns with her master's best clothes in a bundle. She dresses his hair for the evening, glancing surreptitiously the while at a print she has just obtained of a young actor famous for his rôles as a lover with whom she compares Sanza to his advantage. Sanza surprises her in the act and realizes her feelings for him. He catches her hand and feels her shiver at his touch. Since after tonight he may never see her again, he makes love to her, but O Kuni bursts into tears, accusing him of mocking at her ugliness. She denies that she loves him until Sanza discovers on her arm the tattooed words "My master." Then she admits the truth. Sanza, much moved, leads her away to his sleeping room. Matahei, who has been off on his own business, has stolen a man's belt and has narrowly missed capture by the police, returns and is found in the living room by O Kuni. He is in such a state of nerves

that, to calm him, she gives him some of her master's *sake*.
It is only after they have both drunk a cup that Matahei
recalls that the wine is poisoned. O Kuni realizes that there
has been treachery. She accuses Matahei of having a hand
in it, and he tries to kill her. O Kuni manages to wrest the
knife from him and stabs him mortally. The lamp is extinguished in the struggle. Sanza comes from the next room
prepared to go out and seek Banzaemon. He calls to O
Kuni for a drink of water and his sedge hat. In the darkness he does not realize that she is dying. She gives him
what he needs and collapses as, without a further word, he
goes out into the night. (The rôles of O Kuni and Katsuragi are played by the same actor.)

Act III

*The Encounter from Rivalry for Love in the Licensed Quarter
(Date Kiso Kuruwa no Sayaate).*

(This scene is a piece of virtuosity by the actors. Danjuro VII and Kikugoro III, who first played it, introduced
references to their personal crests into the dialogue on the
hanamichi. These references were retained by their descendants Danjuro IX and Kikugoro V when the text was revised
on their behalf. Two *hanamichi* are used. *Nagauta* music.)
The Naka-no-cho of the Yoshiwara. The tea-houses are gay
with lanterns and loud with music. The cherry blossoms are
in full bloom. Two fire watchmen do their rounds. Banzaemon, wearing a wicker travelling hat and a kimono with
a pattern of thunderbolts, enters by the main *hanamichi*;
Sanza, in a similar hat and wearing a kimono patterned
with swallows in flight, enters by the other. They recite
alternate lines (see page 429). Banzaemon boasts that he
is known to all; he is of the White Hilts (the *hatamoto* or
personal retainers of the Shogun) and his sword is named
"Thunder." Sanza announces that his nickname is "Gut-
ter-rat" and his sword is called the "Amorous Swallow."
They both praise the beauty of the Yoshiwara, "the gate of
Paradise," backed by the hills of Ueno and Mount Fuji
rising beyond. As they approach the stage, the chorus
sings: "In the Yoshiwara it is luck which counts above
all. These two have been rivals for three years."
Banzaemon and Sanza come onto the stage, pass, and
become aware of each other as their sword scabbards touch.
Banzaemon seizes Sanza's scabbard, demanding why he did

not greet respectfully one who has long frequented the licensed quarter and is known as "the daijin." Sanza retorts that he indeed recognized him by the pattern of his kimono as the spendthrift whose sword is called "Thunder," adding that he should remember there are other people in the world besides himself. He, Sanza, will even go so far as to guess that this spendthrift's real name is Banzaemon. At that Banzaemon recognizes Sanza's voice. Both remove their hats and disclose themselves, crying, "We meet again!" Banzaemon boasts that he intends to ransom Katsuragi. Sanza answers that as her husband he will not allow it. Banzaemon threatens him with his "Thunder," but Sanza claims that his "Swallow" will be swifter. They draw and are about to fight, when **O Fuku,** the mistress of a neighbouring tea-house, rushes between them. Banzaemon and Sanza shout to her to stand aside, but she refuses to move because they are both good customers. They lower their swords. O Fuku begs them not to quarrel over Katsuragi, but to find themselves other courtesans. Neither will agree to this, although she persuades them to consider a temporary truce. Banzaemon swears that he cannot now tamely sheathe his sword "which thirsts for blood." O Fuku suggests that they should exchange swords, each keeping his own scabbard (see "Gosho no Gorozo," page 301.) This they do and the swords are found to fit perfectly. Both regard this as an omen that for the moment Katsuragi is not for either of them. They undertake to meet again and settle their quarrel.

YADONASHI DANHICHI SHIGUREGASA (*The Fish-monger Danhichi*). *Sewamono.* — Written by Namiki Shozo.

In this typically violent Osaka story we have the standard situation — the search for a lost sword, a samurai in disguise, rivalry in love, and several crossplays of loyalty and hatred. The plot is loosely put together, but has several popular situations. The hero is **Danhichi Mohei,** the son of a respectable samurai called Utagawa Jingoemon of the Minatogawa clan. He is a noted swordsman and wrestler, but is equally renowned for the shortness of his temper which has frequently brought him into troublesome situations. When the play starts, he is in disgrace for having

lost a precious short sword called Niji Yoshimitsu entrusted
to him by his feudal lord. To eke out a living, he has become an auctioneer in the fish market at Sakai, where his
powerful personality, no less than his distinctively checked
kimono, has made him a prominent figure. His enemy
is one **Takaishi Kazuemon** who, out of jealousy for Danhichi's father, has in fact caused the precious sword to be
stolen and (need it hardly be added?) is the choleric fish
auctioneer's rival for the favours of the courtesan **O Tomi**.

Act I

Sc. 1. *The fish market at Sakai.* Danhichi and his fellow
fishmongers are gossiping at the end of the day's work.
Danhichi tells them his story and laments that his cursed
temper has so far ruined every effort he has made to
re-establish his fortunes. In a fit of depression, he tattooes
himself on the arm as a constant reminder of the danger of
giving way to his instinct for violence. At this point, **Jisuke,** the owner of the Iwai bathhouse, who has been listening
to Danhichi's tale, reveals that he is in possession of a short
sword which seems to answer the description given by Danhichi. This revelation is not, however, as innocent as it
seems. Jisuke knows all about Danhichi and, furthermore,
he has no real intention of helping him. He knows that
the sword is useless without the proper accompanying
certificate. Having obtained possession of the sword, he
aims at using Danhichi to find the certificate which he
suspects is in the hands of Takaishi Kazuemon. He then
plans to make off with both sword and certificate and collect
the reward. The ingenuous Danhichi is delighted with this
discovery and decides to leave for Osaka to prosecute the
search for the certificate.

Sc. 2. *Before the theatre in Sakai.* **Gombei,** a brothel-
keeper, is in need of funds and has decided to sell his rights
in the courtesan O Tomi to Takaishi Kazuemon, Danhichi's
rival. The affair is arranged by Jisuke. O Tomi is surrendered and leaves with Jisuke to go to her new master.
In the meantime **Kyuhichi,** a former servant of Kazuemon,
but now employed in a brothel, is conspiring with various
shady characters — **Jumonji Kumoemon,** a *sumo* wrestler,
and **Tora** and **Hachi,** both professional gamblers — to attack Danhichi, beat him up, and thereby earn Kazuemon's
gratitude. The trouble is that none of them knows Danhi-

chi very well by sight. They know, however, that he always wears a certain boldly checked kimono and finally decide that that should be enough for purposes of identification. O Tomi returns to the theatre where she hopes to find her lover Danhichi and acquaint him with her news. She is accosted by the *sumo* wrestler, **Manriki no Ichiemon,** who tries to snatch her purse. The purse falls down a well, O Tomi runs away, and Ichiemon climbs into the well to retrieve the prize. Danhichi enters seeking O Tomi, but is at once apprehended by **Kawakyu,** the owner of the Naniwa tea-house, to whom he owes money. Armed by the law, Kawakyu seizes Danhichi's clothes off his back as part payment of his debt. The fishmonger, resolved not to lose his temper, catches sight of Ichiemon's bundle of clothes near the well and covering his nakedness with them, goes off to find O Tomi. The wrestler emerges from the well with the purse. To his chagrin it contains nothing but two play bills — not even an advertisement for the *sumo* matches in which he is competing. He then discovers the loss of his clothes, but seeing Kawakyu with a bundle of garments, seizes them from him. He has hardly put them on, however, when he is attacked by Kyuichi and his fellow villains. Danhichi observes the scene from afar and, realizing the significance of it, makes off in high spirits.

Act II

Sc. 1. *The Iwai Bathhouse.* O Tomi is under pressure from Jisuke and his wife **O Kaji** to break with Danhichi completely. They hope to use her in their plot to recover the certificate and are sufficiently indiscreet as to give her some hint of their real purpose. She pretends to comply with their wishes and, when presently Danhichi finds her, she plays her part with commendable skill. The fishmonger boils with rage at this infidelity, but, although he does not realize it at the time, this is the second occasion on which his self-control is to further his search.

Sc. 2. *The interior of the house of Namiki Shozo, the playwright* (by tradition one of the inventors of the revolving stage). Namiki Shozo is writing when Danhichi enters. He knows the story of Danhichi's misfortunes and makes no difficulty about lending him money to continue his search in Kyoto. Two actors, **Arashi Sangoro** and **Sawamura Kunitaro,** call on Shozo and, in an attractive scene, discuss with him a forthcoming production in which the heroine is to be murdered. Danhichi, who has been shaving Shozo's head, finds this conversation altogether too suggestive and, secreting a razor in his bosom, abruptly leaves to the astonishment of all present.

Sc. 3. *The Iwai Bathhouse.* Kazuemon comes to claim O Tomi and hand over the sword certificate to Jisuke. Danhichi bursts in, intending to kill O Tomi, but seeing Kazuemon attacks him instead. A desperate fight develops.

Sc. 4. *Behind the Bathhouse at the northern end of the Tazaemon Bridge.* The fight continues in the moonlight. Danhichi slays Kyuichi and another of Kazuemon's jackals, called **Sahei.** Then he kills Kazuemon himself. In his subsequent reaction, he thinks of committing suicide, but his hand is stayed by Jisuke, who, struck by Danhichi's gallantry, has suffered a change of heart. He gives Danhichi the sword, the certificate, and O Tomi and sends the two lovers off to start a new life together.

YANONE (*The Arrowhead*). *Juhachiban.* — This play was first staged by Ichikawa Danjuro II in 1729 and is still very popular. It belongs to the "world" or cycle of plays dealing with the adventures of the Soga brothers (see page 462). The plot is slight, but there are several poses and moments of emphasis which make the play an evergreen favourite.

The scene consists of an open room. There is a backcloth with a formalized Mount Fuji in the centre. The room is set about with stands in which are stacked huge arrows. There are two long swords in a rack in the centre. The play is performed in the most extravagant *aragoto* style.

Argument : It is New Year's Day. **Soga Goro** is seen sharpening a double-tipped arrow, as long as himself, on a great whetstone. He is making preparations against the day when he and his brother Juro can strike at their enemy, Suketsune, who murdered their father some eighteen years previously.

As it is the season of gifts and congratulations, a friend brings Goro a painting of a treasure ship on silk. It used to be the belief that if you slept with this beneath your neck-rest, the first dream of the New Year would bring good luck. Goro accepts the gift and, in due course, retires to rest with it under his head. In his sleep, Goro sees Juro come to him, imploring him to hasten to him, as he is in mortal danger. Goro awakes and leaps to the door where he makes a celebrated pose. Outside a seller of radishes (*daikon*) passes, leading his horse by the bridle. Goro asks for the loan of the horse and, when this is refused, struggles with its owner whom he overcomes. He then mounts the horse and gallops down the *hanamichi* using a huge radish for his whip.

YASUNA. *Shosagoto.* — A dance drama with *kiyomoto* accompaniment. The portrayal of madness through dancing is a feature of the Japanese stage, both Noh and Kabuki. This dance, which has no particular plot, is considered a great test of the dancer's ability.

Argument : **Yasuna,** the favourite pupil of the great astronomer Yasunori, was betrothed to his master's daughter. Both his fiancée and his beloved teacher died suddenly within a few days of each other, and Yasuna went mad with grief. In this dance he wanders through the spring country-side carrying his lady's wedding robe and living again his past happiness and his present sorrow. Two men-servants try to persuade him to return home, but he escapes from them and continues on his aimless way.

YOIKOSHIN (*The Eve of the Koshin Festival*). *Sewamono.* — Written for the puppets by Chikamatsu Monzaemon in 1722, when he was in his seventieth year. The play is based on an incident which scandalized Osaka. The affair was considered particularly tragic, because the young wife was expecting a child, and she and her husband were driven to suicide by the cruelty of his mother. Four days after their death Chikamatsu Monzaemon's rival, Ki no Kaion, staged a puppet play on the subject at the Toyotake-za. It was entitled *The Double Suicide of the Two Girdles.* A fort-night later Chikamatsu produced his version at his own theatre, the Takemoto-za.

Act I

The village of Ueda. The old farmer, **Shimada Heie-mon,** is bedridden and is cared for by his elder daughter

O Karu. His other daughter **O Chiyo,** who is very lovely, has had many misfortunes. First she married a man who lived such an evil life that she was forced to seek a divorce. She married again, but her second husband died within the year. She has now become the wife of a prosperous young Osaka greengrocer named **Hanbei.** This is a great joy to her father and sister, for Hanbei is known to be an excellent young man.

When the curtain is drawn, O Karu is going about her household tasks. A palanquin arrives and, to her astonishment, O Chiyo alights from it. She welcomes her, thinking she has come to visit their sick father, but O Chiyo explains that she has come home, once more, for good. Hanbei has gone to visit his father's grave at Hamamatsu, for he is only the adopted son of the proprietors of the greengrocery. In his absence, his adopted mother has given O Chiyo a letter of divorce in his name and has driven her from the house. (It is hinted that the old greengrocer finds his daughter-in-law too attractive.) Both sisters lament this new misfortune. **Kinzo,** a local farmer who has always been in love with O Chiyo, appears at the door, having heard of her return. O Karu tries to pretend that her sister is only here to see their father, but he says he knows the truth and adds his feelings are unchanged : O Chiyo " shall never be lonely while he is above ground." O Karu sends O Chiyo to take their father his medicine. The old man receives her tenderly. So far as he is concerned, he cares nothing for scandal, and will receive her " not merely three times, but a hundred times if necessary." O Chiyo is much affected and remains with him, reading aloud.

Another visitor arrives — Hanbei himself, come to visit his father-in-law on his way home from Hamamatsu. He has brought presents for him and O Karu. He is amazed to find his wife in the house and horrified when O Karu tells him the reason. Hanbei is of samurai stock, although adopted into a merchant family. His honour has been besmirched, and, begging Heiemon to forgive him for allowing O Chiyo to be treated in such a way, he draws his sword with the intention of killing himself. O Karu disapproves of both Hanbei and O Chiyo's behaviour, but his death is the last thing she desires. She persuades him to desist, and O Chiyo, rushing into the room, adds her entreaties. Heiemon points out that the young man will be dishonouring his adopted parents, if he commits suicide. Hanbei agrees this is true. He swears he never had any intention of divorcing O Chiyo; she shall be his wife for ever. Never again shall she be forced to return to her father's house; even should she die, her body shall not return there. He takes O Chiyo's hand, and they set out for Osaka. O Karu sets a fire at the gate as is done after a death, as an augury that O Chiyo shall never again need to return to her old home.

Act II

The greengrocery Aburakake-cho, Osaka. Hanbei's adopted mother, **O Mine,** has refused to have O Chiyo in the house, and he has been forced to lodge his wife with an aunt at the Yamashiroya.

It is the evening before the Koshin Festival at the beginning of the fourth month. When the curtain is drawn, O Mine is browbeating her maids and the apprentices in the shop. One of them returns from an errand and is scolded for having given Hanbei a message from O Chiyo begging him to go to her. Hanbei returns from O Chiyo and is abused by O Mine for his unfilial conduct. He is in a desperate frame of mind. He loves his wife, but he also recognizes the debt of gratitude he owes his adopted mother, whom he knows to be genuinely devoted to him and to have arranged for him to inherit her husband's business, although she has a nephew of her own whose claim she ought to have supported. He suffers her railing in silence. The old greengrocer, **Iemon,** comes out of his room asking crossly what all the noise is about. He goes off to the local temple to prepare for the festival accompanied by the parish priest who has come to fetch him. He asks O Mine to go with them, but she has not yet finished with Hanbei. Hanbei, in the meantime, has come to a decision. He now tells O Mine firmly that she must allow O Chiyo to return home. O Mine cannot believe her ears, but he explains that it is a reflexion on the honour of their house that O Chiyo should have been sent away, not by her husband, but by her mother-in-law. It is the husband's business to divorce a wife. He therefore wishes O Mine to invite O Chiyo to return and he will then himself give her the letter of divorce. O Mine is delighted, but, knowing how much Hanbei loves his wife, doubts whether he will be able to bring himself to carry out his plan. She therefore makes him swear to divorce O Chiyo, threatening to kill the girl with a kitchen knife if he does not. She leaves, saying she will herself invite O Chiyo to return home before going to the temple.

Left alone, Hanbei writes a letter which he hides in his breast. He fetches his short sword and hides it in a pile of empty vegetable baskets outside the shop. O Chiyo appears, radiantly happy. She cannot think what has happened to her mother-in-law, for she has not spoken so kindly to her for months. She does not notice Hanbei's silence, but runs from one familiar object to another, saying how glad she is to be back, but shocked to find dust on the top of the cupboard and other signs of incompetent housekeeping. She puts on her apron and will soon have everything set to rights. O Mine returns and speaks to her with false sweetness, calling her " my pretty daughter." At the same time she reminds Hanbei that he must now fulfil his promise. Hanbei bids O Chiyo sit down and gives her the letter of divorce. She cannot understand, and Hanbei refuses to give her any explanation of his sudden change towards her. O Mine, hardly able to conceal her delight, pretends to try to make him change his mind and then goes off to her private oratory saying she will pray to God to pardon so cruel a husband. Hanbei and O Chiyo are left in tears.

Hanbei takes the letter of divorce from O Chiyo and tears it up ; he never intended to break his oath to her father nor does he wish ever to be separated from her. But he can no longer stand his mother's persecution. There is only one solution ; they must die together. O Chiyo consents. Hanbei leaves his letter of farewell on the shop counter and the two creep out of the house. Night has fallen. He gropes among the baskets for his sword and taking O Chiyo's hand, begs her pardon for this sad end to their happiness together. For herself, O Chiyo answers, she has no regrets ; her only sorrow is for their unborn child. Tenderly they embrace and go on their way to seek happiness in another life.

YOSHITSUNE SEMBONZAKURA (*The Thousand Cherry Trees.*) *Jidaimono* of the Heike-Genji Cycle (see page

418). — Written by Takeda Izumo, Miyoshi Shoraku, and Namiki Senryu for the puppets. First staged in 1747. Adapted for the Kabuki soon afterwards. The cherry tree stands for martial valour. This play is no more than a series of short plays loosely linked together. The protagonists are: a) **Minamoto Yoshitsune,** who is escaping from his brother's vengeance ; b) **Shizuka Gozen,** Yoshitsune's concubine, who is bent on joining her lover in exile ; c) **Taira Koremori,** a general of the defeated Taira army, in hiding ; and d) **Taira Tomomori,** Koremori's uncle and second-in-command of the Taira army, also in hiding. In the play the two generals are made to survive the total defeat of the Taira at the battle of Dan-no-Ura, and the responsibility for their escape is laid upon Yoshitsune. According to the *Heike Monogatari,* however, although Koremori and Tomomori escaped from the first great battle at Ichi-no-Tani, they were both dead by the time of Yoshitsune's final triumph, as was also the little Emperor Antoku.

Act I

Sc. 1. *The Horikawa Palace in Kyoto.* (This scene is rarely performed.) **Kyo-no-Kimi,** Yoshitsune's wife, has been ailing, and to entertain her a musical party has been arranged. Two of Yoshitsune's most devoted retainers, **Kataoka Hachiro** and **Ise no Saburo,** arrive late. They explain that they are troubled because **Benkei,** the warrior-priest who was one of Yoshitsune's earliest adherents, is in disgrace. He accompanied their lord to the Imperial Court and insisted on wearing full war-harness. Some of the courtiers laughed at him, since now there is peace everywhere, and there has been a quarrel. Kataoka Hachiro and Ise no Saburo appeal to Kyo-no-Kimi to intercede with Yoshitsune on Benkei's behalf.

Shizuka Gozen, who is a dancing girl of great skill, comes to perform before Kyo-no-Kimi. After she has danced, she also appeals to Kyo-no-Kimi to help Benkei. Kyo-no-Kimi suggests that they all go to Yoshitsune together. Benkei is summoned and appears, still armed to the teeth.

Another of Yoshitsune's retainers, **Shinohara Tonai,** arrives with disturbing news. He has heard that a party of samurai from Kamakura, the headquarters of Yoshitsune's brother Yoritomo, has arrived in Kyoto ostensibly to visit the shrines, but in reality to attack Yoshitsune. They are

led by **Unno no Taroyukinaga.** At this moment, another
Kamakura lord has presented himself at the palace and
wishes to speak to Yoshitsune. He is **Kawagoe Taro Shi-
geyori.** Kyo-no-Kimi directs that he must be admitted,
adding that, since he is related to her, there is nothing to fear.
She and Shizuka Gozen go out accompanied by Benkei,
who is delighted at the prospect of a good fight.

Yoshitsune and Kawagoe enter, in formal dress. After
courtesies have been exchanged, Kawagoe announces that he
comes as Yoritomo's ambassador. As such, Yoshitsune yields
him the place of honour. Kawagoe has three questions to
ask Yoshitsune. The first is : does Yoshitsune bear resentment because Yoritomo refused to receive him when he came
to Kamakura ? Yoshitsune replies that as a younger brother
he has no right to question or resent the decisions of his
senior. The second question is : why did Yoshitsune send
to Kamakura three false heads purporting to be those of the
Taira princes, Tomomori, Koremori, and Noritsune? Yoshitsune replies that no one knows the fate of these men, although they are thought to have thrown themselves into the
sea. Although the country is now at peace, there is still a
strong Taira faction. If it were rumoured that these princes
still lived, this faction would be greatly strengthened. Therefore he sent the false heads so that it should be generally
believed that they were killed in battle. Then, says Kawagoe,
it is not true that Yoshitsune is plotting treason ? It is said
in Kamakura that Yoshitsune has received from the ex-
Emperor Go-Shirakawa the gift of a precious drum as a
pledge of support, should Yoshitsune attempt to overthrow
Yoritomo. At this Yoshitsune becomes angry and hotly
denies the charge, saying that the drum was a gift of friendship and, in any case, he himself has never made use of it. The
third question is : Why has Yoshitsune married Kyo-no-
Kimi, the daughter of Taira Tokitada ? Yoshitsune replies
asking whether Yoritomo himself has not taken a wife from
the house of Hojo, vassals of the Taira ? In any case, he
adds, Kawagoe is the last person who should ask him such
a question, since Kawagoe knows that Kyo-no-Kimi is his
own daughter and only adopted by the Taira. Is Kawagoe
afraid that if he acknowledges Yoshitsune as his son-in-law,
he will lose Yoritomo's favour ?

Kawagoe admits the truth of Yoshitsune's accusation, and,

deeply shamed, wishes to commit suicide. But Kyo-no Kimi rushes into the room in time to prevent him. She seizes his sword and stabs herself, saying that, if she is the cause of this quarrel between brothers, she will put an end to it. Kawagoe praises her for her courage and devotion while Yoshitsune mourns bitterly. Kyo-no-Kimi promises him that they will be happier in another life; then telling her father to carry " this Taira head " to Kamakura to appease Yoritomo, she dies.

There are sounds of fighting outside. Yoshitsune guesses that Unno no Taroyukinaga must be attacking the palace with his force. He is about to join his followers, when Kawagoe begs him to do all he can to prevent bloodshed, lest it make a permanent breach between him and Yoritomo. Yoshitsune calls to Benkei to give him this order, but is told that Benkei has already gone to engage the enemy. Yoshitsune sends Shizuka Gozen after him, but almost immediately Kataoka Hachiro and Ise no Saburo return to announce that Benkei has killed Unno no Taroyukinaga.

Kawagoe remarks sadly that now Kyo-no-Kimi has died in vain. Yoshitsune tells him that, since he does not intend to fight against his brother, he will leave Kyoto secretly with only a small following. Kawagoe takes the precious drum from the alcove and gives it to Yoshitsune, bidding him take it to bring him good fortune.

Sc. 2. *Before the gate of the Horikawa Palace.* **Tosanobo Shoshun,** another warrior-priest, enters with his retinue. He has been sent by Yoritomo to capture Yoshitsune. He is opposed by Benkei, and a spectacular fight ensues. Benkei cuts off everyone's head, including Tosanobo's. Benkei then realizes that the palace is empty and his lord and the rest have gone. He flings Tosanobo's head from him, saying it will lead him in the direction in which Yoshitsune has gone. Then he poses triumphantly with the rest of the heads.

Act II

Before the Inari Shrine at Fushimi. (This act is performed in *aragoto* style.) Inari Myojin, the God of Grain, is always depicted as attended by fox-spirits and the fox is sacred to him. In Japanese folklore the fox, who has magical powers, is a benevolent creature, well disposed towards mortals. He can assume human shape at will.

Yoshitsune has decided to make for the island of Shikoku

in spite of the pleas of his retainers who wish to fight the army Yoritomo has sent against them. He arrives at Fushimi, from whence he intends to take ship. There he is joined by his concubine, Shizuka Gozen, who begs to be allowed to go with him. Yoshitsune is persuaded by Benkei that their journey is too perilous for a woman. Yoshitsune has with him the precious hand-drum given him by the ex-Emperor, on the understanding that he should only make use of it if he were fighting against Yoritomo. He now gives the drum to Shizuka Gozen as a love token to protect her while they are apart. Shizuka Gozen is so desperate with grief that Yoshitsune's followers are compelled to tie her to a tree to prevent her running after them. Yoshitsune and the rest leave.

Hayami Tota, a general of Yoritomo's army who is searching for Yoshitsune, appears upon the *hanamichi* with his escort. (He is a stock comic character of Kabuki). He approaches Shizuka Gozen and recognizes her. He is delighted to find such a prize and intends to carry her off. He snatches the drum from her and is about to leave in triumph with his prisoner when, mysteriously, one of Yoshitsune's most devoted retainers, **Sato Tadanobu,** appears to bar the way. Tadanobu was absent at the time of the flight from Kyoto. Tadanobu overcomes Tota, and wrests the drum from him. He frees Shizuka Gozen. Yoshitsune, who has observed all this from afar, now returns and welcomes Tadanobu, praising him for his valour. He bestows upon him as a tribute the name of Yoshitsune Genkuro and gives him a suit of his own armour. He then commits Shizuka Gozen to his care and once more sets out on his journey.

Shizuka Gozen, carrying the drum, makes her way down the *hanamichi*. When she has disappeared, the sound of the drum is heard. At once Tadanobu appears to undergo a change. He is, in fact, not Tadanobu, who is ill, but a fox-spirit in disguise (his fox nature is indicated by his *kumadori* make-up). The skin on the drum is that of his parent and whenever the drum is struck he is irresistibly drawn to it. Now he follows Shizuka Gozen, executing an elaborate *roppo* down the *hanamichi*, in which his true self is revealed in the animal quality of his bounds and gestures.

Act III

Sc. 1. *Before the Shop of Tokaiya Gimpei (Tokaiya no*

Ba). (Although in the original play the child-emperor Antoku appears in this scene in person, it was customary at one
time to change the character to that of a little princess of the
Imperial House called Antoku-hime.)

A group of sailors and young women are talking in front
of the shop. The sailors are idle because of bad weather.
Sagami Goro, a samurai of Yoritomo's faction, appears in
travelling dress with his retainer. He calls for **Gimpei,** the
master of the shop, but is told he is away. He is received
by Gimpei's wife and tells her he has been sent in pursuit
of Yoshitsune, who is believed to be making for Kyushu.
Owing to violent storms he has so far been unable to cross
the sea. Now the storm is abating, and he wishes to hire
Gimpei's boat at the earliest possible moment. Since he is
on urgent business for the Shogun, he demands precedence
over all other travellers. Gimpei's wife demurs, explaining
that they have another client, also a samurai, who has been
waiting in their house for two days for a break in the bad
weather. Goro becomes angry and declares that he will see
this client himself. Gimpei's wife fears a quarrel and tries
to calm him down. Goro grows suspicious; from her behaviour he guesses that this client must be either a Taira
outlaw or someone of Yoshitsune's party. He attempts to
force his way into the house.

Meanwhile, Gimpei returns. He carries an umbrella because it is raining heavily. As he stands by the gate he hears
Goro abusing his wife. When Goro tries to force his way
into the inner room, Gimpei catches his arm, saying he is
the master of the shop. Goro tells him peremptorily that
he has need of Gimpei's ship. When Gimpei replies that
it is already promised to people of importance, Goro attacks
him. Gimpei fends him off, telling him sternly that a
samurai's sword is to defend men, not to kill them. Goro
shouts that he will not be insulted by a common merchant
and again attacks Gimpei with the help of his retainer. Gimpei beats them off, and they take to their heels, Goro vowing
vengeance.

Gimpei returns to the house, telling his wife that they
must make haste and get their guests away as they are in
danger. He will go and prepare the boat. After Gimpei has
left, Yoshitsune comes from the inner room with his followers. Yoshitsune praises Gimpei's spirited manner of

dealing with Sagami Goro. He promises that if ever he, Yoshitsune, comes into his own again, he will make Gimpei a samurai. Gimpei's wife thanks him and gives him her husband's message. Kataoka Hachiro asks doubtfully whether it is really possible to sail in such weather. Gimpei's wife answers proudly that in all matters concerning the sea her husband is to be trusted. She brings *sake*. They drink to a propitious journey and leave, putting or straw raincoats against the downpour.

Gimpei returns, accompanied by his little daughter, **O Yasu.** He is now in full armour and carrying a halberd. He reveals that he is in reality Taira Tomomori, the son of Kiyomori and second-in-command of the Taira forces. Now, since his elder brother is a captive, he is the head of the Taira clan. He sets the little girl in the place of honour, saying that she is the Emperor, Antoku-Gimi. His wife, **Suke-no-Tsubone,** was the child's foster-mother. Antoku-Gimi was believed to have been drowned, but Tomomori saved him and disguised him as his daughter. Tonight, he says, they will at last have an opportunity to be revenged on the hated Minamoto, for Yoshitsune is at their mercy.

Suke-no-Tsubone says, fearfully, that Yoshitsune is a fighter of almost superhuman skill and cunning. Tomomori replies scornfully that Yoshitsune will be taken unawares. The incident with Sagami Goro was arranged deliberately to convince Yoshitsune that 'Gimpei' is his friend. The supposed Goro was in fact a retainer of Tomomori. He adds that this bad weather will play into his hands, because it will be believed that Yoshitsune and his party have been drowned in the storm. In this way he can keep the secret of his own identity and that of Antoku-Gimi. He swears that he will bring back Yoshitsune's head, but warns his wife that, should he himself be killed, all the lights on the ship will be extinguished. If she sees that signal, she is to put Antoku-Gimi to death as all hope will be gone. They drink to Tomomori's victory over Yoshitsune. Tomomori leaves accompanied by his boatman.

Act III

Sc. 2. *Daimotsu Beach.* (*Daimotsu Ura no Ba*). The first part of this scene takes place before Gimpei's house. Antoku-Gimi and Suke-no-Tsubone appear in full court dress with their attendants. They are awaiting the outcome of Tomomori's stratagem and thinking joyfully of the time, now they hope not far distant, when the Taira will return to power.

A messenger arrives from Tomomori. It is the same man who appeared earlier disguised as Sagami Goro. Tomomori sends word that all is not going as easily as they had expected. The storm is very violent and Yoshitsune has somehow had warning of the plot against his life. Suke-no-Tsubone is desperately anxious and sends the messenger back for further news. She and Antoku-Gimi open the doors that give upon the sea and sit looking out. From there they can see Tomomori's ship and hear shouting. At first, the lights on the ship are burning brightly; then they see to their consternation that slowly they are being extinguished. It is Tomomori's signal of defeat. With the dying of the last light all is silence.

Irie Tanzo, Tomomori's retainer, approaches, wounded. He salutes Antoku-Gimi and tells the women that Yoshitsune and his followers have the upper hand. They are pressing Tomomori hard. When Tanzo last saw him, he was surrounded by enemies and by now may already be dead. He bids Suke-no-Tsubone prepare Antoku-Gimi and herself; he has returned to die with them and serve as guide for them on the road of death. Suke-no-Tsubone and her ladies lament. The Emperor is too young to understand and asks on what journey they are going. Suke-no-Tsubone explains that they are going to a better land below the waves where Antoku-Gimi's grandmother and many noble members of the Taira clan are waiting for them. Antoku-Gimi asks whether he must go on this journey alone. Suke-no-Tsubone assures him that she is coming with him, and the child is reassured. Suke-no-Tsubone tells him to turn towards Ise and salute his ancestors. Joining his hands, Antoku-Gimi does so while the ladies weep. The maids-in-waiting throw themselves into the sea. Suke-no-Tsubone takes Antoku-Gimi in her arms and, going down to the shore, is about to follow them when Yoshitsune and his retinue appear. Yoshitsune seizes the child from her. *The stage revolves.*

The scene shows the beach at Daimotsu with rocks and a great anchor. Yoshitsune enters with Antoku-Gimi and Suke-no-Tsubone. Suddenly Tomomori, mortally wounded, appears before them. He tells his wife that he is dying, and they will be able to die together. Then he catches sight of Yoshitsune who has been hidden by a rock. Tomomori cries out to him to prepare himself for death. Making no effort to defend himself, Yoshitsune looks with admiration at his enemy, saying how greatly he respects Tomomori's loyalty, particularly his stratagem of concealing the Emperor Antoku disguised as a girl. He explains that he and Benkei over-heard Tomomori telling Suke-no-Tsubone of his plans and so they were able to forestall them by throwing the boatman into the sea. He bids Tomomori have no fear for the safety of the Emperor, since his person is sacred even though he has Taira blood in his veins. Tomomori will not be mollified; although he recognizes Yoshitsune's nobility, he still regards him as his enemy. He rushes upon him with his spear, but Benkei intervenes, throwing his rosary at him. Tomomori angrily shouts that he has no desire to be a monk; he only wants revenge. Antoku-Gimi begs Tomomori to realize that Yoshitsune is a friend. Tomomori wavers in his resolution and at that moment Suke-no-Tsubone takes her life, bidding them put aside all enmity. Tomomori is overcome by this double appeal and commits the Emperor to Yoshitsune's care.

Tomomori prepares to throw himself into the sea, beg-ging Yoshitsune to tell the world that not the living Tomo-mori, but his ghost, attacked him. Yoshitsune swears he will care for the child and bids Tomomori die in peace. He takes the little Emperor by the hand and is about to leave. Tomo-mori watches them, saying : " Yesterday's enemy is today's friend." As they pass along the *hanamichi,* Tomomori ties the rope of the anchor about his waist and, lifting the anchor on high, flings it into the sea.

Act IV

The Lower Village of Ichimura (Ichimura no Ba). Taira Koremori, since the death of Tomomori the head of the clan which so short a time ago was all-powerful, is believed to have survived the holocaust at Dan-no-ura. His wife, **Waka-ba no Naishi,** and their son, **Rokudai,** are escaping from Yoritomo's vengeance and hoping to join him. With them is a faithful retainer, **Kokingo.** Rokudai is not well and they stop before a tea-house to rest. Wakaba-no-Naishi asks the mistress of the tea-house for medicine for the child, but the good woman has none and goes off with her own little boy to get what is needed. While she is gone, her husband **Gonta** appears. He is a gambler and a rogue, although the son of respectable parents. He plays for a while with Roku-dai, but presently, when no one is looking, he surreptitiously substitutes a bundle he has with him for Kokingo's and makes off. Presently he returns, pretending he has only just dis-covered his mistake. He recovers his own bundle and, opening it, cries out that his money, twenty *ryo*, has been stolen. Kokingo becomes angry and he and Gonta come to blows. They are stopped by Wakaba-no-Naishi who reminds Kokingo that they must not make themselves con-spicuous in any way. Kokingo, fearing he may have endangered his charges, hastily gives Gonta the money he claims. Wakaba-no-Naishi, Rokudai, and Kokingo go on their way, leaving Gonta triumphant. He intends to wheedle more money out of his old mother and has even greater hopes, for he has discovered the identity of the travellers from something he found in Kokingo's bundle and has betrayed them to the police. He expects a fat reward.

Gonta's wife, **O Sen,** and his son, **Zenta,** return. O Sen is horrified when Gonta shows her the money which, he says, he won gambling. She implores him to mend his ways for their son's sake. She asks him to stay at home, but is scan-dalized when Gonta, to pass the time, teaches Zenta to throw dice. They go off in the direction of their house.

Evening is falling, and a temple bell tolls. A party of police appear searching for the fugitives and hide themselves as Wakaba-no-Naishi with her son and Kokingo are seen approaching. They are surrounded and, despite Kokingo's efforts, Rokudai is captured and carried off. Wakaba-no-Naishi rushes after her child and Kokingo is left alone, still fighting. *The stage revolves.*

The scene shows a pine-bordered road. **Inokuma Dai-noshin** enters. He makes himself a spear from a bamboo and hides in the neighbouring thicket. Kokingo and a mem-ber of the police party enter still fighting. Kokingo beats off his antagonist, who takes to his heels, but, while Kokingo stands trying to regain his breath, Inokuma Dainoshin at-tacks him from behind, wounding him with the spear. Ko-kingo turns and they fight. Kokingo defeats his enemy (Inokuma has been following him from Kyoto for a private vendetta), but sinks down exhausted from loss of blood.

Wakaba-no-Naishi reappears, having rescued Rokudai. She goes to Kokingo's assistance, but he tells her he is dying and they must continue their journey alone. They are, he says, close to the temple of Mount Koya. Koremori has lately felt an overwhelming desire to become a priest, and Kokingo believes he may be at the temple. He instructs Rokudai to take his mother to the nearby village of Upper Ichimura where there lives a loyal and devoted supporter of the Taira, **Yazaemon.** He is to leave his mother there and then go alone to the temple and ask for the new priest. He warns the boy not to mention that he is a Taira. Rokudai does not wish to leave Kokingo, but the faithful servant insists, telling the child he will follow shortly. When Wakaba-no-Naishi and her son have gone, Kokingo falls dead as the temple bell tolls again.

A party of villagers appear, among them old Yazaemon. They are discussing the search for Koremori and his family and the fine reward offered for news of them. They pass Kokingo's body and, when no one is looking, Yazaemon secretly cuts off the head and carries it away with him wrapped in an old kimono.

Act V

The Sushi Shop (Sushiya no Ba). (This act is the most frequently performed of the whole play and ranks as one of the great " loyalty " plays of Kabuki and the puppets.)

Yazaemon is Gonta's father. He keeps a *sushi* shop in the village of Upper Ichimura. He makes and sells those confections of cold boiled rice served with fish, pickles, etc., which are such a feature of Japanese life. He is a humble but devoted supporter of the Taira, and it is in his cottage that Koremori has found refuge. Koremori is disguised as an apprentice and goes by the name of **Yasuke.** Yazaemon has given out that he intends to adopt this young man, since his own son has turned out so unsatisfactorily, and marry him to his daughter. Koremori aquiesces somewhat re-luctantly in this deception.

The scene shows the interior of the *sushi* shop with a row of wooden tubs containing the stock-in-trade and a large press which Yazaemon uses as his till standing against the wall. Koremori comes in with a supply of fresh *sushi.* The daughter of the house, **O Sato,** who does not know his real identity, has fallen in love with him and cannot understand why he is so unresponsive, since her father has given her to understand that today they are to be married. While Koremori is trying to escape from the young woman's attentions, Gonta returns home. His old mother welcomes him warily.

Since Rokudai and Wakaba-no-Naishi have not been captured, he has not received the promised reward and he has come to squeeze money out of his mother. When he has her to himself, he tells her a pathetic story to make her stop scolding him and have pity on him. She tries to open the press to give him some money, but it is locked. While she is out of the room looking for the key, Gonta picks the lock and helps himself. He hears steps approaching and, looking round for a place in which to hide the money, puts it in the bottom of one of the *sushi* tubs. Then he hastily disappears into the back of the shop.

Old Yazaemon enters by the *hanamichi* in a great state of agitation, carrying something wrapped in a kimono. Koremori comes out to greet him, as a good apprentice should, but Yazaemon sends him hastily on an errand and, when he is alone, takes a human head (that of the retainer Kokingo) from his bundle and pushes it into the *sushi* tub next to the one where Gonta has hidden the money.

When Koremori returns, the old man tells him that he is in great danger. A search party looking for him is actually in the village and suspects his whereabouts. However, Yazaemon still hopes to save him. He has come upon the body of a samurai killed in a recent fight and has taken the head, hoping to pass it off as Koremori's.

When the shop is again empty, Gonta creeps out, seizes the tub containing the head and runs off down the *hanamichi*. O Sato comes in and prepares the bridal bed by the lamp, hidden by a low screen. Koremori enters and, to O Sato's surprise, makes his bed in the lower room. Koremori's wife and son appear at the door. They are joined by Koremori and relate their several adventures. They talk sadly of the future, which looks very black, but at least they are together. O Sato, who has woken and overhears their conversation, realizes now the hopelessness of her love.

Koremori and his family go out to find a hiding place. They have hardly left when **Kajiwara Kagetoki,** the general charged by Yoritomo with the extermination of Taira Kiyomori's family, stalks down the *hanamichi* with his retinue. He has come to demand Koremori's head. He is suspicious of Yazaemon and impatient. The old shop-keeper places before him the tub in which he believes the false head to be hidden. His wife, who has watched Gonta steal his father's money and put it in that very tub, does her best to hold up proceedings. While they are struggling over the tub, Gonta hurries down the *hanamichi* with the tub containing the head under his arm. He offers it for inspection. His wretched father, who still thinks that the false head is in the tub he himself holds, is forced to the conclusion that Gonta has killed Koremori for the sake of the reward. Gonta now produces a woman and a small boy, gagged and bound, saying they are the wife and child of Taira Koremori. He treats them with great roughness and scorn. Yazaemon is now sure of his son's perfidy. Since Gonta has previously laid information which put Yoritomo's troops on to the track of Koremori's family and, through them on to Koremori himself, Kajiwara has no reason to doubt that the head and the prisoners are authentic. He formally inspects the head and declares himself satisfied. Gonta watches him with a curious expression, but his face remains impassive when the woman and child are led away and Kajiwara presents him with a robe as a reward for his services.

When the procession has disappeared, Yazaemon, overcome with horror at his son's treachery, draws his sword and stabs Gonta mortally. Gonta confesses that, although it was indeed he who betrayed Rokudai and his mother, he has since made atonement. He overheard his father telling Koremori that the search party was upon them, and his father's loyalty made him deeply ashamed. He was sure Kajiwara would see through his father's stratagem, so he had purposely taken the false head. The woman and child were his own wife and son whom he had sacrificed to save those he had betrayed. With his remaining strength he blows a whistle at which signal Koremori and his family come from their hiding-place. The old people weep over their son. Koremori unfolds Kajiwara's gift and from it falls a priest's gown. They all then realize that Kajiwara has not been deceived. To save Koremori, whom he loved in the days when he served the Taira, he has accepted the false head, but has sent this hint that it would be safest for Koremori to retire to a monastery. Koremori puts on the gown as Gonta dies.

Act VI

Travel-dance (*Michiyuki Hatsune no Tabi*), with *kiyomoto* music. Yoshitsune has failed in his attempt to raise support in Shikoku and has returned to the mainland. He is now making his way towards the mountains of Northern Japan, where he grew up.

Shizuka Gozen is determined to rejoin him. She and the fox-Tadanobu travel through the mountains where the cherry trees are now in full bloom. They reach Mount Yoshino. There in a forest glade Shizuka Gozen rests and idly begins to play on the drum given her by Yoshitsune, thinking as she does so of her love. At the first notes of the drum the fox-spirit, whom she still believes to be Tadanobu, appears at her side. She is surprised, for she thinks him away on a foraging expedition. They dance together while the singers tell the tale of the adventurous journey Shizuka Gozen is making for her lover's sake. The thought of Yoshitsune makes her grow sad. To cheer her the fox-Tadanobu sets up the suit of armour presented to him by Yoshitsune, and the two of them salute it as if it were the prince himself. Then to distract her further, the fox-Tadanobu describes for her in a mimed dance the heroic death in battle of Tsugunobu, the real Tadanobu's elder brother. Shizuka Gozen's courage is revived by this noble example and they continue their search for Yoshitsune. (The death of Sato Tsugunobu is described in the *Heike Monogatari*. During the battle of Yashima a notable Taira bowman was determined to kill Yoshitsune. But the latter's bodyguard guessed his purpose. A number of them, including Benkei and the Sato brothers, formed themselves into a living shield before their lord. Ten of them were shot down, including Tsugunobu, who fell from his horse pierced by an arrow from one shoulder to the other. Yoshitsune leapt from his horse and, with his master's arm about him, Tsugunobu died while Yoshitsune wept, pressing the sleeve of his armour to his face. When Yoshitsune's followers saw this, they were moved to tears and said; "For the sake of a lord like this, who would consider his life more than dust or dew?")

As the fox-Tadanobu finishes his narrative, Hayami Tota, still on the track of Shizuka Gozen, appears on the *hanamichi* with his retinue. When Tota sees that Tadanobu is there to defend her, he has not the courage to attack. He is taunted by the fox-Tadanobu who springs towards the *hanamichi* with animal bounds and drives Tota and his retainers away.

Act VII

Kawazura Hogen's palace on Mount Yoshino. Yoshitsune has at last found refuge with of the priests of the neighbouring temple, but his presence is causing apprehension to some of these dignitaries who fear Yoritomo's vengeance.

Yoshitsune's host, **Kawazura Hogen,** has just returned from a meeting at the temple. His wife, **Asuka,** enquires whether Yoshitsune's presence was discussed. Hogen replies that, although the greater part of the priests supported Yoshitsune, he himself and some few others declared themselves for Yoritomo, because he was convinced that Yoshitsune had no chance of escaping his brother's long arm. To prove his point, he shows his wife a letter from her brother, who is a retainer of Yoritomo in Kamakura. The letter makes it clear that Yoritomo is perfectly aware of Yoshitsune's whereabouts. In these circumstances, Hogen considers that the best course will be to murder Yoshitsune and win a large reward by carrying his head to Kamakura. Asuka is dumbfounded. Then, weeping, she declares she did not realize how little confidence her husband has in her. It is true that her brother is a supporter of Yoritomo, but she herself would never betray Yoshitsune. Yet it is clear this is what Hogen suspects. She draws her dagger and is about to kill herself when her husband stays her hand. He praises her loyalty, telling her that the letter is a forgery made to test her. The doors open, and Yoshitsune appears. He tells Hogen and Asuka that he has overheard them and thanks them for their devotion. (The scene usually opens here.)

A samurai enters, announcing the arrival of Yoshitsune's retainer, Sato Tadanobu. Tadanobu enters, deeply moved to be once more in the presence of his lord. He asks Yoshitsune's forgiveness for not being at his side when the latter had to fly from Kyoto. Yoshitsune asks why Shizuka Gozen is not with him. Tadanobu looks mystified and explains that he has this moment arrived from his home where he has been tending his sick mother. Yoshitsune repeats that Shizuka must be with him and, when Tadanobu again denies it, grows angry. He cries out that Tadanobu is lying; he must have sold Shizuka Gozen to Yoritomo and has now come to betray himself. He orders Tadanobu to be taken prisoner, but

Tadanobu indignantly refuses to be bound and defends himself against those trying to seize him.

At this moment another servant announces the arrival of Shizuka Gozen and Sato Tadanobu. Tadanobu angrily asks who has taken his name. Shizuka Gozen appears, carrying the precious drum wrapped in a silken cloth. Yoshitsune welcomes her tenderly and asks her forgiveness for his harsh treatment at their last meeting. He enquires after Tadanobu. She replies that he was with her a moment ago. Yoshitsune then confronts her with the real Tadanobu whom she does not recognize. After some thought she says that, although this man resembles the Tadanobu she knows exactly, there is a difference in the pattern of their kimono. Everyone is astonished. Shizuka Gozen remarks that, if ever on her journey she beat upon the drum, Tadanobu would not fail to appear mysteriously at her side. If they now beat the drum, perhaps he will appear again. Yoshitsune cannot himself touch the drum, but he tells the real Tadanobu to hide himself and then bids Shizuka Gozen beat it, first giving her a sword in case of need.

Yoshitsune retires behind the bamboo blind of the neighbouring room. As soon as Shizuka Gozen strikes the drum, the fox-Tadanobu appears. Shizuka Gozen tells him that Yoshitsune commands his presence, but the fox-Tadanobu is unwilling to obey. Frightened by his appearance, Shizuka Gozen thrusts at him with the sword, but the fox leaps aside. Shizuka Gozen tells him that she knows he is not what he seems and begs him to confess who he is.

The fox-Tadanobu then tells his story. Some years ago there lived in Yamato a pair of old foxes. One season there was a terrible drought and the farmers were at their wits' end. They captured one of the foxes and with its skin made a drum with which they were successfully able to invoke rain. This drum was named *Hatsune no Tsuzumi* and preserved as a great treasure. He himself is a son of that fox from whose skin the drum was made.

Shizuka, terrified, cannot believe that her former companion is really a fox. Then, before her eyes she sees him change into his true shape. He tells her that, because of his love for his parent, he has followed the drum everywhere. It was to be near it that he assumed the shape of the absent Tadanobu. Now he is deeply grieved that he should have caused Tadanobu to fall into disgrace. He will go back to his earth and trouble the world of men no longer, but, because of the honour done him by Yoshitsune when the latter bestowed upon him the name of Yoshitsune Genkuro he will always call himself Kitsune Genkuro (The Fox Gen-kuro). The fox then bows low to the drum, telling it with tears that he must go away. Shizuka Gozen, greatly moved, calls to Yoshitsune who emerges from his place of concealment and speaks kindly to the fox. But the fox, after saluting him, leaves them without a word, his eyes fixed to the last on the drum. Yoshitsune bids Shizuka Gozen strike the drum to call him back, but when she does so, no sound comes from it and Shizuka Gozen remarks sadly that it is sorrowing for its child. Yoshitsune compares the fox's loyalty with his own hard treatment at his brother's hands.

Suddenly the fox reappears. Yoshitsune thanks him for his care and protection of Shizuka Gozen and adds that he wishes to give him the drum as a reward. The fox is over-come with joy and gratitude. He warns Yoshitsune that certain of the priests at the temple are plotting to attack him that very night, but he, the fox, has placed a magic guard about the house to defeat them. Six armed priests rush upon the scene to kill Yoshitsune, but the fox fights with them and drives them off. He then disappears behind a cherry-tree with his beloved drum. *A curtain is lowered.*

(This scene is usually omitted.) The landscape is lit by strange fox-fires. Four priests who have been bewitched by the fox's magic appear and perform a comic dance. *The curtain is once more drawn aside.*

The ringleader of the wicked priests, **Yokawa no Kaku-han,** is lying in a trance. He awakes and, realizing he has been bewitched by the fox, swears vengeance. Yoshitsune's voice is heard shouting; "What, Noritsune!" Kakuhan goes towards the *hanamichi,* but is stopped by Tadanobu who rushes upon the scene. Yoshitsune and his retainers enter calling for Noritsune and shouting their names and titles, as before a battle. Kakuhan pretends he does not understand, but, when challenged again, flings off his disguise and pro-claims himself Taira Noritsune. Yoshitsune refuses to take advantage of his enemy and they swear to meet again and engage in mortal combat.

YOTSUYA KAIDAN (*The Ghost of Yotsuya*). *Sewamono.*
—Written by Namboku Tsuruya (1755—1829). Yotsuya
was a village near Edo, but is now part of the city.

Act I

The house of Iyemon. Iyemon, a *ronin* turned paper-
umbrella maker, has a pretty young wife called **O Iwa,**
who has just given birth to a child. Iyemon is a handsome
man, and **O Ume,** the daughter of his wealthy neighbour,
has fallen in love with him. The parents of this young
woman know that Iyemon loves his wife and conspire to
make him turn against her by sending her a medicine which
will spoil her beauty. O Iwa, still weak from her confinement, drinks the medicine gratefully. When the poison
begins to work, the only person with her is an old blind
masseur who does not know what is wrong with her. When
Iyemon returns home and finds his wife transformed into a
hideous creature, he is horrified and rushes from the house.

Act II

Sc. 1. *The house of Iyemon's neighbour.* Iyemon takes
refuge with his new friends who console him and bring him
food and *sake.* Iyemon drinks a good deal, and presently
it is suggested to him that, since his wife is now abhorrent
to him, he should divorce her and marry his host's daughter. Iyemon hesitates, but then remembers O Iwa's appearance when last he saw her and finally consents.

Sc. 2. *The house of Iyemon.* When Iyemon returns
home, he has not the courage to tell O Iwa that he intends
to divorce her, but deliberately begins to treat her as badly
as possible, hoping she will leave him of her own accord.
He refuses to give her money for the housekeeping, takes
away her best clothes, saying he intends to sell them, and
even pretends to pawn her mosquito net. His faithful
servant **Kohei** pleads with him and begs for money to buy
medicine for O Iwa, but Iyemon will not hear of it. The
two quarrel, and Iyemon ties Kohei up and shuts him in a
cupboard. Iyemon goes out, and while he is away O Iwa,
in despair at her changed appearance and her husband's
cruelty, kills herself with his sword. When Iyemon returns
he has some twinges of conscience at the sight of his wife's
body. But it is too late for regrets, and he is committed to
his new bride. He realizes that Kohei is the only witness
of O Iwa's ill treatment and despair. He therefore drags

the faithful servant from the cupboard and kills him. The two corpses are tied to a plank and bundled into the neighbouring river by a gang of hired ruffians. The house is then set in order for the reception of O Ume. She arrives in state, wearing her wedding dress and head-covering. When Iyemon approaches her and removes the white silk hood, he sees not the face of O Ume, but that of O Iwa. Completely unnerved, he draws his sword and slashes at her, only to find that he has killed his new bride. He rushes from the house and at the gate meets what he takes to be the ghost of Kohei. He runs the apparition through and finds that he has murdered his father-in-law.

Act III

The river bank. Iyemon is wandering along the river bank like a man in a dream. Suddenly from the water rises a plank with the body of O Iwa tied to it. She raises her head and calls beseechingly to her husband. He thrusts the plank down into the river, but it rises again. This time it shows the body of Kohei on the under side crying in tragic tones: "Master, medicine!" — the words he used when begging help for his mistress. (The rôles of the two ghosts are played by the same actor.) Iyemon, in despair, flings himself into the river.

YOUCHI SOGA KARIBA NO AKEBONO (*The Soga Brother's Revenge*). *Jidaimono* of the Soga Cycle (see page 462). — Written by Kawatake Mokuami. First performed at the Murayama-za in 1874. Acted in the classical manner with *joruri* accompaniment.

Act I

The house of Manko, the mother of the Soga brothers. **Soga Manko** lives with her second son, **Suketoshi,** who is blind and has become a priest. One night her two other sons, **Juro Sukenari** and **Goro Tokimune,** come to tell her that at last they hope to be able to avenge their father.

Manko has trained them to believe that this is the dominant purpose of their lives, but now that the moment has come, her mother's heart is stricken at the thought of sending these two young lives to almost certain extinction. She begs Juro to go alone. He is the eldest; let him do the deed. So may his brother be spared. But Goro will not tolerate this. His wild and passionate nature is set upon vengeance. The blind brother also pleads to go with them so that he too may prove his devotion. Juro, knowing it would break Goro's heart to be denied, pleads with his mother who at last reluctantly gives her consent. But Suketoshi is told that he must remain behind.

Bitterly mortified, Suketoshi takes his own life. Juro and Goro leave to carry out their vengeance, disguised in peasant hats and straw raincoats.

Act II

Before Kudo Suketsune's hunting lodge. It is night. Juro and Goro enter by the *hanamichi*, carrying torches. They identify the pavilion where Suketsune is sleeping and retire, extinguishing the torches, to purify themselves before their act of vengeance. This they do by moistening their lips with rain-water. The door of the house is pushed open and a courtesan emerges with a taper in her hand. She is **Tsurukame Kisegawa** who loves the brothers and intends to help them. She has heard their stealthy approach and now utters a few words, as though to herself, to let them know she is aware of their presence. She goes back into the house, but leaves the door unbarred. Juro creeps after her. He is followed by Goro. A moment later the alarm is given, and Suketsune's retainers rush upon the scene. The shutters of Suketsune's room are thrown down, and the two brothers are seen in the act of killing their enemy. They are attacked on all sides but, leaping from the room, drive their assailants before them. They are separated from each other in the mêlée. *The stage revolves.*

Another part of the camp. Juro fights manfully until he is attacked by the great warrior **Nitta Takatsuna**. Takatsuna is reckoned to be without his equal in combat and Juro is already weary with much fighting. Twice Takatsuna disarms him and twice he chivalrously returns him his sword. The third time Juro's weapon breaks and he is wounded. Takatsuna can no longer spare him and reluctantly prepares to cut off his head. *The stage revolves.*

Another part of the camp. Meanwhile Goro has driven off those who surrounded him and is desperately searching for his brother. Suddenly he hears the voice of Nitta Takatsuna proclaiming that he has killed Soga Juro Sukenari. In anguish, Goro rushes away. He makes for the lodging of

the Shogun, Minamoto Yoritomo. *The stage revolves.*
Before the Shogun's lodging. Goro intends to break into
the Shogun's room and kill him in order to avenge his
brother's death. The door of the room is pushed open by
a figure which, in the darkness, he takes for that of a
woman, since it has a woman's cloak over its head. Goro
disregards this person who slips behind him and then
catches him in an iron grip. It is **Gosho no Goromaru**
(or Gorozo), a member of Yoritomo's household, who,
although little more than a boy, is famous for the strength
of his arms. He overcomes Goro and makes him his
prisoner.

Act III

The Shogun's lodging, the following morning. The Shogun's
councillors are assembled as he has expressed his intention
of judging Goro's case himself. **Kajiwara Kagetaka** is
opposed to the young man's being questioned at all and
considers that he should be executed out of hand for making an attempt on the Shogun's life.

Gosho no Goromaru enters with Goro bound. He and
Kajiwara almost come to blows about the prisoner, but are
prevented by the arrival of **Yoritomo.** Goromaru presents
his capture. Goro maintains a haughty silence and refuses
to answer anyone but the Shogun himself.

Yoritomo is impressed by the young man's bearing and
offers him a skin mat to sit upon, since the ground is soaked
with rain. Goro is surprised and moved by this unexpected
attention. He answers the Shogun's questions in a straight-
forward manner and describes his father's murder by Kudo
Suketsune, the brothers' long wait before they could carry
out their plan of revenge and their final triumph. Yoritomo
is moved by the story and realizes that Goro has come with
no premeditated intentions against himself. He tells Goro
that his brother is dead, which Goro knows already, but he
is deeply affected by confirmation of the news. Yoritomo
causes Goro to be unbound and offers to let him see his
brother's head for the last time. Nitta Takatsuna enters
bearing the head and places it before Goro who mourns over
it, eulogizing his brother. He asks how he came to be killed.
Nitta describes the fight and produces the broken sword in
evidence of Juro's great valour.

Inubomaru, Kudo Suketsune's little son, rushes onto

376

the scene with a riding whip in his hand. He attacks Goro,
crying out that he will avenge his father's death. Goro at
first frightens him off, but then looks at him sadly and tells
him to strike harder. Inubomaru finds that his desire for
revenge has left him. He sinks down onto the ground
beside Goro and bursts into tears. Goro bids him take his
revenge while he can. He himself knows how bitter it is to
nurse the desire in one's heart. He has waited eighteen
long years. He offers to let Inubomaru beat him as much
as he likes, if it will relieve his sorrow. Inubomaru is now
most unwilling, but eventually gives Goro a couple of half-
hearted cuts across the shoulders.

Yoritomo, more impressed than ever by Goro's character,
offers to release him. But Goro refuses the Shogun's
clemency. He declares that, since his brother now awaits
him upon the road of death, he wishes only to hasten after
him. The Shogun therefore makes him his personal
prisoner, binding him with a silken cord, and declares he
will honour him by executing him with his own hand.

YOWA NASAKI UKINANO YOKOGUSHI, commonly
called *Genyadana,* or *Kirare Yosa,* or *O Tomi. Sewamono.*
— Written in 1853 by Segawa Joko III. The whole play
(nine acts) is hardly ever performed, but the third act is
considered one of the greatest plays of the *sewamono* group.
The first and second acts are staged occasionally and are
briefly summarized.

Background: **Izuya Yosaburo** is an extremely good-
looking young man and the adopted son of a wealthy Edo
family. Since his adoption, a son has been born to the
house and Yosaburo feels that it is wrong for him to
continue as heir. In order to give the family an excuse for
disinheriting him, he takes to dissipation, but his health
breaks down and his parents send him to the seaside at Kisarazu to recover. At Kisarazu lives **Genzaemon,** chief of a
powerful gang of gamblers. He has ransomed an Edo geisha,
O Tomi, and installed her as his mistress.

Act I

The Scene of the First Meeting. Yosaburo comes down to
the beach at Kisarazu and is followed there by his adopted
parents' old servant **Kingoro,** who has been sent from Edo

to try to persuade him to give up his evil ways. While they are arguing, O Tomi appears with a group of friends. One of the party, who is an acquaintance of Yosaburo's, stops to speak to him. Yosaburo and O Tomi suddenly become aware of each other, their eyes meet, and they fall instantly in love. O Tomi continues on her way, dazed by this new emotion ; pretending to gaze back at the sea, she murmurs, "How beautiful !" Yosaburo stands at the water's edge equally oblivious of his surroundings. His coat slips from his shoulders without his noticing. Kingoro picks it up and tries to attract the young man's attention. Yosaburo takes it from him and puts it on, muttering, "I know...I know... (*shitte iru yo*)" but never notices that the garment is inside out.

Act II

Yosaburo and O Tomi, who have met in secret and are more in love than ever, are betrayed to Genzaemon by one of the gambling gang, **Matsugoro,** who has himself made advances to O Tomi but has been repulsed. Genzaemon plans his revenge. He pretends to go on a journey, but returns with Matsugoro and his gang to discover the lovers in the most compromizing circumstances. O Tomi escapes, but is pursued by Matsugoro, who catches up with her on the seashore and tries to compel her to return. She frees herself from him and leaps into the sea. Meanwhile Yosaburo is tortured by Genzaemon and his confederates, who disfigure his beauty with knife cuts. They are prevented from killing him by Matsugoro, who returns with the news of O Tomi's death and persuades Genzaemon that it will be a greater punishment to Yosaburo to live than to die and be united in death with O Tomi.

Off the seacoast an Edo merchant, Tazaemon, is enjoying the cool night air in his boat. He sees something floating in the water and recognizes it as the body of a young woman. He and his servants drag O Tomi, unconscious rather than dead, into the boat. Tazaemon searches for something that might identify her and finds upon her person a small charm bag. As he examines it he starts : he has recognized the bag and realizes that O Tomi is his sister. He decides, however, to conceal the truth from her and from the world and merely tells the boatmen to make at once for the shore.

Act III

The Genyadana Scene. The scene shows the gate of the

discreet house in the Genyadana district of Edo occupied by
O Tomi. **Tohachi,** a shop clerk, is sheltering there from the
rain when O Tomi and her maid come back from the public
baths. O Tomi's hair is undressed and she carries dangling
from her mouth a little red bag containing the ground rice
husks used as soap. She invites Tohachi to come indoors
till the storm is over. They all enter, and, while O Tomi
completes her toilet, Tohachi tries to find out from her
whether she expects to become the official wife of her protector, Tazaemon. When she positively assures him that she
expects no such thing, Tohachi bribes the maid to leave
them alone, and makes advances to O Tomi which she
evades with good humour. While this is going on, Yosaburo (now called Kirare Yosa or Carved-up Yosa) enters by
the *hanamichi* accompanied by another petty criminal, **Yasu-
goro,** nicknamed "**Komori**" (Bat) because of the bat
tattooed on his cheek. Komori has come across O Tomi
and guessed that there is some scandal in her past history.
He proposes to try to blackmail her with the help of Yosa.
The two come to the gate, and Komori enters the house to
prepare the ground. Yosa waits outside, rather bored by
the whole affair which is just another job to him. Komori
spins a story about his poor sick friend who needs money to
convalesce at a hot-spring resort. He calls in Yosa, who
takes up a modest position near the door, without speaking
or looking at anyone. O Tomi at first refuses. Komori
makes insulting insinuations about her, and Tohachi intervenes, but is swiftly cowed. O Tomi, to get rid of her
unwelcome guests, finally gives Komori a small sum, one
bu. Yosa, who has been getting restive, turns and sees O
Tomi. (This is one of the great moments of the play and
the actor must indicate his sudden change from indifference
to intense emotional excitement.) He refuses to allow Komori to accept the money. Rising, he goes quickly over to
O Tomi, saying ironically : "Great lady — madam — O
Tomi-san — once it was O Tomi ! It is a long time since
we parted." Then, twitching off his head-covering, he looks
into her face, adding : "You did not recognize me ?"

(The speech that follows, with its accompanying poses, is
the most famous passage in the play and therefore a version
of it is given here. It is the key to Yosa's character and
state of mind. He is a man of education and sensibility,

but in his present bitter mood he wants to hurt and shock O Tomi. He says the cruellest things to her, interlarding his speech with the slang of the thieves' quarter.)

"Love and passion have been my worst enemies. In Kisarazu the cable of my life was almost snapped. Fate made me wander aimlessly for three years, disinherited by my parents in Edo, finding no help among my former friends in Kamakura and unable to return to my native place. Fortunately I was able to make use of this wound-scarred mug of mine. I took the name of Carved-up Yosa (Kirare Yosa) and learned all the tricks of blackmail and intimidation. Then suddenly what do I come across? In this quiet backwater of Genyadana, behind a high fence, in a neat garden set about with trelliswork, what do I find but O Tomi — who I thought was dead? God Himself could have been no wiser that I. I find you here, what's more, with a strapping great husband too!" (Turning to Komori) "So you see, Yasu, this one *bu* won't do, will it? We can't be fobbed off with that!

"When I was in Kisarazu, O Tomi, I knew you had a patron, but I was fool enough to think I could get away with loving you. If I'd had any luck, I might have done so. But it fell out otherwise. Your patron committed the vilest outrage on my body. Instead of killing me outright, he cut me about in thirty-four places. For whose sake did I get these wounds? — tell me that! For whose precious sake? You were safe in Kisarazu, it seems, while I believed

Yosaburo

you had thrown yourself into the sea. When they said you had drowned yourself, all sorts of vivid memories welled up in my heart. I murmured a broken-hearted prayer for your soul. Now I hear you've got another fine, strong man to look after you. That's not very decent of you, is it?"

O Tomi, completely shattered, protests that she is neither wife nor mistress. Yosa is sceptical. He and Komori agree that no man would be likely to keep a fine girl in luxury and leave her to her own devices. Yosa swears he will either have her again or get enough money to mend his broken heart. He and Komori set about bullying Tohachi to find out the name of O Tomi's protector. When he escapes from them, Yosa turns back to O Tomi herself. At this moment Tazaemon enters. Komori recognizes him as his father's former employer and tries to hide from him. Yosa, however, asks Tazaemon insolently how he comes to be O Tomi's patron. Tazaemon tells him that he saved her from drowning but, when pressed, asserts that there is nothing between them. Yosa is still sceptical. O Tomi tries to explain his presence and questions by saying he is her brother, to which Yosa adds: "Yes, a brother of unusually deep connections." Tazaemon then turns upon the cowering Komori and upbraids him for his evil life. When he has reduced him to abject shame, he mildly offers to let O Tomi go away with her relative, if she wishes. She is free whenever she chooses; but not tonight, he adds, that would not be convenient. He offers Yosa a considerable sum of

O Tomi

money to set himself up in business. Yosa refuses it, but
in the end decides to accept it. Komori is anxious to get
out of the house. He drags away Yosa who is loth to leave
Tazaemon and O Tomi alone together. Perplexed and off
balance, Yosa is slowly making up his mind.

Outside the gate the two halt, Yosa bidding his companion go home ahead of him; he has a call to make. Komori
begs for a share of the money. Yosa laughs and gives him
some to get rid of him.

(Here the act ends. The rest of the story is as follows:
Yosa hid near the house until he saw Tazaemon leave.
Then he went back to O Tomi. But Tazaemon's intentions
were less benevolent than he gave out. He had guessed
what Yosa would do and returned with a posse of policemen.
Yosa had too many petty crimes to his discredit to hope
for mercy and was banished to a distant island.)

YUKARI NO MURASAKI ZUKIN (*The Purple Head-
cloth*), commonly called *Rancho the Clown.   Sewamono.* —
Rancho belongs to the big group of "double-suicide"
stories. It is not particularly distinguished in itself, but is
often performed for the sake of the music written for it.
This ballad (*shinnaibushi*) was so popular at one time that it
is alleged to have driven young lovers to commit suicide in
emulation of Rancho and Konoito. Indeed, at one period the
Government forbade its performance. Another feature of
the play is that the rôles of Rancho and his wife O Miya are
usually played by the same actor.

Sc. 1.   *A street in the Yoshiwara.*   Various itinerants cross
the stage, including a fortune-teller, by the light of whose
lantern Rancho tries to read a letter from the courtesan
Konoito. Sakuragawa Rancho is a professional clown in
the licensed quarters. He is in reality a samurai called
Ageha Saburo and is searching for a precious heirloom of
his lord's (a valuable tea-caddy) which was entrusted to him
and which, needless to say, he has lost. Impoverished and
disgraced, he leads his present mode of life in order to
retrieve the heirloom and be reinstated in his lord's favour.
His search has been complicated, however, by his falling in
love with Konoito, a famous beauty of the Wakagiya. Rancho always wears a purple cap and is known by it.

Sc. 2. *Konoito's room in the Wakagiya.* Maidservants remove a large screen revealing Rancho and Konoito. Although he has come in response to her letter, Konoito reproaches Rancho for his neglect of her. He rehearses the reasons for his absence, and a mild lovers' quarrel takes place. He goes out, and Konoito receives a visit from the mistress of the house, who tries to persuade her to give up her association with Rancho. He has no money, he wastes Konoito's time, courtesans have no business to fall in love, and, if this goes on, the end can only be suicide together. The maids announce that a lady has called and wishes to see Konoito. The courtesan, doubly wretched, goes to receive her visitor.

Sc. 3. *A reception room in the Wakagiya.* Konoito's visitor is Rancho's wife, **O Miya** who pleads with her to give up her lover. O Miya dilates on Rancho's disgrace, the need to find the missing heirloom, and the fatal distraction which Konoito has proved to be. In a highly emotional scene, the courtesan agrees that she must take the step of breaking with Rancho. O Miya retires, leaving Konoito in tears. Rancho returns hoping to be reconciled to his love, but Konoito plays her part well and attempts to cast him off. Rancho grows desperate and, when Konoito proves obdurate, threatens suicide. Konoito breaks down and agrees to die with him.

Sc. 4. *Behind the Wakagiya.* It is raining. People pass to and fro, gossiping as they go. Rancho and Konoito steal out of the house and, after bidding each other farewell in this life, go hand in hand along the *hanamichi* in search of release from their cares.

YUKI KURETE IRIYA NO AZEMICHI, commonly called *Naozamurai. Sewamono.* — Written by Kawatake Mokuami and first staged in 1881. This play is the second half of *Kochiyama to Naozamurai,* but the two parts are rarely, if ever, played together and are so tenuously linked that they must be considered as separate plays. The first part, *Kochiyama,* will be found on page 207. The second part takes place some months after the first, and the only link between them is that the hero is a member of the gang of criminals headed by Kochiyama. He is the type of charming scoundrel which fascinated the playwright Moku-ami and is one of his most attractive creations.

Act I

A noodle-shop at Iriya, near the Yoshiwara, Edo. **Kataoka Naojiro** is a *ronin*, as is indicated by his ironic nickname **Naozamurai,** " the Faithful Samurai." He is in hiding since the hue and cry is out against him and he has hardly enough money to buy himself a meal. He intends to get out of Edo that very night, since he believes that for the moment he has shaken off the pursuit.

It is a bleak winter evening. Snow is falling heavily. Two men approach the mean little shop and enquire the way to the Oguchi-ro, a house belonging to the proprietor of one of the most fashionable establishments of the Yoshi-wara. When they have gone on their way, Naozamurai comes cautiously to the door of the shop and enters, mak-ing sure that there is no one there but the proprietor and his wife. (Naozamurai's entrance is considered a test of fine act-ing. He must convey both the bitter cold and his anxiety as a fugitive.) He goes to the brazier to warm himself and orders a bowl of noodles and some *sake*. While he is eating he asks, with careful casualness, the way to the Oguchi-ro. Nihachi, the proprietor, gives him directions, mentioning that he is not the first to ask this evening. Naozamurai is taken aback and would enquire further, but at that moment another client enters and he hastily shrinks back behind a screen. The newcomer is an old blind man, **Joga.** He buys a dish of noodles and, while he is eating it, explains that he is a masseur on his way to the Oguchi-ro. The principal courtesan of the house, **Michitose,** is ill, and everyone knows it is because her favoured lover has stopped visiting her. Naozamurai, listening behind the screen, is, of course, the lover in question. He has been in two minds whether to attempt to see his mistress before leaving the city. Now, hearing of her illness, he decides he must do so and hastily scribbles a note to her, warning her of his coming. When Joga leaves the shop, Naozamurai goes after him and accosts him in the street, asking him to deliver the note to Michitose. Joga recognizes his voice, but is told curtly to mind his own business. When Joga has gone, Naozamurai runs into a member of his gang, **Ushimatsu,** who tells him he had better clear out of Edo as fast as he can for the police are close at his heels. (The two men who came to the shop at the opening of the play are, in fact, police agents on their way to keep watch on Michitose's house in the hope of catching her lover.) Ushimatsu says that he himself intends to leave shortly, since life has become impossible. Naozamurai agrees. When he goes on his way, Ushimatsu watches him thoughtfully. He knows how anxious the police are to catch Naozamurai, and it crosses his mind that, if he should put them on the right track, he might save his own skin. His loyalty to the gang struggles for a while with his self-interest. Finally he follows Naozamurai stealthily.

Act II

The inner room of the Oguchi-ro, giving on the garden. Naozamurai comes to the back gate and knocks. Michitose's two maids, courtesans of lesser degree, are waiting for him and admit him. Ushimatsu watches him enter and goes off, sure of his prey.

Naozamurai is sitting by the brazier, drying his drenched kimono, when Michitose comes into the room. He is shocked by her altered appearance. The two maids tell him how ill she has been through worry on his account. Michitose says that now he has come back she is quite better. She asks him reproachfully why he has been away so long. Naozamurai, throwing a significant glance towards the maids, answers that he will tell her later. The others, with studied tact, leave the room. Michitose is about to throw herself into her lover's arms, but he gently wards her off, saying that first he has a confession to make. He is not the wealthy samurai she believed him. He is no better than a common criminal and must flee from Edo or face execution. He takes from his breast a letter in which he has written a full confession, meaning to send it her after his departure. Michitose accepts it, but does not read, or appear much interested in, it. Naozamurai presses her to do so at once, but she tells him that there is no need. She has always known who he really is and has planned, if he were caught and executed, to die at the same moment so that they might be born again together. She implores him to take her with him. When he refuses, saying the life he must lead would be too hard for her, she begs him to kill her before he goes. At intervals throughout the love scene which follows she reiterates her plea. This scene (which is considered one of the most tender and moving of the Kabuki stage) takes the form of a mimed dance with *kiyomoto* accompaniment.

Michitose and Naozamurai are interrupted by the unexpected arrival of another of the courtesan's clients, a samurai called **Kaneko Ichinojo.** This man is known to be practically blind and cannot see clearly in a dimly lit room, so Michitose hides her lover behind a screen and reluctantly prepares to receive him. Ichinojo tells Michitose that he has ransomed her and intends to take her away the same night. Michitose, who while talking with Ichinojo is quietly attending to the comfort of Naozamurai to whom the maids bring food and drink, flatly refuses to be ransomed; she prefers to remain a courtesan. Ichinojo loses his temper and says he knows it is because of her infatuation for Kataoka Naojiro. His main reason for ransoming her is to get her away from her "miserable lover." He adds: "Not that you'll see much more of him in any case. The police are after him, you know. They've got this very house surrounded." Michitose refuses to listen. Ichinojo becomes more and more offensive in his remarks about Naozamurai, who has greater and greater difficulty in suppressing his fury. Finally he can bear it no longer and emerges from behind the screen saying he will make Ichinojo eat his words. Ichinojo replies that he guessed Naozamurai was there all the time and asks whether he can deny anything that has been said. Michitose begs her lover to control himself and remember that Ichinojo is blind. Naozamurai attempts to do so, but is so provoked by his rival that he draws a knife and attacks him. Ichinojo, who has a blind man's quick ears and is renowned for the strength and skill of his hands, knocks the knife out of Naozamurai's grasp with his fan and, catching him by the neck, holds him down on the floor. Naozamurai, utterly shamed, begs Ichinojo to kill him outright and Michitose asks to die with him. But the samurai refuses scornfully; he would not soil his sword with such blood. He rises to go, while Michitose clings to her lover, and as he leaves he turns to Naozamurai and says bitterly: "You are like a scavenging alley-cat, always after other people's leavings. You covet the mouse I wanted myself. Well, I'll leave you my mouse, since you've mauled it already. Get away, both of you, while you

386

can." With that he flings a packet at their feet and goes. Michitose opens the packet and finds in it some money and the papers confirming her release from the brothel. There is also a letter from Ichinojo explaining that he is really her brother and wishes to ransom her to save her from the inevitable consequences of her association with Naozamurai.

The maids beg the two to escape together since Michitose is now free to go where she will. They have made up their minds to do so when the police burst into the room. Naozamurai escapes through the garden and makes off, leaving Michitose wildly calling his name as the curtain is drawn.

(Naozamurai was captured and executed. Michitose, true to her promise, committed suicide.)

NOTES

NOTES

ACTORS AND RÔLES. Although the Kabuki theatre owes its origin to a woman, the celebrated temple dancer O Kuni, by the middle of the 17th century the tradition had become established that all rôles should be played by men and boys, as in the English Elizabethan theatre. This tradition has persisted to this day. At first certain families specialized in female rôles, the actors wearing feminine dress and living as women off the stage. They even entered the public baths by the ladies' door! As a result we know comparatively little about these early *onnagata*, since they carried their art to the extreme of effacing themselves in the conventional manner expected of Japanese women. However, during the last century the great actors began to play both male and female rôles and there have been many outstanding exponents in the present century. Some actors, notably the Ichikawa family, have always tended and still tend to devote themselves to male rôles. On the other hand one branch of the Nakamura family tends to specialize in female characterization.

Much could be written about the merits and demerits of the *onnagata* tradition, but it is not the authors' intention seriously to enter the lists. The Kabuki stage is firmly traditionalist despite its pulsing life, and to replace the *onnagata* by actresses now would be as meaningless as substituting falsettos for the prima donnas of Italian opera. *Onnagata* are not always as lovely as cinema-poisoned Western audiences might require, though some are astonishingly attractive. Again their voices may sound forced to Western ears. From a purely mechanical point of view, it is doubtful whether actresses could stand up to the immense physical strain to which the *onnagata* are exposed on the boards. Not only may they be required to carry wigs weighing twenty pounds, but very often they have to switch from playing a lovely young girl to the portrayal of an animal spirit or an evil ghost performing complex dances of a semi-acrobatic nature (see *Kagami Jishi, Musume Dojoji*, etc).

The late Matsumoto Koshiro VII once declared that if actresses were now introduced they would do no more than imitate the *onnagata* of the last three centuries. He was probably right. Certainly the geisha throng the theatres today in order to learn from the *onnagata* how a woman of distinction should dress and behave.

The original eternal triangle — man, woman, and clown — of the primitive drama developed with the growth of Kabuki into a more complex dramatic structure in which certain stock rôles came to predominate. These are the hero, the villain, the woman, the clown (*dokeyaku*), the old man (*oyaji-kata*), the old woman (*kyasha-gata*), the young man (*wakashu-gata*), and the child. Tradition has accorded to each of these rôles particular attributes of dramatic scope, gesture, make-up, voice, and costume which make it possible for the intelligent playgoer with no knowledge of Japanese to identify them and make a rough guess at the part they will play. But the combinations are infinite — hence the spell of the Kabuki stage.

Heroes (*tate-yaku*) may be sub-divided into supermen (*aragoto-shi*), handsome young lovers (*wagoto-shi* or *iro-otoko*), men of judgment (*sabaki-yaku*), and martyrs (*shimbo-yaku*). For the first, the reader is referred to the note on *aragoto*. The second needs little explanation beyond saying that the Japanese audience likes a lover to be slightly effeminate, usually shy, and frightened of violence, but capable of being roused to feats of unexpected bravery or passion, and often with a streak of moral softness which is the cause of the predicament of which the play treats. The man of judgment is much admired. He is handsome, skilled in all military arts, a scholar, and a poet. He is invariably faced with some impossible problem occasioned by the division of his loyalties between his overlord and his family. A whole series of famous plays deal with just this situation and represent for the Japanese the sort of dramatic conflict typified for the Western world by Macbeth or Coriolanus. The martyr is in many ways no more than a variant of the man of judgment. He suffers the rude blows of fortune with patient endurance and usually gives his life for the cause he has espoused. He is a regular figure of the *sewamono* plays which often depict the latent class-struggles of the 18th and 19th centuries.

Villains may be classified as arch-villains (*kuge-aku*), inveterate rogues (*jitsu-aku*), degenerate young criminals (*iro-aku*), small-time crooks (*ha-gataki*), and comic villains (*hando-gataki*). The first are the Lucifers of the Japanese stage, plotters against the Throne, great and ambitious lords interpreting the generally accepted codes of behaviour in their own perverted way. The inveterate rogues are not unsympathetically portrayed — their lust for money or revenge may have been roused by fortuitous circumstances outside their own control. They may often have started as good men with no more than the usual human failings, but, having become the victims of accident or plotting, give up hope of redeeming themselves and yield wholly to a life of crime (see *Tenga-jaya, Izayoi Seishin,* etc.). They sometimes repent of their misdeeds and attempt to make restitution on their death-beds or, rather, they reveal as they die that they have just accomplished some noble act. This is called *modori* (see *Yoshitsune Sembonzakura, sushiya* scene). The young degenerate should be distinguished from the young lover who succumbs to human weaknesses. He is usually good-looking, resolute, and often of good family. He may have been a temple page who has found the temptations of drink, gambling, and women too hard to resist. He is very often the instrument of the young lover's first fall from grace. The minor and comic villains are self-explanatory. They may play an important rôle in relaxing dramatic tension at the proper moment.

Female rôles fall roughly into the classes of courtesans (*oiran* or *keisei*), young girls (*musume-gata*), princesses, i. e., the daughters of high-born or wealthy persons (*ohime-sama*), wives (*sewa-nyobo*), and victims of cruel circumstance (*hatahazushi no yaku*). The courtesan is the most popular rôle. She was of interest to the lower, middle and aristocratic classes alike. Courtesans throughout the Edo period were much admired for their beautiful clothes, their education in all the arts, their wit, and their unique status in society. Available both to samurai and commoner, provided they had the money to pay for her favours, the courtesan inevitably became the subject of countless tales of romance and adventure. She was, moreover, no lay figure in the tangles of intrigue and revenge. Usually of fine moral fibre, she was capable of great decisions and sacrifices. In the plays of Chikamatsu Monzaemon it is invariably the courtesans who take the lead in cutting the Gordian knot of circumstance. Tearful and shy though they may appear to be, they have no hesitation in proposing double suicide and often force their more fearful lovers into it. They in their own world are often the victims of divided loyalties. The standard situation depicts them as falling hopelessly in love with some handsome, but morally unstable, young man on whose behalf they begin to neglect the duties of their profession. This causes dissatisfaction in the establishment to which they belong with embarrassing consequences to all and sundry. Courtesans were often of good family, the wives of impoverished samurai engaged in the heart-rending business of rehabilitating themselves in their overlords' eyes. It was no dishonour for such a wife to sell herself into a brothel in order to raise the funds needed for her husband's purposes (see *Tenga-jaya, Gosho no Gorozo*). It was apparently even conceivable that a wife should sell herself into prostitution in order to help her husband to ransom a courtesan with whom he was incurably in love (see *Tenno Amijima*). Young girls are usually portrayed by the younger *onnagata* and lack the glamour af the courtesan or the princess. Nevertheless, they can be very rewarding parts, especially in *sewamono* plays. Princesses are of the stuff of dreams. The Japanese play-going public of the 17th and 18th centuries had so little conception of what a real flesh and blood princess was like that they attributed to her all manner of extravagant qualities. Always beautifully attired and wearing a characteristic jewelled headdress and red kimono, she must be incredibly lovely and frail (so much so that she cannot lift heavy objects such as helmets and armour, but must drag them on her sleeves — an action known as "nezumi-hiki" or "dragging like a rat"), capable of unquestioning sacrifice ir causes she barely understands and armed with a virtue of Caesarean purity, although, being a great lady accustomed to obedience, she is by no means slow in making advances to the object of her affections. The most lovable character of the Kabuki stage is, however, the faithful wife. Whether she be of high or low degree, she has all the domestic virtues and is utterly devoted to her lord and master. She is, however, by no means a subservient chattel. Her influence on husband and children is considerable. In *sewamono* plays her intervention in a crisis may be decisive — it is she who suggests the stern course of duty, she who tries to save her man from the bottle and takes his head between her knees when, sick and penitent, he crawls to her for comfort on the morrow, she who sends him back to his mistress so that he may regain his own faith in himself, and lastly she it is who willingly immolates herself to save the honour of the family or satisfy the demand of duty. (See *Terakoya, Banzuin Chobei, O Tsuta, Goju no To,* etc.)

Old people (*fuke-yaku*) are not neccessarily only secondary rôles, though they tend to be so. There has long been a school of specialists in character parts of all kinds — old priests, old boatmen, old masseuses, old brothel-keepers, and the like. The respect shown by Japanese to their elders ensures an honourable place for parents in the Kabuki world and often the old father or mother will play a big part in the development of a plot (see *Kajiwara, Kojiro Hakata Namimakura, Tenno Amijima,* etc).

Children (*ko-yaku*) are important members of the troupe. The sons and nephews of the older actors, they start their apprenticeship the hard way at the age of five. They play little girls and boys and slowly graduate to the bigger parts as they grow up. Yet even their childhood rôles may be important, since often in the parts they play they will be called upon to sacrifice themselves for their parents or their lord's child (see *Moritsuna Jinya, Terakoya*). Their acting is conventionalised except that Japanese children in real life tend to behave in this way — they sing their lines on the same high note and they use traditional gestures for weeping, entreating, and so on. It is always a pleasure to watch them, particularly if their real parent is on the stage at the same time. The Japanese, with their great love for children, do not stint their praise.

ACTORS' NAMES. The principal acting families have each a number of traditional " given " names of varying degrees of honour. The young actor is given one of the minor names on making his *début* (perhaps at the age of five) and as he progresses he is promoted to names of greater honour. As he inherits a name he adds to it a number which is personal to him and which his admirers may shout at the appropriate moments during the performance. A name is not automatically given to some other actor of the same family on the death of its holder ; there may be long gaps before anyone worthy of the bigger name is judged fit to inherit. A great name may be given to a gifted pupil rather than to a less gifted son. The tradition of art is more important even than that of blood, although blood counts for a great deal. There are many " given " names in the leading families. The principal ones will be found classified at the end of this note.

The ordinal number used is in the " -daime " form, thus " rokudaime " (the sixth) or " juhachidaime" (the eighteenth). When two actors are performing together and both earn applause, the enthusiasts shout a combination of their numbers, as " roku-shichidaime " (sixth and seventh).

During the early days of Kabuki, the actors acquired family names, many of which survive to this day, even though it was illegal for anyone but the samurai class to have more than a " given " name. Many acting families, such as the Ichikawa, the Onoe, and the Nakamura sprang from samurai stock and so had family names already, although they had forfeited the right to use them. The actors' " given " and family names were always displayed outside the theatres, but if the police chose to apply the law strictly, these family names could be removed and the actors' yago substituted. The yago is not a nickname but a title, often founded on some local association ; Naritaya, the yago of the senior branch of the Ichikawa, comes from a particular association of that family with the great Fudo Shrine at Narita ; Otowaya, the yago of the Onoe, is derived from the family name of their ronin acestor ; Yamatoya, the yago of the Bando, from the part of Japan from which the family originated. The " ya " in these titles is the same as the " ya " in the names used by merchants, who substituted their " tradenames " (yaoya — greengrocer, kamiya — paper-seller, etc.) for family names much as medieval tradesmen in Europe called themselves " Smith " or " Gardener." Any member of an acting family can be called by the yago of his family, but traditionally it is always particularly associated with the senior members. To shout an actor's yago is the most popular way of applauding.

Beginning on the following page is a chart of actors' names, yago, and crests. The Roman numeral after a name indicates the number of the present holder; an asterisk by such a numeral indicates it to be the number of the last holder, the title being in suspense at the time of going to press.

Name	Yago	Crest
Ichikawa (Tokyo) Danjuro IX * Sansho Ebizo IX Komazo X Somegoro VI[2]	Naritaya Kuraiya Kuraiya	 Three rice measures.[1]
Ichikawa (Osaka) Jukai III* Sumizo VI * Raizo	Naritaya	 Prawn in the shape of a breaking wave
Ichikawa (Tokyo) Chusha VIII Yaozo IX	Tachibanaya	 Peony
Ichikawa (Tokyo) Ennosuke II Danshiro III Danshi	Omodokaya	 Monkey toy
Ichikawa (Tokyo) Sadanji III Omezo VI *	Takashimaya	 Ivy leaf

[1] The three rice measures are used as a family crest by the junior branches of the Ichikawa family. The senior branch uses both the prawn and peony when more than one crest is required.

[2] In spite of his name, Ichikawa Somegoro is the heir of Matsumoto Koshiro and uses his crest and *yago*. The families are very closely connected.

Name	Yago	Crest
Ichikawa (Tokyo) Shocho IV	Wakamatsuya	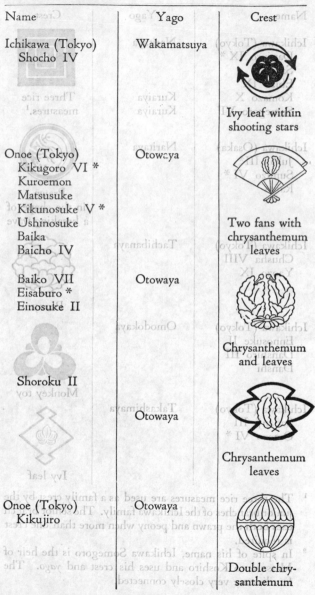 Ivy leaf within shooting stars
Onoe (Tokyo) Kikugoro VI * Kuroemon Matsusuke Kikunosuke V * Ushinosuke Baika Baicho IV	Otowaya	Two fans with chrysanthemum leaves
Baiko VII Eisaburo * Einosuke II	Otowaya	Chrysanthemum and leaves
Shoroku II	Otowaya	Chrysanthemum leaves
Onoe (Tokyo) Kikujiro	Otowaya	Double chrysanthemum

1 The three rice measures are used as a family crest by the ——— children of the Ichikawa family. The ——— prawn and peony when more than the crest

2 In spite of his name, Ichikawa Samegoro is the heir of —— Koshiro and uses his crest and yago. The ——— very closely connected

Name	Yago	Crest
Onoe (Tokyo) Taganojo III Kikuzo VI	Otowaya	Crane
Okawa (Tokyo) Hashizo II	Otowaya	Chrysanthemum leaves
Nakamura (Tokyo) Utaemon VI Shikan VI * Takesaburo I *	Narikomaya	Two song-books
Fukusuke VII Kotaro *		Reversed plum-blossom
Nakamura (Tokyo) Karoku * Kichiemon I * Mannosuke I Tokizo III Shibajaku VI Kasho II Kinnosuke I Matagoro II Kichinojo	Harimaya	Butterfly Nakamura Tokizo uses the same crest with the colours reversed.

Name	Yago	Crest
Nakamura (Tokyo) Kanzaburo XVII Moshio	Nakamuraya	Fan
Nakamura (Osaka) Ganjiro II Senjaku III	Narikomaya	Four characters
Nakamura (Osaka) Tomijuro IV	Tennojiya	Arrow flights
Nakamura (Osaka) Baigyoku III * Fukusuke V	Takasagoya	Three sparrows
Matsumoto (Tokyo) Koshiro VIII (Somegoro VI) Kintaro *	Kuraiya	A diamond of flowers
Bando (Tokyo) Mitsugoro VII Minosuke Yasosuke IV Keizo II Shucho IV	Yamatoya	Chinese character for greatness

Name	Yago	Crest

Bando (Tokyo)
    Hikosaburo VII *
    Kamesaburo IV
	Otowaya
	(this family is
	connected with
	the Onoe)
		
		Stork

Bando (Osaka) Juzaburo I *	Toyodaya	Wood-sorrel

Ichimura (Tokyo)
    Uzaemon XVII
    Kakitsu XVI
    Matsusaburo *
    Takematsu
	Tachibanaya
	(orange tree)
		Orange and
		leaves

Morita (Tokyo) Kanya XIV	Kinojiya	Wood-sorrel

Kataoka (Osaka)
    Nizaemon XIII
    Gato IV
    Hikondo *
    Roen V*
    Daisuke I
	Matsushimaya	Character for two

Kataoka (Tokyo) Ichizo V	Matsushimaya	 Gingko leaf

Name	Yago	Crest
Iwai (Tokyo) Hanshiro X	Yamatoya	Three fans
Kawarazaki (Tokyo) Gonjuro III Gonzaburo IV*	Yamazakiya	Good-luck symbol
Otani (Tokyo) Tomoemon VII Hirotaro	Akashiya	Cross
Sawamura (Tokyo) Sojuro VIII Tossho V Yoshijiro Gempei VI * Tanosuke V Tosshi VIII Gennosuke V	Kinokuniya	First character of the Japanese syllabary

APPLAUSE. While the custom of showing approval by clapping is common in Japan, it is much more typical of the Kabuki theatre to shout the actors' numbers or *yago* (see page 396) or some other encouraging remark such as *Matte imashita* (That's what I have been waiting for), *Edokko no kamisama* (The idol of Edo), *Go kyodai* (Well done the brothers), *Iro otoko* (What a man for the girls), *Nipponichi* (The best in Japan), *Go ryo ni* (Well done, both of you), and so forth. Such remarks may sometimes be a good deal less formal, to the delight of the audience.

The correct time to applaud is just before the curtain is drawn (to show general anticipatory enthusiasm), just before the entry of a popular actor (to show you know the play and the cast), during a particularly effective pose, especially on the *hanamichi* (to express sheer admiration of a difficult feat well done), or when some praiseworthy sentiment or well-known line is uttered. Once the *johiki-maku* is drawn at the end of the play applause is wasted. Japanese actors never take curtains.

ARAGOTO. *Aragoto* (" rough stuff " or " bombast ") is a style of acting. It was conceived and perfected by the great Ichikawa Danjuro I. It is an attempt to portray the superman and has historical origins in the legends, ballads, and plays about a mythical hero-giant called Kimpira. The Japanese admire this kind of robust, aggressive masculinity just as they are moved by the tender wistfulness of the young lover. Indeed Danjuro's creation was in some sort a riposte to the " soft " style of Osaka acting, then much in vogue. It also gave theatrical shape to the popular *otokodate* (see page 448) of the day who were renowned for their skill in the manly arts, wore extravagant clothing, wrote elegant verse, played the flute hauntingly, and strutted about picking quarrels with the equally overbearing samurai.

In *aragoto* everything is on the grand scale. The actors are the chosen exponents of the exit along the *hanamichi* known as *roppo* (lit. " six directions," but also involving the covering of the distance in six hops), a particularly athletic form of progress. Make-up is worn in the same spirit and the style called *kumadori* goes with the extravagant costumes of brilliant colour and huge patterns. Movement is always deliberate and colossal. The voice is torn to shreds to produce an effect and there is a whole vocabulary of meaningless words, such as " *tsu-go-mo-ne,*" " *i-ya-sa,*" " *yattoko totcha untoku na,*" which merely serve to give emphasis.

It follows from the foregoing that the *aragoto* style is only appropriate in certain plays and, first of all, of course, in the Ichikawa family collection, the *Juhachiban*. This technique of acting was so popular, however, that it was soon adopted in many other plays, notably those derived from the puppets. One point of interest is that today in some of the surviving puppet plays the *aragoto* style of declamation is used by the *joruri* singers. The wheel has come full cycle.

ARMOUR (*Yoroi*). Armour is an important element in the spectacle of the Kabuki theatre. Magnificent suits of armour are worn in many *jidaimono*. It is recorded that Ichikawa Danjuro VII was heavily fined for appearing on the stage in a suit which had belonged to a samurai.

Japanese armour is made of small, overlapping plates of metal or rawhide, lacquered over with black, or occasionally with gold, silver or red. The plates are laced together with coloured silk braid, or leather thongs, called *odoshige*. Armour is classified according to the pattern and colour of the *odoshige* and these patterns and colours always follow certain recognized rules. Two fine examples of armour may be seen in Acts III and IV of *Yoshitsune Sembonzakura*. Tomomori wears a splendid suit of white-laced armour, with silver lacquered plates, called *ginkozane shiroi no odoshi* and Yoshitsune wears *murasaki sosogo,* armour laced with purple, the colour graduating from deep to light. In the Amagasaki scene of Ehon Taikoki the armour worn by Jujiro is called *hi odoshi,* laced with scarlet. Kumagai in *Kumagai Jinya* wears *kurokawa no odoshi* (black leather).

A suit of armour consists of: a breastplate (which may be of plates laced together or of a single piece of leather sometimes covered with brocade or patterned in black or indigo); shoulder pieces of laced plates so arranged as to leave the arms unencumbered for drawing the bow; leg and forearm protectors of wadded brocade; a skirt of laced plates divided into four sections for the convenience of the mounted warrior; a helmet of metal, with a wide neck piece to protect the back of the neck and shoulders, adorned with tall, gilded " horns " said to derive from the deer's antlers which ancient warriors wore in their helmets; padded gloves and either coloured *tabi* and straw sandals or fur shoes. Under the helmet is always worn a "sweat band" against which the rim of the headpiece rests.

Common soldiers wear a small, conical metal headpiece called a *zingasa*, painted with the *mon* of their clan.

BEASTS, BIRDS, AND BUTTERFLIES. The Japanese stage seems never to have contemplated the use of live animals in the way we sometimes see patient old horses on the boards in the West. The Kabuki stage horse is a work of art, a splendid structure of wood and velvet borne by two specialist assistants. These assistants have exercised a monopoly for generations and there is very little about the behaviour of horses that they do not know and reproduce. Their beasts toss their heads, paw the ground, back away from obstacles and fret at the bit like any thoroughbred. Trotting is a proud speciality and the authors have even seen a gentle canter. The actor who rides such horses must give a tip known as "hay money" to the artists if he does not wish to risk an undignified fall — the pleasing tradition persists at least, even if present-day stage discipline militates against any such calculated mishaps.

Lesser beasts — dogs, foxes, boars, monkeys — are played by small boys in skins, while dragons, serpents, sea monsters, and other such monstrosities are direct borrowings from the popular animal dances of Chinese origin and may require the co-ordinated efforts of several assistants.

Birds make frequent appearances either as omens or as bearers of messages. They are more or less realistic and are manipulated by the *kurombo* who waves them on long rods called *sashigane*. This technique is also used for butterflies (which are much in demand for enraging lions) and for bouncing balls in games. Rats and other small animals can be made to run about the stage in this way.

COSTUME. The spectacular quality of Kabuki depends to a large extent upon the magnificence of its costumes, but it is a fallacy to think that all Kabuki plays use gorgeous costumes. In every programme there is at least one *sewamono* or *kizewamono* play, in which the actors wear everyday clothes of the period, the men usually very plainly dressed.

Kabuki costumes fall roughly into four groups, according to the type of play in which they are worn ; (1) those plays written in the last hundred years which concentrate upon historical accuracy ; (2) the classical *jidaimono,* which were originally staged in "modern dress," i. e., in the dress of the period between 1673 and 1735 (loosely termed Genroku), and continue to be staged in these costumes ; (3) *sewamono* and *kizewamono,* which were modern plays at the time at which they were written (the 17th, 18th, and 19th centuries) and use costumes similar to those of the first production ; and (4) dances requiring special costumes.

1. Historical Costumes

a. The Heian Period. Careful recreations of the dress of this period are frequently seen on the stage. The kimono is already the basic garment for both men and women of all classes. Ordinary men wear over it a rather scanty version of the *hakama* (see page 415), which is gathered into leggings for outdoor wear, giving something of the effect of " plus-fours." Women have not yet evolved the elaborate stiff obi, but wear a soft, narrow sash wound round the waist and tied in front. Court dress figures largely in these plays and consists, for the men, of a surcoat (*uwagi*) with voluminous hanging sleeves (*osode*), buttoned on the right breast and worn over at least five kimono. With it are worn trousers, sometimes gathered in at the ankle. At the back of the surcoat, which is belted, is a long train which can be looped up over a special attachment on the belt. Women wear long, trailing trousers over anything up to twelve kimono and a trailing outer coat called *uchikake,* usually of brocade. On ceremonial occasions an additional train of fine embroidered muslin is attached at the back.

b. Other modern historical plays set in the pre-Tokugawa era show small differences of detail, but on the whole resemble the classic Genroku costume.

c. The " crop-hair " plays (see page 476). In these can be seen an amusing re-evocation of the first years of Meiji enlightenment, with bowler hats (known as " chapeaux ") Inverness capes, button boots, and gold watch-chains alongside kimono and *haori.*

d. *Kizewamono* written since the Meiji Restoration, but set in an earlier period. Here the costumes are designed in strict accordance with historical accuracy.

2. Costumes of the Genroku Period

These are the costumes which most people have in mind when they speak of " colourful Kabuki." Since the principal characters in *jidaimono* are almost always men and women of rank, their dresses are made as rich as possible. When not in armour, the men usually wear brocade *hakama* and *kataginu* (see page 415) over a number of kimono. For very formal occasions, such as the reception of their overlord (see *Omi Genji Senjin Yakata*, and *Ichi-no-Tani Futabagunki*), they wear the long, trailing *hakama* known as *shitatare*. In the first act of *Kanadehon Chushingura* the daimyo wear the linen *kataginu* and *shitatare* which were *de rigueur* at the Shogun's Court. Imperial Court dress, worn by the *kuge* in Kyoto, remains unaltered from that described in the Heian Period (see Act III, Sc. 2 of *Yoshitsune Sembonzakura*). The long *haori* may replace the formal dress at home, those of princely rank wearing a special *haori* with an upstanding pleated collar. Occasionally warriors are seen in a garment called the *yoroihitatare*, which has cords at the ankles of the *hakama* and an upper part with flowing sleeves having cords at the wrist. This dress is meant to be worn under armour, and the cords pull up the sleeves and *hakama* to fit into the arm and leg pieces. The retainers and servants of the great lords of *jidaimono* wear a plainer version of their master's dress. They sometimes tuck up their *hakama* creating an effect not unlike the puffed trunks of Elizabethan costume. Emissaries of the Shogun or a great lord also wear the tucked-up *hakama* and a surcoat called *suo* with wide sleeves. One sleeve is usually tucked out of sight, the other, the left one, ornamented with the lord's crest (*daimon*), is stiffened with bamboo splints and looks like a shield. This costume is called *ryujin maki*. Servants often wear a short kimono with a fringed and embroidered apron underneath. Small pads are worn tied to the leg just below the knee. The same sort of fringed garment, but calf-length and skirt-like, is often worn by young retainers who are sent to report on battles and other events. This is known as *yoten*. Ladies wear the long kimono which sweeps the ground, unless they are on pilgrimage, or otherwise required to walk, when the kimono is kilted up to reach only to the ankle. Their obi are tied differently according to whether they are unmarried girls, who usually wear the two ends hanging down behind almost to the ground, or married women, who have a severe bow sticking out horizontally just below the shoulder-blades. Another style for young girls consists of a long cylindrical bow worn diagonally with one loop peeping over the shoulder. Over the kimono they almost always wear a trailing brocade *uchikake*. Young *o hime sama* (princesses) are dressed as splendidly as possible, in scarlet kimono and *uchikake* embroidered with gold. Maid-servants, as distinct from ladies-in-waiting, do not wear the *uchikake* and have kimono and obi of plain colours, the latter arranged in a simple bow. Priests and nuns may be recognized not only by their shaved heads, but also by a special over-garment (*koromo*) of transparent material on top of which they wear the *kesa*, a cape of many pieces sewn together, worn *under* the right and *over* the left arm. White is the colour of mourning, usually worn with an obi, or *hakama* and *kataginu*, of pale, watery tourquoise. Black, pale grey, and dun colour can also be mourning colours, but there is no real Japanese equivalent of the black crêpe of the Western world. Mourning is a private matter and is indicated rather by certain personal mortifications of the flesh such as fasting and light summer clothing in winter. White is also the colour of the death robe which is often worn concealed beneath ordinary dress by courageous men and women undertaking some dangerous mission. The same white death robe forms part of the ceremonial dress of the bride, who arrives at her husband's home wearing it to indicate that she has died to her own family. Beneath she wears a kimono of scarlet, the colour associated with infants, to show she is being born again into her husband's family.

A variant of the man's *jidaimono* costume is the exaggerated dress worn by actors performing in the *aragoto* style. They wear heavy wadded kimono covered with big designs, *shitatare* of abnormal length, and the *kataginu* or *suo* so exaggerated that the shoulder-pieces turn into great wings.

3. Sewamono Costume

The samurai who figures in many *sewamono* wears basically the same costume as the heroes of *jidaimono*, except that in his case the material is plain silk and the colours subdued and suitable to his age and station. At home he will often lay aside his *kamishimo* and appear simply in kimono and *haori* or only in kimono. Young boys of the samurai class often wear the brilliant colours reserved for girls. Ladies wear a soberer version of the dress of the ladies of *jidaimono*, but unless at a wedding or some similar ceremony, such as paying or receiving calls, they do not cumber themselves with the *uchikake*.

The ordinary man of *sewamono* wears kimono and *haori* of sober coloured silk, but youths of fashion daringly choose powder blue or lime green, never anything brighter. Cotton kimono are only for the very poor. This applies also to the light informal summer kimono, called *yukata*, which are usually patterned in blue and white. The *yukata* of the well-to-do are of silk. The merchant and his son wear *hakama* for formal occasions but not *kataginu*. When travelling they kilt their kimono to the knee and protect their shins with cloth leggings. A mark of elegance is a black collar band (*eri*) to the under-kimono (*juban*) which is often in this case sea-blue. This collar gives much the same effect as the black stock of the Regency buck and accentuates the white skin of the handsome young man.

Brilliant colour is brought to the *sewamono* stage only by the dresses of young girls, children and, of course, geisha and courtesans. Married women wear discreet, respectable colours, not unlike those chosen by their husbands. Indeed elderly men and women wear almost identical shades, usually dark grey and brown. This gives, by contrast, an added brilliance to the pinks, reds, oranges, and purples of the beautiful courtesans who are the focal point of so many *sewamono*. The devoted wife who becomes a courtesan for her husband's sake turns from a moth to a gorgeous butterfly. The courtesan of the first rank wears the trailing *uchikake* as part of her uniform, and her obi is tied in front instead of at the back, giving her the voluminous silhouette familiar from the prints of Utamaro and Toyotomi. The obi knot of the Edo courtesan is looped so as to fall in superimposed folds. It is covered, on full dress occasions, by a stiff length of material falling to the ground which is heavily fringed and embroidered.. The courtesan of Osaka or Kyoto wears her obi tied in a large bow. Her lowlier sisters, however, often tie the obi in the ordinary way, and their profession is indicated merely by the bright colours they wear and a certain air of studied elegance.

Kizewamono Costume. This differs very little from that of

the common man and woman of *sewamono* except that, since the characters are generally of a very low stratum of society, the cotton kimono is more in evidence. Long cotton trousers are often worn under it by the men. In plays with a summer setting both men and women wear *yukata*. No man in *jidai-mono* or in most *sewamono* would think of revealing what he wears under his kimono ; but in *kizewamono* he is not so reticent, and the loincloth, or *fundoshi,* is an excellent costume in which to show off the physique of a handsome young man whose clothes have been seized by an angry creditor. Fish-mongers wear a black apron under their kimono which covers the chest as well as the thighs. This is to protect their bodies when at work in the fish-market where they take off their kimono to keep it from getting torn and soiled. Carpenters and the like carry their small tools in a bundle attached to the back of the obi along with their pipe and tobacco pouch. Apprentices wear a short cotton jacket called a *happi* with the *mon* (crest) of their master printed on the back. The *happi* is also worn by firemen.

Apart from courtesans, certain other rôles in *sewamono* and *kizewamono* are associated with a particular type of costume, notably the *otokodate* or " chivalrous commoner " (see page 448) who can always be recognized by the bold pattern (in one case skulls, in another dragons) upon his kimono. A similar type of kimono is worn by the five bandits in *Benten Kozo* who choose to regard themselves as *otokodate* who " steal from the rich to give to the poor." Danhichi, an *otokodate* among fishmongers, the hero of several dramas, always appears at some time during the play in a *yukata* with big checks called the " Danhichi check."

Straw raincoats (*mino*) are worn only by the very poor, unless used as a disguise.

4. *Shosagoto Costume*

In a great many *shosagoto* the dancer simply wears the costume suitable to the character he is portraying. In certain dances of Noh origin costumes similar to those of the Noh are worn. These are always of great richness, even a mere fisherman being wrapped in brocade. The Noh costume is based on the Heian court dress described earlier, but with exaggerations suited to the theatre. The Kabuki version of these dresses is often even more exaggerated. The Noh *hakama,* called *seigo no mizugoromo* with its enormous width across the back, is worn by most male characters, unless they wear the formal linen *shitatare*. Servants in comic dances wear ordinary *kamishimo* over a checked kimono. Women wear the closely wrapped kimono, which does not trail on the ground, with a belted over-dress.

5. Footwear

In plays of the Heian period the actors go barefoot indoors. Those playing noblemen's parts wear boat-like black shoes out of doors, such as are worn today by priests in ceremonial dress. Poor men go barefoot all the time or make themselves clumsy shoes of straw.

Tabi (socks), *zori* (sandals), and *geta* (wooden pattens) are worn with costumes of the Genroku period. The commonest footwear is the straw sandal, worn by every class. Travellers and foot-soldiers tie on their sandals with strings. Officers of high rank, when in armour, wear elaborate skin shoes with the fur outside. High *geta* often indicate a man of violent character (see *Sukeroku, Gosho no Gorozo,* and Gimpei in Act III of *Yoshitsune Sembonzakura*). Courtesans of the first rank wear special lacquered *geta*, a foot high, to keep their finery out of the dust or mud. These *geta* are so tall that the lady needs to lean on the shoulder of an attendant to keep her balance ; they require skilful management to be able to walk in them at all.

CURTAINS. Curtains are an important stage property. The characteristic Kabuki curtain which is used to denote the end of an act or of the play (the word for " act " and " curtain " is the same — *maku*) is now made of broad stripes of green, terra-cotta and black and is called the *johiki-maku*. In former times, the different theatres had each its own distinctive curtain. The Nakamura-za had black, brown, and white stripes ; the Ichimura-za, black, brown, and green ; and the Morita-za, green, brown, and black. This curtain is drawn, never raised and lowered, and can be used to blot out part or all of the stage while an actor makes an exit along the *hanamichi*. It may be drawn from either side according to the needs of the play.

In order to achieve some particular surprise effect on the stage, a pale blue curtain (representing the sky) is often suspended in front of the set by a Heath-Robinsonian contraption of a batten and strings. This may be done merely to keep the audience guessing a little longer, even after the *johiki-maku* has been drawn, or while a short introductory scene is played. At the appropriate moment it is whisked away. A black curtain may be used in the same way, if the action is at night. On a smaller scale, scarlet curtains may be held up by stage-hands to mask the entry of an actor either through the wings or by the *seriage*. At the right moment, the stage hands run away with the curtain revealing the newcomer to the audience.

Much use is made in built-up sets of rolling, split-bamboo curtains or blinds. After an interior scene has finished, these can be lowered and the action continues elsewhere on the stage.

DICTION. The Japanese actor is required to have very wide powers of voice production. If he plays *onnagata* rôles, he must be able so to pitch his voice that it gives a convincing imitation of a woman, whether old or young. This is easier, of course, if he habitually acts as a woman — some of the great *onnagata* have very beautiful voices — but many actors have to play both male and female rôles. The male voice must also be flexible. A young lover is required to speak in a high voice of light tenor quality; the mature man has a smooth baritone; the bad man speaks in a hoarse bass. This mechanical trick can be put to effective dramatic use; a hero who has hitherto spoken in the appropriate calibre of voice can indicate that he has decided to take to evil ways by suddenly dropping his voice several tones (see *Izayoi Seishin*).

In *sewamono* plays, as one would expect, the standard of diction approaches very nearly to that of ordinary speech. But in *jidaimono*, and particularly if they are acted in the *aragoto* style (see page 403), it is necessary for the actor to use a declamatory delivery. A form of this used to be common until recently in Japanese public speaking, but few speakers today can do it. One may, nevertheless, hear echoes of it in the addresses made by guides on sight-seeing trips, particularly if these are priests. The declamatory style developed of course from the sonorous chanting of the Noh. It is, in fact, a form of singing which permits of placing unusual emphases on words in ordinary speech. The ideal of spoken Japanese is to place an equal emphasis on every syllable, and this is one of the major stumbling blocks to the foreign student. The theatre, however, clearly requires a more broken and emphatic line, and this is achieved by protracting vowel sounds, giving exaggerated definition to labials and dentals, and exploiting, wherever possible, the juxtaposition of k's and t's and k's and s's. "Kutabirete", for instance, will sound like "ktabirete" and "kusuri" like "ksuri." These effects are further heightened in *aragoto* where many meaningless, exaggeratedly explosive sounds are used and, by western standards, the voice is torn to shreds (see page 403).

Japanese actors, like actors anywhere else in the world, must be able to speak the various dialects of Japanese. This is particularly important if the plays are of Osaka or Tokyo origin. Chikamatsu Monzaemon's dramas should be played in the Kansai dialect, whether the actors be from Osaka or Tokyo. The *sewamono* of Kawatake Mokuami, on the other hand, call for an Edo accent. An amusing example of the use of country dialect may be found in the play *Gotaiheiki Shiraishi Banashi*.

FANS. The folding fan (*ogi*) is so much a part of everyday Japanese life that it needs little introduction to Westerners. No well-dressed man or woman should be without one. In the old days, after seating yourself, you took out your fan and laid it before you, taking it up whenever you wished to speak. This custom is still observed by *nagauta* singers.

On both the Noh and Kabuki stages a special thick paper fan (*maiogi*) with broad folds is used. This fan is perhaps the most important stage property of all and is in constant employ in dances and *monogatari* (see page 443). It may represent a sword, a bow, an arrow, chopsticks, a staff, a halberd, or a letter. When opened it may be water, a turning wheel, a fluttering leaf, a tea-cup, a *sake* saucer, a bottle, wind, or the waves of the sea. Apart from these esoteric uses, it is an integral part of the dance, an element of line and colour and shape. It is, as the teachers say, an extension of the arm and fingers. The manipulation of one or more fans in dancing is known as *ogi no sabaki* and is a difficult art for the practice of which long training is a requisite.

Military iron-ribbed fans (which were used on the field of battle for signalling to, or rallying, troops) appear in the appropriate historical plays and are convenient weapons for striking enemies on the forehead (see *Meiboku Sendai Hagi* and *Toki wa Ima Kikkyo no Hataage*). The ordinary fan is also often used in self-defence by men and women skilled in *judo* for parrying attacks with swords or halberds.

The rigid, square or oblong fan (*uchiwa*) is a stage property in the restricted sense, appearing only when its use is naturalistic, i. e. *sewamono* with a summer setting or plays set in China.

FILIAL PIETY. One of the principal mainsprings of Japanese behaviour (on and off the stage) is *ko* which may be translated as " duty to one's parents or ancestors." This has nothing to do with affection, though it does not exclude it, and is merely the repayment of the obligation put upon one by one's parents (*oya on*) in bringing one into the world and caring for one throughout life. This form of duty comes into the category called *gimu* which implies that the fullest repayment one can make is never more than partial and there is no time limit in which to do it. *Ko* has the same quality as *chu* which covers loyalty to the Emperor, the law, and Japan. It must not be confused with *giri* which is a duty or debt which can and should be repaid with calculated precision within recognized time limits.

Filial devotion is constantly in conflict with *giri* (to one's feudal lord, to one's more distant relatives, to one's name, etc.) in the Kabuki world and so constitutes the plot of many a popular play. *Ko* usually triumphs, being the greater virtue, but at great personal cost. A famous example is afforded by the heroine of *Kamakura Sandaiki,* who is required to avenge her husband's death on her own father ; she solves the dilemma by arranging for her father's assassination and then substituting herself for him. To avenge one's murdered father or elder brother is a very common theme. In *Moritsuna Jinya* the young boy Koshiro commits suicide in order to further his father's stratagem. Other examples will be found in the pages of this book.

Filial piety is, in short, a prime determinant of behaviour and will express itself in a variety of small ways. In *Ikutama Shinju,* for example, Koheiji prefers to hang himself rather than cut his throat with the sword which his father gave him for more worthy purposes.

FORMAL DRESS. Formal dress (*kamishimo*, literally " above and below ") is now rarely worn in ordinary life in Japan, but it will often be seen on the stage. Actors wear it, both in plays and on formal occasions such as *kojo* (see page 431); the singers and instrumentalists always wear it and so do the *koken* (see page 432).

Except in the case of singers and musicians who some-times wear special *kamishimo* designed to go with the set, only sober colours are used — greys, dark browns, and blues. For *kojo*, certain colours are associated with particular acting families, i. e., the Ichikawa wear terracotta red, the Onoe, slate blue. Over the *montsuki*, the black kimono with five crests, are worn *hakama*, (more correctly *hambakama*) a kind of divided skirt reaching to the ankles and made of stiff silk. The *hakama* of formal court dress (*shitatare*) used to be very long, covering the feet and trailing on the floor behind the wearer. These are often seen on the stage, and their manipula-tion is no mean feat. The other element of formal dress is the *kataginu*, a sort of cape which gives an exaggerated width to the shoulders and is considered very manly. *Mon* (see page 441) are always worn with formal dress.

GENROKU. The official era of Genroku, corresponding to 1688 to 1703 of the Christian era, is frequently mentioned in connexion with the Kabuki theatre and calls, perhaps, for some brief explanation. Historically the Genroku era was part of the reign of the Emperor Higashiyama and of the shogunate of Tokugawa Tsunayoshi. The term in the theat-rical sense is usually understood to include as well the two eras of Empo and Kyoho, making in all a total of sixty-two years, from 1673 to 1735.

The Genroku era represents the high-water mark of the development of Kabuki. The country was at peace and was tolerably prosperous. While the distinctions between classes were scrupulously observed, there were significant changes in values. The merchant was no longer to be despised. The samurai's credit did not stand as high as it had. It was an exuberant period of middle-class development in the social, political, commercial, and, most important, artistic worlds. It was the age of the great actors, Ichikawa Danjuro I, Sa-kata Tojuro, Mizuki Tatsunosuke, and Yoshizawa Ayame ; of musicians such as Takemoto Gidayu ; of the playwrights

Chikamatsu Monzaemon and Ki no Kaion; of the *haiku* poet Basho; and of the painters Hishikawa Moronobu, Ogata Korin and Hanabusa Itcho. It was an age when the public demanded the best and usually got it.

HAIKU (*Japanese Verse*). Such frequent mention is made of *haiku* in Kabuki plays that some explanation seems necessary, even though a knowledge of Japanese is essential for a full understanding.

The Japanese are great lovers of poetry and like to write and hear it on suitable occasions, such as family gatherings, cherry-blossom or full-moon viewing parties, and so on. The standard form of verse is alternate lines of five and seven syllables. There is no rhyme in the Western sense. A common form of poem is the *tanka*, consisting of five lines of five, seven, five, seven, and seven syllables. The most popular form, however, is the *haiku* of three lines of five, seven, and five syllables.

The *haiku* should attempt to express a single thought, the simpler the better. This does not mean that the same thought may not have a number of symbolic, allegoric and anagogic interpretations. Thus the *haiku*

Tsuyu chikaku

Midori fuku maru

Sanae kana

literally means : " The rainy season is at hand, the green (of the fields) darkens, a rice-shoot." But the poem has many other meanings which only a knowledge of the circumstances in which it was written would elucidate. That, however, is not the point. The reader is free to adapt the words to any meaning he wishes. Some *haiku* are primarily descriptive, as, for example :

Aoyagi ni

Komori tsutau

Yubae ya

which means : " The bats are flitting amongst the willows in the evening glow." We are not, however, prepared to say that even this simple verse does not mean more than it seems.

The *haiku* sould be terse and well-turned. It is symbolic of Japanese reticence and politeness. It should be able to convey a message without dotting the i's and crossing the t's. The intimacy established in this way is infinitely more precious than the hard, gem-like detail of, say, Petrarch's sonnets. The *haiku* should have visual appeal also. It should be written on good paper in the traditional shape (*tanzaku*) and, of course, with a brush. The characters should be chosen for their intrinsic beauty—a factor which has great influence on the content of the poem itself.

HANAMICHI. The "flower-way" is a raised passage from the rear left of the auditorium to the stage which it joins down right. According to one theory it is the descendant of the *hashigakari* of the Noh theatre which joins the stage (up right) at an oblique angle from the actors' green-room situated on the audience's left and behind the stage-line. This theory is rejected by some on the grounds that in the Kabuki theatre the area up-stage right is still called the *hashigakari* and the *hanamichi* traverses the auditorium and joins the stage at a right-angle, perhaps following in this respect the form established in the *sumo* wrestling ring, but more probably being a development of the steps leading down from the front of the Noh stage into the auditorium on which admirers placed flowers in tribute to the actors' talent. It is said that a roped-off passageway used to be kept clear for these admirers, and the actors came to realize how much the attention of the audience was focussed upon them as they approached the stage. A subsidiary *hanamichi* called the *kari-hanamichi* existed in former times on the audience's right, but it is now rarely, if ever, used. The *hanamichi* covers a corridor from back-stage to a curtained entrance (*agemaku*) at the back of the auditorium. It is fitted with footlights, and spotlights are usually also played on the actors while performing on it. Before the introduction of electricity, candles borne on long flexible wands (*sashidashi*) were held by stage-hands to illumine the actors' faces. This may still happen if the electric supply fails and is done in any case in a few plays. The *hanamichi* is equipped with a lift and trap (*suppon*) at a place (*shichi san*) three-tenths of the way from the stage. During dance plays the *hanamichi* is covered, like the rest of the stage, with specially smooth flats (*shosabutai*). At other times it may be covered with white cloth (to represent snow) or blue cloth (to represent water).

Actors enter by the *hanamichi* and the effect is heightened first by the turning up of the footlights and then by the rattle of the curtain's being drawn at the back of the auditorium. All heads turn to look at the new arrival. This human failing may be exploited to good effect if it is desired to produce a really dramatic entry on the main stage—while attention is fixed on the curtain, the actor slips up through a trapdoor on the stage unobserved. The *hanamichi* is much used for the entry of processions and groups. Actors pause on the *hanamichi*, declare their identities, or engage in conversation with those on the stage. Traditionally the first actor to enter in this way must be a male rôle. Sometimes a number of actors will play a whole scene on the *hanamichi* while an entirely different scene is in progress on the stage. During dance plays it is customary for the performers to leave the stage and pose on the *hanamichi* at some time or other. The " valiant man " will chase his numerous assailants in stamping confusion along it. An actor will sometimes go to the foot of the *hanamichi* and summon another character by addressing himself to the curtained exit from which may come responding shouts. Whereas any actor may enter by the *hanamichi*, only the more important ones leave by it (except in the case of a group exit). This is a great honour which goes therefore only to the best actors. They will usually pause and look at the stage or the audience. This was done at the *shichi san* in the old days, but is now done nearer the stage so that those in the back seats of the top gallery may see. If the exit is a hurried one, the actors will stumble (in the case of women, youths, or old people). In *aragoto* plays, the principal actor has an important pose to perform at the end of the *hanamichi*. The main curtain is drawn across the stage, but held back sufficiently to allow the musicians in the wings down right to see the performer. The actor then poses and leaves by the *hanamichi*, executing a *roppo*. As will be clear, the *hanamichi* is devised in order to heighten dramatic effect by bringing the actors into the midst of the audience who no longer feel they are spectators, but become part of the show. The most sought after seats are those near the *hanamichi*, the seats from which in the old days indignant spectators would pinch the legs of the villain as he made his exit. The best moment for applauding an actor is when he acts on the *hanamichi*.

HEIKE-GENJI CYCLE. This cycle or " world " included

originally a number of plays selected for quite arbitrary reasons. Such plays have, therefore, been omitted from this book. Those given are all directly inspired by the legends which surround the hero Minamoto Yoshitsune, or are from such sources as the *Heike Monogatari*, a twelfth-century account of the overthrow of the Heike (or Taira) by the Genji (or Minamoto) clan.

From the seventh to the twelfth centuries, Japan was ruled, under the Emperor, by the great clan of Fujiwara. Towards the end of that period two other clans grew in strength and importance. These two, the Heike and the Genji, ousted the Fujiwara and plunged the country into civil war. At first the Genji prevailed, but they were not strong enough to hold down their rivals, and in 1159 the Heike rose against them. They defeated them in battle, pursued and killed the Genji leader Yoshitomo, executed his eldest son, and ruled in Kyoto.

The Heike dominion lasted for twenty-three years, mainly because of the ability and personality of one man, Taira Kiyomori. He became Chancellor of the Empire and, despite various abortive rebellions organized by the remnants of the Genji, ruled until his death in 1181. Kiyomori, however, made one serious error. When the Genji were overthrown, he allowed himself to be persuaded to spare the lives of the remaining sons of Minamoto Yoshitomo. Of these, the eldest, Yoritomo, and the youngest, Yoshitsune, were eventually to exterminate his family. Yoritomo was fourteen at the time of his father's death. He was placed in the custody of the Hojo family. He secretly married his jailer's daughter and bided his time until his faction was strong enough to try conclusions again with the Heike.

As a result of the proscription of their clan, Minamoto Yoritomo and his outlawed followers were rude, wild men compared with the exquisite warriors of the Heike, brought up in the gracious atmosphere of the capital. Only Yoshitsune, Yoritomo's youngest half-brother, seemed to belong to neither world. It is his career which largely supplies the material for these plays.

Yoshitsune was an infant at the time of the Genji defeat. His mother, Tokiwa, was a great beauty. To save the lives of her parents and three little sons, she consented to become Taira Kiyomori's concubine. He stipulated, however, that

419

the children should all enter the priesthood. In spite of her beauty, it seems that Kiyomori did not find Tokiwa as attractive a companion as he expected. Their relationship lasted a comparatively short time, and she was eventually married off to a Fujiwara nobleman, Kiyomori's Minister of Finance.

Yoshitsune spent his childhood in the company of the boys of Kiyomori's family. His " boy's name " was Ushiwakamaru, and he is called by this name in the various Noh and Kabuki plays. He is said to have been conscious always of the fact that there was a gulf between himself and his companions. Everything was done to encourage in him a meek disposition suitable to one destined to take holy orders. But secretly he learnt the use of arms from a mysterious personage disguised as a *yamabushi*, a sect of mountain priests who fought as fervently as they prayed. So great did Yoshitsune's fame as a soldier later become that it was said that this *yamabushi* must have been a *tengu,* a sort of goblin of great strength and cunning with red hair and a long nose. (This incident is discribed in a *dammari* or pantomimed dance called " *Kuramayama no Dammari.*")

Yoshitsune remained throughout his life of small stature, slightly built, with a fair, girlish complexion. Perhaps it was partly his appearance which made his captors underestimate him. He was sent to a temple to become a novice, but, finding himself at last free of his jailers, he immediately ran away. He was then twelve years old. He had many adventures. On one occasion, when he was in Kyoto, he happened to hear that a giant warrior-priest had erected a barrier across the Gojo bridge and was forcing those who crossed to give up their swords on the pretext that he was collecting a thousand as a contribution towards the rebuilding of his temple. Yoshitsune, although still hardly more than a child, fought twice with the priest and twice overcame him, stunning him the second time with his fan. The priest became his devoted follower, the Benkei of so many stories. (The incident is described in a dance-drama of Noh origin called *Hashi Benkei* —Benkei at the Bridge).

Yoshitsune was joined by the two Sato brothers and various other secret adherents of the Genji faction including another pair of brothers, Yoshioka Kijiro and Yoshioka Kisanta who figure with Yoshitsune in a youthful escapade. Eventually he made his way with his little band to the moun-

tains of northern Japan, where they were befriended by Fujiwara Hidehira of Mutsu.

Yoshitsune was twenty-one when the news came that his
half-brother, Yoritomo, had escaped from the Heike. When
Taira Kiyomori died shortly afterwards, Yoritomo and his
party were already in open rebellion. They were joined by
Yoshitsune and a cousin, Minamoto Yoshinaka, nicknamed
Kiso because he had won the first Genji victory at the Kiso
River.

Yoshinaka was a figure as heroic as Yoshitsune himself.
He was the typical fierce and ruthless Genji warrior so much
dreaded by the people of Kyoto. With good reason, for it
was he who, after the battle of Kiso, marched upon the capital. The Heike fled before him, taking the six-year-old Emperor, Antoku, with them. Yoshinaka's soldiery did considerable damage to the city. Antoku's baby brother, Go
Toba, was named Emperor, and Yoshinaka had himself
proclaimed Shogun, or Commander-in-Chief.

It did not at all suit Yoritomo's plans that Yoshinaka
should be making and unmaking emperors in Kyoto. During
the next three years the fact that these two repeatedly quarreled, were reconciled, and then quarreled again brought
the Minamoto war effort practically to a standstill. Yoritomo
remained in Kamakura, where he had set up his headquarters.
Yoshinaka lorded it in Kyoto. The Heike did their best to
consolidate their position on the islands of Shikoku and Kyushu where their fleet was in support.

Finally Yoritomo realized that Japan was not big enough
to hold both himself and Yoshinaka. Using as a pretext
the protests made by the Imperial Court against Yoshinaka's
high-handed methods, he sent an army against him led by
Yoshitsune and his half brother Noriyori. Yoshinaka was
defeated at the battle of the Uji River and was killed trying
to leave the field. Yoshitsune sent his head to Yoritomo
and decided, since he now had a free hand, to follow up his
victory by an attack on the Heike army.

The Heike, encouraged by the bickering in the Genji
camp, had crossed to the mainland and lay in what was considered an impregnable position at Ichi-no-Tani, between
present-day Shioya and Kobe, then a strip of sea coast below
steep cliffs, accessible only from the sea or along one well-
defended road. Yoshitsune decided that, since the only way

he could hope to take the Heike by surprise was down the cliffs, down the cliffs he would go. With a picked band of volunteers he worked his way round behind the enemy position while the main bulk of the army, under Noriyori, attacked along the coast road. Led by a lad who was accustomed to hunt in these hills, Yoshitsune and his followers reached the top of the cliffs and looked down on the Heike camp. Their guide told them that only the deer ever went down that way, but Yoshitsune declared that where the deer could go, a horse could go. He and his companions plunged down the cliff face, which was so steep that the stirrups of the man behind struck against the helmet of the man in front! All reached the bottom safely. The Heike were taken completely by surprise and routed. They were driven into the sea where their warships took off a great part of the army. Yoshitsune's victory was by no means decisive. Nevertheless, the Genji took more than two thousand heads in the battle, including those of a number of members of Taira Kiyomori's immediate family.

Yoshitsune returned to Kyoto anxious to continue the fight before the Heike had time to recover. He wished to be appointed commander-in-chief, but to this his brother Yoritomo would not consent. Noriyori was made titular commander-in-chief of the army and another of his generals, Kajiwara Kagetoki, was sent to command the fleet. Kajiwara had defected from the Heike and joined Yoritomo. As a result of these slights, Yoshitsune did not travel north to Yoritomo's stronghold at Kamakura, but remained in Kyoto. Here he found favour at the Imperial Court because of his gentle manners and attractive appearance. The most important person in the Imperial Family was the Retired Emperor Go-Shirakawa, who had become a priest and was known by the title of Ho-O. He had exercised such power as was left to the Emperor, through his sons and grandsons, for the past thirty years, and by skilful trimming had remained on terms with both the Heike and the Genji. When at last Yoshitsune succeeded in goading the indolent Noriyori into action, he persuaded the Ho-O to name him Lord High Constable and Special Envoy so that he could ignore the appointments made by Yoritomo. This did not endear him to his brother, particularly as Yoshitsune had, apparently out of sheer obstinacy, married a girl of Taira blood, Kyo no Kimi, a niece of Taira Kiyomori. Yoritomo began not only to hate Yoshitsune as a rival, but to suspect him as an intriguer.

The Heike fleet, on which the army was embarked, was sheltered in the bay of Yashima off the island of Shikoku. One night, when, because of stormy weather, the Heike leaders felt particularly secure, Yoshitsune decided that the time had come to attack. In spite of the violent opposition of Kajiwara, he set sail with five ships and a picked contingent from the army, including his personal following. The storm was so fierce that the wind carried them across the straits in six hours, whereas usually the crossing took three days. They landed on a deserted strip of coast and secretly, riding by night, made their way towards Yashima. The first warning of their approach came to the Heike when they saw the blazing houses of the neighbouring town of Takamatsu. They imagined that they were being attacked by a great host and, in panic, took to their ships. Yoshitsune, whose force was only about eighty strong, divided up his horsemen into small groups and made them ride down onto the beach shouting and galloping to and fro, kicking up the spray, while a herd of bullocks with torches lashed to their horns added to the general scene of tumult. He himself rode down into the surf and shouted out his name and honours. His companions followed suit so that the Heike were more than ever convinced that this was the van of a great army. By the time they discovered that, in fact, they outnumbered their attackers by more than ten to one, it was too late to retrieve the position. A contingent of five hundred of the Heike landed and attempted to drive off the Genji, but the latter were steadily being joined by groups of sympathizers and renegades so that the forces were about equal. The Heike bowmen made great efforts to shoot Yoshitsune, but his faithful bodyguard formed themselves into a protective phalanx before him. Sato Tsugunobu, one of his earliest adherents, fell pierced by an arrow and died in Yoshitsune's arms. Again and again the Heike attempted to drive off their adversaries, but failed. Finally a charge of the Genji horsemen, headed by Yoshitsune himself, sent them flying back to their ships, the pursuit continuing until the Genji were in the sea up to their saddles. Yoshitsune fought among the ships and only escaped death by a miracle. Finally the Heike were compelled to withdraw from their carefully prepared anchorage and put to sea.

As a result of the battle of Yashima, many nobles who were wavering in their allegiance now sided with the Genji, whose forces increased until they were superior to those of the Heike. The final battle was fought from ship to ship at Dan-no-ura a few weeks later. This time the Genji outnumbered the Heike by three to one. The Heike fought grimly, but everything was against them. As it became increasingly plain that they were doomed, more and more of their supporters went over to the other side. Finally, seeing that defeat was inevitable, the widow of Taira Kiyomori, who was the little Emperor's grandmother, took the child in her arms and leapt into the sea where they were both drowned. His mother did likewise, but was rescued. One after the other the great princes of the House of Taira followed the Emperor into the sea. Taira Tomomori, the great general, put on double harness that he might sink the faster. Only the commander-in-chief, Taira Munemori, hesitated. Ashamed of his lack of courage, some of his samurai pushed him overboard, upon which his son jumped in after him. Both were without weights and could swim. When Munemori saw his son captured by the Genji, he too surrendered.

Yoshitsune returned to Kyoto and then set off for Kamakura, taking Munemori and his son as a peace offering. Yoritomo, however, was by now deeply jealous of his brilliant young brother, in whom he saw a rival more dangerous than Yoshinaka. He refused to allow Yoshitsune to enter Kamakura. Yoshitsune waited three weeks at a village about two miles from the city. He wrote a moving letter to Yoritomo before going back to Kyoto. From there he appears to have protested against the ruthless policy of extermination pursued by Yoritomo against the surviving Heike. Yoritomo's reply was to demand the head of Yoshitsune's Taira wife. This was the last straw. Yoshitsune sent his family into hiding. Yoritomo attempted to have him assassinated but he escaped and, with the connivance of the Ho-O, tried to get together an army to oppose his brother. Before he could do so, Yoritomo was marching on Kyoto. Yoshitsune fled with his faithful band of retainers. The Ho-O, bowing as usual to the inevitable, welcomed Yoritomo and outlawed Yoshitsune.

Yoshitsune at first made for Shikoku, the island from which he had driven the Heike. His brother's forces were hard at his heels so he returned to the mainland. Finally, after many adventures and escapes, he made his way once more to Mutsu, where the Fujiwara chieftain had given him a home in his boyhood. Here his old friend, who was now over ninety, sheltered him in his castle and here he was joined by his wife and children. However, a few months later old Fujiwara died, and his son, threatened by Yoritomo with the confiscation of all his property, betrayed Yoshitsune and led a contingent of Yoritomo's forces to surround the castle.

Yoshitsune and his handful of followers defended the place as long as they were able. One after another the friends who had been with him in victory and defeat fell in the hopeless fight. At last Yoshitsune knew they could keep the enemy out no longer. He killed his wife and children with his own hand rather than leave them to the mercy of Yoritomo. Then he took his own life. Benkei, the warrior-priest, last of the band to survive, set fire to the castle and also committed suicide.

Yoshitsune was barely thirty when he died. Almost immediately legends sprang up that he had, in fact, survived the holocaust. One has it that he escaped to Mongolia and eventually became the great Gengis Khan himself.

HEIRLOOMS. The Japanese, despite, or perhaps because of, their notion of the impermanence of chattels (pots, pans, cups, jugs, and so on, which are usually made of cheap and fragile materials), have the greatest respect for real works of art, particularly if they are old. Age in any case is a thing venerable in itself. Most Japanese families have one or two precious pieces of porcelain or bronze which are only withdrawn from the store-house on special occasions. The utensils of the tea-ceremony come into this class. Unlike the Middle East (and Europe, formerly), it is ill-bred not to admire such treasures and praise them warmly to your host.

Many Kabuki plays, both *jidaimono* and *sewamono*, treat of the loss of, and search for, such heirlooms. These objects of great value and beauty include swords, cups, bowls, incense-burners, figurines of the Buddha, and *nishiki* (painted scrolls). The great daimyo, of course, were the natural owners of such treasures and they had the charming, if somewhat disconcerting, habit of entrusting an heirloom to the safe-keeping of a retainer. This was considered a great favour. It immediately brought into play the whole complex of loyalties which the Western mind sometimes finds it hard to disentangle. If the retainer lost the heirloom through palpable carelessness, he might well lose his head and certainly his property as well. If there were some doubt about the loss, i. e. when there was evidence that an enemy had stolen the heirloom in order to ruin him, his responsibility for the loss remained, but he might, if his lord was clement, be given the chance to find it again. In the meantime, he would be dismissed from his lord's service, and his property would be confiscate to his lord. This is the situation round which the action of many plays revolve (see *Tengajaya, Sayaate, Danhichi,* etc.). The disowned samurai, penniless and vilified, prosecutes a seemingly hopeless search. If he is married, his wife may sell herself into a brothel to help him (see page 440). If he is not he will almost certainly become involved with some light-of-love in the licensed quarter who impedes his search just as much as she helps it. The enemy, concealed or otherwise, is usually also the samurai's rival in love. There are infinite variations on this well-worn theme. One major variant is the story of a lost or disputed heirloom in a *jidaimano* setting. Here the dilemma may often be expressed in the formula " Surrender the heirloom or your son's (or daughter's) head." There is an element of this in the search for the famous Book of Tactics in *Kiichi Hogen San-ryaku no Maki.*

HIKINUKI (*Costume Changes*). The playgoer will very soon be struck by the number of times an actor may be required to change his costume in the course of a Kabuki play. Quite apart from the removal of the right (sword arm) sleeve, or even the whole top, of the outer kimono before engaging in a fight or any manual labour, an actor may make a complete change between two scenes in which in point of time the action is continuous. The reasons for this are purely decorative, being conditioned by considerations of colour and pattern. There is a further and more dramatic form of change which calls for a complete transformation in a matter of seconds and, before the public, on the stage. This happens when a character is in disguise and has to reveal his true identity or is unmasked by his enemies. Such changes are achieved by the technique known as *hikinuki*. The outer garment is kept in place during the first part of the scene by threads. At the right moment the actor's dresser, or a *kurogo*, rips out these threads and the outer kimono either falls to the ground or is neatly turned inside out to reveal a new (and usually more splendid) costume. The turning inside-out process is known as *bukkaeri*. Notable examples of this are found in *Ichijo Okura Monogatari, Tsumoru Koi Yuki no Seki-no-To* and above all *Dojoji*.

HITOGOROSHI (*Murder*). Murder, either premeditated or accidental, became increasingly popular on the Kabuki stage from the beginning of the 18th century onward. Violence of one sort or another is implicit of course in earlier plays, even the Noh, but its actual portrayal on the stage was eschewed. With the settled conditions of life enforced by the Tokugawa Shogunate, however, the public seems to have begun to hanker for theatrical sensationalism, and the stage murder became one of the regular climaxes of the Kabuki play, particularly the *sewamono*. Such murders are more or less realistically performed according to the type of play and the tastes of the producer. They may be simple, mimed affairs which are quickly over. They may be long agonies—this often happens when the victim is a woman — which have a hideously nightmare quality about them. Very often they are something of an anti-climax, a mere shuffling off of the the human coil, for the real tragedy of the heart and mind will have preceded the act, emptying the audience of all emotion ; the blood-letting is then but the writing of the full-stop at the end of the sentence.

Murder may be committed by a just man, goaded beyond bearing by a villain. It may be no more than a phase in a long-standing vendetta. It may be done from a sense of duty or sacrifice, as when a father kills his child for some high motive. Many murders are accidental, the result of scrimmages in the dark, mistaken identities, or errors of judgment. There are also wanton killings when the murderer runs amok and slays all around him. Into whatever category murder falls, the killer is always brought to justice in the end. Virtue always had to triumph in Tokugawa Japan. We sometimes see the murderer struck down before our eyes, but generally Japanese audiences are not interested in the theatrical depiction of the workings of justice. It is known that the villain received his deserts in the end. Or sometimes the curtain is drawn as the police surround the killer and form with him a final Hogarthian pose as they arrest him.

JIDAIMONO. *Jidaimono* or *jidai-kyogen* is the name given to plays in the classical style. Most of them are adapted from puppet plays and were given their present form during the late Genroku Era, i. e. in the first half of the eighteenth century. Such plays treat of historical subjects, though it would be too much to call them historical dramas. They usually relate some particular incident, often of doubtful authenticity, but long enshrined in popular legend. In addition, owing to the strict censorship imposed by the Tokugawa Shogunate, incidents within living memory were deliberately disguised, as were the names of the people concerned. They may be historical only in the sense that the principal character is a historical one used as a peg on which to hang some anecdote. They reflect the natural curiosity of the Japanese public about the doings of the princes and nobles whom they were not permitted to see in the flesh, much as Shakespearean audiences loved " sad stories of the death of kings."

The formal distinction of these plays is rather in the style of acting which calls for great clarity of diction and purity of gesture. The stylization of movement has something of the quality of ballet and is intended primarily for the plastic and colour effects it can produce on the stage. Poses and changes of costume (see page 426) are designed with this end in view. This is not to say that natural movement is barred, but theoretically a *jidaimono* can be performed without movement on the part of the actors other than their entrances and exits, the whole action being contained in the dialogue and the gestures that accompany it. This stylization is due to the puppet origin of *jidaimono,* the actors imitating the jerky, restricted movements of the dolls.

The costumes and wigs are very elaborate. The musical accompaniment is an integral part of the action and is usually of the *joruri* variety (see page 444). The language is classical Japanese, and is sometimes not easily intelligible to modern audiences.

JUHACHIBAN. The "Eighteen (Best Plays)" (*juhachiban*) are a collection made by Ichikawa Danjuro VII (1791–1859) from the best plays performed by the Ichikawa family since the days of Danjuro I. They are copyright in the family and may only be performed with the family's permission. Even when they are performed by others than the Ichikawa, the musicians, singers and stage assistants (*koken*) must wear the Ichikawa *mon* (see page 397) and formal costumes of the characteristic brick-red colour of the family.

The plots are generally slight, the emphasis being put on the spectacle and style of acting. They are excellent vehicles, as one would expect, for *aragoto* (see page 403).

The 18 plays are : *Kanjincho, Shibaraku, Sukeroku, Gedatsu, Yanone, Kagekiyo, Narukami, Kamahige, Kenuki, Fudo, Fuwa, Kanu, Nanatsumen, Zobiki, Oshimo Doshi, Wuranari, Wirouri,* and *Jayanagi.* Most of these plays are never now performed. Synopses of the first seven only are given in this volume.

KAKEAI (*Antiphonal Dialogue*) A well established convention is the form of antiphonal dialogue known as *kakeai,* although this term is now only properly used of such passages in the plays of Kawatake Mokuami. The similarity with a comparable device of the classical Greek theatre is superficial, but nevertheless striking. The language used is highly poetic and describes some incident in the life of, or some attribute of, the actor who is speaking. A and B recite alternate lines, capping, as it were, each other's flights of oratory. A famous example occurs in *Date Kiso Kuruwa no Sayaate* where Nagoya Sanza and his rival and enemy Banzaemon meet in the licensed quarter and speaking, one from the *hanamichi* and the other from the *kara-hanamichi,* boast of their respective prowesses. This form of dialogue may be elaborated into an exchange between two teams, A and B being accompanied by their respective henchmen or retainers who recite alternate lines, sometimes singly, sometimes in unison (see *Gosho no Gorozo*). The pattern is then something like the following : A, B, A1, B1, A2, B2, A3, B3, A1–5, B1–5, A, B, A1, B1, A2, B2, A3, B3, and so on. This device is known as *tsurane.*

KATSUREKI GEKI (*Historical Plays*). Ichikawa Danjuro IX, the most popular actor of the second half of the last century, was a rebel against many of the conventions and traditions of the Kabuki stage. In particular he disliked the performance of plays on so-called historical subjects which in fact were not only inaccurate, but often wholly imaginary (see page 428). In collaboration with the playwright, Kawatake Mokuami, he produced a series of plays which he called " plays of living history " (*katsureki geki*). These dramas dealt with historical incidents and were produced with all the accuracy of detail which scholarly research could suggest. They were never very popular, though Danjuro's acting carried them through. Such plays are still written and produced today, usually with moderate success, and are called " new classical plays " (*shin-jidaimono*). The language used is everyday Japanese and the style of acting differs little from that of the modern stage. Little or no use is made of music or dancing, but the producers enjoy firing off cannon and beating war-drums.

KI AND TSUKE (*Clappers*).

Ki are a pair of clappers of hard *kashi* wood 8 inches by $2\frac{1}{2}$ by $2\frac{1}{2}$. They are struck together by one of the stage assistants (*kyogenkata*) to mark the drawing of the curtain at the beginning or the end of a scene. The striking starts some minutes before the curtain is drawn, at first isolated clicks at longish intervals, then more frequently and, finally, in a continuous clatter.

Another form of *ki* called *tsuke* is used during the play to call attention to moments of climax when an important pose is struck or something special is said or decisive action is taken (such as a hurried *hikkomi* or "withdrawal down the *hanamichi* "). In this case the *kyogenkata* makes his appearance and kneels down stage left. This is always a sign that something of moment is going to happen. At the proper time he beats the *tsuke* on a flat board, making a wild cascade of sound. The *tsuke* are also made of *kashi* wood and are slightly smaller than *ki*, being 6 inches by 2 by 2. The board is an oblong 2 feet by 1 foot.

KISERU (*Pipes*).

Smoking is one of the many bits of stage business in which Japanese actors delight. There is always a fire-box (*hibachi*), a receptacle holding glowing charcoal, in all interior scenes, and much play is made with lighting the long-stemmed Japanese pipe (*kiseru*) at it. The bowl of the *kiseru* is only large enough to take two pinches of powdery tobacco and two or three puffs will consume this amount. The ash is then carefully knocked out and the pipe refilled or put away. A Japanese man always carries his own pipe in a sheath attached to his tobacco pouch and hung at his obi. Smoking is enjoyed by both sexes and old women in particular indulge in it. In a house of any pretensions pipes and tobacco will be found next the fire-box. One of the duties of a courtesan is to prepare and offer a pipe to her clients. A great deal of significant acting can be put into this simple action. It is polite to polish the mouthpiece of the lighted pipe with the sleeve of the kimono and offer the pipe through the folded sleeve. Lovers will, however, forego these little niceties. A famous courtesan going on a visit or to an assignation will have a special attendant to carry her pipe and tobacco for her.

KIZEWAMONO (*Late Sewamono*). This term is applied to domestic plays of the last century of Edo origin. Such plays, broadly speaking, deal with the less reputable elements in Japanese society—the gamblers, petty criminals, prostitutes, confidence men, *ronin*, gang bosses and so on of 19th. century Edo. They were always written for the live stage, never being derived from the puppets. The great playwrights are Tsuruya Namboku (1755—1829) and Kawatake Mokuami (1816—1893). Good examples are *Kozaru Shichinosuke, Tengajaya, Ippon Gatana Dohyo-iri,* and *Irezumi Chohan,* all of which are summarized in this book.

The sets usually represent miserable dwellings or familiar public places (i. e., the bridges over the Sumida River). Such plays are interesting as affording evidence of the tensions which existed in the Japanese social structure of the time. The impoverished samurai and the *ronin* are familiar figures, trying to keep up appearances, strutting and bullying, often descending to petty crime to make ends meet. The demi-monde of the licensed quarters is shewn to be unglamorously squalid. The upper classes are not sympathetically portrayed.

KOJO (*Announcement*). The programme, or even the play, may be interrupted by a *kojo* or " announcement " that such and such an actor has been awarded another of his family's names or has been adopted into a different family (see page

395). Child actors may be introduced to the public in this way. Famous actors or playwrights or even popular heroes such as Sakata Sogo may be commemorated in this form of ceremony. A *kojo* is not only of interest for this reason, but because it affords the public an opportunity of seeing what the actors look like in a "straight" make-up, what their *mon* are, their various families' characteristic hair-dressing styles and the colours they use for formal dress.

The curtain is drawn to disclose a formal set of screens and one or more lines of actors prostrating themselves to the audience. A *kurogo* calls for silence and then the senior actor raises his head and announces the change of name or whatever it is. Others of the troupe may add a few words of commendation. The actor thus introduced thanks the public for its support in the past and promises to do his best to be worthy of this new honour. The senior actor occupies the central place and the others take station on either hand in strict order of precedence. They all wear formal dress with *mon*. An actor who habitually plays *onnagata* rôles wears the traditional purple head-band of former days (*murasaki boshi*) and speaks in a falsetto voice. This custom dates back to the time when the authorities ruled that all adult male actors should have their boys' forelocks shaved in order, it was claimed, to safeguard handsome youths against immoral temptations. The actors retorted by using the head-band.

If the *kojo* is made during a play, the actors of course will be wearing the costume of the rôle they portray and the ceremony will hardly interrupt the action.

KOKEN (*Stage Assistant*). The *koken* is the equivalent of the *kurogo* (see page 433) and is usually to be seen in dance-dramas, particularly those derived from the Noh. He is the stage-assistant whose duty it is to help the actor while he is on the stage. Unlike the *kurogo*, however, he is visible and wears formal dress (see page 415). He should wear the *mon* (see page 441) of the actor he serves. Traditionally his black silk kimono is presented to him by the actor, but his *hakama* and *kataginu*, if he wears it, are the property of the theatre. When not assisting his principal, he discreetly kneels upstage with his back half-turned to the audience. The *koken* is often a younger actor, a pupil of the actor performing.

KUBIJIKKEN (*Head-Inspection*). The deceptions which could be practised as a result of *mi-gawari* (see page 439) gave rise in due course to the ritual of head-inspection. The severed head of an enemy was brought in a wooden head-box to a retainer or official to whom the deceased was personally known and who was then required to identify it and so testify to his superior. The etiquette of such an inspection is described in full detail in *Moritsuna Jinya*. Such a situation is, of course, fertile ground for theatrical exploitation. Not only may the actor have to portray repugnance, pity or sorrow, but he may also, if the head is a false one and he knows it, be called upon to give a moving performance expressive of divided loyalties and conflicting emotions. The effect will be heightened still further if the head is that of his own child which he is trying to pass off as that of someone else (see *Terakoya, Kumagai Jinya,* etc.).

An interesting off-shoot of *kubijikken* is the art of carving severed heads (*kirikubi*). An actor might appear in the early acts of a play and his *kirikubi* be brought in during the great final scene. The ideal therefore was to carve a head resembling that of the real actor as closely as possible. The actor " sat " for his death-mask for three weeks, or rather the carver sat in the actor's dressing-room for that period of time and unobtrusively studied his subject. He then carved the head and the actor was expected to come specially to view and praise it. One can only guess at the feelings of the actors. The Fujinami family of Tokyo who have made hand properties (*kodogu*) for the Kabuki theatres for generations now have an interesting collection of old heads, some of which are considerable works of art in their own right and form a fascinating portrait gallery of the old actors.

Kirikubi are made of paulownia wood if they are to be prominently displayed. Heads of minor importance are carved in persimmon wood or are even made of bamboo and newspapers.

KUROGO (*Assistant Stage Manager*). The *kurogo* or *kurombo* (lit., " black man ") is an assistant stage-manager. He is clothed entirely in black and wears a black veil over his face in order to suggest that he is invisible. Minor manipulators in the puppet theatre are similarly clad. It is in fact most extraordinary how quickly one stops noticing them.

The *kurogo's* duties are to assist the actors on the stage. He prompts them if they forget their lines. He produces stools (*aibiki*) on which they can, and must, rest, if they are wearing heavy costumes. He hands them fans, swords, paper or anything else they need and removes such properties when they have served their purpose. He changes scenery. He very often " shadows " a child actor to make sure that he does not forget his part.

If the scene is set in snow, the *kurogo* is then dressed in white. If the set represents the sea, he may be needed to push boats around, in which case he will be tastefully dressed in blue and white stripes. He is still, however, called a " *kurombo*."

KYOGEN (*Interlude*). The word *kyogen* means " play " nowadays and is interchangeable with *mono* — thus, *sewamono* or *sewakyogen*. Its original meaning is said to be " mad words " and the term was used to designate the comic interludes in Noh programmes. There would usually be two such *kyogen* sandwiched between three full-length Noh or, in a shorter programme, one between two Noh. These interludes afforded comic relief from the solemn tragedy of the Noh and were always popular. They were never committed to writing and only survive today by oral transmission. Most of them relate the adventures of a slightly ridiculous daimyo and his quick-witted and rascally servant who is always called Tarokaja. There may be another servant named Jirokaja.

On the Kabuki stage, *shosagoto* plays (see page 460) based on Noh subjects still retain the *kyogen*, partly as comic relief and partly to give the principal actor time, as in the Noh, to change his costume (see *Funa Benkei*). Isolated *kyogen* of the *daimyo*-Tarokaja type are frequently given (see *Suo Otoshi*).

LIGHTING. In its origins the Japanese theatre was a daytime performance held out of doors. The aristocratic Noh plays were given in courtyards, only the actual stage being protected by a roof. The early Kabuki plays were performed on temporary stages put up in dry river-beds. Even today the proper time to go to the theatre is in the morning. Evening shows are a recent innovation. Hence the problem of lighting is comparatively new. As in the Elizabethan theatre, candles were for a long time the only subsidiary source of light. The stage and the *hanamichi* were illuminated by shielded candles. If it was necessary to focus attention on an actor's face, the *kurogo* (see page 433) held candles on pliant bamboo rods (*sashi-dashi*) in front of him while he danced or delivered his lines. When he made an important exit by the *hanamichi* (*hikkomi*) the *kurogo* unobtrusively ran alongside with their candles. This practice is still retained in certain plays, notably in the dance *Shinobi Yoru Koi wa Kusemono*.

Except in such isolated cases, all this has, of course, gone by the board with the introduction of electricity. Japanese producers yield place to none in the skilful use of modern lighting. Nevertheless, there are one or two interesting relics of the old days which call for some explanation. In the first place, except in modern plays, the house-lights are not put out in the Kabuki theatre. This has its practical advantages, since a Japanese audience has its own life to lead, whether there is a play in progress or not, and it would be unnecessarily complicated to have to lead it in the dark. Secondly, many important scenes, particularly in the *sewa-mono*, turn on the fact that they are supposed to take place in the dark. Mistaken identities and nocturnal confusions are of the very stuff of Kabuki drama. It is essential that the audience should realize what is happening, but it is equally essential that the players should seem to be, literally, in the dark. Another point of interest is that the naked flame is the rule on the Kabuki stage. Lamps are most usually lit by striking flint and steel on tinder (to all appearances!). An electric light switch would offend.

LOYALTY. The loyalty theme is of equal importance in the Kabuki world with the "filial piety" motive (see page 414). Indeed the two are invariably intertwined in some way or other. According to Miss Benedict's admirable classification, loyalty to one's feudal lord, distant relations, or persons who have put an obligation on one (*on*) belongs to the *giri* category, a debt which has to be repaid "with mathematical equivalence to the favour received" and within reasonable time limits. This definition seems somewhat too tight, unless it can be argued, for instance, that duty to one's lord can be aetherialized into something like *chu* or duty to the Emperor (see page 414) which is a permanent and boundless obligation. Certainly the Kabuki retainer will go to quite inordinate lengths in the service of his lord (see Kumagai in *Kumagai Jinya*). The whole subject is very complex, and the working out of the theme provides one of the major interests of the Kabuki stage. For example, the celebrated 47 retainers of the great masterpiece *Kanadehon Chushingura* may be dismissed as blindly carrying out the last injunction of their dying lord in an unquestioning trans-port of feudal loyalty. But if one looks more closely, one soon realizes that their action sprang less from devotion to their lord than from a genuine conviction that they must somehow protest against a system which ruined him unjust-ly. That their protest and subsequent self-sacrifice were not in vain is attested by the ever-green popularity of the play and the hundreds of humble citizens who burn incense at their graves at the Sengakuji every year on December 14th.

MAKE-UP. The Japanese attitude to make-up is funda-mentally different from that familiar in the Western theatre. The actors of the early Japanese stage wore masks, and the principal actor (*shite*) of a Noh play still usually does. The Japanese mask (*men* or, more professionally, *omote*) is justly famous for its beauty and exquisite craftsmanship. Its most extraordinary characteristic is its mobility of expression; by holding his head at various angles the actor can create the illusion that the expression of the mask has changed. The object of make-up in the Kabuki theatre seems to be just the opposite — to give the human face a permanence of ex-pression indicative of the real nature of the character portrayed. Hence the approach to the problem is rot, as with us, to improve on Nature by accentuating existing traits to counterbalance the effects of distance and high light. It is, if possible, to obliterate the physical personality of the individual actor and reduce his facial expression to that traditionally associated with the rôle he plays. This is why at first all Japanese actors seem so very like one another — there are of course, as it happens, many close blood relation-ships, but the make-up tends to level out any personal peculiarities altogether. The essential point to grasp is that make-up has nothing to do with realism; it is a part of the father and be killed in error for them (see Toki-hime in *Kamakura Sandaiki*). A cunning general may contrive to pass off a dead warrior as himself in order to lull enemies into a feeling of false security (see *Moritsuna Jinya*). A loyal retainer may offer himself in the heat of battle to draw the enemy's fire from his lord (see the story of Tsugunobu in *Yoshitsune Sembonzakura*). Dramatic pathos is often created by substituting one's child for that of one's lord, either as an act of penance or as an unsolicited gesture of loyalty (see *Terakoya*).

MI-URI (*The Selling of Human Life*). The "selling of human life" was (and sometimes still is) a practice familiar in many Oriental countries. It had its origins in stern economic necessities. In times of famine the poor farmer was incapable of feeding his family and, rather than that all should die of starvation, one or more of the children would be sold to rich landowners for money or grain. This transaction meant that the farmer and his wife could afford to eat, while the children became the responsibility of their new masters and were probably not less well treated than if they had remained at home. Since in the feudal system everyone was bound to someone or other, the change was often not as terrible as Western minds are prone to think. Boys were usually sold as servants or labourers. Girls, however, if they were at all attractive, were generally sold into brothels or tea-houses, where they were trained for their future duties as courtesans and waitresses. Given the high social standing of the *tayu* in 18th-century Japan, such a change in a girl's fortunes was by no means despised. The traffic in human life was not however exclusively confined to children. A wife or a daughter might make the sacrifice in order to raise money for a husband or father engaged on some difficult quest — usually that of rehabilitating himself in the eyes of his feudal lord. Such a *mi-uri* was considered very honourable, although the husband or father was usually an unwilling party to it. If the lady was of good family, her success would be considerable, since her good looks and delicate upbringing would at once assure her of a wide and appreciative *clientèle*. In this way she could be of great help to her male dependant. (See *Tengajaya, Sayaate, Gossho no Gorozo*, etc.)

pattern just as much as the costume, the scenery or the pose.

Ladies and handsome young men wear a pure white, flat make-up without lines. This tradition springs from the admiration which all Japanese ladies feel for a white skin because it permits of a wider range of colour schemes in clothing. A white skin has also, as with us, the connotation of gentleness of birth. Conversely, dark make-up indicates someone who labours in the open and is therefore of humble origin. The whiteness of the face is sometimes accentuated in women and young men by painting the mouth black to give a characteristically haughty line. Married women or women with permanent lovers may have their teeth stained black according to an old fashion. Other colours are used in obedience to certain rules. Briefly, various shades of red indicate brave, choleric, passionate, or obstinate characters. Light blue suggests calmness, and grey, melancholy. Indigo and black signify villainy, gloom, or fear. Green may be used for ghosts, evil spirits, and such visitants from the other world, or to indicate tranquillity. Purple is the mark of nobility or haughtiness, and dark brown of selfishness or low spirits.

An actor will sometimes change his make-up on the stage. This often happens in *sewamono*, where an actor lying apparently in a state of hopeless inebriation will contrive to rouge his cheek-bones to give the effect known literally in Japanese as "red face" (*akai kao*). Bleeding wounds are similarly applied. Again, an actor playing the part of a great lord in disguise will, at the moment of revealing his true identity, quickly pencil in the black patches above the eyebrows which in *jidaimono* signify blue blood.

The *aragoto* style of acting produced a special kind of make-up known as *kumadori*. The technique probably came from China, but differs from the Chinese practice in that it is the bony and muscular structure of the face which is boldly accentuated, the object being to throw the nose, cheek-bones, forehead and chin into high relief. The colouring varied in accordance with the rules mentioned above. The technique could be used all over the body, the arms, legs, chest or belly being decorated with broad lines of colour to outline the muscles. This, however, is not now done with make-up; the actors wear flesh-coloured tights on which the lines have been painted. (Certain tradesmen are often portrayed as being elaborately tattooed on the shoulders, arms and thighs. This coloration is applied in the same way, but has nothing to do with *kumadori*. It is *sewamono* realism.) *Kumadori* which was originally intended to suggest anger or hatred — emotions difficult to express facially for very long — became very elaborate in the heyday of Kabuki. Some 115 variants have been recorded, but hardly more than a dozen are used today. Ichikawa Danjuro IX prophesied (wrongly) that *kumadori* would not survive himself. He may have felt that the advent of the bright, harsh light made possible by gas and electricity would ruin what had originally been conceived for weak candlelight. Indeed the effect is somewhat lost today and some adaptation seems to be required. Despite its outlandish extravagance, *kumadori* has still a practical value on the stage; it lets the audience into the secret of the true character of the actor, while the other characters who do not wear it remain unaware of this revelation.

In the old days it was usual for an actor who had just played an *aragoto* rôle to press his face into a *tenugui*, leaving thereon the lines of his extravagant make-up, sign it and send it to a patron. The practice, though not extinct, is less common now, but any theatre-goer may buy a *tenugui* stamped with the *kumadori* of the hero of *Shibaraku* and so feel that he has somehow managed to reach across the gulf from the present to the exuberance of the Genroku era.

Japanese actors always do their own make-up (even the most complicated), unless they are small boys — when their fathers do it for them.

MEDICINES. Until the opening of Japan, the practice of medicine was not far removed from witchcraft and herbal remedies. Various specifics, including the famous but ruinously expensive *ginseng*, were common. It was the custom for everyone to carry his own personal panacea around with him in case he should be taken ill, seized with stomach pains or fall into a swoon. It was then up to some charitable passer-by to come to his aid, using the medicine which he would find on the person of the sufferer. Such a situation is dramatically very important, because, while groping for the medicine, the would-be Good Samaritan may find that the sufferer is carrying a good sum of money

on him and then temptation may triumph. Valuable medicine may be given as a present, particularly to someone suffering from an incurable disease or blindness. Medicine on the stage is invariably wrapped neatly in special paper, silvered on the inside, and kept in a case called *inro*. It is administered either in dry powder form or by solution in water or *sake*. The most popular preparation, however, is mixing in human blood, newly shed; a loyal servant can gain much merit by committing suicide in order to provide the blood which with the precious medicine will restore his lord's sight. However such medicine is taken, it always has miraculously revivifying effects.

MICHIYUKI (*Journeys*). A "journey" (*michiyuki*) is a dance interlude in a long play. The travellers are most often a pair of young lovers, but mothers and daughters and brothers and sisters may also be the principals. The *michiyuki* was an integral part of many of Chikamatsu Monzaemon's plays (see *Tenno Amijima, Koi Hakke Hashiragoyomi* etc.), carrying the plot forward as the lovers eloped together or fled from the police or other enemies. The set invariably represents a road or path. The lovers dance and recite to musical accompaniment and singing. Sometimes there are interruptions, generally of a comic character, by casual passers-by or the pursuers (see the *michiyuki* of *Kanadehon Chushingura*). Particularly famous *michiyuki* are often performed in isolation as individual dance numbers in the day's programme.

The term is also applied to dance plays such as *Musume Dojoji*.

MI-GAWARI (*Substitution*). The substitution of one person for another (*mi-gawari*) is a theatrical device as popular in Japan as in the West. The Kabuki theatre makes frequent use of it. Such substitutions may be either miraculous or human. In the first category, the Buddha or a benevolent spirit will assume human form in order to rescue the hero or heroine from death or danger. Examples of this are to be found in the Domyoji scene of *Sugawara* and the Tadanobu sequence in *Yoshitsune Sembonzakura*. The second category includes cases of substitution of oneself or of one's children. A girl may disguise herself as her lover or her

MON (*Crests*). The *mon* corresponds to the crest in European heraldry. It may represent a leaf, an insect, a Chinese character, or any object which lends itself to formal design. Most of the old Japanese families have their distinguishing *mon* and use them in various ways, but particularly in dress. On formal occasions, a Japanese gentleman or lady wears "five *mon*," i. e. on each lapel of the kimono, on each sleeve and at the nape of the neck. On less formal occasions, three *mon* are worn.

On the stage, *mon* are frequently seen in *jidaimono* plays. The great lords (daimyo) wear them on their kimono and use them to decorate the sliding doors of their rooms and the walls of their tents. Historical characters, where they are identifiable, wear the correct *mon* of their families, e. g. the Minamoto, the Tokugawa etc., and it is interesting to note that, when political censorship required the playwright to give his characters fictitious names and set the time of the action in a different age, the practice grew up of giving the characters, nevertheless, the correct *mon* of the persons about whom the play was written. Thus in *Kanadehon Chushingura*, the lord Enya Hangan (a fictitious name) always wears the crossed feather *mon* of Asano Takumi-no-Kami Naganori, daimyo of Ako, the subject of the famous scandal in 1701 on which the play is based.

The actors of the Kabuki theatre, being the chief repositaries of old Japanese tradition, proudly wear their personal *mon* with formal dress. These *mon* are also used on lanterns, stage hangings, the liveries of servants and dressers and so forth. The souvenir shops in the theatres sell all kinds of attractive gewgaws decorated with the *mon* of famous actors. Some of the better known *mon* are shown on p. 397.

MONEY. Money is the root of all evil on the Japanese stage as it is everywhere else in the world. Particularly in the *sewamono* it may be the mainspring of the action. Its loss and the subsequent attempt to replace it are a variant of the heirloom theme (see page 425). In many of Chikamatsu's plays we find that the hero has embezzled his firm's money in order to be able to cut a figure in the licensed quarter. In due course he will be overtaken by his particular Nemesis. Robbery with or without violence is a common motive in *kizewamono* plays. There is a whole group of them dealing with the adventures of gangs of thieves of which the most famous are *Benten Kozo* and *Sannin Kichiza*.

An interesting facet of the money motive is the hold which the adventures of a given sum of money had on the imagination of such playwrights as Kawatake Mokuami. For example, Jihei, a fan-maker, needs the sum of one hundred *ryo* for his old mother, O Kun, who is ill. Jihei's brother, Sanza, whom he has not seen since early childhood, has somehow or other collected this precise amount and has entrusted it to O Sen, his courtesan mistress. Moemon, an old servant of O Kun and the father of O Sen, is also anxious to raise the money for the sick old lady. He learns that O Sen has the exact amount and tries to borrow it from her. When she refuses he kills her in his anger. Moemon takes the money from his daughter's body. It is stolen from him by a thief called Dembichi. Sanza seeks out Moemon to avenge O Sen's death and recover the money. Only when he has killed the old man does he learn who Moemon is, why he wanted the money, and that it is lost. Sanza commits suicide in his remorse and despair. In the meantime, Dembichi, the thief, gambles the money away to Jihei, and they quarrel. In the ensuing struggle Jihei kills Dembichi and is arrested by the police. Thus Jihei, Sanza, Moemon and O Sen, four innocent people wishing to serve O Kun, are ruined by the self-same sum of a hundred *ryo*. This is not a real plot, but it might well be. It is no more fantastic than those of *Benten Kozo, Kozaru Shichinosuke, Izayoi Seishin,* and many others.

A word should perhaps be said about the currency of the Kabuki stage. The unit is the *ryo*, a gold coin worth in the early nineteenth century about £ 1 or $ 4 at par. The most convenient piece for stage purposes is the *ryo* coin which is oval in shape and was called *oban* if newly minted and *koban* if worn with use. A *ryo* was divided into four *bu* and a *bu* into four *shu*. These coins were silver. There was also a brass coinage with holes punched in the centre. The unit was the *mon* of which there were anything from one thousand to six thousand six hundred to the *ryo*. The *mon* could be subdivided into ten *bun* and one hundred *rin*. Silver was also used as a separate currency, but the denominations were by weight. The *kan* of one thousand *momme* varied in value with the fluctuations of the gold/silver exchange rate.

Money on the Kabuki stage is always carefully wrapped in a cloth or purse and carried next to the skin. Its discovery on the bodies of strangers taken ill or otherwise at a disadvantage often leads to unpremeditated crime. Money is invariably wrapped in paper before being offered as a present or in payment to equals or superiors.

MONOGATARI (*Narration*). *Monogatari* literally means "tale" or "chronicle" (cf., *Genji Monogatari, Heike Monogatari,* etc.). On the Kabuki stage it has a special meaning : it is a dramatic recital accompanied by miming of some incident which happened in the past. In this it has close similarities with the "episode" of Greek drama. Some of these *monogatari* reach a high level of literary excellence and at the same time afford the actor wide opportunities for demonstrating his skill. Amongst the most famous are those from *Kumagai's Camp* where Kumagai relates the story of Atsumori's death at his own hands and *Kajiwara's Feat of Stone-cutting* in which Kajiwara tells how his sword-arm was stayed by divine intervention when he had Minamoto Yoritomo at his mercy.

MUSIC. Music plays an essential rôle in Kabuki. Its importance cannot be overemphasized. Only the most modern plays attempt to do without it. By music must be understood anything from the big orchestras and groups of singers to sound effects in the ordinary theatrical sense. As the earliest form of Japanese theatre consisted of mimed songs, it is only to be expected that singing and instrumental accompaniment should form an integral part of the older plays, but even the productions of the late nineteenth century rely heavily on some form of musical setting for the unfolding of the story.

The Kabuki theatre inherited the singers and instrumentalists of the Noh stage, namely a chorus and an orchestra (*hayashi*) consisting of a flute (*yokobue*), hand-drums (*tsuzumi* and *kotsuzumi*), and a stick drum (*taiko*). A Kabuki play derived from the Noh will always use this combination, plus the *samisen*, but will probably increase the number of performers and may add a big Chinese drum and cymbals. (See *Kanjincho, Suo Otoshi, Shojo.*) Dance plays usually employ the same combination, though generally on a smaller scale. Plays derived from the puppets use the chanter-*samisen* combination (*chobo*) of which mor ewill be said below. *Sewamono* plays are usually accompanied by *samisen* music and singing, even if these have nothing to do with the action. Sound effects in general are produced by the *geza* — a group of musicians in a box in the wings down right. The rôle of the *geza* is most important, since on them depends the timing of all the music and much of the acting. Various sizes of drums are used and other devices to simulate the noise of rain, waves, thunder, wind and so on A hanging bell, cymbals, and gongs are important items. Recourse is now being had in modern plays to recordings amplified electrically. In certain plays use is made of the three-stringed violin (*kokyu*), a singularly nostalgic instrument.

There are various schools of music and the appropriate ones should be used for the particular play. The style known as *nagauta* (" long song ") is largely derived from the Noh technique. It was evolved by the Kineya family, but the school has long since broken up into several off-shoots of which the principal ones are the Yoshizumi, the Fujita, and the Yoshimura. As in the Noh theatre, the singer learns his part by heart using no text or score. He is accompanied by a *samisen* player. His only equipment is a fan which he takes up before beginning to sing and lays down when he has finished. If for some reason it is absolutely necessary for him to have a text before him, it is placed upon a small, inconspicuous wooden stand or he holds it, if standing, in the hand. A *nagauta* orchestra is called *debayashi* and sits at the back of the stage, facing the audience on a red-draped rostrum. The style known as *joruri* or *gidayu* or *takemoto* is described as chanting rather than singing. The performer chants or recites from a text which is supported on a lacquer stand before him. He is accompanied by one or more *samisen* players whose instruments are somewhat heavier than those used in *nagauta*. They sit down stage left, at a slight angle to the audience on a revolving platform called *degataridai*, but sometimes they are concealed behind a blind in a little box above the stage entrance down left. This style takes its name from the first recorded *samisen* ballad which told of the loves of the Princess Joruri and Minamoto Yoshitsune. Takemoto Gidayu made it famous at his puppet-theatre, the Takemoto-za, (and it is still primarily puppet ballad music), while Kineya Kisaburo introduced it to Edo audiences. Of the same *katarimono* style is *tokiwazu* music which is more refined in quality and content and relies rather on the voice than the instruments. This style was evolved by Miyakoji Bungojo and was at first known as *bungo-bushi*. It was very popular, being romantic and sentimental. The authorities considered that it was having a bad effect on public morals and in due course proscribed it. Bungojo's adopted son, Mojidayu, elaborated in process of time a new, more restrained style which he named after the bridge near his house, the Tokiwabashi. Perhaps the most beautiful style is *kiyomoto* which, like *tokiwazu*, is derived from *gidayu* and is primarily singer's music. Most people find it superior in quality and form to any other style and it can be very moving. It is somewhat higher in pitch, since one of its early exponents had an exceptionally light and beautiful tenor voice. Another style known as *ozatsuma* is a robust and rhythmic accompaniment suitable for *aragoto* acting. Orchestras other than *debayashi* are called *degatari*. *Tokiwazu* and *kiyomoto* musicians sit downstage right on a rostrum.

It is extremely difficult in the compass of this brief note to describe satisfactorily the subtle differences of style. The regular playgoer will soon come to recognize them for himself, since it is not only a question of singing and playing, but also of dancing to a dancer, for example, *tokiwazu* means a certain kind of dance. The mainstay of all these styles is, however, the *samisen* and the tuning of this instrument has much to do with the style. Thus the basic key (*honchoshi*) is associated with moods of sincerity and solemnity. *Niagari* ("second string up"), another of the three principal keys, suggests cheerfulness and brilliance. *Sansagari* ("third string down") expresses sweet sadness and tranquillity. Rhythms, of course, also vary with the style.

While the use of singers is self-evident in the puppet theatre, their use on the live stage needs some general explanation. The Noh technique, of course, consists essentially of dialogue between the principal actors and their supporters and a chorus which comments, gives advice, fills in gaps, and very often recites the actors' lines as well. The Kabuki theatre, which re-emerged after the puppet theatre had had its day, reverted to the Noh tradition in that the singers now act as a sort of Greek chorus for the benefit of the audience. But the Kabuki substituted the ever popular *joruri* songs for the plain chant of the Noh, thus getting the best of both worlds.

This note ends, as it began, with a restatement of the supreme importance of music in Kabuki, whether it be *geza* or any of the styles described above. Not for nothing is the character for music — ka — the first in the Kabuki trinity.

NOH. The Noh, the classic lyrical drama of Japan, is familiar to the Western world from the works of Arthur Waley, Ezra Pound, and Noel Péri. Brief mention is made of it here only because it was the direct progenitor of the Kabuki. The subject matter, the shape of the stage, the costumes (but not the make-up), the style of delivery and the music of the Kabuki theatre are borrowed more or less directly from the Noh. Frequent mention is made in these pages of the conventionalized Kabuki version of the Noh set, the pine-tree and bamboo, (see particularly under *shosagoto*). Other direct debts are also indicated, where appropriate.

The Noh flourished at its best in the second half of the fourteenth and the first half of the fifteenth centuries. Its similarities with the classical Greek drama have been the subject of frequent comment. In essence, a Noh play is a dramatic recital with music and dancing of an event which took place before the play starts, but there are elaborations. The language is highly poetic and is not immediately intelligible to modern Japanese. The philosophical background of Noh is predominantly Buddhist. The Noh theatre was primarily the preserve of the samurai, but public performances were given from time to time at which the lower classes were permitted to be present. The Kabuki drama was the retort of the common people. It was, and still is, the really popular theatre of Japan. Even today it more than holds its own with the modern stage and, one notices with some relief, the cinema. (It is significant that the most popular films, called *chambara*, are about samurai adventures and offer at a cheap price the sort of entertainment the more wealthy can enjoy at the Kabuki-za.) The Kabuki theatre became popular because it translated the Noh into an idiom which even the common people could understand. The language was their own, the songs were familiar to them and the story was unfolded before their eyes on the boards, not recounted after the event. The Kabuki is vulgar where the Noh is refined, but that suited the popular taste (which is not saying that, in stage matters, the popular taste in Japan should be confused with the popular taste elsewhere). In fine, the Kabuki adaptation of the classical theatre made available to the common people the riches of the store-house of Noh.

NUREBA (*Love Scenes*). Love scenes are called *nureba* ("wet scenes") because they reduce the audience to tears. "They cried so much that their sleeves dripped into the aisles," as one old account relates. The Japanese lady, like her Western sister, loves nothing so much as a good cry. Even male eyes are not always immune.

Japanese lovers are always unhappy in their love. The stock situation is the courtesan of repute and great beauty who has lost her heart to an attractive but morally weak youth of good family. Brothel-keepers and parents intervene to end the affair, and between them usually drive the unhappy couple to double suicide. In *jidaimono* the princess replaces the courtesan, and the same sort of situation is developed when she falls in love with someone not of her parents' choice.

The delicacy with which love scenes are played is one of the charms of the Kabuki. Physical contact is kept to a minimum — the public was horrified, for instance, when Ichikawa Ennosuke tried to introduce the kiss into the Kabuki theatre. Nevertheless, all that needs be said of tenderness, devotion, or passion can be more than adequately conveyed to those who know the signs. It is customary for the young man to seem to take no notice of his lady; indeed, her presence fills him with embarrassment. It is she who makes all the first moves. The lovers will start from opposite sides of the stage, backing towards each other until they collide gently. They then spring guiltily apart and the process is repeated until they get used to each other and agree to sit together. They will cry a great deal as they talk, either for sheer happiness or for the weight of their woes. The young man will bow constantly as he appeals to his lady and will reinforce his arguments with hot weeping.

Hands may be pressed or a hand may respectfully be placed on the other's arm or thigh. The lady may shew the intimacy of her love by combing her lover's hair. The lighting and offering of a pipe (see p. 430) and the handling of *tenugui* and fans can be given many erotic twists. Just before leaving to commit double suicide, the lovers may be permitted to hold each other close for a moment. Anything more than this would be considered (and indeed is) an offence against good taste.

OBI-HIKI *(Sexual Violence)*. As distinct from the true love-scene (*nureba,* see page 447), the *obi-hiki* (" pulling off the obi ") indicates sexual violence. This convention has its origins in the nature of Japanese feminine attire. On the obi-string depends the whole complex structure. Hence, the voluntary loosening of the obi-string has come to mean acceptance of a lover's advances. Contrariwise, if it is the man who pulls at the obi, we have a situation similar to that of tearing off a woman's dress in the West. Villains of the Kabuki stage enjoy the pursuit of love in this lusty fashion. A conventionalized struggle with the lady will usually end in the unwinding of her obi; the villain will strike a triumphant pose grasping the end of the obi, sometimes between his teeth, during which time he will hold the big toe of his right foot in a transparently erotic gesture. A milder suggestion of violence is conveyed by pulling at the long sleeve of a woman's kimono, but this may only indicate a desire to prevent someone leaving.

OTOKODATE *(Chivalrous Commoners)*. The *otokodate* or " chivalrous commoner " was the special product of Tokugawa Edo. In the three centuries of Japan's isolation from the outside world, society settled down into a pattern of rigid class distinctions and the strict observance of feudal codes of behaviour. But because this period was one of static peace, the warrior class of the samurai had no occupation to justify its existence. Protected by privilege, its members fell into evil ways. Many of them ran into debt as a result of gambling and other dissipations and took to abusing their rank in order to make ends meet. Others were naturally arrogant, domineering, swashbuckling, or cowardly at heart. Such are many of the villains of the Kabuki stage.

While the samurai degenerated, the lower classes, and particularly the merchants, improved their standing both socially and economically. A rich merchant was more than a match for a samurai in the licensed quarter, where all men were equal. Yet, in law, he had no redress against a samurai who ill-treated or cheated him. In practice, he did not equal the samurai in the art of defence or offence. Consequently, there grew up a class of "chivalrous commoners" (*otokodate*) who took it upon themselves to defend the interests of the lower classes against the braggart samurai. They were skilled in the use of arms and in the science of *judo*. They were often noted poets and musicians. They attracted to themselves groups of young disciples whom they trained in various professions and hired temporarily to respectable employers. In time these gangs became almost as much a menace as the samurai and their followers. But in the Kabuki world, the *otokodate* are heroes and the champions of the common people. They are invariably the sons of samurai fathers who have renounced their privileges in order to side with the oppressed. They wear only one sword and attire themselves in spectacular kimono. They carry flutes to advertise their artistic ability. Their skill at arms, their personal strength, and their courage are unmatched. The most famous of them all was Chobei of Banzuin, an historical figure about whom many plays have been written and whose story is told in Mitford's *Tales of Old Japan*.

PAPER. Paper of varying qualities is much used by the Japanese for many purposes. It is a prominent accessory for the actor. Each individual should carry his own supply in the bosom of his kimono. This supply may be kept in a neat silk-embroidered satchel or just loose in a big fold. It is used for blowing the nose, cleaning the fingers, drying tears (though women generally use their sleeves, and more particularly the sleeves of the under-kimono, for this all too frequent need), writing notes, covering the neck-rests which were the Japanese equivalent of a pillow, wrapping up money or gifts and cleaning swords, daggers, severed heads, and so on. If an object for inspection is of special value, for instance a gift of sweetmeats from the Shogun or a valuable sword, it is thought discourteous to breathe on it, and the inspector therefore takes his own fold of paper and holds it between his teeth while he is examining the object. Paper which has been used is rolled into a ball between the palms of the hands and secreted in the sleeve of the kimono. A daimyo, after cleaning a sword with a whole fold of paper, will however toss it negligently away. This is a mark of great wealth, since the ordinary Japanese is economical in his use of paper and deplores unnecessary waste. To say that a man "uses three sheets of paper to blow his nose" is as much as to say that he is very extravagant. If a woman needs a piece of paper, she will take the fold from her bosom with the right hand, hold it between her teeth and then replace the fold leaving one sheet only between her lips. A popular *onnagata* may do this several times on the *hanamichi*, throwing the sheets bearing the faint imprint of his lips to admirers in the audience. If a woman is attacked one of the first things she will do is to throw her fold of paper in the face of her assailant in order to confuse him.

PLAY TITLES. One of the greatest stumbling-blocks for the foreigner trying to learn about the Kabuki stage is the length and complexity of the names of plays. When he has learnt them, he will find that they are usually untranslatable; *Sugawara Denju Tenarai Kagami,* for instance, means "Sugawara's School Calligraphy Mirror"—not, one would have thought, a very impelling title. The famous *Kanadehon Chushingura* means "The Alphabetical List of the Treasury of Loyal Servants," which makes some sort of sense, but not much. The reason is that the names of plays were chosen largely for the beauty of the Chinese characters in which they were written. These characters are, of course, suggestive of the theme or themes of the play, but it would be foolhardy to say more than that.

The earnest student should not, however, be discouraged. Even the Japanese actors themselves cannot remember the names of most of the plays they act. They refer to them by a shorter and more practical title or by the name of the chief character in the play. Thus *Omi Genji Senjin Yakata* is generally called *Moritsuna Jinya* (Moritsuna's Camp), this being, in fact, the title of the most important act, and *Amimoyo Toro no Kikukiri* is known as *Kozaru Shichinosuke.* Sometimes, particularly in Chikamatsu love-suicides, the title in common use is compounded of the names of the lovers or even of the first syllable of their names. Thus *Shimban Uta-zaemon* is often called *O Some-Hisamatsu* and *Meido no Hikyaku, Umechu* from Umegawa and Chubei.

The authors have tried to remove some of the stumbling-blocks by compiling a joint list of the full titles and the short titles arranged in alphabetical order. This should make cross reference easier. There is, however, one other considerable complication. Of many of the older and longer plays only one or two favourite acts are now regularly performed. An instance of this is *Moritsuna Jinya*, quoted above; again, of the original eleven acts of *Ehon Taikoki* only Act X, the so-called *Amagasaki Scene,* is usually given at the present time. While there are performances every year of the whole of *Kanadehon Chushingura,* isolated acts are frequently put on at other times. The authors have, therefore, included in their list the names of famous scenes with a cross reference to the parent play. The playgoer who reads in the press that there is to be, for example, a performance of *Yoshitsune Sembonzakura* should ascertain which act or acts are being given and he should then be able to find the relevant synopses without further difficulty.

POSE. Given the dance origins of the Japanese theatre, it is not surprising that poses should be an important ingredient of all plays. A Japanese producer arranges his grouping much as a Western choreographer conceives a ballet. The main important difference is that, while the choreographer seeks to keep the line in continual motion, the Japanese producer freezes it at climactic moments into a rigid pose. Yet this rigidity and its subsequent relaxation should be achieved as imperceptibly and as smoothly as water becomes ice and ice water. It is a difficult art and not many actors now are capable of it. Such poses are known generically as *mie.* They are advertised to the audience by the beating of the *tsuke* (see page 430), although there is one celebrated *mie* in *Kanjincho* where this does not happen. While the principal actors are posing, all other movement on the stage is stopped and the lesser actors even seek to efface themselves by turning their backs. This "freezing" of all movement nevertheless has a curious quality of tension and is, indeed, called *hippari no mie,* a " pulling *mie,*" in Japanese.

The old colour-print portraits of actors usually shewed them holding a pose and this is the reason why so much is known about the technique today. The pose is conceived as an opportunity for the actor to impress himself on the audience with all the resources under his control. In a *deba* pose, the actor enters by the *hanamichi* and executes several poses thereon before stepping onto the stage. A famous example is the first entrance of Sukeroku (see page 324). Poses on the stage are struck at climactic moments and take a variety of forms. The principal actor or actors may pose while sitting, either on the floor, the *san dan* (see page 464) or a tall stool, but poses are usually struck while standing and are more effective as a result. The actor may divest himself of the upper half of his kimono or tuck up its skirts to expose his thighs (*hadanugi*). The arms are flung out sideways, palms outward and fingers crooked. The muscles of the face and neck are tensed and the head is rolled in a circular motion called *senkai*. In the old version the head finishes over the right shoulder, the right leg is bent under the body and the left leg is thrown out. Onoe Kikugoro VI evolved a softer technique in which the head finishes over the left shoulder and the limbs are re-arranged accordingly. While this is being done, the actor may open his eyelids and at the critical moment slowly cross one pupil in the direction to which he wishes to call attention. This glaring is called *nirami*. At the same time the actor may either pull down the corner of his mouth in an exaggerated sneer or protrude a red-stained tongue. Female characters may also " cut a *mie*," but the *senkai* motion is much modified and they never perform *nirami*. What is known as the Genroku *mie* is an exaggerated form of pose such as should be expected in *aragoto* plays. It is seen only in the plays of the Ichikawa family collection (see page 429), two notable examples being *Shibaraku* and *Kanjincho*.

The pose is the right moment for applause and, in particular, the shout " *Matte imashita* " (" This is what I have been waiting for ").

PUPPETS. The influence of the marionette theatre on the development of the Kabuki drama was such that a short note is justified here.

Traditionally the Kabuki theatre was founded by a temple dancing-girl, called O Kuni, who in 1586 gave popular performances on a stage erected in the dry bed of the Kamo River at Kyoto. The plays which were evolved by this lady and her collaborators had their roots in the classical Noh, the singing of historical legends and ballads, the *kyogen* (see page 434) and the early dance forms known as *gigaku*, *dengaku* and *sarugaku*. O Kuni's theatre did not, however, survive her. It gave way to the " Women's Kabuki " (*Onna Kabuki*) which in turn became the " Pleasure Women's Kabuki " (*Yu-jo Kabuki*). These forms were in due course banned by law on the grounds of morality and women were forbidden to act in public. The next phase was the " Young Men's Kabuki " (*Wakashu Kabuki*) which suffered the same fate for the same reasons. Out of this grew the " Men's Kabuki " (*Yaro Kabuki*) which is the basis of the present theatre.

In the meantime, however, great progress had been achieved in the puppet theatre (*ningyo-shibai* or, more commonly, *bunraku*). The mechanical improvement of the dolls was accompanied by big developments in the writing of the ballads (*joruri*) which were an essential part of the plays. The music and singing were revolutionized, moreover, by the introduction of the three-stringed *samisen* from China through the Ryukyu Islands. (It should be remembered that only the instrument was introduced and not the way of playing it; the Japanese worked out their own technique.) The Kabuki theatre seemed to have died a natural death. The official persecution of the actors and the actors' own temperamental bowdlerizing of scripts made the Kabuki an unsound economic proposition for any clear-headed theatrical manager. It was safer to invest in the puppets. The foundation of the Takemoto-za in Osaka in 1685 set the seal on their success. The playwright Chikamatsu Monzaemon (1653–1724), who had begun as a writer of Kabuki plays and had been discouraged by the absurdly pretentious demands of the actors, transferred his allegiance to the puppets and, in collaboration with Takemoto Gidayu and other famous chanters, wrote the great plays of which some are described in this book. Literary genius came into its own and contributed more than its share to the overwhelming success of *bunraku*.

In the course of time, the actors of the Kabuki theatre

began to understand that the story and its artistic presentation were as important as the acting. They therefore started
to borrow the plays of the puppets and adapt them to the
live stage. They imported the *joruri* chanters as well as their
scripts and themselves evolved a style of acting suggestive
of the dolls. This style of acting became an art in itself and
is greatly appreciated by the connoisseur. The Kabuki theatre
had reached a great turning point and many of the most
popular plays even today are adapted puppet pieces (called
maruhommono). The two theatres developed from now on
along similar lines. The puppet theatre even borrowed the
Kabuki technique in such matters as the use of *aragoto* (see
page 403). The Kabuki theatre rapidly overhauled the puppets during the nineteenth century and is now securely en-
trenched. The *bunraku* continues as a form of art, but cannot
hope for further development. The only regular theatre now
is the Bunraku-za at Osaka which is well worth many visits.
The company comes regularly to Tokyo.

Anyone who wishes to appreciate to the full the skill and
beauty of the " puppet style " acting in such plays as *Moritsuna Jinya, Meiboku Sendai Hagi,* and *Asagao Nikki* should
study the dexterity with which the dolls are manipulated in
the original puppet plays. Occasionally today we see live
plays with a puppet interlude (*ningyo-buri*). The actor, supported by others dressed as the manipulator (*tsukai*) in formal
dress or as *kurogo,* will play a scene with doll-like movements
and expressionless face. The rhythm is beaten out by a
kurogo wearing thick-soled *zori* who stands down right and
marks time with his foot. These formal interludes are rarer
than the looser " puppet style " acting and are well worth
seeing.

RANKS. Early Japanese society was in theory divided into
lords, soldiers, priests, farmers, and merchants. This arbitrary classification was borrowed from the Chinese system
and probably had little authority in fact. By the end of the
tenth century society was to all intents and purposes divided
into the samurai and the rest. This conception is familiar
to the Western world, but it is not generally realized that
there were grades among the samuraï themselves. These
grades were immutable under the feudal system. A samurai
of a lower grade could never hope for promotion; he must

always expect to perform only the duties proper to his grade ; he could not even be adopted into a samurai family of higher rank. He could, however, surrender his status by becoming a priest or being adopted into a merchant family. It was no shame f r a samurai to become a *ronin* (masterless retainer). He could become a *ronin* as the result of the extinction (physical or judicial) of his master's family, or of his own free will. A samurai could be created by the Shogun, and even foreigners were sometimes so honoured (cf. Will Adams of Gillingham).

A samurai was a retainer owing personal, but not legal, allegiance to an overlord. In return for a salary expressed in terms of bales (*koku*) of rice, he undertook to perform certain duties for his lord in peace-time and to fight for him in war. He might own a house and personal property, but he could not own land. Only the leading families, heads of clans, could do this, holding their estates in direct fief from the Emperor. Such families were known as daimyo (literally " big names "), a class which corresponded very closely to what in Europe is understood by a peerage. During the Tokugawa era, the title of daimyo came to be used for any wealthy man and even rich merchants were sometimes so called. The title of *kuge* was only given to high-ranking samurai serving the Emperor at court. Later in the Tokugawa era, the Shogun created a class of *hatamoto* lords (literally " bannerets," or, as in England, " baronets ") who were his personal followers and in a sense corresponded to the Imperial *kuge*. A *hatamoto* could be created from any class, but was usually a samurai. To be created a *hatamoto* was one of the few ways open to a samurai to improve himself.

A samurai was in theory a mounted soldier and numbered foot-soldiers (*ashigaru*) among his dependents. In practice he was sometimes so poor that he had no servants at all. However reduced he might be, he had certain inalienable privileges—having a family name and crest, wearing two swords, paying no taxes, and so on. He had certain limitations, too—he was not supposed to go to the Kabuki theatre or to the licensed quarter ! If he did so he went in disguise which usually meant that he covered his face with a straw travelling-hat.

SEMEBA (*Torture*). Scenes of "pressure" are popular climactic passages in Kabuki plays. The hero or heroine is portrayed as being at some disadvantage and is hard pressed by enemies to reveal a secret or to renounce a lover or a claim. The pressure applied may be physical or mental (see *Kagekiyo*). There is of course an element of pressure in all "double-loyalty" plays (see *Moritsuna Jinya, Kajiwara*, etc.), but the term *semeba* should only properly be applied to plays in which the "torture" itself is the primary object for the actor's powers of portrayal.

SEPPUKU (*Suicide Scenes*). The practice of disembowelling oneself (*seppuku*) is sufficiently well known to foreigners (who generally refer to it vulgarly as harakiri) not to require much comment here. The serious student will find detailed accounts in Mitford's *Tales of Old Japan* where both the underlying philosophy as well as the etiquette of this form of suicide are conscientiously described. It may not be realized, however, that *seppuku* could be either voluntary or involuntary. In the first case, a man might immolate himself as an act of atonement for some wrong done, in protest against an injustice, in error or even as a gesture of bravado. He might kill himself in cold blood after the proper ceremonies had been observed or spontaneously on the spur of the moment. Involuntary suicide was a form of execution —it was carried out as the result of an order or a sentence. The most honourable form permitted the victim to disembowel himself and die entirely at his own hand ; i. e. by cutting his jugular vein, since disembowelling in itself is not a quick death. A second category took the form of beheading by a second after the victim had made the first incision. A third variety, and the least honourable, consisted of offering the victim a wooden dirk with which to disembowel himself and, as he leaned forward to take it, quickly striking off his head.

Seppuku scenes are of frequent occurrence in Kabuki and are performed with more or less good taste according to the style of acting. In Tokyo such tragedies are invariably played out with great and moving dignity. The Osaka school, however, is somewhat given to a too liberal use of stage blood. The *seppuku* of Lord Enya Hangan in the celebrated *Kanadehon Chushingura* is the most outstanding example of the

Kabuki stage and never fails to move the audience to tears. There are, however, many other suicides on a less elaborate scale which are no less compelling. (see Sakura-maru's *seppuku* in *Sugawara*).

Contrary to general belief in the West, women do not commit *seppuku*. They stab themselves under the heart with their dirks or perhaps their huge hair-pins.

SERIAGE (*Trap-Doors*). Normally there is a large lift and trap in the middle of the (revolving) stage and another smaller one on the *hanamichi*, called the *suppon*, at the spot known as the *shichi san* (see page 417). These contrivances are technically known as *seriage*. They were once operated by hand, but are now powered with electricity. Nevertheless, the pleasing tradition persists that an actor mounting by the *seriage* should tip the operator in order to forestall any undignified hitches in the ascent. The main stage lift is large enough to accommodate a group of actors and is thus used for introducing them in a set pose at the beginning of a scene. It is also the main factor in the theatrical *tour de force* known as *ozeri* when a whole building may rise from, or sink into, the ground. There are also smaller traps elsewhere in the stage or in the sets erected on it, and these are much used for surprise entrances and exits. The *suppon* is usually reserved for supernatural effects — the entry of a witch or an evil spirit, the re-emergence of an actor thrown into the sea on the main stage, the transformation of an animal on the stage into its human shape (or *vice versa*). In some modern plays the *suppon* may be converted into a flight of steps and thus serve as a supplementary exit in the heart of the auditorium.

SERIFU (*Speeches*). All speeches are, broadly speaking, called *serifu*, but the term is generally understood in a more restricted sense. The principal actor is sometimes allowed to break into the action of the play with a passage in high-flown poetic language which is not strictly connected with the development of the plot, but explains his character and attributes as an actor. One single example will suffice to explain more exactly what is meant and, as it is a famous one, no apology is made for giving it in full. In *Shibaraku*, one of the Ichikawa family's " 18 Favourite Plays," the hero Gongoro Kagemasa interrupts the action to relate in language saturated with references to the Ichikawas why this particular rôle he is playing is important. "The Chinese sages tell us that water, like virtue, is given to all without discrimination. The Genji samurai used to purify themselves in the waters of the Tamagawa (by the headwaters of which river the Ichikawas had their first home). I am Kamakura Gongoro Kagemasa, a samurai, the ninth (interpolated by Danjuro IX and so a reference to his personal number) of the rice-measure crest (the general *mon* of the Ichikawas). In this month of the *kaomise* ("face-showing" performance) we give this play from the "18 Favourites" and my *kumadori* (see page 437) is like the flower of the peony in winter time (the peony is another *mon* of the Ichikawas). The colour of my dress is the hue of the persimmon (the brick-red colour of Ichikawa formal dress) and my acting has a deep, subtle flavour like that of the fruit. It is the speciality of my family. I shall shew you the splendour of our *aragoto* acting (see page 403), the pride of the leading actors of Edo. I speak with all respect." Two or more actors may contribute to such a passage which is then known as *warizerifu*.

SEWAMONO (*Common-People's Plays*). Plays dealing with the lives of ordinary people are called *sewamono* or *sewakyogen*. They began to be written in the early 18th century for the Osaka stage, particularly the puppet theatre. (The first recorded *sewamono* was, however, written for the live stage in 1679 ; see *Yugiri Izaemon*, page 210). The father of the *sewamono* was Chikamatsu Monzaemon (1653–1724) often, though somewhat facilely, called the Shakespeare of Japan. He wrote over a hundred plays, most of which are *jidaimono*, but his greatest claim to fame lies undoubtedly in his domestic pieces which are still regularly performed.

In such plays the dialogue and acting are naturalistic, although certain conventions are observed, and no Japanese producer would neglect the telling effects which can be achieved by daring combinations of colour and pose. The language is simple and easily intelligible to modern Japanese. Scenery and costumes strive after realism and are therefore generally more subdued than in the classical plays. Careful attention is paid to the familiar details of daily life—the preparation of food, the changing of clothes, the drinking of tea and wine, the cries of night-watchmen and street-vendors, the singing of birds, or the croaking of frogs. The music varies with the date and kind of play, ranging from puppet-ballads (*joruri*) to simple *geza* accompaniment.

It is possible to subdivide the *sewamono* into groups according to subject matter, although two or more subjects may, and often do, overlap. *Edosewakyogen* have their settings in Edo and *Kamigatasewakyogen* in Kyoto and the neighbourhood, a distinction which at first sight seems superficial but is, in fact, fundamental, as anyone who compares *Kirare Yosa* (see page 377) with *Shinju Tenno Amijima* (see page 268) will at once realize. Plays about thieves (e. g. *Sannin Kichiza* see page 251) are called *shiranamimono* (" white wave " plays, after the pseudonym of a famous band of Chinese robbers). Plays derived from the puppets are classified as *maruhommono*. A good example is *Nozaki-mura* (see page 262). *Otokodate* plays are called *kyokakumono* and one at once thinks of *Gosho no Gorozo* (see page 300) and *Suzugamori* (see page 8). A popular theme was divorce or the breaking of an engagement (usually for motives of loyalty to one's lord) and there is a large group of these *enkirimono* in the repertoire of which *Ise Ondo* (see page 107) is a fair example. Ghost stories have always had a great vogue and are known as *kaidammono* after the most successful of them all, *Yotsuya Kaidan* (see page 373). Another popular group, called *dokufumono*, deals with the adventures of evil women and consists largely of " female " versions of plays already popular in their own right (i. e. *Kirare O Tomi* taken from *Kirare Yosa* and *Onna Sadakuro* based on the Sadakuro story in *Chushingura*). There are also cross classifications, such as *shinjumono* (" double-suicide " plays).

For " new " *sewamono* see under *kizewamono*.

SHINJU (*Double Suicide*). The *sewamono* plays of Chikamatsu Monzaemon (1653–1724) served, amongst other things, to popularize in Japan the concept of the union of lovers in death familiar to the West in such legends as *Tristan and Isolde* and *The Flying Dutchman*. The double suicide (*shinju*) is more readily intelligible to Japanese than to Western minds because the underlying philosophy of Buddhism has as its cardinal tenet the doctrine of reincarnation. Hence, if two unhappy lovers decide to commit suicide together, they not only escape their present weight of sorrow, but stand an excellent chance of being reborn together in a better life. Death is by no means a leap into the unknown. There may be a little temporary discomfort, but, provided the proper forms are observed, rebirth in happier circumstances is a certainty. Belief in this doctrine became so widespread as a result of Chikamatsu's plays that double suicides at one time became epidemic and the authorities had to take repressive measures. Such suicides are not uncommon even today.

The *shinju* allows for, probably, the highest range of emotional tension on the stage. The actual suicide is committed off-stage and in itself is of little interest compared with the agony of indecision which precedes it. In Chikamatsu's plays, more especially, the hero is usually a young man of weak moral stamina whose defects have got him into the plight from which there is now no escape. The heroine is a beauty of the licensed quarter, frivolous and mercenary to the world, but devoted to her real love and of exceptional moral courage. It is she who first suggests suicide and she often has no little trouble in persuading her lover to agree. Once he has made up his mind, it is her turn to have momentary qualms about the darkness of the road they must travel together. Her relapse may have discouraging effects on her partner, in which case her maternal instinct will reassert itself. It is all done with a sincerity of pathos which cannot fail to move.

SHOSAGOTO (*Dance Plays*). Dance plays or *shosagoto* are an essential part of the Kabuki repertoire and are, of course, direct lineal descendants of the earliest Japanese theatre (traditionally the somewhat *risqué* performance of the goddess Ame no Uzume no Mikoto before the cave retreat in which the Sun Goddess, Amaterasu O Mikami, was sulking.)

Such plays fall roughly into three large groups, but the distinctions are sometimes hard to make owing to the mixture of styles and conventions. To relieve the dramatic tension in long plays there may often by a dance interlude (see page 439) which will be performed in the style appropriate to the play. In *sewamono* and neo-Kabuki pieces, dances performed by geisha in a tea-house or by peasants at a village festival may be integrated into the story.

The first main group of dances is usually derived directly

from the Noh of which the influence is readily apparent. The actors use the sliding step of the Noh (*suri-ashi*) and wear Noh costumes. The set is invariably the same — a backdrop of cream-coloured boards painted with an ancient pine tree and bamboos at the two sides. The curtains at the end of the *hanamichi* and at the entrance down right are Noh curtains in broad stripes of (usually) purple, red, green, ochre, and white and are hung on a red rope. They are lifted by sticks at the lower corners, as in the Noh theatre. There is a "hurry-door" (*kirido*) up left for the musicians and stage-hands which is also sometimes used by the actors. The singers and *samisen* players (*debayashi*) remain on the stage throughout and sit on rostra (*yamadai*) covered in red cloth and stretching right across the back of the stage. The other musicians—flute, big and small hand-drums and a stick-drum — sit on the ground in front of them, the stick-drummer sitting sideways to the audience, the others facing the audience. Stage properties are few— a portable wooden gate, if needed, one or two stools (*aibiki*), serving tables, *sake* saucers, and lacquered barrels (*katsura oke*) used both for sitting on and for the deeper draughts of wine! There is dialogue, but the action is mainly developed by the dancing, with a commentary by the singers.

Manzai

(See *Suo Otoshi, Migawari Zazen, Hige Yagura, Shojo, Funa Benkei*, etc.)

The second group differs from the first in the sets, costumes, and style of dancing. The sets are often elaborate and realistic. Quick scene changes are a feature and clever use is made of lighting. The costumes are of the same order— the actors may have to change them several times, even on the stage, in order to achieve dramatic effect. The style of dancing is freer and more suggestive—the dancer may have to convey the idea, while still in human form, that he is a serpent or a fox. The singers and musicians may be *degatari* orchestras and their platforms are sometimes rolled off the stage, at a change of scene or at some other break in the acting, to yield place to others. The basic structure of such dances is a first part in which the principal dancer appears as a normal human being, followed by a light comic interlude and a second part in which the dancer appears as his true self, human, animal or demon. (See *Kokaji, Kagami Jishi, Musume Dojoji, Momiji Gari, Shinobi Yoru Koi wa Kusemono, Tsumoru Koi Yuki no Seki no To,* etc.) To this group belong the interlude dances called *michiyuki* (see page 439).

The third category is called *fuzeku mitate mono*. These dances are usually solo performances intended to portray a character—a beggar, a tumbler, a young girl in love, a man or woman driven mad by grief. There is often no particular story. The set is designed to create the right sort of atmosphere, the music is appropriately violent or sentimental, and the dancer works out a mood. Notable examples are *Fuji Musume, Yasuna, Kuruma Jishi*, etc.

Mention should perhaps be made here of *dammari* which may be translated " mime " or " dumb show." *Dammari* may be a separate item at the beginning or end of the programme or may be interpolated into a play. Traditionally it is a dance in the dark, in which a number of people weave in and out of each other in a " grand chain." It is often used as a means of introducing " new " actors to the public (see page 431). *Sewa-dammari* is a similar dance in the dark performed by the actors in a *sewamono* play. Very often it takes the form of the preliminary to a fight.

SOGA CYCLE. The plays of the Soga " world " are inspired by an incident which occurred in 1193. It was popular with the ballad-makers even before it reached the stage. There are a number of Noh plays written round the subject and, apart from the numerous puppet and Kabuki plays of the seventeenth, eighteenth, and nineteenth centuries, more than one contemporary Kabuki playwright has made use of the theme.

It is a simple story of revenge and filial piety. Two young samurai, Soga Juro Sukenari and Soga Goro Tokimune, avenged the death of their father who had been killed eighteen years previously in a private quarrel. Their enemy had risen to be a powerful daimyo and a councillor of the Shogun, Minamoto Yoritomo. Their task was not therefore an easy one. Both brothers were killed after they had accomplished their purpose.

Most of the old plays are known to us only by name. Chikamatsu Monzaemon wrote at least three puppet plays: *The Round Fan of Soga*, *The Revenge of the Soga Brothers* and *The Five Soga Brothers*. This last was a far-fetched innovation since the Soga brothers at no time numbered more than three. The first Kabuki play was performed by Ichikawa Danjuro I in 1655 and is one of the two plays summarized in this book. This play, because of its setting, became and has remained ever since a traditional New Year play. As a result of its success numerous variants, with or without New Year themes, were put on in January. Scenes from them may be seen depicted in the colour prints of the period ; "The Soga Brothers' Bow Bent to the Full" by Tsuruya Namboku and "The Soga Brothers' Journey" by Segawa Joko II are good examples. In a play named *Soga no Goro*, Danjuro I wore for the first time worked upon his kimono the three rice measures he later adopted as the Ichikawa crest. These plays are no longer seen in the theatres, although two of the *Eighteen Favourites* of the Ichikawa family, which were grafted onto the Soga story, *Sukeroku* and *Yanone*, are often performed. But Danjuro I's own play holds its own and the actual story of the revenge is told in an excellent play by Kawatake Mokuami. It is one of his more successful historical dramas.

STAGE. The Kabuki stage is wide and not very deep. It is, however, fitted with a circular revolving stage which permits frequent and rapid changes of scene. The revolving stage (*mawaributai*) is of at least eighteenth-century invention and many writer-managers, including Namiki Shozo, are credited with its introduction. The revolving stage is equipped with a *seriage* (see page 457) and there may be subsidiary traps elsewhere on the stage proper. The revolving stage may be used as part of the action—the characters will walk on it and be carried round into the next scene as if they are on a journey. In the play *Hakata Kojoro Namimakura*, where the first set consists of a ship about to make sail, the revolving stage swings round with telling effect as the vessel alters course.

The most characteristic Kabuki set is the *niju-butai*, a raised platform in the centre of the stage which represents a house, castle, camp, palace, etc. It is approached by three steps (*san dan*) of which great use is made at climactic moments. The rest of the stage is known as the *hira-butai* which may represent the garden surrounding the house, the sea or a lake, or may just be free acting space. It can be divided into zones by the use of lighting or curtains. Portable gates or fences may also be used to indicate the limits of particular areas.

The stage normally consists of bare boards, but in elaborate productions it will be covered with cloths to represent grass or snow or water. In interior scene strips of *tatami* (straw matting) are laid on the stage. In *shosagoto* plays it is always covered with a special smooth flooring which gives extra resonance to the stampings of the dancers (*oki-butai* or *shosa-butai*).

Our stage left is called *higashi* (east) or *kamite* (up-stage) and stage right is called *nishi* (west) or *shimote* (down-stage), whatever the real orientation of the theatre. The usual English terms are used in this book.

SWORDS, DAGGERS, AND KNIVES. The curved,
double-handed Japanese sword (*Nihon-to*) is often called the soul of the samurai and enjoys a remarkable degree of veneration. In the West there are many stories of magic swords, as, for instance, that of the Germanic hero, Siegfried. The anthropologists suggest that such swords were " natural accidents "—in other words, in the early Iron Age, some fortuitous circumstance in the process of forging turned them into steel blades which were therefore tougher and more

prized than the ordinary run of weapons. There are traces of similar legends in Japan, but from very early times Japanese craftsmen seem to have evolved techniques which left little to chance and so brought the art of forging to a quite exceptional level of excellence. As a result an almost religious attitude towards swords of all kinds was (and still is) preserved. Forging was restricted to duly qualified experts and partook of the nature of a ritual. The swordsmith was not a common artisan, but of honorary samurai rank. The forging was carried out according to strict and secret rules of procedure, the area round the anvil being purified and protected by prayer ropes and papers and the proper invocations addressed to the gods (see *Kokaji*). The smith wore ceremonial dress and had to be assisted by a qualified apprentice. (See Mitford's *Tales of Old Japan* for fuller details of the manufacture and the makers.)

The Japanese sword combines toughness and sharpness with perfect balance. On the stage it is always supposed to be miraculously sharp (see *Kajiwara Heiza Homare no Ishikiri*) and heads, trees, and bodies are severed with a truly astounding economy of effort. The sword may not, however, be used indiscriminately. In the first place, only a samurai is entitled to wear two swords. It used to be a punishable offence for a commoner to carry more than the short sword. An *otokodate* (see page 448), although often of samurai rank, carried only one sword. Swords may only be used in a worthy cause, for they are the symbols of peace and order, not weapons of war (see the Tokaiya scene in *Yoshitsune Sembonzakura*). Hence swords will only be drawn in a fight with a worthy foe. Assailants of low class will be beaten off with the scabbard or a fan or tricks of *judo*. It is a mark of great honour to be beheaded by a sword, particularly if it is a famous one. A sword is ritually cleansed with water before being put to such uses. It is always most carefully wiped after use. When it is returned to the scabbard, the user holds the mouth of the scabbard in his left hand, passes the back of the blade from hilt to point between the thumb and first finger of the left hand and then clicks the sword into the scabbard with a flowing movement. The samurai is never parted from his sword. On entering a house on a social call, it is correct to remove the long sword from the obi and carry it in the hand. If the samurai sits, the sword is placed beside him on the floor ; if he moves from room to room, or even across the room, the sword moves too. A great lord will have a sword-bearer constantly in attendance or at least there will be a sword-rack within reaching distance. The short sword remains in the obi as it does not get in the way when sitting on the ground. A samurai on duty, i. e., bearing a message from a superior, will, however, not remove his long sword on entering the house of the recipient of the message. He will sit on a high stool or a lacquer tub while he discharges his mission. Thereafter, he may sit on a cushion to partake of refreshment or enter into less formal conversation, in which case he will remove his long sword in the usual way. In certain places—the theatres and houses of assignation in the licensed quarters—swords are supposed to be left outside in order to minimize the risk of quarrels with fatal results.

For the significance of the sword as an heirloom, see page 425.

Some famous blades, particularly those made by Muromasa, were " bad " or " bloodthirsty " swords. Once they were drawn, their appetite for blood took a long time to assuage and the wielder had very little say in the matter (see *Ise Ondo Koi no Netaba*).

The samurai sometimes carries a short throwing knife (*kozuka*) in the hilt of the long sword. Ordinary knives are never carried in sheaths except in the case of the dagger used for *seppuku*. Rogues and thieves who employ such weapons wrap them in *tenugui* and usually carry them next to the skin. The *naginata* is a sort of halberd consisting of a long blade (often very valuable and in the heirloom class) mounted on a long shaft. When not in use, the blade is protected by a leather sheath. The *naginata* is the preferred weapon of the samurai wife but, of course, men use it also.

TACHIMAWARI (*Stage Fights*). The swordfight (*tachimawari*) which often provides the dénouement in plays of violence is basically a dance interlude and a relic of the old art of tumbling. The movements of the fighters are very stylized and superbly co-ordinated. The combatants aim blows at each other, clinch, fall apart, manoeuvre for position, return to the attack, parry, side-step, and feint with a precision which only long years of training can give. A samurai engaged with police or common soldiery will perform feats of gallantry single-handed. He passes through their ranks, parrying their clumsy thrusts with seeming indifference. His victims execute the most daring somersaults (*tombo*) as he tosses them aside. They retire from the fight for a moment, being counted as despatched, but return presently to shout " Nao " in his ear and suffer the same Herculean treatment. Anon panic will fall on the whole craven throng and the hero will chase them pell-mell along the *hanamichi* in utter rout. Sometimes these fights will take place on rooftops or up and down ladders. Then all the thrills of the circus are added to those of the stage. The ballet usually crystallizes into a pose and may seem inconclusive to the Western spectator, but the end of the story is well known to a Japanese audience and does not need to be worked out to the last dreg of realism. Such fights are never skimped—each assailant has his turn at the principal and the pace may seem at times a little slow. There are no mass attacks, for it would be outside the convention to permit the principal to be borne down by " human wave " tactics. The reason for this is partly that the individual assailants are afraid of the principal and partly that the fight is seen only from the latter's point of view—as soon as one attacker is cut down, another takes his place, and every second seems like an hour. This "slow motion" treatment, both in fights and murder scenes, is very characteristic and has even been used, with varying success, in modern Japanese films. It seeks to emphasize the enormity of the moment from the point of view of the person attacked.

TAIKO CYCLE. By the middle of the sixteenth century the Shogun, once the supreme secular ruler of Japan, had become a mere puppet, and the country was in chaos as a result of the wars between the great feudal lords. At length there emerged from among their number Oda Nobunaga who, although a comparatively insignificant daimyo, was able by his military genius and his choice of subordinates to gather into his hands more power than any single man since the days of Minamoto Yoritomo. He was murdered, however, before he was able to bring all Japan under his sway. He left behind him two most able generals who each in turn carried on his work. The first was Toyotomi Hideyoshi, a man of peasant origin but immense ability, who had been

Nobunaga's right hand. Like Nobunaga he never succeeded in seizing the shogunate for himself, but he finished Nobunaga's task of pacifying the country. He also had large ideas of conquest overseas. He was given the title of Taiko (meritorious prince).

When Hideyoshi died, leaving only a six-year-old son to succeed him, the power was seized by his colleague, Tokugawa Ieyasu, just as Hideyoshi had seized the power from Nobunaga's heirs. But Hideyoshi's young son, Hideyori, had powerful supporters and held the strongest fortress in all Japan, Osaka Castle. For more than twenty years Hideyori's party remained a thorn in Ieyasu's flesh and, although on the death of the hereditary Shogun the Emperor bestowed this title upon Ieyasu and subsequently, when Ieyasu went into nominal retirement, upon his son, Ieyasu never felt easy in the possession of his power until he had destroyed Hideyori and razed Osaka Castle. This he was finally able to do. The siege was the last great military operation which set the seal on the absolute dominion of the Tokugawa family.

When written before the Meiji Restoration, plays dealing with this period use fictitious names and set the time in some remote epoch, in deference to the strict Tokugawa censorship laws. Such plays, strictly speaking, belong to the Taiko Cycle. A number of new plays about Toyotomi Hideyoshi and Tokugawa Ieyasu were staged after 1868 and use the real names of the characters. Most of these are "Plays of Living History" (see page 429) and, although they are still occasionally revived, have little dramatic appeal. Such plays are, for instance, *Daitokuji* by Kawatake Mokuami which shows how Toyotomi Hideyoshi seized power after the death of Oda Nobunaga by declaring Nobunaga's infant grandson heir to the Oda honours and himself his principal guardian; *A Paulownia Leaf* by Tsubouchi Shoyo, about the constant hidden warfare between the supporters of Tokugawa Ieyasu and those of young Toyotomi Hideyori; and *Iyeyasu and Lady Kasuga* by Ochikoji Fukuchi, which concerns a private feud within Ieyasu's own family circle.

TENUGUI (*Towels*). The Japanese, before the Meiji restoration and still today in many cases, have no use for handkerchieves in the Western sense. Paper (see page 449) replaces the handkerchief for most purposes, but Japanese in kimono usually also carry about their persons a small cotton towel called *tenugui*. This valuable piece of equipment serves many ends, apart from the obvious one of drying the hands, face or feet after washing. It may be used for wrapping up money or a letter or some other object. (In the upper classes, a special purple cloth is used for this). When a man of the lower classes has a job of work to do or is preparing to fight, he will roll his *tenugui* into a string and tie it round his head so that his hair shall not come undone and fall in his eyes. Again, if it is raining, he will cover his head with his *tenugui* or, if he does not wish his face to be seen, he will arrange it over his forehead, nose and mouth. Women use their *tenugui* in a variety of ways, usually to indicate embarrassment or coyness. Often they will take them out of their bosoms, fold them carefully and then tuck one end into their obi, ready for use. A very attractive pose is made by holding one corner of the *tenugui* in the teeth and pulling gently on it with the right hand ; this is usually done by a woman trying to choke down her emotion. The *tenugui* may also be used as an important accessory in the dance, when the actor frequently has his *tenugui* printed with his own *mon*. These crested *tenugui* are sold in the theatres and are a popular form of souvenir.

VENDETTA. The vendetta was practised in Japan, as in many European countries, from very early times. It had the moral support of the Confucian ethic and a large measure of legal sanction. A vendetta had to be conducted according to certain rules. In the first place, the avenging party had to serve official notice on his intended victim that he was engaged in a vendetta against him. An extension of this concept required at a later date that the avenging party should not take any unfair advantage of his enemy, i. e. killing him when he happened to come upon him unawares or when he was at an obvious disadvantage. In short, the vendetta could only be carried out on terms comparable with the European code of duelling. Finally, a vendetta could not be settled without giving due official notice to the governor of the district in which the act of revenge was to be attempted. The governor could withhold his assent if he thought that the cause was unjust or other considerations militated against a disturbance of public order and security (i. e., if the Emperor or a great prince were in the neighbourhood). In such a case it was a criminal offence to act in that area. If the governor gave his consent, however, it was his duty to see that the rules of the code were observed by both parties. Once the act of revenge had been committed, the feud could not be carried further (as happened in the notorious Corsican vendetta), i. e., the family of the dead man could not then be revenged on the avengers. Mitford (*Tales of Old Japan*) gives full details.

The foregoing rules were not, of course, always kept. There were villains who took mean advantages and sometimes circumstances imposed involuntary breaches of etiquette. It is these fortuitous twists which often form the subject of Kabuki plays in which the vendetta theme is the dominant motif. A very celebrated example is, of course, *Kanadehon Chushingura,* in which the avengers deliberately failed to notify their intention, thus placing themselves in the position of common criminals. An equally celebrated example of a vendetta, but conducted with due formality, may be found in the numerous plays concerning the Soga brothers (see page 462), but there are many others.

WIGS AND HEADDRESSES. The wig is an essential part of the Kabuki actor's make-up. No actor ever appears without one. The wigs are prepared by a special department of wig-makers and dressers (*tokoyama*) who have charge of them up to the moment they are put on the actor's head and again as soon as they are removed. Except for actors in crowd scenes and such small fry, each wig is modelled to the head of the wearer and is specially made for that one particular series of performances. At the end of the run it is taken to pieces and the hair is cleaned and returned to store. Only real human hair (*honke*) is used and this is largely obtained from " combings " which are thriftily preserved by Japanese women and sold by the bagful. The method of making the wigs is complicated. The wig-maker measures the actor's head anew for each wig, that is to say, every month unless the actor is not appearing for some reason. From these measurements he cuts a number of thin strips of copper which are bent and moulded to fit the head exactly. On this foundation, which is drilled with holes and covered with paper or silk, the hair is sewn. In the case of women's hair-styles and those of boys and some men, the front hair is sewn onto a silk band one hair at a time. The completed wig is to all intents and purposes a head of hair, which is then dressed in the required style by equally skilled dressers. These also tidy and if necessary re-dress the wig during the run of the play. In the case of men's wigs, the shaved crown is not part of the wig but is applied upon a separate head covering (*habutae*) and is part of the make-up. In various kinds of " trick" wigs, the hair can be made to fall down on the release of a cord. These wigs are much used in death scenes, to portray jealousy or anger in women, or to mark the change from woman to witch or spirit.

The style of hair-dressing varies according to the period in which the play is set and the rank and condition of the character the actor is portraying. It should, however, be borne in mind that most of the *jidaimono*, particularly those of puppet origin, were originally performed, as were Shakespeare's plays, in "modern dress," i. e. the dresses and hair-styles of the period at which they were written. In *sewamono* and *kizewamono* the costumes and hair-styles are also roughly those of the period at which the plays were written. Since the greater part of the *jidaimono* and *sewamono* were written at the end of the seventeenth and during the eighteenth centuries, a period rather loosely termed Genroku, the costumes and hair styles belong to that period. In *kizewamono*, whose greatest exponent was the nineteenth century playwright Kawatake Mokuami, the styles are those of the last years before the Meiji Restoration. Occasionally one of the "crop-hair" plays (see page 476) launched by Onoe Kikugoro V is revived and shows the characters wearing the first Japanese equivalent of Western hair dressing.

The Heian Period and the Kamakura Period. Modern plays about these eras and some of Ichikawa Danjuro IX's "plays of living history" (see page 429) show the early simple hair-styles which are familiar from ancient picture scrolls. The men wear the hair drawn back and plainly tied behind (*nadetsuke honke*). In the case of the *kuge* or nobles, who naturally figure largely in these plays, the queue (*mage*) is tightly bound so as to make it stand upright. All men of this epoch wear their heads covered both indoors and out, except for priests, who shaved their heads then as they do today. The *kuge* wear for formal occasions the *kammuri*, a small black hat, held in place by a bar which serves as a hatpin, with a hollow compartment rising at the back to receive the queue. On special ceremonial occasions connected with the Imperial Court, a crest of woven horsehair (*ei*), like a broad, stiff ribbon, is attached at the back, its angle varying slightly according to the rank of the wearer. The *ei* of a minor official who has to hurry about a lot is rolled up. Only the Emperor wears an upright crest. On informal occasions the *kuge* wear the conical *eboshi* (sometimes called *tateboshi*), which is also worn by those of lower rank. This hat is worn by officials of the Shogun's Court, when it is secured to the head by a white ribbon (*hachimaki*) tied round the temples and knotted at the back. In the case of the very poor the *eboshi* is replaced by a triangular piece of black silk or even paper, tied on with strings. The *samurai-eboshi*, a flat headdress with a triangular, upstanding crest, is reserved for the military caste.

Women of this period wear the hair loose and very simply dressed, on ordinary occasions caught at the back of the neck with a ribbon. The court-lady wears it unbound and increases the length with false hair or black silk fringe.

The Genroku Period. During the constant wars that preceded the establishment of the Tokugawa Shogunate, the samurai found that a full head of hair made the helmet unduly hot. It therefore became customary to shave the top of the head, bringing the tightly bound queue over the crown to support the weight of the helmet. The *eboshi* went out of fashion for indoor wear, since the warrior wished to be always ready to put on his harness. The shaved crown was gradually adopted by all classes except for the *kuge* who retained the full head of hair, the *kammuri*, and *eboshi*.

In the peaceful Genroku period depicted in so many plays, however, the samurai alone continue to affect the austerely tied back side-locks (*bin*) and the simple queue of their forefathers. The young merchants and men of fashion who figure so largely in the *sewamono* plays of Chikamatsu Monzaemon and his contempories have evolved all sorts of elaborate hairstyles with long, curving side and back locks and carefully arranged queues such as the "tea whisk" queue (*chasengami*) supposed to resemble the split bamboo whisk used in the tea ceremony. Some even grow the hair on top of the head and wear a rather feminine crest in front. Neither the samurai nor the ordinary man wears a hat at this epoch. The only exceptions are the old fashioned *eboshi* which is worn by daimyo at certain functions at the Shogunal Court and the various large hats of wicker-work or sedge worn by all classes for travelling. These latter are the *kasa* which is really a sort of parasol or umbrella ; the *ame-gasa*, a sort of circular wicker basket worn by the samurai ; and the *suge-gasa*, a flat sedge hat worn fore and aft, which is preferred by the ordinary man. The most common form of head covering is some kind of scarf. In the case of a man of rank it is usually of purple silk and is worn either tied round the head to keep the hair in place or like a hood. The man of the people makes use of the *tenugui* (see page 468) for the same purpose.

Women of the Genroku period, if neither ladies of the Imperial Court (who retain the simple Heian hair-style) nor courtesans of the first rank, wear their hair in three main styles, each style varying, of course, with the rank, character, and mood of the wearer.

The *momo-ware* (peach cut in two), a style for very young girls. The name is derived from the shape of the *mage* or knot which is round and wound over a red or pink scarf which shows through the hair like the stone of a peach. With this are worn small, gay hair-ornaments, often of tinsel.

The *shimada-mage*, a style for young, unmarried women in which the long, curved knot is tied with a cord or ribbon. This style has an enormous number of variants and can be very elaborate or quite simple. It is also worn by geisha and by young courtesans who are not yet considered to be at the top of their profession. It is ornamented with a comb in front of the knot and with decorated pins but not with a bar through the knot. The *taka-shimada* is a very elaborate variant and is worn by brides and on formal occasions.

The *maru-mage* (round knot), a style for married women of all ages, particularly in *sewamono*. In *jidaimono* ladies of rank favour the very similar *katsuyama*. It is heavier and more severe, with a smaller, rounder knot, as the name implies. This knot is supported by a roll of coloured silk. With it are worn the *kogai*, or bar, and such pins as the lady considers appropriate to her age, station, and costume. A variant of this form, the *ichogaishi* (gingko leaf), is worn by older women of the servant class and poor men's wives.

The knot is much flatter and closer to the head and is considered too informal for anyone with any pretension to rank or fashion.

Boys under the age of fifteen wear the *mae-gami*, a long lock of hair at the front of the scalp which is trained back over the shaven crown. With very small boys, whose hair is being allowed to grow after the head-shaving common to all Japanese infants, this lock is represented by a little, tied-up tuft. The *mae-gami* is not quite universal, for little boys of the lower classes sometimes have their heads completely shaved except for a band of hair to be trained into the queue.

The bride of good family wears over her head a large white silk hood, rather like a pillow-case. The bride of lesser degree contents herself with a white silk band shading the eyes, such as is also worn by ladies going on pilgrimage. Ladies traveling protect the front lock (which is heavily greased) from dust with a small piece of purple silk (*murasaki boshi*) and carry large, circular wicker hats. Old ladies also wear a strip of material, (*baba boshi*), in a suitable elderly colour, over the top of the head to conceal thinning hair.

The Kabuki has evolved two special women's head-dresses of its own. One is the enormously exaggerated style associated with the top-ranking courtesan, adorned with great loops

A high-ranking courtesan

of false hair, huge pins, scarves and gold tassels at the back. These wigs are called *hyogo-mage* and are extremely heavy, weighing up to twenty-five or thirty pounds. The other is the head-dress of the princess or young lady of high rank. This is a pure Kabuki invention, since no costume designer of Genroku had seen a real princess. She wears a form of *taka-shimada*, known as *fukiwa*, the long, looped knot supported by a glittering bar shaped something like the *tsuzumi*, or hand-drum. In front, in place of the comb, is a wreath of silver flowers with a dangling silver fringe.

Special mention must here be made of the head-dresses worn by actors in *aragoto* plays. These are exaggerated in the same way as the actors' speech, gestures, and make-up are exaggerated. Daimyo and *kuge* in these plays often display great manes of hair, and samurai of lower rank develop curious tufts and loops, stiffly lacquered headdresses that hardly resemble hair at all (*Kuruma bin*).

Wigs, like everything else in classical Kabuki, are ruled by tradition, but often not even the wig-makers known their origin. Thus Moritsuna in *Moritsuna Jinya* always wears a stiffly lacquered wig with the top of the head covered by a black velvet pad. Matsuo in *Terakoya* wears a great bush of hair, like a fur hat, on the crown of his head. This shews that he is a sick man and has not been able to have his head shaved. The white paper band keeps it out of his eyes. A similar bush of hair is worn by the wicked samurai Toma in *Tenga-jaya* who in the earlier part of the play is in hiding from his enemies. On the other hand, the mops of hair worn by Imakuni in *Imoseyama Onna Teikin* and Mitsuhide in *Ehon Taikoki* indicate virility.

The Genroku hair-styles survived with modifications until the Meiji Era. Those seen in *kizewamono* are usually simplified versions since the characters in these plays belong to the lowest strata of society. In these plays the men often appear with the crown of the head heavily darkened or covered with short hair, indicating that they have neglected to have it shaved. This is technically known as *kuma no fukige*, from the bear's fur used for the crown. When one of these men is anxious to escape notice, for he is almost always a petty criminal, he puts his *tenugui* over his head, tying it across his face under the nose and so creating a sort of mask.

Shosagoto. In most dance-dramas the wigs correspond with those worn in straight plays. But in certain dances based on the Noh, ghosts and animal spirits wear the great manes worn by these characters on the Noh stage. The huge white wig worn by the dancer in *Kagami Jishi* is a Kabuki exaggeration of this Noh wig. Women in dances of Noh origin wear their long hair loose and tucked inside the upper surcoat. Round their heads they have the silk band which in a Noh play supports the mask.

ZANGIRIMONO (*Crop-Hair Plays*). Just as Ichikawa Danjuro IX attempted reforms in the historical drama (see page 429), Onoe Kikugoro V tried his hand at emancipating *sewamono* by putting on the so-called " crop-hair plays " (*zangirimono*). This name reflected the upheaval of the Meiji Restoration by calling attention to the levelling of social distinctions as exemplified by the abolition of the top-knot, (see page 472). These plays were no more successful than Danjuro's *katsureki geki*. They are still occasionally performed and the appearance of bowler hats and elastic-sided boots on the Kabuki stage causes genuine, if only transient, amusement.

ZORI-UCHI (*Striking with Footwear*). All visitors to Japan must very soon be struck by the abhorrence with which the Japanese regard street dirt. The removal of footwear before entering a *tatami* room is compulsory. In Kabuki plays *geta* (clogs) or *zori* (sandals) are conscientiously removed at the *genkan* (porch) of houses built on the stage or, if the actor is barefoot, he will wash his feet before entering a room. It follows from all this that to strike someone with one's sandal (*zori-uchi*) is the worst of insults. There are several tense scenes in which this studied form of outrage is given dramatic expression. (See, for example, *Sukeroku*.)

Aston, W. G. *A History of Japanese Literature.* London, 1907.

Bowers, F. *Japanese Theatre.* New York, 1952.

Ernst, E. *The Kabuki Theatre.* New York, 1956.

Fujinami, M *Kodogu* (Hand Properties). Tokyo, 1954.

Haar, F., and Ernst, E. *Japanese Theatre in Highlight: A Pictorial Commentary.* Tokyo, 1952.

Inouye, J. *Chushingura, or the Treasury of Loyal Retainers.* Tokyo, 1910.

Kawatake, S. *Nihon Koten Zensho: Kabuki Juhachiban Shu* (Annotated Texts of the Favourite Eighteen). Tokyo, 1954.

Kawatake, S., Takeshiba, K., and Atsumi, S. *Nihon Gikyoku Zenshu* (Texts of the Japanese Theatre), Vols. 1–32. Tokyo, 1930–32.

Keene, D. *The Battles of Coxinga.* London, 1951.

Kincaid, Z. *Kabuki: The Popular Stage of Japan.* London, 1925.

Kusano, E. *Weird Tales of Old Japan.* Tokyo, 1953.

Maybon, A. *Le Théâtre Japonais.* Paris, 1925.

Mitford. *Tales of Old Japan.* London, 1871.

Miyake, S. *Kabuki Drama.* Tokyo, 1953.

Miyomori, A. *Tales of Old Japanese Dramas.* London, 1915.

Miyomori, A. *Masterpieces of Chikamatsu.* London, 1926.

Murdoch, J. *A History of Japan.* London, 1949.

O'Neill, P. G. *A Guide to No.* Tokyo, 1953.

Papinot, E. *Dictionnaire Japonais-Français des Noms Principaux de l'Histoire et de la Géographie du Japon.* Hong Kong, 1899.

Pound, E. *The Translations of Ezra Pound.* London, 1953.

Sadler, A. L. *The Ten Foot Square Hut and Tales of the Heike.* London, 1928.

Sansom, G. B. *Japan: A Short Cultural History.* London, 1931.

Satchell, T. *Hizakurige: A Shanks' Mare Tour of the Tokaido,* translated from the Japanese of Ikku Hippensha. Tokyo, 1951.

Scott, A. C. *Genyadana: A Japanese Kabuki Play.* Tokyo, 1953.

Scott, A. C. *Kanjincho: A Japanese Kabuki Play.* Tokyo, 1953.

Scott, A. C. *The Kabuki Theatre of Japan.* London, 1955.

Scott, A. C. "Kodogu no Kirikubi: Death Masks of the Kabuki Theatre." *Journal of Oriental Studies,* Vol. II, No. 1. Hong Kong, 1955.

Shaw, G. W. *Tojuro's Love and Four Other Plays by Kikuchi Kwan.* Tokyo, 1925.

Shively, D. H. *The Love Suicide at Amijima.* Cambridge, Mass., 1953.

Toita, K. *Kabuki Mesaku Sen* (Texts of Popular Kabuki Plays). Tokyo, 1953.

Waley, A. *The Noh Plays of Japan.* London, 1921.

Boldface type indicates titles and alternate titles of plays or parts of plays. Italicized page numbers indicate principal references.

Please order from your bookstore or write directly to:

CHARLES E. TUTTLE CO., INC.
Suido 1-chome, 2–6, Bunkyo-ku, Tokyo 112

or:

CHARLES E. TUTTLE CO., INC.
Rutland, Vermont 05701 U.S.A.

Other TUT BOOKS available: